The Implementation and Effectiveness of International Environmental Commitments: Theory and Practice

Global Environmental Accord: Strategies for Sustainability and Institutional Innovation

Nazli Choucri, editor

Global Accord: Environmental Challenges and International Responses
Nazli Choucri, editor

Institutions for the Earth: Sources of Effective International Environmental Protection
Peter M. Haas, Robert O. Keohane, and Marc A. Levy, editors

Intentional Oil Pollution at Sea: Environmental Policy and Treaty Compliance
Ronald B. Mitchell

Institutions for Environmental Aid: Pitfalls and Promise
Robert O. Keohane and Marc A. Levy, editors

Global Governance: Drawing Insights from the Environmental Experience
Oran R. Young, editor

The Implementation and Effectiveness of International Environmental Commitments: Theory and Practice
David G. Victor, Kal Raustiala, and Eugene Skolnikoff, editors

The Implementation and Effectiveness of International Environmental Commitments: Theory and Practice

edited by
David G. Victor, Kal Raustiala, and Eugene B. Skolnikoff

International Institute for Applied Systems Analysis
Laxenburg, Austria

The MIT Press
Cambridge, Massachusetts and London, England

Library of Congress Cataloging-in-Publication Data

The implementation and effectiveness of international environmental commitments: theory and practice / edited by David G. Victor, Kal Raustiala, and Eugene B. Skolnikoff.
    p.   cm.—(Global environmental accord)
    Includes bibliographical references and index.
    ISBN 0-262-22057-1 (hardcover: alk. paper)—ISBN 0-262-72028-0 (pbk.: alk. paper)
    1. Environmental law, International. I. Victor, David G. II. Raustiala, Kal.
III. Skolnikoff, Eugene B. IV. Series: Global environmental accord series.
K3585.6.I555   1998
363.7 0526—dc21   97–36845
                                                    CIP

Contents

Contributors

Steinar Andresen
Fridtjof Nansen Institute
Lysaker, Norway

Juan Carlos di Primio
International Institute for
Applied Systems Analysis
Laxenburg, Austria

Owen Greene
Department of Peace Studies
University of Bradford
Bradford, UK

Ronnie Hjorth
Department of Political Science
Linköping University
Linköping, Sweden

Vladimir Kotov
School of Business Management
Academy of Transport
Moscow, Russia

John Lanchbery
Verification Technology Information
Centre (VERTIC)
London, UK

Elena Nikitina
Institute of World Economy
and International Relations
Russian Academy of Sciences
Moscow, Russia

Kal Raustiala
Harvard Law School
Harvard University
Cambridge, MA, USA

Alexei Roginko
Institute of World Economy
and International Relations
Russian Academy of Sciences
Moscow, Russia

Jon Birger Skjærseth
Fridtjof Nansen Institute
Lysaker, Norway

Eugene B. Skolnikoff
Department of Political Science
Massachusetts Institute of Technology
Cambridge, MA, USA

Olav Schram Stokke
Fridtjof Nansen Institute
Lysaker, Norway

David G. Victor
International Institute for
Applied Systems Analysis
Laxenburg, Austria; and
Council on Foreign Relations
New York, NY, USA

Jørgen Wettestad
Fridtjof Nansen Institute
Lysaker, Norway

Preface

Implementation—translating intent into action—is vital to effective public policy. The implementation process is especially important to international agreements that regulate complex behavior. Until implementation actually begins, it is often unclear exactly what changes in behavior will be required to meet international commitments. Differences in national circumstances abound, suggesting that there is no single way for a country to put its international commitments into practice. National efforts sometimes are nonexistent or fail; yet the international mechanisms for identifying and responding to implementation failures are few and often weak. Given the many complexities and difficulties of implementing international environmental commitments, is it possible to draw any systematic conclusions about the implementation process and ways to enhance implementation?

This book suggests some answers. It is a product of a three-year research project on the Implementation and Effectiveness of International Environmental Commitments (IEC) conducted at the International Institute for Applied Systems Analysis (IIASA) in Laxenburg, Austria. The main element of the IEC Project was the preparation of historical case studies. Many of the studies are presented in this book.* The Project and book offer a foundation for how to think about and analyze the implementation of international commitments.

Our focus on implementation complements existing research on international environmental institutions, which has emphasized the formation of international regimes and especially the process of negotiating legal commitments. We concentrate on how those commitments are translated into practice—whether and how they actually influence behavior in a way that helps to solve environmental problems. Our concern with the practical effect of international commitments is part of the growing attention by scholars to the ways that institutions influence social behavior—often termed "the new institutionalism." We hope that scholars working in this area, and in international environmental law and politics more broadly, find useful the key concepts, context, and methods that we employ. In addition, teachers can use our case studies to focus

*For a complete list of products from the IEC Project, see www.iiasa.ac.at/Research/IEC

students of law, public policy, and political science on the practical effects of international agreements and institutions. Our studies also suggest ways to make the regulation of international environmental problems more effective, which should be of interest to policymakers and international lawyers.

Through 14 case studies we examine how international commitments are implemented at the international and national levels. The following are among our many findings:

- Monitoring, verifying, and enforcing international commitments depend on the availability of data. Overall, national reports, which are the main source of these data, are becoming more complete, but the accuracy and comparability of data remain low in most cases. Mechanisms for reporting and using data often take a decade or longer to build up, which suggests that when creating a regulatory regime, one of the first priorities should be building the data systems that will be needed in the future.

- Many analysts believe that failures to implement international commitments are largely unintentional and the best responses are entirely "soft" measures such as dialogue and financial assistance. We find that some implementation failures are intentional and that "harder" measures, such as sanctions, are available and sometimes necessary. As cooperation deepens, the need for "hard" measures may increase.

- Active participation by industry and other targets of regulation often makes the implementation process more effective: the regulated targets typically have the best information on feasibility and costs, and their inclusion might give them a larger stake in the success of the regulation. "Regulatory capture," a frequently cited fear of target participation, has not been widespread, but we show how it can be reduced further.

- In most areas of international environmental law, public interest groups are increasingly vocal during negotiations to form new legal instruments but have been surprisingly inactive during the implementation process. Contrary to conventional wisdom, we find that it is rare for such groups to serve as "watchdogs" to verify that nations have implemented their international commitments. This inactivity reflects that few groups devote the resources needed to build expertise and gather information to enable them to perform such functions during the implementation process.

- Financial transfers from West to East could help countries in transition from central planning to implement their international environmental commitments. The need is especially severe in Russia, which is the largest of the transition countries. In practice, few transfers to Russia have taken place because compatible domestic institutions are weak or nonexistent. This casts doubt on the more sanguine predictions for schemes such as "joint implementation," which envision solving global and regional environmental problems through extensive transfers and "pollution trading."

• The increased use of nonbinding legal instruments could make international environmental governance more effective. Many analysts and practitioners believe that binding treaties are the most effective legal instruments. We find that compliance with binding treaties is high because they often contain only modest, easily implemented regulatory commitments. Nonbinding agreements frequently contain more ambitious commitments—they are often marked by low compliance but higher influence on behavior. We suggest ways that binding and nonbinding instruments can be used in tandem to maximize effectiveness.

These findings, and many others, are presented more fully in the chapters that follow. In organizing the book, we have employed some devices to make it user-friendly. Chapter 1 gives a compact overview of our approach, the existing literature, and our main results. Details on the relevant literature and the propositions that we examine in this book are discussed in the two short texts that introduce the two parts of the book—one on international mechanisms for monitoring and reviewing implementation, which we term systems for implementation review (SIRs), and the other on national implementation. This two-part organization has made it easier for the studies in this book to focus on common research questions. In turn, that focus has made it easier to identify general conclusions concerning some (but certainly not all) of the main issues related to implementation of international environmental commitments.

The introduction to each of the case studies is written to provide an overview of the main results. Although each study contributes to the broader analysis of implementation issues, each is also written to be self-contained. We have eliminated many details from the case study chapters, most of which are excerpted from longer research studies. For more detailed assessments, readers are referred to the notes. The final chapter reiterates main conclusions and briefly speculates on the implications of our work for international law and society.

We thank especially IIASA and its member countries for funding the Project, which began under the leadership of Director Peter de Jánosi. We are grateful to him and to IIASA's current director, Gordon MacDonald, for support during the vital final stages. Other activities that were part of the IEC Project also contributed to the IEC case studies presented here. In particular, the IEC "regimes database" team of Helmut Breitmeier, Marc Levy, Oran Young, and Michael

Zürn helped those of us writing case studies to sharpen our hypotheses and findings. The Project's Advisory Committee—Abe Chayes, Gueorgui Golitsyn, Peter Sand, and Arild Underdal—provided invaluable critical feedback. So did several colleagues who have collaborated on IEC-related activities, notably Jesse Ausubel, Dan Bodansky, Ted Parson, Julian Salt, Chris Stone, and especially Tom Schelling. Bob Keohane and another, anonymous reviewer provided invaluable comments on the whole manuscript. Many people also contributed to individual studies, and they are thanked in the appropriate chapters.

Much credit is due to Eryl Mädel's publications department at IIASA, which produced the manuscript. Ellen Bergschneider managed the process and edited with great patience and skill; Anka James and Lilo Roggenland tirelessly produced figures and typeset the manuscript. At The MIT Press, we are grateful to Larry Cohen and Madeline Sunley, who initiated publication of this book, and to Clay Morgan, who joined at the final stages. The IEC Project was much happier and more productive for the assistance of Cara Morris, who kept the research on track with grace, charm, and insight that helped IEC navigate at home in Austria and Central Europe. Many early drafts of these chapters were also advanced by her editorial skill. We are also grateful for the assistance of Nina Drinković, Anna Korula, and Hua Dong. The IEC Project was located at IIASA, but most of the scholars involved worked primarily from their home institutions. We thank these institutions for encouraging participation in this IIASA endeavor.

November 1997

David Victor
Laxenburg, Austria

Kal Raustiala, Eugene Skolnikoff
Cambridge, Massachusetts, USA

Abbreviations and Acronyms

AOX	chlorinated organic substances
BAT	best available technology
BBPRU	Belarus, Bulgaria, Poland, Russia, and Ukraine (first ad hoc cases under the Montreal Protocol's Non-Compliance Procedure)
BEP	best environmental practice
BIMCO	Baltic and International Maritime Council
BOD	biochemical oxygen demand
BPO	Baltic Ports Organization
BSEP	Baltic Sea Environment Proceedings
CAA	Clean Air Act (UK)
CBD	Convention on Biological Diversity
CC	Combatting Committee (HELCOM)
CCB	Coalition Clean Baltic
CCC	Chemical Coordinating Centre (EMEP)
CEFIC	Conseil européen de l'industrie chimique (European Chemical Industry Council)
CEGB	Central Electricity Generating Board
CEIT	countries with economies in transition
CFCs	chlorofluorocarbons
CI	Consumers International (formerly International Organization of Consumer Unions–IOCU)
CIA	Chemical Industries Association (UK)
CIS	Commonwealth of Independent States
CITES	Convention on International Trade in Endangered Species of Wild Fauna and Flora
CMA	Chemical Manufacturers Association
CMS	Convention for the Conservation of Migratory Species of Wild Animals
CO_2	carbon dioxide
COCP	Conference of Contracting Parties
COP	Conference of the Parties
CRE	Standing Conference of Rectors, Presidents, and Vice Chancellors of European Universities
DANW	Directorate for Air, Noise and Waste
DDT	dichlorodiphenyltrichloroethane
DGD	Decision Guidance Document

DNA	Designated National Authority
EAP	Environmental Action Programme for Central and Eastern Europe
EB	Executive Body (LRTAP)
EBRD	European Bank for Reconstruction and Development
EC	European Community
ECAT	Environmental Centers for Administration and Technology
ECE	(United Nations) Economic Commission for Europe
EEA	European Environment Agency
EEC	European Economic Community
EEZs	exclusive economic zones
EFMA	European Fertilizer Manufacturers' Association
EHC	Environmental Health Criteria
EIB	European Investment Bank
EMA	Environmental Management Act (Netherlands)
EMEP	Cooperative Programme for Monitoring and Evaluation of the Long-Range Transmission of Air Pollutants in Europe
ENGO	environmental nongovernmental organization
EPA	Environmental Protection Act (UK)
EQO	environmental quality objectives
EU	European Union
EURO CHLOR	European Chlor-Alkali Industry
ExCom	Executive Committee (Montreal Protocol)
FAO	United Nations Food and Agriculture Organization
FCO	Foreign and Commonwealth Office
FI	financial intermediary
FIFRA	Federal Insecticide, Fungicide and Rodenticide Act
FinRep	Project for Preparation of the Final Report on Implementation of the 1988 Ministerial Declaration
FOE	Friends of the Earth
FRG	Federal Republic of Germany
FSU	former Soviet Union
GATT	General Agreement on Tariffs and Trade
GCPF	Global Crop Protection Federation (formerly Groupement international des associations nationales de fabricants de produits agrochimiques–GIFAP)
GDP	gross domestic product
GDR	German Democratic Republic
GEF	Global Environment Facility
GIFAP	Groupement international des associations nationales de fabricants de produits agrochimiques (renamed Global Crop Protection Federation–GCPF)

GLP	good laboratory practice
GNP	gross national product
GTZ	German Technical Assistance Agency
HBFC	hydrobromofluorocarbon
HCFC	hydrochlorofluorocarbon
HELCOM	Helsinki Convention Baltic Marine Environment Protection Commission
HLTF	High Level Task Force (Baltic Sea environment protection regime)
HMIP	Her Majesty's Inspectorate of Pollution (UK)
HOCEC	House of Commons Environment Committee (UK)
IA	implementing agency (Montreal Protocol MLF)
IAEA	International Atomic Energy Agency
IBSFC	International Baltic Sea Fishery Commission
IC	Implementation Committee (Montreal Protocol)
ICBP	International Council for Bird Protection (now Birdlife International)
ICCA	International Council of Chemical Associations
ICES	International Council for the Exploration of the Sea
ICI	Imperial Chemical Industries
ICLEI	International Environmental Agency for Local Governments
ICP	international cooperative programs
ICRW	International Convention for the Regulation of Whaling
IFIs	international financial institutions
IGO	intergovernmental organization
IGPRAD	Inter-Governmental Panel of Experts on Radioactive Waste Disposal at Sea
IIASA	International Institute for Applied Systems Analysis
ILO	International Labor Organization
IMO	International Maritime Organization
IMP	indicative multi-year programs
INC-PIC	Intergovernmental Negotiating Committee for an International Legally Binding Instrument for the Application of the Prior Informed Consent Procedure for Certain Hazardous Chemicals and Pesticides in International Trade
INGOs	industrial nongovernmental organizations
INSCs	International North Sea Conferences
IOC	Intergovernmental Oceanographic Commission
IOCU	International Organization of Consumers Unions (renamed Consumers International)
IPCS	International Program on Chemical Safety
IPM	integrated pest management

IRPTC	International Register for Potentially Toxic Chemicals
IUCN	International Union for Conservation of Nature and Natural Resources (renamed the World Conservation Union)
IWC	International Whaling Commission
IWRB	International Waterfowl Research Bureau
JCP	Joint Comprehensive Environmental Action Programme (Baltic Sea)
JI	joint implementation
JMG	Joint Monitoring Group (North Sea environment protection regime)
JMPIC	FAO/UNEP Joint Meeting of Experts on Prior Informed Consent
JMPR	WHO/FAO Joint Meeting on Pesticide Residues
LCP	large combustion plant
LRTAP	(1979 ECE Convention on) Long-Range Transboundary Air Pollution
MA	Management Authority (CITES)
MAC	maximum allowable concentrations
MAEs	maximum allowable emissions
MAFF	Ministry of Agriculture, Fisheries and Food (UK)
MC	Maritime Committee (HELCOM)
MFA	Ministry of Foreign Affairs (Norway)
MLF	Multilateral Fund (Montreal Protocol)
MOP	Meeting of the Parties
MOU	Memorandum of Understanding
MPC	maximum permissible concentrations
MPE	maximum permissible emissions
MRLs	maximum residue limits
MSC-E	Meteorological Synthesizing Centre-East (EMEP)
MSC-W	Meteorological Synthesizing Centre-West (EMEP)
NAMMCO	North Atlantic Marine Mammals Commission
NATO	North Atlantic Treaty Organization
NCP	Non-Compliance Procedure (Montreal Protocol)
NEFCO	Nordic Environment Finance Corporation
NEPP	National Environmental Policy Plan (Netherlands)
NGO	nongovernmental organization
NIB	Nordic Investment Bank
NMP	New Management Procedure (ICRW)
NO_x	nitrogen oxides
NRA	National River Authority (UK)
NSTF	North Sea Task Force
OAS	Organization of American States

OAU	Organization of African Unity
OCS	Ocean Combustion Services (UK firm)
ODS	ozone-depleting substance(s)
OECD	Organisation for Economic Co-operation and Development
OEWG	Open-Ended Working Group (Montreal Protocol)
OFWAT	Office of Water Services (UK)
OPS	Office of Project Services (United Nations Development Programme)
OSCOM	Oslo Commission (North Sea)
OSI	on-site inspection
OSPAR	Oslo and Paris Conventions (replaced by 1992 Paris Convention)
PAN	Pesticides Action Network
PARCOM	Paris Commission (North Sea)
PCA	Pollution Control Act (Norway)
PCBs	polychlorinated biphenyls
PCEs	provisionally coordinated emissions
PCTs	polychlorinated terphenyls
PHARE	Assistance for Economic Restructuring in the Countries of Central and Eastern Europe
PIC	prior informed consent
PITF	Programme Implementation Task Force (Baltic Sea regime)
PJP	Prior Justification Procedure (Oslo Commission)
PLC	Pollution Load Compilation (Baltic Sea regime)
PMUs	PHARE management units
POPs	persistent organic pollutants
PPP	polluter pays principle
QSR	Quality Status Report (North Sea regime)
RIVM	State Institute for Public Health and Environment Protection (Netherlands)
RMP	Revised Management Procedure (ICRW)
SACSA	Standing Advisory Committee for Scientific Advice
SC	Standing Committee
SciCom	Scientific Committee
SEP	electricity producing companies
SIR	system for implementation review
SO_2	sulfur dioxide
SO_x	sulfur oxides
SPCA	State Pollution Control Authority (Norway)
SPREP	South Pacific Regional Environment Programme
STC	Scientific Technological Committee (HELCOM)
SVV2	Second Transport Structure Plan

SWAP	Surface Waters Acidification Programme
TBq	terabecquerel
TC	Technological Committee
TC/EC ASMOP	TC/EC Ad Hoc Expert Group to Assess National Reports on Measures to Reduce Discharges and Emissions of Heavy Metals and Persistent Organic Pollutants
TC/EC ASNUT	TC/EC Ad Hoc Expert Group to Assess National Nutrient Programmes
TEAP	Technology and Economic Assessment Panel (Montreal Protocol)
TF	task force
TFEI	Task Force on Emission Inventories
TOC	Technical Options Committee (Montreal Protocol)
TPEs	temporary permissible emissions
TRAFFIC	Trade Records Analysis of Fauna and Flora in Commerce
TSCA	Toxic Substances Control Act
TWG	Technical Working Group
TWh	terawatt hours
UBC	Union of the Baltic Cities
UESs	uniform emission standards
UN	United Nations
UNCED	United Nations Conference on Environment and Development
UNDP	United Nations Development Programme
UN/ECE	United Nations Economic Commission for Europe
UNEP	United Nations Environment Programme
UNIDO	United Nations Industrial Development Organization
UNITAR	United Nations Institute for Training and Research
VAK	Environmental Protection Club (Latvia)
VOC	volatile organic compound
VROM	Ministry of Housing, Physical Planning and Environment (Netherlands)
WCMC	World Conservation Monitoring Centre
WG	working group
WHO	World Health Organization
WMO	World Meteorological Organization
WTMU	Wildlife Trade Monitoring Unit
WTO	World Trade Organization
WWF	World Wide Fund for Nature

1

Introduction and Overview

David G. Victor, Kal Raustiala, and Eugene B. Skolnikoff

Introduction

Many environmental problems are international—their causes or consequences cross political borders. Combatting these problems requires coordination among states. In nearly every case, states have organized their responses to transboundary environmental problems via international agreements. The pace of adopting such agreements has been swift and is increasing. More than half of the 170 multilateral environmental agreements on the United Nations Environment Programme's list have been adopted in the past 25 years.[1] In only the past decade have problems such as trade in hazardous wastes, global warming, and depletion of the stratospheric ozone layer become the subjects of international agreements.

The rapid proliferation of international environmental agreements has led most analysts to focus on their formulation, negotiation, and content. Indeed, international accords are being developed so rapidly that some analysts now raise the specters of "treaty congestion" and insufficient coordination among agreements.[2] Yet little empirical analysis of the implementation of these accords has been undertaken.[3] This book helps to fill that gap by examining how international environmental agreements are put into practice. Our concern is effectiveness: the degree to which international environmental accords lead to changes in behavior that help solve environmental problems. Our focus is implementation at both the domestic and international levels. Implementation, for our purposes, is the process by which "intent gets translated into action."[4]

Our interest in implementation—following more than a decade of research focused on negotiation—reflects a similar development in research on national environmental policy. The 1960s and 1970s were decades of rapid growth in public concern about environmental quality. Regulatory laws expanded greatly, and with them attention to their results. Three decades and hundreds of studies later, scholarship has unequivocally shown that it is not legislation alone, but rather the implementation process that determines whether a commitment has any practical influence.[5]

This study is intended as a foundation: it offers ways to think about and examine the process of implementing international environmental commitments. We employ 14 case studies to examine a wide array of implementation experiences in 8 major areas of international environmental regulation (see table 1A.1 in the appendix to this chapter).[6] In most of those areas, regulated behavior has changed markedly in the past two decades. For example, the consumption of ozone-depleting substances has declined sharply since the mid-1970s: the most potent ozone-depleting substances have been all but eliminated in nearly all industrialized countries, and declines are now evident in developing countries as well. Emissions of sulfur dioxide (SO_2), a leading cause of acid precipitation, have fallen by half or more in most European countries; emissions of nitrogen oxides (NO_x), another acidifying pollutant, have roughly stabilized. All industrialized countries have banned or severely restricted the use of certain hazardous chemicals and pesticides. Exports of these substances to developing countries have soared and are now regulated under an international scheme with active voluntary participation by manufacturers; management of these hazards in developing countries appears to have improved. The catch of whales has fallen from nearly 40,000 in the early 1970s to a few hundred per year in the late 1990s. Virtually all marine dumping of high-level radioactive waste appears to have stopped, although Russia still disposes of some nuclear waste in the sea. In the North Sea, dumping has stopped and the discharge of most major pollutants has been cut roughly in half in only a decade, though progress in cutting agricultural pollution has been somewhat slower. In this book we ask, How many of these changes in behavior are the consequence of efforts to implement international commitments?

Implementation is not the only factor that affects behavior, but we expect that it is one of the most important. International environmental agreements are typically regulatory in nature—they aim to constrain not just governments but a wide range of actors, including firms, individuals, and agencies whose behavior does not change simply because governments adopt international commitments. Thus implementation is central. Putting such accords into practice often entails a complex process of forming and adjusting domestic policy to conform with international standards, plus the added complexity of coordinating activities among many governments implementing different policies in parallel.

Because implementation is a vast subject, we have not attempted a comprehensive assessment. Indeed, efforts to synthesize a comprehensive theory of domestic policy implementation have generally failed.[7] Moreover, broad generalizations provide little useful information for theory or decision makers. Rather, these 14 studies examine the implementation process from two perspectives:

1. We look at *systems for implementation review* (SIRs): institutions through which the parties share information, compare activities, review performance, handle noncompliance, and adjust commitments. SIRs operate at the international level, but they focus on implementation activities at the national level.

2. We look at and compare *implementation at the national level.* National implementation is extraordinarily complex and, as we show, there is no single pattern by which international commitments are put into practice within countries. Thus we focus on two aspects of national implementation: (a) Because regulatory commitments affect a wide range of actors, we examine how *participation* has shaped the implementation process. We examine how patterns and modes of participation by government agencies, industry associations, environmental groups, and experts have changed over time. And we examine whether policies designed to expand participation, such as the requirement to provide access to information, have made a difference. (b) We trace how international environmental commitments are implemented in countries with *economies in transition, mainly Russia.* Some of our studies examine how the transition from central planning to a liberal, market-based society has influenced the implementation process and its practical results. These countries receive special attention in the book because of the complexity of their political and economic transitions, and because their environmental impacts are so important—Russia, for example, emits roughly as much carbon dioxide (CO_2), a key greenhouse gas, as all of Western Europe combined. The compliance of countries in transition has been a central focus of SIRs in several regimes.

This book is divided into two parts that reflect these two perspectives. Each part begins with a short description of the main issues to be examined in the case studies. The case studies appear in the part of the book for which they are most relevant, though most contribute to both perspectives. The final chapter of the book draws together major findings, especially those that cut across the two research areas; it offers implications and prescriptions for policy and speculates on broader implications for international law and politics.

In this introduction we present and illustrate the process of implementation and the critical concepts used in the book. We briefly describe the range of factors, beyond implementation, that affect behavior and determine the effectiveness of international accords. We then introduce the two perspectives on implementation—SIRs and national implementation—that organize the book as well as some of the major conclusions from the study. We close by describing our research methods.

The Implementation Process

Implementation is a loose process that is not easily defined. An influential study of domestic policy defined *implementation* as "those events and activities that occur after the issuing of authoritative public policy directives, which include the effort to administer and the substantive impacts on people and events."[8] Our approach is to apply this common-sense definition to the implementation of international environmental commitments. Implementation, for our purposes, comprises the myriad acts of governments, such as promulgating regulations and new laws. But it also includes the activities of non-state actors—such as firms, scientists, consumer and environmental pressure groups, and trade associations—whose activities are stimulated and redirected by an international agreement. Implementation also includes the activities of international institutions, such as monitoring and assisting national governments as they put international commitments into practice.

The ultimate aim of environmental agreements is to influence the behavior of those who cause or can ameliorate the problem at hand. *Targets* are those actors whose behavior an accord ultimately aims to change, including firms emitting wastewater, ships dumping radioactive materials, individuals driving their cars, or industries designing new and cleaner technology. Targets are typically organized by sector and through industry associations, and thus we focus on *target groups*.

Changes in target behavior are what matter in the end, but international commitments usually must go through several stages or levels before they influence the target group.[9] International decisions are normally binding only for states.[10] In turn, states are typically expected to put into place at the national level programs or legislation that transmit international commitments

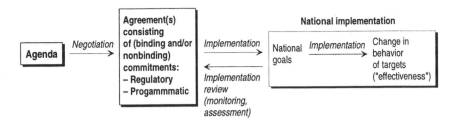

Figure 1.1
Schematic view of the formation and implementation of international environmental agreements

into action domestically. National administration, review, enforcement, and sometimes litigation lead to actual changes in the behavior of polluters, fishers, farmers, and other targets. One reason implementation of international environmental commitments is so complex is that the paths to the targets' doors frequently weave through many intermediate actors and institutions. Figure 1.1 provides a schematic view of international environmental governance, from the agenda to negotiation to successive stages of implementation.

Implementation can at times be swift and direct. Following a 1972 ban on marine dumping of high-level radioactive waste, most governments were able to halt the offensive activities immediately, primarily because only a few organizations were engaged in the dumping and most were militaries under direct government control. Similarly, the whaling industry is small and easy to regulate; governments have generally found it administratively easy to implement whaling restrictions.

In other cases, implementation is not required at all. Sweden has persistently pushed for tougher standards on Baltic Sea pollution, but domestic Swedish standards for water quality have consistently exceeded many standards adopted as part of the Baltic Sea accords. As is often true for leaders in international environmental regulation, the adoption of these standards has in practice required little additional action by Sweden.

More typically, however, implementation of international environmental commitments is a long process that follows varied paths in different countries. The outcome is often uncertain. In 1988, 25 European nations agreed to freeze their emissions of NO_x, a major cause of acid precipitation. Twelve leaders, including the Netherlands and Norway, also signed an ambitious nonbinding

Declaration to cut NO_x by 30 percent. The Netherlands sought to meet international commitments by adopting new technical standards for automobiles, its largest source of NO_x. In Norway, much of the effort has been directed at the burgeoning shipping industry, a major NO_x source. In neither case is it clear exactly what impact these policies will have on emissions. At the outset of the NO_x negotiations, Norway was unaware that emissions from ships were so high as to require regulatory priority.

Our case studies trace other long, often unplanned paths of implementation. In many instances the implementation process appears never-ending. Commitments are adopted; efforts are made to implement them; the commitments are adjusted. Problems are managed rather than eliminated—implementation is part of a perpetual cycle of policy that is driven by new information, experience, and political pressures.

Central Concepts

Our ultimate concern is *effectiveness*. We define effect as the extent to which the accord causes changes in the behavior of targets that further the goals of the accord. We do not equate an accord's effectiveness with its ability to eliminate the environmental threat at hand.[11] For example, the accords to limit the pollution that causes acid precipitation in Europe have had an influence on the behavior of polluters. As a consequence, emissions of some pollutants are lower than they would be without the accords. Nonetheless, the accumulation of acid in European ecosystems continues and environmental impacts compound, albeit at a slower pace than without the accords. We focus on behavioral change because that is the means by which international commitments achieve environmental objectives. However, we are mindful of the different types of behavioral change that contribute to the ultimate environmental objectives of the accord.[12] In some cases, the link between behavioral change and environmental objectives is partial or indirect. For example, regulating trade in toxic pesticides only indirectly contributes to the objectives of limiting the exposure of people and ecosystems to pesticide hazards. We are also mindful that some accords contain conflicting goals—participants in the whaling regime disagree whether the objective is to manage a profitable whaling industry or to stop whaling altogether. Table 1A.1 in the appendix to this chapter summarizes the main goals of the accords and commitments analyzed in this book.

We also do not assess effectiveness by whether behavior conforms with the letter of an international commitment, which is the traditional definition of *compliance*.[13] International environmental law is filled with examples of agreements that have had high compliance but limited influence on behavior. For much of its history the International Whaling Commission (IWC) set catch quotas at very high levels. Until the 1960s the Commission had little effect on the number and types of whales caught, but compliance remained nearly perfect throughout the period.[14] Our studies suggest that there may even be an inverse relationship between effectiveness and compliance with some types of standards. The nonbinding standards in the North Sea regime, for example, have not enjoyed perfect compliance, but as Chapter 8 shows, they have been more effective than earlier binding standards where formal compliance was much higher. All else being equal, more compliance is preferable to less compliance.[15] But it is important to stress that compliance is an artifact of the standard embodied in a commitment. Standards can be too weak, too strong, inefficient, or completely ill conceived. In short, although attention to compliance can be fruitful, compliance must be understood and evaluated in context. Several of our case studies highlight the importance of noncompliance—and the procedures that exist to address it—as a vehicle by which effectiveness is enhanced. Compliance is not an end in itself but rather a means to achieve effectiveness, which is in turn a means to manage environmental stresses.

In summary, we go beyond merely analyzing the output of laws and regulations but stop short of tracing the impact of particular commitments on the natural environment. We look for evidence of effectiveness—actual behavioral change by target groups that is caused by and that furthers the goals of the accord.[16] Our studies observe behavioral changes and then examine—through careful historical research—whether (and how) such behavior is the result of international commitments. Thus, when we assess effectiveness we isolate only those changes that are the result of the commitment.[17]

Finally, this is a study of the effectiveness of international environmental *commitments*—particular obligations to enact programs, change behavior, and conform to standards. We refer broadly to *programmatic* and *regulatory* commitments. Our focus is on regulation—the commitments that require changes in the behavior that leads to environmental problems. However, we show that programmatic activities are often a crucial part of the total effort to identify and address international environmental problems. For example, programs to monitor and model environmental processes often help to improve the quality of data on emissions and implementation and make it easier to set regulatory priorities.

Most commitments are packaged with other commitments, institutions, and expectations; thus regulatory and programmatic commitments must be studied in this larger context. Political scientists have employed the useful concept of a *regime*.[18] A regime exists when widely accepted principles and norms govern behavior. International regimes almost always have at their core an accord (also known as an agreement) that establishes specific rules, commitments, and decision-making procedures to aid in the process of governance. Such accords form the core of international law.[19] We look at two main forms of international accords: *treaties*, which are binding instruments under international law; and *nonbinding instruments*. The practical significance of a commitment's being "binding" under international law is a hotly debated topic. But objectively there is a qualitative difference in the ways states recognize and negotiate binding and nonbinding instruments. Compared with nonbinding instruments, treaties undergo much more extensive review before adoption, leading to delays and perhaps to their being taken more seriously. Nonbinding instruments are more flexible and less cumbersome than binding instruments, but may be less effective. Our studies examine both forms; their relative influence is considered again in the final chapter, where we suggest that regimes may be most effective when they combine the two types of legal instruments.

Other Factors that Influence Behavior

This book is not intended as a comprehensive study of the factors that influence the behavior of target groups. Nor is it a comprehensive account of how international agreements influence behavior—that is, their effectiveness. Rather, we focus on one critical determinant, implementation of international agreements. It is important, however, to be aware of other factors that influence behavior and the effectiveness of agreements. Failure to do so could lead the analyst to conclude that implementation was important when in reality other factors caused the observed change in behavior. Failure to be aware of other factors could also easily lead to conclusions about ways to improve the implementation and effectiveness of international commitments that are not valid under some conditions. In other words, when there are many factors at work, a study that focuses on some variables (related to implementation) must be aware of other variables that are omitted from the model and/or that interact with the particular variables under scrutiny.

Our account of such other factors will touch on only some of those that have been identified as important by other scholars. Exactly which factors are most important, and under what conditions, remains controversial because the role of international law itself is controversial. Law plays a central role in regulating social behavior, but even in domestic settings, where legal institutions are well established and enforcement powers are readily available, there is debate about what leads to effective laws. Even less is understood about the influence of international law. The independent influence of international law is often weak—some would argue nonexistent. Thus it is especially important to be aware of other influences that affect behavior within international society and thus might influence the effectiveness of law embodied in international agreements.[20]

The *nature of the problem* at hand is one factor that influences the effectiveness of international agreements. Some problems are easier to address than others, and thus some international agreements will be easier to implement than others. Three general aspects of problems are significant: the ratio of costs to benefits, the distribution of those costs and benefits, and "strategic" considerations such as international economic competitiveness.[21] Some problems are marked by clear and significant benefits of change, which can be effected at low costs. For instance, for many substances the halt to dumping in the North and Baltic Seas led to significant environmental benefits at a low cost because inexpensive disposal alternatives were available. Other problems exhibit a different pattern: costs are high and target groups are well aware of what they might be compelled to pay; benefits may be tenuous and diffuse. Many efforts to regulate environmental problems begin in this way—environmental benefits are unclear and at least some of the polluters are easily identified and face concentrated costs of regulatory action. Those polluters often organize themselves and oppose stringent policies. Such opposition can often be blunted by dispersing costs to less organized and less politically powerful actors. For instance, Norway partially subsidized projects to control sulfur at large power plants, thus shifting some costs from the plant owners, who otherwise might have blocked the sulfur policy, to a more diffuse group, the taxpayers.[22]

Solutions to environmental problems can affect issues in other areas, such as competitiveness, and as a result deter unilateral action and encourage governments to seek to act in concert. A state may be reluctant to implement policies to address an environmental problem unless it is confident that its economic competitors will do the same.[23] The first agreement to control European sulfur emissions (the 1985 Sulphur Protocol) illustrated few such strategic concerns because the commitments had few economic consequences; the NO_x Protocol (1988) entailed higher costs for countries, and thus strategic considerations were more important. The inclusion of a noncompliance procedure in the second (1994) Sulphur Protocol partially reflects that such strategic considerations, including fear of "free riders," have risen even further as regulatory commitments have become more stringent. When numerous states are involved, such interdependencies may make it especially difficult to reach agreements that require costly action.

Configurations of power may shape effectiveness: powerful states may be able to use threats or inducements to ensure that favored agreements are implemented. The USA, for instance, has engaged in extensive "enforcement" of many international environmental commitments, using its market power and the threat of sanctions to alter the behavior of other states.[24] US threats of sanctions have reduced the number of whales caught by Norway and stopped whaling by Iceland, though the exact influence of US sanctions is contested. (The nongovernmental organization [NGO] Greenpeace has played a similar role as a unilateral enforcer—it leveraged its power through consumer boycotts of Icelandic and Norwegian products in other markets, notably in Germany and the USA; in turn, vulnerable exporters in Iceland and Norway became more opposed to their countries' whaling programs.)[25] Conversely, powerful states rarely face sanctions themselves. This dynamic explains why some consider international law and institutions a facade and a tool of the strong. Some analysts argue that international agreements reflect the interests of the powerful and have no independent effect; when underlying power structures or interests change, regimes may collapse or change to reflect the new configuration of power. Compliance is either meaningless (for the strong) or coerced (for the weak).[26] In some cases, the existence of very powerful states may preclude

the need for elaborate international agreements altogether; the "theory of hegemonic stability," for example, is based on the notion that leading states can
provide for important collective goods in the international system either by
themselves or through international institutions (e.g., the United Nations, the
North Atlantic Treaty Organization, and the Organisation for Economic Cooperation and Development).[27] An international accord backed by a powerful
state may appear to be effective when, in fact, its influence is at best possible
only with the hegemon in the shadows.

Extensive research has shown the many ways that international *institutions*
can lead to more effective international cooperation. Institutions are established
principles and processes for making decisions; they can yield decisions that
affect behavior directly, and they can shape expectations, which also influence
behavior. Under this definition, institutions are not simply organizations but
include established norms and mechanisms for cooperation; thus some scholars
equate institutions with regimes. Institutions are often formalized into international organizations, agreements, and commitments; this book attempts to
isolate the influence of those formal commitments on behavior, but the larger
institutional context also influences behavior directly and in tandem with international commitments. For example, growing concern about the environment
has spawned a wide array of international negotiating procedures; in addition,
virtually every international agreement, itself, includes the commitment to meet
periodically and review the adequacy of existing regulatory efforts. Together,
perpetual reassessments and growing norms to "protect the environment" have
probably increased the extent to which international commitments are adopted,
strengthened, and implemented.

Institutions reduce the costs of negotiating commitments and coordinating
behavior, they help elicit useful information, and they help induce reciprocal
behavior through repeated interactions, which may make parties to agreements
more willing to honor their commitments.[28] By making nations and groups
more aware of their "interests," institutions can facilitate cooperation (or undermine it).[29] Such general influences of institutions on behavior and international
cooperation operate in tandem with the particular regulatory and programmatic
commitments at work in a particular area. Our study examines the influence of
a particular type of international institution—SIRs—but institutions can have
many other forms and influences.

More specifically, existing national and international *organizations*, which are physical entities, also influence behavior and the effectiveness of international commitments.[30] Organizations typically manage the programmatic activities, help oversee and implement the commitments, and organize the meetings where decisions are made. For example, expertise and local contacts built up by the United Nations Food and Agriculture Organization (FAO) over the decades contributed to the success of training programs that have helped officials in developing countries implement restrictions on trade in hazardous chemicals and pesticides (Chapter 6).

The *nature of commitments* may have a strong bearing on effectiveness as well. Previous studies have argued that how an international agreement is constructed—the exact commitment, its scope, clarity, application, and so forth—can be critical for its success.[31] In the international regime for oil pollution resulting from normal ship operations, for example, rules on allowable discharges of oil failed to influence the tanker captains, whose behavior could not be easily monitored on the high seas. Far more effective were rules requiring tanker owners and manufacturers to install particular equipment to limit oily discharges.[32] The equipment rules succeeded by ensuring that required changes were easy to verify and difficult to reverse, and needed to take place only once.[33] Thus the way rules are written and the activities they address can enhance or diminish the effectiveness of commitments.

Commitments and accords can also be effective in changing behavior if they create *linkages with other issues and objectives*. In the 1970s and 1980s the USSR and Western powers used environmental (and human rights) cooperation as a means to interact peacefully during the Cold War.[34] Arguably the main reason that accords adopted to regulate transboundary air pollution had any influence on Soviet behavior was that compliance with these accords was linked with the broader foreign policy climate of East-West relations. Linkages can also occur domestically. Most policies to limit land-based pollution flowing into the Baltic and North Seas also help to reduce local water pollution, which has made it easier to gain local support for costly policy action. Often regimes may appear effective because other domestic policies—aimed, for example, at deregulation, energy efficiency, or local health concerns—dovetail with the requirements of international commitments. Most European countries cut emissions of sulfur precipitously in the 1980s; the existence of international sulfur commitments provided additional impetus for some countries to control sulfur, but most of the reduction can be traced to policies designed to limit local pollution, where sulfur was also a major hazard. Because few international environmental problems are completely isolated from the rest of the economy and society, linkages are commonplace. They offer opportunities for political entrepreneurs but hazards for researchers, because it is often difficult to assess whether and how international commitments have influenced behavior.

Exogenous factors can have a strong impact on behavior, though they are not caused by international environmental institutions. As the chapters on Russia demonstrate, much of the reduction in pollution that has taken place in that country is due to economic collapse, not to the implementation of international regulatory commitments. Economic collapse or recession can result in compliance with commitments, but the commitments are not therefore effective: the correlation between commitments and pollution abatement is spurious, an artifact of the economic situation rather than a sign of efforts to implement commitments.

Other exogenous factors can have an impact as well—for example, individual leaders and political entrepreneurs who play major roles in regime formation and implementation,[35] and strong "focusing events" like the discovery of the Antarctic ozone hole or the extensive and mysterious seal deaths in the North Sea.[36]

Often the most important factor in determining whether international regimes can be effective is *public concern.* Public concern can contribute to the implementation and effectiveness of international agreements. For example, international environmental accords may provide normative benchmarks for good and bad behavior, which domestic groups can then use to assess and criticize the behavior of their own governments or that of other governments. When public concern is high, such domestic scrutiny can yield public pressure to alter behavior and multiply the influence of international agreements. Thus international environmental accords may induce behavioral change through a sort of regulatory competition at the domestic level. Environmental leaders who have already adopted stringent standards can use institutions to diffuse those standards to other countries, thus expanding the scope of environmental protection and leveling out the economic impact. These effects help explain the demand for institutions as well as their pervasiveness in international affairs.[37] Public concern is also a function of the many factors identified above. International institutions can act as focal points for domestic political pressures, as demonstrated in the whaling regime (Chapter 10). Institutions can also provide information on environmental hazards, which in turn helps fan public concern about declining environmental quality.[38] As Chapter 8 shows, increased public concern following the seal deaths in the North Sea made it easier for governments to implement the costly regulatory commitments that were needed to limit pollution. Some public concern about the environment is independent of international institutions—environmental concerns are in endless competition with other public concerns, often rising and falling in cycles.[39]

In short, many factors influence the implementation and effectiveness of international environmental commitments. This makes research such as ours—which aims at tracing cause and effect—particularly difficult. At the end of this chapter we present the methods employed in the case studies to examine whether and how international commitments are implemented and influence behavior, and to isolate implementation from other factors at work.

Because these many factors interact in complex ways, we often cannot make definitive claims as to which factor is decisive in a particular case. However, we expect the process of implementation to be a central factor determining the effectiveness and operation of international environmental accords. These accords often demand extensive regulatory actions that impinge upon diffuse and often private actors, including firms, NGOs, local governments and agencies, and individuals. The process of elaborating, transmitting, monitoring, adjudicating, and enforcing decisions—in other words, implementation—is fundamental to the purpose and process of regulatory law. Not all agreements make such demands—military alliances, for example, are largely aimed at governmental actions, and most arms control agreements are aimed at government weapons stocks. Implementation of most decisions made in the early rounds of the General Agreement on Tariffs and Trade (GATT) was relatively simple: customs officers merely had to be instructed to lower the duties assessed on incoming goods. Although implementing such accords is by no means automatic, in comparison the process of implementation associated with most environmental accords is much more complex. For example, putting the NO_x agreement into practice requires an extensive array of rules and changes that impact many societal actors, down to the level of individual automobile owners. This aspect of environmental accords—the involvement of many private actors in the process of implementation—is the reason participation is a major theme that runs through the case studies.

Increasingly, in fact, implementation is becoming central to the success of many types of agreements, not just those concerning environmental protection. The newest GATT rules require extensive domestic actions, and recent arms control accords, such as the international agreement to regulate chemical weapons, require detailed actions by disparate actors that must be monitored and assessed. New international narcotics control treaties require extensive domestic implementation because they regulate chemical precursors and production equipment, which are mainly in the hands of private actors. Thus the concerns that motivate this study and the conclusions we draw are not limited to the realm of environmental cooperation. Implementation is likely to become an ever more important part of all international cooperation.

Two Perspectives on Implementation

Many factors influence the effectiveness of international environmental accords, but implementation is the central process that turns commitments into action. Despite its importance, implementation is remarkably understudied. No tractable and coherent study can assess in detail the full range of factors that influence outcomes. Thus we investigate implementation from two perspectives: (1) how governments and non-state actors use international institutions and procedures to monitor and review implementation and to handle problems of poor implementation; and (2) how international commitments are translated into action—or are implemented—at the national level. Within each of these two perspectives, which define the two parts of this book, our case studies focus on specific propositions concerning how implementation activities contribute to the effectiveness of international commitments. Below we give an overview of the two perspectives, as well as some major findings. (The short texts that introduce each part of the book provide additional detail and references.)

These perspectives and propositions are not the only ones worthy of investigation, but they meet four important criteria:

- They reflect a central attribute of the implementation process.
- We expect that they help to explain which commitments are most effective—the conclusion to this book reviews these expectations as well as our findings.
- They are sufficiently narrow to allow case studies that focus on specific issues that are amenable to change through policy.
- They have not been adequately explored by existing research.

The case studies appear in the part of the book for which they are most relevant, although both perspectives on implementation—international review and national implementation—are present in most of the case studies. The analysis in this book is structured differently from that in most other books in the field, which present cases according to media (atmosphere, oceans, living resources, etc.) and geography (global, regional). Our approach helps to clarify general conclusions and allows more focused comparisons across cases. However, this approach is not so rigorous that it excludes other issues. Thus the case studies stand on their own, in addition to their contributions to the book's analytical goals.

Implementation Review

The first perspective concerns the operation of specific institutional structures at the international level, what we term *systems for implementation review*. SIRs comprise rules and procedures by which the parties to international agreements (as well as interest groups, administrative bodies, and the like) exchange data, share information on implementation, monitor activities, assess the adequacy of existing commitments, and handle problems of poor implementation. We treat these many functions together under the single rubric "SIRs" because our preliminary research suggested that although such functions are typically performed by many different actors and organizations, in practice they constitute a single system.[40]

We look at the design and operation of SIRs, how they influence the implementation of commitments at the national level, and finally, how they influence effectiveness. We investigate whether the existence of an SIR improves the effectiveness of an agreement by making parties more accountable for the implementation of their commitments, by helping to direct assistance that facilitates implementation, by penalizing parties that do not implement international commitments, and by providing information and assessments that make it easier to adjust agreements over time. The potential importance of SIRs to the effectiveness of agreements prompts us to examine them in detail. Moreover, our research on SIRs contributes to the rapidly growing literature in the social sciences termed the "new institutionalism," which has emphasized how institutional structures and designs can play central roles in shaping and structuring complex social processes.[41] SIRs represent a salient institutional design feature that directly engages implementation and its assessment.

We examine long-term trends in the existence and use of formally established SIRs. Chapter 2 documents how SIRs have evolved in that area of international environmental law with the longest history: the many agreements that deal with fauna and flora. Over time, SIRs have become more prevalent in those agreements; moreover, their particular form has evolved in a way likely to lead to greater influence and effectiveness. Today, the "standard" international agreement on fauna and flora includes regular reporting by parties, reviews of these reports, and often on-site inspections; many agreements also include procedures that allow for some enforcement of international commitments. Still, there is no single pattern by which SIRs develop; in some cases the elements of an SIR are "present at the creation," whereas in others—such as in the Ramsar Convention on wetlands protection—procedures are developed later, after the accord is in operation and in response to demand for the function of implementation review.

The studies also examine how SIRs operate in three regimes: stratospheric ozone depletion (Chapters 3 and 4), protection of the Baltic Sea environment (Chapter 5), and trade in hazardous chemicals and pesticides (Chapter 6). In each, we show that the functions of the SIR are performed by a wide array of institutions, only some of which are formally dedicated to such tasks. By looking only at activity within the formal, dedicated procedures, one could derive the erroneous conclusion that little implementation review occurs in a particular regime and that the review that does occur has only a minor influence on behavior. Viewing the functions of implementation review as a system is crucial to an accurate assessment of how such functions contribute to the implementation and effectiveness of an international agreement.

Our studies suggest that these decentralized systems work well because they distribute tasks according to capacity; significant coordination problems caused by decentralization have not emerged. In the Montreal Protocol on Substances that Deplete the Ozone Layer, for example, most funding to address problems of poor implementation comes from the Protocol's Multilateral Fund, but the financing necessary for Russia and several other states to comply with the Protocol flows from the Global Environment Facility (GEF), a separate entity. In practice the GEF has made its funding contingent upon the prior approval of the parties to the Protocol. When noncompliance by Belarus, Russia, and Ukraine became apparent, the GEF required those countries to have implementation plans approved via the Protocol's Non-Compliance Procedure before funds were disbursed. The GEF's conditionality has, in turn, induced Russia to supply data after years of refusal. These data have made it easier to assess Russia's compliance, to track emerging problems such as illegal trade in ozone-depleting substances, and to assess the overall effectiveness of the Montreal Protocol. In essence, the GEF acted as a critical part of the SIR, ensuring that the system operated well. The Montreal Protocol's SIR includes the GEF, although the Protocol's legal commitments do not formally empower the GEF.

These studies also explore how SIRs contribute to the adjustment of commitments, thus allowing international cooperation to be dynamic and responsive to new information. Of particular interest is how SIRs contribute to the effectiveness of nonbinding agreements. Nonbinding instruments are often more flexible and more rapidly revised than treaties or other binding instruments; thus the effectiveness of a nonbinding instrument should be especially enhanced by the existence of an SIR. Chapter 6 shows how the nonbinding system of prior informed consent (PIC) for trade in hazardous chemicals and pesticides was easily adjusted as the major firms, governments, and environmental NGOs identified and solved many implementation problems. All these actors served certain functions within the SIR, though the PIC system did not contain a formal procedure for reviewing implementation and assessing the adequacy of commitments. Similarly, extensive implementation review coupled with flexible nonbinding agreements in the North and Baltic Sea regimes allowed relatively rapid assessment and adjustment of regulatory commitments (see Chapters 5, 8, and 14). A common fear is that nonbinding commitments will be taken less seriously than legally binding accords; SIRs are one means of enhancing transparency and accountability and thus reducing the tendency for parties to ignore implementation of their nonbinding commitments.

In all these studies on SIRs we give special attention to how data are gathered and assessed. Many observers have noted that few environmental agreements have overcome the chronic problem of poor data reporting.[42] Yet data are the backbone of SIRs; when data are absent the SIR is unable to function. Chapter 7 examines the system for reporting and using data on air pollution in Europe, which has developed over two decades in connection with the Long-Range Transboundary Air Pollution (LRTAP) agreements and related activities by the European Community. The study shows that even in this "best case," the SIR rarely has the data it needs to function well as a compliance and verification system. Although the SIR falls short of the ideal, the study shows that international institutions can substantially enhance data quality and comparability. The requirement to report and compare data on a regular basis, along with active efforts to model the transport and impacts of air pollution, led to steady improvements in the quality and quantity of data reported by nations. (The Baltic Sea regime [Chapter 5] illustrates the same synergy of regular reporting, review, and environmental modeling.) An interesting finding from the European air pollution regime is that the need to harmonize data collection and analysis systems can pose serious problems, even for developed states that are typically thought to have high capacity. In practice, those states have the most elaborate and entrenched systems, which therefore may be the hardest to change.

The analysis of SIRs allows the investigation of many other propositions about how institutions such as SIRs contribute to more effective international environmental commitments. For example, our cases offer a mixed message for the debate over whether "managerial" or "enforcement" approaches to controlling compliance are better.[43] We find that SIRs appear to operate primarily by "managing" implementation problems—they provide incentives such as funding for capacity building that help states overcome implementation problems. The management approach is often effective, especially when the obstacle to implementation is low domestic administrative capacity and resources. But "enforcement" of commitments with penalties such as withdrawal of funding or other treaty benefits, while rare, can be highly influential, especially when management efforts have failed, as in the case of Russia's noncompliance with the Montreal Protocol.

Throughout this book we stress that our focus is on the factors that influence *implementation.* Conformity with international commitments—compliance—is often not the same. Our assessment of SIRs underscores why compliance is nonetheless important. Both the "management" and "enforcement" approaches are, in practice, more prevalent and effective when poor implementation leads to a case of noncompliance. It is difficult to mobilize the resources and diplomatic pressure needed for "management" unless a situation of noncompliance exists or is imminent. Noncompliance acts as a trigger for management efforts. "Enforcement" is especially difficult in the international system and thus is unlikely unless a party persistently fails to comply.

Our studies thus allow an assessment of which legal and organizational forms are most effective. Most debate by theorists and decision makers over how international commitments are monitored, managed, and enforced has focused on formal, centralized procedures, such as the Non-Compliance Procedure of the Montreal Protocol. We find that monitoring, reviewing implementation, and handling implementation problems are also conducted through decentralized and informal processes. In the Baltic Sea case explored in Chapter 3 and the PIC case in Chapter 6, implementation review has been almost entirely informal. One lesson for policy is that what is most important is that implementation review occurs; extensive formalization is less important and can sometimes be damaging.

In short, SIRs are a crucial aspect of practical and effective international environmental governance. Review, assessment, and "verification" have been studied extensively in other areas, notably arms control, but so far have received little attention in environmental agreements.[44] Yet, as these case studies show, environmental agreements illustrate extensive, and increasing, efforts to monitor and review performance.

National Implementation

Studies in the second part of the book focus mainly on domestic implementation processes. They examine implementation of international commitments within industrialized, democratic, high-income countries (Chapters 8 to 10) and within industrialized countries (mainly Russia) undergoing the transition to a liberal market-based society (Chapters 11 to 15). We do not focus on implementation in developing countries, although studies on the Montreal Protocol (Chapters 3 and 4) and on trade in hazardous chemicals and pesticides (Chapter 6) address some issues of importance to developing countries, such as financial transfers and other activities to build the administrative capacity needed to comply with commitments to report data and regulate trade. Other projects have examined implementation in developing countries in more detail.[45] Our focus on industrialized countries reflects that they are often the largest polluters and are expected to make the most extensive (and costliest) changes in their behavior.

These two issues—participation and transition—are not the only ones that influence national implementation in these countries. Below we explain why focusing on these two issues is important for theory and policy, and we outline the propositions related to each issue that are investigated in the case studies.

Participation. The studies on implementation in the West give special attention to whether and how patterns of participation influence the making and implementation of international environmental commitments. A striking feature of international environmental politics in the past two decades is the sharp rise in participation, notably by NGOs such as environmental groups and industry associations. Recent declarations and agreements invoke the need for ever wider and more intensive participation.[46] All new major international environmental agreements include rules of access that allow NGOs to participate, often as observers but in practice allowing participation in other ways beyond passive observation. Three decades ago, even such simple provisions were often quite controversial.[47] At the national level participation has also expanded. Stakeholders—individuals or groups with a special interest in a particular problem or solution—regularly participate in making, implementing, and enforcing policies, including policies that implement international commitments. They often have expanded rights of access to the legal system and to public information, which allows them to participate with potentially greater influence than in the past. Some theorists argue that expanded stakeholder participation marks the emergence of a global civil society—a form of international democracy—characterized by broad participation and deliberation among all social groups.[48] In short, there is good reason to believe that patterns of participation are a major part of the implementation process, and hence could be an important determinant of effectiveness.

We investigate two broad topics: how participation influences outcomes, and the factors that affect participation itself. Participation is thus examined both as an independent variable—a factor that explains important policy decisions and behavior—and as a dependent variable—something that depends on other factors.

First, we examine whether and how the participation of different actors influences policy decisions and behavior. Of special interest is how participation by target groups affects the quality of decisions and the process and extent of implementation. Scholars and practitioners have long hypothesized that the involvement of target groups can lead to decisions that are based on better information about what can be implemented.[49] That hypothesis led the

World Bank in the 1970s (and today other multilateral lending institutions) to involve the targets of aid projects more extensively in the process of project design.[50] Similarly, many national governments now ensure that target groups have access to and are consulted during the process of formulating policies.[51] The intended results are higher-quality policies, the development of a target group "stake" in the process and its outcome, and more democratic decision making. In short, while some suggest that efforts to include industrial groups and regulated parties will lead to capture and a weakening of commitments, an increasingly influential view declares that decisions made through participatory processes are likely to be more democratic, stable, and effective.

Many of the chapters that address the participation theme examine this debate over the efficacy of expanding participation during the formation and implementation of international environmental commitments. Some of the cases suggest that the involvement of stakeholders, notably target groups, leads to better decisions that are implemented more thoroughly. Indeed, the participation of target groups is not a threat, but rather leads to more realistic and ultimately more effective accords. In the North Sea accords, implementation problems have been notably severe; in Chapter 8, these problems are traced in large part to the failure to involve stakeholders in the agriculture sector more extensively in the formulation of North Sea goals and policies. The experience with Soviet implementation of the London Convention on dumping (Chapter 11) confirms that target group participation can be helpful, because target groups provide vital information, but only when balanced by participation of other interests. Similarly, in the Montreal Protocol, target groups have provided information that has improved implementation of the "essential uses" exemption (Chapter 3). Scientists and other experts have played similar roles in providing sober assessments of policy needs and options. But, as often noted, expertise can be politicized or marginalized (or both).[52]

These observations raise as many questions as they answer. For example, does expanded participation frequently lead to gridlock as an ever-expanding array of actors vie for influence? The studies provide little evidence of this. Does participation of target groups inevitably dilute commitments and perhaps lead to "regulatory capture"—regulatory control in the hands of the regulated? Our research shows that participation by target groups often weakens commitments and policies, but whether an accord actually influences target group behavior also depends on whether countervailing pressures exist. In the case of NO_x control, for instance, extensive stakeholder participation in Norway led to preferences for a scaled-back but realistic commitment that is influencing the behavior of targets in Norway. In contrast, extensive consultation but limited enforcement in the Netherlands led to a more ambitious commitment that remains only a distant goal. Often the active participation of environmental groups balances target group interests and reduces regulatory capture. Ultimately what matters most is not merely the level of participation but also the balance of participating interests.

A *second* topic we examine is the factors that shape participation: rules of access, actor interests, and ability of actors to participate. Most policy attention has focused on rules of access. As noted above, rules of access have expanded considerably in recent years, as has participation, especially for non-state actors. Open access rules are a necessary condition for formal participation. However, our studies suggest that policies to open access rules have as much followed as facilitated the rising influence of non-state actors.

More important in determining patterns of participation are actor interest and actor ability. ENGOs that are most active and influential during the implementation process are often specialized, having worked continuously and built expertise over long periods of time. High participation by target groups frequently reflects these groups' strong interest in the outcomes. This is especially evident in nonbinding agreements, which are frequently marked by high levels of target group participation and extensive efforts to make the agreements effective lest binding and less flexible regulations ensue. In the PIC system for trade in chemicals and pesticides, for example, industry worked hard to implement the voluntary international commitments because it feared that failure would lead to less flexible and more costly binding regulations. Similar patterns are also evident in the use of voluntary instruments at the national level.[53]

On balance, we find that participation during the negotiation of international commitments and the making of national implementing policy is high, but it often has proved difficult to expand participation during the implementation phase. Policymakers have opened rules of access. However, our studies suggest that, especially for public interest groups, a more serious barrier to participation during the implementation process is the difficulty of obtaining useful information and providing timely analysis. Expanding access to information has helped in some cases; but, as we show, often the quality and utility of information is initially low. SIRs, which are discussed in the first part of the book, also increase the availability of useful information. Those groups with the most influence during the implementation process are specialized and often have expert knowledge from working continuously on the topic for long periods of time. Although target groups often find it strongly in their interest to develop such implementation expertise, the cost-benefit calculation of public interest groups often is less favorable.

Societies in Transition.   Chapters 11 to 15 explore how the process of economic and social transformation within formerly centrally planned countries influences the ways that these countries, Russia in particular, implement international environmental commitments. The studies trace how the devolution of power has affected the ability to control targets, which is necessary to implement international commitments. They also evaluate how new structures for property rights and regulation influence the incentives of individual enterprises, especially those newly exposed to market forces. As Chapter 14 on implementation of Baltic Sea commitments in the former Soviet Union shows, as a result of privatization, massive state enterprises have split into many smaller firms, which has increased the number of stakeholders and swamped the new and weak regulatory authorities in the St. Petersburg area in Russia. The former system of centralized power in fact facilitated implementation by limiting discretion and shortening chains of delegation from Moscow to the regional, oblast, and local levels. Destruction of the system of totalitarian control and the difficulties in creating a viable new system have severely impeded implementation.[54]

In general, the former Soviet government viewed environmental cooperation as a useful means of maintaining good relations with the West. The centralized Soviet structure meant that the state could act as single, strategic unit in the negotiation and implementation of international accords. The USSR achieved formal compliance with LRTAP's 1985 Sulphur Protocol, for instance, by shutting down polluters in the western part of the country but not in the interior. In effect, compliance with the Protocol shifted pollution from western areas to the Soviet interior and the Arctic. The situation today is far more complicated, and as a result, implementation is often quite incomplete and plagued with administrative problems.

The form of privatization that has taken place in Russia has left the managers of enterprises with de facto control. In most cases, the managers (and workers) have maximized the short-term flow of revenue rather than the long-term accumulation of capital. Yet pollution control often requires precisely the opposite approach—capital investments in cleaner technologies with long payback periods as well as continued investment to maintain existing pollution control equipment. The failure to invest today will have consequences for plant infrastructure that will last long after the period of transition ends. A system of pollution charges has been in place in Russia since 1992, but in practice charges have not kept pace with the high rates of inflation engendered by economic restructuring. Moreover, officials often waive charges to avert bankruptcy or layoffs. In some cases, such as with Norilsk Nickel, the massive Russian nickel-smelting complex on the Kola Peninsula, the firm itself wields enormous power in the surrounding region and regulatory authorities are loath to take any actions that might reduce its output or local employment. The result of all these factors is limited—often nonexistent—implementation.

The studies also explore the role of financial and technology transfers in improving the incentives for environmental protection, the relative roles of international financing versus domestic resources, and the ways in which international financial packages are assembled and implemented. Such transfers are often essential if downwind and downstream countries want polluters to change their behavior and implement international commitments. Our study of the attempt to fund the reduction of pollution from Norilsk Nickel illustrates some of the difficulties associated with West-East financial transfers. This extreme case suggests sobering lessons for related funding schemes, such as current proposals to jointly implement international commitments to slow global warming or to limit acid rain. While in theory "joint implementation" can yield significant efficiency gains, in practice "implementing" joint implementation can be highly complicated under conditions of transition, such as unstable property rights and poor enforcement of contracts. The Norilsk Nickel case documents a decade-long course of false starts and intense bargaining, with little actual change even today. In contrast, in Poland financial transfer arrangements have worked better, as Chapter 15 describes. In all the cases of West-East financial transfers analyzed in this book, a substantial part (typically more than half) of the total cost of implementation is supplied by domestic sources. Financial transfers can aid implementation of international environmental commitments but domestic interests, resources, and activities are dominant.

Our focus is mainly on Russia. Although the Russian experience may offer few generalizable conclusions, Russia is a crucial part of most international environmental agreements. Russian noncompliance with the London Convention on dumping (Chapter 11) and the Montreal Protocol (Chapter 4), for example, represent extremely serious failures to implement international commitments. Russia's sheer size and central role in international politics make it a major contributor to many international environmental problems and a major player in any cooperative solution. Hence dramatic changes in the structure of the Russian economy and society are likely to have a significant impact on the effectiveness of environmental accords. In general, the cases show that while transition has not led to rampant Russian noncompliance with its international commitments, this is often a result of "compliance without implementation." The dramatic reduction in economic activity in Russia has caused a drop in pollution. However, it appears that pollution intensity (per unit of gross domestic product) has risen. For example, official statistics show that economic activity in St. Petersburg has dropped by 50 percent, but pollution output is down by only 10 percent. Thus our analysis is quite pessimistic. As the economy recovers, pollution will also rebound unless the new regulatory structures take hold. In cases where environmental projects require substantial investments, as in the case of Norilsk Nickel or in Russian implementation of the London Convention, economic recovery and/or carefully directed financial or technology transfers may be an essential condition.

This pessimistic scenario is not inevitable however; our study of Poland shows that transition there has been accompanied by relatively well-functioning regulatory systems. These have allowed Poland to achieve admirable progress in implementing the Baltic Sea accords.

Methods

Our work is both descriptive and theoretical. The implementation of international environmental agreements is an underexplored aspect of international relations. We aim to describe how it works in practice, to compare and contrast cases and issues, and to analyze how the implementation process influences and shapes the effectiveness of international agreements.

As noted earlier in this chapter, implementation of international environmental commitments is not the only factor that determines behavior. The complexity of many factors interacting during the implementation process makes it difficult to isolate which factors, under what conditions, explain effectiveness. We address this problem in three ways.

First, the authors of the case studies are sensitive to the full range of the other factors, discussed above, that influence effectiveness either directly or by interacting with the implementation processes that are the focus of our study. As a group, prior to writing the case study reports, the authors agreed to give special attention to these other explanatory factors while focusing on the process of implementation and the particular issues and propositions related to SIRs and national implementation. In most of our case studies, the implementation of international environmental commitments is not directly responsible for most changes in behavior. Other factors are typically more important.

Second, each study employs the "process tracing" method. The chapters unpack the often elaborate sequence of events that make up the implementation process and trace the connections between the individual events that constitute the complex story of cause and effect.[55] Historical process tracing is aided by selecting only cases where the international commitments have been in place long enough to observe objectively how they have been implemented and to plausibly unravel cause and effect. Thus none of our studies concerns the implementation of the Framework Convention on Climate Change or the Convention on Biological Diversity—both topics of high political salience today, but neither with sufficient history for analysis of implementation.[56] Many of the chapters also employ *counterfactual* descriptions.[57] Counterfactuals are stories of what, in the judgment of the author, would have happened under different conditions. Such thought experiments do not add any empirical information, but they do aid in the description of how a particular factor or institution has been influential. Posing counterfactual questions clarifies the causal pathways suggested by the author's analysis.

Third, we improve process tracing through our selection of cases. In part, where possible, we have selected cases that allow comparisons. We take advantage of convenient "quasi-experiments," such as the ability to compare implementation of the Baltic Sea accords in the former Soviet states of Russia, Estonia, Latvia, and Lithuania with implementation of the same accords in Poland (Chapters 14 and 15). The studies on pollution in the North Sea and on NO_x policies also allow us to hold "constant" the international context and observe how national differences influence outcomes. Our studies also allow us to take the national context in the Netherlands, Norway, and the UK as a constant while comparing the influence of different international commitments (Chapters 8 and 9). Comparisons across cases are an imperfect and hazardous method because despite efforts to hold many factors constant, much still changes. Thus process tracing remains our main method.

Our selection of case studies spans a range from cases where implementation is complex, costly, and difficult (NO_x, and North and Baltic Sea pollution) to cases were implementation is relatively easy (i.e., the whaling case, which affects a small and declining industry). However, the aim of this book—a foundation that unpacks the implementation process—is furthered by selecting cases where implementation review and national implementation are likely to be important. Thus we have focused on implementation of the policy concerning NO_x emissions—which often requires costly changes by many targets—rather than that concerning sulfur emissions, which flow from a small number of well-defined sources. (Sulfur has also been the subject of earlier, extensive research on acid rain policy implementation.)[58] Similarly, we focus on land-based sources of pollution in the North and Baltic Seas, rather than ocean dumping, which is easier to control (and thus has largely been stopped). Our study on marine dumping of nuclear waste focuses on Russia, the only country that has not fully implemented the international ban. In the whaling case, we focus on Norway—the only country that has not implemented the IWC's whaling moratorium—and on Iceland—the country that is leading the effort to build an alternative organization to the IWC.

Our selection also ensures that the factors (independent variables) we examine vary across the cases. For example, in the studies on SIRs, we have investigated one regime that includes formal procedures for implementation review (the Montreal Protocol), one where the level of formalization is very low (the Baltic Sea regime), and one where no review procedures were included in the original agreement (trade in hazardous chemicals). In the studies on participation, we examine implementation of international commitments concerning the North Sea and NO_x policy in three countries with markedly different patterns of participation—the open Dutch system, the closed UK system, and the Norwegian policy process, which lies in the middle.

Though the assessment of causal relationships is difficult, we present coherent and well-supported causal arguments whenever possible. The dangers of wrongly ascribing causation are especially severe when using information that correlates the existence of institutions with observed behavior. Correlation does not prove cause and effect. For example, many observers have celebrated the fact that since the signature of LRTAP's 1985 Sulphur Protocol, which requires parties to cut sulfur 30 percent below 1980 levels by 1993, emissions across Europe have dropped sharply. However, studies that take a closer look, tracing cause and effect, find that the Protocol had little effect on most of its signatories, who for other reasons were already reducing sulfur emissions.[59] Our distinction between implementation and compliance helps to focus on causal relationships and not just correlation.

Concluding Thoughts

Despite its centrality to international cooperation and the operation of international regimes, implementation has been little studied in detail. Implementation is a complex process that, as domestic scholarship demonstrates, is ill-suited to the construction of parsimonious theories. Yet implementation is what turns grand principles and commitments into actual practice, and hence it is an essential part of international environmental (and other) affairs. We tackle this topic via a variety of structured case studies. We show how commitments have been implemented in different countries and reviewed by international institutions, and we assess whether and how these implementation activities have influenced the behavior of target groups.

Practitioners and scholars interested in how commitments have been implemented and how international environmental governance can be improved should find much of interest in this book. The concluding chapter presents major findings. It also explores issues that cut across the many case studies, such as which types of international legal instruments are most effective and how to design international institutions to allow more extensive international environmental cooperation. In the final chapter we also explore some implications for international cooperation and international law. We ask whether it matters that the most extensive activities for implementing international environmental commitments are found in liberal states—those with democratic decision-making processes, independent judiciaries, and market-based economies. Our case studies mainly focus on liberal states and states undergoing a transition to liberalism. We argue that liberal characteristics lead to special forms of cooperation where non-state actors play central roles, international and domestic politics are increasingly intertwined, and governments often do not know whether they can comply when they adopt international commitments. We argue that international institutions such as SIRs play an increasing role in scrutinizing "behind" national borders and looking beyond formal compliance, both of which are necessary when effective international cooperation requires changing the behavior of private actors.

Appendix to Chapter 1: Table 1A.1

Fourteen case studies of international cooperation on eight environmental issues: summary of objectives, international commitments, and behavior. The studies examine whether and how international commitments caused changes in behavior in accordance with the relevant objectives.

Regime and case study	Chapter (authors)	Objectives of international agreements	Regulatory and programmatic commitments examined in the case study	Observed behavior
European Air Pollution Regime (Long-Range Transboundary Air Pollution [LRTAP] Convention and related policies of the European Community)				
Implementation of NO_x controls in the Netherlands, Norway, and the UK	9 (Wettestad)	Reduce NO_x emissions to sustainable levels.	Binding LRTAP agreement to stabilize NO_x emissions by 1994 at 1987 levels (or at a different specified baseline; nonbinding and less inclusive agreement to cut NO_x emissions by approx. 30% by 1998 (baseline can be chosen as any year from 1980–1986). (The UK did not join the nonbinding agreement; Norway recently anounced that it would not comply with the nonbinding agreement.)	Between the mid-1980s and 1994, all three countries reduced NO_x emissions by a few percent.
Implementation of LRTAP Sulphur and NO_x Protocols in the USSR and Russia	12 (Kotov and Nikitina)	Reduce SO_2 and NO_x emissions (or transboundary fluxes) to sustainable levels.	Binding agreement to cut SO_2 emissions by 30% from 1980 levels by 1993; binding agreement to stabilize NO_x emissions by 1994 (see above).	Emissions of SO_2 down by about 50% (1980–1993); NO_x emissions down 13% (1987–1992).
Implementation of SO_2 pollution controls at the Norilsk Nickel facilities on the Kola Peninsula	13 (Kotov and Nikitina)	Reduce SO_2 emissions to sustainable levels.	Binding agreement (LRTAP Protocol): cut SO_2 emissions 30% from 1980 levels by 1993. Nonbinding agreement (bilateral accords with Finland): cut SO_2 emissions along the common border by 50%. Nonbinding agreements (bilateral accords with Finland and Norway): reduce air pollution, notably from Kola smelters.	Emissions have declined by 38% at the two Norilsk facilities on Kola; recent plans to install less-polluting equipment are stalled.
The LRTAP data, review, and modeling system	7 (di Primio)	Improve information on emissions, deposition, and models of transboundary pollution.	All parties to LRTAP are required to report data on emissions. Participants in the EMEP network report data on deposition and participate in modeling. National officials compare and improve national statistics through LRTAP activities and related programs of the European Community, such as CORINAIR.	Quality of data (accuracy and comparability) has improved over two decades; models have been developed, allowing innovative approaches to pollution control such as "critical loads."

Regime and case study	Chapter (authors)	Objectives of inter-national agreements	Regulatory and programmatic commitments examined in the case study	Observed behavior
North Sea/northeast Atlantic pollution regime (nonbinding Ministerial Agreements, 1972 Oslo Convention, 1974 Paris Convention, and 1992 Paris Convention)				
Implementation of North Sea pollution controls in the Netherlands, Norway, and the UK	8 (Skjærseth)	Prevent and eliminate pollution in the North Sea.	Binding technology standards. Nonbinding agreements: 50% cut in nutrients and 36 pollutants flowing into the North Sea from rivers and estuaries. Nonbinding and binding commitments: stop dumping and incineration, and adopt best available technologies.	Dumping is nearly stopped; the UK still dumps sewage sludge in accordance with relevant commitments. Land-based emissions have declined substantially.
Baltic Sea environment protection regime (nonbinding Ministerial Agreements, Joint Comprehensive Programme, and 1974 and 1992 Helsinki Conventions)				
The Baltic regime's system for implementation review	5 (Greene)	Eliminate dumping into the Baltic and reduce shipborne, airborne, and land-based pollution sources (e.g., agricultural runoff and sewage) to restore the Baltic Sea's ecological balance.	Nonbinding agreements (Ministerial Agreements and Joint Comprehensive Programme): stop dumping; cut organic toxins, heavy metals, and nutrients by 50%. Binding agreements (Helsinki Conventions and decisions of the Helsinki Commission): technology and effluent standards. (Many countries have opted-out of many binding standards and thus are not formally bound by them.)	Projects to install, e.g., wastewater treatment facilities are under way; dumping is being regulated.
Implementation in the former Soviet Union (Russia, Estonia, Lithuania, Latvia)	14 (Roginko)	Same as above.	Same as above.	Effluents sharply lower since collapse of economies; few policies being implemented, but situation may be improving.
Implementation in Poland	15 (Hjorth)	Same as above.	Same as above.	Emissions declined with economy in early 1990s; new policies and projects, such as completion of wastewater treatment plants, should keep emissions low in future.

Regime and case study	Chapter (authors)	Objectives of international agreements	Regulatory and programmatic commitments examined in the case study	Observed behavior
Stratospheric ozone depletion regime (Montreal Protocol)				
The Montreal Protocol's system for implementation review	3 (Greene)	Eliminate consumption of ozone-depleting substances (ODS), returning the ozone layer to its natural state.	Eliminate production of the most noxious ODS by the mid-1990s and phase out others over long periods. Developing countries are allowed a time delay to implement most commitments. Industrialized countries must contribute to the Multilateral Fund. All countries must report data on production, trade, and consumption.	Industrialized countries, except Russia and other transition countries (see below), have virtually eliminated the most noxious ODS. Some developing countries have eliminated ODS ahead of schedule.
The Montreal Protocol's Non-Compliance Procedure	4 (Victor)	Same as above.	Same as above. Study includes analysis of failure of Belarus, Bulgaria, Poland, Russia, and Ukraine (BBPRU) to comply with the commitment to phase out ODS and report data.	Data reporting initially poor but improving. BBPRU nations now phasing out ODS and reporting data as required.
Marine dumping of radioactive waste regime (London Convention, 1972)				
Implementation of controls in the USSR and Russia	11 (Stokke)	Reduce hazardous dumping in the oceans.	Binding commitments: eliminate dumping of hazardous substances, including high-level radioactive waste; regulate dumping of less hazardous substances, including low- and medium-level radioactive waste. A 1983 voluntary moratorium on dumping of all radioactive waste was prolonged in 1985 and superseded by a binding prohibition in 1993. Russia filed a reservation to the prohibition and is not legally bound by it.	USSR dumped high-level radioactive waste as recently as the late 1980s, in violation of the London Convention; the latest dumping of Russian low-level radioactive waste occurred in 1993.

Whaling regime (International Convention on the Regulation of Whaling [ICRW] and moratorium on commercial whaling adopted by International Whaling Commission)

Trade in hazardous chemicals and pesticides regime (nonbinding system for prior informed consent [PIC] under the UNEP *London Guidelines* and the FAO *Code of Conduct on the Distribution and Use of Pesticides*)

Conservation and preservation of fauna and flora regimes (sample of 36 binding and nonbinding agreements)

Regime and case study	Chapter (authors)	Objectives of international agreements	Regulatory and programmatic commitments examined in the case study	Observed behavior
Regulation of whaling in Iceland and Norway	10 (Andresen)	Two views. "Conservationist": conserve whales to allow the "orderly development of the whaling industry" (ICRW preamble). "Preservationist": stop all killing of whales.	International Whaling Commission's binding moratorium on commercial whaling starting in 1985–1986 and fully implemented by 1989. (Norway lodged a reservation and thus is not formally bound by the moratorium.)	Nearly 40,000 whales caught in early 1970s; a few hundred killed annually in the 1990s, and catch is gradually increasing.
The implementation and evolution of the nonbinding PIC system	6 (Victor)	Increase the ability of developing countries to regulate imports of hazardous chemicals and pesticides.	All countries must report national regulatory actions, which are used to determine which chemicals and pesticides are hazardous and thus eligible to be put on the PIC list. Importers must decide whether they want future imports of substances on the PIC list. Subsequently, exporters are expected to obey the decisions of the importers.	All exports of PIC substances appear to conform with the PIC system. Most countries have supplied most of the requested information.
Long-term trends in systems for implementation review	2 (Lanchbery)	Preserve and conserve fauna and flora.	Various. Study focuses on requirements of parties to report data and, increasingly, to submit to intrusive reviews of national performance.	Various. Breadth and depth of reporting and implementation review is increasing, which should lead to greater influence on behavior (a hypothesis that is examined in depth in case studies in the first part of this book).

Notes

We thank Jesse Ausubel, Dan Bodansky, Helmut Breitmeier, Abe Chayes, Wendy Franz, George Golitsyn, Robert Keohane, Marc Levy, Gordon MacDonald, Peter Sand, Chris Stone, Arild Underdal, Oran Young, and the authors of the case studies in this book for discussions and comments on earlier drafts. We are especially grateful to Tom Schelling and Michael Zürn for detailed comments on a draft.

1. United Nations Environment Programme (UNEP), 1993, Register of International Treaties and Other Agreements in the Field of the Environment, Nairobi, Kenya.

2. Brown Weiss, E., 1993, "International Environmental Law: Contemporary Issues and the Emergence of a New World Order," *Georgetown Law Journal* 81:675–710.

3. Exceptions include two studies on implementation conducted in parallel with the present study: on implementation of the international accords to regulate acid rain, see Hanf, K., *et al.*, 1996, "The Domestic Basis of International Environmental Agreements: Modelling National/International Linkages," Erasmus University, Rotterdam, Netherlands; on implementation of five international accords in nine countries, see Brown Weiss, E., and Jacobson, H.K., eds., 1998, *Engaging Countries: Strengthening Compliance with International Environmental Accords*, The MIT Press, Cambridge, MA, USA (forthcoming). Researchers have given some attention to the effectiveness of international environmental agreements (see below for definition of terms), which has of course required giving attention to issues of implementation. In particular, see Haas, P.M., Keohane, R.O., and Levy, M.A., eds., 1993, *Institutions for the Earth: Sources of Effective International Environmental Protection*, The MIT Press, Cambridge, MA, USA; Sand, P.H., ed., 1992, *The Effectiveness of International Environmental Agreements*, Grotius Publishers, Cambridge, UK; Rittberger, V., and Mayer, P., eds., 1993, *Regime Theory and International Relations*, Clarendon Press, Oxford, UK; and Wettestad, J., and Andresen, S., 1991, *The Effectiveness of International Resource Cooperation: Some Preliminary Findings*, R:007-1991, Fridtjof Nansen Institute, Lysaker, Norway. For a review of the literature see Levy, M.A., Young, O.R., and Zürn, M., 1995, "The Study of International Regimes," *European Journal of International Relations* 1:267–330. An important early study considered the topic of effectiveness but was completed in the early 1980s, when few of the issues investigated had been the subject of international cooperation for long—there were few international commitments to implement and a quite limited track record for assessing whether international institutions had been effective; see Kay, D.A., and Jacobsen, H.K., eds., 1983, *Environmental Protection: The*

International Dimension, Allanheld Osmun & Co., Totowa, NJ, USA. Useful earlier studies that focus mainly on international decision making and the impact of international commitments on national legislation, rather that the influence on the ultimate targets, include Schwebel, S.M., 1971, "The Effectiveness of International Decisions," papers of a conference of the American Society of International Law and the proceedings of the conference, Sijthoff, Leyden, Netherlands, and Oceana Publications, Dobbs Ferry, NY, USA; Cox, R.W., and Jacobson, H.K., 1973, *The Anatomy of Influence: Decision Making in an International Organization*, Yale University Press, New Haven, CT, USA; and Leive, D.M., 1976, *International Regulatory Regimes: Case Studies in Health, Meteorology, and Food*, Lexington Books, Lexington, MA, USA.

4. Rein, M., and Rabinovitz, F.F., 1987, "Implementation: A Theoretical Perspective," in *American Politics and Public Policy*, edited by W.D. Burnham and M.W. Weinberg, The MIT Press, Cambridge, MA, USA, p. 308.

5. See, for example, Pressman, J., and Wildavsky, A., 1973, *Implementation*, University of California Press, Berkeley, CA, USA; Derthick, M., 1972, *New Towns In-town: Why a Federal Program Failed*, Urban Institute, Washington, DC, USA; Elmore, R.F., and Williams, W., eds., 1976, *Social Program Implementation*, Academic Press, New York, NY, USA; Bardach, E., 1977, *The Implementation Game: What Happens After a Bill Becomes a Law*, The MIT Press, Cambridge, MA, USA; Lipsky, M., 1980, *Street-Level Bureaucracy*, Russell Sage Foundation, New York, NY, USA; Mazmanian, D.A., and Sabatier, P., 1983, *Implementation and Public Policy*, Scott, Foresman & Co., Chicago, IL, USA; Downing, P., and Hanf, K., 1983, *International Comparisons in Implementing Pollution Laws*, Kluwer/Nijhoff Publishing, Boston, MA, USA; Goggin, M., *et al.*, 1990, *Implementation Theory and Practice: Towards a Third Generation*, Scott, Foresman & Co., Glenview, CA, USA. Related case studies include Friedland, M.L., ed., 1990, *Securing Compliance: Seven Case Studies*, University of Toronto Press, Toronto, Canada. Much of the literature on policy implementation has been motivated by a desire to explain why policy fails. Recent exceptions include Jänicke, M., and Weidner, H., eds., 1995, *Successful Environmental Policy: A Critical Evaluation of 24 Cases*, Ed. Sigma, Berlin, Germany. Also relevant to the study of "implementation" is analysis of how organizations and institutions affect behavior, and how they can be changed; for a review see March, J.G., and Olsen, J.P., 1989, *Rediscovering Institutions: The Organizational Basis of Politics*, Free Press, New York, NY, USA. We apologize to the many dozens of authors whose work on implementation we do not have space to cite.

Current surveys of environmental policy implementation include Weale, A., 1992, *The New Politics of Pollution*, Manchester University Press, Manchester,

UK; and Rosenbaum, W., 1995, *Environmental Politics and Policy*, 3rd edition, Congressional Quarterly Press, Washington, DC, USA.

6. This empirically oriented strategy follows the advice of Robert Keohane and Joseph Nye's seminal study on international politics: it expands the number of case studies that trace in detail how countries weigh and implement international commitments and balance international obligations with other interests and pressures, as well as the roles that international institutions play in effective international cooperation. See Keohane, R.O., and Nye, J.S., 1989, *Power and Interdependence*, 2nd edition, Scott, Foresman & Co., Glenview, CA, USA; pp. 259–260.

7. For example, see Van Meter, D.S., and Van Horn, C.E., 1975, "The Policy Implementation Process," *Administration & Society* 6(4) (February):445–488; Sabatier, P.A., 1986, "Top-down and Bottom-up Approaches to Implementation Research: A Critical Analysis and a Suggested Synthesis," *Journal of Public Policy* 6(1):21–48; Goggin, M.S., *et al.*, 1990, *Implementation Theory and Practice: Toward a Third Generation*, Scott, Foresman & Co., Glenview, IL, USA. See the critical review in Najam, A., 1995, Learning from the Literature on Policy Implementation: A Synthesis Perspective, WP-95-61, International Institute for Applied Systems Analysis, Laxenburg, Austria.

8. Mazmanian and Sabatier, op. cit., note 5.

9. The ultimate target is often defined by the problem at hand. For example, efforts to control NO_x ultimately aim to influence (in part) the technologies used by individual automobile owners, such as catalytic converters. But the policy process often focuses on some intermediate target, for example automobile manufacturers. Often the behavior of intermediate targets is concentrated and highly leveraged—their decisions affect the behavior of the ultimate targets—and thus it is a highly efficient focus of policy. Often the politics of the issue determine the targets that are selected, notably symbolic targets. North Sea campaigns by environmental groups devoted much attention to activities of particular dumping ships, which were highly visible; the campaigns did not focus on diffuse land-based pollution sources, although they are also serious contributors to North Sea pollution. Some targets are selected for indirect activities. The US government has threatened to apply sanctions and antiwhaling groups have focused boycotts on exports from Iceland, Japan, and Norway in the hope that these countries will stop whaling.

10. For the most part, public international law—law between states—cannot directly bind individuals or private organizations such as firms. States must implement and enforce international treaty commitments. One exception is universal human rights, which bind and give rights to individuals even if states do not ratify the relevant international agreements. Some scholars make similar

claims for customary international law—that is, principles that are law because they are widely followed (see note 19). Our studies examine nonbinding instruments as well as binding treaties (see below). For nonbinding instruments the distinction of who is "bound" may be less important and thus the succession of stages, from international commitment to national law to target behavior, may be less evident. In the PIC case, for example, industry in many countries voluntarily implemented international rules without those rules being formally translated into domestic law.

11. Various definitions of effectiveness are discussed in Young, O., 1994, *International Governance*, Cornell University Press, Ithaca, NY, USA.

12. We are also mindful that accords may cause changes in behavior that contravene the ultimate environmental goal. One such example is Soviet implementation of international accords to limit acid precipitation, which in essence shifted some pollution from western USSR to the Arctic: although technically outside the scope of the European acid rain regime, the Arctic was nevertheless vulnerable to acid precipitation. Accords often include very broad objectives and thus increasingly refer to the need to achieve environmental protection in a least-cost manner. Thus even when an accord causes changes in behavior that protect the environment, such changes may not be fully consistent with the goals of the accord. At times it is very difficult to determine precisely which changes in behavior would be consistent with an accord's goals. In practice, such choices are made by the analyst on the basis of the written goals and the expectations of the parties to an accord. Where expectations do not converge, the analyst must explain the differences.

13. Compliance with international environmental commitments is a major focus of legal scholars; see, for instance, Cameron, J., *et al.*, eds., 1996, *Improving Compliance with International Environmental Law*, Earthscan, London, UK; in particular the chapter by Mitchell, R.B., 1996, "Compliance Theory: An Overview"; Chayes, A., and Chayes, A.H., 1996, *The New Sovereignty*, Harvard University Press, Cambridge, MA, USA. Some analysts have defined the term "compliance" very broadly such that it comprises both the narrow traditional concept (i.e., conformity with a legal standard) as well as changes in behavior (which we call "effectiveness"). Notably, see Brown Weiss, E., and Jacobson, H., 1995, "Strengthening Compliance with International Environmental Accords," *Global Governance* 2(2) (May–August). We do not adopt the broad definition because, as we show, compliance and effectiveness are often not the same. Moreover, using "compliance" broadly conflicts with its common meaning. Compliance is a useful concept, but we argue that research designed to uncover whether and how international accords help solve environmental problems must look beyond compliance (see Chapter 16).

14. Birnie, P., 1985, *International Regulation of Whaling*, 2 volumes, Oceana Publications, Dobbs Ferry, NY, USA.

15. See, for example, Mitchell, op. cit., note 13, p. 6.

16. We do not evaluate implementàtion in the sense of comparing it with an ex ante standard for "good," "full," or "complete" implementation. Rather, we describe the implementation that has actually occurred. We then assess the degree to which this observed activity is a result of the accord and, most important, the extent to which it has resulted in behavioral changes by target groups that further the goals of the accord.

17. We look to the activities of target groups to assess effectiveness, but because target groups are an integral part of the implementation process, we are careful when drawing conclusions that link implementation with effectiveness.

18. See Krasner, S., 1983, *International Regimes*, Cornell University Press, Ithaca, NY, USA.

19. Other possible sources of international law include "customary law" (the custom of nations), the decisions of international courts and tribunals, and the writing of jurists. See Bodansky, D., 1995, "Customary (and Not So Customary) International Environmental Law," *Indiana Journal of Global Legal Studies* 3(1):105–119.

20. For more on the role of law in international society, see Bull, H., 1977, *The Anarchical Society*, Columbia University Press, New York, NY, USA.

21. There are other dimensions to the nature of the problem as well. Some goods, such as power, are relational—gains by one party are losses for another. Other goods are absolute. Some problems are conflicts over values and ideas. Others involve direct material concerns, and thus compensation schemes are more readily available to change the structure of costs and benefits. For a well-structured overview of some elements of problem structure, see Efinger, M., and Zürn, M., 1990, "Explaining Conflict Management in East-West Relations: A Quantitative Test of Problem-Structural Typologies," in *International Regimes in East-West Politics*, edited by V. Rittberger, Pinter, London, UK, pp. 64–89.

22. For a discussion of the magnitude and distribution of costs and benefits, see Underdal, A., 1987, "International Cooperation: Transforming 'Needs' into 'Deeds'," *Journal of Peace Research* 24(2):167–183. Much analysis of the diffuse versus concentrated distribution of costs and benefits can be traced to Olson, M., 1965, *Logic of Collective Action*, Belknap Press/Harvard University Press, Cambridge, MA, USA. James Q. Wilson addresses the issue in Wilson, J.Q., 1973, *Political Organizations*, Basic Books, New York, NY, USA; and Wilson, J.Q., ed., 1980, *The Politics of Regulation*, Basic Books,

New York, NY, USA; he points out that the diffuse beneficiaries are often represented by environmental groups, whose actions to mobilize public opinion and pressure help strengthen commitments that would otherwise be diluted by industry, which bears concentrated costs of regulation. For an application of these concepts—the distribution of costs and benefits—to the formation of domestic policies to implement international commitments, see Hanf, K., and Underdal, A., 1995, "Domesticating International Commitments: Linking National and International Decision-Making," in *The International Politics of Environmental Management*, edited by A. Underdal, Kluwer, Dordrecht, Netherlands. For the Norwegian example of compensation, see Laugen, T., 1995, *Compliance with International Environmental Agreements: Norway and the Acid Rain Convention*, R:003-1995, The Fridtjof Nansen Institute, Lysaker, Norway.

23. On "strategic" considerations, see especially analysis using game theory. For example, see Stein, A., 1990, *Why Nations Cooperate*, Cornell University Press, Ithaca, NY, USA. Whether the situation being addressed is a coordination game or a collaboration game can matter as well. Coordination games are those in which rules are self-enforcing—for example, the rule to drive on a particular side of the road needs little enforcement once a choice is made. Compliance is likely to be very high. By contrast, collaboration games are those in which deviation from the rules makes sense for an individual actor. Collaboration game problems are far more difficult to address and less likely to yield marked behavioral change than coordination game problems. Coordination situations, however, are rare in international affairs and virtually nonexistent in international environmental affairs.

24. Charnovitz, S., 1994, "Encouraging Environmental Cooperation through the Pelly Amendment," *The Journal of Environment & Development* 3(1): 3–28; DeSombre, E.R., 1995, "Baptists and Bootleggers for the Environment: The Origins of United States Unilateral Sanctions," *Journal of Environment and Development* 4(1):53–75. More generally on sanctions see Hufbauer, G.C., Schott, J.J., and Elliott, K.A., 1990, *Economic Sanctions Reconsidered: History and Current Policy*, Institute for International Economics, Washington, DC, USA; Martin, L.L., 1992, *Coercive Cooperation*, Princeton University Press, Princeton, NJ, USA.

25. See Chapter 10 for a discussion of how the threat of US sanctions and consumer boycotts affected the internal politics, and thus the behavior of whalers, in Iceland and Norway.

26. Downs, G.W., Rocke, D.M., and Barsoom, P., 1996, "Is the Good News about Compliance Good News about Cooperation?" *International Organization* 50(3):379–406.

27. Keohane, R.O., 1980, "The Theory of Hegemonic Stability and Changes in International Economic Regimes: 1967–1977," in *Change in the International System*, edited by O. Holsti, Westview Press, Boulder, CO, USA, pp. 131–162.

28. For example, see Krasner, op. cit., note 18, Keohane, R., 1984, *After Hegemony*, Princeton University Press, Princeton, NJ, USA; Oye, K., ed., 1986, *Cooperation Under Anarchy*, Princeton University Press, Princeton, NJ, USA; Stein, op. cit., note 23; Ruggie, J., ed., 1993, *Multilateralism Matters*, University of California Press, Berkeley, CA, USA.

29. We are mindful of at least two competing views on the use of information. One argues that cooperation is easier when information is abundant because it is easier to negotiate and monitor contracts; see, for example, arguments on how international institutions improve the "contractual environment": Haas, P.M., Keohane, R.O., and Levy, M.A., 1993, *Institutions for the Earth: Sources of Effective International Environmental Protection*, The MIT Press, Cambridge, MA, USA. An alternative view emphasizes the benefits of uncertainty (incomplete information)—behind a "veil of uncertainty" parties are less aware of their specific interests and thus more willing to negotiate fair and robust agreements; see Young, O.R., 1989, "The Politics of International Regime Formation: Managing National Resources and the Environment," *International Organization* 43(3) (Summer):349–375.

30. For a more detailed discussion of the differences between institutions and organizations see Young, O.R., 1989, *International Cooperation: Building Regimes for Natural Resources and the Environment*, Cornell University Press, Ithaca, NY, USA.

31. Virtually all policy-relevant analysis on international environmental law makes arguments (sometimes indirectly) about how particular designs for commitments could be more effective. Of particular interest, see Sand, P.H., 1990, *Lessons Learned in Global Environmental Governance*, World Resources Institute, Washington, DC, USA.

32. Mitchell, R., 1994, "Regime Design Matters: Intentional Oil Pollution and Treaty Compliance," *International Organization* 48(3) (Summer):425–458.

33. Ibid. pp. 427–428.

34. Rittberger and Mayer, op. cit., note 3; Chossudovsky, E.M., *East-West Diplomacy for Environment in the United Nations*, UNITAR, New York, NY, USA, pp. 23–25.

35. For example, Mostapha Tolba of UNEP is frequently mentioned as a critical influence on the development of several international environmental regimes.

36. Kay and Jacobsen, op. cit., note 3.

37. Keohane, R.O., 1983, "Demand for International Regimes," in *International Regimes*, edited by S. Krasner, Cornell University Press, Ithaca, NY, USA.

38. Levy, M.A., 1993, "European Acid Rain: The Power of Tote-Board Diplomacy," in *Institutions for the Earth: Sources of Effective International Environmental Protection*, edited by P.M. Haas, R.O. Keohane, and M.A. Levy, The MIT Press, Cambridge, MA, USA.

39. Downs, A., 1972, "Up and Down with Ecology—The Issue-Attention Cycle," *The Public Interest*, Summer, pp. 38–50.

40. Victor, D.G., *et al.*, 1994, Review Mechanisms in the Effective Implementation of International Environmental Agreements, WP-94-114, International Institute for Applied Systems Analysis, Laxenburg, Austria. Victor, D.G., 1996, "The Montreal Protocol's Non-Compliance Procedure: Lessons for Making Other International Environmental Regimes More Effective," in *The Ozone Treaties and Their Influence on the Building of Environmental Regimes*, edited by W. Lang, Federal Ministry for Foreign Affairs, Vienna, Austria.

41. March, J.G., and Olsen, J.P., 1989, *Rediscovering Institutions*, The Free Press, New York, NY, USA; Weaver, R.K., and Rockman, B.A., eds., 1993, *Do Institutions Matter?* The Brookings Institution, Washington, DC, USA.

42. GAO (General Accounting Office), US Congress, 1992, *International Environment: International Agreements Are Not Well Monitored*, GAO/RCED-92-43; Ausubel, J.H., and Victor, D.G., 1992, "Verification of International Environmental Agreements," *Annual Review of Energy and Environment* 17: 1–43.

43. Chayes and Chayes, op. cit., note 13; Downs *et al.*, op. cit., note 26.

44. Earlier work includes Fisher, W., 1991, *The Verification of International Conventions on Protection of the Environment and Common Resources: A Comparative Analysis of the Instruments and Procedures for International Verification with the Example of Thirteen Conventions*, Programmgruppe Technologiefolgenforschung, Kernforschungszentrum Jülich, Germany; Ausubel, J.H., and Victor, D.G., 1992, "Verification of International Environmental Agreements," *Annual Review of Energy and Environment* 17:1–43; Sachariew, K., 1992, "Promoting Compliance with International Environmental Standards: Reflections on Monitoring and Reporting Mechanisms," *Yearbook of International Environmental Law* 2:31–55, Graham & Trotman/Martinus Nijhoff, Boston, MA, USA.

45. An issue of special importance is the role of financial transfers to developing countries. On how such transfers are mobilized and implemented, see

44   *David G. Victor, Kal Raustiala, and Eugene B. Skolnikoff*

Keohane, R.O., and Levy, M.A., eds., 1996, *Institutions for Environmental Aid: Pitfalls and Promise*, The MIT Press, Cambridge, MA, USA. Chapters 2 and 4 of this book briefly explore the effect of participation by developing countries on the effectiveness of SIRs. The study of implementation and compliance led by Brown Weiss and Jacobson includes case studies on Brazil, Cameroon, China, and India; see Brown Weiss, E., and Jacobson, H.K., eds., 1998, *Engaging Countries: Strengthening Compliance with International Environmental Accords*, The MIT Press, Cambridge, MA, USA (forthcoming). Few international environmental agreements require substantial behavioral change in developing countries. Very little of the research on national policy implementation has focused on developing countries. For a pertinent review, see Najam, op. cit., note 7. For one of the few studies on developing countries, see Ayee, J., 1994, *An Anatomy of Public Policy Implementation*, Avebury, Sydney, Australia.

46. Principle 10, "Rio Declaration on Environment and Development, The United Nations Conference on Environment and Development," 1992.

47. But see the MARPOL negotiations, where participation by target groups was quite high; Mitchell, R.B., 1994, *Intentional Oil Pollution at Sea*, The MIT Press, Cambridge, MA, USA. Also, in the International Labor Organization (ILO), participation by non-state actors (labor unions and industry) has been high since its creation seven decades ago; see Romano, C.P.R., 1996, *The ILO System of Supervision and Compliance Control: A Review and Lessons for Multilateral Environmental Agreements*, ER-96-1, International Institute for Applied Systems Analysis, Laxenburg, Austria. Also, industry has been heavily involved in fisheries and marine management. See Østreng, W., and Andresen, S., 1989, *International Resource Management: The Role of Science and Politics*, Belhaven Press, London, UK; and Floistad, B., 1990, *The International Council for the Exploration of the Sea (ICES) and the Providing of Legitimate Advice in Fisheries Management*, R:003-1990, Fridtjof Nansen Institute, Lysaker, Norway.

48. Dryzek and other theorists imagine a social dialogue among groups of stakeholders; advocates of "direct democracy" imagine a similar deliberation but one that uses technology to empower individuals, not only groups, to participate. For references and further discussion, see notes to the introductory text for the second part of this book.

49. For a more complete discussion of participation, see the introductory text and references for the second part of this book.

50. For example, see the review article Korten, D.C., 1980, "Community Organization and Rural Development: A Learning Process Approach," *Public Administration Review* (September/October):480–510.

51. Fiorino, D.J., 1996, "Environmental Policy and the Participation Gap," in *Democracy and the Environment*, edited by W.M. Lafferty and J. Meadowcroft, Edward Elgar, Cheltenham, UK; Baker, S., 1996, "'Environmental Policy in the European Union: Institutional Dilemmas and Democratic Practice," in *Democracy and the Environment*, edited by W.M. Lafferty and J. Meadowcroft, Edward Elgar, Cheltenham, UK. In the 1980s, the Netherlands, among many other countries, adopted policies to promote participation by target groups (see Chapters 8 and 9). For additional citations, see the introductory text and references for the second part of this book.

52. In the whaling case, scientific input has been both politicized and marginalized: the debate has been oriented primarily around ethical issues of whale preservation, an area in which scientists have little influence.

53. For example, for an overview and discussion of the main issues surrounding voluntary agreements and other interactive modes of policy-making in a European context and an initial assessment of the roughly 150 such agreements in Austria, Denmark, and the Netherlands—whose small, neo-corporatist structure makes them perhaps most likely to employ these negotiated instruments successfully—see Mol, A.P.J., Lauber, V., Enevoldsen, M., and Landman, J., 1996, "Joint Environmental Policy-Making in Comparative Perspective," presented at the Conference on the Greening of Industry, Heidelberg, Germany, November. See also Liefferink, D., and Mol, A.P.J., 1996, "Voluntary Agreements as a Form of Deregulation? The Dutch Experience," in *Deregulation in the European Union: Environmental Perspectives*, edited by U. Collier, Routledge, London, UK. The relevant literature on voluntary agreements, and more generally the role of the state and other stakeholders in negotiating environmental standards rather than simply imposing standards on firms, is huge. For one review, with emphasis on voluntary agreements at the local level, see Rehbinder, E., 1994, "Ecological Contracts: Agreements Between Polluters and Local Communities," in *Environmental Law and Ecological Responsibility: The Concept and Practice of Ecological Self-Organization*, edited by G. Teubner, L. Farmer, and D. Murphy, John Wiley & Sons, Chichester, UK, pp. 147–165. Voluntary agreements are one aspect of a general approach to policy-making that emphasizes extensive participation, negotiation, communication, and mutual adjustment. For an influential assessment of the role of public administration in this spirit, see Stewart, R., 1975, "The Reformation of American Administrative Law," *Harvard Law Review* 88:1667–1813. For one of many more recent treatments see, for example, Majone, G., 1989, *Evidence, Argument and Persuasion in the Policy Process*, Yale University Press, New Haven, CT, USA. See also note 3 of the short text that introduces the second part of this book.

54. Darst, R.G., 1997, "The Internationalization of Environmental Protection in the USSR and Its Successor States," in *The Internationalization of Environmental Protection*, edited by M.A. Schreurs and E. Economy, Cambridge, University Press, New York, NY, USA (forthcoming).

55. In other words, these studies are firmly in the tradition of "qualitative research" that is designed to uncover cause and effect as described by King, G., Keohane, R.O., and Verba, S., 1994, *Designing Social Inquiry: Scientific Inference in Qualitative Research*, Princeton University Press, Princeton, NJ, USA.

56. However, this research has sponsored analyses of the prospects of the climate and biodiversity conventions that focus on implementation and employ aspects of this approach. See Victor, D.G., and Salt, J.E., 1994, "From Rio to Berlin: Managing Climate Change," *Environment* 36(10):6–15, 25–32; Victor, D.G., and Salt, J.E., 1995, "Keeping the Climate Treaty Relevant," *Nature* 373:280–282; Raustiala, K., and Victor, D.G., 1996, "Biodiversity Since Rio," *Environment* 38(4):16–20, 37–45.

57. Fearon, J.D., 1991, "Counterfactuals and Hypothesis Testing in Political Science," *World Politics* 43:169–195; Biersteker, T.J., 1993, "Constructing Historical Counterfactuals to Assess the Consequences of International Regimes," in *Regime Theory and International Relations*, edited by V. Rittberger and P. Mayer, Clarendon Press, Oxford, UK.

58. Hanf *et al.*, op. cit., note 3.

59. Levy, op. cit., note 38.

I

Systems for Implementation Review

Most international agreements require governments to report on their efforts to implement the agreement. Many contain specific procedures for reviewing these reports. Often these reports and reviews contribute to assessments of the adequacy of existing commitments. A few agreements also include procedures for managing cases of poor implementation. In practice these many activities of reporting, reviewing, assessing, and promoting implementation are typically conducted in synergy, even when actually performed by many different actors and institutions. We call these activities a *system for implementation review* (SIR).

By increasing the flow of information that is relevant to managing an environmental problem, an SIR can lower transaction costs and enhance international cooperation.[1] By promoting transparency, SIRs may also make it easier for actors such as environmental nongovernmental organizations (ENGOs) to identify implementation problems and to pressure their governments to implement commitments more fully.[2] Transparency may also help build confidence, which can facilitate deeper and sustained international cooperation. SIRs can aid the process of working out the many detailed issues that inevitably arise when complex international commitments are implemented in different domestic settings. SIRs may also help avoid unproductive disputes. SIRs focus attention and resources on implementation and thus may be especially important when international cooperation requires complex changes within countries— that is, when implementation of international commitments is both demanding and crucial to the effectiveness of international commitments.

The case studies in this part of the book analyze how SIRs operate and explore the ability of SIRs to promote more thorough implementation and greater effectiveness of international commitments. They assess how SIRs help to perform four functions that plausibly lead to more effective regulatory commitments:

- Coordinating and assisting the reporting of data on implementation.
- Reviewing and assessing implementation.
- Handling implementation problems such as noncompliance.
- Providing assessments of needed adjustments to international commitments.

Although some studies have examined particular functions such as data reporting and responding to implementation problems, empirical research on implementation review remains limited.[3] Moreover, no study has examined how the functions of implementation review are performed by many different actors and procedures operating together as a system. These studies show that the synergies of the system are crucial; they help explain, for example, how and why the functions of implementation review are performed even when no formal procedures exist to do so.

Through six empirical studies, we examine SIRs in three ways. *First*, we explore trends in how the functions of SIRs are actually specified in environmental agreements. In Chapter 2, John Lanchbery investigates historical trends in SIRs by analyzing a set of three dozen accords on fauna and flora. The study shows that the pace at which SIRs have developed has quickened in recent decades, in part because early systems are used as models for later agreements. Moreover, all the case studies presented in this part of the book show that even when the functions of SIRs are not built into an initial agreement, they are often constructed later. Often, extensive SIRs have developed in response to growing pressure from parties and nongovernmental organizations (NGOs) that want to ensure that international commitments are more fully implemented. Although in some cases it has taken more than a decade to build even rudimentary systems, in all cases examined in this part of the book the trend is toward greater capacity to report and review data on implementation, address problems of noncompliance, and assess the adequacy of existing commitments. SIRs are becoming more prevalent and sophisticated.

Second, we examine the ways that SIRs operate and contribute to effectiveness in several regimes. Owen Greene investigates how problems implementing the Montreal Protocol on Substances that Deplete the Ozone Layer have been addressed (Chapter 3). He examines how many actors and institutions have operated together as a system to review and enhance the Protocol's implementation—he shows that the practice of implementation review extends far beyond the few procedures that are formally dedicated to the task. David G. Victor focuses on how the Protocol's dedicated Non-Compliance Procedure has addressed both minor implementation problems and the first major violations of the Protocol, which concern Russia and several other countries undergoing transition from central planning (Chapter 4). The Non-Compliance Procedure is one of the few examples of a formal process for handling implementation problems in international environmental law; we study it because often it is cited as a model, and thus it is crucial to understand why it has been effective. Greene also applies a systems perspective to implementation review in the Baltic Sea environment protection regime (Chapter 5). Whereas the Montreal Protocol includes a dedicated procedure for performing implementation review (i.e., the Non-Compliance Procedure), the Baltic Sea regime has not had one until recently; nontheless, in practice, implementation review has been extensive. Victor examines the SIR in the joint Food and Agriculture Organization/United Nations Environment Programme scheme for prior informed consent (PIC), which regulates trade in hazardous chemicals and pesticides (Chapter 6). The PIC system contains no formal procedures for implementation review, but in practice some functions of review have emerged as needed. Industry and ENGOs have played leading roles both in providing data needed to implement PIC and in reviewing implementation. Comparisons of these cases allow us to speculate about which functions are best performed formally, as part of an agreement's programmatic commitments and legally codified procedures, and which are more effective when performed by mechanisms that operate informally and/or external to the legal agreement.

We also explore how SIRs contribute to assessing the adequacy of commitments. Such assessments may lead to the dynamic adjustment (and expansion) of commitments.[4] Because SIRs increase the flow of information about implementation activities, we expect that they will result in commitments that better reflect what parties can put into practice. In turn, more realistic commitments are likely to be more effective. Of special interest is whether the ability of SIRs to yield adjustments depends on the legal form of an international commitment. In particular, we explore whether *nonbinding instruments* may be more effective than binding instruments because they do not require ratification, and thus can be more easily adjusted in light of new information, and because they are more likely to embody ambitious commitments. This issue is explored in the study of the nonbinding PIC system. (Cases in the second part of this book—on North Sea pollution and nitrogen oxides regulation [Chapters 8 and 9]—also include analysis of nonbinding instruments. In the conclusion we suggest some ways that nonbinding agreements can be used to make international environmental cooperation more effective.)

All the studies examine data reporting and other sources of information on implementation records. We devote extensive attention to this topic because information on implementation is obviously the backbone of the implementation review process. Most international environmental accords require data reporting by states—in essence, they oblige governments to report on their own successes and failures. In some cases, third parties such as NGOs and international organizations provide additional, more independent data on implementation. Yet the quantity and quality of data reported are often low; independent data sources are few. We assess the factors that explain poor data reporting as well as efforts to improve it. Juan Carlos di Primio's study, presented in Chapter 7, focuses on the data reporting system in the European air pollution regime, which consists of both the dedicated data and modeling programs of the Convention on Long-Range Transboundary Air Pollution (LRTAP) and the related, parallel activities of the European Community. Together they constitute one of the most active data reporting and exchange mechanisms in any international environmental regime. Often the European air pollution regime is used as a model, but few have analyzed the elaborate data and modeling system that has allowed the expansion and adjustment of LRTAP commitments over time. The other chapters explore cases with more typical and mixed experiences with eliciting and using data on implementation. All of the studies examine the effectiveness of efforts to improve both the quantity and quality of data.

All of the studies show that conceiving of implementation review as a *system* is crucial to an accurate picture of how implementation review actually takes place in environmental agreements. Few agreements rely mainly on dedicated and centralized procedures to perform the functions of implementation review. Instead, those functions are performed by a decentralized array of institutions. Formal and dedicated mechanisms, such as noncompliance procedures, perform only some of the wide range of interlocking SIR functions. The systems view opens the way to exploring how both dedicated and non-dedicated, formal and informal, and state and non-state processes work together as a single, decentralized institution.

Third, although the chapters in this section primarily examine the operation of SIRs, they also explore how SIRs exert influence on the behavior of actors and thus contribute to the effectiveness of international environmental accords. Five major pathways to behavioral change are considered.

(a) *SIRs can assure reluctant participants.* Under some conditions, parties to international agreements will not implement commitments unless they are confident that others will do the same. The fear of "free riding" is one manifestation of the phenomenon that some types of cooperation involve strategic, interdependent choices—that is, what one party does depends on its expectations of the behavior of other parties. Institutions that help identify when and how parties are implementing commitments can help build confidence that agreements are, in fact, being put into practice. Such benefits of confidence-building are often discussed in arms control. SIRs could provide similar functions for environmental accords. The demand for SIRs should rise as cooperation deepens and the need for assurance increases.[5]

(b) *SIRs can redistribute power to actors that favor implementation and compliance.* SIRs can make it easier for actors that favor thorough implementation to influence policy debates. Such actors can use the existence of international scrutiny to strengthen their influence on domestic policy. It is often easier to push the adoption of domestic policies that are needed for compliance with international commitments if the implementation record will be scrutinized. The existence of an SIR affects who participates in international institutions—typically in favor of experts and others who support thorough implementation. SIRs can also make more transparent and comparable information on state behavior (e.g., current and future emissions of pollutants) that would otherwise be expensive or impossible to gather. In turn, such information may allow government agencies and NGOs that favor more regulation to influence domestic and international policy debates on an informed basis. More useful information on environmental problems may also change the collective "interests" of a country by highlighting the implications of an environmental problem and feasible policy options, which in turn could change the types of agreements that a country is willing to adopt.[6]

(c) *SIRs can help manage noncompliance.* One school of legal thought argues that implementation problems must be "managed" rather than "enforced." According to this view, strict enforcement and deterrence are not possible in the international system because there is no superior enforcement body. Moreover, most failures to implement agreements are not willful violations; rather, they result from ambiguous commitments and low capacity to implement commitments.[7] According to this school of thought, SIRs can influence behavior less by facilitating the application of sanctions than by identifying and publicizing particular problems of noncompliance and working with the delinquent party to help it implement its commitments. SIRs can even help target the transfer of financial and technical resources to assist nations to implement commitments.

(d) *SIRs can help enforce commitments.* A second way of approaching implementation problems emphasizes "enforcement" of commitments. Proponents of this view argue that as international commitments become more costly and difficult to implement, the incentives for willful violations rise. Enforcement, though difficult in the international system, is necessary for such agreements. Enforcing commitments may also deter others from violating commitments. The enforcement approach presumes that failure to implement commitments is a conscious choice that can be influenced by the use of penalties.[8] Within this school of thought, SIRs can help identify and sanction parties that do not implement their international commitments. Our studies show that SIRs operate and are effective in both the "management" and "enforcement" roles.

(e) *SIRs can promote learning.* At least three major modes of learning are possible: (1) negotiators could learn to make better international agreements; (2) governments could learn to better implement their commitments by dealing with specific implementation problems or by observing how others implement their commitments; and (3) societies could learn more about their interests, because when useful information is readily available public debates on the need to address international environmental problems are likely to be more focused on realistic policy options.[9] When serious international environmental problems are at stake, learning should lead to more cooperation. Participants and societies will learn how to define and solve common problems—the "problem" itself may even be redefined. It may also be that individuals and organizations will learn that costly international commitments are not needed or justified. All three of these learning modes are likely to be more influential when supported by abundant information about implementation and when specific implementation problems are being handled; that is, when an SIR is in operation.

We are unable to test each of these pathways in detail, but their diversity underscores the many possible avenues of influence of SIRs. In the conclusion (Chapter 16) we offer a brief assessment of the extent to which of these five pathways explain how SIRs contribute to more effective international commitments.

To close, we note that research on SIRs has direct implications for policy. In major areas of international cooperation—such as arms control, trade, monetary policy, narcotics control, and the environment—the need for implementation review appears to be growing. The rising demand for these functions is most notable where international commitments are complex, where implementation is a challenging task, and where the economic and political stakes are sufficiently high that parties are concerned about whether other parties also implement their international commitments. Indeed, the parties to international agreements increasingly demand SIRs and provide for them in the agreements. Our studies show that those functions are well developed in some aspects of international environmental cooperation, and lessons from the cases presented in this book can contribute to designing even more effective agreements and SIRs.[10]

Notes

The editors and authors of case studies thank Abram Chayes, Peter Sand, Arild Underdal, and Oran Young for comments on earlier drafts.

1. Keohane, R.O., 1983, "The Demand for International Regimes," in *International Regimes*, edited by Stephen D. Krasner, Cornell University Press, Ithaca, NY, USA, pp. 141–171; Haggard, S., and Simmons, B.A., 1987, "Theories of International Regimes," *International Organization* 41:491–517; for a collection of papers on international institutions, see Young, O.R., ed., 1996, *The International Political Economic and International Institutions*, 2 volumes, Edward Elgar, Cheltenham, UK.

2. The many pathways by which review mechanisms can lead to more effective international agreements are reviewed in Victor, D.G., Greene, O., Lanchbery, J., di Primio, J.C., and Korula, A.J., 1994, Review Mechanisms in the Effective Implementation of International Environmental Agreements, WP-94-114, International Institute for Applied Systems Analysis, Laxenburg, Austria.

3. Ausubel, J.H. and Victor, D.G., 1992, "Verification of International Environmental Agreements," *Annual Review of Energy and the Environment* 17:1–43; Fisher, W., 1991, The Verification of International Conventions on Protection of the Environment and Common Resources: A Comparative Analysis of the Instruments and Procedures for International Verification with the Example of Thirteen Conventions, Programmgruppe Technologiefolgenforschung, Kernforschungszentrum Jülich, Jülich, Germany; Sachariew, K., 1992, "Promoting

Compliance with International Environmental Legal Standards: Reflections on Monitoring and Reporting Mechanisms," in *Yearbook of International Environmental Law*, Volume 2, edited by G. Handl, Graham & Trotman, London, UK, pp. 31–52. Chayes, A., and Chayes, A.H., 1996, *The New Sovereignty*, Harvard University Press, Cambridge, MA, USA; Greene, O., 1993, "International Environmental Regimes: Verification and Implementation Review," *Environmental Politics* 2(4):156–177. Relevant to our concept of implementation review is the process of performance review, in which the OECD organizes in-depth reviews of the policies of its member states in areas such as science and technology, energy, and now also environment. See Lykke, E., ed., 1992, *Achieving Environmental Goals: The Concept and Practice of Environmental Performance Review*, Belhaven Press, London, UK. Also relevant is research on international financial institutions since they are often used to finance implementation of international environmental commitments. See Sand, P.H., 1996a, "The Potential Impact of the Global Environment Facility of the World Bank, UNDP and UNEP," *Enforcing Environmental Standards: Economic Mechanisms as Viable Means?*, edited by R. Wolfrum, Springer-Verlag, Heidelberg, Germany; and Sand, P.H., 1996b, "Institution-Building to Assist Compliance with International Environmental Law: Perspectives," *Zeitschrift für ausländisches öffentliches Recht und Völkerrecht* 56(3):774–795.

4. In other terms, SIRs may contribute to "adaptive management" of ecosystems. Detailed design and application of adaptive management has focused within national, regional, and local political systems. See Holling, C.S., ed., 1978, *Adaptive Environmental Assessment and Management*, John Wiley & Sons, Chichester, UK; Walters, C., 1986, *Adaptive Management of Renewable Resources*, Macmillan Publishing Company, New York, USA; Lee, K.N., 1993, *Compass and Gyroscope: Integrating Science and Politics for the Environment*, Island Press, Washington, DC, USA; and Gunderson, L.H., Holling, C.S., and Light, S.S., eds., 1995, *Barriers and Bridges to the Renewal of Ecosystems and Institutions*, Columbia University Press, New York, NY, USA. For related concepts and analysis see Ostrom, E., 1990, *Governing the Commons: The Evolution of Institutions for Collective Action*, Cambridge University Press, Cambridge, UK. The present study analyzes how SIRs can provide a feedback of information that leads to practical adjustments and improved effectiveness of international governance. For analysis of such issues from a legal perspective see, for example, Gehring, T., 1994, *Dynamic International Regimes: Institutions for International Environmental Governance*, Lang, Frankfurt am Main, Germany.

5. For reasons of simplicity, in this text our discussions of "assurance," "enforcement," and "management" have not included discussion of the type of problem that is the subject of coordination (see Chapter 1). For example,

whether assurance affects behavior will largely depend on the type of problem the parties are confronting—truly interdependent problems should require such assurance, but problems involving mere coordination may require little assurance for all parties to find it in their interest to comply. Similarly, enforcement problems presumably will not exist in coordination cases, because all parties will find it in their rational interest to comply. Not all the modes by which SIRs operate will be evident in all problem types.

6. Müller has explored how security regimes (including institutions that we would label SIRs) empower actors that favor implementation of and compliance with international norms: Müller, H., 1993, "The Internalization of Principles, Norms, and Rules by Governments: The Case of Security Regimes," in *Regime Theory and International Relations*, edited by Volker Rittberger with Peter Mayer, Clarendon Press, Oxford, UK. In the case of acid rain, the argument is made more generally by Levy, M.A., 1993, "European Acid Rain: The Power of Tote-Board Diplomacy," in *Institutions for the Earth: Sources of Effective International Environmental Protection*, edited by P.M. Haas, R.O. Keohane, and M.A. Levy, The MIT Press, Cambridge, MA, USA. In the case of Rhine River pollution, it has been argued that information and institutions for international cooperation shifted power to environmental ministries, which favored stronger international commitments (and implementation): Bernauer, T., and Moser, P., 1996, "Reducing Pollution of the River Rhine: The Influence of International Cooperation," *Journal of Environment and Development* 5:389–415.

7. Chayes and Chayes, op. cit., note 3.

8. See Downs, G.W., Rocke, D.M., and Barsoom, P., 1996, "Is the Good News about Compliance Good News about Cooperation?" *International Organization* 50(3):379–406.

9. This brief discussion of learning is intended only to illustrate ways that information and assessments provided by SIRs can change the ideas and interests that, in turn, affect which commitments and policies are adopted, the behavior of targets, etc. We do not here delve into the important details, such as how learning by individuals leads to changes ("learning") by organizations.

10. The research project from which these case studies are drawn has contributed some insights into the need for and design of procedures for reviewing implementation and handling noncompliance under the Framework Convention on Climate Change; Romano, C.R.P., 1996, *The ILO System of Supervision and Compliance Control: A Review and Lessons for Multilateral Environmental Agreements*, Executive Report ER-96-1, International Institute for Applied Systems Analysis, Laxenburg, Austria; Victor, D.G., 1996, *The Early Operation and Effectiveness of Montreal Protocol's Non-Compliance Procedure*,

Executive Report ER-96-2, International Institute for Applied Systems Analysis, Laxenburg, Austria; Victor, D.G. and Salt, J.E., 1995, "Keeping the Climate Treaty Relevant," *Nature* 373:280–282.

2

Long-Term Trends in Systems for Implementation Review in International Agreements on Fauna and Flora

John Lanchbery

Introduction

Mechanisms for reviewing the implementation of international agreements may enhance the agreements' effectiveness by identifying, or offering the prospect of identifying, instances of noncompliance. For this reason, international agreements usually contain many mechanisms and processes that contribute to implementation review; these elements typically function as a system. International agreements also typically include means of adjusting commitments, often strengthening and expanding them. Such adjustment mechanisms can make agreements more effective, because they facilitate changes made in the light of new information and political opportunities. The presence of both systems for implementation review (SIRs) and adjustment mechanisms should contribute greatly to the effectiveness of agreements: SIRs can provide information on needed adjustments, and adjustment mechanisms allow that information to be used. This chapter examines trends in the inclusion of SIRs and of mechanisms that permit the growth and adjustment of commitments.

In exploring these trends, the chapter examines a sample of 34 fauna and flora agreements. The first of these treaties was concluded more than 100 years ago (see table 2A.1 in the appendix to this chapter). Using such a large set of agreements that span a long period of time is essential for identifying significant historical trends in the inclusion and development of SIRs. Flora and fauna agreements were selected for analysis because they are a coherent subset of environmental agreements and their history is the longest of all the environmental agreements.

This chapter demonstrates that formal SIRs are becoming more common in fauna and flora agreements and that the types of SIRs these agreements contain are increasingly likely to enhance effectiveness. Provisions that might facilitate the adjustment of commitments are also increasingly common. The research suggests that negotiators have increasingly become aware of the potential benefits of SIRs and commitment-adjustment mechanisms, and have deliberately included them in agreements.

The existence of a rising trend does not, however, reveal whether there is a similar trend in the operation of SIRs. Therefore, to see whether SIRs and adjustment mechanisms are used in practice, the chapter briefly examines a sample of three global fauna and flora preservation treaties from the 1970s: the Convention on International Trade in Endangered Species of Wild Fauna and Flora (CITES); the Convention on Wetlands of International Importance Especially as Waterfowl Habitat (the Ramsar Convention); and the Bonn Convention for the Conservation of Migratory Species of Wild Animals (CMS).

Analysis of these three accords shows that extensive SIRs were created after the agreements came into force. Moreover, many informal procedures, often operated by nongovernmental organizations (NGOs), also arose in response to the demand for implementation review. The original, formal procedures incorporated in agreements provided a basic framework for implementation review; however, in the three cases examined here, that initial framework proved inadequate.

The chapter begins by briefly examining some characteristic features of fauna and flora agreements. It then looks at how formal treaty-based provisions for implementation review and the adjustment of commitments have changed over time. Finally, it examines the SIRs in three selected global fauna and flora agreements.

Fauna and Flora Agreements

This section gives a brief background on the origins and aims of fauna and flora agreements. It focuses on how the nature of their commitments has changed. The ways in which the SIRs in these agreements have also changed are examined in the next section.

The first international treaty on flora was concluded in Bern, Switzerland, in 1889. It concerned measures to be taken against *Phylloxera vastatrix* (see table 2A.1, agreement 1), a disease that at the time posed a massive threat to European vineyards. All subsequent agreements concerning flora alone have likewise tended to concentrate on preventing the spread of disease and maintaining healthy stocks of cultivated plants, either by limiting trade or by setting up gene banks (see table 2A.1 for a list of flora agreements). The preservation of plants in their natural habitats is almost invariably covered by treaties that govern both plants and animals, such as CITES and Ramsar.

International agreements about fauna alone also initially concentrated on resource management.[1] Early agreements concerning marine animals, for example, were solely about managing resource stocks, as was the 1902 Convention for the Protection of Birds Useful to Agriculture (table 2A.1, agreement 10), which indirectly aimed to protect cultivated plants by protecting those birds that prey upon the "pests" that destroy them. However, since the early 1970s, agreements have tended to focus on species preservation.[2] They typically cover species that migrate across national boundaries or that are, as in the case of marine fauna, a "common-pool resource." Such agreements are generally highly species-specific and invoke a very limited range of mechanisms for protecting animals. Their commitments are usually confined to limiting or banning the killing or capture of animals, although the Convention for the Conservation and Management of the Vicuña (table 2A.1, agreement 17) also establishes reserves, and the Schedule to the International Convention for the Regulation of Whaling (table 2A.1, agreement 11) has long included the concept of limiting whaling in certain geographical areas.

Agreements concerning both fauna and flora have always been concerned with the preservation of species for their own intrinsic worth, rather than for their usefulness to mankind. The seminal treaty in this area, which never entered into force, is the 1900 London Convention Relative to the Preservation of Fauna and Flora in Their Natural State (concerning fauna and flora in Africa), which arose, even then, from a concern that fauna and flora on the African continent were rapidly disappearing.[3] The treaty set up parks and reserves in which the killing or taking of animals was strictly regulated. In 1933, a second London Convention concerning fauna and flora in Africa (with the same name as the first; table 2A.1, agreement 24) was concluded. The Convention kept the concept of parks and reserves, but also banned certain types of killing and taking of species on the grounds that they were cruel. In addition, it banned or limited international trade in endangered species. Almost all subsequent treaties on both fauna and flora bear striking similarities to the 1933 London Convention. Most, for example, borrow the concept of easily changeable annexes or appendices and establish parks or reserves. Many also seek to limit trade in species and their products, particularly CITES.

Historical Trends

This section explores whether there is a historical trend toward including more formal, treaty-based provisions for SIRs and whether there is a similar trend toward including formal provisions for the adjustment of treaty commitments.

The Historical Development of SIRs

The formal SIRs included in the texts of the 34 fauna and flora agreements covered here can be ranked in terms of their complexity. A six-part scale used to rank the SIRs is shown in table 2.1.[4] At the bottom of the table are treaties that have no formal provisions for reporting data on implementation or for reviewing implementation. At the top are those that contain many such provisions, including reviews of the adequacy of commitments, which facilitate commitment adjustment (see discussion below). This ranking reflects the hypothesis that agreements that have more extensive sources of information about implementation and that regularly review implementation will be more effective than those that do not. All else being equal, one would, for example, expect a treaty whose main review mechanism allows only states to report to operate less effectively than one that also provides for independent monitoring. (This hypothesis is examined in more detail later in this chapter and in Chapters 3–6.) The decades in which the agreements opened for signature are displayed laterally across table 2.1. Each agreement is indicated by an asterisk.[5]

Table 2.1 shows that the historical trend is for fauna and flora agreements to increasingly contain provisions for SIRs. The trend holds for all fauna and flora agreements outlined in the previous section and for both resource management and preservation treaties. Nearly all recent agreements have provisions for regular reviews of both implementation and the adequacy of commitments; most also have reporting systems that are not completely dependent on self-reporting by states. Since the 1950s, the only agreements for which this is not the case are those whose only participants are developing countries.[6]

Table 2.1 Trends in Systems for Implementation Review in 34 Fauna and Flora Agreements

Complexity and presumed effectiveness of agreement	Types of SIRs	Decade agreement concluded								
		1900	1910	1920	1930	1940	1950	1960	1970	1980
Most complex (most effective)	Regular implementation and adequacy review; reporting by states, regime, and experts; OSI					*			***	*
	Regular implementation and adequacy review; reporting by states, regime, and experts						***		***	***
	Regular implementation review; reporting by states, regime, and experts						**		***	***
	Regular implementation review; reporting by states				*			*	*	
	Some implementation review; reporting by states			*		*		*		
Least complex (least effective)	No reviews; no reporting	**		*		*	*	*	*	

Notes: OSI = On-site inspection; that is, independent observers or those of other parties can inspect sites, ships, etc. Each asterisk respresents an agreement opened for signature during the given decade.

Historical Development of Factors That Facilitate Adjustment

In table 2.2 the factors that facilitate the adjustment of commitments in the 34 agreements on fauna and flora are ranked on a five-point scale. The ranking reflects the hypothesis being tested here that specific formal mechanisms which enable parties to easily change the commitments in an agreement can help that agreement to take into account new knowledge and changing circumstances, thereby enabling it to become, or remain, effective.[7]

At the bottom of table 2.2 are agreements that are difficult to change because they make no provisions for meetings of the parties, such as the 1950 International Convention for the Protection of Birds, which came into force but never functioned. The next two categories have provisions for meetings of the parties: in one category conferences of the parties are set up, but are not obliged to meet regularly; in the other the parties are obliged to meet regularly. At a fourth level are treaties with clearly delineated, usually quite short, lifetimes, at the end of which they either cease to operate or are renewed by the parties; these were designated "renewable" treaties. Finally, there are treaties that are specifically designed to change over time. These can be subdivided into three types, although they are listed in the same general category in table 2.2. First, there are agreements that are conventionally known as "frameworks"; among the many well-known examples is the Convention for the Protection of the Ozone Layer. Such treaties are designed to be changed through the addition of protocols or amendments. Second, there are agreements that contain annexes, schedules, or appendices which include commitments (and sometimes review mechanisms) that can be completely altered by resolutions of the meetings of the parties. Examples of this type of agreement are CITES and the International Convention for the Regulation of Whaling. This type of agreement is referred to as an "annex" agreement. Third, there are agreements that are set up with the specific aim of spawning subagreements, such as the CMS. Strictly speaking, this type of legal instrument is a framework agreement; however, as is described later, such treaties do have certain distinct peculiarities. This type of agreement is referred to as a "flexible breeder."

The categories in table 2.2 are listed in order of decreasing complexity, with the greatest presumed effectiveness toward the top of the table. The decades during which the agreements were opened for signature are listed across the top. Each agreement is represented by an asterisk.

Table 2.2 Trends in Factors That Facilitate Adjustment in 34 Fauna and Flora Agreements

Complexity and presumed effectiveness of agreement	Factors facilitating adjustment	Decade agreement concluded								
		1900	1910	1920	1930	1940	1950	1960	1970	1980
Most complex (most effective)	Regular meetings of parties; "framework," "annex," or "flexible breeder" treaties				*	*	***		***	***
	Regular meetings of parties; "renewable" treaties								**	***
	Regular meetings of parties						**		***	*
	Irregular meetings of parties					*		*		
Least complex (least effective)	No conference of parties	**		*		*	*	*	*	

Note: Each asterisk represents an agreement opened for signature during the given decade.

Table 2.2 shows that there is a historical trend for fauna and flora agreements to increasingly contain provisions for adjusting commitments. As is shown later, in the three cases analyzed in depth here, this trend was prompted by a desire to enable the regimes as a whole to develop in light of the experience gleaned from their operation, and thus become generally more effective over time. All recent agreements contain adjustment-promoting mechanisms of the sorts coded in the top three categories of the table, except for some regional agreements whose memberships are made up of developing countries only.[8]

SIRs in Three Fauna and Flora Agreements

The previous section identified clear trends in SIRs and mechanisms for adjusting the commitments in 34 agreements. Because the sample was large and the goal was to provide a systematic assessment, the analysis only identified trends in the formal, treaty-based provisions for SIRs and commitment adjustment. It would be useful to examine in detail the actual operation of SIRs and adjustment of commitments. Although this is primarily the task of the other studies in this part of the book, a selection of 3 of the 34 agreements is briefly examined here. The three agreements, Ramsar, CITES, and CMS, were selected in part because of all recent fauna and flora agreements they have attracted the most attention from governments and NGOs, which are the actors most engaged in their implementation. They should thus exhibit the most implementation-related activity and give the most attention to implementation issues. Also, all three agreements were adopted in the 1970s, thus they contain extensive SIRs but are old enough to permit historical research on the actual operation of the SIRs. In short, they represent the "state of the art" in implementation review and contain the most extensive systems for implementation review. Moreover, they are global in their memberships, thereby hopefully eliminating biases of a purely regional nature.[9] In addition, their aim is to preserve the species per se, rather than to manage the resource for consumptive use. Thus there may be less need to disentangle biases arising from commitments based on commercial interests from those based on more altruistic goals.

Here, the focus is on SIRs that have been developed since the three agreements entered into force. Table 2.3 summarizes the commitments, SIRs, and provisions for adjustment included in the original agreements. Attention is given to how information is gathered, such as through national reports; how

Table 2.3 Main Commitments, SIRs, and Adjustment Mechanisms Included in the Ramsar, CITES, and CMS Treaty Texts

Convention	Types of commitments	SIRs	Adjustment mechanisms
Ramsar	To create protected areas (Ramsar Sites) nominated by parties; to protect Sites through domestic legislation	Triennial COPs; reporting to COPs by contracting parties; reviews of changes to Sites	Site-alteration process ("annex"); regular meetings of parties
CITES	To ban or limit trade in species listed in three revisable "appendices" through a system of import/export permits issued by parties	Biannual COPs; reporting by parties on issuance and receipt of trade permits and domestic legislation; reviews of implementation and adequacy of commitments	Appendix alteration processes ("annex"); regular meetings of parties
CMS	To protect migratory species using two "appendices." In Appendix I, parties protect species through domestic legislation. In Appendix II they do so by concluding new, discrete, subagreements called AGREEMENTs on particular species	Triennial COPs and a scientific council; reporting and review by parties on implementation of commitments relating to Appendix I; review of adequacy in form of possible new AGREEMENTs.	Appendix alteration processes ("annex"); regular meetings of parties

Note: COP = Conference of the Parties.

it is assessed; and how it contributes to the adjustment of commitments. The extent to which formal procedures for implementation review have shaped the ways that SIRs actually operate is also considered.

In these agreements, as in fauna and flora agreements in general, NGOs have played major roles, both in raising awareness of the issues at stake and in performing certain functions of implementation review. The NGOs that played a key part in the fauna and flora agreements of the 1970s were large professional organizations, such as the International Union for Conservation of Nature and Natural Resources (IUCN) and the World Wide Fund for Nature (WWF). In 1994, the IUCN had an annual budget of nearly 57 million Swiss francs and a staff of more than 500.[10] (Here the United Nations' classification is followed and the IUCN is referred to as an NGO, although its members include both states and non-states.) The WWF is financially supported by over 5 million contributors. The nationally based NGOs have similarly impressive credentials: Britain's Royal Society for the Protection of Birds has more than a million members, far more full-time professional ornithologists than the British government, and the Queen of England as its Patron.[11]

Ramsar.   The first of the 1970s era fauna and flora treaties to be negotiated was the Ramsar Convention.[12] The activities that led to this international treaty to protect wetlands date back to the 1950s and 1960s, notably an international project on the conservation of wetlands. The main participants were the IUCN, the International Council for Bird Protection (ICBP, now Birdlife International), and the International Waterfowl Research Bureau (IWRB)—all three of which are NGOs. At the final project conference in 1962, an international convention on wetlands was proposed.

The IWRB took the lead in developing principles for the Convention; in 1966 it gave the task of drafting the nascent treaty to the Dutch government. This draft version was revised at an IUCN meeting, with the ICBP and IWRB and some state representatives present, and at a series of other meetings. An International Conference on the Conservation of Wildfowl and Wetlands was eventually called, and 18 prospective parties convened in January 1971 in Ramsar, Iran, to sign the Convention on Wetlands of International Importance Especially as Waterfowl Habitat (the Ramsar Convention).

The Ramsar Convention primarily aims to preserve waterfowl by preserving their wetland habitat. The treaty requires parties to list one or more wetlands as "Ramsar Sites," to make "wise use" of those Sites, and to supply information on implementation of policies at them. The treaty commitments are adjusted by alterations to the so-called List of Ramsar Sites.

Ramsar's supreme decision-making body is the Conference of Contracting Parties (COCP), established by the Convention. All other treaty-related bodies were created by COCP decisions more than 10 years after the agreement came into force. A secretariat, called the Ramsar Bureau, was set up in 1987 together with a Standing Committee (SC) to oversee the operation of the Convention between COCP meetings. The SC meets once a year and has regular biannual "cooperative meetings" with the principal NGOs: the IUCN, the IWRB, the

ICBP, and the WWF. Indeed, the SC is constituted so as to include "advisors" from the IUCN and the IWRB, and it regularly invites other expert NGOs to its meetings. Both formal and informal technical information concerning the Convention is assessed by a Technical and Scientific Review Panel, which meets twice a year; the Panel, like most of the other treaty-related bodies, was set up long after the agreement came into force.

Information on implementation is supplied through "national reports," which are submitted to the COCP via the Bureau by national administrative authorities. There is an agreed format for national reporting to the COCP. About two-thirds of the reports are submitted on time and with complete contents, although whether the data they include are reliable is questionable. The Ramsar database officer expressed concern about the quality of "official" data at the most recent (1996) COCP meeting in Brisbane, Australia. There is no formal mechanism for resolving disputes about the accuracy of information submitted by the parties; they are normally resolved informally between the parties, or between parties and NGOs.[13]

Although the COCP cannot force parties to list wetlands as Ramsar Sites, it does publish "recommendations" in which the Conference expresses concern about a party's wetlands. In 1990 the COCP called on Poland to protect parts of the Vistula River and on Vietnam to designate the Melaleuca Forest as a Ramsar Site. It also made recommendations concerning Germany, Greece, Hungary, Jordan, Spain, the USA, and Yugoslavia, as well as praising some states for making listings.[14]

To help handle data on the 500 or so Ramsar Sites, the Bureau—with the help of the IUCN, the IWRB, and World Conservation Monitoring Centre (WCMC)—set up a computerized database in 1990.[15] Additional informal information on implementation and adequacy of commitments enters the review system in many ways. NGOs serving in an official capacity on Ramsar committees supply a lot of the information, but much information on implementation is also accumulated by the Bureau—often from NGOs that approach its staff, and sometimes vice versa. This information is retained by the Bureau, which frequently acts on it; interestingly, however, the information is not part of the public record, unlike the national reports from the parties.[16]

Much of the background information on wildfowl and wetlands is provided by NGOs in the form of inventories and directories. For example, in 1982 the IWRB produced a 784-page tome on wetlands in Central and South America.

In 1984 they launched a similar project on Asia, followed by studies of Africa and Oceania. Some of the parties conduct extensive studies on their own, such as the US National Wetlands Inventory Program begun in 1977. In addition, "Shadow Lists" of wetlands that could be included as Ramsar Sites have been produced by key NGOs.[17]

Monitoring of existing Sites has been strongly linked to the development of inventories. By the time the third COCP was held, 29 Ramsar Sites were reported by parties or NGOs to be undergoing "undesirable" changes.[18] The Conference gave the SC the task of identifying a way to reverse the trend. In 1990 the SC proposed a "Monitoring Procedure," which the Conference adopted. At the same time the COCP also adopted the so-called Montreux Record, a published list of Ramsar Sites where "undesirable" ecological changes are either occurring or seem likely to occur on the basis of both formal and informal information received by the Bureau.

The Monitoring Procedure is presented as a scientific, technical, and management assistance process rather than as a noncompliance procedure, thereby making it more acceptable to some parties.[19] Indeed, the Procedure's mandate makes it clear that its purpose is not to "detect noncompliance" but to "assist implementation."[20] As provided for in the Procedure, if the Bureau finds that a Site is changing adversely, or is likely to do so, it can ask the party concerned for more information and propose applying the Monitoring Procedure.[21] If a solution cannot be found, the Bureau must notify the SC, which then also seeks a solution. The Committee can in turn refer cases to the COCP. The Bureau is required to periodically review progress on the conservation status of Sites that come to its attention; results of these reviews are published in the Montreux Record. The reports from the Monitoring Procedure are also published after the party in question has had the opportunity to comment on the entry in the Record. In spite of its intrusiveness (subject to prior permission, teams of experts make long visits to the Sites), the Procedure has gained almost universal acceptance. It has been applied to Austria, Bolivia, Greece, Iran, Pakistan, Romania, Russia, Trinidad and Tobago, UK, Uruguay, Ukraine, and Vietnam.

In summary, Ramsar's formal, treaty-based SIR has undoubtedly provided the parties with some of the information that has enabled them to make the agreement more effective. However, the parts of the SIR that have been developed since the treaty was adopted, such as the Monitoring Procedure, have proved more effective. These processes, developed largely in the light of experience and often informally, have also provided the majority of the information needed for the commitment-adjustment mechanism (the List of Ramsar Sites) to operate effectively. The List has, for example, been greatly influenced by the shadow lists of the NGOs.

The conception and subsequent development of the Ramsar Convention has largely been due to a few key NGOs with an interest in waterfowl. The formal, treaty-based part of the SIR played a part in making the Convention effective, but the formal and informal mechanisms that have developed over time have generally had a greater effect than those written into the Ramsar Convention at the outset and have provided much of the information for the commitment-adjustment mechanism.

CITES.   Substantive negotiations on CITES and the Ramsar Convention began at about the same time, and the origins of CITES as a global agreement again date back to the 1950s.[22] During that decade there was growing public awareness in developed countries of the uncertain chances of survival of many species of wild animals and, to a lesser extent, of their habitats. Interest in the topic was promoted both by the increasingly powerful fauna and flora NGOs and by books and television documentaries about animals.[23] In 1963, the General Assembly of the IUCN called for "an international convention on regulating the export, transit and import of rare or threatened fauna and flora species or their skins and trophies."[24] Progress in drafting an agreement was slow until 1972, when the Stockholm Conference echoed the IUCN's original call for a treaty, adding a proposal that it include plants as well as animals. By March 1973 CITES was negotiated and signed by 21 states.[25]

CITES seeks to preserve fauna and flora solely by limiting or banning international trade in endangered species or their products. Species are listed in one of three appendices. Trade in items listed in Appendix I is essentially banned; regulation of trade in items listed in the other appendices is less stringent. The parties can and do routinely change listings in the appendices depending on the conservation status of the species.

From its inception, CITES was seen as the flagship of the fauna and flora preservation treaties. There was a far greater impetus from both parties and interested non-state actors to get the agreement under way than was the case for either Ramsar or the CMS. The agreement came into force in 1975, just over two years after it opened for signature. The first Conference of the Parties

(COP) was held in 1976. Likewise, the membership of the Convention has grown rapidly, from just 10 parties in 1975 to 124 by the beginning of 1995.

CITES has set up a far more elaborate committee structure than the Ramsar Convention for carrying out functions related to reviewing implementation and the adequacy of commitments. But like Ramsar, its committees were set up after it came into force. For example, a Standing Committee (SC) was established at the first COP to oversee the operation of the Convention between COPs.

Information about implementation enters CITES via the reporting processes established in the original agreement.[26] The parties are still required to report on all trade in species listed in Appendices I and II, on the number and types of permits issued, and on other factors such as the enactment of domestic legislation. However, the national reporting processes have been tightened in a series of COP resolutions. There are now strict deadlines for the submission of annual reports on trade and well thought-out guidelines for reporting, the latest of which were prepared in 1994.[27] Indeed, the guidelines for reporting would result in excellent information on implementation if the parties followed them. Many national reports are, however, submitted very late and are frequently incomplete. By mid-1992, for example, only 25 of 119 parties had submitted the reports due 31 October 1991. Poor reporting has constantly vexed the SC, and there have been many COP resolutions regarding the problem. Most recently, the SC exhorted the parties to report on their trade in plants, about which many states do not report at all.

In some countries poor reporting is due to a lack of resources. The treaty is implemented at the national level by Management Authorities (MAs), many of which do not have adequate resources and have low levels of expertise. Consequently, the Secretariat now runs training schemes for MAs. However, reporting and implementation problems occur more often with developed countries than with developing ones, and in some cases noncompliance is deliberate.[28]

Trade information from the parties is compiled in a database at the Wildlife Trade Monitoring Unit (WTMU) in Cambridge, UK, which is part of the WCMC. The WTMU began in the 1970s as part of Trade Records Analysis of Fauna and Flora in Commerce (TRAFFIC) International; it became the WTMU when it joined with the WCMC (then the CMC) around 1980.[29] The WTMU continued to manage the work of the TRAFFIC network until about 1990, when the WWF and the IUCN made TRAFFIC International a separate body. Like the WTMU, TRAFFIC monitors trade in fauna and flora and has an extensive network of NGOs working at the domestic level. One of the network's functions is to keep national authorities informed of illicit trade. In spite of the fact that the WTMU, TRAFFIC, and the IUCN are nominally separate bodies, they continue to have offices in the same building in Cambridge and keep in close contact, much as the Ramsar Bureau, the WWF, and the IUCN do in Gland, Switzerland. The WTMU is nominally completely independent of CITES; in fact, however, it manages data under contract for the Secretariat.

The WTMU database currently contains about 2.5 million trade records dating back to 1975; new records are added at a rate of about a quarter of a million per year. The database allows import and export records from the parties to be cross-matched to identify anomalies. Where the records do not match, or where parties report possible illicit trade, the WTMU informs the Secretariat.[30] (Under the terms of their contract with the CITES Secretariat, the WTMU is obliged to report all instances of potentially illegal trade and any more general problems.) Considerable informal information from NGOs concerning infractions enters the system through two different but parallel routes: first, in reports from NGOs directly to the Secretariat, and second, in reports from states to the Secretariat that are based on NGO information. TRAFFIC, for example, directly informs the Secretariat of any noncompliance that it identifies. However, TRAFFIC normally also works directly with national authorities via its regional offices to stop illicit trade at the source. Those authorities also report to CITES infractions that were originally reported to them by TRAFFIC.

The Secretariat compiles lists of infractions, which have grown considerably since the listing process was instigated by a resolution of the first COP.[31] All confirmed infractions are published and tabled in the Alleged Infractions Report at each COP. At the 1994 COP, the list ran to over 100 pages. Some Infractions Reports have clearly led to improvements in the effectiveness of CITES. For example, in 1989 the Secretariat notified Italy's MA of "serious and repetitive problems concerning its implementation of CITES ... ."[32] The Secretariat and the SC then repeatedly urged Italy to improve matters. In June 1992, the Committee concluded that Italy had not fully addressed the problems that had originally been raised. The SC therefore urged the parties not to issue any more CITES documents to Italy and not to accept any CITES documents issued by it until specific measures had been taken to improve the situation.[33] Most parties obliged and thus all legal trade with Italy concerning endangered fauna and flora was in effect suspended until Italy came into line.

Cases such as this are rare, although six major cases were cited in the 1994 Alleged Infractions Report and similar action was taken against Thailand and the United Arab Emirates. The SC also restricted trade with El Salvador and Equatorial Guinea, which were not parties at the time but later joined CITES. Although CITES implementation is far from ideal, these cases clearly show that parties modify their behavior in response to the agreement. The bans on fauna and flora trade with Italy and Thailand were not lifted until those countries modified their behavior. Indeed, the fact that the trade ban was imposed at all is indicative of the seriousness with which the parties take CITES. The treaty text contains no such provisions for enforcement, so the SC devised one—and it worked.[34]

Most infractions listed in the Reports are comparatively minor. The many infractions cited by the Secretariat at each COP indicate both the extent of the illicit trade in fauna and flora and the fact that much is done by CITES to prevent it.

In terms of information about the conservation status of species, the formal reporting system established by CITES does not provide the information the regime needs to establish whether species are endangered, and thus whether the existing commitments are adequate or need to be adjusted. There is no clear obligation for parties to provide information concerning the conservation status of species, and the information that is provided varies considerably from party to party. Some parties, such as the USA, usually have copious, high-quality information on their endangered species, whereas others, such as some states of the former Soviet Union, currently provide very little information. To supplement the information on the conservation status of endangered species supplied by parties, a considerable amount of data is provided by the United Nations Environment Programme (UNEP) and especially by NGOs such as the IUCN and the WWF. Thus, in practice, a very influential system has evolved for acquiring basic information on which to base decisions concerning listings in the appendices. Intergovernmental organizations (IGOs) and NGOs are usually particularly good at highlighting species whose conservation status is very poor. The IUCN publishes its Red Data Books listing endangered species of plants and animals; both NGOs and parties contribute to the Red Books, which are invaluable for CITES delegates.

In summary, the practice of CITES has changed considerably since the agreement was adopted in 1973. In terms of reviewing the adequacy of its commitments, CITES has built considerably on the basic adjustment mechanism of the appendices: the statuses of the species are assessed and the appendices are revised regularly. The mechanism of revisable appendices, in conjunction with regular reviews, requires the parties to focus on the contents of those appendices and on making regular changes to them. Abundant information on the adequacy of commitments flows into the regime, but the process is informal and decentralized. Much of the information is provided by NGOs. The mechanisms for implementation review that have been developed since the agreement came into operation, which are largely informal and involve extensive NGO participation, have been at least as important as those formally included in the Convention.

CMS. As with both Ramsar and CITES, the IUCN played a major role in creating the Bonn Convention for the Conservation of Migratory Species of Wild Animals (CMS). Serious international attention was originally drawn to the problems associated with migratory species in the early 1960s by the IUCN. (At that time the IUCN called for a treaty on migratory species, which many governments thought was a "crazy" idea.)[35] In 1979 West Germany organized the meeting at which the agreement was concluded.[36]

As in the other two agreements, the negotiations for the Convention gave special attention to learning from the failures of past agreements. In particular, the CMS is designed to allow expansion and revision of commitments. In this case, it was envisioned that the CMS would provide a framework for the negotiation of species-specific subagreements that would address the problems unique to particular migratory animals.

The CMS has two appendices, but they serve a completely different purpose than those in CITES. The first (Appendix I) lists species that the countries within the natural range of the migratory species ("Range States") are obliged to protect. The second (Appendix II) lists species for which the parties are required to set up completely new subagreements (called AGREEMENTs).

The main business of the Conference of the Parties (COP), the supreme decision-making body of the CMS, is listing Appendix I species and receiving reports on implementation from the parties. Most of these reports are late and few are sufficiently comprehensive to be useful. Reporting by states has been improving since 1983 when the CMS came into force; by the 1994 COP almost half of the parties had submitted reports of varying quality. Because of the rather loose reporting requirements, most national reports are brief and merely list domestic legislation, action plans, Range State status, and national focal points in two or three pages. In 1994 the only substantial reports were submitted by France, Myanmar (Burma), the Netherlands, South Africa, the UK, and to a lesser extent, Australia and India. In practice, therefore, meaningful reviews of domestic implementation of obligations regarding Appendix I species are difficult because the information needed to conduct them is absent. However, most parties do appear to have enacted appropriate domestic legislation. In other fauna and flora treaties information on implementation comes in large part from NGOs, but NGOs are much less active in the CMS than in the other treaties. NGO attendance at the COP has fallen steadily, from 30 organizations in 1985 to only 10 in 1994, including the ubiquitous IUCN and IWRB.

After the third COP in 1991, the SC set up a working group on "the strategy for the future development of the Convention," which was meant to tighten up the reporting and review processes. As a consequence of the poor reporting standards, at their fourth meeting, in 1994, the parties decided to adopt guidelines that if followed will result in a far higher reporting standard and include information from surveys and monitoring exercises as well as simple lists of the type mentioned earlier.

The CMS has made significant progress in listing new species in Appendix I and in concluding separate AGREEMENTs for species in Appendix II, although progress in the latter was painfully slow at first. At the first COP it was decided that AGREEMENTs should be concluded concerning four sets of animals: European species of bats, the white stork, small cetaceans in the North and Baltic Seas, and ducks and geese in the Western Palearctic. (At the time there was already a draft treaty for preserving seals in the Wadden Sea.) By the second COP, in 1988, all of the AGREEMENTs were at different stages of drafting, some at very early stages, and it was agreed not to try to conclude any more until the first batch were well under way. In 1991 the first AGREEMENT (on Wadden Sea seals) was concluded. This was followed by the small cetaceans AGREEMENT and the European bats AGREEMENT. The Western Palearctic AGREEMENT was concluded in 1995, as was the AGREEMENT on African-Eurasian migratory waterbirds.

Because of the long time needed to conclude AGREEMENTs, which are full legal treaties in the same sense as the CMS itself, it was decided at the third COP to try to get around the delays associated with ratification by concluding Memorandums of Understanding (MOUs) instead. These are more in the nature of "soft law" agreements. They are easier to conclude and have no restrictions concerning either ratification or the numbers of parties that must sign them. Also, they need not have separate secretariats and can make use of the CMS Secretariat, although this may be a mixed blessing because the Secretariat is chronically underfunded and its two staff members are hard put to keep up with their current work.

So far, two MOUs have been concluded: one on the Siberian crane (in 1993) and one concerning the slender-billed curlew. More AGREEMENTs or memoranda are being developed.

Apart from the process of concluding AGREEMENTs, which has been time-consuming, one of the main reasons for the CMS' slow pace has been a lack of interest by many states.[37] Countries in both North and South America have failed to join it (with the notable exceptions of Chile and Argentina), as have many Asian states. Some of these countries preferred to enter directly into bilateral or multilateral agreements concerning migratory species without using the CMS; the USA and Canada have had this attitude, for example. During the late 1980s and early 1990s, many states also took the view that the issues covered by the CMS would be better addressed by other agreements. Many states still see it as competing with the Convention on Biological Diversity (CBD) and, in the case of Europe and North Africa, with the regional Bern Convention on European Wildlife and Natural Habitat.[38]

Ironically, the CMS COP and Secretariat have spent considerable time co-ordinating their operations with the Bern Convention, the Whaling Convention, CITES, and increasingly with the CBD as well. Representatives from the agreements attend one another's meetings and there appears to be consensus among them that the agreements are complementary rather than mutually exclusive. Nevertheless, it is a fact that many states have been lukewarm toward the agreement, as have most NGOs. NGO publicity boosts, which are a prominent feature of CITES, are noticeably absent in the CMS.

In summary, it is still too early to say whether the CMS is effective or not because its main means of implementation, subagreements on particular species, have only entered into force over the past few years and MOUs are a recent innovation. Likewise, the state of implementation of Appendix I is difficult to assess without detailed information, which parties generally fail to provide in their reports. However, it is clear from COP reports that most of the parties enact domestic legislation in line with the terms of the agreement, even if it is less obvious whether they enforce it.

The formal mechanisms for implementation review codified in the CMS provided a framework; however, because they were inadequate, they changed once the agreement was under way. Today's SIR is much more elaborate than that formally created in the original agreement. Unlike in other fauna and flora agreements, however, these changes have not been brought about largely, or even partly, by NGO pressure. Nor have the NGOs, other than the IUCN, helped to provide much in the way of information. In the CMS, the movement for more rigorous SIRs seems to be driven mainly by states and by the UNEP.

Conclusions

The historical trend is for fauna and flora agreements to contain an increasing number of potentially more effective formal provisions for SIRs. Likewise, these agreements increasingly contain provisions for adjusting commitments. These trends are apparent in both global and regional agreements, and in both preservation and resource-management agreements. The only exceptions to the trends in SIRs over the past four decades have been a small number of agreements whose memberships are made up of developing countries only; this is probably because of heightened sensitivity to monitoring and implementation review in general (see Chapter 4). However, many developing countries that actively participate in global fauna and flora agreements concluded in the 1970s have, for example, welcomed the application (to them) of intrusive implementation review processes such as the Ramsar Monitoring Procedure, which includes on-site inspections.

Similarly, negotiators have long included provisions for adjusting agreements in the light of experience. As long ago as 1933, the London Convention allowed for adjustment by means of its system of appendices, a feature that was later included in CITES, the CMS, and the Ramsar Convention. An upward trend is also evident on closer examination of how the functions of implementation review are actually performed within agreements. This study briefly reviews the evolution of the SIRs in three of the most prominent fauna and flora agreements adopted in the 1970s. Within each agreement, attention to implementation review has increased over time; new procedures have been developed in response to the increased demand for implementation review. In two cases—Ramsar and CITES—NGOs have played major roles in supplying information on implementation and in identifying needed adjustments to substantive commitments in the light of such information and implementation reviews. Indeed, substantial reporting processes have been set up and operated entirely by NGOs in support of the regimes, with few formal links to them. The development of these informal processes was not usually prompted by the existence of formal mechanisms; they generally evolved in spite of formal processes in response to the perceived information requirements of the regimes. In practice, these NGO-dominated informal procedures have operated in synergy with the formally established procedures.

In summary, SIRs have become common and extensive, both in the full set of fauna and flora accords and in a sample of three major agreements adopted in the 1970s. As the three more in-depth studies show, despite this rising trend, once an agreement is adopted the formal provisions for SIRs are at best only a guide. In all three cases, the actual practice of implementation review was substantially elaborated after the agreement came into force. In some instances, elaborate informal procedures have also arisen. In short, while a trend is strongly evident, there is no substitute for in-depth analysis of case studies to show how SIRs operate and contribute to the effectiveness of agreements.

Appendix to Chapter 2

Table 2A.1 Thirty-four Agreements Concerning Fauna and Flora

Name of Agreement	Date and place of opening for signature	Geographical scope (no. of parties)	Type of treaty	Type of commitments	Reporting and review Processes	Monitoring
Agreements Concerning Flora						
1. International Convention regarding Measures to be taken against *Phylloxera vastatrix*	1889 Bern	Regional	Immutable	–	None	None
2. International Convention for the Protection of Plants	1926 Rome	Global	Immutable	Limits on trade	None	None
3. International Plant Protection Convention	1951 Rome	Global (81)	Regular COP; breeder	Limits on trade	Implementation and adequacy review; reporting by states	Self reporting by states; regime
4. Convention for the Establishment of a European and Mediterranean Plant Protection Organisation	1951 Paris	Regional (23)	Regular COP; annex; establishes Organisation to oversee and prevent spread of pests and diseases	Specified by Organisation but could limit trade	Implementation and adequacy review; reporting by states	Self reporting by states

5. Phytosanitary Convention for Africa South of the Sahara	1954 London	Regional set up under 1951 Plant Protection Convention	Regular COP (commission)	Limits on trade	Implementation and adequacy review; reporting by states	Self reporting by states; regime
6. Plant Protection Agreement for the South East Asia and Pacific Region	1956 Rome	Regional set up under 1951 Plant Protection Convention	Regular COP (committee)	Limits on trade	Implementation and adequacy review; reporting by states	Self reporting by states; regime
7. Agreement Concerning Co-operation in the Quarantine of Plants and their Protection against Pests and Diseases	1959 Sofia	Regional (10) Eastern Europe	Regular COP; annex	Limits on trade	Implementation and adequacy review; reporting by states	Self reporting by states
8. International Tropical Timber Agreement (ITTA)	Geneva 1983 (renewed 1994)	Global (50)	Regular COP; renewable	Limits on trade	Implementation and adequacy review; reporting by states and experts	Self reporting by states; regime
9. International Undertaking on Plant Genetic Resources[39]	1983 Rome (FAO)	Global (111)	Regular COP	Gene banks	Implementation and adequacy review; reporting by states and experts	Self reporting by states; regime; NGOs

Agreements Concerning Fauna[a]

Name of Agreement	Date and place of opening for signature	Geographical scope (no. of parties)	Type of treaty	Type of commitments	Reporting and review processes	Monitoring
10. Convention for the Protection of Birds Useful to Agriculture	1902 Paris	Global—in practice European	Immutable	Limits or bans on activities	None	None
11. International Convention for the Regulation of Whaling	1946 Washington	Global (40)	Regular COP; framework annex	Limits or bans on activities	Implementation and adequacy review; reporting by states and experts	Self reporting by states; regime; NGOs; OSI[40]
12. International Convention for the Protection of Birds	1950 Paris	Global (10)—in practice applied to Europe	Immutable	Limits or bans on activities	None	None
13. Convention for the Conservation of Antarctic Seals (part of the Antarctic Treaty System)	1972 London	Regional (11)	Regular COP; annex	Limits or bans on activities	Implementation and adequacy review; reporting by states and experts	Self reporting by states; regime; NGOs; OSI
14. Agreement on the Conservation of Polar Bears	1973 Oslo	Regional (5)	Regular COP; renewable	Limits or bans on activities	Implementation review—informal via IUCN	Self reporting by states; regime; NGOs
15. Convention on the Conservation of North Pacific Fur Seals[41]	1976 Washington	Regional (4)	Regular COP; renewable	Limits or bans on activities	Implementation and adequacy review; reporting by states	Self reporting by states; regime; OSI
16. Convention for the Conservation of Migratory Species of Wild Animals (CMS)	1979 Bonn	Global (42)	Regular COP; annex breeder	Limits or bans on activities	Implementation and adequacy review; reporting by states and experts	Self reporting by states; NGOs

[a]Early regimes concerning marine resources are omitted because they only concerned consumptive use.

17. Convention for the Conservation and Management of the Vicuña	1979 Lima	Regional (5)	Regular COP; renewable	Limits on activities; limits on trade; reserves	Implementation and adequacy review; reporting by states	Self reporting by states
18. Convention on the Conservation of Antarctic Marine Living Resources	1982 Canberra	Regional (29)	Regular COP; framework	Limits or bans on activities	Implementation and adequacy review; reporting by states	Self reporting by states
19. Agreement on Seals in the Wadden Sea (concluded under CMS)	1988 Bonn	Regional	Regular COP; annex	Limits or bans on activities	Implementation and adequacy review; reporting by states	Self reporting by states
20. Agreement on the Conservation of Bats in Europe (concluded under CMS)	1991 London	Regional	Regular COP; annex	Limits or bans on activities	Implementation and adequacy review; reporting by states	Self reporting by states
21. Agreement on Small Cetaceans in the Baltic and North Seas (concluded under CMS)	1992 Bonn	Regional	Regular COP; annex	Limits or bans on activities	Implementation and adequacy review; reporting by states	Self reporting by states
22. Agreement on Western Palearctic Waterbirds (concluded under CMS)	1995	Regional	Regular COP; annex	Limits or bans on activities	Implementation and adequacy review; reporting by states	Self reporting by states
23. Agreement on African-Eurasian Migratory Waterbirds (concluded under CMS)	1995	Regional	Regular COP; annex	Limits or bans on activities	Implementation and adequacy review; reporting by states	Self reporting by states

Agreements Concerning Both Flora and Fauna

Name of Agreement	Date and place of opening for signature	Geographical scope (No. of parties)	Type of treaty	Type of commitments	Reporting and review Processes	Monitoring
24. Convention relative to the Preservation of Fauna and Flora in their Natural State	1933 London	Regional (9)	Regular COP; framework annex	Reserves and parks; trade restrictions	Implementation review; self-reporting	Self reporting by states
25. Convention on Nature Protection and Wildlife Preservation in the Western Hemisphere	1940 Washington	Regional (17)	Immutable	Reserves and parks; trade restrictions	Occasional review by OAS	Self reporting by states
26. African Convention on the Conservation of Nature and Natural Resources	1968 Algiers	Regional (27)	Immutable	Reserves and parks; trade restrictions	Occasional review by OAU	Self reporting by states
27. Convention on Wetlands of International Importance especially as Wildfowl Habitat	1971 Ramsar (plus Regina Amendments and Paris Protocol)	Global (80)	COP	Reserves and parks	Implementation and adequacy review; reporting by states and experts	Self reporting by states; regime; NGOs
28. Convention on International Trade in Endangered Species of Wild Flora and Fauna (CITES)	1973 Washington	Global (120)	Regular COP; framework annex	Trade restrictions	Implementation and adequacy review; reporting by states and experts	Self reporting by states; NGOs
29. Convention on the Conservation of Nature in the South Pacific	1976 Apia	Regional (4)	Immutable	Reserves and parks	None; maybe review by SPREP	Self reporting by states

30. Convention on the Conservation of European Wildlife and Natural Habitat	1979 Bern	Regional (31)	Regular COP; framework annex	Reserves and parks; trade restrictions	Implementation and adequacy review; reporting by states and experts	Self reporting by states; NGOs
31. Protocol to Amend the Convention on Wetlands of International Importance (Protocol to Ramsar—see Agreement 4 above)	1982 Paris	See Ramsar—see Agreement 4 above	Introduces regular COP to Ramsar	As for Ramsar	As for Ramsar	As for Ramsar
32. Protocol Concerning Protected Areas and Wild Flora and Fauna in the East African Region (Protocol to the Convention for the Protection, Management and Development of the Marine and Coastal Environment of the East African Region)	1985 Nairobi	Regional	Regular COP; annex part of a framework convention	Reserves and parks; limits or bans on activities	Implementation and adequacy review; reporting by states	Self reporting by states
33. ASEAN Agreement on the Conservation of Nature and Natural Resources	1985 Kuala Lumpur	Regional	Regular COP; framework annex	Reserves and parks; limits or bans on activities; gene banks	Implementation and adequacy review; reporting by states	Self reporting by states; experts
34. Convention on Biological Diversity	1992 Rio de Janeiro	Global	Regular COP; framework annex	Gene banks; other; complex	Implementation and adequacy review; reporting by states	Self reporting by states

Note: OAS = Organization of American States; OAU = Organization of African Unity; OSI = On-site inspection; SPREP = South Pacific Regional Environment Programme.

Notes

The author would like to thank all the people who made helpful comments and contributions to this chapter, including Peter H. Sand, Dwight Peck (Ramsar Bureau), Jonathan Bardzo (CITES Secretariat), Arnulf Muller-Helmbrecht (CMS Secretariat), Kal Raustiala (Harvard Law School), and David Victor (IIASA).

1. The earliest accord concerning fauna was a resolution of the twenty-sixth General Assembly of German Agriculturists and Foresters in Vienna, Austria, in 1868. See Lyster, S., 1985, *International Wildlife Law*, Grotius, Cambridge, UK, p. 63. This book was used extensively in the research for this chapter.

2. The Conventions on the Conservation of the Vicuña and Antarctic Marine Living Resources are the main exceptions to this "rule," but both pay regard to preservation as well as to conservation for consumptive use.

3. See Lyster, 1985, op cit., note 1; Sands, P., 1995, "Framework, Standards and Implementation," in *Principles of International Environmental Law*, Vol. 1, Manchester University Press, Manchester, UK.

4. The categories used here are broad; reviews of the adequacy of commitments are included among the SIRs. Nevertheless, the categories reflect the grouping of provisions for SIRs found in treaty texts.

5. Recent agreements (those concluded since 1990) were excluded from the study on the grounds that they had an insufficient history of development; in general, they would fall into the top category of the table, with the possible exception of the Convention on Biological Diversity.

6. The agreements in question are the 1968 Algiers Convention (Africa) and the 1976 Apia Convention (South Pacific); see table A.1. Developing countries tend to be opposed to "monitoring" and processes associated with it, such as implementation review. This opposition sometimes arises because the countries view such processes as intrusive and as an infringement of their national sovereignty; see Lanchbery, J., 1994, "Verification of Environmental Agreements," in *Verification after the Cold War*, edited by J. Altmann, T. Stock, and J-P. Stroot, VU University Press, Amsterdam, Netherlands.

7. For further details see Victor, D.G., Greene, O.J., Lanchbery, J.F., di Primio, J.C., and Korula, A., 1994, Review Mechanisms in the Effective Implementation of International Environmental Agreements, WP-94-114, International Institute for Applied Systems Analysis, Laxenburg, Austria; Victor, D.G., Lanchbery, J.F., and Greene, O.J., 1994, An Empirical Study of Review Mechanisms in Environmental Regimes, WP-94-115, International Institute for Applied Systems Analysis, Laxenburg, Austria.

8. The agreements in question are the 1968 Algiers Convention and the 1976 Apia Convention.

9. It was suspected at the outset of this work that there might be regional biases for or against including provisions for implementation in treaties, with developed countries generally being in favor of including them and developing ones tending to be against it. This suspicion later proved to be at least partially true.

10. There are some 140 people based at the IUCN headquarters and about 400 "outposted staff," including consultants. See Bergesen, H.O., 1995, "A Global Climate Regime: Mission Impossible?," *Green Globe Yearbook*, edited by H.O. Bergesen and G. Parmann, Oxford University Press, Oxford, UK.

11. Information about the Royal Society for the Protection of Birds was collected by the author at the 1994 Annual General Meeting of the Society in London, UK.

12. For a more detailed description of this agreement and its origins, see in particular Matthews, G.V.T., 1993, "The Ramsar Convention on Wetlands: Its History and Development," Ramsar Convention Bureau, 28 rue Mauverney, CH-1196 Gland, Switzerland. See also Navid, D., 1989, "The International Law of Migratory Species: The Ramsar Convention," *Natural Resources Journal* 29(4) Fall; Lanchbery, J., 1996, "The Role and Development of Implementation Review Mechanisms in the Convention on Wetlands of International Importance: The Ramsar Convention," in *Verification 96*, edited by J.B. Poole and R. Guthrie, Westview Press, Boulder, CO, USA.

13. Dwight Peck, Ramsar Bureau, personal communication with the author.

14. Recommendations are not always censures. In the 1990 COCP report, a proposal by the USSR on designating new Sites was "warmly welcomed."

15. The WCMC is discussed in greater detail in the following section on CITES.

16. Dwight Peck, Ramsar Bureau, personal communication with the author.

17. For further information on the documents mentioned here, see Matthews, op cit., note 12.

18. Much of the information concerning the sites came from NGOs, such as the IUCN and the IWRB. The IWRB has organized annual waterfowl counts since 1967 and maintains a computerized database of waterfowl counts in 101 countries.

19. Since the 1996 COCP in Brisbane, Australia, the monitoring procedure has been called the Ramsar Management Guidance Procedure, both to better

reflect its real function and to avoid the widely disliked term "monitoring," which connotes unwanted intrusiveness.

20. Peter Sand, personal communication with the author.

21. The Monitoring Procedure is funded by grants from both parties and NGOs and "enables the Bureau to work directly with government officials to seek solutions to problems facing Ramsar Sites"; 1990 Montreux COCP Proceedings, p. 246.

22. Lyster, op. cit., note 1; Burns, W.C., 1990, "CITES and the Regulation of International Trade in Endangered Species of Flora: A Critical Appraisal," *Dickinson Journal of International Law* 8(2):203.

23. As evidenced by television documentaries and books published at the time, for example Bernard Grzimek's *Serengeti Shall Not Die* and Jacques Cousteau's numerous films and other publications.

24. The proposal for a trade treaty was made by Wolfgang Burhenne at the IUCN's Environmental Law Centre in Bonn, Germany, of which Burhenne is now the director. Personal communication with the author.

25. For more details on this process, see Sand, P.H., "Commodity or Taboo? International Regulation of Trade in Endangered Species," in *The Green Globe Yearbook*, edited by H.O. Bergesen, Oxford University Press, UK (forthcoming).

26. Much of the information in this chapter this is taken from Wijnstekers, W., 1994, *The Evolution of CITES: A Reference to the Convention on International Trade in Endangered Species of Wild Fauna and Flora*, 4th ed., International Fund for Animal Welfare, Geneva, Switzerland. I have also used COP reports and have had considerable help from John Caldwell at the WTMU and Jonathan Bardzo at the CITES Secretariat.

27. Reports on legislative and other issues are submitted every two years.

28. Personal communication from the WTMU. This is also mentioned in Secretariat Infractions Reports. For a truly damning report see WWF, 1986, The EEC Annual CITES Report for 1984: A Preliminary Assessment of CITES in the European Community, Gland, Switzerland.

29. Nearly all information cited here concerning the WTMU and WCMC was supplied in a series of personal communications from John Caldwell, the Senior Research Officer at the WTMU. The NGO TRAFFIC was formed in 1978.

30. John Caldwell, WTMU, personal communication with the author.

31. This increase can be seen by simply comparing the contents of the second, third, and ninth COP reports on infractions.

32. Ninth COP, Doc 9.22, summaries of alleged infractions.

33. Notification to the parties No. 675, 30 June 1992.

34. Peter Sand, former head of the CITES Secretariat, has argued that the actions of the Standing Committee are covered by the text of the Convention, which states that the parties have the right to take "stricter measures" individually or collectively; personal communication with the author.

35. Arnulf Muller-Helmbrecht, CMS coordinator, personal communication with the author.

36. Arnulf Muller-Helmbrecht, CMS coordinator, personal communication with the author.

37. Arnulf Muller-Helmbrecht, CMS coordinator, personal communication with the author.

38. Although the regional Bern Convention nominally concerns Europe, it is increasingly incorporating African states.

39. The Undertaking is a "soft law" agreement but was widely implemented much as a hard law agreement, certainly before the Convention on Biological Diversity came into force. (The Biodiversity Convention covers many of the same issue areas as the Undertaking.)

40. The term OSI (on-site inspection) is here used mainly in the context of boarding ships.

41. This agreement is a successor to a series of older regimes dating back to 1911, and was reconstituted in 1957. The agreement mentioned is thus the latest in a series which lapsed in 1984–1985 when it was not renewed.

3

The System for Implementation Review in the Ozone Regime

Owen Greene

Introduction

The ozone-layer protection regime is widely regarded as one of the success stories of international environmental regimes and as a model for tackling other global environmental problems. It has proved to be dynamic and relatively flexible, and has achieved a great deal.[1]

Since the initial 1985 Vienna Convention for the Protection of the Ozone Layer and 1987 Montreal Protocol on Substances that Deplete the Ozone Layer, commitments have regularly been reviewed and revised in the light of new scientific advice on the threat of ozone-layer depletion and of further opportunities to phase out ozone-depleting substances (ODS).[2] Controls on ODS have been strengthened and expanded, particularly through the revisions agreed upon in 1990 (London), 1992 (Copenhagen), and 1995 (Vienna) (see figure 3.1). Between 1987 and 1995 global consumption and production of the main ODS stopped expanding and began to decrease. By early 1996, 156 states had ratified the Protocol. Most developed countries had substantially phased out consumption of chlorofluorocarbons (CFCs) and halons. Helped with resources from the Protocol's Multilateral Fund (MLF), most developing countries had devised programs to do likewise in the first decade of the 21st century.[3] Meanwhile, controls had been extended to hydrochlorofluorocarbons (HCFCs), methyl bromide, and other ODS.

There is little doubt that the regime's rules, institutions, and mechanisms have contributed substantially to these achievements. Much of its effectiveness can be attributed to its capacity to develop and adapt.[4] This capacity is closely related to its institutional design. For example, the advantages of being based on a "framework" convention, designed to facilitate the negotiation of additional protocols and amendments, have been widely noted.[5] This chapter examines the ways systems for collecting, exchanging, reviewing, and using

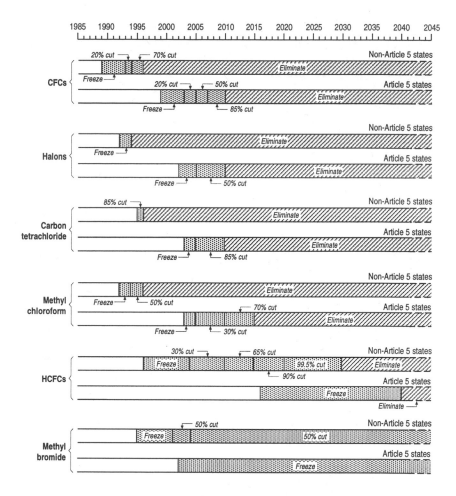

Figure 3.1
International commitments to regulate the consumption of ozone-depleting substances

information about implementation and compliance have enabled the regime to identify and respond to problems and lessons arising from the implementation process. Whereas the significance of regular scientific reviews (and of transnational "epistemic" communities) is now widely appreciated,[6] the significance of the Protocol's system for implementation review (SIR) has been relatively neglected until recently.[7]

This examination of implementation review systems in the Montreal Protocol focuses on the regime in operation since 1990, particularly after 1992 when implementation problems were coming to the fore alongside debates about further commitments. By the mid-1990s, there were serious concerns about compliance, loopholes, black-market trading, and trends in production and trade in some developing countries.[8] The effectiveness of the regime depended on its capacity to learn about and tackle such challenges and to take advantage of emerging opportunities. In principle, implementation review processes can contribute to these efforts by, for example, promoting transparency, learning, and accountability; building mutual confidence; deterring noncompliance; and facilitating timely responses to problems.[9] This chapter examines how SIRs have promoted the implementation and development of the ozone regime.

The chapter takes a systems perspective; implementation review in the Montreal Protocol is examined as part of the whole system of institutions and processes. Previous studies of SIRs in environmental regimes typically focused on the operation of mechanisms that are formally dedicated to implementation review or dealing with compliance problems.[10] This chapter, however, shows that such a focus can be too narrow. Several implementation review processes in the Montreal Protocol operate through a variety of international institutions; these include the MLF, the Global Environment Facility (GEF), the Technology and Economic Assessment Panel (TEAP), and the European Union (EU), as well as the formal reporting system and noncompliance procedures. Moreover, the chapter shows that these institutions have started to operate as a system, linking themselves in reinforcing ways. This decentralized implementation review system was not planned at the outset, but has evolved through both formal and informal processes.

Furthermore, the systems perspective emphasizes the importance of interactions between implementation review bodies and other mechanisms and institutions associated with the regime. The roles of the MLF and GEF in creating incentives for states to cooperate in the Montreal Protocol's Non-Compliance Procedure have been noted in previous studies,[11] and are discussed in Chapter 4 by David G. Victor. These interactions, however, are widespread, generating the complex decentralized system that has been important for the operation and effectiveness of the ozone regime. This chapter argues that implementation review must be seen as an integral part of the operation of the regime and as a factor promoting capacity for adaptive management practices.

The chapter first identifies the main components of the ozone regime's SIR and then focuses on how these have operated as a system in response to key challenges to the regime. The next section examines the development of implementation review activities of several different institutions and their individual operation and significance, and the following section shows how these institutions have linked together to tackle two major implementation and compliance problems in the mid-1990s. The final section draws conclusions and discusses some implications for institutional design and effectiveness.

Systems for Implementation Review in the Montreal Protocol

Several institutions have been established for the Montreal Protocol, and other international bodies have become formally linked with it. The supreme decision-making body is the Meeting of the Parties (MOP), supported by the Ozone Secretariat, the Open-Ended Working Group (OEWG)—a less formal negotiation group open to all parties which meets two or three times a year between MOP sessions—and numerous other bodies. These institutions and their allocated functions and relationships are summarized in figure 3.2.

Two mechanisms dedicated to implementation review have been established in the Montreal Protocol: the data reporting mechanism and the Non-Compliance Procedure. In addition, several other institutions have, in practice, developed important implementation review mechanisms, but have not been formally recognized within the regime. This section first outlines the two dedicated mechanisms and then examines the development and significance of the most important "non-dedicated" review mechanisms.

Dedicated Systems

The Montreal Protocol established a comprehensive system for reporting national data. Each party must provide statistical data on its production, imports, and exports of each controlled substance for the relevant baseline year (e.g., 1986 for CFCs and halons) and for every year since becoming a party to the Protocol.[12] The annual data must be submitted to the Secretariat within nine months of the end of the year.

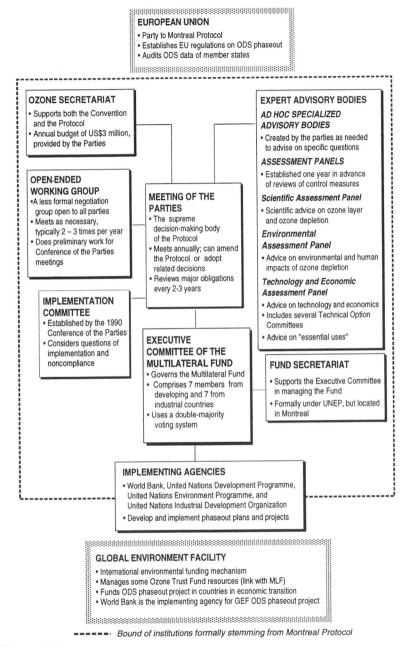

Figure 3.2
The institutional structure of the ozone regime

Formal implementation review is largely based on these national reports. The Secretariat prepares a report on implementation for each meeting of the MOP—the supreme review body. In this report, data from national reports are compiled into tables showing each party's annual consumption and production of ODS.[13] These publicly available tables make it easy to compare annual production and consumption with baseline figures and thus to assess whether a party is in compliance. ODS consumption per capita is also listed in the reports, along with data on reporting rates and brief analyses of trends and activities of various groups of parties.

Up to 1996, these compilations of national data have indicated good overall progress in implementing commitments—mostly in advance of Protocol obligations—and have revealed no significant compliance problems except with the reporting obligations themselves. As with several other environmental agreements, parties— even Organisation for Economic Co-operation and Development (OECD) states—were slow in reporting their data.[14] They have improved, but problems continue into the late-1990s, with many developing countries or states from the former Soviet Union (FSU) submitting late reports.

The Secretariat's reports on national data make noncompliance with reporting obligations transparent: states whose data are late or incomplete are clearly identified. However, no substantial review of the quality of submitted data (versus completeness of data) has developed.[15] Discussions of the reports at the MOP focus on overall trends, guidelines, and reporting rates, rather than on the performance of individual countries. Since 1992, such specific issues have instead been referred to the Implementation Committee (IC), which was set up to manage the Montreal Protocol's Non-Compliance Procedure adopted in 1990 and established in 1992.

Since then, the Non-Compliance Procedure and the IC as the standing committee associated with it have constituted the core of the "dedicated" implementation review system in the Montreal Protocol.[16] The IC regularly reviews specific compliance issues arising from the data reporting system or that are referred to it by the MOP. Its task is to guide the Secretariat on these issues and to make recommendations to the MOP. It also considers specific reports of possible noncompliance. Meetings are closed, but detailed proceedings of each meeting are available shortly afterward.[17]

The IC has avoided highly politicized issues and has established itself gradually and cautiously. It has tried to gain confidence among the parties in its procedures and operations and to promote compliance in a nonconfrontational, nonjudicial, and transparent way.[18] Until 1994, it limited itself to considering data reporting problems, for example, recommending that MLF financing be made available to developing countries for capacity-building projects to enable them to provide timely and accurate reports.

By 1994, sufficient confidence and precedents had been established that the IC began to make states, including developing countries that had received assistance but that still had not provided appropriate data, accountable for their reports.[19] This effort resulted in additional reports and established good cooperation between the IC and the Secretariat, as well as among the MLF bodies. In 1995, the IC considered its first formal submission on possible noncompliance by named parties (Belarus, Bulgaria, Poland, Russia, and Ukraine [BBPRU]). This action presented a key challenge, to which the IC was widely deemed to have responded effectively.[20]

"Non-dedicated" Systems for Implementation Review

In practice, a number of institutions, mechanisms, and actors have become involved in the collection, exchange, and review of information on implementation of and compliance with the Montreal Protocol even though they have not been officially assigned to such tasks. Of these, the most important are TEAP; the MLF, the GEF, and their implementing agencies; the EU; and nongovernmental organizations (NGOs).

The Technology and Economic Assessment Panel.   The significance of expert panels for the negotiation and early development of Montreal Protocol controls is widely known. They provided a direct institutional link between scientific or expert communities and the negotiation process, and contributed significantly to the development of commitments.[21] The Montreal Protocol specifically provides for convening panels of experts to prepare reports for major reviews of control measures by the MOP.[22] Thus, the Panel for Scientific Assessment, the Panel for Environmental Assessment, and TEAP were established to prepare reports for MOP sessions in 1990, 1992, and 1995.[23]

The role of TEAP has developed and expanded in the 1990s. TEAP reports provide detailed assessments of technical issues, such as technical options and alternative practices for reducing ODS consumption; the technical feasibility and economic implications of possible controls; the feasibility of identifying products to restrict trade; and the availability of ODS substitutes.[24] At the three main review conferences, these reports helped to shape policy debates and clarify that some further control measures were more feasible and less costly than had been feared. What is more important, TEAP became central to the management of important aspects of the regime. In practice it became closely involved with implementation and implementation review processes.

TEAP carries out its duties through three major implementation review mechanisms: the Technical Options Committees (TOCs); the essential-use procedure; and TEAP ad hoc working groups, particularly the working group on implementation problems in countries with economies in transition.

TEAP established several TOCs to examine technical options relating to particular sectors of ODS use, such as solvents, refrigerants, aerosols, foams, halon fire-extinguishing agents, and (more recently) methyl bromide applications.[25] TOCs play a key role in the operation of the regime. Much of the effectiveness of TOCs has been ascribed to their members and the rules by which they operate. The members are selected by the chair of the relevant TOC (in consultation with TEAP members) from lists of nominees provided by the parties. In addition, the chairs add their own nominees.[26] At an early stage, a precedent was established that members would not be drawn from ODS-producing industries on the grounds that such individuals may find it particularly difficult to focus on identifying feasible options for alternatives or substitutes, and would not have relevant user expertise.[27] Instead, members have overwhelmingly been drawn from key ODS industrial and other user groups or regulators and standard setters in the sector.[28] TOC members are volunteers who serve as independent experts. They pledge not to present the views of their countries or employers during deliberations, and not to take instructed positions on votes. Reports and technical recommendations are normally adopted by consensus (in only two instances between 1989 and 1996 was it necessary to present a minority perspective).

TOCs have the capacity to monitor and review implementation by their respective user groups and to take their findings into account in subsequent recommendations or activities. TOC members are generally people with direct influence and involvement in implementing the recommended alternative practices or ODS substitution programs. Their involvement ensures that their recommendations take detailed account of concerns and practical constraints of user industries or domestic regulators and raises the credibility of the TOCs' recommendations among "target" groups. It also means that well-placed champions are disseminating information and promoting implementation of all recommendations (even before they are formally adopted internationally). In practice, therefore, TOCs have become actively involved in informal implementation review as an inherent part of their adopted role of promoting the introduction of relatively ozone-friendly substitutes or alternative practices within their sector. This is in line with the "just do it" philosophy of TEAP and its TOCs.[29]

The activities and role of the Halons TOC illustrate these points.[30] Halons are primarily used in fire extinguishers, for which they have long been regarded as uniquely well-suited in several key roles. Thus there was strong resistance among fire fighters in the mid-1980s to proposals to reduce or phase out halon production. This resistance was reflected in government positions during negotiations for the 1987 Montreal Protocol. Nevertheless, by 1990 agreement had been reached to phase out halon "consumption" within 10 years.[31] In industrial countries phaseout dates were subsequently brought forward to 1994, and implementation has been reasonably successful. The Halons TOC played a key role in bringing about this success and in managing the ongoing halon-banking and halon-recycling systems.

Controls on halons are essentially implemented by a community of producers, users, and regulators of fire-fighting equipment. The 30 or so members of the Halons TOC are all prominent members of this community, many having a direct role in setting standards or regulations within their country or industry. Their recommendations for reducing or phasing out halon consumption thus carry high credibility among the groups that are to implement them. The TOC thus led the development of the complex set of controls, rules, guidelines, and exemptions that has been adopted by the MOP and that is in line with what is considered implementable by the fire-fighting community and domestic regulators.

Since the establishment of the broad framework of the Montreal Protocol controls, national regulators and the fire-fighting community have tended to go directly to the TOC and its reports for guidance on recommendations and regulations.[32] In fact, the Halons TOC recommendations have often led directly to changes in domestic or industrial practices and regulations, irrespective of MOP endorsement.[33] For example, TOC members from the oil and gas industry were able to change fire-fighting practices first within their own company

(British Petroleum) and then in other major oil companies using links within the industry. Similarly, the greatly reduced use of halons by US, UK, and Canadian armed forces was due to the involvement of senior military fire-fighting officers in the Halons TOC.[34] Military forces have been major halon consumers because of the high priority they give to regular fire-control training, and they stimulated the establishment of a Military-Use Subcommittee in the TOC to investigate military practices and needs.

Moreover, the Halons TOC has undertaken substantial implementation review as part of its efforts to contribute to effective management of the halon management and control regime. In 1994, for example, the TOC reviewed halon-bank management, supply and use of recycled materials, implementation within various industries and sectors, and the incentives to comply among fire-fighting equipment producers and users.[35] On the basis of this review, the TOC made a set of detailed recommendations (which were adopted) to improve the operation of the halon-control regime. These covered issues such as purity standards for recycled halons in international transfers, regulations and reporting systems for recycling facilities and product labeling, and clarifications of how the Basel Convention applies to trade of used and recycled halons.[36]

Further, the Halons TOC developed cogent arguments for the appropriate international framework for managing halon banks. In particular, the TOC strongly opposed proposals by the EU and some European states to establish programs to destroy stocks of used or recycled halons. It argued that such programs would send the wrong signals on the future of halon banks and reduce incentives to conserve or recycle halons. The ensuing debates and the successful lobbying on this issue by the TOC and TEAP co-chairs at 1995 meetings of the OEWG and the MOP clearly illustrate that in practice the Halons TOC (and TEAP) not only has taken a central role in managing and reviewing the operation of the halon-control regime, but is able to mobilize support to enable it to resist pressures from a strong actor like the EU.

The essential-use exemption system is the second important dimension of TEAP's implementation review activities. Provisions for essential-use exemptions enabled agreements to be achieved in 1990 and 1992 to phase out most categories of ODS because they provided a "safety valve." Countries and interest groups that doubted that satisfactory substitutes or alternatives were available for all uses of banned ODS were reassured that their case for continued use after phaseout could still be considered. Each phaseout commitment in the Protocol includes a sentence that states that the parties may "decide to permit such production and consumption that is necessary to satisfy uses agreed by them to be essential."[37]

Such exemptions could have created damaging loopholes. To avoid this, the 1992 MOP established criteria and a well-developed procedure for assessing applications for essential-use exemptions.[38] Each application for an essential-use exemption is referred to TEAP for detailed examination by the relevant TOCs. The MOP decides on the basis of TEAP's evaluation.

There is a presumption against granting exemptions unless TEAP reports that a strong technical case has been made and the criteria have been met. For example, applications were made in 1994 for exemptions for uses of halons, CFCs, carbon tetrachloride, and 1,1,1-trichloroethane (methyl chloroform). Each application was evaluated by TEAP. In its 1994 report, TEAP recommended exemptions for some uses of aerosol metered dose inhalers (MDI); certain applications in the manufacture of rocket motors for the space shuttle; and some laboratory/analytical uses. TEAP did not support any other applications. The MOP accepted TEAP's advice in each case.[39]

In practice, a key function of the essential-use mechanism is to focus attention on areas where there may be implementation problems and to stimulate international review and problem-solving responses. In essential-use applications, parties highlight areas where they expect compliance to be difficult or impossible. This function has received little attention from observers, but it has proved important for the effectiveness of the regime.

The application process can help governments to review the feasibility of substitutes and alternatives: applicants are required to provide detailed information on specific uses and why they consider alternatives to be infeasible. Once the application is submitted, the combined expertise of the TOC members is directed toward reviewing existing practices, identifying feasible alternatives and substitutes, and discussing these with the applicants. This process frequently involves visits by TOC members to the sites of manufacture or use and holding seminars and in-depth meetings with both national officials and target user groups. There are no detailed formal guidelines for such activities, but applicants are expected to cooperate fully with TEAP reviews, since the onus of proof of an essential-use requirement is on them. As a result of such activities, denial of an exemption is accompanied by detailed and expert guidance and assistance on how to implement the phaseout.[40]

Exemptions granted by the MOP are for specific quantities of ODS for specific uses; permitted quantities are reviewed annually. Every two years TEAP reviews whether the use still qualifies as essential. Thus TEAP and the relevant TOC regularly review implementation of any exemptions to check that ODS use is at a minimum and to determine whether alternatives have become available.

The essential-use mechanism performs a number of important functions in the Montreal Protocol. It allowed the negotiation of phaseout commitments in the early 1990s. It has proved to be an important safety valve for compliance with commitments, providing for flexibility in obligations where implementation of phaseouts is truly technically impractical. By referring application to TEAP expert committees, the MOP was able to resist some political pressure for exemptions so that essential uses were kept to a minimum. However, as stated earlier, the essential-use mechanism allowed TEAP to become centrally involved in implementation review and promoting compliance in areas where parties found implementation of phaseout commitments most difficult.

The TEAP Ad Hoc Working Group on Countries with Economies in Transition (CEIT) Aspects provides the third main dimension of TEAP's implementation review activities. It was established in October 1994 to examine and report on emerging compliance problems in countries in Eastern Europe and the FSU.

The role of this working group in reviewing and responding to implementation and compliance problems in these states is discussed in detail in the next section. From mid-1995, its reports (and the advice of its members) served as a reference point in discussions and decisions on these issues in the ozone regime. The working group and its consultants repeatedly visited national officials and user and supplier groups in former Soviet bloc countries, building on links established through TOCs and other TEAP panels.[41] In this context, it was perhaps the key body in monitoring and advising on progress toward implementation (or lack of it) in these countries. It also contributed to the formulation of international assistance programs. Moreover, the working group reviewed the situation in transition economies (such as Kazakstan, Georgia, and Tajikistan) that were not yet parties to the Montreal Protocol, but whose use of ODS and close trading relationships with Russia made their activities and plans an important factor.

The establishment and role of the TEAP Ad Hoc Working Group on CEIT Aspects established an important precedent for the future. For the first time, TEAP expert groups were explicitly assigned to review implementation and compliance problems in specific countries.

The Multilateral Fund and Its Implementing Agencies. The MLF was established in 1990 to help developing countries meet their commitments to phase out ODS by funding the "incremental costs" they incur in implementation and assisting with the transfer of non-ODS technologies to these countries.[42] By 1995, MLF funding had been approved for over 1,000 projects and activities in developing countries.[43] Funded activities include preparation of country programs for ODS phaseout; technical cooperation programs; training and information dissemination; promotion of bilateral and regional cooperation; and ODS phaseout investment projects.

The MLF is run by the Executive Committee (ExCom), supported by the MLF Secretariat, with four implementing agencies (IAs)—the World Bank, the United Nations Development Programme (UNDP), the United Nations Environment Programme (UNEP), and the United Nations Industrial Development Organization (UNIDO)—responsible for disbursing MLF funds and for working with developing country partners to design and implement projects. ExCom reports to the MOP, which sets overall policies and funding levels and reviews highly political issues such as whether donor countries have contributed as expected. ExCom continuously monitors and evaluates the operation of the MLF, including project implementation.[44] For this purpose, review systems were established in 1994 and have been greatly improved over the years.

In practice, the MLF has provided the main system for reviewing the development and implementation of country programs for phasing out ODS in developing countries. Since Article 5 countries negotiated a 10-year grace period, making 2010 their first phaseout date, the question of reviewing their compliance with Montreal Protocol phaseout commitments is unlikely to arise in the 1990s. However, MLF recipients must enter into contracts that entail near-term obligations. For example, of the 60 Article 5 countries with ExCom-approved country programs in 1995, 46 have agreed to a complete phaseout of specific substances ahead of their Montreal Protocol deadlines.[45] All 60 countries are committed to implement some MLF-funded projects within a few years.

Not surprisingly, in the MLF's first years of operation, reviews of funding applications were more important than implementation review. Any proposal for an MLF-funded project must go through several stages of international review before it is accepted.[46] It is reviewed by the implementing agency in the course of being prepared; by the Fund Secretariat;[47] and by the ExCom Subcommittee on Project Review, which then makes its recommendations for the full ExCom meeting where decisions are made. In practice, the review by the Fund Secretariat is usually the most detailed and rigorous, often including reports from commissioned expert consultants on the technical details.[48] IAs have developed expert groups to review their proposals before submission.[49] However, they often appear to act more as an agent of the requesting party than of the ExCom, and they are not yet trusted by ExCom to be consistently rigorous in their own review of project applications.[50] In contrast, the Fund Secretariat's support for a proposal is normally critical to its success. ExCom has only rarely approved projects against the recommendations of the Secretariat.

The system for evaluating MLF applications also provides a mechanism for identifying and addressing important issues raised by the developing countries' project proposals. The Fund Secretariat systematically notifies ExCom of any application that raises broader policy questions, because MLF guidelines are mainly developed through precedent-setting cases. Through this mechanism, questions have systematically been raised about India's programs to develop existing and new CFC production facilities and about China's plans to build an HCFC production plant. ExCom has found it difficult to agree on MLF guidelines for projects that will increase ODS production.[51] Nevertheless, the debates have not only resulted in important changes in producer countries' plans, but have also stimulated negotiations at the MOP on rules on the production, use, and export of controlled substances in Article 5 countries.[52]

By the mid-1990s, sufficient MLF projects were under way that the development of effective review systems for project implementation was becoming a priority. Until then, ExCom relied on IA progress reports that were based on each agency's standard procedures for monitoring projects—designed mainly to check that funds were properly accounted for and used efficiently. It was not until 1994 that specific guidelines and procedures for reviewing implementation of country programs and MLF-funded projects began to be developed in earnest, in the context of a major official review of the overall operation and effectiveness of the MLF.

In March 1995 the final report of this review concluded that, now that the MLF was established, "the essential issue facing the Financial Mechanism as an institutional system is less its capacity to develop, review and approve projects than its ability to implement approved projects in a timely manner."[53] This implied a need for the IAs to develop effective project monitoring and evaluation systems within standardized guidelines set by ExCom. Further, the report recommended that

> the ExCom and the implementing agencies, supported by the Fund Secretariat, collaborate on the development of practical guidelines for post-project monitoring and evaluation encompassing monitoring for verification of phase-out and disposal of phased-out equipment and monitoring for safe application of technology. Operational responsibility for carrying-out ex post monitoring and evaluation may remain with governments, financial intermediaries or the implementing agencies but the agencies themselves, in co-operation with ExCom, have a responsibility for ensuring that an appropriate level of monitoring takes place and that the information is fed back to the ExCom.[54]

The need for verification of ODS phaseout and disposal of phased-out equipment are stipulated in MLF funding eligibility guidelines. These guidelines require that no project establishing a new facility for producing ODS substitutes may be funded unless the original ODS-producing facility is shut down. For example, if "ABC" powder plants are to receive funding for producing all-purpose fire-fighting powders that substitute for halons, then the halon-production facilities in operation must be closed down. Project approval is dependent on the cooperation of the national government as well as the local project partner, because the company wishing to set up the powder plant may not be associated with the national halon producer that is to close. In addition, conversion projects must properly dispose of the redundant equipment and close down replaced facilities.

As of early 1995, MLF systems for verifying ODS phaseout and disposal of phased-out ODS-consuming or ODS-producing equipment were still incomplete.[55] Implementing agencies were formally responsible for such verification, but did not have the systems to carry out this task adequately. UNIDO was not enforcing proper disposal of redundant ODS equipment, arguing that this was the responsibility of the recipient governments. The World Bank implements its projects through government-approved financial intermediaries (FIs), which are normally banks. In principle, the World Bank expected FIs, in association with the local executing agency, to take the leading role in such verification. In practice, most FIs had limited interest in or capacity to go beyond financial disbursement and auditing; clearly, this arrangement did not lead to adequate verification.[56] Finally, the UNDP's Office of Project Services (OPS) had a system whereby, through its sector and national consultants, confirmation was required from the recipient plant that the old machines had been scrapped or destroyed. However, the OPS relied on government assistance to verify such certifications, but many developing country governments did not yet have adequate institutional capacity or interest to carry out such tasks reliably.[57]

ExCom accepted the main recommendations arising from the 1994–1995 MLF review and set about developing more effective implementation review systems. It had already begun the process by adopting (in July 1994) requirements for reporting on the implementation of country programs,[58] involving annual reports by Article 5 countries to the Fund Secretariat.[59] In November 1995, ExCom established guidelines for monitoring and evaluating project implementation, including post-project reviews and procedures to check that phased-out ODS plants and materials have been destroyed.[60] The IAs remain responsible for much of this task, providing regular reports to ExCom. In addition, the Fund Secretariat should establish an independent system for checking completed projects from each agency to ensure that "consistent and objective evaluation standards are being applied."[61]

To meet these responsibilities, in 1994 and 1995 the World Bank developed new systems for reviewing project implementation, focusing particularly on ODS phaseout projects.[62] For such projects, "Every grant and subgrant agreement . . . should establish guidelines by which equipment disposal/conversion will be verified. Equipment disposal/conversion should be monitored throughout implementation."[63] For all but the smallest projects, such verification involves in-depth reviews, site inspections, and spot checks, mostly carried out by local or international consultants, who are normally hired by the local executing agency (normally the FI); one restriction is that institutions carrying out evaluations should not be involved with project implementation. These new World Bank guidelines provide a basis for standardized monitoring and evaluation systems to be used by all IAs.[64]

Thus, by early 1996, a relatively well-developed implementation review system was being put into place within the MLF, the World Bank, and other implementing agencies. It was primarily developed as a way to facilitate timely responses to implementation problems and to learn from the past. However, it also specifically includes more effective systems for verifying phaseout and disposal of ODS-consuming equipment. Although it remains to be seen how it will actually operate, the system has been built upon rigorous reviews of project applications. By 1995 the system already involved levels of independent monitoring and evaluations of country programs and ODS phaseout projects. Such activities probably could not have occurred in the context of a dedicated Montreal Protocol verification or noncompliance procedure. The MLF will provide the primary system for reviewing implementation of ODS phaseout programs in developing countries for several years to come.

The GEF and Its Implementing Agencies. The MLF's review systems apply only to the development and implementation of MLF projects and ODS phaseouts in developing countries. Only countries that meet Article 5 criteria qualify for such funding. However, the new World Bank procedures outlined above also apply to the review of GEF projects and country programs in countries in economic transition.[65] The World Bank is the sole implementing agency for GEF-supported ODS phaseout projects in such countries. Moreover, a substantial proportion of these projects have been under development since early 1995; from the outset the new World Bank monitoring and evaluation guidelines have been thoroughly integrated into ODS phaseout projects in countries in transition.

In April 1996 the GEF Council adopted the GEF Operational Strategy, with a chapter on ozone regime funding, which strengthened GEF monitoring and evaluation procedures for its Ozone Trust Fund and brought them in line with those established by ExCom for the MLF.[66] Similarly, it made its IAs—preeminently the World Bank in this context—responsible for carrying out many implementation monitoring tasks, post-project verification, and evaluations of projects of the GEF Ozone Trust Fund.

In funding projects that help countries in economic transition comply with the Montreal Protocol, the GEF has added some new elements to its role in implementation review. In May 1995, the GEF Council decided that funding should be withheld from eligible parties that fail to meet their obligations under the Protocol.[67] Thus approval for additional funding for ODS phaseout projects in countries in economic transition such as Belarus, Russia, and Ukraine would be conditional on their abiding by Montreal Protocol procedures, including the

Non-Compliance Procedure. In practice, this stipulation makes GEF financing of projects in these countries conditional on their having satisfactory ODS phaseout programs that have been agreed with the IC. At the IC meetings in autumn 1995, the GEF representative made clear his concern about imminent noncompliance in several countries in transition.[68]

Once agreement is reached between the IC and each noncompliant state on plans for compliance, the IC carries out regular reviews of progress toward implementation. Thus, in practice the IC has become involved in reviewing implementation of GEF projects in several countries in economic transition.[69] Conversely, the GEF and World Bank systems directly monitor compliance with the Montreal Protocol Non-Compliance Procedure.[70] This is discussed further later in this chapter.

The European Union.   The EU is a party to the Montreal Protocol, as is every EU member. Thus the EU occupies a unique position as an international institution. Since 1990, EU regulations have tended to impose more stringent obligations on EU member states than the Protocol itself.[71] Simultaneously, the EU has emerged as a leader in strengthening the global regime. Its special position in the regime has allowed it to play a major role in reviewing implementation in EU states, which in turn has supported and extended implementation review in the Montreal Protocol.

Several EU member states have refused to supply fully disaggregated national data to the Ozone Secretariat on grounds of commercial confidentiality and that the system of collection and reporting of national data goes against the objectives of the single European market. Instead, all EU states supply full data to the EU Commission on conditions of confidentiality; the Commission then reviews the data and sends them to the UNEP in aggregated form. Thus, the Ozone Secretariat cannot fully monitor implementation in EU states individually, but relies on the EU Commission to do this.

In fact, the EU has established a system for thoroughly auditing the data supplied to it.[72] This system involves examining the books of commercial producers, traders, and users and dealing directly with the sources of national data rather than working through national authorities. Partly because several businesses and member governments lack confidence in the ability of Commission officials to maintain confidentiality, much of this task has been contracted out to a private auditing company—the accountancy firm KPMG Peat Marwick.

The task has reportedly been carried out with the detail and rigor that would be expected of a financial audit, with the auditors having full access to invoices, production records, shipping papers, and so on of each relevant company involved. Although the contract for this work is periodically put out to tender, the contract has been awarded to KPMG Peat Marwick throughout the 1990s. Thus, this firm has gained substantial experience and knowledge. Reportedly, the EU Commission, EU governments, the Chemical Industry Federation (CEFIC), and the companies themselves have become confident that the reports have been compiled rigorously and in strict confidence.[73]

After the data are audited and revised as deemed appropriate, KPMG Peat Marwick prepares a summary report for the EU Commission (DG XI). This report contains partially aggregated data on production, consumption, and international trade of each controlled substance within the EU, together with data aggregated according to individual countries and analyses (such as time series) to provide a basis for reviewing implementation and compliance. Data in this report are presented in a way that protects commercial sensitivity. The data remain confidential and are viewed only by the Commission and the Ozone Management Committee established by the Council of Ministers to facilitate implementation of Montreal Protocol obligations and associated EU regulations.[74] KPMG Peat Marwick also provides separate confidential information on how it compiled the data for each country and what problems and issues were raised. Apparently, KPMG Peat Marwick has on occasion reported doubts about the reliability of certain company records. In these cases DG XI raised the matter with national members of the Ozone Management Committee, who have, in turn, stimulated remedial action by domestic regulators. Thus, whereas no substantial review of the *quality* of submitted data has developed in the global regime, the EU has established a detailed system for reviewing and promoting data reliability—for baseline data as well as for annual data.

The EU data compilation and auditing system has had to adjust to new controls on new substances such as methyl bromide. These adjustments required input from new groups of producers, distributors, and consumers. Patterns of trade, distribution, and use of these new substances were different from those of CFCs and halons. Moreover, the agricultural use of methyl bromide was a particular concern of southern European states such as Italy, Greece, and Spain. These countries consumed relatively small amounts of other ODS, thus previous auditing and review activity had not focused on them. Initial reported baseline data for methyl bromide turned out to be full of serious inaccuracies, discrepancies, and double counting. KPMG, assisted by DG XI, had to embark on a detailed paper-trail exercise. The exercise began with an audit of the shipping orders of all major methyl bromide producers (producers outside the EU also cooperated), continued with an investigation into importer and wholesale distributor records, and ended with an examination of final users. Only then were the baseline data considered reasonably accurate.

DG XI and the Ozone Management Committee have cooperated in coordinating implementation of new EU regulations on ODS. The Commission reviews and revises existing EU regulations, standards, and licenses relating to ODS production, trade, and use. Implementation problems or requests for exemptions are considered on a case-by-case basis. For example, after much deliberation channel tunnel trains were granted a special exemption from a ban on HCFC air-conditioning units in new railway equipment on the grounds that it would be disproportionately expensive to implement the ban while maintaining the special fire-prevention standards for these trains. Just as for any state, the EU's task of achieving implementation has involved a complex process of implementation review and adjustment.

By 1994 the problem of illegal use and smuggling of controlled ODS had become a major concern throughout much of the world. There were substantial seizures of illicit CFCs by customs authorities in OECD states. Russia and other former Soviet republics were the main source of these CFCs, though there were suspicions that some ODS might have originated in developing countries such as India. Concerns also grew about imports of recycled or recovered CFCs and of feedstocks. These imports are permitted, but much of the recycled CFCs imported from Russia were suspected to be virgin CFCs that had been mixed with water or other pollutants to gain an import license. There is doubt that CFC-recycling facilities even exist in several regions from which the recycled chemicals were supposed to have come.

National governments traditionally are responsible for preventing illegal use and gray- and black-market trading. However, here too, the EU occupies a special position as an international institution in the ozone regime. Several industries and other enterprises in Europe report to the EU on possible noncompliance, particularly by competitors or traders. For example, in Western Europe, issuance of quotas and licenses for imports of ODS is an EU rather than a national process. By 1994 chemical companies such as Imperial Chemical

Industries (ICI), Elf Ata-Chem, Hoechst, and Solvay were complaining that trade in illicit CFCs was widespread, undermining demand for their legitimate substitutes.[75] They reported many instances of such trading, and increasingly sought to provide firm documentation or photographs of such practices to help police or customs investigators. Similarly, the EU permitted some trade in used CFCs so that surplus CFCs could be returned to manufacturers for disposal. However, import quotas for used CFCs were also given to a range of companies that turned out to be in the business of repackaging CFCs in new products instead of disposing of them. Finally, the import of CFCs for chemical feedstocks—where they are consumed during the chemical production process and thus pose no threat to the ozone layer—is also legally permitted. However, the definition of a feedstock had been stretched by many importers to include manufacture of expanded polyurethane foams and repackaging for use in refrigeration.[76] In 1994 the EU Commission set quotas of 16,000 tons of CFCs for use as feedstocks, whereas the major legitimate user in the EU of CFCs as feedstocks (Zeneca, which uses CFCs in pesticide production) required only about 1,500 tons.[77]

EU institutions were central in responding to these problems and concerns. Whereas customs inspections and policing remained under national control after the Maastricht Treaty, the EU institutions played a key coordination and standard-setting role. To tackle gray- and black-market trading, the Commission tightened its licensing systems and regulations, requiring detailed reviews of ODS imported as feedstocks by individual companies.[78] Customs controls were improved through the efforts of the Commission and the Ozone Management Committee. Reports of illicit trading were used to review EU licenses and were sent to relevant national authorities for investigation. The EU worked with the USA to enforce controls (though with limited success), as well as to raise the issue at the MOP and to clarify or develop Montreal Protocol controls that were ambiguous. These efforts included the MOP request that all countries provide a list of ODS-recycling facilities to help in policing false labeling.

Nongovernmental Organizations. Nongovernmental organizations can broadly be classified as environmental or industrial organizations (ENGOs or INGOs). ENGOs have devoted some attention to monitoring implementation. In April 1995, for example, the Spanish NGO, CODA, accused two Spanish firms of importing CFCs from Russia, adulterating them, and selling them to manufacturers as reclaimed substances.[79] In the UK, Greenpeace and Friends of the Earth focused attention on ICI's plans and activities in the late 1980s and early 1990s, particularly in relation to its promotion of HCFCs as substitutes.[80] ENGOs have good access to most international bodies associated with the Montreal Protocol, and many have taken advantage of this access. However, although several can draw on substantial resources and expertise, ENGOs have been surprisingly uninvolved in implementation review at the international level, preferring to focus on the development of OECD commitments.

INGOs have sometimes played an important informal role in monitoring and reviewing implementation of controls on ODS. Commercial producers and users of controlled ODS have detailed knowledge of the implementation process and often have a clear interest in reporting any problems or noncompliance that might affect their commercial competitiveness. In general they report problems to the relevant national authorities, who then either tackle the issues nationally or pursue them through international channels.[81] In addition to their activities in TEAP, representatives of industry have been active at the MOP and have participated in other bodies of the Montreal Protocol as observers or national delegates. For example, they have circulated reports relating to black-market trading and lobbied for remedial action. Similarly, they have lobbied within the EU. For example, when Austria joined the EU, several EU refrigerant manufacturers argued that Austrian companies were reporting suspiciously high stockpiles of CFCs which, if accepted, could legally permit Austrian refrigerant producers to use CFCs in new equipment and thus gain a commercial advantage over competitors required to use more expensive alternatives.[82]

The System in Action: Linkages and Synergies in Response to Implementation and Compliance Problems

The practice of implementation review goes far beyond the Montreal Protocol mechanisms that are formally dedicated to such tasks: the data reporting system and the Non-Compliance Procedure involving the Implementation Committee. In addition, the MLF, the GEF, and their implementing agencies have developed major implementation review systems, as has the EU. TEAP has also become involved in implementation review through three mechanisms: the activities of its TOCs, its role in the essential-use exemption system, and its Ad Hoc Working Group on CEIT Aspects. ENGOs and INGOs have also played a significant role. Since 1992, the implementation review activities of each body have developed gradually, as key actors responded to existing or new challenges. The development process has accelerated since 1994, contributing considerably to regime effectiveness.

In principle, interactions among these bodies could increase the overall effectiveness of implementation review, and thus perhaps the effectiveness of the regime as a whole. Links between them could be mutually reinforcing or provide useful redundancy in case of obstacles to the operation of one of the bodies or mechanisms. Important questions for our purposes are whether such *linkages and interactions* have developed to establish a larger *system* for implementation review, and whether and how this development has helped to tackle some of the major challenges that confronted the regime in the mid-1990s. This section addresses these questions by considering the significance of linkages between bodies involved in implementation review in the response to the two most important noncompliance issues that have arisen so far: data reporting problems and noncompliance of some countries in economic transition.

Responding to Data Reporting Problems. Developed states were slow to comply with their data reporting obligations. Initially, the Secretariat was the main body involved in pestering states to provide data, supported by periodic requests from the MOP. After the IC was established in 1992, it gradually established a close working relationship with the Ozone Secretariat. Together, they focused on improving the reporting of data. In 1993, the IC called some OECD states such as Italy and countries in economic transition such as Russia, Belarus, and Ukraine to appear before it to account for their noncompliance.[83] This action had some effect. Italy provided its baseline data, and by 1994 so had nearly all other OECD states.[84] Most non-FSU East European states had also supplied at least some data by that time, though baseline data from the Czech Republic were overdue. Belarus partially met its obligations by providing data for 1986 and 1992, but data were still missing from Ukraine, Russia, and other states of the FSU.

The rate of reporting among developing countries was also poor. As previously mentioned, the IC and the Secretariat initially ascribed this to a lack of institutional capacity to prepare reports in such countries. They were able to mobilize MLF capacity-building assistance to address this problem. By 1994, however, reporting rates of developing countries remained low: over 40 recipients of such assistance still had not provided their baseline data. The IC decided in July 1994 to invite some of the offending parties to appear before its next meeting in October to explain. Significantly, representatives of the MLF Fund Secretariat, the World Bank, the UNDP, the UNEP, and UNIDO were also invited to attend the meeting as observers and to provide relevant project information.[85] Their presence put pressure on the parties appearing before the IC to provide accounts to the IC that were consistent with their project commitments and their reports on project implementation and to provide the required data as soon as possible. In fact, several of the missing reports were supplied over the summer, and at the IC meeting in October 1994 several other states promised to furnish reports in the near future.[86]

The involvement of MLF bodies in the proceedings of the IC has been useful in encouraging data reporting. Since 1994 they have been invited to all IC meetings, consolidating links between all of the bodies, with the GEF also attending since 1995. More generally, these links between the IC and the funding bodies helped by emphasizing that cooperation with the IC had potential benefits as well as penalties.

The MOP also contributed to this system in important ways. In October 1994, the MOP decided that a developing country would no longer be given Article 5 status (which is necessary to qualify for MLF funds and for the grace period for phaseouts) if it did not report baseline data within a year of approval by the MLF ExCom of its country program and institutional strengthening project.[87] Further, it decided that countries that had yet to ratify the (amended) Protocol could only gain special exemptions from trade restrictions if they had fully met the Montreal Protocol reporting requirements. Countries in economic transition were particularly affected by this—several were slow to become parties after the breakup of the USSR or to ratify the 1992 Copenhagen amendments. For example, Poland was stimulated to provide full data to gain an exemption.[88]

Responding to Compliance Problems of Countries in Economic Transition. The implementation and compliance problems in Eastern Europe and the FSU that emerged in the mid-1990s posed perhaps the greatest challenge to the regime since phaseouts were first agreed to in 1990. These countries have been struggling with profound economic, political, and social transitions. Several had made virtually no effort to implement Protocol obligations. Several of the new FSU states had yet to become parties to the Protocol; only Belarus, Russia, and Ukraine automatically became parties to the Protocol after the breakup of the USSR.[89]

Two key functions of SIRs are to identify implementation and compliance problems in a timely way, and to stimulate effective international responses. Throughout the early 1990s, representatives from countries in economic transition often referred to their difficulties at MOP or OEWG sessions: most often in the context of requests for essential-use exemptions or explanations for delays in data reports or financial contributions to the MLF. Other parties tended to respond with sympathy, reminders that international assistance was available through the GEF, and expectations that the countries would nevertheless adhere to their commitments. Discussions of implementation problems in countries in economic transition became routine and predictable. In this context, it was uncertain whether additional international measures to address likely noncompliance of these countries would be seriously considered in time to prevent a crisis.

The Ozone Secretariat and TEAP were the first two institutions to become fully aware of the large-scale noncompliance in some countries. The activities of TEAP and its TOCs and the Secretariat's role in the data reporting system meant that they were relatively well informed of the situation.[90] They joined together to push the issue up on the MOP's agenda. In its report to the MOP in October 1994, TEAP reported that

many of the successor states [of the USSR] had no legislative basis for either ratifying or implementing the Montreal Protocol and there are no institutions and authorities to manage the phase-out of ODS or even to report consumption data and to establish the baseline consumption level. . . . Their [economic transition countries'] resources are mostly inadequate for a timely ODS phase-out. . . . It seems inevitable that noncompliance will occur in several states.[91]

TEAP gained permission from the MOP to form the Ad Hoc Working Group on CEIT Aspects (discussed earlier) assigned to examine emerging compliance problems in countries in economic transition.

Meanwhile the chair of the IC, the Secretariat, and others consulted on whether and how to invoke the Montreal Protocol's Non-Compliance Procedure so that the IC could address the problem of likely noncompliance by countries in transition. This was a delicate issue. There were few precedents for using noncompliance machinery in international environmental regimes. States may react very badly to accusations of noncompliance, and it was not at all clear how Russia and other FSU states would respond. It was important that compliance problems be dealt with as cooperatively as possible and that the process be initiated at an early stage—without waiting for positive evidence of substantial noncompliance after the January 1996 phaseout date.

In May 1995, Belarus, Bulgaria, Poland, Russia, and Ukraine (BBPRU) submitted a joint statement to the OEWG declaring that they did not expect to be able to comply with phaseout obligations by the end of 1995; they requested a four-year extension of their phaseout deadline, an exemption from their contributions to the MLF, and international assistance for measures to phaseout ODS over several years.[92] They made it clear that they wanted to resolve this issue politically at the MOP.

However, other parties at the OEWG decided that the MOP would not consider any proposals on noncompliance by transition countries except on the basis of recommendations from the IC. Moreover (as discussed in the section above), the GEF Council had decided that further funding for ODS projects in these countries would be conditional on their cooperation with appropriate Montreal Protocol procedures. Thus, when the Secretariat chose to interpret a letter sent by the Russian prime minister on May 26 (combined with the earlier BBPRU statement) as a submission under paragraph 4 of the Non-Compliance Procedure, the BBPRU governments decided to accept that the process could go ahead within this framework.[93] This meant that they officially invoked the Procedure themselves, rather than being accused of noncompliance by other parties, thus resolving the earlier diplomatic dilemma.[94]

The matter was considered by the IC at two meetings in August 1995 and at a third meeting at the end of November 1995.[95] Briefly, the IC adopted a constructive but rigorous problem-solving approach. It ruled out any extension of treaty deadlines. However, provided that the BBPRU governments complied fully with all data reporting requirements and presented a detailed plan to come into compliance with phaseout obligations as soon as possible, the IC was prepared to examine such phaseout plans in detail. Once satisfactory plans were agreed, they would be recommended for GEF support. Implementation would then be monitored and regularly reviewed by the IC, on the basis of detailed annual progress reports, until the countries came into compliance.

This overall approach was accepted by the BBPRU governments, and each country's situation was considered separately. For example, a way was found for Poland to comply fully by the end of 1995. Bulgaria arrived at the August IC meeting with its data and with a detailed phaseout plan showing how it could, with GEF assistance, come into compliance by 1997. Belarus and Ukraine had provided most of their data in time for the August meeting of the IC, but did not provide national phaseout plans until the November IC meeting (at which they also confirmed, as requested, that they had no ODS production, recovery, or recycling facilities). The IC requested further information on Belarus's phaseout plan and additional time to review Ukraine's national program, with a view to achieving acceptance by early spring 1996. At the IC in August Russia continued to argue that it was not possible to provide baseline data or annual data before 1995, a feasible phaseout plan, or information on its ODS recycling or recovery facilities. At the November meeting, Russia provided acceptable baseline data, but a detailed phaseout plan and other requested information were still missing. Russia was asked to provide an in-depth phaseout program by the end of January 1996 for consideration at a special intersessional meeting in the spring. In practice it took several further efforts to obtain the required information from Russia during 1996; ultimately, however, the IC was able to approve a phaseout plan with Russia by early 1997 and to recommend it for funding.

All of these arrangements were presented as recommendations at the MOP in December 1995, where they were accepted.[96] The IC also included recommendations to ban all trade of ODS from Russia to developed states, except to approved Commonwealth of Independent States (CIS) for domestic use. Russia opposed this recommendation, and became even more unhappy when the MOP expanded the restrictions to exports to developing countries.[97] Nevertheless, these recommendations were also ultimately accepted.[98]

The IC and the Non-Compliance Procedure clearly played a central role in the formulation and development of the institutional response to noncompliance problems of the countries in economic transition, particularly after August 1995 (the specific operation of the Non-Compliance Procedure is examined in detail in Chapter 4). In doing so, they established important precedents for the future. However, it is important to note five dimensions of the involvement of the other review bodies and of the links between them.

First, TEAP played a key role, together with the Secretariat and other non-dedicated review bodies, in clearly identifying the emerging noncompliance problems in countries in economic transition and putting them on the MOP's agenda. The EU also contributed here by funding a 1994 study by private consultants COWIconsult on ODS phaseout in Russia and informing TEAP of the results (and subsequently also funding the TEAP Ad Hoc Working Group on CEIT Aspects).[99]

Second, these other institutions directly contributed to the operation of the IC. In addition to the 10 members of the IC and the Ozone Secretariat, representatives of the MLF-implementing agencies (the World Bank, the UNEP, the UNDP, and UNIDO) and the Fund Secretariat were present at the meetings, together with a representative from the GEF and the co-chairs of the TEAP Ad Hoc Working Group on CEIT Aspects.[100] The TEAP Ad Hoc Working Group's draft reports were central to the discussions. Its co-chairs not only provided key advice to the Committee, but also played a major role in questioning, assessing, and evaluating the information and draft phaseout programs submitted by the BBPRU governments.[101] The GEF stood ready to provide funds. Moreover, its refusal to consider project proposals from the BBPRU without IC approval was critical to the initial decision by Russia and others to accept that this issue would be dealt with through the noncompliance mechanism. Firm restatements of GEF policy during the IC meetings in autumn 1995 by the GEF representative helped to keep the process on track, particularly in relation to the difficult discussions with Russia at the November IC meeting.[102] Further, the involvement of World Bank and GEF representatives, in particular, ensured that the phaseout programs under negotiation had realistic expectations of GEF funding and followed funding guidelines.

Third, in practice the reviews of implementation of each BBPRU country's phaseout program will depend on several institutions. The establishment of systems to carry out these reviews was clearly critical to the effectiveness of the approach adopted to deal with compliance problems in transition economies. Formally, the IC conducts the reviews and reports to the MOP. However, as discussed earlier, the contracts for GEF funding of ODS phaseout projects include provisions for detailed monitoring and review by the World Bank and the GEF, including on-site inspections and verification of destruction of phased-out equipment and production facilities. The Ad Hoc Working Group on CEIT Aspects is to continue monitoring and providing advice on the situation in the non-compliant states and countries in the CIS that are not yet parties to the Montreal Protocol. The IC and the MOP can draw on these review systems as well as on the reports provided by the parties. Moreover, these bodies are expected to help solve problems during the implementation process.

Fourth, the non-dedicated review bodies helped the BBPRU governments meet the requests of the IC in time for the Vienna MOP in December 1995. TEAP, particularly the members of the Ad Hoc Working Group, helped the Russian government to prepare baseline data for the IC meeting in November 1995. Without TEAP's support, it is doubtful whether Russia would have been able to proceed along the track proposed by the IC that autumn, which would have undermined the credibility of the overall approach and increased the risk that Russia would withdraw from the process. The reliability of the submitted Russian baseline data was questionable, but the involvement of TEAP members in the compilation process both improved data quality and provided reassurance to IC members that the data were as good as could be expected under the circumstances.[103] The IC accepted the judgment of the TEAP Working Group co-chairs on this point.[104]

The World Bank, as the GEF-implementing agency responsible for ozone projects in transition countries, advised Bulgaria and Belarus on the development of their phaseout programs. Informally, the Ad Hoc Working Group members, the Secretariat, and the IC chair tried to alert the BBPRU governments over the summer of 1995 to the approach likely to be taken by the IC. They prompted Bulgaria to prepare a detailed phaseout proposal for the August IC meeting. The Ukrainian phaseout proposal, tabled at the end of November, was prepared by COWIconsult, which had close and well-established links with both TEAP bodies, the MLF and GEF funding institutions, and the EU. The TEAP Ad Hoc Working Group and the Ozone Secretariat played the lead role in alerting countries in the CIS that were not yet parties to the Montreal Protocol about the requirements for exemption from ODS trade restrictions.

Fifth, the non-dedicated review institutions also addressed some noncompliance issues outside the Protocol's Non-Compliance Procedure. The GEF, through the World Bank, was already funding ODS-related projects in several countries in economic transition before 1995. This situation allowed the World Bank to provide advice on the project proposals for ODS phaseout in countries in economic transition. Members of the relevant TOCs and the TEAP Ad Hoc Working Group, which had already considered aspects of compliance problems in transition economies, were a source of technical advice on these plans. Their efforts went beyond the development of a plan for IC approval.

Similarly, the issue of possible noncompliance by Poland was largely addressed outside the IC.[105] Poland had associated itself with the Russian statement because of the possibility that it would have difficulties in complying in 1996 if its essential-use nomination for 100 tons of CFC-12 for servicing refrigeration equipment were to be turned down. Despite strong Polish lobbying, TEAP had firmly and repeatedly advised the parties at OEWG meetings in May and August 1995 that the Polish application did not fulfill the appropriate essential-use criteria.[106] Polish concerns remained unresolved at the August IC meeting. However, TEAP members, particularly those involved in the Refrigeration TOC, subsequently persuaded the Polish government that Poland's needs could be met by recycling domestically available CFCs. In addition, they arranged for the EU to confirm that access to EU-recycled stocks would be available as a backstop. Although this was all done in the context of the essential-use exemption system, internal TEAP communications meant that TEAP and TOC members were aware of the importance of these activities for efforts to address the noncompliance problem of the countries in economic transition.[107]

Whether or not the compliance problems in Russia and other countries of the FSU are indeed resolved remains to be seen. However, there is no doubt that a range of the mechanisms and institutions associated with the Montreal Protocol played an important part in the international response that at least promises to be effective. Moreover, they have combined to form a mutually reinforcing overall implementation review system. The Secretariat, TEAP, the IC, the GEF, the World Bank, the EU, independent consultants, and the MOP sessions all were important in addressing the challenge and promoting a constructive and rigorous response.

Conclusions

The effectiveness of an international regime depends on the way in which its norms, rules, and institutions directly or indirectly affect societies and the behavior of a wide range of relevant actors. Institutions or mechanisms for reviewing implementation and responding to problems can play an important role in promoting implementation and increasing the capacity of environmental regimes to develop and adapt. This chapter has identified and discussed numerous examples of this for the ozone regime in the 1990s.

The chapter has shown that implementation review in the ozone regime takes place through several institutions, and not only through mechanisms that are formally dedicated to such tasks. In addition to the dedicated institutions—the data reporting system and the Non-Compliance Procedure—several non-dedicated bodies have developed substantial implementation review functions and procedures since 1992. The most important of these are TEAP (particularly through its role in the essential-use exemption system and the activities of its TOCs and the Ad Hoc Working Group on CEIT Aspects); the MLF, the GEF, and their implementing agencies (including the World Bank and the UNDP); the EU; and NGOs (particularly INGOs). In some of these bodies the review systems became well-developed in the mid-1990s and were contributing substantially to the implementation, development, and effectiveness of important aspects of the ozone regime.

The formal and informal implementation review activities of these bodies evolved over time according to need, as perceived by key actors in the regime. This shows that the ways in which institutions actually operate and develop in a regime can be very different and more complex than would be supposed from a study of legal provisions or "dedicated" institutional functions or roles. It is important to examine regimes in operation, rather than only formal arrangements and decisions, to understand their effectiveness and their capacity to cope with challenges.

The existence of *several* different implementation review institutions may in itself increase the overall effectiveness of the implementation review process. It provides the advantages of redundancy, as well as wider and more timely access to relevant data and review procedures. The risk that effective review could be paralyzed by a blockage in one link or mechanism is reduced. There are also more potential sources of information than simply those available to the dedicated reporting and review mechanisms. For example, the information gathered and used through the MLF, the GEF, TEAP, and the EU review processes extends far beyond that required in the Montreal Protocol's dedicated data reporting system. Moreover, the fact that several review mechanisms are non-dedicated or informal could increase flexibility.

Further, the interactions between different bodies involved in the monitoring and review processes can create synergies that increase the overall effectiveness of implementation review. Together these bodies can operate as linked components of a larger SIR. This linkage is occurring in the ozone regime. Particularly since 1994, the numerous institutions have linked up in mutually reinforcing ways. This is evident, for example, in the efforts to resolve the two major compliance problems of the mid-1990s: poor data reporting rates and noncompliance in some countries in economic transition. These linkages were not planned, but rather have evolved through the efforts of a variety of institutions and actors to actively manage the regime to address problems and seize opportunities. The system has increased the capacity of the regime to cope with implementation and compliance problems and with major challenges to its operation and effectiveness.

The development of implementation review functions *within* the ozone regime's bodies or mechanisms that are officially dedicated to other roles (such as TEAP, the MLF, the GEF, or the EU) has promoted close links between systems for reviewing implementation, responding to implementation problems, and revising and developing rules and institutions. The benefits of such organic links are clear, for example, in the role of TEAP in the essential-use exemption system. This system combines an important safety-valve procedure for adjusting obligations with a de facto mechanism for focusing attention on areas where there may be compliance problems and for stimulating review and problem-solving responses. Similar benefits may be seen in the development of systems in the MLF for reviewing implementation of ODS phaseout projects or the activities of the Halons TOC. The regime's effectiveness has also benefited from the linkages *between* implementation review bodies and institutions with other functions, as illustrated by the mutually reinforcing interactions between the IC and the funding bodies in tackling noncompliance problems since 1994.

An important theme of this book is that participation can substantially affect outcomes. The involvement of a variety of bodies and mechanisms may increase both the number and types of participants in the implementation review process. Each institution or mechanism has its own set of formal and operational rules concerning access to and participation in its review activities. For example, the participation in and style of the IC, TEAP, the ExCom, the World Bank, the Secretariat, the MOP, and the NGO reviews of ODS phaseouts differ greatly. The selection of one mechanism over another for reviewing a particular aspect of implementation affects which actors participate and how they do so. Moreover, some mechanisms offer more scope for managing participation than others. Such management is widely regarded to be a critical ingredient in the success of TEAP and several of its TOCs, and since 1994 the IC has shown that it can manage participation of observers in its meetings in order to promote its goals.

Thus, one aspect of the systems perspective is that it highlights the ways in which many different actors can participate in implementation review processes and how rules of access and participation (and the policy levers they provide) can be much more flexible or complex than it would appear from a study of dedicated implementation review mechanisms alone. The availability of a variety of bodies or mechanisms for implementation review increases the ability of policy entrepreneurs, regime leaders, and others to use them to recognize problems and opportunities and to stimulate timely responses, as illustrated in the process of responding to the compliance problems of countries with economies in transition.

The contribution of the SIR to the overall development and effectiveness of the ozone regime is intrinsically hard to evaluate. Clearly, the SIR did not have a considerable impact before the 1990s, since most of its key components were not operational until after 1992. Even so, the combination of state and EU monitoring and enforcement systems, the capacity and interest of major commercial ODS producers and users to monitor and report on the performance of competitors, and the prospect of an effective SIR in the future made some contributions even at that early stage.

By the mid-1990s, however, implementation issues had come to the fore in the operation of the regime. This chapter has provided numerous examples of where the SIR has made important contributions to the regime's capacity to promote implementation and respond to problems. Moreover, each dedicated and "non-dedicated" implementation review mechanism is developing rapidly; only recently have the mechanisms begun to link up to form an overall system. The relative importance of that system in the operation and effectiveness of the regime increased in the mid-1990s, and continues to increase. However, evaluations of factors determining the effectiveness of established regimes should focus not only on individual components of their rules and institutions, but on the way they combine to form a system. The ozone-layer protection regime in operation in the 1990s is a complex system, and must be understood as such.

This analysis raises a number of policy-relevant issues for institutional design relating to the development of SIRs and to their place within the regime. It emphasizes that mechanisms for monitoring and implementation review (or for other important functions in a regime) can be effectively, if informally, developed in institutions that have been established for other purposes. Moreover, it suggests that there are important advantages to this type of development: creation of several mechanisms available for key functions, additional institutional resources, and potential advantages of redundancy and synergy.

Given the experience of the Montreal Protocol, it is neither feasible nor necessary to try to preplan the development of a set of mutually reinforcing implementation review mechanisms in detail. In fact, the effort would probably be counterproductive, causing negotiation problems and leading to inflexible and inappropriate systems. The important factor in the ozone regime has been that several institutions and mechanisms associated with it have a sufficiently flexible mandate allowing implementation review mechanisms to be formally or informally developed, linked, or used as needed, without great fuss. Moreover, outside institutions, such as the EU and ENGOs and INGOs, were also available to play important and somewhat systemic roles.

There are well-known dangers in drawing up broad, permissive, or overlapping mandates for institutions within a regime. These types of mandates can lead to confusion, battles over authority, and inadequate attention in each institution for the development of its core roles and procedures. Moreover, overreliance on non-dedicated or informal mechanisms can result in systems that are not sufficiently robust or that lack sufficient legitimacy or procedural clarity to cope with serious challenges.

In the ozone regime, it is significant that the main role of each institution of the Montreal Protocol was reasonably clear and well delineated. Furthermore, it was not until the mid-1990s that several such institutions developed substantial informal or non-dedicated implementation review activities—that is, *after* they had become well established in their core roles and the regime was in operation for some years. Moreover, they extended and developed their activities with caution and attention to due process, in order to contribute to solving real problems for the regime. The lesson for institutional design that can be drawn from the ozone regime is not that subsidiary institutions should be given vague or overlapping mandates or encouraged to engage in implementation review activities for which they were not established. Rather, mandates should be drawn up so that institutions can develop and pursue their roles according to needs and in a way that recognizes that implementation review activities are likely to become an important dimension of the operation of most aspects of an effective regime. Once a regime becomes established, there should be close links between the processes of reviewing implementation, responding to implementation or compliance problems, and developing or revising regime rules and obligations.

Moreover, experience from the Montreal Protocol also demonstrates the advantages of establishing institutions or mechanisms that are *dedicated* to implementation review mechanisms, alongside developing non-dedicated or informal systems. Dedicated systems can provide legitimacy and formally recognized precedents or reference points. For example, as a standing committee of elected parties that met regularly and had established certain precedents and procedures, the IC was a key institution for considering and coordinating responses to the compliance problems of countries in economic transition. It provided an important anchor for the SIRs in this context. Evidence from the ozone-layer protection regime shows that a mixture of dedicated and non-dedicated implementation review institutions and mechanisms, which can function autonomously, but which can also link together with other bodies in the regime, works best.

Care must be taken in any attempt to apply aspects of the Montreal Protocol regime to other issue areas or regimes: the effectiveness of institutions and rules can be very sensitive to the context and to the characteristics of an issue. Nevertheless, there are useful lessons to be learned. Overall, the ways that the norms, rules, and institutions of the ozone regime have developed and operated appear to have contributed substantially to the effectiveness of international efforts to limit stratospheric ozone depletion.

This is not to imply that international institutions have on their own been largely responsible for what has been achieved. Of critical importance to the operation of the regime since the late 1980s is that most states and most industrial producers of ODS have had a strong interest in making the regime work, and that awareness of and support for the main principles and objectives of the regime have become widespread throughout much of the world. However, the ozone regime has played an important role in constituting and shaping the development of these interests and concerns. Moreover, the institutions of the ozone regime have been allowed to develop and operate effectively. They have often been able to draw on political support to have an important impact on the behavior of relatively powerful actors and to induce such actors to comply with inconvenient or uncomfortable measures. This chapter shows that SIRs can develop and contribute to regime effectiveness when parties genuinely want to tackle an international environmental threat.

Notes
1. For an examination of the achievements of, and challenges for, the ozone protection regime in the 1990s, up to early 1995, see Parson, E., and Greene, O., 1995, "The Complex Chemistry of the International Ozone Agreements,"*Environment* 37(2):16–20, 34–43, March. For an examination of the operation and development of the regime in 1995, see Greene, O., 1996, "The Montreal Protocol: Implementation and Development in 1995," in *Verification 1996: Arms Control, Environment and Peacekeeping*, edited by J. Poole and R. Guthrie, Westview Press, Boulder, CO, USA. For an examination of the development of the ozone-layer protection regime in its early phases (up to 1992), see, for example, Benedick, R., 1991, *Ozone Diplomacy: New Directions in Safeguarding the Planet*, Harvard University Press, Cambridge, MA, USA; Litfin, K., 1994, *Ozone Discourses: Science and Politics in Global Environmental Co-operation*, Columbia University Press, New York, NY, USA; Rowlands, I., 1995, *The Politics of Global Atmospheric Change*, Manchester University Press, Manchester, UK; Greene, O., 1993, "Limiting Ozone Depletion: The 1992 Review Process and the Development of the Montreal Protocol," in *Verification 1993: Peacekeeping, Arms Control and the Environment,* edited by J. Poole and R. Guthrie, Brassey's, London, UK.

2. See references in note 1. See also Parson, E., 1993, "Protecting the Ozone Layer," in *Institutions for the Earth*, edited by R. Keohane, P. Haas, and M. Levy, The MIT Press, Cambridge, MA, USA; Makhijani, A., and Gurney, K., 1995, *Mending the Ozone Hole: Science, Technology and Policy*, The MIT Press, Cambridge, MA, USA.

3. These countries are covered by Article 5.1 of the Montreal Protocol. Article 5 countries are developing countries whose annual consumption of CFCs was less than 0.3 kg per capita when they joined the regime. In 1990, it was agreed that such countries would have a 10-year grace period (to 2010) before they were obliged to phase out CFCs, halons, carbon tetrachloride, and methyl chloroform, though numerous developing countries (such as Mexico, China, and Thailand) have unilaterally announced earlier phaseout dates.

4. See Gehring, T., 1994, *Dynamic International Regimes: Institutions for International Environmental Governance*, Peter Lang Publishers, Frankfurt, Germany; and Parson and Greene, op. cit., note 1.

5. The potential advantages of a "framework" convention approach to regime development are discussed, for example, in Sebenius, J., 1991, "Designing Negotiations Toward a New Regime: The Case of Global Warming," *International Security* 15(4):110–148; Gehring, T., 1990, "International Environmental Regimes: Dynamic Sectoral Legal Systems," in *Yearbook of International Environmental Law*, Vol. 1, pp. 35–56, edited by G. Handl, Graham & Trotman Ltd., London, UK; and Greene, O., 1995, "Environmental Regimes: Effectiveness and Implementation Review," in *The Environment and International Relations*, edited by J. Vogler and M. Imber, Routledge, London, UK, pp. 196–214.

6. See, for example, Haas, P., ed., 1992a, special issue on "Knowledge, Power and International Policy Co-ordination," *International Organization* 46(1); and Haas, P., 1992b, "Banning Chlorofluorocarbons: Epistemic Community Efforts to Protect Stratospheric Ozone," *International Organization* 46(1):189–224.

7. See Victor, D.G., Greene, O., Lanchbery, J., Di Primio, J., and Korula, A., 1994a, "Review Mechanisms in the Effective Implementation of International Environmental Agreements," WP-94-114, International Institute for Applied Systems Analysis, Laxenburg, Austria; Greene, O., 1996, "Environmental Regimes: Effectiveness and Implementation Review," in *The Environment and International Relations*, edited by J. Vogler, and M. Imber, Routledge, London, UK; Victor, D.G., Lanchbery, J., and Greene, O., 1994b, "An Empirical Study of Review Mechanisms in Environmental Regimes," WP-94-115, International Institute for Applied Systems Analysis, Laxenburg, Austria; Greene, O., 1994, "On Verifiability, and How it Could Matter for International Environmental Agreements," WP-94-116, International Institute for Applied Systems Analysis, Laxenburg, Austria; Lanchbery, J., 1995, "Reviewing Implementation of Biodiversity Agreements: An Historical Perspective," in *Verification 1995: Arms Control, Environment and Peacekeeping*, edited by J. Poole and R. Guthrie, Westview, Boulder, Co, USA; Ausubel, J. and Victor, D., 1992, "Verification of International Environmental Agreements," *Annual Review of Energy and the Environment 1992* 17:1–43; Greene, O., 1993, "International Environmental Regimes: Verification and Implementation Review," *Environmental Politics* 2(4):156–177. See also introduction to the first part of this book.

8. See Parson and Greene, op. cit., note 1, and Greene, op. cit., note 1, respectively, for a discussion on the situation since early 1995 and for an examination of the debates and responses to these problems in 1995 and 1996.

9. See Victor et al., 1994a, op. cit., note 7; Greene, 1996, op. cit., note 7; Greene, 1993, op. cit., note 7.

10. See, for example, Baratt-Brown, E., 1991, "Building a Monitoring and Compliance Regime Under the Montreal Protocol," *Yale Journal of International Law* 16:519–570; Greene, O., and Salt, J., 1993, "Verification Issues in the Development of an Effective Climate Change Convention," *World Resources Review* 5(3):271–285; Katscher, W., Stein, G., Lanchbery, J., Salt, J., eds., 1994, *Greenhouse Gas Verification: Why, How, and How Much?*, KFA Jülich, Germany; Lanchbery, op. cit., note 7; and Széll, P., 1995, "The Development of Multilateral Mechanisms for Monitoring Compliance," in *Sustainable Development and International Law*, edited by W. Lang, Graham & Trotman Ltd., London, UK, pp. 97–109.

11. See, for example, Victor, D.G., 1996, "The Montreal Protocol's Non-Compliance Procedure: Lessons for Making Other International Environmental Regimes More Effective," in *The Ozone Treaties and Their Influence on the Building of Environmental Regimes*, edited by W. Lang, Austrian Foreign Policy Documentation, Austrian Ministry of Foreign Affairs, Vienna, Austria; Parson and Greene, op. cit., note 1; Greene, op. cit., note 1.

12. Article 7, Montreal Protocol; see Ozone Secretariat, 1993, *Handbook for the Montreal Protocol on Substances that Deplete the Ozone Layer*, 3rd ed., United Nations Environment Programme, Nairobi, Kenya. Imports and exports of each substance are reported separately, as are the amounts used as feedstocks and the compounds recycled or destroyed by approved technologies. Annual data on national population are also required for assessing a country's Article 5 status.

13. A recent report, for example, is "Report of the Secretariat on Information Provided by the parties in Accordance with Articles 4, 7, and 9 of the Montreal Protocol on Substances that Deplete the Ozone Layer," UNEP/OzL.Pro.7/6, UNEP, 25 September 1995.

14. "Report of the Secretariat on Information Provided by the parties of the Montreal Protocol on Substances that Deplete the Ozone Layer," UNEP/OzL.Pro.4/6, UNEP, 26 August 1992.

15. See Chapter 4; Parson and Greene, op. cit., note 1; Greene, op. cit., note 1.

16. For a detailed examination of the early development and operation of the IC and the noncompliance procedures of the Montreal Protocol, see Chapter 4 of this volume. See also Victor, D.G., 1996, *The Early Operation and Effectiveness of the Montreal Protocol's Non-Compliance Procedure*, ER-96-2, International Institute for Applied Systems Analysis, Laxenburg, Austria. See

also Széll, P., 1995, "The Development of Multilateral Mechanisms for Monitoring Compliance," in *Sustainable Development and International Law*, edited by W. Lang, Graham & Trotman Ltd., London, UK; Széll, P., 1996, "Implementation Control: Noncompliance and Dispute Settlement in the Ozone Regime," in *The Ozone Treaties and Their Influence on the Building of International Environmental Regimes*, edited by W. Lang, Austrian Foreign Policy Documentation, Austrian Ministry of Foreign Affairs, Vienna, Austria; Schally, H., 1996, "The Role and Importance of Implementation Monitoring and Noncompliance Procedures in International Environmental Regimes," in *The Ozone Treaties and Their Influence on the Building of International Environmental Regimes*, edited by W. Lang, Austrian Foreign Policy Documentation, Austrian Ministry of Foreign Affairs, Vienna, Austria; Greene, op. cit., note 1.

17. See the UNEP/OzL.Pro/ImpCom series, United Nations Environment Programme, Nairobi, Kenya.

18. Many parties had serious reservations about establishing such a procedure, which might be used to embarrass parties deemed to be performing unsatisfactorily (interviews with Patrick Széll and Hugo Schally, Autumn 1994). See Széll, 1996, op. cit., note 16; Schally, op. cit., note 16. See also Chapter 4 in this volume. Some international legal authorities worried that the establishment of nonjudicial and nonconfrontational mechanisms for addressing noncompliance problems threatened to undermine the principle of compliance with international law and the ability to enforce agreements; see, for example, Koskenniemi, M., 1992, "Breach of Treaty or Noncompliance? Reflections on the Enforcement of the Montreal Protocol," *Yale Review of International Environmental Law* 3:123–162.

19. See relevant *Reports of Implementation Committee Under the Non-Compliance Procedure for the Montreal Protocol*, published by the United Nations Environment Programme, Nairobi, Kenya, in its series UNEP/OzL.Pro/ImpCom; see also Parson and Greene, op. cit., note 1.

20. For a detailed discussion of this case, see Chapter 4 in this book; Victor, op. cit., note 16; and Greene, op. cit., note 1.

21. See, for example, references in notes 1, 3, and 4.

22. Article 6, Montreal Protocol, op. cit., note 12, p. 16.

23. In fact, four panels of experts were established in 1989 to advise the 1990 MOP. Subsequently, the Panel for Technical Assessment and the Panel for Economic Assessment were merged to form TEAP.

24. Technical Assessment Panel, Report of the Technology Review Panel: Technical Progress on Protecting the Ozone Layer, August 1989; TEAP, Report of the Technology and Economic Assessment Panel: Montreal Protocol

1991 Assessment, December 1991; TEAP, 1994 Report of the Technology and Economics Assessment Panel: For the 1995 Assessment of the Montreal Protocol, UNEP, 1994; TEAP, Report to the parties, Parts I–IV, UNEP, November 1995.

25. TOCs were first established in 1989. Their number and topic of analysis have varied over time, as deemed appropriate by TEAP. In 1995, there were seven TOCs: 1. Aerosols, Sterilants, Miscellaneous Uses, and Carbon Tetrachloride; 2. Economic Options; 3. Flexible and Rigid Foams; 4. Halons; 5. Methyl Bromide; 6. Refrigeration, Air Conditioning, and Heat Pumps; and 7. Solvents, Coating, and Adhesives.

26. Stephan Anderson, TEAP co-chair, interview with the author, August 1995. The members of the panels have overwhelmingly been from OECD countries (though representation from developing countries increased during the mid-1990s), with the USA particularly well represented. This has lead to concerns about and occasional accusations of bias. However, TOC reports are nevertheless highly regarded as authoritative and relatively objective.

27. This precedent, however, has not always been followed. For example, for several reasons, the Methyl Bromide TOC included some members from producer industries (as well as from NGOs). As consequence, this TOC reportedly had more problems completing its work and arriving at consensus than the other TOCs (interview with Jonathan Banks, chair, Methyl Bromide TOC, August 1995, and with Stephan Anderson, ibid.).

28. The main exception to this is the Economic Options Committee, whose members are mainly academics or officials from national ministries, to which much of the subsequent discussion in this section does not apply.

29. Interviews with Stephan Anderson, Gary Taylor, David Catchpole, Nick Campbell, and Jonathan Banks (chairs and members of various TOCs) in August and November 1995.

30. In addition to the Halons TOC reports, reports of the OEWG and the MOP, and other documentary sources, this brief discussion of the role of the Halons TOC draws substantially from interviews in 1995 with Gary Taylor (co-chair), David Catchpole (TOC member), and Stephan Anderson (TEAP co-chair).

31. In the Montreal Protocol "consumption" is defined as "production plus imports minus exports minus approved destruction."

32. Interviews with Gary Taylor, David Catchpole, and Stephan Anderson, December 1995.

33. Interviews with David Catchpole, Gary Taylor, ibid.

34. Effects on the home institutions of TOC members are, of course, not automatic; it is unclear whether the TOC has had great effect on the practices in the Russian or Israeli forces (members of which were also in the Military-Use Subcommittee of the Halons TOC).

35. See, for example, Report of the Halons Technical Options Committee, 1994, United Nations Environment Programme, Nairobi, Kenya.

36. Ibid. See also Report of the Sixth Meeting of the Parties to the Montreal Protocol, 1994; Report of the Seventh Meeting of the Parties to the Montreal Protocol, UNEP/OzL.Pro.7/12, 27 December 1995; Reports of the Tenth, Eleventh, and Twelfth OEWG.

37. See Articles 2A–2G of the Montreal Protocol, as amended in 1990 and 1992, Ozone Secretariat, op. cit., note 12.

38. Decision IV/25, Fourth Meeting of the Parties, 1992, see Ozone Secretariat, op. cit., note 12; Technology and Economic Assessment Panel, 1994, *Handbook on Essential Use Nominations*, United Nations Environment Programme, Nairobi, Kenya. A use can qualify as essential only if it is necessary for the health and safety or is critical for the functioning of society and if no available technically and economically feasible alternatives are acceptable from the standpoint of environment or health (not economic costs). Moreover, production or consumption of a controlled substance for essential use is permitted only if all economically feasible steps have been taken to minimize the essential use and any associated emission of the controlled substance and if existing stocks of banked or recycled controlled substances are not adequate to needs.

39. See TEAP, 1994, "Report of the Technology and Economics Assessment Panel," United Nations Environment Programme, Nairobi, Kenya. In one case, the OEWG felt that TEAP's initial recommendations might be too generous to applicants, and referred the matter back for further consideration by TEAP. The Aerosol Products TOC and TEAP initially recommended exemptions for all aerosol MDI applications. After further review of the evidence, TEAP identified possible non-ozone-depleting alternatives for some MDI uses, with the result that exemptions were granted only for orally inhaled drugs for asthma and Chronic Obstructive Pulmonary Disease and for a single category of anticancer drug.

40. Interviews with TOC chairs. See also *Handbook on Essential Use Nominations*, 1994, United Nations Environment Programme, Nairobi, Kenya.

41. Lambert Kuijpers and Laszlo Dobe, respectively, chair and committee member of the Ad Hoc Working Group, interviews with the author, December 1996.

42. See references in note 1, and Sand, P., 1995, "Trusts for the Earth: New International Financial Mechanisms for Sustainable Development," in *Sustainable Development and International Law*, edited by W. Lang, Graham & Trotman Ltd., London, UK, pp. 167–188; and DeSombre, E.R., and Kauffman, J., 1996, "The Montreal Protocol Multilateral Fund: Partial Success Story," in *Institutions for Environmental Aid*, edited by R. Keohane and M. Levy, The MIT Press, Cambridge, MA, USA, pp. 89–126.

43. Multilateral Fund, 1995, *Working Together to Protect the Ozone Layer: The Multilateral Fund for the Implementation of the Montreal Protocol*, Multilateral Fund, Montreal, Canada. See also World Bank, 1995, *The World Bank Portfolio of Montreal Protocol Investment Projects*, World Bank, Washington, DC, USA, October.

44. "Terms of reference of the Executive Committee," UNEP/OzL.Pro.4/15.

45. Multilateral Fund, op. cit., note 43.

46. For a detailed discussion of the ExCom review process of project applications, see COWIconsult, 1995, *Study on the Financial Mechanism of the Montreal Protocol*, United Nations Environment Programme, Nairobi, Kenya, March.

47. The Fund Secretariat aims at resolving any problems through negotiation with the implementing agency before the ExCom meeting. The revised proposal is then sometimes checked with the requesting party in the developing country before submission to ExCom. In many cases, however, the revised proposal agreed upon between the Fund Secretariat and the implementing agency is simply communicated later to the requesting party as the "best deal" that the implementing agency could achieve. Different implementing agencies have tended to adopt different practices in this regard. The UNDP, the UNEP, and UNIDO have been less inclined to risk delays by checking with the recipient before making a deal on its behalf, whereas the World Bank has been more inclined to insist on checking that the revised proposal is acceptable to the prospective recipient even if this delays approval. Ibid., chapters 5 and 6.

48. The Secretariat reviews issues such as whether the proposed alternatives or substitute technologies meet TEAP requirements; whether the project appropriately and efficiently contributes to ODS phaseout with clear contractual guarantees that are in line with the country programs; and whether satisfactory provisions for monitoring and evaluations are included.

49. For example, the World Bank established its Ozone Operations Resource Group for this purpose; this group has become well respected for its expertise. The UNDP and UNIDO have established a roster of experts, and the UNEP makes use of its Informal Advisory Group and of TEAP and TOC members.

50. COWIconsult, op. cit., note 46, chapter 6. See also reports of the ExCom's seventeenth and eighteenth meetings in 1995, "Report of the Eighteenth Meeting of the Executive Committee of the Multilateral Fund for the Implementation of the Montreal Protocol," UNEP/OzL.Pro/ExCom/18/75, 24 November 1995. Interestingly, the World Bank is the implementing agency which is perceived to be too lenient toward applicants and which occasionally supports proposals that are not completely in line with Montreal Protocol priorities or MLF guidelines: it is perceived to have fought for projects with inflated costs or ineligible components or both; COWIconsult, op. cit., note 46, paragraph 366.

51. ExCom works by consensus, and members can argue and vote on projects in which they have a direct interest.

52. For example, ExCom decided to consider guidelines relating to the transitional substances on a sector-by-sector basis and set up an Expert Group on the Production of Substitutes for Ozone-Depleting Substances to provide advice (UNEP/OzL.Pro.6/6, 9 August 1994, para 39d). Progress has been slow, but in 1995 it was agreed that there should be a presumption against HCFCs in projects relating to domestic refrigerants (UNEP/OzL.Pro.7/7, 25 November 1995, paragraph 58). After a difficult debate, ExCom decided not to consider any projects to convert any ODS production capacity installed after 28 July 1995 (UNEP/OzL/Pro.7/7, paragraph 63). In spite of the difficulty of agreeing upon general guidelines, agreement was achieved with China on several projects relating to ODS production, incorporating numerous guarantees and constraints that were not present in the initial proposal. The questions of whether and how to develop further rules on such issues were high on the agenda of all Meetings of the Parties during 1995.

53. COWIconsult, op. cit., note 46, Executive Summary, paragraph 33.

54. COWIconsult, op. cit., note 46, Executive Summary, paragraph 87.

55. COWIconsult, op. cit., note 46, paragraph 395; also interviews with Fund Secretariat and World Bank, August 1995.

56. Moreover, allowable payments by the World Bank to FIs for their services for MLF projects have been strictly constrained, leading to difficulties in finding FIs in some cases and strong pressure from FIs that results in the payments barely covering the minimal costs of disbursement and auditing. Interview, World Bank, August 1995.

57. The 1995 MLF review noted that "it is also difficult to see how the re-use of old ODS equipment and construction of new enterprises/production lines based on traditional ODS consuming equipment can be prevented or even contained unless there is not only national legislation and commitments by government, but also national institutional capacity to identify, develop, and

implement projects . . ." [COWIconsult, op. cit., note 46, paragraph 394]. Thus
the development of effective MLF-implementing agency verification systems
in this context also has implications on the design of institutional strengthening
programs.

58. ExCom, "Format for Presentation of Information on Progress of Implementation of Country Programs," UNEP/OzL.Pro/ExCom/13/47 Annex II.

59. UNEP/OzL.Pro.6/6, paragraph 18.

60. "Report of the Eighteenth Meeting of the Executive Committee of the
Multilateral Fund," UNEP/OzL.Pro/ExCom/18/75, paragraph 47, (i)–(viii).

61. The Fund Secretariat also reports on the performance of each implementing
agency, according to criteria agreed upon by the EU.

62. World Bank, "Guidelines on Monitoring and Evaluation," UNEP/OzL.Pro/
ExCom/17/53, July 1995.

63. World Bank, "Monitoring and Evaluation Guidelines for ODS Phase-out
Investment Projects," UNEP/OzL.Pro/ExCom/17/Inf.4, 30 June 1995, p. 12.

64. At its eighteenth meeting in November 1995, ExCom gave the Fund Secretariat the task of preparing standard technical guidelines for monitoring and
evaluation activities for all implementing agencies, based on the guidelines
developed by the World Bank in 1994 and 1995. Interviews with Fund Secretariat, December 1995, plus Report on the Eighteenth Meeting of the Executive
Committee.

65. UNEP/OzL.Pro/ExCom/17/Inf.4, op. cit., note 63, p. 1.

66. Report of Council Meeting of Global Environment Facility, April 1996.

67. Council Meeting of Global Environment Facility, 3–5 May 1995, Washington DC, Joint Summary of the chairs, paragraph 10 (work program Russia),
quoted in Sand, P., 1995, "The Potential Impact of the Global Environmental
Facility of the World Bank, UNDP, and UNEP," paper presented at Symposium on Enforcing Environmental Standards: Economic Mechanisms as Viable
Means, Heidelberg, Germany, 5–7 July.

68. See, for example, statement at the twelfth IC meeting; UNEP/ImpCom/
12/3, 1 December 1995. See also reports of the tenth and eleventh meetings,
August 1995.

69. Ibid. Also, interviews with Hugo Schally (chair, IC), Lambert Kuijpers
(co-chair TEAP CEIT Ad Hoc Committee), December 1995.

70. Interviews with Andrew Steer and Robert Rahill, Global Environment
Co-ordination Division, World Bank, December 1995.

71. For example, the EU Regulation on Ozone Depleting Substances, No. 3093/94, came into force on 23 December 1994. This regulation pushed forward Montreal Protocol phaseout dates for CFCs by one year and imposed relatively restrictive controls of HCFCs and methyl bromide.

72. Much of the information in this discussion was obtained from interviews with John O'Neill, DG XI, EU Commission, March 1995, and subsequent personal communications.

73. Background interviews.

74. The committee's official name is the Management Committee for Council Regulation 3093194 on Substances that Deplete the Ozone Layer.

75. See, for example, "Loophole Opens up Black Market in CFCs," *New Scientist*, 19 March 1994, p. 6. For further discussion of gray- and black-market issues and the Montreal Protocol in the mid-1990s, see Parson and Greene, op. cit., note 1; Greene, op. cit., note 1; and Brack, D., 1996, *International Trade and the Montreal Protocol*, RIIA, London, UK.

76. For example, a French foam manufacturer was allocated an EU quota to import from Russia 225 metric tons of CFC-11 as feedstock. In this case, the French Ministry of Environment became aware of the situation, and action was taken to intercept the delivery by European Customs authorities. See "Importing New of Used ODS," *Ozone Action* 11(July 1994):6.

77. *New Scientist*, 19 March 1994, p. 6.

78. DG XI interview, 1995.

79. *Global Environmental Change Report*, VII:9, 12 May 1995, quoted in Brack, op. cit., note 75.

80. Interview with Tracy Heslop, Greenpeace International, February 1995; Nick Campbell, ICI, 1995.

81. Interviews with Nick Campbell (ICI Klea); O'Neill, (DG XI, EU Commission); British delegation at the OEWG and the MOP, August and December 1995; personal observations at the MOP and the OEWG.

82. In this case, once the Austrian government confirmed the existence and legitimacy of the stockpiles, the EU Commission felt obliged to accept them. Nevertheless, INGOs had played a significant role in the monitoring and review processes.

83. "Report of the Implementation Committee under the Non-Compliance Procedure for the Montreal Protocol upon the Work of its Seventh Meeting," UNEP/OzL.Pro/ImpCom/7/2, 16 November 1993.

84. Nevertheless, baseline data from Monaco, Liechtenstein, Luxembourg, and Israel (relating to 1986 or 1989) have yet to be submitted; "The Reporting of Data by the parties to the Montreal Protocol on Substances that Deplete the Ozone Layer: Report of the Secretariat," UNEP/OzL.Pro.6/5, 15 July 1994, p. 2.

85. Interviews with Hugo Schally, August 1995; Fund Secretariat, August 1995.

86. IC meeting, October 1994, report UNEP/OzL.Imp series.

87. Special temporary exemptions were granted by the Meeting of the Parties; Ozone Secretariat, "Report of the Sixth Meeting of the Parties to the Montreal Protocol on Substances that Deplete the Ozone Layer," UNEP/OzL.Pro.6/7, 10 October 1994.

88. Report of the MOP in October 1994.

89. Russia was the legal successor state to the USSR. Ukraine and Belarus were formally treated as independent states for UN purposes throughout the Cold War, and thus remained parties after the breakup of the USSR.

90. The Ozone Secretariat's involvement in efforts to stimulate submission of data reports from countries in economic transition and its role in preparing its annual report on implementation and data reporting, together with its other activities, required it to be in regular contact with relevant officials in these countries. As far as TEAP is concerned, several TOCs were closely involved in the situation in several countries in transition as part of their de facto implementation review activities discussed earlier. TEAP members were also aware of the findings of COWIconsult (with whom some had good personal links), which had just completed a study (funded by the EU TACIS program) on ODS phaseout in Russia (COWIconsult, 1994, "Phaseout of Ozone Depleting Substances in Russia," final report, EU TACIS Program, August).

91. Technology and Economic Assessment Panel, 1995, *1994 Report of the Technology and Economic Assessment Panel: 1995 Assessment*, United Nations Environment Programme, Nairobi, Kenya.

92. Statement by countries with economies in transition that are parties to the Montreal Protocol (Belarus, Bulgaria, Poland, Russian Federation, and Ukraine) circulated at the eleventh meeting of the OEWG of the parties to the Montreal Protocol, May 1995.

93. There is no dispute that the Secretariat's interpretation was technically legitimate. Nevertheless, this was an important example of an international secretariat using its discretion to push a politically charged process forward in a particular direction. A more cautious secretariat might have asked for

clarification of the prime minister's precise intentions in sending the letter before proceeding further. Had this been done, it seems likely that an important opportunity to invoke the Non-Compliance Procedure within a cooperative framework would have been missed. Russia would probably have stated that the letter was not intended to invoke the Non-Compliance Procedure (paragraph 4). At best, this would have led to delays while Russia was being persuaded to change its position. At worst, it would have forced either another party to invoke the Non-Compliance Procedure by raising accusations of noncompliance or the MOP to deal with the issue itself in a less systematic and more politically charged atmosphere. Either option would have resulted in considerable damage to the ozone regime.

94. The way in which the Non-Compliance Procedure was officially invoked is confirmed in "Report of the Implementation Committee under the Non-Compliance Procedure for the Montreal Protocol on the Work of Its Tenth Meeting," UNEP/OzL.Pro/ImpCom/10/4, 30 August 1995, paragraph 31.

95. The following summary is based on reports of the tenth, eleventh, and twelfth Implementation Committee meetings (UNEP/OzL.Pro/ImpCom/10/4, 30 August 1995; UNEP/OzL.Pro/ImpCom/11/1, 14 September 1995; and Report of the Implementation Committee under the Non-Compliance Procedure for the Montreal Protocol on the Work of Its Twelfth Meeting, UNEP/OzL.Pro/ImpCom/12/3, Ozone Secretariat, 1 December 1995); interviews with several participants in the IC meetings. The story is told in Greene, op. cit., note 1.

96. Implementation Committee, "Decision VII/12; Implementation of the Protocol by the parties," Draft Recommendations, 1 December 1995.

97. In fact, the language of the extension of restrictions to exports to developing countries was sufficiently ambiguous that Russian direct exports to Article 5 countries to meet their "basic domestic needs" does not appear to have been banned. See discussion in Chapter 4.

98. Ozone Secretariat, Report of the Seventh Meeting of the Parties to the Montreal Protocol on Substances that Deplete the Ozone Layer, UNEP/OzL.Pro.7/12, UNEP, 27 December 1995.

99. See discussion in note 90.

100. At that time, the 10 countries elected to serve on the IC were Austria (chair), Bulgaria, Burkina Faso, Chile, Jordan, the Netherlands, Peru, Russian Federation, United Republic of Tanzania, and Slovenia.

101. Interviews with participants at IC meetings, autumn 1995.

102. See Report of the Twelfth Meeting of the Implementation Committee, UNEP/OzL.Pro/ImpCom/12/3, Ozone Secretariat, 1 December 1995.

103. Interview, Lambert Kuijpers (co-chair) Ad Hoc Working Group, December 1995.

104. Interview, Jan-Karel Kwisthout, Dutch IC representative.

105. This account is based on information from interviews with the TOC co-chair, proceedings of the August OEWG meeting, and discussions at tenth and eleventh meetings of the IC.

106. Effective and accepted alternatives were available for use in servicing refrigerators, and the argument that the financial resources were not available in Poland to adopt them was not acceptable under the essential-use criteria. Report of the twelfth meeting of the OEWG of the parties to the Montreal Protocol, UNEP/OzL.Pro/WG.1/12/4, 18 September, paragraph 65.

107. Communications within and between TEAP and its TOCs and working groups tend to be detailed and frequent, helped by regular meetings, communications between chairs, and informal personal links. In this case, coordination was further enhanced by the fact that the chair of the Refrigeration TOC, Lambert Kuijpers, was also co-chair of the Ad Hoc Working Group and of TEAP itself.

4

The Operation and Effectiveness of the Montreal Protocol's Non-Compliance Procedure

David G. Victor

Introduction

Many international environmental agreements have developed systems for implementation review (SIRs): procedures for gathering data, reviewing implementation, handling cases of noncompliance, and adjusting commitments. All of the agreements that are assessed in this book have developed at least a rudimentary SIR; none has an extensive system for implementation review, and the extent to which SIRs have contributed to making agreements effective has varied. Often even basic functions, such as data reporting, are performed poorly.[1] In general, the least developed function of SIRs is the most controversial: handling of specific instances of noncompliance.

Chapter 3 examines how the functions of implementation review in the ozone regime are performed by many institutions that operate in concert, forming an integrated, synergistic system for implementation review. This chapter focuses on the main institution in the ozone regime formally charged with reviewing implementation and responding to implementation problems, the Non-Compliance Procedure (NCP) of the Montreal Protocol on Substances that Deplete the Ozone Layer, which is one of the few formal mechanisms in international environmental law for identifying and handling problems of noncompliance.[2] It consists of two interlocking components. The "regular" component is managed by a standing committee, the Montreal Protocol Implementation Committee (IC). The IC reviews specific cases of noncompliance, debates general matters related to implementation of and compliance with the Protocol, makes recommendations to other bodies, and issues a publicly available report after every Meeting. The Committee also operates a second, "ad hoc" component that allows parties to the Montreal Protocol to file "submissions" about alleged noncompliance by other parties or about problems with their own compliance.

Although the chapters in this part of the book emphasize that SIRs often consist of many institutions that are not formally dedicated to implementation review, where formal dedicated procedures do exist they can play a special role of focusing the wide array of implementation review activities. Because the NCP is one of the few examples of this type of formal procedure in operation, close analysis of the specific ways that it has contributed to the effectiveness of the Montreal Protocol is especially important. Indeed, although only in operation since 1990, the Procedure is already the leading model for similar procedures in other multilateral environmental agreements. Yet the literature on the NCP is limited;[3] this study is the only analysis of how all aspects of the NCP's operation have contributed to the effectiveness of the Montreal Protocol.

The study assesses whether and how the NCP has influenced the behavior of parties that are not complying with the Protocol—whether it has been *effective*. It finds that the Procedure alone has been influential mainly when it has handled instances where parties have found it relatively easy to comply. In more difficult cases—such as the persistent failure of some countries to report data and of Russia to comply with the Protocol's regulatory commitments—the Procedure has induced parties to comply with the Protocol only when it has been able to connect a country's performance with rewards and penalties provided by other institutions. Especially important has been funding from the Protocol's Multilateral Fund (MLF) and funding from the Global Environment Facility (GEF). By itself, the NCP is relatively powerless.

Because the NCP is a pioneer, it offers one of the few mechanisms for examining how noncompliance problems are addressed in international environmental regimes. This study explores whether the NCP's Implementation Committee "manages" noncompliance problems—a process that relies on dialogue and diplomatic pressure and providing positive incentives for countries to comply—or whether tougher "enforcement" approaches, such as sanctions, are necessary. Advocates of the management approach, such as Abram Chayes and Antonia Chayes, underscore that most noncompliance problems are unintentional, and sanctions are often not available under international law. Advocates of the "enforcement" approach, such as George Downs and colleagues, argue that when international commitments require costly changes in behavior, incentives to violate commitments will be high and tough sanctions will be needed to influence the behavior of parties that consider defection. In this view, the unavailability of sanctions is both the cause and consequence of the fact that international cooperation has not been demanding.[4]

This study demonstrates that the IC has been most effective when it blends the two approaches. Management avoids the most severe and unproductive antagonism, but the credible threat of tougher actions, including sanctions, helps ensure cooperation, especially when dealing with parties who are unswayed by management alone (e.g., Russia's noncompliance). So far the only "stick" wielded under the procedure in response to noncompliance has been the threat to cut off MLF and GEF funding. Tougher measures, such as trade sanctions, have been ambiguously threatened but never clearly applied in any of the instances of noncompliance handled by the IC.

Although a leading model for other agreements, the Procedure operates in a special context. It reviews compliance with highly specific commitments to report data and *eliminate* consumption of major ozone-depleting substances (ODS). Thus whatever the Procedure does to improve compliance is largely synonymous with greater effectiveness of the Montreal Protocol and of cooperation to limit depletion of the ozone layer. In contrast, when assessing the effectiveness of international agreements that *manage* pollution and resources—rather than eliminate environmental problems—compliance and effectiveness are not necessarily the same. Indeed, as shown in the North Sea and nitrogen oxide (NO_x) cases (Chapters 8 and 9), compliance and effectiveness need not be related. This relationship makes it difficult to draw general lessons about how such noncompliance procedures contribute to the effectiveness of all types of legal regimes. If a noncompliance procedure leads to more compliance it may not enhance effectiveness if commitments are weak or inappropriate. Even in the Montreal Protocol there is evidence, as Patrick Széll has argued, of an inverse relationship between the stringency of the Procedure and the commitments the parties have been willing to adopt. In other words, any assessment of whether noncompliance procedures enhance an agreement's effectiveness must examine how the existence and operation of such procedures influence the standards that are adopted. That topic is considered in the conclusion, which speculates on how such institutions can be designed to avoid some of the conservatism that has made parties hesitant to adopt both stringent procedures and stringent commitments.

This chapter reviews the origins and legal basis of the Procedure and evaluates the experience with the two components of the NCP. The regular component has actively addressed many general and specific issues of noncompliance. The ad hoc component has already dealt with a few formal submissions of noncompliance concerning five countries in economic transition (Belarus, Bulgaria, Poland, Russia, and Ukraine—BBPRU). The chapter also provides a systematic and quantitative analysis of trends in the Committee's work load; the analysis demonstrates that over its short life the Committee has evolved from a body that considers only general issues to one that handles specific problems of noncompliance faced by specific parties. By handling specific cases, the Procedure supplies a unique and important function that has increased the effectiveness of the Montreal Protocol.

Origins and Modalities of the Montreal Protocol's
Non-Compliance Procedure

The Montreal Protocol's negotiators knew that the treaty would probably face problems of noncompliance and might need a procedure for handling them. The USA proposed an elaborate noncompliance procedure in the final stages of the negotiations.[5] With neither time nor consensus to work out the details, the Protocol was adopted in Montreal in 1987 with only a short and loosely worded Article 8 that deferred the formation of a noncompliance procedure until later.[6] The first Meeting of the Parties (MOP) of the Montreal Protocol, in 1989, established an ad hoc Working Group of Legal Experts to develop proposals for a noncompliance procedure.[7] The Working Group developed a procedure, which was adopted only on an interim basis in 1990 because some parties, led by Norway, thought a tougher system for noncompliance would be needed.[8] In 1992 an expanded (but similar) final procedure was adopted.[9] The procedure that the Working Group developed was designed, from scratch, to perform the function of handling noncompliance problems; no particular precedent was used as a model.[10]

Most countries were not heavily involved with the design of the NCP, which probably benefited from their benign neglect. Australia and a few European participants (Austria, the European Commission, the Netherlands, Norway, and the UK) led the negotiations.[11] The USA participated actively, but in 1990 it became less supportive of a strong NCP as it was also fighting battles on the MLF and did not want a procedure that could find the USA in noncompliance with the delicate agreement for industrialized countries to contribute to the MLF, which would help compensate developing countries for the costs of complying with the Protocol.[12] A few active developing countries, primarily from Latin America, were active in the negotiations and suspicious of a stringent process. The participation of the countries that were concerned about their ability to comply with the Protocol weakened the Procedure that was ultimately adopted.

The deliberations and thoughts behind specific elements of the NCP and its overall legal context are discussed in more detail elsewhere.[13] The objective was to create a multilateral mechanism that would build confidence through nonconfrontational discussion rather than adjudication.[14] Considerable effort was made to ensure that amicable solutions would be sought "on the basis of respect for the provisions of the Protocol" (paragraph 8 of the NCP). The procedure was developed to be completely independent of the Protocol's dispute resolution system (which has never been used).[15]

The NCP that was finally adopted consists of two major components, each of which is managed by the IC. First, in what is referred to here as the regular component, the Committee meets on a regular basis even when it has no formal submissions on its agenda. The Committee also acts as a standing body to hear compliance-related issues that parties to the Protocol, the Secretariat, other institutions of the Montreal Protocol, and Committee members think are important.

The second component is a system for handling "submissions" about noncompliance. A party may submit its concerns about another party's implementation. A party may also enter a submission about itself if it cannot comply with the Protocol. The Secretariat has an ambiguous obligation to inform the IC if it becomes aware of possible noncompliance.[16] The Procedure includes basic instructions and timetables for communicating information about such submissions to the parties, the Secretariat, and the IC.[17] Collectively, these procedures are referred to here as the ad hoc component.

The Committee consists of 10 members who serve as representatives of their countries (i.e., not in their personal capacities). Membership is roughly balanced between industrialized and developing countries. Participants who represent developing countries are offered assistance from a trust fund for travel and local costs associated with the meetings.

The Procedure's rules explicitly allow only three groups to participate in the Committee's deliberations: members of the Committee, the Secretariat, and any party involved in a submission. The Committee invites other participants as needed.[18] Because funding is often important for addressing problems of noncompliance, representatives from the MLF and its implementing agencies are regularly invited to attend IC meetings. The IC's president also attends the meetings of the Executive Committee of the MLF. A representative of the GEF or the World Bank (which is the GEF's implementing agency in the BBPRU countries) has attended every meeting of the IC since the ad hoc system was first invoked for the BBPRU cases. None of the BBPRU countries are eligible for MLF funding; thus they rely on the GEF to provide the financial assistance they need to comply with the Protocol.

There are no provisions for attendance at the Committee's deliberations by other international organizations, countries that are not parties to the Protocol, or nongovernmental organizations (NGOs). However, several non-parties— including Armenia, Georgia, and Kyrgystan—have been invited to discuss their situations with the Committee because they would be affected by the handling of Russia's noncompliance, with whom they have close trading relationships. But participation largely remains controlled and limited. A request from an environmental NGO to attend an IC meeting was denied on the basis that confidential, delicate, and sensitive information might be discussed and the presence of an NGO could limit frank discussion.[19] Although they currently do not participate in meetings, in principle, NGOs can raise issues for discussion by working through the Secretariat or sympathetic members of the Committee; so far, however, this has never happened.

Operation and Effectiveness of the Regular Component

During its first five years, until 1995, all work of the IC was done under the regular component. This section answers two central questions about the operation of the Committee: How do issues reach the agenda? Once an issue is on the agenda, how is it handled?

The Committee's Agenda

The issues that can arrive on the Committee's agenda reflect the primary responsibilities and benefits of membership in the Montreal Protocol: reporting of data, operation of the MLF, and regulation of ODS.

Data Reporting.   All parties to the Montreal Protocol are required to submit baseline and annual data on production, imports, and exports of each controlled substance.[20] Until 1995 most of the Committee's work load concerned inadequate reporting of baseline data and problems related to assessing and revising reported data. Placement of most of these issues on the Committee's agenda was due to the Secretariat's efforts to compile all reported data and identify parties that have failed to supply the required data.[21] The Secretariat identifies problem cases, some of which the Committee handles in detail.

Problems with data reporting have arisen in all types of countries—rich industrialized members of the Organisation for Economic Co-operation and Development (OECD), countries with economies in transition, and developing nations. Problems in OECD nations have been minimal. The European Union (EU), which is a party along with each individual member of the EU, had difficulty compiling data on consumption of ODS because of trade between EU members and the desire to protect confidential business information.[22] Italy encountered severe bureaucratic problems in preparing its data reports. In the countries in economic transition, especially in the former Soviet Union (FSU), data-reporting problems have been severe. The FSU republics only recently became independent countries and immediately faced the need to develop statistical systems that account for production and trade according to new political borders. Poor data reporting by Belarus, Russia, and Ukraine has often been on the Committee's agenda, especially because these countries have also been in front of the IC for failure to comply with the Protocol's regulatory commitments (see ad hoc cases below).[23]

Problems of missing data have been most extensive in developing countries. For example, by 1994 baseline data were overdue from 51 developing countries and only 1 OECD member.[24] Data are especially important for determining eligibility for the two major benefits that developing countries receive under the Protocol: financial assistance from the MLF and lenient provisions for controlling consumption of ODS, such as a 10-year delay in the requirement to phase out major chlorofluorocarbons (CFCs) and halons.[25] Article 5, which determines eligibility for those benefits, requires that a party must *both* be a "developing country" *and* have consumption of ODS below certain per capita thresholds.[26] There is no single definition of a "developing country," but in 1989 the MOP adopted a list that has since been adjusted slightly.[27] The other half of the Article 5 definition is its most innovative part, but it is impossible to implement without population and ODS consumption data.[28] Initially, the Secretariat estimated which countries would qualify for Article 5 status, but that only temporarily delayed the need for actual data from the countries. Thus, the obligation of all countries, especially developing countries, to report data has often been a topic on the Committee's agenda.

Attention to data reporting has focused exclusively on *missing* data rather than suspected inaccuracies in the data. The Secretariat or any party can formally raise concerns about the veracity of reported data. However, none has done so. Nor has the Committee sought to check the veracity of any data, although it has the mandate to do so if it wishes. Many parties have also submitted estimates of their data, a practice that is explicitly allowed under the Protocol.[29] Presumably estimates could be manipulated, but this issue has not been addressed directly by the Committee.[30] In practice there have been some contradictions between data that Parties report to the Ozone Secretariat, data available from other international sources (e.g., UN statistical agencies), and data that MLF recipients are required to report to the MLF Secretariat and to MLF implementing agencies. The Ozone Secretariat attempts to resolve these data conflicts informally. So far, only one case of conflicting data has formally been resolved by the Committee: Lebanon has submitted population data that are significantly different from UN figures; the IC has ruled that the data supplied by the party must be used.[31]

The Committee's attention to data reporting has also helped to implement a key provision of the Protocol: trade restrictions against non-members.[32] States that are not parties to the protocol can avoid these trade restrictions if they submit data that demonstrate that they are complying with the Protocol's control measures.[33] The MOP is responsible for making a final determination of which parties are exempt from the trade restrictions, but it has asked the IC to review the data submitted by states seeking such an exemption. In this capacity, the Committee has considered data from 22 states; it has accepted 13 as sufficient to qualify for an exemption.[34]

Multilateral Fund Issues.   Because MLF resources help developing countries comply with the Protocol's commitments, the work of the IC and that of the MLF are linked by a common objective: promoting compliance by developing countries. So far, the only significant commitment for developing countries has been to report data. The failure of many developing countries to supply data is due mainly to low administrative capacity and can be addressed only with projects to gather baseline data and to build capacity to report data on an annual basis. The MLF funds such projects, and thus MLF representatives are uniquely able to supply the IC with precise information about projects and problems encountered in developing countries.

Although representatives of the MLF and its implementing agencies are responsive to requests for information on their projects, they have never brought particular instances of noncompliance before the Committee, nor have they actively sought the Committee's advice. This may reflect that the MLF and its implementing agencies are primarily concerned with disbursing funds and often take the perspective of the recipient and the need for stable funding of projects rather than that of the enforcer of compliance. Insofar as the MLF and its implementing agencies review party performance, they do so through their own review procedures and not through the Protocol's dedicated NCP and IC (see Chapter 3).

The Committee has played a role in introducing the principle of conditionality to MLF funding. Prompted by many MLF donor countries, in 1994 the MOP adopted a decision to cut funding to MLF recipients that do not report baseline data within one year of approval of their MLF country program and the implementation of projects to strengthen institutional capacity.[35] Since country programs typically include funding to collect and estimate baseline data, a task often performed by outside consultants, in principle this conditionality should not be too onerous. This is the first explicit linkage between compliance by the parties and the benefits provided under the Protocol, in this case, funding. No such conditionality exists for the annual data that parties are also required to report; these data are chronically late and incomplete.

The obligation to pay funds into the MLF is the only significant commitment under the Montreal Protocol that has never been on the agenda of the IC. This illustrates that flexibility in setting the agenda has allowed the Committee to avoid politically sensitive issues. The legal status of MLF contributions is purposely vague. Most donor countries interpret the obligation to contribute to the MLF as binding; others, including the USA, treat it as voluntary. The text of the MLF agreement specifies neither. None of the donor parties want to raise the issue formally as it may unravel the delicate MLF agreement, which survives through a combination of differing interpretations and the fact that the MLF appears to be working well. Indeed, all major contributors are paying their shares. Clarifying the status of MLF contributions might even be counterproductive. In 1995, for example, of the US$119 million outstanding (22 percent of total "agreed" contributions), half was due from Belarus, Russia, and Ukraine. These countries were also addressing their failure to comply with the Protocol's ODS controls and themselves required financial assistance to achieve full compliance. The issue of their delinquent MLF contributions has been informally set aside and is not part of the resolution of their ad hoc submissions (see discussion below). Facing scrutiny on their MLF contributions while in front of the IC because of failure to implement the Protocol's control measures might have deterred these countries from volunteering to discuss their noncompliance.[36] The Committee's flexibility in setting its agenda is probably not absolute—presumably it must hear any case brought before it under the ad hoc procedure.

Regulation of Ozone-Depleting Substances.   The NCP and the IC may ultimately be judged primarily on their ability to improve compliance with the Protocol's main regulatory commitments:

1. The elimination of the three controlled halons by 1994.
2. The elimination of 15 CFCs, carbon tetrachloride, and methyl chloroform by 1996.
3. The elimination of transitional partially hydrogenated chlorofluorocarbons (HCFCs) by 2030.
4. The elimination of partially hydrogenated bromofluorocarbons (HBFCs) by 1996.
5. A freeze on methyl bromide by 1996.[37]

There are timetables for these phaseouts in most cases, some additional limits within each category, and some exceptions, notably for "essential uses." For developing countries operating under Article 5, each requirement is relaxed, mainly through longer timetables for limiting ODS (see Chapter 3, especially figure 3.2).

The countries to which these obligations apply fall broadly into three categories: developed countries without economies in transition (mainly members of the OECD); countries with economies in transition; and developing countries that exceed Article 5 thresholds. Each category is considered here. Developing countries that are still operating under Article 5 do not yet face stringent requirements concerning the control of ODS, thus their compliance with these regulatory commitments has not been addressed by the IC and is not discussed here.

First, all OECD developed countries appear to be complying with the Protocol, and thus it is unlikely that they will be a source of noncompliance issues to be handled by the IC. Most OECD countries are phasing out ODS more rapidly than is required by the Protocol's commitments.[38] Nonetheless, it is unclear how compliance will fare as the control levels decrease to zero and the list of allowable "essential uses" is pared down. The Secretariat and the IC are aware of some potential cases of noncompliance; however, these cases are not on the Committee's agenda because they are already being handled elsewhere. For example, the United States is prosecuting several cases of illegal trade in ODS.[39] Many similar cases worldwide underscore that the commitments under the Montreal Protocol have made some ODS as valuable as illegal drugs, leading to similar problems of smuggling and enforcement of border controls.[40] Even if the IC wanted to address this issue it would be difficult to do so since it involves the very complicated internal administrative and legal systems of countries. The IC offers no special resource for addressing such problems.

Second, several countries in economic transition are encountering significant problems of noncompliance. None of these countries except Georgia, Romania, and the former Yugoslavia is considered to be a "developing country," and thus none is eligible for Article 5 status, even though some have very low consumption levels of ODS. Five such countries have invoked the NCP's ad hoc component (the BBPRU cases). However, several parties in economic transition had their compliance problems on the Committee's agenda before the ad hoc component was invoked in 1995. Poland forecast its inability to meet domestic demand for CFCs because its supply from the EU was being phased out; it sought from the Committee (but was denied) special treatment that would have allowed CFC imports during 1994 and 1995 in excess of the Protocol's limits in order to meet Polish domestic needs after the EU's 1995 phaseout.[41] Romania sought to transfer some of its production quota to Greek firms, which might have affected Greece's compliance.[42] Russia, followed by Ukraine, predicted its noncompliance with the 1994 halon ban and announced through the IC that it would need additional financial transfers, access to halon banks, and/or lenient treatment from the MOP to remain in compliance.[43] Even after the BBPRU cases were initiated, the IC regularly considered ODS compliance problems in other transition countries. In a letter to the Ozone Secretariat, the Lithuanian prime minister sought a five-year delay in implementing some controls on ODS; late in 1996, Latvia and Lithuania's noncompliance became the second set of cases to be initiated under the NCP's ad hoc component.[44] The Czech Republic recently reported data that showed it violated the halon ban in 1994 but has since complied.[45] In short, nearly all the issues on the Committee's agenda concerning compliance with the Protocol's regulatory commitments have pertained to countries with economies in transition.

Third, developing countries on the borderline of Article 5 status could face sudden problems of formal noncompliance if their consumption of ODS exceeds Article 5 allowances, as well as loss of MLF funding that many need to comply with the Protocol. So far, the issue has not arisen. One reason is the ability of Parties to correct their data. For example, in 1995 five developing countries were classified with per capita consumption above the Article 5 threshold in 1994.[46] Two of them (Kuwait and Lebanon) corrected their data, bringing themselves back below the threshold, and thus avoided the problem of sudden noncompliance. Kuwait claimed that there had been a typographical error in its halon data. Lebanon challenged the population statistics used to calculate per capita consumption (see discussion above). Two of the remaining countries (Cyprus and Slovenia) intend to comply with the Protocol without the need to involve their eligibility for Article 5 status (both also want to join the European Union, none of whose members are "developing countries"). The last of these five countries (the United Arab Emirates) eventually claimed that there had been a mistake in its data; in 1996 it submitted corrected figures that showed it below the Article 5 threshold starting in 1994. It and other parties that return to Article 5 status after a year or more above the threshold are urged not to seek MLF funding in the future.[47] That could limit these countries' ability to comply with the Protocol's commitments in the future, but so far the extent of this potential problem is unclear.

In sum, the issues that have been placed on the Committee's agenda have reflected all of the main obligations of the Montreal Protocol except the requirement to contribute to the MLF. All parties are required to report data;

the failure of many to supply the required data has continuously been on the Committee's agenda. Requirements to phase out ODS went into full effect in 1994 (halons) and 1996 (CFCs), and increasingly the Committee's agenda has included the failure of a few parties to fully implement such controls.

Virtually all issues related to data reporting have reached the Committee's agenda at the initiative of the Committee itself or the Secretariat. In contrast, all the issues related to compliance with the Protocol's obligations to phase out ODS have been put on the Committee's agenda by the affected parties themselves. This style of volunteering to discuss noncompliance may set a pattern for the Committee's work and distinguishes the NCP from accusatory dispute resolution systems. The volunteer method of agenda setting has ensured that, today, most of the Committee's agenda directly reflects the issues that the parties themselves want to address.

How the Committee Handles Issues on Its Agenda
The IC has only a limited number of tools available to address issues placed on its agenda. Formally, it is empowered only to discuss issues, make recommendations to the MOP, and make transparent which parties are in compliance.[48] These three interrelated tools—discussion, recommendations, and transparency—are often described as elements of a "management" approach to noncompliance. While soft, these tools may nonetheless be influential, especially as stronger enforcement techniques, such as sanctions, are often not available or effective under international law.[49] The IC has played a central role in mobilizing other institutions—the MLF and the GEF—to apply stronger responses to noncompliance; thus, in practice, the IC also applies some techniques of the "enforcement" approach to noncompliance. Those stronger responses are also discussed here and, especially, in the next section on the BBPRU cases handled under the ad hoc component.

Discussion and Recommendations. Like any efficient subsidiary body, the ability to discuss issues and make recommendations allows the Committee to serve as a "first-stop" forum for handling matters that ultimately go to the MOP for formal decision. The Committee has increased the efficiency of the Montreal Protocol by preparing some draft decisions for the MOP and efficiently resolving many detailed issues, such as the reclassification of Article 5 countries and the correction of data. It has probably helped to dispose of some potentially cumbersome issues before they grew too large: for example, the question of whether developing countries can transfer production quotas to industrialized countries.

Beyond the benefits of an efficient subsidiary body, there is only limited evidence that discussion about general issues of compliance has influenced the behavior of particular parties. For example, the IC and the Secretariat have stressed that parties that are unable to provide real baseline data can comply with the requirement by supplying estimates. Many parties have now done so, and a few may not have known about that possibility before. However, in the case of the Russian Federation, where the need for some data was extremely urgent because the country is a large producer and consumer of controlled substances, repeated requests even for estimates were not rewarded with data. Russia complied with the request for baseline data only later, when its noncompliance was being handled under the ad hoc system and the IC demanded the data before it would approve the Russian compliance plan; the IC's approval, in turn, was essential to unlocking GEF funding for Russia. Even then, Russia supplied the data only reluctantly. Only in late 1996—more than a year after the BBPRU cases were initiated and after some GEF funding was already flowing—did Russia supply all of its baseline data.

As recently as 1993 the role of the IC within the Montreal Protocol was unclear. Today, it is increasingly accepted as the first forum in which to air compliance issues before other avenues are pursued. For example, Romania asked that its request to transfer production quotas to Greek firms be addressed by the MOP in 1994, but the issue was sent to the IC first. The BBPRU cases began as a Russian appeal submitted on behalf of all five countries to the MOP, but the request was rerouted through the IC. In this role, the Committee has substantially improved the overall efficiency of the Montreal Protocol's system of institutions. If these cases had gone directly to the MOP they might have been more politicized and handled less strictly according to the letter of the Montreal Protocol; the net effect might have been greater production and atmospheric release of ODS.

The IC's recommendations, when adopted, have helped address some problems of noncompliance and have also set precedents that may deter others from noncompliance. Notably, the IC has played the central role in making MLF financing conditional upon reporting of baseline data by implementing the 1994 Decision by the MOP (which the IC helped draft) to terminate funding to developing countries that fail to report data. In the first application of this conditionality, the IC noted Mauritania's persistent failure to supply baseline data and recommended withdrawal of the country's Article 5 status.[50] Within days of that recommendation, with a decision drafted by the IC and ready for imminent adoption by the MOP, Mauritania submitted the necessary data.[51] Following that precedent, a year later the IC noted that 17 countries would lose their Article 5 status for failure to report data; with 2 months all 17 had complied.

Transparency.   The ability to make transparent which parties are in compliance might be influential because delegates and other national officials may fear the embarrassment of representing noncompliant countries and thus be more inclined to do what is necessary to comply. Some officials and NGOs may not even be aware of their nation's noncompliance until a report or official query from the Committee makes the problem transparent; upon learning to noncompliance, these actors might have the power to change the situation.

Of the Montreal Protocol's institutions, the Secretariat plays the most important role in making compliance transparent, notably through its compilation of baseline and annual statistics on the consumption of ODS. These statistics reveal (albeit with self-reported data) which countries are complying with the obligations to limit ODS and to supply data. The Committee and MOP indirectly contribute to these activities by visibly supporting the Secretariat's efforts; when the Secretariat queries delinquent parties about why they have not reported data, the missive has more weight because it refers to the specific mandate given by the IC and MOP.

The Committee has directly increased transparency of compliance in several cases of egregious failure to report data. It publicly invited nine parties to appear before it in 1993 to explain their persistent failure to report baseline data. Six of the countries did so;[52] five brought the data with them or submitted the information shortly before the meeting.[53] Some parties have still persistently failed to report baseline data. The IC repeated the exercise a year later and invited seven countries to explain their situations. Of the five that attended, three reported that they had recently submitted the necessary data. The remaining countries discussed the problems they had encountered and offered timetables for the full reporting of their data.[54] By inviting these delinquent parties to explain their behavior, the Committee provided a strict deadline that helped speed the provision of data.

In none of these cases did transparency alone cause significant changes in the behavior of governments. At the minimum, transparency was backed by critical discussion, which increased pressure on countries to comply. But these tools have only limited influence—they have been effective only when the country and its delegates have been responsive and have found it relatively easy to comply. Some have neither complied nor cooperated with the Committee. For developing countries, the MLF-funded country programs, which include grants for gathering baseline data as well as capacity building to improve the ability of countries to provide data, have had a much greater influence than the increased transparency provided by the IC.[55] In those few cases where MLF funding has not rapidly improved the reporting of baseline data, the 1994 Decision of the Meeting of the Parties to terminate funding has helped to induce compliance. The direct effect of this action was evident in the cases of Mauritania and 17 other countries. Every developing country with a long-standing MLF-funded country program has now reported its baseline data. Nonetheless, in 1995 the baseline data for the main CFCs and halons were more than two years overdue for 15 parties, all of them developing countries.[56] An encouraging sign is that most of the delinquents eventually report their data. Only three countries on the list in 1995 had been on the list in 1994.[57] Only two of the parties that the Committee queried about missing data in 1993 needed to be invited back for another face-to-face inquiry in 1994.

These cases of non-reporting of baseline data are extreme examples. The Montreal Protocol regime faces a much larger, chronic problem of incomplete and late annual data. For example, in 1994 one-third of the parties had not reported the required annual data for 1992.[58] In 1995 about half had not reported data for 1993; in 1996, one-third had not reported for 1994.[59] Developing countries account for most of the missing annual data, but several industrialized countries have also failed to report their annual data on time. If the past is a guide, MLF funding will be most important in the general improvement of data reporting by developing countries. The Secretariat and the IC may play a role in the most delinquent cases; so far the Committee has not been active on this issue, but it is playing a role in harmonizing the data-reporting system which could make data reporting easier. At present, most parties submit up to three regular reports—to the Protocol Secretariat, the MLF Secretariat, and to the relevant MLF implementing agencies.

In at least one case, Committee discussions have made compliance problems transparent to officials who otherwise might be unaware of them—in 1997, data submitted by Russia and ensuing discussions in the IC exposed some problems of illegal exports to Poland. Whether trade controls will change as a result is still unclear.

The limited effectiveness of discussion, recommendations, and transparency is evident in the handling of noncompliance of countries in economic transition. Belarus, Russia, and Ukraine had discussed their impending noncompliance with the Committee before the ad hoc system had been invoked.[60] The result was some airing of views, but there was no change in behavior. Those countries sought an extension for their obligations, but the IC repeatedly underscored that it was a deliberative forum and could not tailor the commitments of the Protocol to the circumstances of particular parties. Thus the IC's deliberation and discussion offered few benefits, nor could it impose many costs on noncompliant parties. The IC's power was enhanced only after the ad hoc system was triggered and GEF funding was made conditional upon the IC's endorsement (see below).

The influence of the IC's efforts to induce compliance could be multiplied by pressure from environmental nongovernmental organizations (ENGOs). Unable to gather timely information about noncompliance on their own, ENGOs that want to pressure governments to comply with the Protocol's commitments must rely substantially on the transparency of official information. ENGOs are excluded from the Committee's deliberations, which may inhibit their activities. However, there is little evidence that such pressure groups have been closely observing the Committee's actions or reading its reports. Thus, when the Committee or the Secretariat makes cases of noncompliance transparent, the ENGOs typically are not waiting in the wings to seize on the information and use it to pressure governments to comply.

The lack of ENGO activity in tandem with the NCP reflects that the Committee has not engaged a single significant issue in a country where ENGOs are active domestically on the stratospheric ozone problem (for example, Germany, the UK, and the USA). The Committee's most difficult cases have concerned countries where ENGOs are not influential or active on the ozone-depletion issue (for example, Russia, Ukraine, and several developing countries). The

Committee has handled some data-reporting problems in the EU and Italy, where interested ENGOs may be more abundant, but these problems reflected difficulties in integrating the EU into a common market and in overcoming domestic bureaucratic obstacles, which are now mostly resolved. Attention from ENGOs probably would not have been very helpful. (Italy has also persistently failed to pay its contributions to the MLF; ENGO pressure might have helped the IC change Italy's behavior in that instance, but the IC has never handled any compliance problems related to MLF contributions.[61]) Further, compliance with data reporting is hardly the type of issue typically championed by ENGOs, especially those that are keen to make public images that attract dues-paying members. Some ENGOs within industrialized countries have been active in the dramatic issue of illegal trade in ODS, but this issue has not been addressed by the IC. In short, the Committee's influence on state behavior has not been multiplied by ENGOs, which is a reflection of the countries and issues that have dominated the agenda thus far and not a suggestion that this mode of influence is ineffective or unavailable.

In sum, when countries have found it relatively easy to reverse their noncompliance, the Committee's regular procedure has been effective in inducing them to do so simply by informing them of their noncompliance with their obligations. In some instances, the embarrassment of being identified and questioned as a noncompliant party by the Committee has probably resulted in countries' reporting data more quickly and completely than they would have otherwise. These powers are limited, but they have grown as the stature of the Committee has grown, especially since 1993 when it began to address specific cases of noncompliance and (since 1995) the difficult BBPRU cases. Its place in the Montreal Protocol has been strengthened by the fact that the decisions adopted by the MOP have never substantially deviated from the IC's recommendations.

Nonetheless, its tools are limited and the Committee can only contribute to improving overall compliance with the Protocol in special ways. Its successes in the most difficult cases—such as inducing Mauritania and Russia to report data—reflect the combination of transparency with political or economic pressure. This history points to the important role of transparency, discussion, and nonconfrontational approaches, but it also underscores the role of critique, confrontation, and even threats. The "soft" mode of compliance management is made more effective by availability of a harder approach for difficult cases.

In addition to its direct and indirect influences, the Committee may have some additional influence by deterring noncompliance. The Mauritania case shows that the threat of applying conditionality is serious. The decisions concerning exemption of trade sanctions show that the Montreal Protocol system is serious about implementing such sanctions against countries that stay outside the regime and do not comply. These examples presumably send credible signals that deter others, but assessing the deterrent value is extremely difficult. A procedure that is never used may be completely ineffective because nobody bothers to use it, or completely effective as a deterrent and thus is never used because it is never needed. Procedures that are used frequently may be ineffective and thus face many undeterred violations, or effective because they often catch minor problems before they become more severe.

By itself the Committee does not have stronger powers to penalize noncompliance or reward compliance. The Procedure includes an "indicative list of measures that might be taken by a meeting of the parties in respect of noncompliance with the Protocol," which mentions strong actions such as sanctions. However, the list has had no effect on the behavior of parties, nor will it in the future. Some parties have referred to it, but only when it serves their interests.[62] The reasons why stronger techniques are not directly available to the Committee are considered elsewhere.[63] The Committee can, however, mobilize other bodies inside and outside the Montreal Protocol to apply stronger response to noncompliance. That has been evident in the role of the IC in making funding from the MLF conditional upon data reporting, and it is especially evident in the handling of the first cases under the ad hoc component of the Non-Compliance Procedure.

The First Cases under the Ad Hoc Component

The IC, with the same tools at its disposal, also handles cases under the ad hoc component. In 1995 that component was invoked for the first time to deal with formal submissions of noncompliance with the Protocol by five countries with economies in transition: Belarus, Bulgaria, Poland, Russia, and Ukraine (the BBPRU submissions). Some observers suspected that prior to 1995 some of these countries, notably Russia, were not complying with the Protocol's interim reduction targets and ban on halon consumption and were also trading in illegal ODS. However, data submitted by all five showed that they were in compliance. Thus the formal submissions applied only to these countries' failure to comply with the Protocol after 1 January 1996, when they were to have eliminated essentially all consumption of 15 CFCs, carbon tetrachloride, and methyl chloroform.

The five parties, led by Russia, originally intended to submit a request for a special five-year grace period directly to the MOP.[64] Instead, their request was rerouted through the IC, which separated the request into individual "submissions" under paragraph 4 of the procedure, which allows a party to make submissions concerning its own noncompliance. In other words, the five countries "accused" themselves of noncompliance.[65] The BBPRU submissions have not yet been fully resolved, but they are receiving an evenhanded assessment based primarily on an objective evaluation of the facts and circumstances of each country. A nonpartisan review might not have been possible had the matter been handled entirely within the more political MOP, as Russia had originally intended.

The IC's approach has been to focus on ways that the countries can achieve compliance with the Protocol as rapidly as possible. Rather than tailor the Protocol to the party, the party is expected to bring its performance back to the Protocol's standards, with periodic reviews along the way. Late in 1995 each party presented its case to the IC. Two of the parties (Poland and Bulgaria) were already on track to comply with the Protocol in 1996; the IC recommended that their cases be reviewed later if the parties actually fail to comply. The other three parties (Belarus, Russia, and Ukraine) were instructed to develop plans to achieve compliance with the Protocol and by early 1996 each country had submitted a plan. However, the IC has deemed each compliance plan inadequate and has asked each party to provide more details on technical aspects and to confirm its political commitment to comply with the Protocol. In all three cases, the IC's requests for further information have been heeded, though Russia took considerably longer. Russia supplied its baseline data only after strong pressure and many delays; the data supplied were only for 1990 although 1986 data were requested and several other former Soviet states had demonstrated that it was possible to make useful estimates for 1986, as the IC had requested Russia to do.

The BBPRU submissions and the planned reviews of each party's situation involve technical issues beyond the competence of the members of the Committee. For these submissions the Committee has received advice from a special Technology and Economic Assessment Panel (TEAP) on countries with economies in transition.[66] TEAP experts have actively participated in the IC's deliberations on these submissions. This panel is one of several expert groups that provide legitimate, useful, and timely advice to the ozone regime.[67]

The IC recommended the plan and review approach to the MOP, which adopted three formal decisions concerning Belarus, Russia, and Ukraine that almost exactly followed the IC's recommendations. The one significant exception involved restrictions on some exports of ODS from Belarus, Russia, and Ukraine. Belarus and Ukraine, with no domestic production of ODS or recovery and recycling facilities, agreed to stop exports. However, as permitted by the Protocol, Russia intended to continue exports to developing countries for "basic domestic needs" and to develop an ODS recovery and recycling industry. Some developing countries, concerned about competition with Russian ODS exports in lucrative markets in the developing world, sought to ban all Russian ODS exports. But the result of their revisions to the decision has been more ambiguous wording that bans the re-export of Russian production through other members of the Commonwealth of Independent States (CIS), including Belarus and Ukraine. Trade among CIS member states is allowed; CIS economies remain closely interlinked, despite the collapse of the USSR.[68] The decision does not explicitly ban Russian exports for the "basic domestic needs" of developing countries. Russia must still submit information on recovery and recycling facilities if such production is to comply with the Protocol's requirements, but this information is required of any party that engages in recovery and recycling. Indeed, the IC (in 1996 and 1997) has recommended that Russia expand its recovery and recycling so that production of new ODS by Russia can be reduced.

These three decisions set a framework for handling likely submissions of noncompliance by other members of the CIS if they become parties to the Protocol. Already the model is being used for noncompliance by Latvia and Lithuania. Estonia has also raised its noncompliance before the IC, but that case has been postponed until Estonia ratifies the Montreal Protocol (and thus is formally in noncompliance). GEF funding for ozone projects in all the transition countries is conditional upon ratification of the London (1990) amendments to the Protocol, which added many ODS to the Protocol's regulatory commitments and also requires all non-developing countries to pay into the MLF. Many transition countries have hesitated to ratify because of this additional cost, although their MLF contributions would be smaller than the funding they will receive from GEF. For now, as in the cases of Belarus, Russia, and Ukraine, the problem of MLF contributions has been informally set aside in favor of ratification.[69] It is important to note that the work of the IC and funding from GEF concerns only the fraction of ODS production and consumption that remains after each country has made substantial efforts to comply with the Montreal Protocol on its own. In Lithuania, for example, 80 percent of CFC consumption (compared with 1986 base year) had been eliminated before Lithuania raised its noncompliance with the IC and sought funding from the GEF to help eliminate the remaining 20 percent.[70]

Although the BBPRU cases are examples of self-accusation, in none of the countries was the submission an entirely voluntary act. Funding needed for those countries to comply has been allocated by the GEF. However, before the GEF would approve additional projects in Belarus, Russia, and Ukraine, it sought broad approval of these countries' compliance plans by the IC and the MOP. Although the GEF has no official role within the Montreal Protocol's system of institutions, in general it sees its role as supporting the funding of projects that contribute to the compliance and effectiveness of relevant global environmental agreements. Because the countries with economies in transition are not considered developing countries, they are not eligible for MLF funding. Thus, the GEF has identified these countries as fitting into its funding niche for stratospheric ozone protection.

Although the GEF provides the funding, the IC continues to play the central role by regularly reviewing progress and dealing with compliance issues as they arise. The decisions pertaining to Belarus, Russia, and Ukraine state that,

> in case of any questions related to the reporting requirements and the actions of Belarus, Russia, or Ukraine, the disbursement of the international assistance should be contingent on the settlement of those problems with the IC.[71]

Speaking to the IC, when the IC developed its recommendations for handling the BBPRU cases, a GEF representative underscored that "GEF funding was subject to the formal processes of the Montreal Protocol for noncompliance." In the case of Russia, which only reluctantly supplied the information requested, the representative added that the "GEF was awaiting the advice of the IC as to the quality of the Russian Federation's submissions . . . before proceeding with a project for the Russian Federation."[72] Thus, in practice the system of institutions that reviews implementation and handles problems of noncompliance extends beyond the formal boundaries of the Montreal Protocol. The Committee serves as the arbiter of conditionality between these countries' compliance and the supply of GEF funding. This model is promising, but it does not indicate how compliance problems will be handled in developing countries, which are suspicious of the conditionality and will draw their funding from the MLF, not the GEF.

By far the most difficult of the BBPRU cases has been that of Russia. Many observers are privately skeptical of the accuracy of the Russian data, but there are no independent means to verify them. An additional concern is that Russia will not implement the full phaseout. But most important is the problem of trade. Russia is the only major CFC producer of the FSU, and it had been planning to recover, recycle, and sell ODS in foreign markets to earn hard currency. The decision by the MOP may limit that lucrative trade. Russia's strong objections to that ban led to the unusual outcome that the decision was adopted "by consensus" with one unnamed party (Russia) dissenting.[73] Whether Russia's dissent matters is unclear. While the decision instructs Russia to control these exports, it might also legitimize efforts by other countries to ban imports from Russia. Given the already lax Russian export controls, it may be the import controls that matter most.

Interestingly, depending on how the ambiguous decision is interpreted, this may be the first time that substantial trade sanctions have been applied within the Montreal Protocol regime. If an importer applied those restrictions, and if Russia were a member of the World Trade Organization (WTO), Russia might initiate a WTO dispute to challenge the trade restrictions. That scenario has long been feared by those who advocate using trade sanctions to enforce compliance with environmental agreements because compatibility of such measures with the free-trade-oriented WTO rules remains unclear. However, this thorny problem does not arise when sanctions are applied against countries that are not WTO members.

By the middle of 1997 the plan and review approach to handing Belarus, Russia, and Ukraine appeared to be working well—all three countries were regulating ODS more than they would have if their cases had not been addressed, and thus all are moving toward full compliance with the Protocol. Most problematic has been the Russian case, in part because Russia has delayed the provision of data and in part because external funding, while substantial, has been partially delayed. By the end of 1996, the GEF had cleared about US$40 million for projects to eliminate ODS in Russia, with a similar amount of funding to be paid by Russia using domestic resources. However, the supply of viable projects to cut Russian ODS production and consumption still exceeds the available external financing; the GEF and the World Bank are attempting to raise the additional needed money. Nonetheless, progress in Russia has been measurable. Russia's planned ODS production for 1996 was only one-quarter of its production capacity in 1990. Since 1995, when the Russian case under the Non-Compliance Procedure was initiated, production has fallen about 40 percent. Russia has implemented a quota system to regulate production and plans to eliminate all production of new ODS by 2000.[74]

Systematic Analysis of the Work of the Committee

In the previous sections the regular and ad hoc components were assessed; arguments were illustrated with particular issues that the IC has handled. Here, an effort is made to analyze the Committee's work systematically and to answer two classes of questions. First, how has the IC divided its attention between the two main types of commitments identified in Chapter 1: Programmatic commitments (mainly reporting of data because the commitment to pay MLF contributions has never been addressed by the IC) and regulatory commitments (controlling consumption of ODS)? Second, to what degree has the IC focused on specific, as opposed to general, problems of noncompliance. Answers to the first question help assess whether the IC has been responsive to the types of potential noncompliance—programmatic commitments have been in full effect since the IC began operation, but the most stringent regulation commitments took hold in 1994–1996. Answers to the second question are especially important because the NCP has a unique role when handling specific cases of noncompliance. The handling of specific instances of noncompliance is the least developed aspect of systems for implementation review, which is the topic of the chapters in this part of this book.

Discussion of substantive matters in each of the reports from the 18 meetings of the Committee—December 1990 to June 1997—was coded into one of four categories:[75]

- Matters related to compliance with programmatic commitments.
  (1) General discussions.
  (2) Country-specific discussions or deliberations initiated by the situation of a specific country.
- Matters related to compliance with regulatory commitments.
  (3) General discussions.
  (4) Country-specific discussions or deliberations initiated by the situation of a specific country.

The number of lines from each report devoted to each category has been tabulated and the results are charted in figure 4.1.

Results and Implications.   Although it is difficult to identify robust trends after only seven years of operation, three findings are evident from the data (see figure 4.1). First, the bulk of the Committee's work has been general and has concerned programmatic commitments (i.e. mainly data reporting). Since the third meeting, the attention given to general matters of data collection has been relatively constant. Most meetings of the IC include a section (of fairly constant length) in which the Secretariat gives the IC a summary of the state of data reporting. The bulk of the Secretariat's report is general; specific countries are mentioned, usually in lists, but most of the discussion does not focus on particular countries or result in an explanation of why countries have not reported their data. The abnormally high totals for the 8th and 17th meetings reflects the committee's debates on how to handle the general problems of data revisions and reclassification of developing countries (8th meeting) and to streamline the Montreal Protocol's three partially separate data-reporting requirements (17th meeting).

Second, whereas general attention to data reporting has been continuous since 1992, attention to country-specific aspects of data reporting has increased (see figure 4.1). The Committee began with a loose mandate; it started by addressing those issues of noncompliance that were most immediate for the Protocol, data reporting, and did so in a general way. But that system has evolved, and the Committee now increasingly handles specific issues as well. This shift to case-specific issues took place in 1993 and 1994, under the regular system and *before* any formal cases of noncompliance were raised. It is plausible that the substantive experience during those two years was useful preparation for handling the more difficult cases under the ad hoc component.

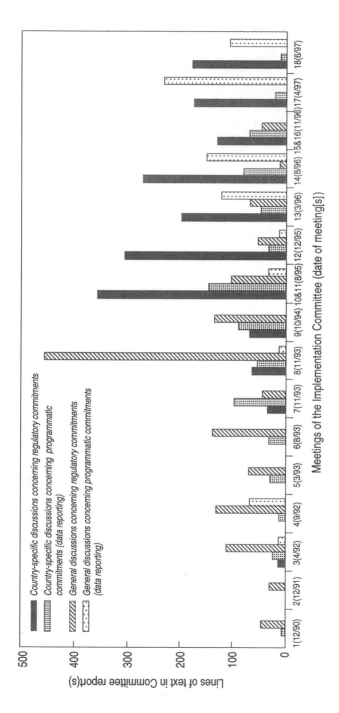

Figure 4.1

Evolution of the Implementation Committee's work load

Figure shows number of lines in Implementation Committee reports devoted to four categories of compliance issues. Reports from meetings that were separated by only a few days were combined.

Third, since late 1993 the Committee has increasingly addressed matters of potential noncompliance with the Protocol's regulatory commitments. Nearly all of this attention has come in the form of country-specific discussions, primarily concerning countries with economies in transition. Since 1995, the majority of the Committee's attention has been devoted to actual or potential cases within the ad hoc component. In sum, today the IC devotes most of its time to its most unique function in international environmental law—handling specific compliance problems. In 1990, when the Committee began operation, it was hardly clear that it would evolve to fill this niche and play a useful role.

Conclusions

Until 1993, the NCP did not have a clear position within the Montreal Protocol's system of institutions.[76] Now its legitimacy and influence are growing. In the past its relative obscurity gave it control over its agenda, but more and more the Committee is being asked by other bodies of the Montreal Protocol system to consider issues. Increasingly, parties also seek the Committee's advice on compliance problems. Today the Committee is the legitimate first-stop forum in any formal discussion within the Montreal Protocol on matters related to compliance.

This study shows that the Committee by itself has had some influence in getting countries to report data as required by the Protocol. But its influence has been most evident when countries have found it relatively easy to comply. Because its powers are quite limited, the Committee has had less success in inducing compliance in cases where gathering and reporting data have been difficult, primarily in developing countries and a few countries with economies in transition, notably Russia. Regarding data reporting from developing countries, the MLF and its implementing agencies now have many projects under way to help these countries improve their capacities to report. Essentially all efforts to identify and manage these projects are made within the MLF, its implementing agencies, and the parties. The IC plays almost no role. The MLF, implementing agencies, and Committee exchange information, but there is little if any change in the projects that the MLF and agencies support as a consequence of the issues brought before the Committee.

Increasingly, the Committee has addressed issues beyond data reporting, notably, compliance with the Protocol's obligations to regulate ozone-depleting substances. Nearly all have consisted of specific concerns about compliance by a particular party. All of those issues have been put on the Committee's agenda by the affected party. The Committee has also addressed some general issues related to compliance with regulatory commitments, such as drafting the reviewing decisions for the MOP, which has contributed to the efficiency of the Montreal Protocol, as would any well-organized subsidiary body. But the Committee has played a unique role and has had its greatest influence on compliance by handling specific cases.

In 1995 the Committee heard the first cases lodged under the ad hoc component by Belarus, Bulgaria, Poland, Russia, and Ukraine. To handle those cases, which are still unresolved, the Committee has adopted a pragmatic, problem-oriented approach. It has focused on ways to achieve compliance, requiring each party that is not in compliance (currently only Belarus, Russia, and Ukraine) to document its plans for complying with the Protocol. The Committee has periodically reviewed these plans and handled issues that have arisen. The plan and review approach demonstrates a useful role for the Committee. However, the parties, especially Russia, have cooperated with the Committee mainly because the GEF, which provides the funds to comply, has made funding conditional upon the IC's approving each party's plan. While the Committee applies mainly the soft management approach to noncompliance, it has been effective in its most difficult cases of noncompliance only because it has access to slightly "harder" tools of conditionality.

The Committee does not interpret (legally or politically) the provisions of the Protocol. Such a quasi-judicial function could lead to a body of "case law" on the application of the Protocol. However, the Fourth Meeting of the Parties (1992) reaffirmed that interpretation of the Protocol "rests with the Parties themselves." In particular instances where it would have been extremely efficient to delegate detailed decision making to the Committee, the Meeting of the Parties has underscored its final authority. In practice the Committee has been developing this quasi-judicial function, as evident in its handling of the threat to cut off MLF funds to Mauritania, its strict application of rules governing the revision of data and reclassification of Article 5 countries, and the "plan and review" approach to handling the cases of noncompliance by Belarus, Russia, and Ukraine. This role has increased the stature and influence of the Committee, which will presumably continue as long as the Meeting of the

Parties (which holds all final powers in the Protocol) follows the Committee's advice.

This essay analyzed the regular and ad hoc components separately in order to explore their differences and to focus on detailed policy-relevant lessons that can be learned. However, there are many commonalities. Both the ad hoc and regular components have the same basis in law (the NCP) and are managed by the same institutions (the Implementation Committee and Secretariat). The tools that the Committee uses to handle both its regular work load and ad hoc cases are the same. These commonalities have been important—the Committee's work as a standing body over five years built legitimacy and competence that improved its ability to handle the first ad hoc submissions. In the future, the Committee's work as a standing body may be more legitimate and influential because it has handled the first ad hoc submissions well.

Throughout its history, the Committee's approach has been pragmatic.[77] Its aim has been to cooperate with parties to find ways to achieve compliance, rather than to adjudicate and apportion blame. This approach is one way it differs from traditional dispute resolution and is part of the reason the Committee and Procedure have been active. They improve compliance by operating in the realm between mere peer pressure (which is often ineffective in ensuring compliance) and abrasive dispute resolution (which is never used).[78] The pragmatic approach raises many questions about traditional concepts of state responsibility for compliance under international law.[79] So far, however, the approach seems to improve the ability of the Procedure to influence the behavior of noncompliant parties.

If the designers of other noncompliance procedures intend to create mechanisms capable of efficiently handling difficult cases of noncompliance, they should use caution in drawing lessons from the operation of the Montreal Protocol's experience. The Protocol's NCP has not often been used to handle difficult problems of noncompliance; experience with its system for ad hoc submissions is limited. Efforts to give it more extensive powers that might be needed to handle difficult cases have been rejected. Links between the Committee and the MLF and its implementing agencies, which could give the Committee more influence and leverage, are relatively weak (but growing stronger). The decision to cut off MLF funding to parties that persistently fail to report data demonstrates one of the Committee's toughest tools at work, but this decision applies only to baseline data, which are relatively easy to report once an MLF program is in place.

This history suggests some detailed lessons for the design of similar procedures in other regimes. Among these is the value of a standing committee that can handle issues even without a formal submission of noncompliance. Backed by an active Secretariat, the committee can operate a regular review procedure that handles easy cases of noncompliance. Moreover, such a committee can build expertise and legitimacy, which are useful assets once difficult issues of noncompliance reach its agenda. Other detailed lessons are discussed in other essays based on this study (see acknowledgment note).

Finally, this analysis speculates on how review mechanisms improve international cooperation. Most observers see the Protocol's stringent targets for abatement of ODS, wide participation of industrialized and developing countries, prohibition against reservations, and the inclusion of trade sanctions as reasons why the Protocol has been effective. Yet these strong commitments may be directly responsible for the weakness of the IC's mandate. Széll, chair of the ad hoc group that designed and elaborated the NCP, suggests that the experience of the Montreal Protocol illustrates an inverse correlation between the strictness of supervision and the stringency of its substantive obligations.[80] The analysis here supports that claim. The weak NCP stems mostly from the participation of countries that were unsure whether they would be able to implement the substantive obligations, and thus were wary of adopting a stringent supervision mechanism. The commitments and institutions that countries are willing to accept must be seen as a package.

This inverse relationship need not repeat itself in other regimes: strong commitments can and often must go hand in hand with strong compliance controls. For example, over four decades the General Agreement on Tariffs and Trade (now the WTO) has evolved a more stringent supervision system alongside more detailed commitments that require greater changes in domestic policy. But so far the experience in environmental agreements is limited, and the results have been mixed. Although weak, the Procedure has played an important and unique role in handling specific problems of noncompliance— without the Procedure, many problems would go unaddressed, although other institutions could informally or formally handle them.[81]

Some institutional reforms might help limit the inverse relationship that has been evident in the case of the Montreal Protocol. First, the Montreal

Protocol has established a pattern of agreeing to simple legal texts (in this case Article 8 of the Montreal Protocol) and deferring nearly all of the debate over the function and form of such procedures until later. In the spirit of viewing commitments and institutions explicitly as a package, it might be more useful to develop the form of review mechanisms alongside the commitments and not to defer institutional design until after commitments are accepted. When dealing with regimes that manage pollution, such a reform may be especially important because it is likely that there will be significant trade-offs and synergies between the stringency of commitments and review mechanisms that require a more integrated negotiation.

Second, when the NCP was negotiated, parties seem to be especially wary of untested compliance mechanisms that could find them in noncompliance but offer few ways out. In the case of the NCP, such wariness has abated over time because the Committee has been responsive to the interests of the parties and has mainly applied positive incentives to handling cases of noncompliance such as funding and technical assistance. But wariness remains. If the NCP model is used in other regimes, it might be valuable to allow some form of relief from commitments once the implementation committee has gone through a series of direct exchanges with the relevant party. Such an arrangement may increase the willingness of parties to expose their problems of noncompliance and to adopt stringent noncompliance procedures by offering an ultimate escape for parties. To some degree, "temporary relief" has been the IC's pragmatic approach in the BBPRU submissions. As long as the parties are implementing their agreed plans to comply with the Protocol as soon as possible, less attention is being focused on whether the parties are formally in compliance and apportioning blame for the failure to comply. Such an approach partially deflects the most onerous cases of noncompliance; it is not a recipe for gaining the most from law and compliance supervision, but it seems to work.

Notes
This chapter is excerpted from a longer version: Victor, D.G., 1996a, *The Early Operation and Effectiveness of the Montreal Protocol's Non-Compliance Procedure*, ER-96-2, International Institute for Applied Systems Analysis, Laxenburg, Austria. The author would like to thank Gilbert Bankobeza, Hugo M. Schally, and Patrick Széll for interviews and comments on that manuscript. Thanks also go to Abram Chayes, Winfried Lang, Cesare Romano, Peter

Sand, Jacob Werksman, and two anonymous reviewers for many helpful discussions and comments, and to Ellen Bergschneider, Cara Morris, and Lilo Roggenland for their help in the preparation of the manuscript. The Ozone Secretariat (Nairobi) was extremely helpful and provided many documents. The author thanks Kal Raustiala for editorial support in producing this shorter version. Another excerpt, with additional analysis applied to possible designs of noncompliance procedures in other legal regimes (notably the Framework Convention on Climate Change), is published as part of the proceedings of a workshop held in conjunction with the Seventh Meeting of the parties to the Montreal Protocol on Substances that Deplete the Ozone Layer, 4 December 1995, in Vienna, Austria. See Victor, D.G., 1996b, "The Montreal Protocol's Non-Compliance Procedure: Lessons for Making Other International Environmental Regimes More Effective, in *The Ozone Treaties and Their Influence on the Building of Environmental Regimes*, edited by W. Lang, Austrian Foreign Policy Documentation, Austrian Ministry of Foreign Affairs, Vienna, Austria.

1. For a review of monitoring and enforcement in environmental treaties, see Ausubel, J.H., and Victor, D.G., 1992, "Verification of International Environmental Agreements," *Annual Review of Energy and the Environment* 17:1–43; Sachariew, K., 1992, "Promoting Compliance with International Environmental Legal Standards: Reflections on Monitoring and Reporting Mechanisms," in *Yearbook of International Environmental Law*, Volume 2, edited by G. Handl, Graham and Trotman, London, UK.

2. In addition to the Montreal Protocol's Non-Compliance Procedure, Sand's comprehensive review of international environmental agreements mentions two other systems with similar functions: the infractions system under the Convention on International Trade in Endangered Species (CITES) and the European Union's enforcement of the Single European Act. Each procedure is substantially different from the Non-Compliance Procedure. See P.H. Sand, 1992, ed., *The Effectiveness of International Environmental Agreements*, Grotius Publishers, Cambridge, UK.

3. One study documents the origins and design of the Procedure. See Széll, P., 1995, "The Development of Multilateral Mechanisms for Monitoring Compliance," in *Sustainable Development and International Law*, edited by W. Lang, Graham and Trotman, London, UK. See also Széll, P., 1996, "Implementation Control: Non-Compliance Procedure and Dispute Settlement in the Ozone Regime," in *The Ozone Treaties and Their Influence on the Building of Environmental Regimes*, edited by W. Lang, Austrian Foreign Policy Documentation, Austrian Ministry of Foreign Affairs, Vienna, Austria. Other studies discuss aspects of the early experience under the Procedure as well as legal issues. For reflection on the early experience under the Non-Compliance Procedure by the president of the Implementation Committee, see Schally, H.M., 1996, "The

Role and Importance of Implementation Monitoring and Non-Compliance Procedures in International Environmental Regimes," in *The Ozone Treaties and Their Influence on the Building of Environmental Regimes*, edited by W. Lang, Austrian Foreign Policy Documentation, Austrian Ministry of Foreign Affairs, Vienna, Austria. For an assessment of the handling of the Russian case see Werksman, J., 1996, "Compliance and Transition: Russia's Non-Compliance Tests the Ozone Regime," *Zeitschrift für ausländisches öffentliches Recht und Völkerrecht (Heidelberg Journal of International Law)* 56:750–773. For discussion on some important legal implications, see Koskenniemi, M., 1993, "Breach of Treaty or Non-Compliance? Reflections on the Enforcement of the Montreal Protocol," in *Yearbook of International Environmental Law*, edited by G. Handl, Graham and Trotman/Martinus Nijhoff, London, UK. In addition, one other article addresses this topic, but the article is substantially less informative than accounts provided by Széll and Koskenniemi; see Trask, J., 1992, "Montreal Protocol Non-Compliance Procedure: The Best Approach to Resolving International Environmental Disputes," *The Georgetown Law Journal* 80:1973–2001.

4. On the management versus enforcement approaches, see Chayes, A., and Chayes, A.H., 1995, *The New Sovereignty: Compliance with International Regulatory Agreements*, Harvard University Press, Cambridge, MA, USA. They argue that the enforcement approach is typically not feasible. For a critique from the "enforcement school," see Downs, G.W., Rocke, D.M., and Barsoom, P., 1996, "Is the Good News about Compliance Good News about Cooperation," *International Organization* 50(3):379–406.

5. Background interviews.

6. Article 8 states, "The Parties, at their first meeting, shall consider and approve procedures and institutional mechanisms for determining noncompliance with the provisions of this Protocol and for treatment of Parties found to be in noncompliance."

7. Decision I/8.

8. Széll, interview with author, London, 20 June 1995. To allow continued consideration of the issues, both the Second and Third Meetings of the Parties gave the ad hoc group a mandate to keep working on a revised, final Non-Compliance Procedure (Decisions II/5 and III/2).

9. Decision IV/5.

10. Széll, interview with author, London, 20 June 1995.

11. Széll, interview with author, London, 20 June 1995.

12. Background interviews.

13. See primarily Széll, 1995, 1996, op. cit., note 3, and Koskenniemi, 1993, op. cit., note 3.

14. Patrick J. Széll, interview with author, London, 20 June 1995.

15. The Montreal Protocol does not have its own dispute resolution system but rather relies on that in the Vienna Convention—the parent agreement of the Protocol. All parties to a protocol to that Convention must be parties to the Convention (Article 16 of the Convention); the provisions of the Convention that relate to its protocols apply to the Montreal Protocol (Article 14 of the Montreal Protocol); and the Convention's dispute resolution system applies to its protocols (Article 11.6 of the Convention).

16. The Secretariat does not have a strict obligation to report possible noncompliance. If the Secretariat becomes aware of possible noncompliance,

it may request the party concerned to furnish necessary information about the matter. If there is no response from the party concerned within three months or such longer period as the circumstances of the matter may require . . . then the Secretariat shall include the matter in its report to the Meeting of the Parties . . . and inform the Implementation Committee accordingly.

The Secretariat has never formally asked a party for information about its noncompliance under this paragraph of the Non-Compliance Procedure. Thus, although the Secretariat (and everyone) is aware of some noncompliance, it has never requested the "necessary information"; therefore, the Secretariat has not been compelled to initiate the Procedure.

17. Paragraph 2 of the Non-Compliance Procedure.

18. No party involved in a matter being considered by the Committee may participate in the elaboration and adoption of related recommendations by the Committee.

19. Background interviews.

20. Most of the Protocol's control measures apply to a *group* of substances (e.g., Group I of Annex A), but data are required for each controlled substance individually because compliance with the group target is computed by weighting consumption (production, imports, and exports) of each controlled substance according to its ozone-depleting potential. Parties are also required to submit data on the amounts used for feedstocks, amounts destroyed by approved technologies, imports from and exports to parties and non-parties, and imports of some recycled substances.

21. At present, the most recent of the Secretariat's annual reports on data (required by Article 12.c of the Protocol) is UNEP/OzL.Pro.7/6, 25 September 1995.

22. The Protocol was amended in 1990 to allow the EU and other "Regional Economic Integration Organizations" to report only imports and exports between the Organization and states that are not members of the Organization (see Chapter 3).

23. Data reporting by Belarus, Italy, and Ukraine was discussed at the seventh meeting. See UNEP/OzL.Pro/ImpCom/7/2, 16 November 1993, pp. 2–5.

24. See UNEP/OzL.Pro.6/5, 15 July 1994.

25. Article 10 mentions financial assistance from the MLF for developing countries. Article 5 mentions lenient provisions for controlling consumption of ODS.

26. The main definition is in paragraph 1 of Article 5. The paragraph sets a consumption threshold at 0.3 kg per capita for the core five CFCs and three halons (listed in Annex A and weighted according to ozone-depleting potential) on the date of entry into force for that particular party or any time thereafter until 1 January 1999.

27. Decision I/12 E. This list consists of all countries of the UN minus OECD members (in 1989), minus a few special cases (e.g., Israel, Liechtenstein, Monaco, and South Africa), and minus all the economies in transition (except Albania, Romania, and Yugoslavia, which are perhaps economies in transition but are included on the list). Georgia, which is considered "developing" by the OECD and the World Bank, was added to the list in 1996 (Decision VIII/29). Turkey, an OECD member but classified as a developing country by the World Bank and the United Nations Development Programme (UNDP), was added to this list in 1991 (Decision III/5). Mexico and South Korea are on the list although they have since joined the OECD. The Meeting of the parties requested that a working group further define criteria to determine what is a "developing country" (Decision III/5). That group made little progress, and the MOP has decided to handle requests for developing country status on a case-by-case basis (Decision IV/7).

28. Population data are mid-year estimates derived from the UN (UNEP/OzL.Pro/ImpCom/4/2, 6 October 1993, pp. 2–3). UN data are drawn from reports submitted by UN member countries.

29. Parties that do not have actual data for a year may use "the best possible estimates" (Articles 7.1 and 7.2).

30. However, the "sense" that data had been manipulated for the purpose of putting a country below the threshold identified in paragraph 1 of Article 5 led some members of the IC to argue strongly that rules about data correction be established to protect against such manipulation, especially where

changes in data would modify the status of a country under Article 5. See UNEP/OzL.Pro/ImpCom/8/3, 4 July 1994, p. 10.

31. Twelfth Meeting of the Implementation Committee, UNEP/OzL.Pro/ImpCom/12/3, 1 December 1995, advance copy, p. 9. The Lebanese challenged the UN data by presenting alternative population estimates from the World Bank (Decision VII/20). That precedent may be applied in the still unresolved case of Kuwait, which has also challenged its population data (see UNEP/OzL.Pro/ImpCom/15/3, 18 November 1996, p. 6.

32. The specific trade restrictions in Article 8 have been expanded in tandem with the addition of new controlled substances in the 1990 and 1992 amendments to the Protocol. Thus the specific application of the trade restrictions depends on the specific substance as well as the applicable amendment.

33. This formal exception is listed in Article 4.8 and elaborated in Decision IV/17 C.

34. UNEP/OzL.Pro/ImpCom/6/3, 26 August 1993, p. 5.

35. Decision VI/5.

36. The status of fund contributions is derived from the report of the MLF's Executive Committee: UNEP/OzL.Pro/ExCom/18/75, 24 November 1995, Annex I.

37. The provisions are given, respectively, in 1. Article 2B and Group II of Annex A; 2. Article 2A and Group I of Annex A (the core five CFCs), Article 2C and Group I of Annex B (an additional list of 10 CFCs), Article 2D and Group II of Annex B (carbon tetrachloride), and Article 2E and Group III of Annex B (methyl chloroform); 3. Article 2F and Group I of Annex C; 4. Article 2G and Group II of Annex C; and 5. Article 2H and Annex E.

38. Parson, E.A., and Greene, O., 1995, "The Complex Chemistry of the International Ozone Agreements,"*Environment* 37:16–20, 35–43.

39. Ibid.

40. Brack, D., 1996, *International Trade and the Montreal Protocol*, Earthscan, London, UK.

41. UNEP/OzL.Pro/ImpCom/9/2, 5 October 1994, p. 7.

42. Romania thought that it potentially possessed excess quotas, in part because it was treated as a developing country under Article 5 and thus had lenient controls on ODS and found it easy to comply beyond the requirements. The case was deferred to the next meeting of the Committee, but it was never raised again by Romania or Greece and has not yet been resolved. See UNEP/OzL.Pro/9/3, pp. 6–7.

43. UNEP/OzL.Pro/ImpCom/7/2, p. 5.

44. In 1995, when the Prime Mister made his request, the IC requested more information from Lithuania and pointed out that Lithuania would not gain assistance from international financial institutions for projects concerning ODS unless it ratified the London Amendment. The GEF has made membership in and compliance with relevant international agreements a condition for receipt of GEF money. See UNEP/OzL.Pro/ImpCom/12/3, 1 December 1995, pp. 9–10. The Latvian and Lithuanian cases are being handled in the same manner as Belarus, Russia, and Ukraine. (See below and see Decisions VIII/22 and VIII/23 of the Meeting of the Parties.)

45. The IC recommended, and the MOP decided, that no significant response was needed because the Czech Republic was now in compliance. Decision VIII/24 of the Meeting of Parties.

46. Cyprus, Kuwait, Lebanon, Slovenia, and the United Arab Emirates. UNEP/OzL.Pro/ImpCom/10/4, 30 August 1995, pp. 3, 5–6.

47. UAE was also requested to pay its MLF contribution for 1994. The policy of urging reclassified parties not to seek MLF is based on MOP Decision VI/5. For the application to UAE, see UNEP/OzL.Pro/ImpCom/13/3, 18–19 March 1996, p. 13.

48. The Committee also makes recommendations to the Executive Committee of the MLF, the only other body within the Montreal Protocol that has decision-making authority.

49. These arguments are developed at length in Chayes and Chayes, 1995, op. cit., note 4.

50. UNEP/OzL.Pro/ImpCom/12/3, 1 December 1995, p. 2, with reference to Decision VI/5.

51. See the report from the Seventh Meeting of the Parties: UNEP/OzL. Pro.7/12, 27 December 1995, p. 23.

52. The Maldives did not appear, but a representative from the United Nations Environment Programme (UNEP, one of the MLF-implementing agencies) reported that the relevant data had just been submitted to the Secretariat through a country program in the Maldives. Trinidad and Tobago did not appear, nor did Togo.

53. Belarus, Iran, the Maldives, Ukraine, and Syria. UNEP/OzL.Pro/ImpCom/ 7/2, 16 November 1993, pp. 2–5.

54. These discussions are excerpted from UNEP/OzL.Pro/ImpCom/9/2, 5 October 1994, pp. 2–3.

55. GEF-funded projects in countries with economies in transition have played a similar role in building capacity to report the required data.

56. See the Secretariat's annual data report for 1995: UNEP/OzL.Pro.7/6, 25 September 1995, p. 2. This report also lists Russia's data for Annex A substances as being more than two years overdue, but Russia provided these data as part of its deliberations with the IC and its name was removed from the list of delinquents. See UNEP/OzL.Pro/ImpCom/12/3, 1 December 1995, p. 8.

57. The list referred to here is that of countries with Annex A baseline data that are delinquent more than two years. For the 1994 list (which contains nine countries—seven developing and two industrialized), see UNEP/OzL.Pro.6/5, 15 July 1994, p. 2.

58. UNEP/OzL.Pro.6/5, 15 July 1994, p. 3.

59. UNEP/OzL.Pro.7/6, 25 September 1995, p. 4; UNEP/OzL.Pro.8/12, 19 December 1996, Decision VIII/2.

60. The statement of the Russian Federation in the eighth meeting (UNEP/ OzL.Pro/ImpCom/8/3, 4 July 1994, p. 12) indicates that Russia intended to request from the MOP a special status until 1998. At that same meeting, Ukraine also sought flexibility in applying the Protocol. At the seventh meeting (UNEP/OzL.Pro/ImpCom/7/2, 16 November 1993, p. 4), Belarus reported that it would have problems meeting some of the requirements of the Protocol, especially the rapid phaseout of halons. Poland's compliance problems, which were also discussed by the Committee long before the BBPRU cases were an issue, related to supply of CFCs after an early phaseout by the European Union. In 1995, Russia submitted its request for leniency to the Open-Ended Working Group that was preparing for the MOP; that request was declared a "self-submission," and the BBPRU submissions were formally under way by the tenth meeting of the IC (UNEP/OzL.Pro/ImpCom/10/4, 30 August 1995, p. 6).

61. UNEP/OzL.Pro/ExCom/18/75, 24 November 1995, pp. 4–7.

62. Notably, Russia referred to the list when complaining about the trade sanctions imposed against exports of Russian-produced ODS. It argued that the milder measures on the list—such as financial assistance and the issuance of cautions—should be employed before harsher measures (i.e., sanctions) are effected (UNEP/OzL.Pro.7/12, 27 December 1995, p. 53). For the full context, see the next section on the BBPRU submissions.

63. See Victor, 1996a and 1996b, op. cit., acknowledgment note.

64. The request, in the form of a statement by Russia on behalf of all five BBPRU countries, as well as three countries that intend to become parties to

the Protocol (Armenia, Georgia, and Kyrgystan), is reproduced in Annex II of the report of the eleventh meeting of the IC (UNEP/OzL.Pro/ImpCom/11/1, 14 September 1995, pp. 13–14).

65. The formal basis for this determination is the declaration by Russia, on behalf of the five parties, that they were unable to meet their obligations under the Protocol. Later, that declaration and a similar letter to the Executive Director of the United Nations Environment Programme were formally defined as "submissions."

66. TEAP Ad Hoc Working Group on Countries with Economies in Transition Aspects, Assessment of Basic Problems Confronting Countries with Economies in Transition in Complying with the Montreal Protocol, United Nations Environment Programme.

67. See Chapter 3 for more on the role of TEAP in reviewing implementation.

68. The final decisions are reported in Decisions VII/15–VII/19 (Poland, Bulgaria, Belarus, Russia, and Ukraine, respectively), UNEP/OzL.Pro.7/12, 27 December 1995, pp. 31–36, 51–54. For the IC proposals, see UNEP/ OzL.Pro.7/9/Rev.1 draft decisions circulated at the MOP.

69. UNEP/OzL.Pro/ImpCom/13/3, 28 March 1996, pp. 8–10; UNEP/OzL. Pro/ImpCom/14/4, 26 August 1996, pp. 2–6.

70. UNEP/OzL.Pro/ImpCom/14/4, 26 August 1996, p. 5.

71. Decision VII/17 (paragraph 7), Decision VII/18 (paragraph 9), and Decision VII/19 (paragraph 7), UNEP/OzL.Pro.7/12, 27 December 1995, pp. 32–36.

72. UNEP/ImpCom/12/3, 1 December 1995, pp. 5–6.

73. UNEP/OzL.Pro.7/12, 27 December 1995, pp. 52–54.

74. UNEP/OzL.Pro/ImpCom/13/3, 28 March 1996, pp. 5–7; UNEP/OzL.Pro/ ImpCom/17/3, 16 April 1997, pp. 5–7; UNEP/OzL.Pro/ImpCom/18/3, 4 June 1997, pp. 7–10; "Funds Needed to Help Russia Phase Out CFCs," *Global Environmental Change Report* 9(12), 27 June 1997.

75. "Substantive matters" excludes all portions of the report concerned with rules of procedure, officers, reorganization of the Committee, and formalities in opening and closing the meeting. Coding was done manually by the author; copies of the coded Committee reports are available for inspection. The number of lines in Committee reports devoted to each category were then counted and tabulated. Raw data for meetings 1–12 are reported in Victor, 1996a and 1996b, op. cit., acknowledgment note.

76. Hugo M. Schally, interview with author, Vienna, Austria, June 1995.

77. Schally, 1996, op. cit., note 3, p. 90.

78. Széll, 1996, op. cit., note 3, p. 45.

79. Koskenniemi, 1993, op. cit., note 3.

80. Széll, 1995, op. cit., note 3, p. 107.

81. See Chapter 3 and Chapter 5 and the conclusions in Chapter 16.

5

Implementation Review and the Baltic Sea Regime

Owen Greene

Introduction

This chapter examines the development of systems for monitoring and reviewing implementation in the Baltic Sea environment protection regime. It shows that substantial implementation review processes have developed in *each* of the main parts of the Baltic Sea regime, particularly since 1989, and that these processes have played a significant role in promoting the implementation and development of commitments. Several of these implementation review processes have been informal, taking place through bodies and mechanisms that are not dedicated to such tasks.

The chapter broadly adopts a "systems" perspective on the operation of implementation review in the Baltic Sea regime. Thus it emphasizes the importance of the fact that implementation review has been decentralized and has mostly functioned as an integral part of the broader operation of the regime, where processes of *learning about implementation* have been closely associated with the development of commitments and programs to protect the Baltic. Similarly, it aims at identifying the links between monitoring and review of implementation.

The character and significance of such links across different areas of an environmental regime can depend significantly on the extent to which they relate to central, dedicated implementation review mechanisms (as illustrated by the Non-Compliance Procedure of the Montreal Protocol; see Chapters 3 and 4). This chapter identifies and examines in detail the emergence of a system for implementation review (SIR) in the Baltic Sea regime during the 1990s, as well as the way that system became a central focus for the regime's key institutions by 1996.

The following section provides a brief overview of the operation of implementation review in the context of the development of the overall regime; it also identifies the key institutions and actors involved. Chapter 14 provides further information on the development of the Baltic regime. The third section discusses the separate operation and development of systems for monitoring and reviewing implementation in each of the main parts of the regime, illustrating their significance for the regime's overall effectiveness. Whereas these systems tended to operate relatively autonomously and often informally, during the 1990s a dedicated and increasingly comprehensive system was developed for reviewing implementation of the ambitious pollution reduction goals declared in 1988. This dedicated SIR is examined in detail in the fourth section. Conclusions are presented in the chapter's final section.

Implementation Review and the Baltic Sea Environment Protection Regime

The Early Years

The Baltic Sea environment protection regime was one of the first regional sea regimes to be established.[1] Its development began in earnest in multilateral discussions among all Baltic littoral states after 1972. These talks were stimulated by Nordic concerns about marine pollution, by the UN Conference on the Human Environment held in Stockholm, Sweden, and by the opportunities presented by East-West détente.[2]

The Convention on the Protection of the Marine Environment of the Baltic Sea Area (1974 Helsinki Convention) was essentially a "framework" convention: it established some goals, principles, institutions, and procedures to provide a framework for the future development of environmental commitments. In the early years, participants largely had to feel their way forward and "learn by doing." There were few shared understandings among participants concerning the environmental problems and appropriate policy responses, and there were no established regional sea agreements to provide precedents. Moreover, the involvement of North Atlantic Treaty Organization (NATO) members, Soviet bloc states, and neutral countries meant that governments were operating in an acutely sensitive political environment.

Officially, systems for reporting and implementation review were established from the beginning in the 1974 Convention.[3] The Helsinki Convention Baltic Marine Environment Protection Commission (HELCOM)—the governing body of the Baltic Sea regime—was given a broad mandate to receive, assess, and disseminate information related to the Convention, and to monitor and review implementation of commitments. Parties had a duty to monitor and exchange data on the state of the Baltic Sea environment, including pollution loads in the sea. They were obliged to establish "national authorities" whose responsibilities include issuing special permits for the discharge of noxious pollutants listed in Annex II and reporting such discharges to HELCOM. Similarly, they must provide detailed reports on any dumping, discharges, or spills at sea, and coordinate and improve their national systems for responding to accidental spills of oil or other pollutants at sea.

Despite the formal existence of these reporting and review systems, however, in practice reporting procedures were uneven and developed only slowly between 1974 and 1988. Apart from the reporting system related to permits for discharges of noxious substances, the most detailed reporting requirements were related to dumping, offshore incineration, and oil spills at sea. Here, the Baltic Sea regime incorporated obligations concerning pollution from ships established in the 1973 International Convention for the Prevention of Pollution from Ships (MARPOL Convention), as modified by the 1978 MARPOL Protocol (MARPOL 73/78).[4] Similarly, commitments (and reporting requirements) on dumping in the Baltic Sea were modeled on the 1972 Convention for the Prevention of Marine Pollution by Dumping from Ships and Aircraft (Oslo Convention) for the northeast Atlantic, to which Sweden, Denmark, and Finland were already parties. In other areas, reporting obligations were often vague. Moreover, reporting rates tended to be quite low during this period.[5] Even when reports were received on progress in implementation, they were often cryptic.[6] Soviet bloc countries were particular culprits, but Finland and other West European parties were not innocent in this respect, either.

Until the 1990s, implementation review was a relatively low priority for HELCOM. Attention was focused instead on maintaining and developing the basic framework for environmental cooperation among Baltic Sea states with profoundly different political systems in the context of the decline of East-West détente.[7] The USSR and its allies were highly secretive: for these governments, concerns about security and sovereignty were dominant. The regime "leaders" (Sweden, Denmark, and West Germany) were content to concentrate on developing East-West cooperation on scientific research and environmental monitoring, using HELCOM to press the USSR and its allies to endorse environmental standards similar to their own.

Nevertheless, some implementation review processes did develop between 1974 and 1989, albeit mainly in an ad hoc or informal way, according to the issues and types of obligations involved.[8] At the most informal level, the intensification of contact between scientists and experts from different countries brought about through HELCOM programs improved understanding of existing practices and laid the basis for more specific East-West exchanges on implementation problems.[9] Furthermore, the meetings of HELCOM committees and working groups of specialists provided nominally technical fora where governmental experts could discuss submitted data on national programs or on discharges, loads, and sources of pollution, as well as any implementation problems reported by the state concerned.[10]

Moreover, during this period it was politically acceptable for HELCOM and its subcommittees to seriously review implementation of agreed reporting obligations. Thus, poor performance in reporting was regularly noted, and guilty parties were systematically reminded of their obligations. In HELCOM's committees of specialists, such problems could often be raised directly with the responsible national officials, frequently inducing belated submission of the relevant national report. Where reporting guidelines were revealed to be inadequate, they were often further developed to induce more useful or comprehensive reports. Perhaps most importantly, the HELCOM subcommittees tasked with developing new HELCOM Recommendations took account of formally and informally available information on existing practices or implementation problems as an integral part of their carrying out their task.

After the Cold War
As the Cold War drew to an end, the Baltic Sea environment protection regime entered a new phase. It is generally agreed that the regime has become more dynamic and effective since 1988. The scope and stringency of its commitments have increased substantially, not least because the USSR, under Mikhail Gorbachev, agreed that the commitments could be expanded to cover territorial seas, internal waters, and land-based sources of pollution, as well as the open sea.

Legally, this new phase is marked by the negotiation of the 1992 Helsinki Convention, which will supersede the earlier Convention when it comes into force (probably by 1998).[11] Politically, this new phase is marked by the introduction of regular Ministerial Conferences, which have promoted the stringency and political authority of HELCOM commitments and energized and developed the regime's institutions.[12] The 1988 Ministerial Declaration pledged states to achieve 50 percent cuts in their emissions and discharges of key pollutants between 1987 and 1995. The 1990 and 1992 Ministerial Conferences established the Joint Comprehensive Environmental Action Programme (JCP) to develop and fund programs to reduce pollution from 132 pollution "hot spots" throughout the Baltic Sea catchment area (that is, including parts of Belarus, Ukraine, the Czech Republic, Slovakia, and Norway, as well as the Baltic Sea littoral states).

Reporting and implementation review activities have also expanded and intensified during the 1990s. Legally, the 1992 Helsinki Convention widened and strengthened the reporting obligations of the regime.[13] However, this Convention will not come into force until 1998 at the earliest. Thus the development of the SIR in the 1990s occurred mainly through political agreements arising from the regime's increased dynamism and strengthened political commitment to the regime, rather than through changes in international law.

The expansion and intensification of review processes was largely due to the reduction of political constraints on such activities. By 1990, there was great concern about the environment in both the East and the West. Governments in Eastern Europe wanted to demonstrate openness and change. They had no great objections to revealing the poor environmental performance of their communist predecessors, particularly if this helped to motivate foreign assistance and investment. Authorities within the Baltic states were keen to assert their autonomy and to use environmental problems to demonstrate the damaging consequences of Soviet rule.[14] By 1989, the Soviet policies of *glasnost* and *perestroika* brought about an openness that only increased after the breakup of the USSR two years later.

Thus reporting and review systems have developed substantially in the Baltic Sea regime since 1989, mainly through legally nonbinding ("soft") Ministerial Declarations and HELCOM Recommendations. For the most part, this process has proceeded relatively autonomously within each of the different areas covered by the regime, leading to a decentralized set of review activities operating at a number of different sites and through several mechanisms (see discussion below). However, during the 1990s a more systematic review process has also developed to review progress in implementing the 50 percent reduction goals announced in the 1988 Ministerial Declaration and to produce a comprehensive assessment of the implementation of these goals (and of all other major regime commitments and programs). The resulting assessment is to be considered at the 1998 Ministerial Conference. This process is examined in the fourth section of this chapter.

Fora for Monitoring and Implementation Review

Before proceeding with the examination of the formal and informal SIRs that have developed in the Baltic Sea regime, it is useful to identify the key types of institutions or actors involved.

HELCOM.   As the regime's governing body, HELCOM has a broad mandate to receive, assess, and disseminate information and to monitor and review implementation. It meets once a year, and decisions are made by consensus by the representatives of contracting parties. The small Helsinki-based Secretariat is tasked with facilitating HELCOM in its work.

In practice, much of the Commission's detailed work is carried out in a number of HELCOM committees, which periodically have been reorganized as the regime's activities have developed. Since 1990, there have been four main HELCOM committees—the Environment Committee, the Technological Committee (TC), the Maritime Committee (MC), and the Combatting Committee (CC)[15]—each of which has been supported by a number of subcommittees and ad hoc working groups. In addition, in 1992 a new Programme Implementation Task Force (PITF) was established to coordinate and promote implementation of the JCP. As discussed below, each of these HELCOM committees and working groups serves as a forum for implementation review, in addition to performing the other tasks related to its specific area of activity.

Lead Parties.   In many international agreements, individual governments can informally take a lead in developing commitments or in monitoring and assessing other participants' environmental performance. In the Baltic Sea regime, however, this has become an important institutional characteristic. It has become established practice in HELCOM and the JCP to nominate "Lead Parties" to play a leading role in the development, management, or review of particular aspects of the regime.

In this practice, which began in the 1970s, a country with an interest or expertise in the pollutant, industrial process, or sector under consideration is nominated to carry out a study of existing practices at home and in other member countries, and to examine possible measures and proposals to improve environmental standards. It then provides background information and drafts proposals for consideration by the relevant HELCOM committees. As the regime has developed and expanded in scope, so too has the role of Lead Parties.

There are Lead Parties associated with many of HELCOM's 164 Recommendations (particularly the 63 Recommendations related to land-based sources of pollution) and with most other major areas of HELCOM activity and concern. Similarly, each of the program elements of the JCP also has a Lead Party responsible for coordinating and developing its part of the program. Lead Parties are expected to take the lead in proposing more stringent yet feasible standards and have been nominated on this understanding.

In practice, Lead Parties typically have a good deal of scope, inter alia, to engage in implementation review.[16] An intrinsic part of their role in developing new Recommendations is reviewing existing national practices, including the implementation of any existing Recommendations that are due to be superseded. Moreover, where Lead Parties are responsible for coordinating a HELCOM or JCP program, they can initiate and coordinate reviews of implementation and stimulate responses to poor performance as they see fit—and in practice they have often chosen to do so. Finally, as formal review systems have developed in the regime, Lead Parties have explicitly been made responsible for compiling national reports and producing reports on progress in implementation of relevant Recommendations or activities.

Nongovernmental Organizations.   A variety of industrial, environmental, and scientific nongovernmental organizations (NGOs) typically participate in environmental regimes and can play a significant informal (and sometimes formal) role in monitoring and reviewing environmental performance. Until the late 1980s, the scope for NGO participation in HELCOM activities was very limited. Efforts by environmental NGOs (ENGOs) such as Greenpeace and Friends of the Earth to monitor or expose polluting activities therefore took place in domestic or broader international political arenas.

However, since 1989 a number of NGOs have been granted observer status at HELCOM and at the meetings of the High Level Task Force (HLTF) and its successor, the PITF. By 1992, Greenpeace, the World Wide Fund for

Nature (WWF), and Coalition Clean Baltic (CCB) had all become active in this context.[17] By 1996 these NGOs had been joined by several others, including some industrial associations such as the European Chlor-Alkali Industry (EURO CHLOR) and the European Fertilizer Manufacturers' Association (EFMA).[18]

As observers, these NGOs have access to the meetings of HELCOM and the PITF and, where they can claim relevant expertise, to the meetings of HELCOM committees and working groups. Greenpeace, CCB, EURO CHLOR, and EFMA, for example, have all played active roles in reporting and review activities, as well as in the development of Recommendations.[19] Indeed, some NGOs (such as the WWF) have actually become Lead Parties.[20]

Links With Other International Institutions. The Baltic Sea environment protection regime operates in a complex institutional environment. In several areas of its operation, links with other regimes and international institutions or programs are of real significance. For example, there are close institutional links with the regimes set up under the Oslo Convention and the Convention for the Prevention of Marine Pollution from Land-based Sources (Paris Convention) to prevent pollution of the North Sea and the northeast Atlantic.[21] Close links also exist with the International Maritime Organization (IMO) and the MARPOL regime to prevent pollution from ships.[22] Various bilateral and trilateral agreements between Baltic Sea states provide additional frameworks for environmental cooperation between Sweden, Finland, Russia, and Estonia. Many international organizations are accredited observers to HELCOM and contribute to a range of activities such as environmental monitoring and preparation of emission inventories.[23] Similarly, numerous multilateral banks (such as the World Bank) and other funding agencies have played an important role through their participation in the JCP.[24]

Finally, the relationship with the European Economic Community (EEC), and subsequently the European Union (EU), has been important throughout the lifetime of the regime. Even when it was not a formal participant in the regime, the EU played an important indirect role through its effects on relevant regulations and activities of member states such as West Germany and Denmark. In the 1990s it became a formal party to the 1992 Helsinki Convention and the JCP. Moreover, all HELCOM members except Russia have become EU members or associate members and are therefore committed (politically if not legally) to adopting and implementing relevant EU regulations and to participating in EU monitoring programs.

This involvement with other institutions can be important for monitoring and reviewing implementation as well as for the broader operation of the regime. Outside institutions can provide many potential sources of information relevant to implementation. They also provide additional fora and mechanisms for monitoring and reviewing implementation, and for responding to implementation or compliance problems. In principle, such outside links could be as important for the regime's effectiveness as links within the Baltic Sea regime itself. In practice, this does indeed appear to be the case in some areas, such as the prevention of oil pollution, as is discussed in the next section.

Reporting and Review in Different Parts of the Baltic Sea Regime

Preventing Pollution from Ships

Measures to prevent pollution from ships are among the most highly developed and specific commitments in the 1974 and 1992 Helsinki Conventions: over a third of the Recommendations adopted by HELCOM relate to this issue. The MC, one of HELCOM's main committees, focuses solely on this issue area.

Yet HELCOM has actually played only a subordinate role to the IMO in developing international regulations for the Baltic Sea in this issue area, and has mainly adopted and endorsed global maritime regulations agreed in MARPOL 73/78 and its subsequent annexes.[25] In this role, it has sometimes adopted MARPOL regulations for Baltic Sea states some years before they came into force globally. Moreover, HELCOM has coordinated member-state activities inside the IMO, particularly to ensure that the Baltic Sea is designated a "special area" in the MARPOL regime, which thus requires that all ships follow particularly strict antipollution requirements.[26] HELCOM has also developed regulations in areas that are not covered by MARPOL—related, for example, to discharges from smaller vessels and pleasure craft.[27]

HELCOM's key role in preventing pollution from ships has not been in developing commitments, but rather in reviewing and promoting compliance with MARPOL regulations in the Baltic Sea area. Mainly through its MC, HELCOM has promoted concern about pollution from ships, increased awareness of relevant MARPOL regulations among relevant national and port authorities in the region, and harmonized and promoted domestic adoption of

MARPOL regulations in Baltic Sea states by refining and adopting them in HELCOM Recommendations.

The MC has also promoted and developed systems for reporting on implementation and compliance. The reporting obligations incorporated into relevant HELCOM Recommendations often have been similar to those included in MARPOL. However, reporting rates for MARPOL have been low, and the IMO has devoted little time and few resources to try to improve reporting rates or to use the information reported for reviewing implementation.[28] In the 1990s, the MC began actively reminding and encouraging parties to submit the required reports. Although this improved reporting rates, the MC found that the submitted reports often were not very revealing about the real state of implementation. Thus, since 1992 the Committee has not only expanded the reporting requirements, but has also taken measures to further investigate actual implementation.[29]

It is difficult to enforce implementation of MARPOL regulations that directly restrict discharges from ships at sea, and compliance with these regulations is thought to be low throughout the world. To deter noncompliance, HELCOM's CC has actively coordinated and promoted systems of surveillance, policing, and penalties (fines, etc.) in the Baltic area.[30] Although it made some progress in this respect in the 1990s, the impact of these efforts on compliance seems limited. International experience has shown that it is more effective to focus on promoting implementation of MARPOL rules requiring installation and use of specific equipment (on ships or in ports) designed to reduce the incentives for operators to discharge oil or waste at sea than it is to focus on regulations restricting such discharges.[31] One reason for this is the relative ease with which the existence and operation of such equipment can be verified, making the rules easily enforceable. The MC encouraged Baltic Sea states to regularly inspect ships arriving at their ports to determine whether they had installed and were using the required equipment (such as separate tanks for sewage or bilge), and to report any violations.[32]

It is important to note that since the late 1980s the MC has focused on reviewing whether adequate "reception facilities" for ship wastes are available at all Baltic ports. MARPOL requires port states to ensure that adequate reception facilities are available at each port, so that ships that have stored their wastes can efficiently dispose of them when they arrive at port. To qualify as a "special area" under MARPOL, all Baltic Sea states must install such reception facilities at every port; thus this requirement was included in the 1974 Helsinki Convention and early HELCOM Recommendations. All Baltic Sea states duly installed reception facilities and reported that they had done so to both HELCOM and the IMO. However, it became clear that many of these reception facilities were inadequate or inconvenient, causing undue delays or expense. Moreover, in several ports, special fees were charged for using such facilities. Thus many ship operators continued to illicitly discharge their wastes at sea.

In the late 1980s, the MC launched a substantial review of existing reception facilities in the region. Governments were asked to provide detailed national reports on their facilities and fee systems; this request was repeatedly followed up until every report had been submitted according to agreed guidelines. The reports were published in 1989 in a HELCOM booklet aimed primarily at ship operators.[33] At the same time, new, more developed guidelines on port reception facilities were created and disseminated, along with a standardized form for ship operators to report any inadequacies encountered.[34] In the changed political context after 1991, the MC initiated another in-depth review of reception facilities in Baltic ports, which revealed that provision of such facilities was grossly inadequate in many ports.[35]

In response to the findings of the 1991 MC report, HELCOM established a working group (MC ReFac) to review the problems throughout the Baltic Sea in detail and propose remedies.[36] This task was carried out in close cooperation with the IMO, for which the exercise was a significant precedent. The IMO arranged "advisory missions" to all major East European and Russian ports. The Baltic Ports Organization (BPO) and the Baltic and International Maritime Council (BIMCO), a ship operators' association, also became actively involved—criticizing each other's evidence.[37] Together, the IMO and MC ReFac found many major problems concerning facilities and administrative systems.[38] They jointly developed a Baltic Strategy for Port Reception Facilities, which was subsequently adopted by HELCOM in 1996.[39]

The MC and IMO continued to work closely to promote implementation of this strategy, which included adoption of common guidelines on the capabilities and operation of reception facilities in the Baltic (including a "no special fee" system), together with a detailed funding program to bring existing facilities in East European ports up to standard. When the MC found that the multilateral funding bodies involved in the JCP were unwilling to provide significant funds (the funds required at each port were typically small, about US$36 million divided among some 16 ports—too small for the main JCP funding bodies to be interested in becoming involved),[40] the IMO turned to the United Nations Development Programme (UNDP), with a more positive response.[41]

Thus, particularly since 1989, HELCOM's MC and its working groups have actively reviewed and promoted implementation of commitments to prevent pollution from ships in the Baltic Sea and have coordinated policy responses to the implementation problems identified. The MC has been particularly active and effective in improving reporting (to the IMO as well as to HELCOM) and in promoting compliance with obligations requiring ship operators and port authorities to install and maintain facilities to contain and dispose of ship wastes, especially reception facilities at Baltic Sea ports. SIRs became quite well developed in these areas in the 1990s, and in practice were closely linked with the development of responses to revealed compliance problems.

In this way, HELCOM has acted as an important institution for reviewing and improving implementation of commitments established in another international regime, MARPOL. Recently it went further and involved the IMO in joint efforts to review compliance and develop responses, which resulted not only in the establishment of an international aid program to tackle implementation problems, but also in a precedent that the IMO now aims at following in other regions. This is a significant example of the importance of links between regimes for the operation and effectiveness of international commitments.

Monitoring the Environment and Pollution Loads

Many of HELCOM's activities during the Cold War concerned programs for monitoring and assessing the state of the Baltic Sea environment or loads or emissions of pollutants in the Baltic Sea area. Within the Baltic Monitoring Programme, launched by HELCOM in 1979, assessments of the state of the Baltic Sea environment have been carried out every five years.[42] In addition, there are ongoing programs to monitor and evaluate airborne deposition of pollutants, radioactive substances, coastal waters, seal populations, and (since 1992) protected natural habitats.

Apart from the intrinsic importance of such scientific assessments, these programs have facilitated informal information exchange and review among experts. They have also generated information related to implementation of HELCOM commitments that can be used for implementation review. In the

Baltic Sea regime, the most important of such programs has been a series of exercises to monitor and evaluate the pollution load entering the Baltic Sea from land-based sources, so-called Pollution Load Compilation (PLC) exercises.

These PLC exercises started in 1985, when work on PLC-1 began. HELCOM itself regarded the results of PLC-1, published in 1987,[43] as very unreliable and difficult to interpret. The states provided data on pollution loads monitored in their coastal waters; however, each state's data were collected and evaluated using different methods, which were of uneven quality and often undefined. The data for 1990, included in PLC-2, were somewhat more comparable and reliable than those in PLC-1, not least because uniform methodological guidelines had been prepared.[44] For the first time the PLC exercise generated detailed statistics on sources and quantities of pollution in the Baltic Sea. Moreover, as a result of increased opportunities for cooperation in coastal monitoring after 1990, improved and more comprehensive data became available late in the project. Despite these improvements, however, many problems remained, and after PLC-2 was finished HELCOM immediately launched programs to intercalibrate monitoring devices and promote data quality.

PLC-3, which covered 1995, was carried out between 1994 and 1996. This exercise was again much more intensive and thorough than its predecessor. The information in PLC-3 was expected to be much more reliable and comprehensive than information in the previous PLC reports, and thus potentially useful for implementation reviews. On the basis of measured pollution loads entering particular parts of the Baltic Sea, it is possible to monitor trends in discharges of pollutants from major land-based sources in a particular region. Thus, data from PLC-3 became a significant resource for the comprehensive review of implementation of the 1988 Ministerial Declaration and linked HELCOM Recommendations (see next section).

Implementing Environmental Standards for Land-Based Sources of Pollution

One of HELCOM's main functions has been to develop Recommendations that set environmental standards to reduce pollution from land-based sources, mainly through the TC.[45] In practice, the development of Recommendations in this area has been carried out in TC subcommittees or working groups of specialists, involving national officials and representatives from relevant international organizations. The Lead Party system has been central to this process.

In the 1990s, for example, 11 priority areas for point sources were identified (such as the pulp and paper industry, the chemical industry, and fish farming), as well as 6 priority areas related to diffuse sources (such as agriculture, and mercury- or cadmium-containing products).[46] Lead Parties existed for each of these areas, operating as described above. In each area, specialist groups developed new Recommendations and definitions of "best available technologies" and "best environmental practice." After the late 1980s, NGOs also became increasingly involved in this process.

Implementation review increasingly formed an integral part of the process of developing Recommendations concerning pollution from land-based sources. The Lead Party in this area typically prepared reports based on reviews of existing practices at home and in other countries, including implementation of existing Recommendations related to reducing land-based pollution. Members of each working group also informally drew on similar information. However, such implementation review processes typically were informal and not comprehensive. Also, although some Recommendations included specific reporting obligations, the reports received often were not terribly revealing, particularly those from Soviet bloc countries. In the 1980s, Western states sometimes actively reviewed one another's reports in the committees, often merely for demonstration purposes; however, a much more cautious and less confrontational approach was used when dealing with reports from the USSR and its allies.

In fact, until the 1990s reporting and review processes related to pollution from land-based sources or inside territorial waters were blocked by a fundamental dispute about how to define pollution standards and environmental performance indicators. Western parties preferred emission standards linked with regulations on emissions from industries, treatment plants, etc. The USSR and its allies preferred ambient environmental quality standards.[47] Thus, in the USSR there was no focus on monitoring and control at the sites of pollution: even large discharges were not reported as "substantial," because they were deemed to be sufficiently diluted when they crossed Soviet territorial waters into the open sea. Technical arguments continued for over a decade, but with little progress as long as Soviet authorities remained unwilling to permit the regime to develop clear standards or effective implementation review in relation to territorial waters or land-based sources of pollution. Only after strong pressure from Sweden, West Germany, and Finland were recommendations on emission standards agreed in the 1980s (e.g., on discharges of mercury from chloralkali plants).

After the 1988 Ministerial Conference, reporting and review processes became much more significant for the TC's work on pollution from land-based sources. A system was established for reporting on implementation of every HELCOM Recommendation in this area, with reports due every three years. HELCOM also decided that, henceforth, all new Recommendations in this area were to be accompanied by specific forms and guidelines for reporting on implementation. Developing the Recommendation and the reporting guidelines simultaneously would not only ensure the establishment of proper reporting systems, it would also mean that requirements for effective reporting and review would be taken fully into account when new standards were being developed.[48] Thus, the development of review processes became an integral part of the development of Recommendations aimed at limiting pollution from land-based sources. This reporting and review system is discussed in more detail in the next section, as it became integrated with the development of a dedicated and comprehensive system for reviewing implementation of the pollution reduction goals in the 1998 Ministerial Declaration.

The development of Recommendations concerning the pulp and paper industry provides an illustrative example of some of the ways in which implementation review processes have become integral to the development of Recommendations in this area, and of the emerging role of NGOs in these activities. Pulp and paper mills were a major pollution source, thus TC working groups focused on developing standards on discharges of chlorinated organic substances (AOX). In the early 1990s, substantial reviews of existing practices in Eastern Europe and Russia took place for the first time, which greatly informed Lead Party reports. However, national representatives of countries with such industries (particularly Finland, Sweden, and Russia) shared a concern that environmental standards would undermine the competitiveness of these industries and thus drew heavily on cautious advice from industry. Greenpeace developed the strategy of releasing its own assessments of discharges from pulp and paper plants at press conferences timed to preempt TC meetings or announcements. The TC found itself constantly on the defensive, forced to respond to Greenpeace data without having systematically compiled their own. Greenpeace's strategy played an important role in stimulating the TC to produce its own regular and detailed compilation of emission estimates, which could then be used to review implementation of HELCOM commitments.[49]

Greenpeace, CCB, and the industrial association EURO CHLOR became involved in the TC working group to develop standards concerning discharges from pulp and paper mills. Greenpeace advocated zero AOX discharges and provided its own arguments as to why this was feasible. Although data from environmental NGOs were not decisive in themselves, they did stimulate thorough and vigorous reviews, as a result of which industry discovered that standards could be raised much more rapidly than it had previously believed. The enhanced data compilation system on discharges from plants promoted learning from best practice. The reductions in monitored discharges from some plants reportedly took participants by surprise in certain cases and stimulated both reviews of best practice and rapid development of stringent Recommendations.[50] Similar illustrations can be found in relation to several other priority areas, such as metal surface treatment, chemicals, and agriculture (fertilizers).

Implementing the Joint Comprehensive Programme
Since its establishment in 1992, the JCP has been a central part of the Baltic Sea environment protection regime. It consists of a coordinated regional program to address major pollution sources within the Baltic Sea catchment area. The program focused on 132 pollution "hot spots," of which 95 were located in Eastern Europe and the former Soviet Union. As outlined above, the JCP formally involves all countries in the catchment area, the European Community, five multilateral financial institutions and individual donor countries, and a number of NGOs and international organizations. The PITF works under the aegis of HELCOM and is responsible for coordinating and developing the JCP.

By 1996, the JCP was widely regarded as an effective program: it had helped to set priorities and mobilize national and international funding for many investment projects to reduce pollution from the listed hot spots.[51] As an international environmental aid program, it lacked the institutional coordination or focus of the Montreal Protocol's Multilateral Fund, for example. However, it compared well with similar programs launched to fund environmental projects in Eastern Europe.[52] The JCP set environmental priorities and standards, involved recipients as well as donors, provided a framework within which "matchmaking" could be facilitated between funding organizations with complementary skills or complementary institutional constraints or preferences, and included structures for coordination and review of implementation activities. It was clear from the 1996 Visby Ministerial Declaration, for example, that the Baltic governments remained committed to maintaining the JCP as the central regional program for reducing emissions of pollutants into the Baltic Sea.[53]

The development and implementation of the JCP has involved many monitoring, reporting, and implementation review processes. The preparatory work between 1990 and 1992 involved an intense national and international review process, as problems and hot spots were identified, national plans were developed, prefeasibility studies and other studies were carried out by a range of donors, consultants, multilateral funding agencies, and international organizations, and the HLTF assessed the results. Since 1992, the PITF has regularly reviewed progress in implementing the JCP, and has reported its findings to HELCOM and to Ministerial Conferences.

In 1994, the PITF accepted Denmark's offer to commission in-depth studies of the status of the 47 "priority hot spots" identified in the prefeasibility studies. These detailed studies included assessments of pollution loads, reports on the status of the projects and the local contexts, and reviews of funding and pollution control programs, both by country and by drainage basin.[54] Lead Parties for JCP program elements have produced similar detailed reports, such as the 1996 Swedish review of the status of hot spots associated with industrial and municipal discharges.[55] Also, each of the international financial institutions has its own internal review procedures and requirements, as do the EU and donor governments. Formal HELCOM review procedures were established for deciding whether to remove hot spots from the list, after environmental NGOs such as CCB protested that the PITF agreed to remove some hot spots in Finland and Sweden simply on the basis of reports from these countries.

In preparing its reports on implementation of the JCP, the PITF can draw on information from a range of sources, including reports from nominated local "contact persons" at each hot spot and status reports provided by the World Bank and other multilateral funding agencies. However, in the early years the PITF Secretariat (made up of a program coordinator and an assistant) found that it was as much as it could do to keep track of the different monitoring systems and evaluation reports from all of the agencies, governments, consultants, and institutions involved.[56] Larger projects tended to involve multiple funding bodies, each with its own review procedures, which were not always coordinated with those of other participants (though the World Bank and the EU tended to take the lead on coordinating procedures where they were involved). Particularly where private enterprises or the European Bank for Reconstruction and Development (EBRD), the European Investment Bank (EIB), or the Nordic Investment Bank (NIB) were involved, there were also significant questions concerning confidentiality. In this context, unless there were major discrepancies, the Secretariat tended to accept the status reports from the local contact point for each project with little questioning.[57]

In spite of all of the monitoring, reporting, and review activities taking place within the JCP, until 1996 systematic or dedicated systems for reviewing implementation of the Programme were being established only gradually. Nevertheless, a great deal of relevant information emerged from these multiple processes. For example, preparatory work for the JCP during 1990–1992 provided a framework for detailed review of past environmental (and reporting) performance and was mainly carried out on the basis of a common understanding of how poor environmental performance had been. This work revealed information that had not been supplied by parties for PLC-2. Thus the JCP review processes improved the other review mechanisms within the regime, including reviews of implementation of HELCOM Recommendations and the 50 percent pollution reductions pledged by the 1988 Ministerial Conference. Moreover, once the information was informally available, governments became more willing to provide it officially for formal review.

The PITF provided a forum where JCP participants periodically reviewed and learned from recent experience. Indeed, participants believe that PITF and Lead Party reviews helped the World Bank, EBRD, and other Western funding organizations to understand what conditions were necessary for successful project development and to change some of the ways they operated (related to the presumed role of markets or the need for grants as well as loans, for example).[58]

In 1996–1997, as the first phase of the JCP was coming to an end, greater coordination and consistency of data collection and review processes within the JCP was being established. In 1996 a comprehensive review was launched by the PITF, other HELCOM committees, and Lead Parties, to assess the JCP's operation and to set priorities for the program's second phase, to be launched in

1998. This review was rather systematic and was linked to the comprehensive review of implementation of the 1988 Ministerial Declaration, discussed below.

One major issue arising from the PITF reviews that has caused increasing concern is the relative neglect of so-called "diffuse" hot spots. Efforts to reduce pollution from diffuse sources, such as runoff from agricultural areas or emissions from motor vehicles, pose relatively difficult project management challenges. To be successful, such efforts must change widespread agricultural or social practices. There is a well-known tendency for funding agencies such as the World Bank to prefer major capital programs and a single site to smaller, more widely dispersed projects. This preference has been reflected in the funding mobilized for the JCP, where projects to tackle "point" hot spots have been favored over those addressing non-point sources of pollution.

The PITF reviews not only raised awareness about this problem, they also stimulated some responses to it. As the Lead Parties for the JCP program elements dealing with agriculture and traffic, Poland and Germany prepared reports and arranged seminars on ways to address diffuse sources of pollution in the JCP. The World Bank initiated a review of ways in which its criteria and procedures should be developed to address this issue more effectively.[59] The importance of tackling diffuse sources of pollution has become a central focus of attention in the design of the JCP's second phase, which will be linked to an initiative to promote the Baltic Agenda 21.[60]

Reviewing Implementation of the 1988 Ministerial Declaration: The Development of a Dedicated Implementation Review Mechanism

The 1988 Ministerial Declaration was an important stimulus for the development of a formal implementation review system in the Baltic Sea regime. In 1989, HELCOM decided that parties should provide detailed national reports on progress in implementing their pledge in the 1988 Ministerial Declaration to reduce by 50 percent their discharges of heavy metals, persistent organic pollutants (POPs), and nutrients by 1995, as well as separate reports on their implementation of every associated HELCOM Recommendation (i.e., those dealt with by the Scientific Technological Committee [STC] and its successor, the TC).[61] All of these reports were to be prepared using detailed standardized reporting forms and were to be submitted every three years beginning in 1990. They would then be compiled and reviewed by relevant Lead Parties and TC working groups of specialists, assisted by the Secretariat. A report on implementation was then to be submitted by the TC to HELCOM for overall review and assessment.

Thus, in 1990 parties (and the three Baltic states)[62] were supposed to submit reports on their progress in implementing the 1988 Ministerial Declaration and each relevant HELCOM Recommendation. In line with previous experience, most of the national reports were late and several were incomplete or did not use the agreed guidelines or reporting forms.[63] However, the new system tied reports to a more systematic and explicit SIR, increasing the pressure to improve reporting rates. The Secretariat, TC chairpersons, and Lead Parties pressured governments to provide appropriate reports in time for the special meeting in November 1990, which was organized to review the reports and prepare the required status report on implementation.[64] Thus parties were given a deadline, by which time each had made at least some submissions, however cryptic or lacking in detail. The report to HELCOM stated that implementation was "incomplete" for nearly all relevant Recommendations (i.e., those relating to land-based sources of pollution).[65] As would be expected at such an early stage in the implementation process, the reports on implementation of the 50 percent pollution reduction goals mostly outlined national plans and intentions. However, progress on establishing the 1987 emissions baseline, against which pollution reductions were to be compared, was also very limited. Some baseline data were provided on discharges occurring around 1987, but they were largely incomplete.

At the HELCOM meeting in February 1991, it was decided that further efforts should be made to fill the gaps in national reports and improve the quality of reported data. The Lead Parties were to revise their reports, taking the opportunity to include any new information reported by parties or data that had become available through the PLC-2 exercise. The new and revised reports were then to be reviewed by the appropriate TC working group (TC Point or TC Diff).[66] To increase transparency and emphasize the importance of the new reporting system, the revised reports were then to be published in the Commission's "Baltic Sea Environment Proceedings" (BSEP) series.[67] In practice, this process was only partially successful. Further information was provided and the review process generated additional requests from the TC to fill gaps or address inconsistencies in the national and Lead Party reports,[68] but by the end of the year reporting was still incomplete. Moreover, some of the information becoming available for PLC-2 looked dubious. For example, some East European countries were suspected of grossly inflating their baseline emissions to make the 50 percent cuts more "achievable" and to stimulate environmental aid.[69] Although the revised reports were made available to HELCOM participants, they were not published.

However, strengthening the operation of the reporting system was regarded as a long-term process. Thus the 1990–1991 round of reporting was set aside and attention was focused on ensuring that the second round, for 1993–1994, would be more successful.[70] Reporting rates did improve: by May 1993 (two months after the requested submission date), only Russia and Latvia had failed to provide any national reports. However, most of the other countries had reported on implementation of only a minority of the relevant Recommendations: only Sweden, Denmark, and Germany covered more than two-thirds of them.[71] Moreover, for several Recommendations, much of the information requested in the reporting forms was not provided. Over the summer, the Secretariat and TC chairpersons managed to induce submissions of more reports, but remaining gaps meant that only an interim report on implementation could be prepared in time for the February 1994 HELCOM meeting. A process for improving, reviewing, and publishing these reports similar to that introduced in 1991 after PLC-1 was therefore established in 1994, with similar mixed results.[72]

In this second attempt to improve the reports, however, the reporting problems were not put to one side. The 1994 HELCOM meeting urged parties to accelerate implementation of pollution reduction measures and to prepare an assessment of their national programs.[73] Lead Parties were explicitly requested to carry out a substantial assessment of implementation, to "spell out clearly the remaining problems of implementing the Commission's decisions," and to draw conclusions for consideration by the TC in November 1994.[74] In response, Lead Parties appeared to give their role in implementation review high priority, and some raised problems with implementation requiring further action. For example, Denmark reported concerns about implementation of commitments on the disposal of PCBs and PCTs.[75] Moreover, the Secretariat and working group chairpersons established a precedent by presenting their own assessment of implementation problems to the TC. The Secretariat distributed a document specifying exactly which data were missing from each country, and the review process went through another iteration.[76] In March 1995, HELCOM established an additional follow-up process for finding all available data for past years at the same time as it launched the next round of the reporting exercise.[77]

The third round of reporting on implementation (1996–1997) was particularly important, because 1995 was the target date for achieving the 50 percent cuts pledged in the 1988 Ministerial Declaration. It was clear from the two previous reporting rounds that the mechanisms for collecting and reviewing relevant data would need further strengthening. On the initiative of the Secretariat, a special Project for Preparation of the Final Report on Implementation of the 1988 Ministerial Declaration (FinRep) was established, under the direction of the executive secretary of HELCOM.[78]

The Final Report on Implementation aims at providing a detailed assessment of the implementation of the 1988 Ministerial Declaration.[79] In fact, it is intended to be a comprehensive examination of the implementation and effectiveness of the entire regime since 1988. The Final Report will

- Evaluate relevant national programs and their results.
- Assess the implementation of all HELCOM Recommendations.
- Examine reductions of pollution loads of nutrients, heavy metals, and POPs (such as pesticides).
- Evaluate observed changes in Baltic environmental conditions between 1987 and 1995 (eutrophication, heavy metals, POPs, endangered species, and the state of living resources).
- Provide conclusions and recommend actions.[80]

Thus the FinRep project will have to integrate and assess information from virtually all aspects of HELCOM activities, including the PLCs, the PITF, Periodic Environmental Assessments, Lead Party reports, and the implementation reports discussed above. The Final Report is scheduled for presentation at the 1998 Ministerial Conference.

An immediate priority of the FinRep project was to collect and assess information on national discharges of nutrients, heavy metals, and POPs in 1995, and to fill in the many gaps in reported data for 1987, 1990, and 1993. Thus during the 1996–1997 reporting round, two ad hoc groups of governmental experts were established to assess the implementation of the 50 percent reduction goals: the joint TC/EC Ad Hoc Expert Group to Assess National Nutrient Programmes (TC/EC ASNUT) and the TC/EC Ad Hoc Expert Group to Assess National Reports on Measures to Reduce Discharges and Emissions of Heavy

Metals and Persistent Organic Pollutants (TC/EC ASMOP).[81] In 1995, priority was given to gathering and assessing information on national discharges of nutrients and on national programs to reduce such discharges. In 1996, the focus was on heavy metals and POPs.

Thus, through 1995 there was a coordinated drive by the Secretariat and HELCOM working group chairpersons to gather national data on national nutrient discharges and programs.[82] As a result, every country except Poland submitted a report in time for the key meeting of TC/EC ASNUT in September 1995, where the main assessment was due to be carried out.[83] This assessment was based not only on the recently submitted national reports, but also on past implementation reports and all other data submitted or gathered through HELCOM activities.[84] Moreover, the technical review group took its task seriously. Information gaps and discrepancies were identified, and every effort was made to resolve these problems during the course of the meeting, with participating government representatives frequently contacting relevant officials or experts in their home countries for clarifications or additional information. At first, assessments regarding Poland and Lithuania were virtually absent, due to inadequate national reports and the fact that the representatives from these countries did not attend the meeting. In the ensuing weeks, however, additional information was obtained from these two countries, as well as from Latvia and Sweden.[85]

It became clear that quite rough estimates of national nutrient discharges often would have to be accepted: reliable data were simply not available in some countries, particularly for the baseline year of 1987. Nevertheless, it proved possible for TC/EC ASNUT to prepare for FinRep agreed drafts of fairly detailed reviews of pollution reductions, national programs, and estimated implementation status in each of the main sectors for each country represented, though with a number of gaps or discrepancies left to be filled in or resolved by September 1997 (when the draft Final Report is to be completed).[86]

Despite uncertainties concerning baseline emissions, countries were prepared to accept the available emission estimates, even though they indicated noncompliance. The draft assessments clearly state that most countries had not achieved the goal of 50 percent cuts in discharges. However, the assessments, which specify national performance on a sector-by-sector basis, also show that most countries managed to achieve 50 percent cuts in at least some sectors. For example, the Baltic states "overachieved" in the agricultural sector, and Poland came within 10 percent of the target.[87] However, only Latvia was judged to have actually achieved the necessary overall cuts by 1995.

Moreover, TC/EC ASNUT's draft review includes assessments of policy: why targets were or were not achieved in each sector, what further actions are planned, and what these actions are expected to achieve in terms of pollution reduction in the near future. Thus, for example, it notes that the Baltic Sea states managed to achieve the 50 percent cuts in the agricultural sector because of "decreased use of fertilizers and decreased agricultural production, . . . mostly caused by structural changes and financial difficulties."[88] It explains that Poland's reductions of about 43 percent for nitrogen and 65 percent for phosphorus were due to the same reasons and notes that the programs in place were not expected to be sufficient to achieve further reductions by 2000. In contrast Sweden and Denmark had programs that respectively were expected to achieve 45 percent and 50 percent cuts in nitrogen discharges from agriculture by the end of the century.

In 1996, HELCOM concentrated on compiling data and similar assessments related to reductions of discharges of heavy metals and POPs. Countries were once again pressed to submit data on emissions and programs (according to detailed guidelines agreed in the spring of 1996) in time for a meeting of TC/EC ASMOP in June. Once again, most national reports arrived just before the meeting. Poland's report was not available until September 1996 (however, this time its representative was present to give an outline of the report); the Danish representative did not attend, and simply reproduced the report Denmark had submitted to the fourth International North Sea Conference a year before (which did not provide data in the form needed by HELCOM). In addition to the Secretariat and national representatives, EURO CHLOR was also invited to participate in the meeting.

The TC/EC ASMOP meeting attempted to prepare draft assessments for the meeting similar to those prepared by the TC/EC ASNUT meeting in 1995. Those tasked with drafting the assessments made use of data available from national reports, supplemented by information from past implementation reports and other HELCOM activities (such as data submitted for PLC-2 and PLC-3) and by information gathered through contacts with relevant officials in home countries or in other international bodies (such as EMEP and relevant European Environment Agency [EEA] Topic Centres). It was immediately clear, however, that even preparing draft assessments was impractical. Although each of the countries had approved the guidelines for the requested emissions data, apparently very few had systems in place to collect the necessary information. Several national reports included no data on emissions of the 39 pesticides and other organic pollutants covered by the 1988 Ministerial Declaration, and those that did (from Sweden, Germany, and the Baltic states) were very incomplete.[89] The situation was a little better for heavy metals: all countries except Poland provided at least some usable data, although each report also had major gaps.[90] Only Sweden and Finland had data for 1987. Russian figures referred only to emissions from St. Petersburg (and the Leningrad region for 1994 and 1995), rather than to the entire Russian catchment area. Only Finland and Germany provided separate figures for waste treatment plants and industrial waste, and Germany alone provided detailed sectoral information. Moreover, only Estonia and Germany gave any information on national measures implemented to reduce emissions of heavy metals.

Because data were poor or incomplete, no attempt was made at the TC/EC ASMOP meeting to assess pollution reductions since 1987 or national measures implemented to reduce discharges of pollutants, except to note that it seemed likely that the promised pollution reductions had not been achieved and therefore additional actions were needed.[91] Luckily, the Secretariat had anticipated problems with obtaining adequate data on heavy metals and POPs. As a contingency plan, it had prepared the groundwork for a special project on Inventory and Emissions of Organochlorine Products in the Baltic Sea catchment area. This project was to study production, use, and emissions of POPs, particularly in Russia and Eastern Europe, employing consultants to carry out the work. Early in 1996 the Danish government agreed to prepare a pilot study on the situation related to POPs and heavy metals in Denmark and Poland. Germany and EURO CHLOR agreed to assist with costs and resources for the more comprehensive special report, and the executive secretary informally approached funding bodies (such as the Nordic Council) for support.[92] As soon as the Secretariat realized that submitted data on heavy metals and POPs were inadequate, the Danish study was circulated to parties and the special project was initiated. The project will draw on data from international bodies and industrial associations such as EURO CHLOR.[93] Where appropriate or comprehensive national reports to HELCOM are not submitted, emission inventories or estimates from such international sources will be used as the default data.

Notably, the TC/EC ASMOP review meeting took place only a month after the 1996 Baltic Sea States summit meeting at Visby, Sweden, where it was declared that "discharges, emissions, and losses of hazardous substances [...including pesticides] will continuously be reduced, towards the target of their cessation within one generation (25 years)."[94] The heads of state and the presidents of the EU Council and Commission present at the Visby meeting thus declared ambitious new targets on heavy metals and POPs, apparently without giving serious attention to monitoring the implementation of existing emission reduction goals—a point subsequently emphasized to national representatives by the executive secretary of HELCOM.[95]

In the summer of 1996, therefore, much remained to be done to prepare the Final Report on Implementation. This FinRep project became a top priority for HELCOM institutions, particularly for the Secretariat, Lead Parties, and TC working groups.[96] By July 1997, much of the draft report had been completed, but there were still major gaps and uncertainties concerning data related to heavy metals and POPs. The FinRep assessment of implementation of the 1988 Ministerial Declaration was emerging as critical and substantial, though it clearly did not include a reliable comparison between all types of discharges in 1987 and 1995, as had originally been hoped. The exact outcome of this process, and the contents of the Final Report, were not clear at the time of this writing.

The preparations for the Final Report have constituted a major strengthening of dedicated mechanisms for reviewing implementation within the Baltic Sea regime. They have involved a concerted drive to induce better and more comprehensive reporting of implementation and to produce substantial assessments of national performance. Moreover, the process has not only focused directly on reviewing implementation of the declared 50 percent cuts in emissions or discharges of nutrients, heavy metals, and POPs; for the first time it has also attempted to seriously review the links between reported cuts in emissions, implementation of recommendations, changes in the measured pollution load, and the state of the Baltic environment.

Judging from the draft assessments prepared so far, the review mechanism is on track to clearly identify (for each country, sector, and type of pollutant) whether or not the 50 percent cuts in discharges pledged in the 1988 Ministerial Declaration have been achieved and the extent to which national policies are expected to significantly improve environmental performance in the near future.[97] Even though in the final analysis a government can insist that its national figures on emissions be officially accepted by HELCOM, however implausible they are, the technical reviews by TC working groups and Lead Parties now mean that any discrepancies will not go unnoticed: questions will be asked and follow-up processes to try to resolve them could be initiated. Moreover, the data used in the Final Report will primarily be based on information from national sources or international bodies, and the political costs of belatedly submitting implausible data indicating compliance are likely to be greater than the costs of accepting that further measures to reduce pollution are needed.

In any case, the postcommunist governments of Russia, the Baltic states, and Poland have become relatively comfortable with admitting problems concerning implementing national environmental targets. They can explain such implementation problems by referring to the problems of managing economic and social transition and to the need for further or better environmental aid. Moreover, it seems clear that every country that has adopted commitments in the Baltic regime will have to admit failures in some areas. In contrast to the early years of the regime, when HELCOM Recommendations were often only difficult for East European countries to implement, the goals of the 1988 Ministerial Declaration were highly ambitious for all parties. Thus the governments of Sweden, Denmark, Germany, and Finland are likely to also have to admit to some implementation problems and noncompliance. Even if they wanted to, these governments would find it hard to disguise such failures: they are highly constrained to provide reasonably reliable and consistent reports, by domestic, EU, and international institutions, traditions of openness, and political culture.

Conclusions

The intensity and significance of implementation review processes in the Baltic Sea environment protection regime have increased as the regime has become more dynamic and effective, and as deadlines for implementing high-profile emission reduction goals have approached.

Some limited formal reporting and review procedures existed prior to 1989, but they had little significance for the effectiveness of the regime. Their operation was highly constrained by secrecy in the Soviet bloc and by the difficulties of maintaining basic cooperation on environmental monitoring and standard setting during the Cold War. Any significant implementation review took place informally in HELCOM technical working groups or through Lead Party activities and was focused on identifying and learning from experiences in Western or neutral parties. To the extent that it occurred, formal review largely addressed reporting rates.

After 1989, the scope of the regime expanded to include land-based pollution sources. The political constraints on reporting and review declined greatly with the economic and political transitions in Eastern Europe and the USSR. During this period concern for the environment was high. Openness also increased, together with a willingness to admit to major pollution problems and to cooperate in tackling them. Implementation review activities intensified rapidly, largely in a decentralized and informal way according to the perceived need in each aspect of the regime. These review activities became an integral part of efforts to clarify and address problems in each area of concern: that is, for the most part they were integrated with all of the other activities in the relevant area of concern, rather than carried out as a formally distinct exercise or by a dedicated body.

Programs for environmental monitoring have indirectly contributed to implementation review. Since the 1970s, such programs have served to promote understandings and informal communications between experts in different countries. Since the late 1980s, HELCOM exercises to monitor the coastal environment and pollution loads have become increasingly valuable in generating information that can contribute to implementation review. Of these, the PLC exercises stand out: PLC-2 generated significant new information between 1990–1992, and in 1996 PLC-3 began to provide unprecedentedly comprehensive and comparable data on 1995 pollution loads from land-based sources.

In relation to pollution from ships, implementation review developed mainly through the activities of HELCOM's MC, aimed at promoting implementation of long-established MARPOL regulations in the Baltic Sea area. The MC actively and successfully worked to improve compliance with reporting obligations, develop the reporting system, promote awareness and harmonized policing of MARPOL regulations related to equipment and facilities on ships, and improve implementation of commitments to maintain adequate facilities for receiving ship wastes in Baltic Sea ports. Of these activities, the systems for reviewing and promoting the provision of port reception facilities have been particularly well-developed and significant, with the MC playing the leading role in identifying major implementation problems and coordinating responses in cooperation with the IMO.

Regarding HELCOM Recommendations to limit land-based sources of pollution, informal implementation review was closely linked to the TC's efforts to develop new standards for land-based sources of pollution and was centered on Lead Party activities in each sectoral area. Information collection and review became more systematic, not only because the TC's efforts became more dynamic, but also in response to activities by ENGOs. Both ENGOs and industrial associations eventually became involved in TC activities. Such informal implementation reviews contributed significantly to effectiveness in several sectors, promoting learning about problems, best practice, and opportunities for rapidly developing relatively stringent standards.

The process of establishing the JCP generated an enormous range of reporting and review activities. Although these activities were not formally concerned with implementation review, they generated a great deal of information related to excessive emissions from land-based sources of pollution, particularly hot spots in Eastern Europe and the former Soviet Union. Reviews of this information by the HLTF defined and developed the priorities of the JCP. Since its inception, a wide range of reporting and review systems have operated through the JCP, involving the PITF, Lead Parties, multilateral funding agencies, the EU, and NGOs. Many of these systems were not formally coordinated, though the PITF has provided a central framework for review and evaluation, which has had significant impacts on policies and activities. The World Bank and the EU have also served to coordinate activities and reviews in some areas.

Thus, reporting and implementation review systems developed in a decentralized and largely informal way after 1989 in each main area of operation of the Baltic Sea regime. In part, this development of SIRs was facilitated by a willingness on the part of newly independent governments in Eastern Europe to reveal poor compliance by the previous communist authorities. The SIRs have also become a key part of the process of knowledge building, agenda setting, and competing for resources for the future. However, some of these SIRs depend significantly on the ways various Lead Parties or other bodies viewed their roles and whether they devote adequate resources to them, and their operation has sometimes been inconsistent and rather ad hoc in nature.

Alongside these decentralized non-dedicated implementation review activities, a formal, dedicated mechanism for reporting and review of implementation has developed in the 1990s. This system began in 1989 as a follow-up to the 1998 Ministerial Declaration, when HELCOM established a triennial system for reporting and reviewing implementation of the Declaration's 50 percent pollution reduction goals and associated HELCOM Recommendations. Reporting rates improved through the combined efforts of the Secretariat, the TC and its working groups, and Lead Parties. These reviews have become progressively more comprehensive and substantial with each round of reporting.

In 1995, this formal SIR was developed further, with the establishment of a special project dedicated to carrying out a detailed assessment of implementation of the 1998 Ministerial Declaration. By the end of 1996, it was clear that the Final Report on Implementation being prepared for the 1998 Ministerial Conference would amount to a comprehensive evaluation of the implementation and effectiveness of the principal parts of the regime. Despite substantial uncertainties concerning 1987 baseline emissions, the review is on track to produce detailed assessments of compliance with pollution reduction goals and with HELCOM Recommendations and of the effectiveness of national and international programs designed to achieve them. It promises to clearly identify noncompliance or inadequacies in performance in several areas for nearly all parties.

During the 1990s, the links between the various bodies involved in information gathering and implementation review were often important for their operation. Between 1988 and 1992, a vast amount of information on pollution sources and emissions in East European and former Soviet Union countries became available—for example, information collected through preparations for the JCP and the PLC exercises became informally available for reviews of implementation of HELCOM Recommendations and the 50 percent pollution reduction goals.

However, it was not until the development of a dedicated mechanism for implementation review, and particularly the FinRep project to assess implementation of the 1988 Ministerial Declaration, that these information sources began to be linked together more systematically and in a mutually reinforcing way. Moreover, links with "outside" institutions, such as EMEP and the EEA, have recently started to become significant in this respect. This is even more true in relation to pollution from ships, where the link with the IMO has in many ways been more important for the MC than links with other bodies within the Baltic Sea regime.

The effectiveness of the system dedicated to reviewing implementation of the pollution reduction goals of the 1988 Ministerial Declaration appears to have depended significantly on this system's place within the overall operation of the regime. In view of the fact that significant uncertainties remain concerning countries' discharges and emissions in both 1987 and 1995, in principle it would be possible for every country to either present emission data indicating full implementation or at least oppose assessments of noncompliance. In fact, there is no substantial evidence that governments tried to do this in 1995–1996. Instead, they accepted rough estimates indicating substantial non-implementation and the assessments of national compliance and performance that this implied. Their acceptance may partly be due to the domestic openness and accountability imposed by democratic systems. Furthermore, the density and complexity of sources of relevant information in the regime in the 1990s may also help to deter such attempts to disguise poor implementation: attempts to manipulate data would generate discrepancies that may now be difficult to disguise. Perhaps most importantly, however, the JCP provides a mechanism whereby identified implementation problems can be linked to efforts to generate further international environmental assistance. Moreover, HELCOM Recommendations and Ministerial Declarations are political agreements and thus are not legally binding; therefore, governments tend to be less sensitive to admitting noncompliance. It may be significant that states have proved more resistant to admitting noncompliance with the few legally binding parts of the Helsinki Convention (the banning of DDT, PCT, and PCBs, and incorporated MARPOL regulations).

It is instructive to briefly compare the SIRs established in the 1990s in the regime to protect the Baltic Sea environment with those established in the ozone regime. Although the Baltic Sea regime was established first, the ozone regime has developed more rapidly and is now in many ways more mature. Both regimes have provisions for regular meetings of their governing bodies (respectively HELCOM and the Meeting of the Parties), with a broad mandate to review implementation, develop and revise commitments, and otherwise manage the regime with the help of a complex set of committees and working groups. Both have compulsory reporting mechanisms (and problems with reporting rates that have recently been addressed by implementation review bodies). In both regimes, implementation review processes have developed over time in a decentralized and often informal way and have been largely integrated with other activities aimed at promoting implementation or developing commitments.

In both cases, environmental assistance programs have provided an important framework for implementation review. However, coordination of the JCP is substantially looser that for the ozone regime's Multilateral Fund: the PITF is a relatively weak coordinating body compared with the Fund's Executive Committee. Consequently, the JCP's review systems are less developed and centrally coordinated.

Both regimes have also developed formal and dedicated implementation review systems, which have only gradually become established. But whereas the Montreal Protocol has a dedicated noncompliance procedure and a dedicated standing body (the Implementation Committee) to address concerns about compliance, the Baltic Sea regime has yet to go in that direction. All HELCOM standing committees involved in reviewing implementation or compliance are also involved with other activities in their own sectors. The dedicated program to review compliance with the 1988 Ministerial Declaration is coordinated by an ad hoc project group created for the sole purpose of preparing an assessment for the 1998 Ministerial Conference. (A similar ad hoc process for implementation review is coordinated by the host country for each North Sea Ministerial Conference—see Chapter 8.)

This ad hoc project group is technically assisted in its task by the Secretariat, Lead Parties, and HELCOM committees, especially TC working groups of specialists. A body of experience and precedents for reviewing implementation and responding to compliance problems has developed in numerous HELCOM bodies through the mid-1990s. Although it has no noncompliance procedure or dedicated standing body to which a case of "noncompliance" would be referred, HELCOM now has a number of committees and mechanisms through which concerns about poor implementation can be and have been tackled. Moreover, the HELCOM Secretariat has generally been allowed significantly wider scope to initiate and coordinate reviews and respond to problems than the ozone regime's Secretariat. It remains to be seen whether HELCOM will find a need for a standing body to deal with noncompliance after the review of implementation of pollution reduction goals is complete in 1998.

Overall, the effectiveness of each regime has been increased by the development during the 1990s of an overall system of implementation review, which links a set of dedicated and informal review bodies and mechanisms together to reinforce one another and yet allows for close integration between review and the other activities in each of the regime's main areas of operation. Links with outside institutions and regimes have been (and remain) important for the functioning and effectiveness of both regimes. For example, these links are important sources of data for reviews. Moreover, HELCOM operates effectively as an institution that reviews and promotes compliance with regulations established in another regime— MARPOL—in the Baltic Sea area.

Notes

1. For a brief review of the development and implementation of the Baltic Sea regime, see Chapter 14. Other useful sources on the development of the Baltic Sea environment protection regime include Hjorth, R., 1992, Building International Institutions for Environmental Protection: The Case of Baltic Sea Environmental Co-operation, Linköping Studies in Arts and Science, No. 81, Linköping, Sweden; Broadus, J., Demisch, S., Gjerde, K., Haas, P., Kaoru, Y., Peet, G., Repetto, S., and Roginko, A., 1993, Comparative Assessment of Regional International Programs to Control Land-Based Marine Pollution: The Baltic, North Sea and Mediterranean, Marine Policy Center, Woods Hole Oceanographic Institution, Woods Hole, MA, USA; Haas, P., 1993, "Protecting the Baltic and North Seas," in *Institutions for the Earth*, edited by P. Haas, R. Keohane, and M. Levy, The MIT Press, Cambridge, MA, USA; Hjorth, R., ed., 1996, Baltic Environmental Co-operation: A Regime in Transition, Linköping Water and Environmental Studies, Linköping University, Sweden.

2. The initial participants, and parties to the 1974 Helsinki Convention, were Denmark, Finland, German Democratic Republic (GDR), Federal Republic of Germany (FRG), Poland, and Sweden. The membership of the European Community was blocked by Sweden (which regarded the European Community as a laggard on agreements to prevent sea pollution) and the USSR (which refused even to officially recognize the European Community until 1987, for broader foreign policy reasons). After 1989, participation changed in response to unification of Germany and the breakup of the USSR: the GDR was incorporated into the FRG, Russia succeeded to the USSR's membership, and newly sovereign Estonia, Latvia, and Lithuania became independent parties. From 1988, the European Union also participated as a participant in Ministerial Conferences and the Joint Comprehensive Environmental Action Programme, and as a party to the 1992 Helsinki Convention.

3. As detailed, for example, in Helsinki Commission, 1994, "Intergovernmental Activities in the Framework of the Helsinki Convention, 1974–1994," *Baltic Sea Environment Proceedings No. 56*, HELCOM, Helsinki, Finland.

4. Annex IV of the 1974 Helsinki Convention incorporated the obligations, including the reporting obligations, of the 1973 MARPOL Convention. The 1978 MARPOL Protocol and later revisions were subsequently incorporated into the Baltic Sea regime through HELCOM Recommendations.

5. Helsinki Commission, 1994, "Intergovernmental Activities in the Framework of the Helsinki Convention 1974–1994," *Baltic Sea Environment Proceedings No. 56*, HELCOM, Helsinki, Finland.

6. For instance, reports often consisted entirely of marks such as "+" or "–," or a one-line statement: see, for example, Maritime Committee, 1994, "Compilation of National Implementation Status of HELCOM Recommendations within the Maritime Field," Maritime Committee 20th Meeting, HELCOM Document MC 20/10/1, 30 May.

7. East-West détente was in overall decline during the mid-1970s, with a "second cold war" between approximately 1978 and 1985. In contrast to the first period of intense bipolar confrontation during the 1950s (the "first cold war"), Europe was not the main focus of antagonism during the "second cold war." Nevertheless, the diplomatic effects of the intensified nuclear arms race and conflicts in the third world spilled over into Europe, testing the newly established frameworks for European détente to the limit.

8. The following observations draw on a number of interviews at HELCOM in 1995, together with an examination of the reports of the meetings of the HELCOM committees and their working groups.

9. Ulf Ehlin, Eeva-Liisa Poutanen, and Vassili Rodionov, HELCOM Secretariat, interviews with the author, June 1995.

10. In this context, representatives of Western parties reviewed one another's reports and raised and discussed some of their own implementation problems to establish precedents and to show how such discussions can be useful and constructive. In practice, such exchanges were primarily for demonstration purposes: any substantive concerns or reviews between these countries during the Cold War normally took place first in other fora or through bilateral arrangements. Ulf Ehlin and Vassili Rodionov, HELCOM Secretariat, and Lea Kauppi, Finnish Environment Agency, interviews with the author, June 1995.

11. Convention on the Protection of the Marine Environment of the Baltic Sea Area, 1992. Note that Sweden and Russia withdrew their veto on EU participation, and the EU is now a party to the 1992 Convention.

12. As outlined by Alexei Roginko in Chapter 14; see also references in note 1.

13. The 1992 Helsinki Convention requires an environmental impact assessment for all projects and installations that may cause transnational pollution; these impact assessments should then be reported and reviewed by the Commission. According to Article 16 of the Convention, the contracting parties should report regularly to HELCOM on their legal, regulatory, and other measures taken to implement the Convention and all HELCOM Recommendations; on the effectiveness of these measures; and on any implementation problems they have encountered. Moreover, in Articles 17 and 18 the Convention states that the public has a right to access information on the details of emission permits granted to plants; water quality objectives; and results of water and effluent sampling (although in practice access often remains restricted on grounds of commercial confidentiality or national security); 1992 Helsinki Convention, reproduced in HELCOM BSEP No. 56, 1994.

14. It should be noted that the Baltic states acquired responsibility for environmental policies and measures in 1989, two years before they gained independence.

15. Initially, there were two such committees: the Maritime Committee (MC), dealing with pollution from vessels at sea, and the Scientific Technological Committee (STC), which dealt with scientific and technological cooperation, monitoring of sea resources, and land-based sources of pollution, dumping, and hazardous substances. In 1990, these were reorganized into four main committees.

16. The character and extent of such implementation review activities have been highly dependent on the priorities and capacity of the particular Lead Party concerned. Within minimum guidelines established by the relevant HELCOM committee, it is for the government concerned to decide how, and how thoroughly, to carry out its Lead Party role. Since 1992, there has been increased reliance on Lead Parties, as member countries have endeavored to restrict funding for HELCOM and its Secretariat as part of an economy drive at the same time that the regime has expanded and developed. Unfortunately, this has coincided with cuts in national environmental agencies and ministries during the 1990s in countries such as Sweden, Germany, and Finland, which have tended to adopt Lead Party roles. This has led to lost opportunities. Nevertheless, overall, Lead Party implementation review activities appear to have continued to increase since the 1988 Ministerial Declaration.

17. Ulf Ehlin *et al.*, HELCOM Secretariat, interviews with the author, June 1995; also Helsinki Commission, 1993, "Activities of the Commission 1992," *Baltic Sea Environment Proceedings No. 52*, HELCOM, Helsinki, Finland.

Coalition Clean Baltic is a coalition of numerous local and national environmental groups from all Baltic Sea littoral states.

18. In addition to Greenpeace and Friends of the Earth, NGOs participating in HELCOM now include BirdLife International, the Union of the Baltic Cities (UBC), the Standing Conference of Rectors, Presidents and Vice Chancellors of the European Universities (CRE), and the International Environmental Agency for Local Governments (ICLEI). In addition to EURO CHLOR, participating industrial associations include EFMA and the Baltic Ports Organization (BPO). Helsinki Commission, 1996, "Activities of the Commission 1995 (including the 17th Meeting of the Commission held in Helsinki, 12–14 March 1996)," *Baltic Sea Environment Proceedings No. 62*, HELCOM, Helsinki, Finland.

19. Vassili Rodionov, TC secretary, interview with with author, June 1995; Tapani Kohonen, TC chairman, interview with the author, September 1996.

20. In December 1994, the PITF nominated the WWF to act as the "Lead Party" in the development of the program element related to Management Programmes for Wetlands and Lagoons. The ICLEI joined Germany as a Lead Party for the program element on Policies, Laws, and Regulations; and the ICLEI, UBC, and Germany were Lead Parties for the Institutional Strengthening and Human Resource Development element, thus officially involving city and local authorities in the process. The CCB was also briefly the Lead Party for the JCP program element on promoting public awareness and environmental education.

21. For example, HELCOM membership overlaps with those of the Oslo Commission (OSCOM) and the Paris Commission (PARCOM), and these bodies regularly liaise with or learn from one another. More generally, these regimes have profoundly shaped one another's development. See, for example, Broadus *et al.*, op. cit., note 1; Haas, op. cit., note 1; Andresen, S., 1996, "Implementation of International Environmental Commitments: The Case of the Northern Seas," *The Science of the Total Environment* 186:149–167.

22. As discussed, the Helsinki Conventions and HELCOM Recommendations have adopted and promoted MARPOL 73/78 regulations to prevent oil pollution from ships, and there have been close interactions between the IMO and HELCOM.

23. Accredited observers to HELCOM include the International Council for the Exploration of the Sea (ICES), the International Baltic Sea Fishery Commission (IBSFC), the United Nations Environment Programme (UNEP), the World Meteorological Organization (WMO), the Intergovernmental Oceanographic Commission (IOC), the United Nations Economic Commission for Europe (UN/ECE), the International Atomic Energy Agency (IAEA), and the World Health Organization (WHO).

24. Important participants include the World Bank, the European Bank for Reconstruction and Development (EBRD), the European Investment Bank (EIB), the Nordic Investment Bank (NIB), and the Nordic Environment Finance Corporation (NEFCO), as well as national funding agencies in donor countries. The EU has also been a major contributor to the JCP, particularly through funds from programs such as Assistance for Economic Restructuring in the Countries of Central and Eastern Europe (PHARE), TACIS, and LIFE.

25. The subordinate role of HELCOM and the Helsinki Convention in this area is not a failure of the regime, but rather a matter of deliberate policy by the parties. See, for example, Helsinki Commission, 1994, "Intergovernmental Activities in the Framework of the Helsinki Convention 1974–1994," *Baltic Sea Environment Proceedings No. 56*, HELCOM, Helsinki, Finland.

26. Specifically, HELCOM coordinated successful applications for the Baltic Sea to be accepted as a "special area" in the MARPOL Annexes dealing with discharges from ships of oil (Annex 1), noxious chemicals (Annex 2), garbage and sewage (Annex 5), and air pollution. In 1995, MC Air (an MC subcommittee) submitted an application to the IMO on behalf of all HELCOM member states, asking that the Baltic Sea area be designated a "special area" in the Annex to MARPOL 73/78 that was being negotiated at the time. This Annex aimed at introducing global regulations governing emissions of sulfur dioxide and other gases from ships, and "special area" status would mean that all ships, under any national flag, would be bound to obey regulations designed to strictly limit their emissions of such gases while sailing in the Baltic Sea: Ad Hoc Working Group on Air Pollution from Ships (MC Air), Report of the Seventh Meeting, Helsinki, Finland, 10–12 April 1995, MC Air 7/6 (particularly Annex 3, reproducing the application to IMO); Maritime Committee (MC), Report of the 21st Meeting, Copenhagen, Denmark, 9–11 Also Adam Kowalewski, MC secretary, interview with the author, June 1995.

27. Adam Kowalewski, MC secretary, interviews with the author, June 1995 and September 1996.

28. Mitchell, R., 1993, "Intentional Oil Pollution of the Oceans," in *Institutions for the Earth*, edited by P. Haas, R. Keohane, and M. Levy, The MIT Press, Cambridge, MA, USA; and Mitchell, R., 1994, *Intentional Oil Pollution at Sea: Environmental Policy and Treaty Compliance*, The MIT Press, Cambridge, MA, USA.

29. Recommendations in this area were among those where parties sometimes simply reported on implementation with a "+" or "–," and more frequently simply made a statement such as "the Recommendation is taken into account" or "the recommendation is applied"; see, for example, MC, "Compilation of

HELCOM recommendations related to the maritime field," MC 20/10/1, 30 May 1994.

30. Adam Kowalewski, Secretary to MC and CC, interviews with the author, June 1995 and September 1996. See also "Activities of CC," in BSEP No. 56 (op. cit., note 25), and minutes of CC and MC meetings throughout this period.

31. Mitchell, 1993, op. cit., note 28.

32. A group of 14 European states, including Denmark, Germany, and Sweden, adopted a Memorandum of Understanding in 1982 whereby participating states pledged to make use of the right to inspect ships established under MARPOL to randomly inspect at least 25 percent of the ships arriving at their port. They established a central facility where any violation or suspected violations could be reported, to be disseminated to other states. HELCOM encouraged the Baltic Sea states to participate in this arrangement, or to at least adopt similar practices.

33. Reception of Wastes from Ships in the Baltic Sea area—a MARPOL 1973/78 Special Area, BSEP Series No. 28, HELCOM 1989.

34. HELCOM Recommendation 10/5, 1989; 10/6, 1989.

35. "Seminar on Reception Facilities in Ports," BSEP Series No. 50, 1993; Adam Kowalewski, MC secretary, interview with the author, June 1995.

36. Ad-hoc Working Group on Reception Facilities in Ports (MC ReFac). HELCOM 15.

37. For example, the BPO provided a report on behalf of port authorities to MC ReFac, arguing that port reception facilities were basically adequate with the exception of a few older ports that required foreign aid for upgrading. However a report by BIMCO provided detailed and critical evidence of pervasive problems; BIMCO, 1994, "Inventory on Reception Facilities," BIMCO, Bagsværd, Denmark.

38. Summarized in MC ReFac, Report to the Maritime Committee, WP.6, June 1995. Examples of the problems found include the separate privatization of the reception facilities within some ports, leading to excessive and uncoordinated fees, and sewage reception facilities that either did not work, were inconvenient, or which discharged the untreated sewage directly back into the sea.

39. The Baltic Strategy for Port Reception Facilities for Ship Generated Wastes and Associated Issues, HELCOM, March 1996.

40. MC ReFac, "Investments to improve reception facilities in the countries in transition in the Baltic Sea region," in MC ReFac 4.5, HELCOM, August 1995.

41. The program now seems likely to go ahead with funds from the UNDP and some Scandinavian donor countries. The World Bank has also agreed to include elements of the proposal in a large ongoing project to develop Polish port infrastructure, Adam Kowalewski, interview with the author, September 1996.

42. For example, BSEP 5 A&B, 1981; BSEP17 A&B, 1986; and BSEP 35 A&B, 1991: the fourth periodic assessment was due in 1996.

43. Helsinki Commission, 1987, "First Baltic Sea Pollution Load Compilation," *Baltic Sea Environment Proceedings No. 20*, HELCOM, Helsinki, Finland.

44. Helsinki Commission, 1993, "Second Baltic Sea Pollution Load Compilation," *Baltic Sea Environment Proceedings No. 45*, HELCOM, Helsinki, Finland.

45. Like its predecessor, the Scientific and Technological Committee (STC), the TC was also responsible for managing the ban on releases of "hazardous" substances (DDT, PCBs, PCTs) and the system of special permits for discharges of "significant quantities" of "noxious" substances.

46. As listed, for example, in BSEP No. 56. pp. 42–43, op. cit., note 25.

47. Laane, A., 1995, Political Impediments to Implementing International Waterway Agreements: The Example of the Baltic States, Tallinn Technical University, Tallinn, Estonia.

48. Report of the 10th Meeting of HELCOM, held in Helsinki, Finland, 14–17 February 1989, HELCOM Document 10/14, paragraph 3.9; Tapani Kohonen, TC chairman (1990–1996), interview with the author, September 1996.

49. Tapani Kohonen, TC chairman, interview with the author, September 1996.

50. Vassili Rodionov, interview with with author, June 1995; TC Point documents 1992–4.

51. See, for example, The JCP Fourth Activity Inventory, HELCOM, April 1996.

52. See, for example, Connelly, B., Gutner, T., and Bedarff, H., 1996, "Organizational Inertia and Environmental Assistance to Eastern Europe," in *Institutions for Environmental Aid*, edited by R. Keohane and M. Levy, The MIT Press, Cambridge, MA, USA.. The authors identify several major weaknesses in environmental assistance programs for Eastern Europe, including unclear priorities and environmental standards; donor domination of the selection process for projects and project development; institutional inertia among funding bodies leading to inappropriate or inflexible lending or granting policies; a

lack of links between funding bodies or lack of cooperation between them; and an absence of structures for overall coordination and review. Surprisingly, the authors do not discuss the JCP in their review of environmental assistance programs in Eastern Europe. Had they done so, they might have revised some of their conclusions and developed their recommendations further. Compared with the program that they identified as being among the most effective—the Environment Action Programme for Central and Eastern Europe (EAP)—the JCP is clearly significantly less prone to the main weaknesses in funding programs that they identify.

53. Presidential Declaration of the Baltic Sea States Summit, Visby, Sweden, 3–4 May 1996, p. 13.

54. KCCV (a consortium of Danish environmental consultants), 1994, Hot Spot Review, Vols. 1–9, Danish Environmental Protection Agency, Copenhagen, Denmark.

55. Swedish Environmental Protection Agency, Lead Party Report on Combined Municipal and Industrial Discharges, Stockholm, Sweden, February 1996.

56. Niels Seeberg-Elverfeld, PITF program coordinator, interview with the author, June 1995.

57. Ibid.

58. Niels Seeberg-Elverfeld, PITF program coordinator, interview with the author, June 1995; Ulrich Kremser, German representative on the PITF, now PITF secretary, interview with the author, September 1996; World Bank, interview with the author, December 1995.

59. Andrew Speer, World Bank, interview with the author, December 1995.

60. Presidential Statement, Ministerial Conference, Visby, Sweden, May 1996.

61. Report of the 10th Meeting of HELCOM, held in Helsinki, Finland, 14–17 February 1989, HELCOM Document 10/14, paragraphs 3.4, 3.7, 3.8. In 1989, the STC of HELCOM was responsible for this area of the regime. In 1990, it was succeeded in this role by the TC.

62. The USSR gave the Baltic states responsibility for controlling their coastal pollution in 1989—over two years before they gained overall sovereignty.

63. Technological Committee (TC), Report of the First Meeting, Gdynia, Poland, 22–26 October 1990, HELCOM Publication TC 1/16, 1990, paragraphs 12.1–12.5; also Vassili Rodionov, TC secretary, interview with the author, June 1995.

64. Ibid.

65. The two exceptions were the bans on discharges of DDT and PCTs, which had been blacklisted in the regime since the early 1980s; HELCOM Document 12/4b/1, HELCOM, 1991. Overall, there were 38 HELCOM Recommendations related to land-based sources of pollution by this stage; Kohonen, J.T., 1991, "Protection of the Marine Environment of the Baltic Sea," *Marine Pollution Bulletin* 23:543. However, some of these were sufficiently vague or lacking in specific obligations so that reporting on implementation was scarcely relevant. In this discussion the focus is on comparatively substantive Recommendations.

66. That is, the Working Group on Reduction of Discharges and Emissions from Point Sources (TC Point), or the Working Group on Reduction of Inputs from Diffuse Sources (TC Diff).

67. Report of the 12th HELCOM Meeting, February 1991, HELCOM Document 12/18, paragraphs 4.11 and 4.12; Vassili Rodionov, TC secretary, interview with the author, June 1995.

68. Report of the First Meeting of the Working Group on the Reduction of Inputs from Diffuse Sources (TC Diff), held in Tallinn, USSR, 23–26 April 1991, HELCOM Document TC Diff 1/13, paragraphs 10.1–10.6; Report of the First Meeting of the Working Group on Reduction of Discharges and Emissions from Point Sources (TC Point), held in Stockholm, Sweden, 13–17 May 1991, HELCOM Document TC Point 1/11, paragraphs 8.1–8.10.

69. Interviews as reported in Roginko, A., 1994, "The Helsinki Convention: A Failure or Success Story?" paper presented to ISA Convention, Washington, DC, USA, March.

70. Reporting forms were elaborated and a timetable was prepared in plenty of time to be used. See, for example, Report of the Second Meeting of the Working Group on Reduction of Discharges and Emissions from Point Sources (TC Point), held in St. Petersburg, Russia, 18–22 May 1992, HELCOM Document TC Point 2/9, paragraphs 6.1–6.7.

71. Third Meeting of TC Point, April 1993; TC Point 3/11, paragraphs 7.1–7.6, and TC Point 3/INF.2/Rev/1; Third Meeting of TC Diffuse, May 1993, TC Diff 3/11, paragraphs 7.1–7.4, Annex 6, and TC Diff3/INF.2/Rev.1.

72. Fourth Meeting of the TC, 8–12 Nov. 1993, St. Petersburg, Russia, HELCOM Document TC 4/15, paragraphs 8.1–8.5. See also Helsinki Commission, 1994, "Activities of the Commission 1993," *Baltic Sea Environment Proceedings No. 55*, HELCOM, Helsinki, Finland, p. 8.

73. HELCOM 15, HELCOM Document 15/18, paragraph 6.1.

74. Report of the Fourth Meeting of the Working Group on Reduction of Discharges and Emissions from Point Sources (TC Point), held in Sopot, Poland, 9–13 May 1994, HELCOM Document TC Point 4/11, paragraphs 7.1–7.6; Report of the Fourth Meeting of the Working Group on the Reduction of Inputs from Diffuse Sources (TC Diff), held in Rostock-Warnemunde, Germany, 18–22 April 1994, HELCOM Document TC Diff 4/11, paragraphs 7.1–7.6.

75. HELCOM document TC Diff 4/11, paragraph 7.5.

76. HELCOM Document TC 5/9a/WP.1; Report of the 5th Meeting of the Technological Committee, Copenhagen, Denmark, 31 October–4 November 1994, HELCOM Doc TC 5/11, paragraphs 9.1–9.3. Another "Interim Implementation Report" was submitted to HELCOM for its March 1995 meeting: Interim Implementation Report, HELCOM Document 15/4/1/Rev 1.

77. Report of the 16th Meeting of the Commission, held in Helsinki, Finland, 14–17 March 1995; BSEP Series No. 60. This process was integrated into the Project for Preparation of the Final Report on Implementation of the 1988 Ministerial Declaration, which is discussed below.

78. HELCOM Secretariat, "Proposal for establishment of a Project for preparation of the Final Report on Implementation of the Ministerial Declaration 1988," submitted to HELCOM 16, 14–17 March, reproduced in HELCOM Document TC Point 5/3/2, 27 February 1995.

79. Specifically, its agreed aim is to provide a "quantitative and qualitative assessment of national action taken to implement the Declaration goals and results achieved; to provide the basis for decision-making with regard to further actions required," ibid.

80. HELCOM Secretariat, "Project Plan," HELCOM FinRep 1/6, Annex 4, September 1995.

81. TC/EC ASNUT began work in the summer of 1995; TC/EC ASMOP started in early 1996.

82. Detailed guidelines on the contents of national reports on these matters had been prepared by the TC the previous year: Technological Committee, "Guide on the Content of National Programmes of Measures to Reduce Substantially the Discharges and Emission of Nutrients," TC 5/11, Annex 4, November 1994.

83. Most reports only arrived within a few days (sometimes minutes) before the start of the meeting. Ulf Ehlin (executive secretary), Vassili Rodionov (TC secretary), and Eeva-Liisa Poutanen (EC secretary), HELCOM Secretariat, interviews with the author, June 1995; Tapani Kohonen (executive secretary and then TC chairman), and Eeva-Liisa Poutanen (EC secretary), HELCOM Secretariat, interview with the author, September 1996.

84. Ibid. It was agreed that reports should focus on waterborne discharges of nutrients (i.e., compounds such as ammonia or nitrates containing nitrogen or phosphorus). It was deemed that airborne deposition of nitrogen was not specifically covered by the 1988 Ministerial Declaration; moreover, HELCOM guidelines on monitoring and assessing it for the Baltic Sea area were still being developed.

85. TC 6/6a/3/Corr.1, 18 October 1995; Report of TC/EC ASNUT to Sixth Meetings of TC and EC, 1995.

86. Briefly, the assessments came in five parts: an overall country-by-country assessment of national programs to reduce nutrient discharges; separate assessments of national programs for each of the main sectors (agriculture, aquaculture [e.g., fish farms], industry, municipalities, transport, and power production); identification of sources of nutrient inputs into identified eutrophication "problem areas" in the Baltic Sea; inputs into regions judged to be "non-sensitive" to nitrogen discharges (i.e., the open parts of the Bothnian Bay); and overall conclusions about the extent to which each country had implemented the goal of 50 percent cuts between 1987 and 1995. Report of the TC/EC ASNUT, TC 6/6a/3 (EC 6/6a/3), 2nd October 1995, Annexes 3,4,5,6,7.

87. Ibid, Annex 4.

88. Ibid, Annex 7.

89. TC/EC ASMOP 96: 3/1; 3/2; 3/3; 3/4; 3/5; 3/6; 3/7 (dates May–June, 1996).

90. See references in note 89; see also HELCOM Secretariat, "Heavy Metals from Municipal Waste Water Treatment Plants as well as Industrial Plants of all CPs [Contracting Parties] within the Baltic Sea Catchment Area," TC/EC ASMOP 96, 11 June 1996. Some data submitted by Denmark (in its report to the Fourth North Sea Conference) were included in this compilation, but with apparent comparability problems highlighted.

91. Ad Hoc Expert Group to Assess National Reports on Measures to Reduce Discharges and Emissions of Heavy Metals and Persistent Organic Pollutants, TC/EC ASMOP 6/1, Pro Memoria, Helsinki, Finland, 10–12 June 1996.

92. Tapani Kohonen, executive secretary, interviews with the author, HELCOM Secretariat, September 1996; letter from Ulf Ehlin to Nordic Council, 20 February 1996.

93. In particular, data from relevant EEA Topic Centres, the Long-Range Transboundary Air Pollution (LRTAP) regime, and the wider (OSPARCOM-HELCOM-ECE [European part]) project to prepare a European air emissions

inventory for heavy metals and POPs. TC/EC ASMOP 2/2; INF.5; INF.7; 4/1; May–June 1996.

94. Op. cit., note 53.

95. Tapani Kohonen, executive secretary, HELCOM Secretariat, interview with the author, September 1996.

96. By November 1996, the Lead Party reports on implementation of HELCOM Recommendations were due from the 1996 reporting round. A special meeting of experts from TC RED (the new TC Working Group on Pollution Reduction, formed in 1996 to replace TC Point and TC Diff) and TC INPUT was organized for the following December to assess the results of the 1996 reporting round (and the 1990 and 1993 rounds); to compare these results with results from the PLCs (including interim results from PLC-3) and other sources; and to prepare a study of the "reasons for changes in pollution load" for the Final Report together with a summary of the Lead Party reports on implementation for each sector. Tapani Kohonen and Eeva-Liisa Poutanen, HELCOM Secretariat, interviews with the author, September 1996. See also Working Group on Pollution Reduction (TC RED), Report of the First Meeting, 20–24 May 1996, HELCOM Document TC RED 1/96.

97. This is certainly the intention of the FinRep project group responsible for drafting the report. Tapani Kohonen, HELCOM executive secretary and "project manager" of the FinRep project, interview with the author, September 1996.

6

"Learning by Doing" in the Nonbinding International Regime to Manage Trade in Hazardous Chemicals and Pesticides

David G. Victor

Introduction

In response to public concern about food safety and environmental quality, since the early 1970s all major industrialized countries have sharply tightened regulations on chemicals and pesticides. Initially those domestic controls did not apply to rapidly growing export markets. In developing countries, in particular, the continued spread of the green revolution and cash cropping led to rising demand for pesticides, including pesticides that had been banned in industrialized countries. Development organizations documented a rising tide of health effects among agricultural workers in developing countries where hazardous pesticides were being imported and used, often with little knowledge of the risks. They blamed multinational corporations for promoting excessive use of pesticides. Developing countries railed against the dumping of these substances on local markets.

Despite intense pressure from governments in developing countries and nongovernmental organizations (NGOs) to address the problems of unregulated trade in hazardous chemicals and pesticides, by the early 1980s few trade controls had been adopted. Major producers of pesticides and chemicals—all located in industrialized countries—had successfully rebuffed pressures for export regulation; some countries had adopted minimal requirements to exchange information about chemical and pesticide hazards with importers, but these were poorly implemented and had little impact on trade patterns.

Within a decade the pesticides and chemical industry had sharply changed course. In 1989 a voluntary system was adopted to ensure that exports of the most hazardous chemicals and pesticides took place only with the prior informed consent (PIC) of importing nations. Producers of chemicals and pesticides have enthusiastically supported this voluntary system and have played a leading role in implementing it.

The PIC system is managed jointly by the Food and Agriculture Organization (FAO) and the United Nations Environment Programme (UNEP). Its objective is to improve the capacity of developing countries to make and implement informed decisions to regulate chemical and pesticide hazards. The PIC system makes useful information on those hazards available to developing countries. In addition, it partially shifts the burden of regulating trade from importers, which increasingly are developing countries, to exporters, which are predominantly rich industrialized countries with high capacity to regulate pesticide and chemical shipments. The first substances formally entered the PIC procedure in 1991; by the end of 1997, 38 pesticides and industrial chemicals were either in the PIC system or soon to be added. Although data for assessing PIC's effectiveness are poor, the system appears to be responsible for a significant increase in regulation of chemicals and pesticides trade between the North and the South, in part because all of the major industry associations have required their members to implement PIC. There have been no known violations of the voluntary PIC system. International training programs to help developing countries to implement PIC have increased those countries' capacity to do so (and to manage hazardous chemicals and pesticides more generally). Although the "PIC list" includes many substances that have been practically banned worldwide and thus are not often traded, over time it has expanded to include many substances that are still widely used. The success of the voluntary PIC system is evident in the fact that PIC did not merely codify what firms and governments were doing already—its scope has widened and its influence on behavior has grown.

This chapter describes the origins and operation of the PIC system and focuses on two factors that help explain PIC's success. First, the study gives special attention to how the type of legal agreement has affected outcomes. PIC is based on two nonbinding instruments, UNEP's *Amended London Guidelines* and the FAO's *Code of Conduct on the Distribution and Use of Pesticides*. In contrast, virtually all studies of international environmental governance have focused on legally binding international accords. Conventional wisdom holds that binding instruments are the most effective mechanisms for international regulation, yet the evidence in this study suggests that the nonbinding PIC system has been highly effective—probably more effective than if a binding system had been adopted in 1989. Because it is nonbinding, the PIC system was embraced by the pesticides and chemical industry, which (correctly) predicted that more onerous and less uncoordinated regulation would result in the absence of a unified, global PIC system. Moreover, the nonbinding format was highly flexible and facilitated "learning by doing" during the implementation process.

Second, this study examines how the PIC system has been dynamic and responsive to new information. The voluntary PIC system includes few formal provisions for gathering and reviewing information about how PIC is implemented at the national level. However, in practice an elaborate system for implementation review (SIR) has emerged, consisting of many decentralized activities of international organizations, national and international funding agencies, national governments, and NGOs. At the center of the SIR has been the FAO/UNEP Joint Meeting of Experts on Prior Informed Consent (JMPIC), which has reviewed experience and evidence. Because PIC is nonbinding, this small group has also been able to make policy decisions that, in practice, have efficiently expanded the PIC system. The presence of the SIR has made learning by doing possible.

This chapter begins with a review of the health and safety regulations in the main industrialized countries. Some elements of the PIC system can be traced to those early regulatory programs and to international efforts, such as through the Organisation for Economic Co-operation and Development (OECD), to promote trade by harmonizing different national and regional regulations. The chapter then reviews efforts by entrepreneurial NGOs and government officials, working through UNEP and the FAO, to tighten trade regulation and improve management of chemicals and pesticides. The joint PIC system was a direct consequence of those efforts. The chapter then examines how the voluntary PIC system has been implemented and traces how several factors—the nonbinding format of the PIC instruments, the Joint Meeting of Experts, and the development of an SIR—contributed to the development and effectiveness of the PIC system. It concludes with speculation that the conversion of the voluntary PIC system to a binding convention, which is currently under way and will be complete in 1998, has been costly and unnecessary.

National Regulation and International Harmonization

Prior to the 1960s, efforts to regulate pesticides focused mainly on protecting brands and consumers by ensuring that products on the market were effective and that trade names accurately described active ingredients. The character and cost of regulation changed dramatically with the environmental movement. Between the late 1960s and early 1970s, public concern about the environment led to dozens of new statutes. Chemicals and pesticides regulators faced common challenges, such as gathering and assessing the mass of toxicological data needed to determine which substances were safe for the environment. However, regulatory rules varied markedly. The resulting patchwork of different chemicals and pesticides regulations caused two international problems that have animated industry and environmental groups since the 1970s. Together they have led to the PIC system and related efforts to manage trade in hazardous chemicals and pesticides. The first problem was harmonizing national systems, which is discussed here; the second was regulating trade, especially trade with developing countries that had low domestic capacity to control imports and limit products on local markets, which is addressed later. The PIC system concerns the latter issue, but the former was a precursor to PIC and strongly influenced the institutions and industry participation that have subsequently influenced the PIC system.[1]

Producers of chemicals and pesticides who traded their products in many markets had a strong incentive to harmonize national regulations. The USA strengthened the Federal Insecticide, Fungicide and Rodenticide Act (FIFRA) in 1972 to require environmental registration of pesticides, and in 1976 it adopted the Toxic Substances Control Act (TSCA), which added strict environmental criteria to chemicals regulation. In the European Community (EC),[2] the other main market for pesticides and chemicals, some harmonization concerning pesticide applications had occurred through the adoption in 1976 of common maximum residue limits (MRLs) for fruits and vegetables.[3] But this harmonization did not affect marketing and trade in pesticides themselves. The EC had more success harmonizing chemicals legislation. With public attention focused by the accident at a chemical plant in Seveso, Italy, in 1976, and with chemical firms concerned that TSCA would limit access to US markets, the EC adopted the "Sixth Amendment" and thus created comprehensive Europe-wide chemicals legislation.[4] A similar scheme to harmonize marketing of pesticides throughout the EC was proposed in 1976 but did not lead to any action.

By the late 1970s both the USA and the EC had well-developed but largely separate schemes for regulating hazardous substances. Chemicals and pesticides were regulated separately, testing standards and registration requirements differed with the substance and market, and firms that sought access to multiple markets were required to submit several different packages of "pre-marketing data" in each market to demonstrate that their products were safe. Because three-quarters of trade took place between OECD member states, the OECD was the logical forum for addressing the problems resulting from poor harmonization of national regulations. Moreover, because the USA was an OECD member it would have a say in the effort, which was not true of the EC harmonization efforts. There were three tangible consequences of the OECD's engagement. First, the OECD established a notification "package" consisting of a minimum amount of data that OECD members could use to assess the hazards of chemicals. That minimum would partially harmonize the expensive testing requirements for new chemical and pesticide products. Second, OECD guidelines required OECD members to accept each other's toxicological data— the most expensive part of chemical testing—provided that they were prepared using agreed standards of good laboratory practice (GLP). The OECD produced guidelines on GLP, which were adopted as the OECD standard in 1981. Third, the OECD adopted principles concerning exchange of confidential data.

The OECD's work approach addressed all of the major concerns of industry, though it did not meet industry's ultimate goal of full harmonization. It did not supplant national decisions on which substances were "safe" for market, but the OECD system did promote coordination that eliminated many costly redundancies, especially in data requirements. In practice, from the late 1970s to the present, harmonization of the national systems of OECD members has been extensive, even when national law has not explicitly required it.[5] In the USA the Reagan administration, for example, implemented TSCA by exempting most of the substances that were exempt under the Sixth Amendment.[6] In other words, by the mid-1980s a regime for roughly harmonized regulation of chemical hazards was in place in OECD nations.[7] To a lesser degree that regime also harmonized pesticide regulation. In 1976 the USA unilaterally developed TSCA. By 1984 no industrialized country would develop and implement new chemicals legislation without reference to data harmonization and OECD standards.

A US General Accounting Office study comparing the data requirements for pesticide registration in 18 OECD countries and the EC found that by the early 1990s the actual data requirements overlapped by 71–83%; a study by the OECD found similar results.[8] By 1993 a group of US chemical industry executives could claim that, "to a large extent, the harmonization of data requirements has already taken place."[9] Experts on European regulation arrived at similar conclusions on the extent to which the EC had harmonized its testing requirements.[10]

Regulation of International Trade in Hazardous Pesticides and Chemicals

The OECD chemicals regime would be the dominant system today and would have remained focused on harmonization of national standards—which industry sought—if environmental, consumer, and development NGOs had not pushed a different agenda: reduction of hazardous exports to developing countries. Many of those public interest groups were well-informed of the hazards of chemicals and pesticides because they had been active in the policy battles to limit registration of those substances within industrialized countries. However, none of the first generation of regulations adopted by OECD nations to regulate the environmental consequences of chemicals and pesticides had a significant impact on exports, except when exports were sent to other countries that had also adopted health and safety legislation. Most exports went to other OECD nations, but a rising fraction of world trade flowed to developing countries. In the 1970s world trade in chemical products rose more than fourfold to nearly US$100 billion, but exports to developing countries rose nearly 500%. By 1980, one-quarter of world trade in chemical products went to developing countries.[11] A higher fraction—one-third—of trade in pesticides flowed to developing countries.[12]

With rising trade in hazardous substances came rising impacts in developing countries. Most efforts to document health and safety problems have focused on pesticides. In the early 1970s, the World Health Organization (WHO) estimated that 500,000 people were accidentally poisoned by pesticides annually, with roughly half the cases occurring in developing countries.[13] David Bull's authoritative study for OXFAM in the early 1980s quoted 375,000 annual accidental poisonings in developing countries, leading to 10,000 deaths.[14] By the early 1990s, WHO data suggested there were perhaps 1.5 million to 3 million annual accidental poisonings worldwide.[15] Some estimates were as high as 25 million.[16] Although only one-fifth of global pesticide application takes place in developing countries, by the 1990s those countries accounted for perhaps three-fourths of the world's poisonings.[17] While the data indicate the scale of the problem, they are imperfect: pesticide-related hazards are practically impossible to measure accurately; despite more than two decades of concern about this problem no reliable data exist.[18]

The dangers of pesticides and chemicals were known, but so were the benefits for food production and social development. Some public interest groups advocated sharp cuts or even elimination of pesticide usage and a halt to exports of such hazardous substances. But a more nuanced view was taken by mainstream development organizations such as OXFAM and the Pesticides Action Network (PAN)—a global network of local NGOs concerned with sharply cutting the usage and ill effects of pesticides, formed in 1982 by the network NGO International Organization of Consumers Unions (IOCU, later Consumers International) with Dutch financial support.[19] None of the major development organizations favored a ban on trade in hazardous pesticides, including pesticides banned for sale in industrialized countries. Although the views of NGOs and developing countries varied, all were unified in their endorsement of integrated pest management (IPM), a concept developed in the late 1960s to describe the use of natural means to limit pesticide applications (e.g., crop rotations that limit the ability of crop-specific pests to survive in fields between plantings) and to minimize total use through targeted application (e.g., only in calibrated dosages and at times when plants are vulnerable to specific pests). Development and environmental organizations all argued in favor of IPM and criticized multinational corporations that promoted excessive use of pesticides. By the mid-1970s, IPM was conventional wisdom in crop management and was increasingly employed by all major field programs that included the use of pesticides. With its incorporation into the first FAO *Code of Conduct* in 1985, IPM became even more widely accepted as "best practice" and thus was incorporated, for example, into the operational directives and guidelines on best practice that govern the funding of World Bank projects.[20] Although some NGOs still charge that Western funding agencies and the FAO promote pesticide usage, in large part the wisdom of IPM had been accepted and put into practice by all major stakeholders by the end of the 1970s.

A few governments modified national policy in response to concerns about the impacts of their hazardous exports. Notably, the Carter administration added export notification requirements to FIFRA in 1978 that required exporters of any pesticide banned, severely restricted, or not marketed in the USA to supply the importing country with basic toxicological information on the hazards. Upon the first shipment of any such substance, exporters were required to obtain a written "acknowledgment statement" saying that the importer had been informed of the pesticide's regulatory status in the USA. Labels were required to indicate that the product was not registered for use in the USA, and manufacturers were obliged to communicate data on production, sales, and trade to the Environmental Protection Agency.[21] By executive order (thus not requiring congressional approval), President Jimmy Carter also strengthened export notification procedures and created a Commodity Control List for regulating hazardous exports.[22] Exports of substances on this list required a license, thus allowing more direct government control on exports.

Most of the Carter administration's limits on exports of hazardous substances were removed early in the Reagan administration as part of the new administration's effort to eliminate regulations that interfered with commerce. Only the FIFRA notification system survived: changing it would have required a legislative act because it was an integral part of FIFRA legislation.[23] The notification system was severely criticized by environmental pressure groups as ineffective; observers inside and outside the administration agreed that notifications often were not received and that recipient agencies in developing countries could make little use of the information they did receive.[24] The practical impact of the US notification system on trade appears to have been limited or nonexistent, although some analysts claim that a few developing countries did ban certain imports after receiving information through the FIFRA notification process.[25] Nonetheless, ever since the FIFRA amendments, "notification" has been enshrined as the minimum acceptable regulation of trade in hazardous chemicals and pesticides. Despite the Reagan administration's hostility to global rules, efforts to develop a global notification system in the mid-1980s proceeded rapidly because the USA had already adopted such a system. Potential opposition from industry, which was already compelled to comply with the US notification system, was blunted.

No other industrialized country adopted a notification system in the 1970s. Members of the EC did not adopt such a notification system in 1979 with the Sixth Amendment legislation on chemicals. (Until the mid-1980s the EC saw its mandate narrowly—to reduce the main barriers to trade between EC members—and notification of exports to non-EC countries fell outside that scope.) The European Parliament did not make its first prominent statement on the need to regulate hazardous pesticide exports until 1983, but that body was nearly powerless. The Dutch government adopted a notification and consent system at the end of 1985 and used its presidency of the EC in the first half of 1986 to press (without success) for an EC-wide notification and export consent system; however, not even a limited form of the Dutch-proposed PIC system was adopted.[26] Only in 1988, after the *London Guidelines* had been adopted, did the EC adopt a system requiring member states to notify importing countries at the time of the first shipment of a banned or severely restricted chemical.[27]

Global Regulation of Trade in Chemicals and Pesticides

By the early 1980s, marginal changes to export regulations in a few industrialized countries, mainly the USA, and improvements in national regulation in developing countries partially limited the problem of unregulated hazardous exports. However, the core of the problem that concerned public interest groups and developing countries remained largely untouched: how would developing countries with low capacity regulate these hazards? Translating concern into action remained problematic. Existing notification schemes seemed ineffective. Training programs to improve pesticide management were under way but were quite limited. Exporters could have limited shipments of hazardous substances, but few did. Outright bans on hazardous exports, especially of products that were not registered for use in industrialized countries, had been proposed by some environmental nongovernmental organizations (ENGOs) but were neither politically feasible nor necessarily in the interests of developing countries—some of the hazardous substances were still extremely useful in developing countries where newer, less toxic formulations were unaffordable or ineffective.

In addition to the two extremes of minimal regulation of trade through existing notification schemes and politically infeasible bans on exports, a third alternative emerged for regulating exports from industrialized to developing countries: prior informed consent (PIC). PIC would be much stronger than the existing notification schemes (which in practice allowed shipments to proceed without ensuring the informed and explicit consent of importing governments) but would not halt trade.

The phrase "prior informed consent" is most often ascribed to OXFAM's David Bull, whose 1982 study on pesticide usage in developing countries was the ENGOs' bible of statistics and arguments.[28] However, PIC was one of many related concepts under discussion in the late 1970s and early 1980s, when industrialized countries were facing the need to regulate exports of many hazards, including chemicals and pesticides.[29] In the USA, the FIFRA system of notification and "acknowledgment statements" was an attempt to promote informed consent. In 1982 the European Commission considered a form of PIC as part of its policy governing trade of hazardous waste among EC members. In 1984 the USA was the first country to adopt a PIC system for exports of hazardous waste, which was implemented in 1986. The 1989 Basel Convention on the Control of Transboundary Movements of Hazardous Wastes and their Disposal explicitly included a PIC system, but in practice the PIC system for hazardous waste was not often used.[30] (Many scholars argue that PIC is an emerging principle of international law to govern trade in hazardous products between countries with markedly different levels of regulatory capacity.[31] Because the Basel Convention's PIC system has not been used much, the experience with PIC for chemicals and pesticides reviewed in this chapter is currently the only guide to how PIC might be implemented and thus is especially important as PIC-like schemes are considered in other areas of international law.)

A PIC scheme was considered (and rejected) by the OECD in 1982–1983. The OECD was involved in the issue to help harmonize domestic rules, testing, and registration. The OECD had no mandate or support for expanding regulation, but it was a small step for the OECD forum to develop (nonmandatory) guidelines on export notification, which the USA had already implemented. In 1984 the OECD Council recommended that OECD members implement a notification system that would inform importing countries of domestic restrictions (i.e., bans or severe restrictions) at the time of the first export of the product, followed by an opportunity for the importing country to request more information.[32] The OECD system did not exactly follow any of the existing systems in OECD countries, although it did largely reflect the existing

US notification system. Rather, the OECD's Recommendation resembled a least-common-denominator compromise among the major hazardous chemical exporters. For example, it did not include notification requirements for exports of substances that had never been registered or had been withdrawn from consideration before a registration decision.

The global response developed on two parallel tracks, one through UNEP and the other through the FAO. UNEP ultimately focused on chemicals and the FAO on pesticides, which reflected these organizations' differing mandates rather than overt coordination. Most of the diplomatic negotiations leading to global regulatory systems, and ultimately PIC, took place under UNEP auspices, but the organization had poor or nonexistent relations with chemical and pesticides producers and little practical experience implementing policies in developing countries. UNEP was catalytic, rather than action oriented; as in many other areas, it spawned agreements and institutions. In contrast, the FAO had extensive experience implementing agricultural projects in developing countries and, after a decade of attracting criticism for promoting overconsumption of pesticides in the 1970s, was implementing pesticides management programs. The activities of these two organizations were joined when the PIC system was created. However, many of the organizational differences persist. The activities of the two organizations are reviewed here, beginning with UNEP. Where possible, the activities of the two organizations and the substances they deal with are considered separately because the two experiences help to illustrate why some organizations and procedures have been effective while others have failed. Although many efforts have been made to establish an integrated PIC system, the differences between "chemicals" and "pesticides" and the roles of UNEP and the FAO have remained distinct.

United Nations Environment Programme
The problem of trade in hazardous substances has continuously been on UNEP's agenda since the mid-1970s, put there by environmental groups and especially developing countries that sought to highlight injustices in the world trading system. Much of the early attention, including many symbolic decisions by UNEP's Governing Council, which was dominated by developing countries, focused on dumping of products that had been banned or severely restricted in the North onto less regulated markets in the South. One of UNEP's first concrete actions was to establish the International Register for Potentially Toxic

Chemicals (IRPTC) in 1976, with the task of compiling and circulating information on chemical hazards. In 1978, the UNEP Governing Council specifically directed IRPTC to focus on providing information on limitations, bans, and regulations that had been enacted in exporting nations.[33] Developing countries pushed the same agenda in the United Nations (UN) General Assembly. Every year, starting in 1979, the UN General Assembly adopted a stronger resolution advocating limits on exports of products that had been banned in industrialized countries and greater information exchange.[34] Led by developing countries, these efforts culminated in a 1982 resolution that created the UN Consolidated List of Products Whose Consumption and/or Sale have been Banned, Withdrawn, Severely Restricted or not Approved by Governments.[35] IRPTC was one of three organizations charged with contributing to that list, which first appeared in 1983 and has since been updated twice. Like the notification system already in place in the USA, the Consolidated List was intended to provide useful information to importers (mainly developing countries) on substances deemed hazardous. Industry reviled the concept, many firms refused to provide information to IRPTC, and the USA (alone) voted against the resolution because the Consolidated List was de facto a blacklist with few controls to ensure its accuracy.

In 1984, in parallel with the OECD's Recommendation on information exchange, UNEP's Governing Council created the Provisional Notification Scheme for Banned and Severely Restricted Chemicals.[36] The Scheme emerged from a working group created by UNEP in 1982 under pressure from the Dutch government. The group was organized to propose nonbinding guidelines for exchanging information related to trade in hazardous chemicals, especially pesticides—in essence, to improve what IRPTC was already doing.[37] Developing countries hoped that the working group would yield trade regulations, which exporters strongly opposed. Failure to agree led to a provisional system modeled on the OECD's information system—some parts were even excerpted verbatim.[38] The Scheme charged IRPTC with developing and managing a database of "control actions," decisions by countries to ban or severely restrict a chemical. IRPTC would circulate the database of these decisions to all UN members; in principle, that information would increase awareness of controls on hazardous substances.[39]

The Provisional Scheme did not go beyond the export notification schemes already in place in the USA or being considered in other major exporting nations. Nor did it tighten procedures to make the existing notification systems more effective. However, the UNEP Provisional Scheme extended the OECD system in two ways. First, the UNEP framework created a universal system open to all members of the UN. Second, it created an explicit institutional structure to manage the exchange of information. It required IRPTC to provide a clearinghouse for information and advice; participating states were asked to name Designated National Authorities (DNAs) to communicate with IRPTC. DNAs were requested to notify IRPTC of all control actions to ban, severely restrict, or withdraw hazardous chemicals and pesticides from the market.[40] Since then, DNAs and control actions have been the cornerstone of every significant attempt to regulate international trade in hazardous chemicals and pesticides.

With the ink barely dry on the Provisional Notification Scheme, UNEP reconvened the working group that developed the Scheme, this time with the mandate to create a more permanent system. As before, ENGOs and developing countries urged inclusion of PIC; as before, industry and the main exporting nations uniformly opposed the idea. In 1987, UNEP adopted the *London Guidelines for the Exchange of Information on Chemicals in International Trade*. Little changed from 1984 to 1987, the *Guidelines* merely augmented the Provisional Notification Scheme with general commitments to promote the sound management of chemicals. Today the 1987 *London Guidelines* are often cited as the beginning of UNEP's notification activities. However, a UNEP notification system could have developed under the Provisional Notification Scheme. It did not because UNEP gave little attention to implementing the Provisional Notification Scheme, focusing its activities instead on negotiating additional legal instruments—a pattern that has since been repeated several times.

In parallel with efforts to implement the Provisional Notification Scheme and the *London Guidelines*, ENGOs put more rigorous systems for regulating trade of hazardous chemicals and pesticides on national government agendas. By the late 1980s virtually all major chemical-exporting nations were considering, and a few had implemented, systems for export notification. A few were also considering PIC procedures. The Netherlands implemented a voluntary PIC system in 1986; however, by 1991 all Dutch production of especially dangerous substances had been stopped, which made PIC largely superfluous for the Netherlands. The USA had an export notification system in place; in the late 1980s it was developing rules for a possible PIC system. Canada was developing a system for export notification of severely restricted chemicals; like Japan, it had banned exports of domestically banned chemicals. The UK put a voluntary export notification scheme in place in 1986. The EC implemented a Regulation in June 1989 for export notification of 21 chemicals (or chemical groups) that had been banned or severely restricted within the Community.[41]

Food and Agriculture Organization

Concern about trade in hazardous chemicals from industrialized to developing countries has historically centered on pesticides. Indeed, it was primarily concern about pesticides that originally motivated the UNEP Provisional Notification Scheme and the *London Guidelines*. The UN's most important activities related to pesticides have been managed by the FAO, which logically plays a key role because its mandate centers on the food production system. Because the FAO implements country-level programs on food production, its involvement with pesticide issues has been extensive. The FAO's approach to pest management was codified in the nonbinding 1985 FAO *Code of Conduct on the Distribution and Use of Pesticides*. Like many other codes and guidelines, the FAO *Code of Conduct* is broad: it establishes guidelines for the marketing and use of pesticides and identifies specific responsibilities for industry and government.

Negotiating the Joint UNEP/FAO PIC System

The PIC system was the result of continuous pressure by entrepreneurial public interest groups and developing countries simultaneously in UNEP and the FAO. Since 1982, public interest groups have uniformly supported PIC, even when they have differed on the extent to which the use and trade of hazardous chemicals and pesticides should be permitted. PIC was on the agenda but was rejected when the Provisional Notification Scheme was adopted. OXFAM's David Bull, the most respected expert in the NGO community that had pressured industry and the FAO to do more to control pesticide risks, was enlisted by the FAO to draft the FAO *Code of Conduct*. His drafts included PIC, which was removed as a result of industry pressure in 1985 when the final draft was adopted.[42] Public interest NGOs and developing countries also pushed for inclusion of PIC in the *London Guidelines*, where it was rejected by a minority of industrialized countries that exported chemicals and pesticides. At the 1987

UNEP Governing Council meeting, where the *London Guidelines* (minus PIC) were adopted, Greenpeace and the Pesticides Action Network (PAN) helped to organize a coalition of developing countries led by Senegal that sponsored a resolution to require a working group to investigate amending the *Guidelines* to include PIC.[43] Only months after the UNEP Governing Council Decision was adopted, the coalition of developing countries forced the adoption of a resolution in the FAO Conference requiring that PIC be incorporated into the *Code of Conduct*.[44] PIC had been struck down by its foes at every turn from the early 1980s to 1987 because advocates were not well organized and opponents tactically favored regulatory alternatives (e.g., export notification) while opposing PIC. Only in 1987 did advocates focus major international policy decisions on PIC itself. The result—two clear mandates to pursue PIC—meant that opponents could scuttle PIC only at great cost. Some form of PIC was inevitable, and industry turned its attention to ensuring that the PIC system adopted and implemented reflected its interests.

Following the mandates of 1987, UNEP and FAO working groups developed procedures for a PIC system. In 1989 the UNEP Governing Council adopted the *Amended London Guidelines*, which included PIC.[45] Later that year, the FAO governing body amended the *Code* to add a compatible system for information exchange and PIC. The definitions of "prior informed consent" in the two documents are identical, except that the FAO's definition refers only to pesticides and UNEP's uses the broader term "chemicals." The procedures for exchanging information in the PIC system are nearly identical in the two documents. The *Amended London Guidelines* give the role of providing secretariat functions to the IRPTC—since renamed "UNEP Chemicals"—and the *Code of Conduct* merely says that the FAO will provide some secretariat functions in coordination with UNEP. A memorandum of understanding between the Executive Director of UNEP and the Director-General of the FAO provides the formal basis for a joint Secretariat and a common effort to implement PIC.[46]

Although the two PIC systems were developed in tandem and implemented jointly, in 1989 it was still unclear whether the UNEP and FAO visions of PIC would be fully compatible.[47] In particular, ENGOs and developing countries active in UNEP feared that the FAO was beholden to agriculture ministries and pesticides producers and would implement PIC reluctantly and poorly. Some charged that the *Code of Conduct*, even without PIC, was already widely abused.[48] Thus UNEP's *Amended London Guidelines* gave UNEP and the FAO joint "operational responsibility ... in accordance with their specialized expertise, with UNEP handling industrial chemicals and FAO handling pesticides . . . ."[49] UNEP would not include pesticides on its list of PIC substances "[i]f the procedures recommended by the FAO Committee on Agriculture prove to be at least equally protective to human health and the environment." If not, UNEP would include them in their part of PIC, with the FAO implementing (presumably a less strict form of) PIC on the same substances.[50] How UNEP would have made this determination is unclear; so far, the problem has not occurred and the division of responsibility between "chemicals" and "pesticides"—between UNEP and the FAO—has been relatively clear. Thus an area of international law that was a prime candidate for conflicts between overlapping legal instruments—"treaty congestion"—in fact illustrates a case of remarkable speed and coordination in adopting new and significant commitments.[51] Speed and coordination are well-known benefits of using nonbinding instruments.[52] As is shown later in this chapter, it was even more important that most of the key elements of the PIC system were not resolved in 1989; rather, they were developed through the process of implementation—learning by doing—which was greatly aided by the flexibility of the nonbinding instruments.

Implementing the Voluntary PIC System

PIC is intended to help governments control imports of hazardous chemicals and pesticides. Both the *Amended London Guidelines* and the amended FAO *Code of Conduct on the Distribution and Use of Pesticides* require all participating governments to name DNAs, who are responsible for regulating chemicals and pesticides (or both). The DNA(s) in each country are expected to notify the joint FAO/UNEP Secretariat of control actions to ban or severely restrict a chemical or pesticide. Those substances are then eligible to be included in the PIC system.

For each substance in the PIC system, the Secretariat prepares (usually by commission) a Decision Guidance Document (DGD) summarizing published (peer-reviewed) scientific information on the hazards of the chemical or pesticide. The DGD is sent to all DNAs, who then evaluate whether and under what conditions to allow future imports. Each DNA summarizes its decision in an Importing Country Response. These Responses are collated by the Secretariat and transmitted to all other DNAs. Thereafter, exporters of PIC chemicals have easy access to information on whether a particular nation allows imports of a particular substance that is part of the PIC system.[53]

If an importer has decided to ban a substance, the exporter should prohibit the export of that substance. If the importer allows imports only with a permit, the exporter must ensure that the proper permit is obtained prior to export. In essence, PIC shifts enforcement responsibilities from importing nations, some of which are developing nations with low administrative capacity, to exporting nations, mainly industrialized countries with high administrative capacity. When information is lacking, the status quo prevails—exporters are expected to make an effort to determine whether the country allows the PIC chemical to be imported. Figure 6.1 summarizes the sequence of events.

Because the PIC system is part of broader efforts to regulate trade in chemicals and pesticides—and to improve management of these hazards generally—figure 6.1 also shows the notification systems codified in US and EC legislation, the 1984 OECD Recommendation, the UNEP Provisional Notification Scheme, the 1985 FAO *Code of Conduct*, and the 1987 *London Guidelines*. The notification systems require exporters to provide information on control actions; most also require notification of exports. The influence of those notification systems will not be considered further here, except insofar as the data required for them to operate (i.e., data on control actions and on shipments) are also needed for the operation and evaluation of the PIC system. In the past, notification systems appear to have had little influence on trade; perhaps by coupling notification with the PIC system the information provided during notification will be more accurate, timely, and useful. Similar requirements for notification can also be found in other binding and nonbinding legal instruments, such as the International Labor Organization (ILO) Convention on Safe Use of Chemicals in the Workplace.[54]

Putting PIC into practice—implementation—has depended on several critical processes at the international and national levels. At the international level, two processes have been particularly important: (1) developing the "PIC list" of chemicals and pesticides that are part of the PIC system; and (2) preparing DGDs. Other international functions such as gathering and distributing Importing Country Responses are also vital, but they have been relatively easy to achieve. Implementation of the PIC system at the national level has been critical to PIC's success. Particularly important national implementation activities include naming DNAs, communication of information by DNAs, and

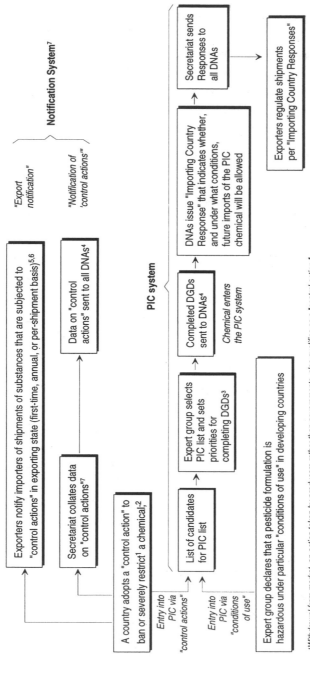

Figure 6.1

Operation of the PIC system of the *Amended London Guidelines* and the FAO *Code of Conduct*

regulating production and trade of PIC chemicals. In this section, each of these critical international and national activities is examined.

International Implementation

Implementation at the international level has required many policy decisions that were unresolved or unknown in 1989 when the *Amended London Guidelines* and the FAO *Code of Conduct* were adopted. Those decisions were made in an expert forum—the FAO/UNEP Joint Meetings on Prior Informed Consent. Thus, before turning to the particular processes that have been required to implement PIC, the origins and operation of the Joint Meetings are reviewed. The flexibility of the joint FAO/UNEP forum and the fact that it was composed of experts in the field are the main reasons PIC has been able to efficiently handle the many problems that have arisen during its few years of operation.

FAO/UNEP Joint Meetings on Prior Informed Consent.   Like all dynamic agreements, the PIC system requires a forum for debating and making policy decisions. In virtually all international environmental agreements the main forum for these activities is a regular meeting of the "parties"—the national governments that have ratified the agreement. PIC is different because it was created with nonbinding instruments. There are no formal parties to nonbinding instruments and thus no automatic need for a formal supreme decision-making body consisting of the parties.[55] Moreover, there was no established pattern for decision-making bodies under nonbinding instruments. Neither the FAO *Code of Conduct* nor the UNEP *Amended London Guidelines* envisioned the need for a body to regularly make significant decisions once the PIC system was in place. Neither provides much guidance on how to create a body to make and review decisions.[56] The supreme decision-making fora were the FAO and UNEP governing bodies—composed of government representatives—which had adopted the PIC system. However, in practice, none of the operational decisions for PIC were made by those bodies, which were large and unwieldy and had many other issues on their agendas.

Because PIC was especially created to regulate pesticides, in the early stages most of the technical capacity for the PIC system came from the FAO. Neither the FAO *Code of Conduct* nor the UNEP *Amended London Guidelines* specified a particular form for policy-making. Therefore, the FAO employed a model it had already used extensively—convening a group of experts on a regular basis to provide guidance on technical questions. The result was the FAO/UNEP Joint Group of Experts, which convened eight times at the FAO/UNEP Joint Meetings on Prior Informed Consent (JMPIC).

The FAO/UNEP Joint Group consisted of about 10 experts, with five chosen by each organization and representation roughly balanced between developed and developing countries. The experts were selected as individuals rather than government representatives. In practice, FAO and UNEP contacts are mainly through governments, and thus most experts were government employees. Governments thus potentially had some influence over outcomes, although so far no group has publicly charged that any of the experts made improper or instructed assessments of any issue that the Joint Group examined. Technical work was done by the Secretariat and consultants, but with the guidance and advice of this expert committee. Other international organizations with active pesticides and chemicals trade programs (WHO, OECD, ILO, and EEC) normally sent observers.

NGOs also participated actively in the work of JMPIC. Near the end of its life, JMPIC adopted formal NGO access rules and limited participation to a pair of experts from each of four organizations—two from industry and two from public interest groups—or eight people in total.[57] In practice, participation was governed more by groups interested in the work of JMPIC than by the rules. Pesticide producers were represented by the Groupement international des associations nationales de fabricants de produits agrochimiques (GIFAP), which normally sent the largest delegation and historically had a close relationship with the FAO. (In 1996, GIFAP changed its name to the Global Crop Protection Federation—GCPF.) Chemical producers in Europe were represented by the European Chemical Industry Council (CEFIC); the Chemical Manufacturers Association (CMA) represented North American producers. In addition, in 1993 the International Council of Chemical Associations (ICCA) was established with CEFIC as its Secretariat; its mandate is to represent the global interests of chemical producers, but so far it has not supplanted the separate North American and European industry associations. Public interests were represented by PAN and the International Organization of Consumer Unions (IOCU), now called Consumers International (CI). The World Wide Fund for Nature (WWF) also participated. Most of the key participants from industry and public interest groups had been active on these issues since before JMPIC began operation and coordinated their work informally. NGO participants were excluded when JMPIC decided particularly sensitive matters, such as which substances were to be on the PIC list because of "conditions of use" in developing countries.

Developing the PIC List.   First, and fundamentally, the FAO/UNEP Joint Group had the task of setting priorities for the pesticides and chemicals to be included in PIC.[58] More than 1,000 control actions existed at the time the PIC system was created.[59] Setting priorities was crucial because a substance could not enter the PIC system until a DGD had been prepared—an expensive and time-consuming process. Negotiators anticipated that the PIC procedure could not be immediately launched for all eligible chemicals; thus the *Amended London Guidelines* include instructions on identifying an initial PIC list, consisting of those chemicals that had been banned or severely restricted in five or more countries.[60] Although that rule could have been helpful for setting priorities during the start-up stage, in practice it was not immediately useful because the inventory of existing control actions had been derived from the IRPTC databases that contributed to the UN Consolidated List of Products Whose Consumption and/or Sale have been Banned, Withdrawn, Severely Restricted or not Approved by Governments—the same list mandated by the 1982 General Assembly Resolution and reviled by industry. The contents of that list could not be easily verified; thus the list was practically useless and the Joint Group of Experts decided it was unreliable.[61] Similarly, IRPTC could have been in a good position to provide information on control actions based on its work to implement the Provisional Notification Scheme and the 1987 *London Guidelines*, but in practice little attention had been paid to implementing those instruments fully or to cataloging control actions using consistent definitions. In short, when JMPIC first considered what would be on the PIC list, the slate was clean.

Developing the PIC list and setting priorities required two major actions, and the Joint Group played the central role in both. First, the types of control actions that qualified under PIC had to be clarified. The *Guidelines* and *Code* state that "bans" and "severe restrictions" qualify as control actions. The FAO conference report, written at the time the *Code* was amended, also clearly states that chemicals rejected for registration or voluntarily withdrawn from registration for health or environmental reasons should be included in PIC. Thus in practice four types of control actions make a chemical eligible for PIC:

"ban," "severe restriction," "rejection," and "withdrawal."[62] Putting those four concepts into operation was not easy.

The Joint Group developed more detailed definitions for each type of control action and has revised the reporting requirements for control actions to clarify when a control action satisfies the new criteria and to improve comparability of national control actions.[63] Consequently, regulators in countries that participate in the PIC system now have access to more useful information about the reasons a particular chemical has been controlled by other countries. In principle, this should improve management of PIC chemicals, although that benefit is understandably not yet much in evidence. Furthermore, the revised reporting scheme includes requests for data on actual production and usage, making it easier to set priorities among chemicals. Much of the Joint Group's early work in setting priorities was based on its expert sense of whether a given chemical was a severe threat; in some cases priorities have been revised after the submission of official data.[64] The new reporting system has helped to increase the probability of decisions being made on a more informed basis from the outset.

In borderline cases, JMPIC evaluated control actions on a case-by-case basis. For example, some substances are severely restricted only in particular geographical locations or agricultural settings. A related problem is that the PIC system is triggered when such bans or severe restrictions apply to a particular use of a chemical—as a pesticide for example. But in practice some national legislation does not control use directly, but rather regulates production, distribution, labeling, or other aspects of pesticide delivery and application.[65] How the Joint Group resolved such ambiguities is illustrated by the case of the pesticide bifenthrin, which the Netherlands allows to be applied only within certain greenhouses because of its toxicity to aquatic organisms. The substance was on JMPIC's agenda as a borderline case because industry had objected to the Dutch government's inclusion of the substance in its export notification scheme, which industry thought would alarm potential importers and disrupt efforts to have the pesticide registered in other countries. In considering the case, the Joint Group agreed that bifenthrin should not be in PIC because it was not "severely restricted" except under conditions relevant in the Netherlands, but that information on such chemicals should be distributed to DNAs on "information data sheets."[66] Information sheets, themselves an innovation of the Joint Group, were intended to provide relevant information on existing or possible regulations that affected pesticides, but they were formally outside the PIC process.[67] The earlier notification schemes—UNEP's Provisional Notification System and the original (1987) *London Guidelines*—did not envision a need for such reporting and data sheets.

In addition to resolving definitions and other issues that have affected PIC, the Joint Group has also been the forum where the PIC list has been adopted. In 1990, when the Joint Group took stock of which chemicals and pesticides with verified control actions qualified for PIC, none had received the minimum five notifications of control actions needed for inclusion, and thus there was nothing on the initial PIC list. Few countries had notified the PIC Secretariat of their control actions, and IRPTC's databases were not reliable. At the meeting, the EC presented its list of restricted chemicals from the appendix to the regulation that established the EC notification system (Regulation 1734/88). Lacking any other candidate lists, the Joint Group accepted the EC list.[68] Because the EC consisted of 12 member states, every substance on its list immediately exceeded the threshold of five control actions. The EC's regulations thus defined the first group of chemicals for PIC. In practice, many such information vacuums have been filled by EC ideas. This may explain some oddities, such as why two chemicals whose use and production had been largely discontinued (endrin and toxaphene) were nonetheless on the PIC list, whereas many other chemicals of greater importance in developing countries initially were not. Late in 1991, DGDs for the first six pesticides were circulated and PIC formally began operation.[69]

The Joint Group also adopted a procedure for removing chemicals from the list, which was developed by implementing the removal of cyhexatin from PIC. In 1989 a review of studies concluded that cyhexatin was teratogenic to rabbits (i.e., caused birth defects). Dow Chemical, the manufacturer, withdrew the substance from sale and five countries notified the PIC Secretariat that they had banned or severely restricted cyhexatin. The substance entered the PIC procedure, and a DGD was circulated to all DNAs. Additional testing showed no teratogenicity, a finding confirmed in a 1994 review by the WHO/FAO Joint Meeting on Pesticide Residues (JMPR). Some countries withdrew their objections; two other manufacturers began sales of the substance, and in July 1995 the Joint Group decided to revise the DGD. A year later, cyhexatin was removed from the procedure.[70]

Soon the number of eligible chemicals grew to many times the capacity of the PIC procedure. The Joint Group declared January 1992 the end of PIC's start-up phase. Since then, as required by the *Amended London Guidelines* and the FAO *Code*, a control action by any *single* country invokes the PIC system.[71] The flood of control actions that could result from this requirement was most vividly illustrated in the case of Austria, which adopted new chemicals legislation that banned or severely restricted 81 chemicals, 70 of which were not in the PIC system.[72] A literal reading of the *Amended London Guidelines* and FAO *Code of Conduct* would require that all these substances be included in PIC. Instead, the Joint Group developed criteria for setting priorities: they emphasized chemicals that were widely used and excluded those no longer in production. Such priorities were never envisioned in the *Guidelines* and *Code*, but in practice they have proved important because the process of bringing a chemical into the PIC procedure is time consuming. By 1995 the list of PIC candidates numbered 127 chemicals and was still growing, but only 17 were in the system.[73] By mid-1997 only 38 chemicals and pesticides were on the PIC list. Priorities, which the Joint Group have explicitly adopted, have been crucial to putting PIC into practice.[74]

Conditions of Use in Developing Countries.   The PIC system is triggered by national legislation. Countries decide how to manage chemicals domestically, and when those national decisions include a ban, severe restriction, withdrawal, or rejection, the chemical is eligible for the PIC list. However, such a scheme potentially misses many substances that are hazardous but widely used in developing countries. Moreover, many substances are considered safe when used under certain conditions (e.g., by workers wearing heavy rubber boots and respirators) and thus are not severely restricted, banned, withdrawn, or rejected. However, these substances may not be safe when applied under conditions that are typical in some developing countries (e.g., where rubber suits are unaffordable or impractical, such as in hot, steamy fields). Of course developing countries could have controlled those substances, which would have triggered PIC, but in practice many did not have the administrative capacity to identify the hazards and develop the necessary control actions. Typically labels warned of the hazards, and in many countries the law formally required that protective gear be worn during application, but in practice directions were not followed and many severe poisonings resulted. Some pesticides did not have known antidotes; for others, antidotes were not locally available. This problem is referred to here as "conditions of use in developing countries," but the formal term is much longer and more complicated to satisfy industry concerns that this list of substances not be interpreted by importers as a ban on use (and thus sales) of the pesticides.[75] Particular concern was focused on especially hazardous formulations of specific pesticides.

The existence of these "conditions of use" hazards has been the focus of efforts to reduce pesticide hazards since at least the early 1970s. Prior to PIC, the WHO, for example, developed a four-tier method of classifying pesticide formulations according to toxicity: Extremely Hazardous (Class 1A), Highly Hazardous (Class 1B), Moderately Hazardous (Class 2), and Slightly Hazardous (Class 3).[76] In principle, that list—especially Class 1A formulations—would allow easy identification of dangerous pesticide formulations that thus might be included in PIC. How, in practice, the PIC system expanded to include "conditions of use" substances illustrates the flexibility of the nonbinding instrument and crucial functions performed by the Joint Group of Experts and by NGOs.

The danger that hazardous pesticide formulations could slip through the cracks of PIC was widely recognized, but the only guidance was a brief mention added to the *Amended London Guidelines* that an expert group should study the issue of "acutely hazardous pesticide formulations to determine if there exists a need for a list of such products to supplement the chemicals already subject to the PIC procedure."[77] The *Amended London Guidelines* direct the expert group to begin by reviewing the hazardous formulations listed by the WHO as "Class 1A," but that list is long, many of the formulations are tightly regulated already, and reliable data on which substances cause the greatest problems are scarce. Environmental groups helped to fill the gaps. At an early meeting, Pesticides Trust presented a survey on implementation of the FAO *Code of Conduct* that it had conducted with members of PAN on the use of 19 hazardous pesticides in 17 countries. It identified nine pesticides that frequently caused problems.[78] The Joint Group used this as the starting point for a new classification of chemicals—termed "Class 1A+"—which were then candidates for the "PIC list."[79] Ten substances were ultimately included: all those identified by the NGOs plus the fumigant methyl bromide.[80]

The creation of Class 1A+ chemicals and their inclusion in PIC was within the mandate of the *Amended London Guidelines* and a similar provision in the

FAO *Code of Conduct*. But the NGO activity ensured that this review took place and that consideration of these substances was based on factual assessment of the hazards. It led (albeit with considerable delay) to inclusion of specific formulations under the Class 1A+ scheme. The list has been adjusted slightly over time.

NGOs were influential in developing the Class 1A+ list because they performed a vital function—the supply of useful and timely information.[81] Similarly, industry representatives have given briefings on the hazards associated with their products, providing information that was difficult or impossible for the Joint Group to obtain from other sources.[82] Not all efforts by NGOs to influence PIC were successful. Greenpeace and the German PAN affiliate urged expansion of the PIC system to include substances that had never been submitted for registration in exporting nations. Such substances could not trigger PIC because they had not been banned, severely restricted, withdrawn, or rejected.[83] The Joint Group deferred the issue and never addressed it again. That the NGO case was not supported by any factual analysis of whether these substances were causing problems probably contributed to inaction. The NGO request went beyond the mandate of the PIC system and was (appropriately) rejected. To date there is no reliable and useful information on whether these substances are problematic, and thus they remain off the agenda.

Although public interest NGOs helped to set the agenda on this crucial issue of "conditions of use," they did not control it for long. Industry argued for a narrow definition of the "conditions of use" problem, which would have resulted in few, if any, substances being included. The Joint Group initiated its own study by circulating a questionnaire to developing countries to obtain more information on substances that caused "conditions of use" problems. The response was poor: after five months only 22% had replied; reminders from the Secretariat elevated the response rate to only 35% after more than a year had passed. Moreover, the responses did not offer much information on the topics of greatest interest, such as the number of poisonings caused by these Class 1A+ substances.[84] Lack of data on such problems continues to be a serious problem. The Joint Group developed a point system that would allow an objective assessment of which formulations would be included under the "conditions of use," but the system was not useful in practice.[85] Industry advocated its own point system that would have required collecting data on poisonings, which would have further delayed implementation of the "conditions of use" provisions. Thus the final decisions on which substances are included in PIC have depended heavily on the expert case-by-case judgment of the Joint Group.

On the basis of all the information it was able to gather, the Joint Group held a rare closed session and selected a total of six pesticides for inclusion in PIC on the basis of hazards caused by conditions of use in developing countries.[86] Five of these pesticides joined the PIC procedure in 1997. Moreover, contrary to industry pressure, the DGDs for these substances cover their *active ingredient*, although the original rationale for adding these substances to PIC was only that specific *formulations* were dangerous: the Joint Group decided that DGDs limited to specific formulations would not be helpful to developing countries that needed to weigh the risks and benefits of pesticides.[87]

Decision Guidance Documents.   If it operates properly PIC could be one of the largest organized transfers of useful regulatory information to developing countries, which in turn could contribute to the ultimate goal of the PIC system—improving management of hazardous chemicals and pesticides. PIC differs from the earlier information exchange systems in the USA, OECD, EC, and UNEP because PIC requires prior consent. Because prior consent potentially delays shipments, it gives both exporters and importers an incentive to ensure that information reaches its destination so that decisions can be made in a timely manner. In contrast, earlier notification systems merely required exporters to send information about chemical hazards to importers; typically that information was not scientifically reviewed or presented in a format that was comparable with information on other chemical hazards or useful for regulatory decisions. Much of the information never even reached importers. In principle, that problem is more easily overcome when consent is explicitly required.

The PIC system supplies information on chemical and pesticide hazards through DGDs that summarize available scientific assessments. A chemical on the PIC list becomes part of the PIC system only when its DGD is completed, approved by the Joint Group of Experts, and sent to all participating countries for their review. DNAs in those countries are requested to respond within 90 days with a decision on whether and under what conditions imports of the PIC chemical will be allowed. (In practice, only a tiny fraction of DNA responses are received within that time limit, but most DNAs eventually do respond.) Thus the availability of DGDs is pivotal to the operation of PIC. Preparing DGDs is time-consuming, which is one reason why PIC is still not fully implemented nearly a decade after the scheme was created and why it took nearly two years for the first substances to enter the PIC system—from 1989, when the *Code of Conduct* and the *Amended London Guidelines* were adopted and JMPIC first met, until late 1991, when the first DGDs for six pesticides were circulated.

The experience of preparing and adopting DGDs has varied enormously for pesticides and chemicals: progress on pesticides has been rapid while only a few chemicals are part of PIC. The first 12 substances to enter PIC were all pesticides, followed by 5 chemicals. Of the 38 substances currently on the PIC list, 28 are pesticides, 5 are pesticides that are hazardous under "conditions of use," and only 5 are chemicals.[88] (PIC distinguishes between "industrial" and "consumer" chemicals; all 5 chemicals in PIC are "industrial.")

The stark differences reflect two factors, one intrinsic to the substances involved and the other a consequence of the organizations that have been involved in the implementation of PIC. The intrinsic factor is that, compared with chemicals, pesticides have a much longer and more extensive history of regulation for their particular health and environmental effects. When PIC began there were many existing control actions on pesticides; governments, international organizations, and NGOs had extensive experience and knowledge of pesticide hazards. In contrast, control actions on chemicals were fewer and more difficult to assess. For this reason, more pesticides than chemicals should be included in the PIC scheme, but the longer history of pesticide regulation does not fully explain the persistent problems in implementing PIC for industrial chemicals. After the PIC system had been in place for three years, 12 pesticides were part of PIC but no industrial chemicals had been added, although more than a dozen chemicals had been identified as PIC candidates by the Joint Group. Part of the explanation for PIC's failure to include many industrial chemicals lies with the organizations and procedures used to implement the PIC system. The central problem in compiling DGDs is gathering information about the hazard—exactly the problem which countries with low administrative capacity have faced for a long time and which motivated the creation of the PIC system. DGDs are most useful to decision makers in those countries when the information is clear, but clarity is difficult to achieve when (as is common) toxicity tests give conflicting results. Thus in practice a crucial condition for efficient preparation of DGDs is the availability of consensual expert information on hazards and/or a legitimate procedure for producing that information.

Although PIC combined the existing activities in the FAO on pesticides and at UNEP on industrial chemicals (as well as pesticides), the two organizations have retained their areas of expertise. The FAO has taken the lead for matters related to pesticides. Its long history of setting standards for pesticide residues and helping countries regulate pesticides gave it extensive in-house expertise, and that capacity was easily applied to the preparation of DGDs. A central factor was the existence of the FAO/WHO Joint Meeting on Pesticide Residues .(JMPR), a permanent group of experts that assesses scientific evidence about pesticide-related hazards and regularly publishes systematic reviews of the literature. Most of the pesticides included in PIC so far have already been addressed by JMPR, and thus the information on hazards that is needed for DGDs is readily available. Moreover, JMPR's long history and reputation help ensure that its findings are not contested. The case of cyhexatin, which was added to PIC in 1992 when its DGD was finalized, illustrates the importance of JMPR's activities. Cyhexatin has been reviewed by JMPR nine times since 1970, thus there was a long series of well-established data available for its DGD. When new tests showed cyhexatin was not a teratogen, the DGD was revised only after JMPR reviewed the test results. The removal of cyhexatin from the PIC list might otherwise have been a controversial decision, or at least a difficult one to make with certainty; the existence of a JMPR review made it a much easier decision.

In contrast, preparation of DGDs for industrial chemicals has taken much longer. UNEP has no regular system for reviewing and assessing data on chemical hazards. The IRPTC has existed since 1976, but its rolé is to facilitate the exchange of information and not to engage in comprehensive expert reviews of hazards data. UNEP is a member of the International Program on Chemical Safety (IPCS), a joint program established by UNEP, WHO, and the ILO to assess and develop criteria for environmental health. But IPCS is young: it has been active only since the 1970s and its activities have been criticized for not being balanced, comprehensive, or timely. In practice, it has supplied information to the PIC system, but the link between IPCS and PIC is weak. Like JMPR, IPCS conducts reviews of the scientific literature on known hazards of particular chemicals, resulting in Environmental Health Criteria (EHC) documents. All five of the industrial chemicals in the PIC system have had at least one EHC. However, the interface between PIC and IPCS is poor. The first EHCs for two PIC chemicals, PBBs and tris (2,3-dibromopropyl) phosphate, were published at least a year after these substances entered the PIC system. The EHCs for two other PIC chemicals, PCBs and PCTs, were first published in 1976, reflecting that these substances had long been a concern of regulators; revised editions were published in 1993, after the initial DGDs for these substances had already been written and were under review.[89] The chemicals that are in the PIC system are among the easiest to assess because they have been subjected to domestic regulation and assessment for long periods of time—they are the best cases for close and timely coordination. The lack of an established assessment mechanism implies that the prospects for including other industrial chemicals in PIC are not bright.

National Implementation

In the simplest sense, PIC is highly successful: interviews by the author confirm that there is not a single documented case of a firm exporting a PIC substance contrary to the PIC procedure. However, that admirable outcome is hardly surprising. Industry associations, fearful of poor public images, have required their members to comply with public regulations, including PIC. Most of the substances initially on the PIC list were already tightly regulated, and in cases where importers do not indicate their regulatory preferences the PIC system explicitly allows the shipment to proceed. Thus, a proper evaluation of how PIC has been implemented at the national level requires looking beyond the simple indicator of compliance to the actions of governments and NGOs, especially within the developing countries that PIC was created to assist. This section evaluates two critical requirements of the PIC system: (1) the need for all participating countries to name DNAs responsible for exchanging information and for making decisions about which PIC substances can be traded; and (2) the need for importing countries to build administrative capacity so that they can make informed decisions and better manage hazardous chemicals and pesticides.

Designated National Authorities and Information Exchange.   PIC aims at changing the behavior of exporters and importers, which it does by strengthening the hand of the government agencies serving as intermediaries (the DNAs). In particular, it aims at strengthening DNAs in importing nations by shifting

Table 6.1 Types of Designated National Authorities (DNAs) Declared by the 143 Countries that Participate in the Voluntary PIC System

Separate DNAs for chemicals and pesticides[a]	59 (41%)
Combined DNA[b]	61 (43%)
DNA for pesticides only	33 (23%)
DNA for chemicals only	0 (0%)
Total number of countries that have named DNAs	143

[a]Countries that have named at least one DNA responsible for pesticides and at least one DNA responsible for chemicals. Several countries in this category have named a combined DNA (i.e., responsible for chemicals and pesticides) as well as a DNA for pesticides.
[b]Countries that have named only one DNA, which is given responsibility for pesticides and for chemicals.
Source: Compiled by author from *Register of Designated National Authorities for the Implementation of the Information Exchange and PIC Procedures of the London Guidelines and the International Code of Conduct* (March 1997).

some of the responsibility for regulating trade to exporters. Thus the establishment and performance of DNAs is crucial to the effectiveness of the whole PIC system.

The PIC system allows governments to declare different DNAs for pesticides and for chemicals, an option most countries have taken. Differences between these two types of DNAs illustrate differences in the national capacity to regulate chemical and pesticide hazards and thus differences in the ability to influence the ultimate targets of PIC—the firms that export. Countries that have decided to name two DNAs have consistently named the DNA for pesticides before naming the DNA for chemicals. This pattern is most evident in developing countries—those the PIC system was created to assist. In the first year of PIC's existence, 40 countries elected to declare separate DNAs for pesticides and for industrial and consumer chemicals. Most named only the DNA for pesticides; all of those were in developing countries. Not one country named a DNA for chemicals but not for pesticides. Table 6.1 summarizes the situation at the end of 1996—143 countries have participated in the voluntary PIC procedures; 33 of the countries that have declared that they will name separate DNAs have so far named only one of the two required DNAs. All of the missing DNAs are for chemicals.

DNAs for pesticides also perform better than their chemical counterparts. Table 6.2 shows the responses for the first two sets of pesticides (12 pesticides, including cyhexatin, which was later removed) and the first set of 5

Table 6.2 Import Responses for Pesticides and Chemicals

	Prohibit	Permit	Total responses	Response rate[a] (%)
Pesticides				
First set of pesticides				
(entered PIC September 1991)				
Aldrin	86	9	95	66
Dieldrin	86	12	98	69
DDT	87	18	105	73
Dinoseb & dinoseb salts	84	6	90	63
Fluoroacetamide	73	14	87	61
HCH (mixed isomers)	86	9	95	66
Second set of pesticides				
(entered PIC November 1992)				
Chlordane	70	11	81	57
Chlordimeform	68	9	77	54
Cyhexatin (later removed from PIC)	54	20	74	52
EDB (1,2-dibromoethane)	73	6	79	55
Heptachlor	69	11	80	56
Mercury compounds (average response				
for 3 mercury compounds)	71	6	77	54
Industrial chemicals				
First set of industrial chemicals				
(entered PIC March 1993)				
Crocidolite (asbestos)	25	15	40	36
Polybrominated biphenyls (PBBs)	5	35	40	36
Polychlorinated biphenyls (PCBs)	27	16	44	40
Polychlorinated terphenyls (PCTs)	24	16	40	36
Tris (2,3-dibromopropyl) phosphate	5	37	42	38

[a] "Response rate" is the percentage of named DNAs that responded (143 for pesticides and 110 for chemicals).

Source: Compiled by author from data in *PIC Circular VI* (July 1996).

industrial chemicals. These 17 substances have been in the PIC system since 1991–1993—long enough to permit meaningful comparisons. The next set of substances (6 pesticides) entered PIC only in January 1997. Responses to the 12 DGDs for pesticides have been much more rapid and complete than responses for the 5 DGDs on industrial chemicals. The stark differences reveal that while administrative capacity varies across countries and is generally lower in developing countries, it also varies considerably by sector. The capacity to participate in PIC is systematically higher for pesticides than for chemicals.

As with the earlier comparison between pesticides and industrial chemicals, some of the difference is explained by the longer history of pesticides regulation. Malaysia, the Philippines, and many other developing countries had pesticides legislation in place in the 1970s; chemicals regulations were generally developed a decade later.[90] Moreover, import decisions for chemicals may be more complicated (and time consuming) because many countries intend to allow future imports of these chemicals; in contrast, roughly 90% of pesticide responses have simply banned future imports.

Differences also reflect the organizations and industries involved. Through its projects, the FAO—which is responsible for pesticides—has a long-standing relationship with agriculture ministries in developing countries. Thus when problems have arisen, the FAO has had an established point of contact and relationship to help resolve the matter. In contrast, those few developing countries that have named DNAs for chemicals have typically given the task to the environmental ministry, which is typically weaker than other ministries in the government. This organizational choice largely reflects that UNEP, whose national counterparts are environmental ministries, is responsible for chemicals. Anecdotal evidence suggests that UNEP's local contacts are not as extensive or powerful as those of the FAO, and thus it has been less able to resolve problems with DNAs. Thus even when DNAs for chemicals are established they do not perform well.

Capacity Building in Developing Countries.   For importing countries, complying with the basic requirements of the voluntary PIC system is relatively simple; the principle obligation is to name a DNA and issue Importing Country Responses. Most countries eventually comply, especially with the most trivial requirement—naming a DNA—which dates back to UNEP's Provisional Notification Scheme. Moreover, over time the quality of information provided by DNAs under the PIC procedure has improved; with experience, the participants have become better able to implement PIC.[91] However, it is worth examining whether the voluntary PIC system is resulting in improved capacity to manage chemical and pesticide hazards in developing countries. Capacity building, the ultimate aim of PIC, goes far beyond naming DNAs and responding to letters from the FAO/UNEP Joint Secretariat. Assessment of capacity building is especially important for this study of a nonbinding instrument; analysts and policymakers have assumed that binding instruments are superior because they are taken more seriously by countries and thus are perhaps implemented more thoroughly. Interest groups that favor better management of chemicals and pesticides may be better able to press their cause when capacity building is part of a binding instrument. Actors who are expected to pay for programs to build capacity (e.g., industrialized countries, industry) might be less likely to shirk responsibility if they face binding commitments. Indeed, one of the only areas where the binding PIC Convention currently under negotiation is likely to differ significantly from the voluntary procedure is the requirement for a binding financial mechanism to transfer resources to developing countries to help build administrative capacity.

These claims about the relative effectiveness of binding and nonbinding instruments cannot be fully tested in this study because the PIC system has operated only on a nonbinding basis. However, the experience under the existing PIC system shows that extensive capacity-building efforts can emerge even with a nonbinding instrument. Moreover, there is suggestive evidence that industry participation under the nonbinding system has been equal to or greater than that which would have occurred with a binding PIC Convention.

Capacity building in the PIC system has principally consisted of three activities, all of which have been coupled to broader efforts to improve chemicals and pesticides management. First, after the *Code of Conduct* was amended in 1989, PIC was immediately added to the FAO's programs to improve pesticides management. Seminars to inform local government officials in developing countries about the PIC system began in 1990, only a year after PIC was adopted. Projects in Asia, the Caribbean, and South America (with Japanese funding), in Central America (with Dutch funding), and in Africa (with United Nations Development Programme and Dutch funding) were initiated through the FAO. In addition to those regional efforts, the FAO's Technical Cooperation Programme added PIC to projects on pesticide regulation—funded by the Rockefeller Foundation and the United States Environmental Protection Agency—in several countries.[92]

Second, the United Nations Institute for Training and Research (UNITAR) launched a two-phase project to implement the *London Guidelines* and thus improve chemicals management in developing countries. In its first phase, started in 1991 with Swiss funding, regional and subregional workshops were conducted with extensive participation by developing countries. An extensive audit of the program, conducted by the Pesticide Service Project of the German Technical Assistance Agency (GTZ), showed that the UNITAR programs have been effective and should be extended.[93] (GTZ itself was extensively involved in funding and conducting PIC and related chemicals and pesticides management activities, and thus was able to give a well-informed evaluation.) At present, that broad first phase is being intensified with UNITAR-supported efforts to help countries develop "national profiles" for chemicals management.[94] Both the extensive and intensive efforts include some attention to PIC. UNITAR has also conducted some regional workshops focused on building capacity to implement PIC.[95] Switzerland, the principal funder of this UNITAR project, has included its support for such activities in its high-profile bid to host the Secretariat of the PIC Convention.[96]

Third, the industry itself conducts some projects to improve pesticides management, often working closely with the FAO. GIFAP, the association of pesticide producers, has required its members to comply with the *Code of Conduct.* GIFAP prepared documents for the FAO/UNEP Secretariat on implementing PIC, and it has added PIC to regional workshops such as those in West Africa.[97] PIC was also one element of GIFAP's US$4 million "Safe Use Project" in three countries—Kenya, Guatemala, and Thailand—completed in 1995. As with the FAO's activities, PIC was added to GIFAP's existing capacity-building activities. Other elements of GIFAP's projects to implement the *Code of Conduct* include education campaigns, development of low-cost protective clothing, and distribution of pesticide antidotes to local hospitals. So far the project has not been extended to other countries, although industry associations and government funding agencies have conducted similar programs on a smaller scale in other countries. GIFAP has had the performance of the Safe Use Project reviewed and found that it has led to measurable improvements in pesticides management.[98] When Danish television crews went to Central America to uncover poisonings caused by Danish-made pesticides, they focused their cameras on Nicaragua.[99] Neighboring Guatemala, where conditions were similar except that the country had been part of GIFAP's Safe Use Project, offered relatively few examples of poor management.

It is difficult to make a precise assessment of how much these activities have contributed to improved capacity in developing countries, how much the improved capacity has led to a more effective PIC system, and how much of this additional capacity has been caused by PIC. Much of the improvement would have occurred anyway as the attention of concerned governments and international organizations turned to the need to manage chemical and pesticide hazards in the late 1980s. However, PIC has added to and benefited from these efforts, a fact most evident from the improved management of pesticides, for which training programs have been extensive and ongoing for decades and where PIC was quickly incorporated. These activities took place without an overarching legal instrument to address all aspects of chemicals and pesticides, nor did it matter that the principal instruments were nonbinding. Rather, the most important factor was that the main participants focused on implementation. In contrast, the succession of UN General Assembly Resolutions and UNEP Governing Council decisions from the late 1970s through the mid-1980s resulted in little practical action on the ground because the supply of legal instruments was not accompanied by implementation efforts.

Analysis of Factors that Explain the Design, Operation, and Effectiveness of PIC

This section reviews the operation of PIC and traces the institutional factors that explain PIC's apparent success. "Institutions" do not explain all of PIC's outcomes. Notably, the interests of stakeholders have been most important. PIC itself was delayed because industry opposed a PIC system; only once some form of additional regulation was inevitable did industry embrace nonbinding PIC as its best alternative. Pressure from public interest groups and governments in a few industrialized countries and in developing countries made such further regulation "inevitable." The existing programs and interests of the FAO and UNEP constrained how these stakeholders expressed their interests and the policy decisions that were made. However, in the larger context of interests and existing institutions, the design of institutions that were particular to PIC had a significant influence on outcomes. Two factors were particularly important: (1) the legal form of commitments (binding or nonbinding); and (2) implementation review. The identification of such particular institutional factors is important because stakeholders that want more effective regulation often have the greatest influence over the design and operation of institutions, although institutions and policy choices often do not explain most of the behavior that is observed.

Legal Status of Agreements

The legal form of the international commitments had a significant influence on policy decisions and outcomes related to PIC. In particular, the use of nonbinding instruments allowed considerable flexibility in the implementation and adjustment of PIC. In 1989, when the FAO *Code* and the UNEP *London Guidelines* were amended to include PIC, it was possible to agree on only the broadest outlines of how the PIC system would operate. Virtually all of the important details—such as which substances would be on the PIC list—were left to be decided later. Two factors that became crucial to PIC's influence—an active meeting of experts that made PIC policy decisions and extending PIC to cover pesticides that were hazardous only under specific conditions of use—had only vaguely been considered in the negotiations that led to adding PIC to the FAO *Code* and the UNEP *London Guidelines*. If PIC had been legally binding, governments probably would have scrutinized the exact legal implications more closely, leading both to delays and to a more restrictive PIC system. If PIC had been restricted, less information would have been transferred to developing countries and PIC would have covered fewer (or none) of the substances that caused the greatest problems in developing countries. Scrutiny of what one signs is important, but in 1989 there was little to be scrutinized; governments wary of uncertain binding obligations would have been especially wary of the ill-formed PIC system if it had been binding.

The benefits of nonbinding agreements can be partially tested using experience from the negotiations under way to convert the nonbinding PIC system to a legally binding PIC Convention, currently taking place in the UNEP/FAO Intergovernmental Negotiating Committee for an International Legally Binding Instrument for the Application of the Prior Informed Consent Procedure for Certain Hazardous Chemicals and Pesticides in International Trade (INC-PIC). This shift is taking place because some European countries, the EC, developing countries, and all public interest groups active in this area believe that a binding convention will be more effective than a nonbinding system.[100] That coalition led UNEP's Governing Council to adopt a decision in 1991 to explore the possible use of a legally binding instrument for PIC;[101] every year since, UNEP has had an active working group or task force considering this issue.[102] The formal decision to pursue a binding instrument was made in the FAO Conference in 1994 and in the UNEP Governing Council in 1995.

When negotiations began, there was widespread agreement on using the voluntary procedure as the basis of the binding Convention.[103] However, none of the groups charged with preparing the negotiations was ever able to consider the lessons learned from the voluntary procedure in detail: they started their work before much had been learned. The final discussion paper from this process, issued late in 1994, was based on work from a task force that had reviewed experience during only the first year of PIC's operation.[104] UNEP established no useful mechanism for gathering and analyzing that experience, beyond the helpful but anecdotal expertise of participants in the meeting and in the UNEP Chemicals Secretariat. UNEP sent surveys to countries that participated in the voluntary procedure, but the response rate was low. Some effort was made to gather data on production and trade of hazardous chemicals—those on the PIC list and/or subjected to a more expansive EC export regulation—but replies were few. The data were only qualitative and gave no indication of whether the voluntary PIC mechanism was failing; the final analysis of the data was completed only in 1995, after the process to convert PIC into a binding instrument was under way.[105]

Thus the process led by advocates of tighter regulation, working mainly through UNEP, has been largely blind to systematic analysis of the experience learned during the voluntary procedure. The premise of their work—that a binding procedure could improve PIC—had not been established before the decision to pursue a binding instrument was made, nor has it been confirmed subsequently. When Elizabeth Dowdeswell, UNEP's Executive Director, opened the first negotiating session for a binding PIC Convention, she said that "[a] legally binding procedure was needed because, as long as compliance was not mandatory, it was susceptible to producing uneven results."[106] The head of the US State Department's team for negotiating environmental agreements, Eileen Claussen, said in an interview conducted after the PIC negotiations began that a PIC Convention was needed because the "voluntary scheme . . . hasn't been terribly successful."[107] Yet the experience appears to have been the opposite: compliance with the nonbinding regulatory commitments in PIC (to make shipments only according to the wishes of importers) has been perfect. Moreover, the voluntary PIC mechanism has been a crucial way to learn through implementation—to learn by doing. Summaries of lessons learned during the voluntary procedure have been regularly supplied to the working groups preparing the negotiations and to the INC-PIC negotiating sessions, but because the voluntary procedure did not operate long, few lessons have been learned; those documents say little beyond what was obvious in 1992 and 1993.[108] From 1991 to 1995, JMPIC repeatedly urged that the voluntary procedure be implemented fully prior to focusing on converting it to a binding instrument. Directly contradicting that advice, in 1994, UNEP's Ad Hoc Group of Experts on the Implementation of the *Amended London Guidelines*—the main UNEP body charged with assessing progress under the voluntary PIC procedure—recommended that PIC be made a binding instrument.[109] Yet 1994 and 1995 marked the first time that the voluntary PIC system was beginning to be widely implemented, making it possible to learn and build upon experience. Only in 1994 did JMPIC start to carefully formalize its rules and procedures and expand beyond the first, simplest, 17 PIC substances.[110] But starting that year the focus, especially in UNEP, began to shift to the negotiation of new, binding instruments. Although implementation of the voluntary procedure has since continued, most efforts (such as preparation of DGDs) were slowed; some activities were stopped. JMPIC—the centerpiece of the voluntary PIC system of learning by doing—has not met since the UNEP Governing Council decided in 1995 to initiate negotiations for a binding PIC Convention.

Not only has the shift to a binding convention stymied implementation, it has also come at considerable financial cost. The joint FAO/UNEP program to implement the voluntary procedure has cost US$1.2 million per biennium.[111] The direct costs of translation, documentation, and meeting support for the negotiations leading to a binding PIC Convention will probably be approximately US$2.5 million (or more) over two years. National delegations have spent double or triple that amount to attend negotiating sessions.[112] Thus the cost of operating the effective voluntary system for several years has been spent on merely converting the system to a binding convention. Often such resources are not interchangeable, but in this case they probably are: the same governments that are paying most of the cost of negotiating the binding PIC Convention (Switzerland, the EU, the Netherlands, and Belgium) have also been the main funders of projects to implement the voluntary PIC procedure. Once in place, a binding PIC system will probably cost twice as much to operate for the same activity (for example, numbers of DGDs, etc.).

In addition to the financial costs, the shift to a binding PIC Convention may have stalled the process of "mutual education" that makes many international environmental regimes effective.[113] Negotiations for a binding system have shifted participation within governments from operational ministries (especially agriculture) that actually regulate pesticide and chemical hazards to foreign ministries. For example, a comparison of attendance lists for all regional workshops on the implementation of PIC in Africa reveals that only 21% of the countries had at least one person from those training workshops on their delegation to the most recent session of negotiations on a binding PIC Convention, despite the availability of financial support to pay for participation of delegates from developing countries.[114] Those people who have gained field experience during the voluntary PIC procedure are not participating in the design of the binding system. The conversion to a binding instrument is resulting in a large loss of information in those countries that PIC was mainly intended to benefit.

System for Implementation Review

When PIC was first adopted, practically no observers articulated the main reason for the PIC system's effectiveness: it allowed learning by doing. The analysis here shows that PIC has been most effective where it has promptly led to efforts to gain practical experience in the field—implementation. However, learning also requires information on what has worked and failed in the efforts to implement PIC. Yet neither the FAO *Code of Conduct* nor UNEP's *Amended London Guidelines* made any provision for regular reporting by participants or for reviews of implementation. By formal design, PIC seems brittle and destined to fail; in practice, it has worked.

In practice, an elaborate system for implementation review (SIR) has emerged around PIC, although little of that system can be traced to the formal provisions in the legal instruments that created PIC. The SIR consists principally of four elements. First and most important is the Joint Group of Experts, which has been the forum for most learning by doing. The Joint Group has assessed the available information and made decisions that have *de facto* adjusted PIC procedures with experience. Where needed information has been absent, the Joint Group has filled gaps with its own expertise. Thus implementation and learning have not been significantly stalled because of inadequate information, a fact most evident in the case of adding "conditions of use" substances to PIC. If a scheme such as the industry-proposed "point system" had been used to identify such substances, rather than the Joint Group's expert judgement, no such substances would be in the PIC system today—the information needed to apply such an objective point system operate did not exist.

Second, international organizations that have conducted field projects on implementation of PIC have also contributed to the SIR. Those projects have produced vital information on which PIC provisions have proved difficult to implement in the field and have made it possible to target resources to implementation problems. In particular, UNITAR, the FAO, and UNEP have conducted a series of regional workshops on implementation of PIC that have helped to identify implementation problems.[115] In turn, these activities are linked to the organizations' broader activities to improve chemicals management, such as under the FAO *Code of Conduct* and the UNEP *Amended London Guidelines*. These links have made both the broader and the PIC-dedicated efforts more effective. In particular, the FAO has conducted two reviews of the broader instrument's effectiveness, which have identified some implementation problems that are now being rectified.[116] UNEP's contribution to the SIR has been less extensive. UNEP's Working Group on Implementation of the *Amended London Guidelines* and its working group and task force that considered ways to strengthen the legal basis of the *London Guidelines* might have helped to review the adequacy and implementation of the voluntary PIC system because they were charged with examining in detail ways to improve the existing voluntary system. They could have formed an active part of PIC's SIR. Indeed, in 1992 the UNEP Secretariat prepared an overview of the main problems with implementation of the voluntary procedure, which the group could have used as the basis for useful assessments and proposed adjustments.[117] (Interestingly, that report did not examine which, if any, of the well-known problems with the voluntary PIC procedure would be ameliorated by conversion to a binding instrument, which by 1991 was a policy change that UNEP was actively considering.) However, in practice these simple and incomplete survey exercises added little value and essentially no new information on PIC's operation. Rather, the UNEP bodies focused on negotiating new instruments.[118] The only substantial suggestion from these UNEP activities to the Joint Group of Experts was to replace "pesticides" with "agrochemicals" in the PIC procedure, which the Joint Group rejected as ill-conceived.[119] Since 1993, this UNEP-sponsored activity has focused on preparations for a binding PIC Convention and has played no significant role in reviewing or improving implementation of the existing procedure.

Field activities and regular reviews by international organizations made it possible to catalog the many (mostly detailed) changes to PIC operation that could improve PIC's effectiveness. PIC training workshops helped to identify pesticides that were hazardous under particular "conditions of use," which in principle would have led to the inclusion of more such substances in PIC if the voluntary procedure had continued.[120] Every session of JMPIC included a briefing on such field activities. Some of the problems identified in the field have led to refinements in the voluntary PIC process, such as improvements in PIC documentation and, most important, pressure to expand PIC from the first group of 5 chemicals and 12 pesticides—which were already heavily regulated in many countries—to other substances that were more widely used. Many of those detailed lessons are in the minds of negotiators converting PIC to a binding instrument, and most come from practical field experience. Indeed, several studies cataloging the problems with the existing PIC procedure were used to identify possible improvements for the binding PIC system; those studies principally relied on the feedback of information from these field programs.

Public interest NGOs provided the third element of PIC's system for implementation review. PAN and IOCU/CI have monitored implementation of the PIC system and, more generally, the *Code of Conduct*. PAN members have conducted case studies on pesticide hazards, especially to farmers and their families, which have helped to illustrate the problems, such as pesticide applications that cause dangers for 99% of cotton pickers (mainly women) in Pakistan and infertility routinely caused by lindane use in Ghana.[121] Extensive local contacts have allowed these NGOs to conduct evaluations of the implementation of PIC and the *Code of Conduct*. While criticized by industry for inaccuracies, these evaluations often have been the only independent assessment of the actual implementation of international rules. The *Code of Conduct* is now slated to be strengthened, in part because these evaluations have highlighted problems and violations of the *Code*. Without NGO pressure, backed by data, the *Code* would not have advanced significantly beyond what was adopted in 1985. As noted, these evaluations also helped to set the agenda for inclusion of "conditions of use" substances. PAN has been the NGO most active and influential in monitoring PIC, but many other NGOs, such as IOCU/CI and the World Wide Fund for Nature (WWF), have also monitored pesticide use while promoting policies that reduce pesticide consumption.[122]

NGOs are much less active in monitoring management of chemicals in developing countries; no comparable review of the *London Guidelines* has ever been conducted, and NGOs have played no significant role in evaluating and proposing chemicals for inclusion in the PIC system.

Industry—the fourth element—has provided vital information on some substances, especially pesticides that are hazardous under "conditions of use." Like the international organizations that conduct field projects, industry has also targeted assistance in some countries, which has improved management of pesticide hazards and probably also implementation of PIC.

In sum, these four elements—the Joint Group of Experts, field programs, public interest NGOs, and industry NGOs—make up a system for implementation review that has made PIC more effective. The activities and interests of the actors in these four elements are different, but together their actions have been partially synergistic. The Joint Group has been able to make decisions mainly because information from industry and public interest NGOs has been available. Improvements to the PIC system, such as refinements to the DGDs, were the result of information feedback from field programs conducted by international organizations (notably the FAO, UNITAR, and UNEP) and, to a lesser degree, industry. The different interests of the main stakeholders have served as a useful balance to each other. Whereas UNEP had been criticized as a handmaiden of environmental interests and the FAO attacked as an advocate of pesticide producers, the joint system with explicitly balanced (and informed) participation from both sides has yielded balanced results. Independent expert review by the Joint Group has also helped to reduce regulatory capture.

Additional synergies are evident when examining the many other legal instruments and activities that govern management of and trade in chemicals and pesticides. OECD's harmonization of laboratory practices has substantially improved the comparability and probably also the accuracy of firm- and national-level data. In turn, this has improved the ability of international organizations to assess chemical and pesticide hazards. As a result, those international bodies—notably JMPR—have been better able to provide useful technical judgements of the risks, which in turn has made it easier to determine which substances should be included in PIC. Accepted procedures for testing and assessing risks have made it easier to evaluate whether chemicals in PIC should remain, as evident in the case of cyhexatin.[123] Few of these procedures and organizations are formally linked, but in practice they work together as a system. Where formal links are being created—notably between the OECD and the UN organizations working on chemical safety (the FAO, ILO, UNEP, WHO)—the links follow much existing informal coordination, they do not lead it.

Conclusions

In the 1970s, public interest NGOs and developing countries pressed for greater control of hazardous exports from industrialized countries. The result was a series of nonbinding resolutions in the UN General Assembly and UNEP. Those resolutions envisioned substantial controls on exports but in practice had little effect on patterns of trade. In UNEP and the OECD, schemes were adopted that urged countries to supply information on exports—"notification systems"—but they merely codified what major countries were already doing and had little effect on behavior.

In 1989 a nonbinding PIC system was adopted by the FAO and UNEP. Although industry and major exporting countries opposed PIC, once it was adopted they embraced the concept as an alternative to more onerous binding rules. The adoption of PIC largely resulted from the efforts of entrepreneurial NGOs, a coalition of developing countries, and an increasingly active handful of European countries that favored tougher export controls, notably Belgium and the Netherlands. The groups had only modest success in tightening EC rules, but through the FAO and especially UNEP they created a global system which, in turn, all industrialized countries have put into practice. Since 1989 PIC has expanded to include more than three dozen substances; so far there has not been a single documented violation of the PIC system.

PIC worked well in part because its nonbinding legal form permitted high flexibility and learning by doing. Many of the key policy decisions for PIC were unresolved or had not even arisen in 1989; a nonbinding instrument allowed those issues to be worked out along the way, without the stifling influence of extensive national review and ratification that accompanies binding legal instruments.

However, while PIC was nonbinding, so were the many failed efforts that preceded it. What set PIC apart was that it marked a pause in efforts, especially those of UNEP, to negotiate numerous legal instruments; instead, UNEP, the FAO, and various NGOs (especially those representing industry) focused on putting PIC into operation. In contrast, earlier nonbinding instruments were merely symbols—they marked aspirations that could not be attained at the time, or they merely reflected the lowest-common-denominator outcome of a negotiated process.

A shift to implementation was necessary for PIC's success. However, learning by doing required extensive efforts to document and review implementation experiences under PIC. Yet the PIC system included no provisions for collecting and analyzing the needed data—to this day, lack of data on production, trade, and effects of hazardous chemicals and pesticides is a critical weakness. Especially problematic is the complete lack of accurate and comparable data on pesticide poisonings in developing countries. Such information is badly needed for setting priorities and monitoring implementation of PIC for pesticides that are hazardous under particular "conditions of use" in developing countries. However, a Joint Group of Experts that met periodically to make PIC policy decisions, various international organizations that implemented projects to build capacity in developing countries (including capacity to implement PIC), public interest NGOs, and industry formed a decentralized SIR. These actors performed functions of implementation review, such as providing information on pesticides that were causing problems in developing countries and identifying needed changes to the PIC system, according to their interests and abilities. The formal provisions for implementation review were almost nonexistent; nonetheless, the SIR has supplied extensive feedback of information, which this analysis shows was crucial to learning by doing in the PIC system.

Notes

This chapter is excerpted from a much more detailed study by the author: Victor, D.G., "Regulating Trade in Hazardous Chemicals and Pesticides: The Origins, Operation and Effectiveness of the Prior Informed Consent (PIC) System," Ph.D. Thesis, Massachusetts Institute of Technology, 3 October 1997, chapter 2. For initial discussions and documents the author thanks Bill Murray (formerly with the FAO, now with the government of Canada), Peter Sand (formerly with the World Bank, now with the University of Munich), and Aase Tuxen (UNEP Chemicals). For documents and background discussions, the author is also grateful to Barbarah Dinham (Pesticides Trust), Birgit Engelhardt (CEFIC), Ronald Macfarlane (Consumers International), Richard Nielsson (GCPF, formerly GIFAP), Jenny Pronczuk de Garbino (WHO), Achim Alexander Halpaap (UNITAR), René von Sloten (CEFIC), and Michael Walls (Chemical Manufacturers Association).

1. The approach taken in this chapter, which identifies the PIC system as emerging from the dual agenda—harmonization and regulation—is consistent with the background to PIC in the account by Pallemaerts: see Pallemaerts, M., 1988, "Developments in International Pesticide Regulation," *Environmental Policy and Law* 18(3):62–69. Other accounts of pesticide regulation, including the origins of PIC, have mainly focused only on regulatory efforts: see, for example, Paarlberg, R.L., 1993, "Managing Pesticide Use in Developing Countries," in P.M. Haas, R.O. Keohane, and M.A. Levy, eds., *Institutions for the Earth: Sources of Effective International Environmental Protection*, The MIT Press, Cambridge, UK, pp. 309–350; and Dinham, B., 1996, "The Success of a Voluntary Code in Reducing Pesticide Hazards in Developing Countries," in *Green Globe Year Book of International Co-operation on Environment and Development*, edited by H.O. Bergesen and G. Parmann, Oxford University Press, New York, NY, USA, pp. 29–36.

2. Throughout, "EC" will be used to denote the European Economic Community (EEC) and European Union (EU), which are different legal and political classifications for the European common market countries.

3. Boardman, R., 1986, *Pesticides in World Agriculture*, St. Martin's Press, New York, NY, USA.

4. The EC approach was to amend an earlier directive on chemicals, rather than create legislation *de novo*. See, for example, Wilkinson, G.B., 1980, "The Sixth Amendment: Toxic Substance Control in the EEC," *Law and Policy in International Business* 12:461–501.

5. For more on US and EC chemicals regulation and harmonization efforts, see two accounts written at the time: Wyman, R.A., 1980, "Control of Toxic Substances: The Attempt to Harmonize the Notification Requirements of the US Toxic Substances Control Act and the European Community Sixth Amendment," *Virginia Journal of International Law* 20:417–458; and Alston, P., 1978, "International Regulation of Toxic Chemicals," *Ecology Law Quarterly* 7:397.

6. An overview of OECD harmonization in the wake of TSCA and the Sixth Amendment is provided in Brickman *et al.*, 1985, *Controlling Chemicals: The Politics of Regulation in Europe and the United States*, Cornell University Press, Ithaca, NY, USA, pp. 281–285.

7. The existence of such a regime is one conclusion from the most authoritative independent comparison of chemicals regulation. See Brickman *et al.*, op. cit., note 6. See also, Ilgen, 1983, "'Better Living Through Chemistry': The Chemical Industry in the World Economy," *International Organization* 37: 647–680.

8. These figures reflect 39 tests identified by GAO on the basis of US testing requirements. Perfect overlap (100%) would be the requirement of each test by each of the OECD nations and the EC (i.e., 19 "countries" × 39 tests = 741 country tests). Figures computed by the author from GAO's survey sent to US embassy officials in the EC and 17 OECD nations. The range reflects all tests as required by law and practice (71%) and all tests except wildlife tests (83%). Because chemical effects depend on the environment in which the chemicals are released, it is understandable that some of the test requirements should vary, notably those concerning wildlife. Some tests must be performed using different procedures—for example, environmental fate tests must be conducted at lower ambient temperatures for countries in cold climates. In those cases, the test is coded as "required" in the relevant countries, but in practice a different test is needed to satisfy the data requirements. GAO also noted that while data requirements are similar, risk assessment, monitoring, and enforcement practices—which also affect the influence of regulations on firm behavior and trade—still vary considerably (see p. 87). GAO briefly reports results from the OECD survey (see pp. 37–38). General Accounting Office (GAO), 1993, *A Comparative Study of Industrialized Nations' Regulatory Systems*, GAO/PEMD-94-17.

9. Based on GAO roundtable meetings (GAO, op. cit., note 8, p. 40). For more on de facto harmonization through implementation, see also Brickman *et al.*, op. cit., note 6.

10. Micklitz, H.-W., 1992, "International Regulation and Control of the Production and Use of Chemicals and Pesticides: Perspectives for a Convention," *Michigan Journal of International Law* 13:653–697.

11. UNCTAD trade statistics for 1981 cited in Norris, R., ed., 1982, *Pesticides, Pills and Profits: The International Trade in Toxic Substances*, North River Press, Croton-on-Hudson, NY, USA.

12. FAO Trade Year Book statistics, 1979, ibid.

13. WHO, 1973, "Safe Use of Pesticides," 20th Report of the WHO Expert Committee on Insecticides, Technical Report Series No. 513, Geneva, Switzerland, cited in Paarlberg, op. cit., note 1, p. 315.

14. Bull, D., 1982, *A Growing Problem: Pesticides and the Third World Poor*, OXFAM, Birmingham, UK.

15. WHO and other data cited in Paarlberg, op. cit., note 1, p. 310. The high number, also based on WHO data, is quoted in Dinham, B., 1991, "FAO and Pesticides: Promotion or Proscription?" *The Ecologist* 21(March/April): 61–65.

16. Jeyaratnam, 1990, "Acute Pesticide Poisoning: A Major Problem," *World Health Statistics Quarterly* 43:139–44, quoted in Dinham, op. cit., note 1.

17. For the fraction of global pesticide application occurring in developing countries, see US AID data cited in Paarlberg, op. cit., note 1, p. 310.

18. No systematic data are collected, and data that do exist typically do not accurately indicate accidental poisonings, which are of interest for the argument here. Many poisonings are intentional because toxic pesticides are an effective means for committing suicide. Data from Paraná, Brazil, for example, show that from 1982 to 1991 approximately 90% of deaths from pesticide poisonings were suicides, with no discernible trend over time; see Tucker, J.C., and Brown, M.A., 1995, "Comparative Analysis of Pesticide Regulatory Programs in the United States and Brazil," *Loy. L.A. Int'l & Comp. L.J.* 18:81–108. Industry data for Nicaragua show that all pesticide-related deaths in 1995 (17 fatalities) and 1996 (27 fatalities) were suicides; see Cheminova, 1997, "Report on the use of Cheminova's products in Central America," 23 May 1997 (report issued in response to Danish TV documentary, see note 99).

19. The role of Dutch financial support in early meetings is mentioned in Paarlberg, op. cit., note 1. Paarlberg also discusses the role of pesticides in food production and views the collapse of world food prices in the early 1980s, and talk of a food surplus, as a critical agenda-setting opportunity. However, research for the present study suggests that this factor was not particularly important; momentum for regulating pesticide use had been under way since the mid-1970s, and the agenda-setting opportunity did not yield much practical action—the legal instruments that followed, until PIC was adopted in 1989, did not have any significant influence on behavior.

20. World Bank, "Operational Directive 4.03" The World Bank Operational Manual, July 1992, Washington, DC, USA; see also World Bank, "Guidelines and Best Practice 4.03", ibid., April 1993. The Directive also requires pesticide management plans, which are similar to the prerequisite for effective IPM and also similar (but narrower than) the country profiles being prepared under UNITAR and IOMC (see notes 94 and 95 below).

21. For extensive discussion of US legislation, especially FIFRA, and related resolutions of UNEP's Governing Council, see Schulberg, F., 1979, "United States Export of Products Banned for Domestic Use," *Harvard International Law Journal* 20:331–383. See also Goldberg, K.A., 1985, "Efforts to Prevent Misuse of Pesticides Exported to Developing Countries: Progressing Beyond Regulation and Notification," *Ecology Law Quarterly* 12:1025–1051.

22. Executive Order 12264.

23. Limits on the president's ability to influence policy, illustrated using the case of Reagan's attack on US pesticides regulation, are analyzed in Hoberg, G., 1990, "Reaganism, Pluralism and the Politics of Pesticide Regulation," *Policy Sciences* 23:257–289.

24. For example, Pallemaerts (op. cit., note 1) cites a 1984 Environmental Protection Agency study on the operation of the US notification system under FIFRA: Halter, F., 1984, How to Improve International Notification Procedures for Pesticides under United States Law, unpublished paper, US Environmental Protection Agency, Washington, DC, USA. The problem of notifications that are never received has improved, but it remains questionable whether the information that is received is useful—for example, the identity of shippers and recipients is typically protected as confidential business information; thus importers are still typically unable to intercept shipments if they want to.

25. Some analysis suggests that Mexico and South Korea were among the countries that stopped importing some substances in response to FIFRA export notifications received from the US: Norris, op. cit., note 11, cited in Goldberg, op. cit., note 21. Surveys cited by Schulberg, (op. cit., note 21, p. 366) show that when export notification was adopted, many countries were keen to receive information: a State Department survey showed that 66% of the responding countries wanted to receive notifications, and a GAO survey found that representatives from developing countries were especially keen to receive notifications because they did not have the capacity to perform hazard analyses comparable to those of the US Environmental Protection Agency.

26. The Dutch PIC system and proposals for an EC PIC system are reviewed in Mehri, C., 1988, "Prior Informed Consent: an Emerging Compromise for Hazardous Exports," *Cornell International Law Journal* 21:365–389.

27. Regulation EEC/1734/88, which applied to member states starting June 1989. It applies only to chemicals listed in an annex, which is adjusted periodically.

28. Bull, op. cit., note 14.

29. For example, in 1975 Japan applied a system of prior informed consent for exports of DDT and BHC. See Pallemaerts, op. cit., note 1.

30. Krueger, J.P., 1996, "Regulating Transboundary Movements of Hazardous Wastes: The Basel Convention and the Effectiveness of the Prior Informed Consent (PIC) Procedure," WP-96-113, International Institute for Applied Systems Analysis, Laxenburg, Austria. The discussion in this chapter does not analyze other links between regulation of hazardous chemicals and pesticides and the Basel Convention. Notably, the line between "hazardous chemical and pesticide" and "hazardous waste" is fuzzy. The line will become even fuzzier as

hazardous chemicals and pesticides become more extensively regulated—for example, under the Convention on Persistent Organic Pollutants, which will be negotiated starting in 1998. Tighter regulation will focus attention on the need to recover, recycle, and properly dispose of organic compounds already in use, in turn leading to transborder industries for that purpose. In general, special efforts have been made to adjust the scope of the PIC Convention so that it will not overlap with the Basel Convention, notably by excluding chemical wastes from the PIC Convention.

31. For a comprehensive survey on the use of PIC up to the late 1980s, see especially Mehri, op. cit., note 26; and Gündling, L., 1989, "Prior Notification and Consultation," in *Transferring Hazardous Technologies and Substances: The International Legal Challenges*, edited by G. Handl and R.E. Lutz, Graham and Trotman, London, UK, pp. 63–82. Mehri and Gündling argue that even in the mid-to-late 1980s, PIC was not a principle of international law. However, today—with PIC having been adopted for trade in hazardous wastes, chemicals, and pesticides—it probably would be classified as a widely accepted principle for regulation of hazardous exports.

32. "OECD Council Adopts Recommendation on Exports of Banned, Restricted Chemicals," *International Environment Reporter*, 11 April 1984, p. 100, cited in Hill, R., 1988, Problems and Policy for Pesticide Exports to Developed Countries, *National Resources Journal* 28:699–720; p. 714.

33. UNEP Governing Council Decision 6/3B, cited in Pallemaerts, op. cit., note 1.

34. GA Resolutions 34/173 (1979), 35/186 (1980), and 36/166 (1981).

35. Resolution 37/137, which urges that banned products be exported only when a "request ... is received from an importing country or when the consumption of such products is officially permitted in the importing country." This development of General Assembly activity is reviewed by Pallemaerts, op. cit., note 1, p. 65. See also Goldberg, op. cit., note 21.

36. UNEP Governing Council Decision 12/14 (1984).

37. UNEP Governing Council Decision 10/24 created the group. For more on the mandate and early negotiations, see "Chemicals and Pesticides in International Trade," *Environmental Policy and Law* 12(3):61–64 (1984).

38. See Pallemaerts, op. cit., note 1, p. 66.

39. For a brief overview of the operation of the Scheme and related activities in the early 1980s, see Goldberg, op. cit., note 21, pp. 1041–1045.

40. Then, as now, "withdrawal" was defined to mean withdrawal for reasons of human or environmental safety. Other withdrawals (e.g., because markets were not profitable) did not constitute a "control action." Bans and severe restrictions were actions taken by governments; withdrawals were made by firms.

41. A selection of national legislation is reviewed in Ad Hoc Working Group of Experts on the Implementation of the *Amended London Guidelines*, first session (15–19 October 1990), UNEP/PIC.WG.3/4.

42. Paarlberg, op. cit., note 1, p. 321.

43. See Pallemaerts, op. cit., note 1. Pallemaerts modestly does not indicate his own role; interviews with others present at the Council meeting suggest that he was instrumental in organizing the coalition.

44. See Pallemaerts, op. cit., note 1, p. 67. For an account of these events that emphasizes that PIC, if adopted, would yield few additional benefits at high cost, see Walls, M.P., 1988, "Chemical Exports and the Age of Consent: The High Cost of International Export Control Proposals," *International Law and Politics* 20:753–775.

45. UNEP Governing Council Decision 15/30 (1989).

46. The relationship was formalized with letters exchanged in November 1992.

47. Even the first FAO/UNEP Joint Meeting of Experts, held in 1989 shortly after the two separate PIC procedures had been adopted, suggested that UNEP and the FAO might even adopt different (but similar) Decision Guidance Documents. The role of the Joint Meeting is discussed below. See Joint Meeting of Experts on Prior Informed Consent (JMPIC), 1989, "Eighth session of the FAO panel of experts on pesticide specifications, registration requirements and application standards, First FAO/UNEP Joint Meeting Report," 18–21 December, p. 8.

48. Pesticides Trust, 1989, *FAO Code: Missing Ingredients*, Zed Books, London, UK.

49. Ad Hoc Working Group of Experts on Prior Informed Consent and other Modalities to Supplement the London Guidelines for the Exchange of Information on Chemicals in International Trade, "Proposed recommendations as presented by the expert from the United Kingdom of Great Britain and Northern Ireland," Second Session, New York, 13–17 February 1989, UNEP/PIC/WG.2/CRP.10.

50. CRP.2.

51. On "treaty congestion" see Brown Weiss, E., 1989, "International Environmental Law: Contemporary Issues and the Emergence of a New World Order," *Georgetown Law Journal* 81:675–710.

52. Notably, many analysts point to the speed at which nonbinding instruments take effect because they do not require ratification and thus do not sit idle during sometimes long periods of "entry into force." On this point, see in particular Sand, P.H., 1990, *Lessons Learned in Global Environmental Governance*, World Resources Institute, Washington, DC, USA.

53. Small shipments (below 10 kg) are excluded. See JMPIC, 1993, Sixth FAO/UNEP Joint Meeting on Prior Informed Consent, 28 June–2 July 1993, p. 12. Shipments of any size for purely research purposes and personal effects are also excluded, as are articles that contain PIC chemicals—the scheme applies only to shipments of the chemicals themselves (ibid., p. 11). There is widespread agreement that similar exemptions should apply to the PIC Convention. See, for example, INC-PIC, 1995, "Comments on the Possible Elements for an International Legally Binding Instrument for the Application of the Prior Informed Consent Procedure for Certain Hazardous Chemicals and Pesticides in International Trade Identified by the Ad Hoc Working Group," Brussels, 11–15 March 1996, UNEP/FAO/PIC/INC.1/3 (8 December), para. 21.

54. ILO Convention #170, adopted in 1990.

55. Indeed, there are no formal "parties" to the PIC agreements. Under international law, countries "adhere to" or "participate in" the PIC system; they do not become parties in the same sense that they become parties to international treaties. This distinction reflects that under international law parties to binding agreements are expected to comply, whereas the moral and legal requirement to comply with nonbinding agreements may be less intense. Whether this assertion is true and its implications for the effectiveness of international agreements are among the subjects considered here.

56. The *Amended London Guidelines* mention an Expert Group in Annex II, but only for the narrow purpose of determining hazardous pesticide formulations. This task has been performed in the identification of so-called Class 1A+ chemicals, discussed below. The *Amended London Guidelines* also mention in passing that "[a]n informal consultative process may be used to assist IRPTC in determining whether the control action meets the definition of the Guidelines." (Article 7.2).

57. The rules adopted to govern access can be found in JMPIC, op. cit., note 53, pp. 21–22.

58. One of the few issues that the Joint Group has not needed to address is the definitions of controlled substances. The standard definitions, codified

in the *Amended London Guidelines* and the FAO *Code of Conduct* are the following: (1) "pesticides," chemicals applied to control pests in agriculture and animal husbandry, disease vectors, defoliants, and plant growth regulators; (2) "industrial chemicals," chemicals used in industrial processes; and, (3) "consumer chemicals," chemicals used for private, nonoccupational purposes. The PIC scheme explicitly excludes other chemicals, such as fertilizers and drugs; the Joint Group also decided to exclude small (less than 10 kg) shipments of consumer chemicals and all chemicals used for laboratory scientific research.

59. JMPIC, op. cit., note 47, p. 3.

60. Annex İİ, *Amended London Guidelines* (1989); no time limit was set for the start-up phase.

61. Industry representatives reported that the list contained many errors, and in 1991 the Joint Group advised that, because of errors and the difficulty of substantiating control actions, the list should be abandoned; JMPIC, 1991, "Third FAO/UNEP joint meeting on Prior Informed Consent (PIC), Report" Rome, 3–7 June, p. 15.

62. The four categories, and explicit omission of a fifth (non-registered pesticides), are reviewed in the first meeting report, JMPIC, op. cit., note 47, pp. 10–11.

63. For discussion and elaboration of the definitions, see JMPIC, op. cit., note 47, p. 5.

64. An example is toxaphene, which was excluded from PIC (although it had been banned in the EC) because the Joint Group thought there was no production. It was later reinstated as a PIC candidate (i.e., recommended for a DGD) when the Group found that production was taking place in a Nicaraguan plant. Similarly, chlordecone was reinstated when it was discovered that the pesticide was produced in Brazil and exported to Africa. JMPIC, 1992, "Fifth FAO/UNEP Joint Meeting on Prior Informed Consent (PIC) Report" 26–30 October, p. 17.

65. JMPIC, 1990, "Second FAO/UNEP joint meeting on prior informed consent, Report," Geneva, 1–5 October, p. 14.

66. The bifenthrin case is reviewed in JMPIC, op. cit., note 65, p. 12.

67. JMPIC, op. cit., note 47, p. 8.

68. The only minor exception is HCH and isomers. The PIC scheme adopts a general term to cover isomer mixtures, "HCH, mixed isomers," whereas the EC regulation specifies fractions of a specific isomer: "HCH containing less than

99.0% of the gamma isomer." The extent to which the lists conform is astounding. Even the bizarre ordering of industrial chemicals on the UNEP/FAO PIC list, for example, reflects the ordering of the list in the Community's regulation, which sorts chemicals by whether they are banned (b) or severely restricted (sr), and within each category lists the compound according to CAS number. For the Community Regulation see EEC Regulation 1734/88. That regulation is superseded by the EC Regulation 2455/92, by which the EC implemented PIC; substances 1–21 of Annex I are the original 21 chemicals and pesticides included in the EC's notification system.

69. Joint FAO/UNEP Programme for the Operation of Prior Informed Consent, "Decision Guidance Documents: Aldrin, DDT, dieldrin, dinoseb and dinoseb salts, fluorocetamide and HCH (mixed isomers)," Rome (1991).

70. See JMPIC, 1994, "Seventh FAO/UNEP Joint Meeting on Prior Informed Consent (PIC) Report" 21–25 March, pp. 19–20; and JMPIC, 1995, "Eighth FAO/UNEP Joint Meeting on Prior Informed Consent Report," Geneva, 6–10 March, pp. 21–22.

71. JMPIC, op. cit., note 61, p. 17.

72. JMPIC, op. cit., note 64, p. 16.

73. JMPIC, 1995, op. cit., note 70, p. 10.

74. For the Joint Group's criteria for setting priorities for the completion of DGDs for PIC-eligible chemicals, see JMPIC, 1995, op. cit., note 70, pp. 12–13.

75. The term currently most widely used in official documents is "acutely hazardous pesticide formulations which have not been banned or severely restricted in any country for health or environmental reasons, but which are causing problems under conditions of use found in developing countries." For the source of this term, see note 79. Industry had documented to the Joint Group that misinterpretations—that is, treating lists of pesticide formulations that were candidates for "conditions of use" inclusion as a "blacklist"—had occurred. Since 1993, this concern of industry has also led the Joint Group to exclude candidate lists from its reports. For similar reasons, an extensive disclaimer has been added to the cover of DGDs for "conditions of use" substances. Moreover, the Joint Group of Experts instructed the Secretariat to make a special effort to explain the purpose of the "conditions of use" inclusion in the PIC system. See, JMPIC, op. cit., note 53, pp. 17–19. In the PIC Convention, these "conditions of use" substances will probably be termed "acutely hazardous pesticide formulations."

76. For the current contents of WHO lists, see International Programme on Chemical Safety, 1996, The WHO Recommended Classification of Pesticides by Hazard and Guidelines to Classification, 1996–1997, WHP/PCS/96.3.

77. *Amended London Guidelines*, Annex II.

78. Pesticides Trust, 1989, FAO Code: Missing Ingredients, London, UK. The NGO list was as follows: aldicarb, carbofuran, dichlorvos, methamidophos, methomyl, moncrotophos, parathion methyl, paraquat, and phosphamidon. Eight were WHO Class 1A or 1B substances; paraquat formulations were listed only as WHO Class 2, but widespread improper use made the substance hazardous.

79. Here and throughout this chapter, the term "PIC list" is used to denote the list of chemicals and pesticides that are in the PIC system (i.e., DGDs have been circulated) or that have been given a priority for inclusion in the PIC system (i.e., DGDs are being prepared and reviewed). However, the author is mindful that the term is controversial because industry fears that it will be viewed as synonymous with a "blacklist." Industry's fears of this, which have been documented, are especially acute in the case of "conditions of use" substances because such substances are not included in the PIC system because of severe regulation. The long and complicated title for "conditions of use" pesticides (see note 75) is also the result of this sensitivity. See, for example, JMPIC, op. cit., note 53, p. 17.

80. Methyl bromide has since been removed as a candidate because it is being regulated under the Montreal Protocol on Substances that Deplete the Ozone Layer. For information on how the 10 substances on this short list were selected, see JMPIC, op. cit., note 64, pp. 8–9. See also, JMPIC, op. cit., note 65, pp. 8–9. Later the closely related substance parathion was added to the list, based mainly on a WHO draft Environmental Health Criteria (EHC) document on parathion. See JMPIC, op. cit., note 61, p. 16. Parathion was not named as a priority according to the NGO survey but was on the WHO Class 1A list and had long been the subject of scrutiny by pesticide experts. It was, for example, part of the Pesticide Action Network's "Dirty Dozen" list.

81. Their role here resonated with an earlier request from the Joint Group that the Secretariat "obtain information on pesticides in the WHO category 1A and any other pesticides regardless of the hazard category, that have been observed to cause problems due to toxicity and under conditions of use in their countries." JMPIC, op. cit., note 47, p. 12.

82. For example, a briefing on paraquat by its producer (ICI) discussed paraquat hazards that were important for the DGD on paraquat, which was being revised at the time. JMPIC, 1992, "Fourth FAO/UNEP joint meeting on Prior Informed Consent (PIC), Report," Geneva, 17–21 February, p. 19.

83. However, many substances in this category were registered elsewhere and then banned or severely restricted, and thus are already eligible for inclusion

in PIC. Some were already on the PIC priority lists, and many did not have sufficient testing data to allow the compilation of a DGD. See JMPIC, op. cit., note 65, pp. 12-13.

84. See JMPIC, op. cit., note 82, p. 9; JMPIC, op. cit., note 64, p. 9.

85. For the point system, which was tested but never used in practice, see JMPIC, op. cit., note 64, Annex 2.

86. Parathion, methyl parathion, monocrotophos (600 g/l formulation and higher), methamidophos (600 g/l formulation and higher), and phosphamidon (1,000 g/l formulation and higher). I also include paraquat in the list, which was on the initial PIC list (see JMPIC, op. cit., note 61, report, Table 1) but has not yet been implemented. The Joint Group reviewed the paraquat decision in 1992 and deferred consideration of the chemical. JMPIC, op. cit., note 64, pp. 17–19.

87. For the decision to write DGDs for the active ingredient, see JMPIC, 1994, op. cit., note 70, p. 19.

88. A list of those 38 substances and priorities developed by JMPIC for the preparation of DGDs is available in JMPIC, 1995, op. cit., note 70, pp. 13–15.

89. The fifth chemical is crocidolite, a form of asbestos; an EHC for asbestos was published in 1986.

90. This general point is illustrated by a UNEP survey of 10 political units—6 industrialized countries, 3 developing countries, and the European Community—conducted in 1990. The three developing countries (Ghana, Malaysia, and Mexico) had no national legislation, registration and licensing, or import policies regarding industrial chemicals; however, all had legislation, registration and licensing, and import policies for pesticides. Each also had prohibitions or severe restrictions on the books for some pesticides, though none of the countries was classified as enforcing those rules. See Ad Hoc Working Group of Experts on the Implementation of the *Amended London Guidelines*, "Review of Activities Related to the Production and Use of Chemicals, Report of the Secretariat," Nairobi, 15–19 October 1990, UNEP/PIC.WG.3/4 (24 September 1990), tables 1–2.

91. Interviews.

92. For a survey, see JMPIC, op. cit., note 64, pp. 3–4; JMPIC, op. cit., note 53, p. 3.

93. Pesticide Service Project, Deutsche Gesellschaft für Technische Zusammenarbeit (GTZ) GmbH, Report on the Assessment of the "UNEP/UNITAR Training Programme on the Implementation of the London Guidelines, Eschborn, Germany (December).

94. UNITAR, Preparing a National Profile to Assess the National Infrastructure for Management of Chemicals—A Guidance Document (no date).

95. These programs are conducted in cooperation with other international organizations, notably through the Inter-Organization Programme for the Sound Management of Chemicals (IOMC) and in particular UNEP. However, the main actor is UNITAR. For an overview see UNITAR, 1997, The UNITAR/IOMC National Profile Capacity Building Programme (February). For more on earlier UNITAR activities directly on PIC, see note 115. The in-depth component has been developed through a pilot program in four countries (Argentina, Ghana, Indonesia, and Slovenia); see UNITAR, Planning and Implementing a National Action Programme for Integrated Chemicals Management (May 1997).

96. For information on its bid, see, for example, Government of Switzerland, "Geneva and PIC," circulated at INC-PIC, 30 May 1997.

97. JMPIC, 1995, op. cit., note 70, p. 3.

98. Information derived from three documents prepared by industry: Safe Use Project (Thailand), Safe Use Project (Kenya), and Plant Protection: Safe Use Projects in Latin America (Guatemala). All three are available from the Global Crop Protection Federation (formerly GIFAP). Additional information from GIFAP briefings at JMPIC meetings. In interviews, none of the other stakeholders has ever questioned the veracity of these reports or the accomplishments of the GIFAP Safe Use Project.

99. The documentary focuses on parathion and methyl parathion poisonings in Nicaragua. TV94, "Made in Denmark," 34 Minutes, Copenhagen, Denmark.

100. Support from developing countries for a binding convention dates back to the late 1970s, although the language of the debate at that time did not employ the "PIC" term, nor was there much focus on the legal status of possible commitments—no significant commitments were forthcoming, as discussed at length in this chapter. EC support is principally due to the entrepreneurial leadership of the Belgian and Dutch governments, which since the late 1980s have thought that a binding convention would be more effective. Support for this position by public interest NGOs is difficult to date; by the late 1980s, several were advocating a binding convention. In 1993, Pesticides Trust and the Foundation for International Environmental Law and Development (FIELD), a legal consultancy, reported results from their review of the legal framework for pesticides, which concluded that an international convention on pesticides was needed. (See Ad Hoc Working Group of Experts on the Implementation of the *Amended London Guidelines*, "Report of the Ad Hoc Working Group on the Work of its Third Session," Geneva, 25–29 January, UNEP/PIC/WG.1/3/5

(23 April), para. 65.) The unity of their position is certainly evident in the INC-PIC negotiations, where Consumers International and PAN have argued, "We strongly support the need for a framework convention . . ." (Consumers International (CI) and Pesticides Action Network (PAN), 1997, "An NGO Submission to the Third International [sic] Negotiating Committee of the International Legally Binding Instrument for the Application of the Prior Informed Consent Procedure for certain hazardous chemicals and pesticides in international trade," Geneva, 26–30 May, notes 1–2).

101. Decision 16/35.

102. In particular, the Ad Hoc Working Group of Experts on the Implementation of the *Amended London Guidelines*. This group established a task force to consider modalities for the development of a legally binding instrument for the mandatory application of the PIC procedure.

103. INC-PIC, 1996, "Comments on the Possible Elements for an International Legally Binding Instrument for the Application of the Prior Informed Consent Procedure for Certain Hazardous Chemicals and Pesticides in International Trade Identified by the Ad Hoc Working Group," Brussels, 11–15 March, UNEP/FAO/PIC/INC.1/3 (8 December), para. 3.

104. Informal Consultative Meeting to Consider Major Issues Related to the Development of a Legally Binding Instrument for the Application of the Prior Informed Consent Procedure, 1994, "Major Issues Related to the Development of a Legally Binding Instrument for the Application of the Prior Informed Consent Procedure," Geneva, 1–2 December 1994, UNEP/PIC/CONS.5/2 (17 November).

105. INC-PIC, 1995, "Study on International Trade in Widely Prohibited Chemicals," Brussels, 11–15 March, UNEP/FAO/PIC/INC.1/9 (22 December 1995).

106. INC-PIC, 1996, "Report of the Intergovernmental Negotiating Committee for an International Legally Binding Instrument for the Application of the Prior Informed Consent Procedure for Certain Hazardous Chemicals and Pesticides in International Trade on the Work of its First Session," Brussels, 11–15 March 1996, UNEP/FAO/PIC/INC.1/10 (21 March), para. 10.

107. Interview, "Claussen: Art of Treaty Negotiation," *Chemical and Engineering News*, 2 June 1997, pp. 22–26.

108. See, for example, INC-PIC, 1995, "Experience in the Implementation of the Prior Informed Consent Procedure," Brussels, 11–15 March 1996, UNEP/FAO/PIC/INC.1/6 (19 December 1995). See also INC-PIC, 1995, "Review of Issues Relevant to the Implementation of the Existing, Voluntary PIC

Procedure: Note by the Secretariat," 11–15 March, UNEP/FAO/PIC/INC.1/5 (19 December). The importance of the voluntary procedure is evident not only in what is included in the PIC procedure, but also in what is excluded. For example, "conditions of use" substances are included, but chemicals that have only handling restrictions are not: in the voluntary procedure, the Joint Group of Experts devised a useful procedure for the former but made little progress on the latter. (See UNEP/FAO/PIC/INC.1/5, p. 7.)

109. Ad Hoc Working Group of Experts on the Implementation of the *Amended London Guidelines*, 1994, "Report of the Ad Hoc Working Group of Experts on the Work of Its Fourth Session," UNEP/PIC/WG.1/4/5 (15 April), para. 89.

110. A stark increase in the formality of JMPIC is evident starting at the Seventh Meeting, where special care was taken to document what the group decided—in essence, to build up the PIC procedures through the accumulation of expert decisions and debates informed by implementation in the field. See JMPIC, 1994, op. cit., note 70.

111. UNEP/FAO/PIC/INC.1/4 (19 December 1995), annex.

112. These figures are estimates made by the author for travel, local, and support costs. The direct costs (to the UNEP/FAO Secretariat) of converting are easier to measure—approximately US$500,000 for translation, meeting space, support, and documents for a 5-day session. PIC is being negotiated through five 5-day sessions, plus a diplomatic conference (in Rotterdam), which may also include a negotiating session.

113. Sand, P., 1990, in Helm, J., ed., *Energy: Production, Consumption and Consequences*, National Academy Press, Washington, DC, USA.

114. Names of delegation members were taken from the published list available at the Third Session, Intergovernmental Negotiating Committee for an International Legally Binding Instrument for the Application of the Prior Informed Consent Procedure for Certain Hazardous Chemicals and Pesticides in International Trade. (These lists are not officially published but are available to delegates and observers.) The workshops were the two UNITAR workshops on PIC in Africa, funded by the European Commission (Directorate-General for Development, DGVII) and the German Technical Assistance Agency (GTZ): UNITAR/FAO/UNEP, "Workshop on the Implementation of Prior Informed Consent (PIC) and the Sound Management of Chemicals for Countries of Southern and Eastern Africa," Johannesburg, South Africa, 4–8 September 1995; UNITAR/FAO/UNEP, "Workshop on the Implementation of Prior Informed Consent (PIC) and the Sound Management of Chemicals for countries of Western and Central Africa," Accra, Ghana, 22–26 July 1996.

115. Ninety-two developing countries have participated in regional and sub-regional workshops on PIC, and there have been seven national PIC workshops (with five more slated for 1997). See UNITAR, 1997, Training and Capacity Building Programmes in Chemicals Management—Information Note, May. For reports from regional workshops see, for example, "Regional Follow-up Workshop on the Implementation of Prior Informed Consent (PIC)," FAO/UNEP/UNITAR, in cooperation with GTZ, Cha-Am, Thailand, 13–16 December 1993, Workshop Report. Workshops were also conducted in Africa (see note 114) and in Latin America. For an early overview of the UNITAR training activities, funded by the Dutch and Swiss governments, see UNITAR/UNEP, 1992, UNEP/UNITAR Training Programme on the Implementation of the London Guidelines—Information Note, 1 March.

116. One in 1986 (published in 1989); the other in 1993 and 1994 (published in 1995): FAO, 1989, *International Code of Conduct on the Distribution and Use of Pesticides: Analysis of Responses to the Questionnaire by Governments*, GC/89/BP.1; FAO, 1995, *Review of the Implementation of the International Code of Conduct on the Distribution and Use of Pesticides*.

117. Ad Hoc Working Group of Experts on the Implementation of the *Amended London Guidelines*, 1992, "Problems Encountered by Governments in the Implementation of the PIC Procedure," Third Session, Geneva, 25–29 January 1993, UNEP/PIC/WG.1/3/3/Add.1 (4 December).

118. The penchant for new law extended to the drafting of model national legislation, although surveys done at the time showed that nearly all countries already had legislation—the weak link was implementation. See Ad Hoc Working Group of Experts on the Implementation of the *Amended London Guidelines*, 1990, "Draft Model National Legislation on the Management of Chemicals for the Implementation of the *Amended London Guidelines*," UNEP/PIC.WG.3/3 (17 September). The author has never seen an analysis of the influence of this draft legislation, nor has the importance of this legislation received any significant attention in any of the documentation related to the voluntary PIC procedure. The working group also contributed to the development of a Code of Ethics, which has not been followed by any implementation activity and appears to have had no influence on behavior; it does, however, mirror what was already under way by reproducing parts of the *Amended London Guidelines*, require firms to comply with the PIC procedure, and echo much of what chemical firms were already implementing through industry programs such as "Responsible Care." See UNEP, "Code of Ethics on the International Trade in Chemicals," agreed at the Informal Consultation on a Code of Ethics on the International Trade in Chemicals (Fourth Session, Geneva, 8 April 1994).

119. JMPIC, op. cit., note 61, p. 20.

120. For example, see the identification of paraquat, aldicarb, endosulfan, fenitrothion 60% EC and 96% EC, fenthion, carbofuran granules, and diazinon in the PIC workshop for Southern and Eastern Africa. Regional Workshop for Southern and Eastern Africa, op. cit., note 114.

121. These examples are cited, for example, in Consumers International (formerly IOCU) and Pesticides Action Network, op. cit., note 100.

122. One American NGO has also analyzed implementation of the *Code*, but the study seems to have had no influence on the *Code*'s subsequent development. See Hansen, M., and Rengam, S., Violating the Code: A Preliminary Survey of Indonesia, The Philippines and Thailand, Institute for Consumer Policy Research, Mount Vernon, New York, NY, USA, cited in Mehri, op. cit., note 26.

123. That only one substance has been removed from PIC is hardly surprising since the standards for inclusion in PIC are stringent. Unlike with other international environmental accords, the removal of a substance from PIC was impressively swift. In contrast, it has proved very difficult to gain agreement to remove species from Annex I of CITES and thus to allow resumption of commercial trade.

7

Data Quality and Compliance Control in the European Air Pollution Regime

Juan Carlos di Primio

Introduction

Most environmental treaties require that the parties inform one another about the progress of implementation, exchanging information by means of national reports issued at regular intervals. Most also require that these national reports be evaluated in an appropriate body where the parties review one another's performance and often take action in response to implementation problems. These procedures are collectively referred to in this volume as *systems for implementation review* (SIRs). Chapters 2 to 6 show that SIRs are a common feature of environmental accords and discuss ways SIRs make accords more effective. The presence and operation of SIRs reflect the parties' desire to know whether others have complied, and continue to comply, with their commitments under a particular agreement. Satisfying that demand fundamentally depends on the completeness and reliability of the information available: the backbone of SIRs is data. This chapter examines the sources, reliability, and uses of data in one case and addresses the question, To what degree are the data of extant SIRs of international environmental agreements sufficient to provide information on whether parties comply with their regulatory commitments?

The case studied here is the European air pollution regime, in particular, the Convention on Long-Range Transboundary Air Pollution (LRTAP). Because of its nearly two-decade history, its complexity, and the character of its membership (most parties are highly industrialized European states), LRTAP is among the regimes most likely to include an extensive system for collecting and reviewing data. Widely regarded as a success, the LRTAP Convention's approach to implementation review provides a model for the design of data systems elsewhere.

Although the LRTAP implementation review system provides a sound basis for verifying compliance, it has not been used for this purpose. Rather, the system has largely focused on improving data quality and the methodologies for data collection and collation; these steps have significantly enhanced the functioning of the SIRs and the regime. In this context, many analysts have pointed to the problem of developing countries' low technical capacity to report data, yet the LRTAP case points to a different problem: assembling a useful integrated international data set has required harmonizing the many divergent and well-entrenched national data collection and collation schemes. The highest degree of entrenchment—and the greatest resistance to full harmonization—is evident in the countries with the greatest existing capacity. The LRTAP system is distinctive in another respect: the monitoring capacity—embodied in the Cooperative Programme for Monitoring and Evaluation of the Long-Range Transmission of Air Pollutants in Europe (EMEP)—existed before the regulatory commitments were in place, though this capacity has been significantly enhanced over the lifetime of LRTAP. Thus the LRTAP commitments were negotiated alongside a well-functioning monitoring mechanism operating on a parallel track. Finally, while formally the data contained in national reports remain unchallenged, as a matter of practice LRTAP and EMEP officials have been aware of compliance problems. The regime is increasingly moving to address noncompliance formally.

The next section treats general aspects of the LRTAP regime, and the third section discusses EMEP. The last section discusses results and presents some conclusions.

The LRTAP Regime

A variety of aspects of the LRTAP regime have been addressed over the past two decades.[1] This section provides a brief overview of the origins of research and policy responses to the acid rain problem, the LRTAP regime, and the SIRs that are part of that regime.

Overview

The acidification of rain was observed long before negotiations began on LRTAP.[2] In Europe, the chemical composition of precipitation was first measured in 1947 in a Swedish network of stations. The network was progressively extended to other European countries during the 1950s, eventually comprising nearly 100 stations. In the early 1960s, many of these stations observed increasing acidity in precipitation. In 1968, S. Odén showed that acid precipitation in Scandinavia was expanding annually; he attributed the increase to sulfur emissions transported from remote sources.[3] These findings were reported to international fora: in 1969 to the Organisation for Economic Co-operation and Development (OECD) and in 1972 at the Stockholm Conference on the Environment, which identified transboundary air pollution as a problem requiring urgent attention in industrialized countries. In the early 1980s forest damage and decline in Central Europe, initially ascribed to acid rain, became an issue of widespread concern.

The first in-depth scientific study of regional acidification started in 1972, under OECD auspices, "to determine the relative importance of local and distant sources of sulfur compounds in terms of their contribution to the air pollution over a region, special attention being paid to the question of acidity in atmospheric precipitations."[4] Coordination responsibilities for measurements and analysis of data were assigned to a central coordinating unit. The OECD study is of special interest because it established the approach that was later to be followed and extended under LRTAP:

> [T]o work out an emission survey based on information from the participating countries and to establish a number of representative ground level stations in each of them. Information on the vertical distribution of sulfur compounds should be obtained through aircraft sampling. The interpretation of the data was to be based on atmospheric dispersion models.[5]

The OECD program began operating in early 1973. An evaluation of available results in September 1973 showed that the "long-range transport of air pollutants was of considerable importance in the acidification of precipitation"[6]— namely, that an extensive exchange of air pollution takes place among all European countries and that about 20 percent leaves the area. Monitoring and evaluation activities were expanded. In 1977, EMEP was established under the auspices of the United Nations Economic Commission for Europe (UN/ECE) in cooperation with the World Meteorological Organization (WMO) and the UN Environment Programme (UNEP), funded by member states' contributions and by UNEP.[7]

LRTAP: Institutions and Commitments

After extensive negotiations within the UN/ECE, LRTAP was adopted in 1979 and entered into force in 1983; by 1995 it had a membership of 39 parties, including the European Union (EU).[8] LRTAP's supreme decision-making assembly is the Executive Body (EB), constituted within the framework of the UN/ECE yet formally independent. Formed by representatives of all contracting parties, the EB meets at least once a year to review the implementation of the Convention. The EB also regularly adopts a work plan that sets priorities for LRTAP, including those related to negotiating new commitments and strengthening existing commitments that are inadequate. The functions of Secretariat have been assigned to the UN/ECE. A number of expert working groups (WGs), international cooperative programs (ICPs), and intergovernmental task forces (TFs) help put the work plan into action.

LRTAP is a framework agreement within which the parties identify problems posed by transboundary air pollution and elaborate protocols for air pollution control and abatement. Five protocols have been adopted.

In its first protocol, LRTAP incorporated EMEP as a principal institution of the Convention and created a funding mechanism for it.[9] Within LRTAP, the main objective of EMEP is to supply governments with information on the deposition and concentration of air pollutants and on the quantity and significance of their fluxes across national boundaries. EMEP is managed by a Steering Body, under which three centers operate: the Chemical Coordinating Centre (CCC) in Norway is responsible for the supervision of the chemical measurement program, data-quality assurance, management, and storage; the Meteorological Synthesizing Centre-West (MSC-W) in Oslo and the Meteorological Synthesizing Centre-East (MSC-E) in Moscow are responsible for modeling the transport and deposition of pollutants.

LRTAP's second protocol, known as the Helsinki Protocol, commits parties to "reduce their national annual sulfur emissions or their transboundary fluxes by at least 30 per cent as soon as possible and at the latest by 1993, using 1980 levels as the basis for calculation of reductions."[10] The Helsinki Protocol also requires parties to report on their annual sulfur emissions and the calculation method and on their national policies and strategies to reduce sulfur emissions or their transboundary fluxes.

The third LRTAP regulatory protocol committed parties to freeze annual emissions of nitrogen oxides (NO_x) or their transboundary fluxes at the level in 1987 (or any earlier year) by the end of 1994.[11] It also requires that parties control NO_x emissions from major stationary sources and apply emission standards to new mobile sources. Reporting is required on annual national emissions of NO_x, as well as on policies to reduce emissions (e.g., emission standards).

A regulatory protocol on volatile organic compounds (VOCs) was adopted in November 1991 but is not yet in force.[12] VOCs are precursors to secondary photochemical oxidants and urban smog; the Protocol principally requires parties to reduce VOC emissions by at least 30 percent by 1999, using the emission level in 1988 (or any year from 1984 to 1990) as the reference.

The Helsinki Protocol concerning sulfur emissions has recently been succeeded by the Protocol on Further Reduction of Sulfur Emissions (the Second Sulphur Protocol). This fifth LRTAP protocol was adopted in June 1994 and is currently in the process of ratification. The Protocol sets reduction obligations so that "depositions of oxidized sulfur compounds in the long term do not exceed critical loads for sulfur, given . . . as critical sulfur depositions, in accordance with present scientific knowledge." This formulation introduces differentiated reduction rates that are guided by a scientific assessment of pollution effects. The requirements of parties to report are similar under the two sulfur protocols.

EMEP has prepared reporting guidelines and recommendations concerning the content, extent, and frequency of national reports on emission data.[13] On several occasions the EB has interpreted the text of the Convention and its protocols—for example, concerning the parties' obligations to report to LRTAP on their fulfillment of requirements under Article 8, in relation to the definition of "transboundary fluxes," and on the continuing commitment of parties to the Helsinki Protocol not to increase their emissions after the 1993 target date.[14]

LRTAP's System for Implementation Review

As in environmental accords in general,[15] LRTAP's formal procedures for reviewing implementation and responding to implementation problems are not extensive, virtually no attention has been given to independent verification, and all data used to evaluate national compliance are reported by the nations themselves. Despite these potential weaknesses, which are common to most international environmental regimes, the following four elements of an SIR can be identified: required national reports on emissions, policies, and strategies; EMEP's monitoring and modeling activities; functions of the Secretariat related to review, especially the preparation of major four-year reviews of national implementation; and yearly reviews of implementation by the EB. The first element concerns activities that the parties are obliged to perform. These are complemented and extended by the second element—the activities of EMEP. The bulk of this chapter concerns the first two elements related to data. However, we now briefly mention the other two elements, which concern the actual implementation review process.

Major reviews of national implementation strategies and policies are undertaken every four years.[16] The only body with the authority to review implementation is the EB, which evaluates information on emissions, national programs, policies, and strategies summarized in the annual and four-year reviews. The EB also approves the work plan drafted by the Secretariat. In addition to drafting the work plan, the Secretariat is entrusted with preparing both annual and major reviews on the basis of national submissions, enhanced with information from other *official* sources, such as EMEP, WGs, TFs, and ICPs. (Although their work is only summarily reported in the reviews, the information provided by official sources is fundamental. Therefore, some activities of these bodies should be seen as an essential part of the LRTAP SIR process.)

The yearly review of implementation at the general EB meetings consists mainly of a perusal of the reports drafted by the Secretariat. No analyses of national strategies and policies, or of compliance, are undertaken at the meetings; nor have any formal disputes arisen. The LRTAP dispute-settlement mechanism has never been used. The VOC Protocol and the Second Sulphur Protocol both create formal procedures, modeled on the Montreal Protocol's Non-Compliance Procedure (see Chapter 4), to review instances of noncompliance; neither has begun operating.[17]

Data on Implementation: The Roles of EMEP and National Reports on Emissions

EMEP engages in a wealth of activities related to data collection, collation, assessment, and use; these activities represent the core of a monitoring system that has no precedents in the field of international environmental regulation.[18] Over time, measures undertaken by EMEP have steadily increased both the quantity and the reliability of data; without these activities, the availability of data adequate for useful modeling would be limited and the capacity to verify compliance with emission targets would be low. EMEP's basic work involves the following activities: collation and evaluation of emission data reported by parties, including the development (with other institutions) of a common methodology for calculating emissions; design, coordination, quality assurance, and control of measurements of air and precipitation quality; and modeling of atmospheric dispersion of chemicals on the basis of emission data and relevant meteorological parameters. These activities are considered below.

Emissions

Anthropogenic emissions are not directly measured, but are calculated.[19] In general terms, estimates are arrived at by multiplying each source's activity rate, such as tons of coal consumed per year, by an appropriate emission factor, such as sulfur dioxide (SO_2) emitted per ton of coal burned. Most of the relevant substances are formed during fossil fuel combustion. There are two main approaches to compiling emission data from the energy sector: a top-down methodology based on aggregated energy statistics that contain energy data and energy balances showing consumption (the activity rate) in the principal economic sectors and a limited number of average emission factors; and a bottom-up approach, in which a selection of several socioeconomic activities (e.g., combustion of fossil fuels at large power plants) requires the identification of a great number of specific emission factors. The estimation of anthropogenic emissions from sources other than energy is based upon a few studies of national situations. The huge amount and variety of statistical information that must be gathered, collated, and assessed, as well as the inherent difficulties in determining activity rates and emission factors, introduces errors into the estimates, whose uncertainty is generally poorly understood.

To date most emission data have been prepared using national methodologies. Many parties, in particular the most industrialized states, have developed detailed methods to determine emission rates that are distinctively different from methods used by other states in a number of ways. For instance, variations in fuel specifications and the definition and composition of the economic sectors (such as the relative shares of different transportation modes) affect corresponding activity rates and emission factors. A number of states have used the top-down approach based on gross activity aggregates and average emission factors. For these reasons, comparability of national emission inventories is poor, so it is difficult to apply a national methodology directly to other country situations.[20] A common methodology would improve the consistency of results and the comparability across countries. It would also improve the reliability of data. Both the EU and the LRTAP regime have taken steps to develop basic methodologies and guidelines for preparing emission inventories. That these two activities have been conducted synergistically, although only EMEP is formally a part of LRTAP, illustrates the importance of viewing data management, and the whole process of implementation review, as a system.

The EU's CORINAIR Methodology.   Concerned by expert views that environmental data in Europe were of low quality, in 1985 the EU established an "experimental project for gathering, coordinating and ensuring the consistency of information on the state of the environment and natural resources in the Community," identified with the acronym CORINE.[21] Within it the CORINAIR project was created to collect and organize information on emissions relevant to transboundary air pollution, including acid deposition. A task force was formed in 1986 with experts from national agencies to develop a common methodology and to calculate a 1985 prototype emission inventory; this was completed in 1990, and has recently been published.[22] A second inventory (CORINAIR 90 for the year 1990) has been compiled, and follow-up activities by the EU European Environment Agency (EEA) aim at developing annual inventories from 1994 on.[23] The methodology follows a bottom-up approach; it uses data on the types of plants or vehicles, emission control equipment, and other factors to estimate emissions. Plant-specific information is required on a number of point sources (power plants, airports, refineries), whereas other smaller and/or more diffuse sources (motor vehicles, agriculture) are treated on an area basis. Common guidelines for estimating emissions were prepared, but countries may use detailed country-specific data if they better reflect particular national conditions.[24] Although CORINAIR allows flexibility in the estimation of emissions from each activity, the CORINAIR methodology also provides for consistency by specifying the main source sectors and subsectors in which each activity is to be quantified. CORINAIR constitutes an important step toward increasing the transparency and comparability of national emission inventories, opening the way for improvements in the quality-control process.

The LRTAP Task Force on Emission Inventories.   The LRTAP Convention does not incorporate any explicit provisions regarding the completeness and reliability of emission information in national reports. The data provided by the parties are stored in databases and, in principle, are accepted unchallenged.[25] However, complaints about data quality and delays in reporting have been voiced at various meetings. These complaints have increased the attention devoted to emission data.

A 1990 EMEP workshop drafted a set of guidelines for estimating and re-porting national emissions which proposed, inter alia, that annual emission data should be provided on the 11 major source categories agreed upon with the CORINAIR project. Thereafter, the EB appointed the Task Force on Emis-sion Inventories (TFEI) "to ensure an adequate flow of reliable information to support the work under the Convention."[26] The TFEI concluded that collabo-ration with other groups that had been engaged in similar activities would save time and prevent duplication. Eight expert panels were established to work out methodological issues, one of which was to deal with the verification of emission inventories.[27] In the same year, the UN/ECE and the EU Commission agreed to adopt a common classification of emission sectors. In 1993 the TFEI proposed the development of an *Atmospheric Emission Inventory Guidebook* that would ensure that "a detailed methodology such as CORINAIR would be required to allow verification of emission data."[28] The first edition of the *Guidebook* was published in 1996.[29]

Analysis of Emission Data.   Parties to LRTAP are required to report data on emissions of major pollutants. Those reports are the primary source of in-formation used to determine whether parties are in compliance with LRTAP's regulatory commitments. Full and accurate reporting of data is also essen-tial for modeling air pollution, such as the modeling work done by EMEP's Meteorological Synthesizing Centres and by independent groups such as the International Institute for Applied Systems Analysis (IIASA). Complete time series of emission data are necessary inputs to long-range dispersion models; any voids must be filled through interpolations, extrapolations, or both, thus increasing the uncertainty of results.

To assess whether reported data are useful for modeling and for determining compliance, two questions must be answered.

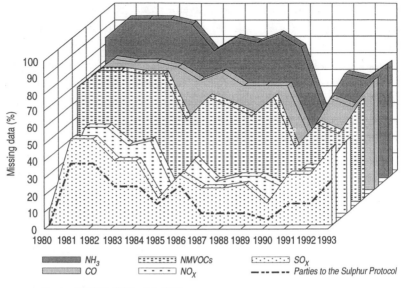

Source: ECE/EB.AIR/44 - July 1995

Figure 7.1
Missing data as percentage of requested data for four major transboundary pollutants
Data here show reporting by all members of LRTAP. For comparison, the dashed line shows reporting rates for sulfur by members of the Helsinki (1985) Sulphur Protocol—it illustrates that reporting rates are higher for members of the corresponding regulatory protocol, but reporting remains imperfect.
Note: NMVOCs = Non-methane volatile organic compounds.
Source: ECE/EB.AIR/44, July 1995.

Are the reported data complete? Most parties to the LRTAP Convention have reported data on SO_2 and NO_x emissions for the Helsinki Protocol's reference year, 1980, and since 1985, but there are many gaps between 1980 and 1985. However, a few parties to the Protocols have reported intermittently during this period. The official record of other air pollutants (e.g., ammonia, VOCs) is much less complete. A comparison of the emission time series published in the LRTAP annual reviews shows that data are reported by parties with a delay of about two years.

Figure 7.1 shows the percentage of data required in national reports that is missing. Of the 20 European parties to the Sulphur Protocol, only 10 have perfect reporting records in the 1980–1993 period; in the case of the NO_x Protocol, this is true for 10 of 22 parties. The reporting records are relatively good for SO_2 and NO_x—the two main sources of acid precipitation and the subject of LRTAP's first two regulatory protocols. The record between 1980 and 1985 is poor; at that time no LRTAP regulatory protocols had been adopted and there were no common reporting standards. The record is best in 1980 (the baseline year for the Sulphur Protocol) as well as in 1985 and 1990 (years of major inventory compilation by the EU's CORINAIR program). Reporting rates have improved over time with improvements in methodologies by the EU and LRTAP and the building of national reporting capacity.

Are the reported data accurate? It is very difficult to objectively assess whether emission figures are accurate because no fully independent sources of data exist. Here, two approaches are taken—both indicate that accuracy is satisfactory and that activities to refine methodologies and to model air pollution have contributed to improvements in accuracy.

First, the parties periodically revise the information on emissions as more knowledge and better ways to estimate energy use and other emission sources become available. An important by-product of this activity is that emission figures for previous years have been, at times, substantially modified. In general, early estimates have been subsequently reduced. With respect to SO_2 data for 1980, the baseline year, estimations made in 1985 are generally quite different from values reported at later dates (with due account being taken of changes in national borders). In the majority of cases, estimates for 1980 emissions have stabilized over time. East European countries show the highest variability. The trends of the NO_x emission time series are similar to those of the SO_2 time series. On balance, it appears that emission inventories are at present more complete and homogeneous than at any previous time, covering the main sources and increasingly introducing common estimation methods. One way to explore whether this view is correct is to compare the figures with estimations performed independently.

Second, it is possible to compare national reports to LRTAP with emissions estimates derived from the EU's CORINAIR system, which employs a comprehensive and elaborate methodology. CORINAIR's SO_2 emission figures are consistent with, and at times lower than, the data most recently reported to LRTAP by the parties. Some eastern and southern European countries have substituted CORINAIR's 1985 and 1990 results for previous estimations: in

294   Juan Carlos di Primio

these cases, the LRTAP and CORINAIR numbers are identical because the source is the same. Although these cases allow no independent analysis of reported data, the adoption of the CORINAIR methodology probably has yielded an improvement of data quality over the previously used national data system.

Transport and deposition models can also help assess whether emission data are accurate (see discussion below). Independent calculations of 1980 SO_2 emissions made at IIASA by the Transboundary Air Pollution (TAP) Project show good agreement with the emissions data reported by countries.

The reported data indicate substantial compliance with LRTAP's regulatory commitments. Over the 1980–1993 period, the parties to the Helsinki Protocol substantially cut their SO_2 emissions, thus surpassing, both individually and as a group, the goal of cutting emissions by at least 30 percent. With respect to compliance with the NO_x Protocol, emissions have in general diminished, remarkably in some cases, over the 1987–1993 period: the intended stagnation has been achieved.

Measurements of Air and Precipitation Quality

In their journeys from sources to sinks, emissions of sulfur and nitrogen compounds are partially transformed through reactions in the atmosphere and under the influence of solar radiation. Thus, new substances join the primary pollutants. This mix of chemicals is discharged from the atmosphere, returning to the surface by dry and wet deposition. Long-range transport models simulate the trajectory, chemical transformation, and deposition of pollution. Such modeling activities are crucial for the air pollution regime, because they help to identify needed changes in regulatory commitments and provide input to policy-oriented models that allow exploration of the costs and benefits of policy options. Moreover, long-range transport models can be used for assessing the accuracy of reported emissions data and compliance, although the LRTAP regime does not (yet) provide a formal mandate to perform this function. Using such models for these tasks depends critically on the existence of both good models and data on deposition to validate them and to set the initial conditions. The types and accuracy of these models have been analyzed elsewhere.[30] Here, attention is given to the sources and accuracy of data on deposition.

Measurement Program. EMEP supervises a continuous monitoring program conducted by national laboratories all over Europe. The deposition of a number of chemicals is measured daily in samples collected at sites that are regionally representative and, as far as possible, unaffected by local pollutant sources. Begun in 1977 and initially designed to measure and analyze sulfur compounds, the EMEP measurement program has gradually been enlarged to assess other air pollutants—today it measures all important acidifying substances as well as ground-level ozone. In parallel, the sampling network has also expanded: 46 stations were working during the first measurement phase of EMEP (1978–1980); by the 1987–1989 period the CCC was receiving data from 102 sites.[31] Currently, about 100 sites take daily measurements; however, by the end of 1993, fewer than 30 had implemented the full measurement program, and information is still incomplete about some airborne substances, particularly nitrogen compounds.[32]

Sampling sites and laboratories in participating countries started with, and some have continued to use, the techniques and equipment that were already in use. A manual with recommended methods to harmonize these elements was issued by EMEP in 1977 and has since been regularly updated.[33] By 1990 most of the laboratories were using the methods described in the manual. The CCC conducts a quality-assurance program that includes field comparison of sampling stations;[34] the results show that the mean of reported values is always close to the expectations.[35] Nonetheless, many deficiencies remain; a few sampling sites are influenced by emissions from nearby sources; others are located at extremely high elevations. Furthermore, the density of the network is not uniform; while in Western and Central Europe the coverage is fairly thorough, it is rather low in Eastern and Southern Europe.

Conclusions and Final Observations

The system of collecting and using emission data that is used under LRTAP is one of the systems that are most likely to permit credible evaluation of compliance. Clear targets allow compliance to be measured. In LRTAP there have been few problems with noncompliance because commitments have generally not been stringent and thus have been easy for most parties to meet.

The analysis here has focused on the sources and uses of data on pollution and deposition; other types of data have not been analyzed. It is important to reiterate that within the official review process little or nothing is done with the parties' reports on strategies and policies undertaken to fulfill LRTAP commitments. Detailed comparisons of such information with reports on emissions would further help to assess domestic implementation. Notably, it would help to build the capacity of the LRTAP system to assess whether a party is on track to comply with regulatory commitments in the future. At present, the only capacity to verify compliance is ex post. This part of SIRs has not been given the attention it merits.

Many functions of implementation review have not formally been part of the LRTAP regime; notably, no mechanism has been in operation to handle cases of noncompliance that arise, in part because the regulatory commitments have been modest and thus noncompliance has not been evident. Whether the current LRTAP verification capacity will become involved in compliance issues will depend on whether there is good reason to examine compliance. In the future, when more stringent protocols will likely lead to increases in noncompliance, the ability to identify (and anticipate) noncompliance will be essential to the operation of the institutions established to handle such problems.[36]

The situation is now changing. Notably, the 1994 Sulphur Protocol explicitly addresses compliance and an Implementation Committee will be appointed when the agreement comes into force. One can expect that the shift from "typical" implementation review activities to true verification of compliance will require additional steps, both of a quantitative (more data, new tasks) and a qualitative (political decisions on regime and institutional structure) nature. Such evolution may pave the way for greater internationalization of institutions.[37] In the Montreal Protocol, the Non-Compliance Procedure and the Implementation Committee have been supported by the expertise of the Technical and Economic Assessment Panels.[38] The LRTAP regime has mature institutions (EMEP and other technical bodies) already available to offer expert advice on compliance matters.

Because the European air pollution regime is an important case—both as a model and on its own terms—observations drawn from this analysis are central to understanding the role and limits of implementation review in other international environmental regimes. This study of the regime's data system suggests seven conclusions:

1. The emission data reporting, pollutant monitoring, and modeling activities that revolve around EMEP constitute a nascent verification system; however, they are not currently used as such. Nor is there a significant

independent capacity to verify compliance—most data are reported by the parties themselves. This situation reflects not only the political sensitivity of verification, but also the fact that LRTAP is judged to be a high-compliance regime.[39] During the past decade the regime's main challenge was to develop regulatory commitments. The nascent verification system arose from efforts to better understand the sources and impacts of acid rain, not primarily to perform functions of implementation review. Thus, the task was less to ensure compliance than to build an effective data collection and assessment system and an appropriate institutional structure. In sum, the existence of a nascent verification capability was a by-product of other related efforts by the parties.

2. Despite the wealth of activity, it is important to realize that the huge amount of data produced throughout Europe does not necessarily constitute a complete and reliable data set. However, EMEP's endeavor to gather and process such an information flood and, along the way, to change or extend the initial approaches to cover the entire area and reach high quality standards, is without equal in the environmental field. The coordination of the measurement program on air and precipitation quality and the modeling of long-range transport of air pollutants provide both support for and constructive criticism of the estimation of emissions. The integration of these information sources into the emission data yields a comprehensive view of the issue area, which is essential for independent verification of the reported emission rates. Although the data and models could be used for verification purposes, this has not been the only reason data collection and modeling have been pursued. Rather, efforts to improve data quality and reporting have been active and effective largely because they directly lead to improved scientific modeling. At best, verification has been only one goal. In the words of one analyst "monitoring and reporting [have] served the dual objectives of tracking compliance and of furnishing information for adjusting the standards set by the international legal instrument."[40]

3. In practice, there has been a close connection between the parties and the institutions responsible for data assessment. This has resulted in a continuous flow of information on domestic implementation and EMEP activities inside the regime. EMEP and LRTAP officials have learned about noncompliance problems as they have developed. However, during the Cold War there was little, if any, discussion of noncompliance. This changed in the early 1990s, and today the opportunities to address compliance formally are better.[41] Both the 1991 VOC and the 1994 Sulphur Protocols include provisions to create a forum for such formal consideration.

4. Starting in the mid-1980s many activities within LRTAP have addressed the incompleteness and incomparability of national emission inventories. Collaboration between the EU's CORINAIR project and

EMEP has helped considerably. The CORINAIR methodology did not completely harmonize the different national systems, but it provided a common approach that increased transparency, comparability, and probably accuracy of the national inventories; in some countries (notably in eastern and southern Europe) the CORINAIR methodology became the basis for the development of national systems. Separating the activities of CORINAIR and EMEP is difficult because often the same experts worked in both programs. Through collaboration of institutions and individuals the EU has taken the lead in developing LRTAP's emission inventory methodology.

5. Data revision has occurred on a regular basis. This is an important part of efforts to improve emission statistics. It does, however, raise the possibility of manipulating (especially baseline) data in order to create the *appearance* of compliance. Independent estimates suggest that these, at times substantial, revisions have mainly been made in the interest of improving data quality, not strategic manipulation of data.

6. The formation of EMEP before the creation of LRTAP (and its attendant protocols) enhanced the ability of the LRTAP system to engage in extensive data collection and analysis. Unlike many other international environmental regimes, LRTAP was able to rely upon an existing data system, though that system underwent significant change as a result of LRTAP's development. Despite the favorable beginnings, it took two decades to develop an active, accurate, and useful data system. Nonetheless, compliance with LRTAP's data-reporting requirements remains imperfect, though it has improved in response to international activities to create and harmonize reporting methodologies. Compliance with data-reporting requirements is lowest for emissions that parties have not historically gathered data on or that are difficult to estimate. The long period required to build data reporting and modeling capacity underscores the need to start early with data collection and modeling activities in environmental regimes so that the capacity is in place when it is needed to verify compliance.

7. Interestingly, many scholars point to low capacity as a reason for inadequate compliance with reporting deadlines by parties, especially developing countries. This study underscores that highly industrialized states face a different but nonetheless serious obstacle to reporting consistent data: namely, harmonization of national methods. Typically, international data-reporting systems stem from already existing national systems, which aggregate and estimate data in different ways. These national differences are difficult to overcome, but this study shows in what ways they have been reduced. Countries with limited-capacity data-reporting systems

have probably been able to harmonize more easily with a single international system (in this case CORINAIR's methodology) than countries with highly developed reporting systems.

Notes

This essay is based on di Primio, J.C., 1996, Monitoring and Verification in the European Air Pollution Regime, WP-96-47, International Institute for Applied Systems Analysis, Laxenburg, Austria. The original essay includes complementary figures and tables and complete references.

1. For recent appraisals see Wüster, H., 1992, "The Convention on Long-Range Transboundary Air Pollution: Its Achievements and Its Potential," in *Acidification Research, Evaluation and Policy Applications*, edited by T. Schneider, Elsevier, Amsterdam, Netherlands; Levy, M.A., 1993, "European Acid Rain: The Power of Tote-Board Diplomacy," in *Institutions for the Earth: Sources of Effective International Environmental Protection*, edited by P.M. Haas, R.O. Keohane, and M.A. Levy, The MIT Press, Cambridge, MA, USA; Levy, M.A., 1995, "International Cooperation to Combat Acid Rain, in *Green Globe Yearbook 1995*, edited by H.O. Bergesen and G. Parmann, The Fridtjof Nansen Institute, Oxford University Press, New York, NY, USA; Wettestad, J., 1996, Acid Lessons? Assessing and Explaining LRTAP Implementation and Effectiveness, WP-96-18, International Institute for Applied Systems Analysis, Laxenburg, Austria.

2. For a historical survey see, for example, Wetstone, G.S, 1987, "A History of the Acid Rain Issue," in *Science for Public Policy*, edited by H. Brooks and C.L. Cooper, Pergamon Press, Oxford, UK.

3. Odén, S., 1968, "The Acidification of Air and Precipitation and Its Consequences in the Natural Environment," *Ecology Committee Bulletin*, No. 1, Swedish National Research Council, Stockholm, Sweden (in Swedish).

4. OECD, 1972, Decision of the OECD-Council of 18 April 1972, C(72)13 (Final), Organisation for Economic Co-operation and Development, Paris, France.

5. OECD, 1979, *The OECD Programme on Long Range Transport of Air Pollutants Measurements and Findings*, 2nd edition, Organisation for Economic Co-operation and Development, Paris, France.

6. Ibid.

7. Gosovic, B., 1992, *The Quest for World Environmental Cooperation: The Case of the UN Global Environment Monitoring System*, Routledge, London, UK; Dovland, H., 1993, "EMEP—The European Monitoring and Evaluation

Programme," paper presented at the Expert Meeting on Acid Precipitation Monitoring Network in East Asia, Toyama, Japan, 26–28 October; Sand, P., 1996, May, personal communication with the author, Laxenburg, Austria.

8. Economic Commission for Europe, 1995, "Strategies and Policies for Air Pollution Abatement, 1994 Major Review," EC/EB.AIR/44, United Nations Economic Commission for Europe, Geneva, Switzerland.

9. The Protocol on Long-Term Financing of the Cooperative Programme for Monitoring and Evaluation of the Long-Range Transmission of Air Pollutants in Europe was adopted in Geneva on 28 September 1984 and entered into force on 28 January 1988. As of 31 May 1995 it had 35 parties, including the EU. The Protocol commits parties to contribute annually to the EMEP budget.

10. The Protocol on the Reduction of Sulphur Emissions or Their Transboundary Fluxes by at Least 30 Percent was adopted in Helsinki on 8 July 1985 and entered into force on 2 September 1987. It had 21 parties as of 31 May 1995.

11. The Protocol Concerning the Control of Emissions of Nitrogen Oxides or Their Transboundary Fluxes was adopted in Sofia on 31 October 1988 and entered into force on 14 February 1991. As of 31 May 1995 it had 25 parties, including the EU.

12. The protocol referred to is the Protocol Concerning the Control of Emissions of Volatile Organic Compounds or Their Transboundary Fluxes.

13. The reports of the EB's annual meetings give full details. See, for example, the documents ECE/EB.AIR/16 (1987), ECE/EB.AIR/24 (1990), and ECE/EB.AIR/29 (1991).

14. Sand, P., 1996, May, personal communication with the author, Laxenburg, Austria.

15. Fisher, W., 1991, "The Verification of International Conventions on Protection of the Environment and Common Resources," KFA Report Jül-2495, Research Center Jülich, Germany; USGAO, 1992, *International Agreements Are Not Well Monitored*, GAO/RCED-92-43, United States General Accounting Office, Washington, DC, USA; Ausubel, J., and Victor, D.G., 1992, "Verification of International Environmental Agreements," *Annual Review of Energy and Environment* 17:1–43.

16. As of this writing three major reviews have been performed, for the years 1986 (ECE/EB.AIR/14), 1990 (ECE/EB.AIR/27), and 1994 (ECE/EB.AIR/44).

17. The 1991 LRTAP VOC Protocol (not yet in force) states that "the parties shall establish a mechanism for monitoring compliance" (Article 3.3). The

1994 Protocol to the LRTAP Convention on Further Reduction of Sulphur Emissions (not yet in force) creates an Implementation Committee (Article 7) "to review the implementation of the present Protocol and compliance of the parties with their obligations." See Széll, P., 1995, "The Development of Multilateral Mechanisms for Monitoring Compliance," in *Sustainable Development and International Law*, edited by W. Lang, Graham & Trotman/Martinus Nijhoff, London, UK.

18. Sand, P., 1990, "Regional Approaches to Transboundary Air Pollution," in *Energy—Production, Consumption and Consequences*, edited by J.L. Helm, National Academy Press, Washington, DC, USA.

19. Emissions of acidifying pollutants stem from human activities as well as natural sources. The Convention focuses on anthropogenic emissions; however, it is important to have records of emissions of natural origin in order to understand the relative significance of those from anthropogenic sources and the limits of abatement measures. Moreover, natural emissions are a necessary input for EMEP's modeling activity. The focus here, and in EMEP, is on anthropogenic sources. Concerning the calculation of anthropogenic emissions, in some countries continuous monitoring of a few pollutants is often implemented at a few large point sources such as power plants and refineries.

20. Klimont, Z., Amann, M., Cofala, J., Gyarfas, F., Klaasen, G., and Schöpp, W., 1994, "An Emission Inventory for the Central European Initiative 1988," *Atmospheric Environment* 28(2):235–246.

21. Council Decision 85/338/EEC.

22. Bouscaren, R., 1995, CORINAIR Inventaire des emissions de dioxyde de soufre, d'oxydes d'azote et des composes organiques volatiles dans la Communauté européenne en 1985, Report EUR 13232, Luxembourg, Luxembourg.

23. The 1990 CORINAIR nomenclature covers about 260 emission-generating activities in 11 main source groups and extends the 1985 list of three pollutants (sulfur dioxide, nitrogen oxides, and VOCs) to eight: sulfur oxides, nitrogen oxides, nonmethane VOCs, ammonia, carbon monoxide, methane, nitrous oxide, and carbon dioxide. The method has been made available to 30 European countries: 15 member states of the EU, 2 from the European Free Trade Association (Norway, Switzerland), 3 Baltic states (Estonia, Latvia, Lithuania), 9 East and Central European countries (Albania, Bulgaria, Croatia, the Czech Republic, Hungary, Poland, Romania, Slovakia, Slovenia), and Russia. Thus, although pursuing the goals of the EU, the CORINAIR project covers most requirements of the LRTAP Convention as well.

24. Complete harmonization of national systems would have been impossible.

25. Data are stored at the UN/ECE International Environmental Data Service (IEDS) and at EMEP's centers.

26. ECE/EB.AIR/29.

27. McInnes, G., Pacyna, J.M., and Dovland, H., 1992, "Proceedings of the First Meeting of the Task Force on Emission Inventories," EMEP/CCC Report 4/92. London, UK, 5–7 May.

28. McInnes, G., Pacyna, J.M., and Dovland, H., 1993, "Proceedings of the Second Meeting of the Task Force on Emission Inventories," EMEP/CCC Report 8/93, Delft, Netherlands, 7–9 June.

29. McInnes, G., ed., 1996, *Atmospheric Emission Inventory Guidebook*, 1st edition, a joint EMEP/CORINAIR production, prepared by the EMEP Task Force on Emission Inventories, European Environment Agency, Copenhagen, Denmark.

30. For a review see di Primio, J.C., 1996, op. cit., acknowledgment note; especially see Eliassen, A., and Saltbones, J., 1983, "Modelling of Long-Range Transport of Sulfur over Europe: A Two-year Model Run and Some Model Experiments," *Atmospheric Environment* 17:1457–1473; Iversen, T., 1993, "Modelled and Measured Transboundary Acidifying Pollution in Europe: Verification and Trends," *Atmospheric Environment* 27A(6):889–920.

31. Hanssen, J.E., Pedersen, U., Schaug, J., Dovland, H., Pacyna, J.M., Semb, A., and Skjelmoen, J.E., 1990, "Summary Report from the Chemical Co-ordinating Centre for the Fourth Phase of EMEP," EMEP/CCC-Report 2/90.

32. Berge, E., Schaug, J., Sandnes, H., and Kvalvagnes, I., 1994, "A Comparison of Results from the EMEP/MSC-W Acid Deposition Model and the EMEP Monitoring Sites During the Four Seasons of 1989," EMEP/MSC-W/CCC Note 1/94.

33. Schaug, J., 1995, June, personal communication with the author, Olso, Norway.

34. Schaug, J., 1988, "Quality Assurance Plan for EMEP," EMEP/CCC Report 1/88, Norwegian Institute for Air Research, Oslo, Norway.

35. Hanssen, J.E., and Skjelmoen, J.E., 1992, "The Twelfth Intercomparison of Analytical Methods Within EMEP," EMEP/CCC-Report 7/92.

36. Schally, H.G., 1996, "The Role and Importance of Implementation Monitoring and Noncompliance Procedures in International Environmental Regimes," in *The Ozone Treaties and Their Influence on the Building of International Environmental Regimes*, edited by W. Lang, Austrian Foreign Policy Documentation, Austrian Foreign Ministry, Vienna, Austria; Victor, D.G.,

1996, "The Montreal Protocol's Non-Compliance Procedure: Lessons for Making Other International Environmental Regimes More Effective," in *The Ozone Treaties and Their Influence on the Building of International Environmental Regimes*, edited by W. Lang, Austrian Foreign Policy Documentation, Austrian Foreign Ministry, Vienna, Austria.

37. Széll, P., 1995, "The Development of Multilateral Mechanisms for Monitoring Compliance," in *Sustainable Development and International Law*, edited by W. Lang, Graham & Trotman/Martinus Nijhoff, London, UK, pp. 97–109.

38. See Chapters 3 and 4 in this volume.

39. See, for example, Wettestad, op. cit., note 1.

40. Sachariew, K., 1991, "Promoting Compliance with International Environmental Legal Standards: Reflections on Monitoring and Reporting Mechanisms," *Yearbook of International Environmental Law* 2:31–52.

41. When asked why the issue of compliance—which has apparently been brewing for a long time—was brought into the open after many years of a quiet buildup of the monitoring and assessment system, an experienced high-level LRTAP official answered that a favorable political situation was required to start a frank discussion. The opportunity arose in the early 1990s with the end of the Cold War.

II

National Implementation

Because the implementation of international environmental agreements centers on national actions—such as the creation of new programs and the promulgation and enforcement of laws and standards—actual implementation experiences are likely to vary widely, perhaps enormously, among countries. For the most part, environmental accords are implemented through extant domestic regulatory apparatuses. These vary significantly, as do political dynamics, interest groups, institutional arrangements, and national "styles" of regulation. Consequently, implementation of international commitments is a complicated enterprise. As two decades of research on national policy has shown, identifying general patterns is difficult.[1]

Whereas the chapters in the first part of the book look primarily at activities undertaken at the international level—specifically, systems that review national and international implementation efforts—the chapters in this part examine the core national-level processes in a broad array of European states. They look at both East and West European experiences, remaining cognizant of the fact that political, legal, and economic differences between East and West are likely to critically influence implementation. Each chapter looks in-depth at national implementation of a set of international environmental commitments. Collectively, the studies address two broad issues: participation within the implementation process, with the primary focus on West European liberal democracies, and the special nature of implementation in East European countries undergoing fundamental political and economic transitions from central planning to a liberal, market-based system.[2] The conclusion to this volume explores how this liberal–nonliberal distinction influences the implementation process and international environmental cooperation more broadly.

These two factors—participation and transition—are not the only ones that affect implementation; nor can they be separated from other factors, such as the level of public concern about and pressure to improve environmental quality. Consequently, each study must describe the full range of factors at work, though analytical attention is focused on only a few. We concentrate on participation and transition because they speak to important theoretical and policy debates. Below we explain why these factors have been selected, and we briefly outline the important theoretical and policy issues and the specific propositions examined in the case studies.

Participation within the Implementation Process

"Participation" is the involvement of stakeholders—actors with a special interest in a given issue—in the making and implementation of policy. The need to expand participation, especially to nongovernmental organizations (NGOs), is virtually a mantra: every major international environmental declaration or treaty endorses wider access for NGOs. Debates over access rules are a regular feature of international and national policy-making. In liberal states, NGOs are granted extensive access to information and to the processes of making and implementing policy; many argue that similar open access should be granted in international fora. Increasingly, theorists argue that higher participation by the public and non-state actors marks a new form of governance—the emergence of an international (increasingly global) civil society.[3]

The studies that concentrate on implementation in the West (Chapters 8–10), as well as the study on Russian nuclear dumping (Chapter 11), give special attention to how patterns of participation have influenced outcomes. These studies describe the actors, interests, and institutions involved in the process of making policy decisions, which takes place at both the international and national levels, and in the process of implementation, which is primarily a national activity. All of the studies in Chapters 8 through 11 focus on national implementation, but each also analyzes the development of international commitments; it is difficult to analyze the former without the context of the latter.

The studies focus on four main types of actors: target groups, environmental nongovernmental organizations (ENGOs), scientists (experts), and government agencies. These actors participate in three modes: (1) voicing interests, for instance by making statements in policy fora such as international negotiations and national policy processes; (2) making public policy decisions, such as negotiating and adopting international commitments and making national policies that translate those commitments into domestic rules; and (3) monitoring and enforcing international commitments and national policies. Not all modes of participation apply to all actors. By definition, government agencies typically have the main responsibility for making public decisions—to negotiate international commitments, to consider whether to join those commitments, to translate commitments into specific national policies, and to enforce those policies. Target groups are directly affected by policies and thus often participate extensively, especially in voicing their interests. Other actors—such as ENGOs and scientists, which are frequently termed "third parties"—often have an interest in outcomes and therefore add their voice. Some also help to enforce standards (e.g., through citizen suits and other forms of private enforcement). Government agencies often also represent the interests of non-state actors; thus even when target groups and ENGOs appear to be absent from the policy process, in practice their interests are often represented by the respective government ministry (e.g., agriculture, transport, environment).[4]

These studies examine several broad propositions about participation. First, and most important, we ask whether patterns of participation influence the international commitments that are negotiated, the national policies adopted in order to give effect to those commitments, and the changes in behavior that ultimately result. We began this study with the simple expectation that if participation is dominated by one interest group then the policy outputs and outcomes should reflect that group's interests more than if participation were more balanced. Moreover, we expected that because decisions made during the implementation phase are crucial, patterns of participation during that phase would be especially important. In contrast, to date the main undertaking of analysts and policymakers has been to document (and promote) expanded participation during the process of negotiation and policy formation.

The proposition that participation influences policy outputs and outcomes is fundamental. If it is invalid then the rationale for much of current environmental policy—which emphasizes the need to open access to non-state actors, especially ENGOs—may be misplaced.

The case studies trace changes in patterns of participation and assess whether and how participation ultimately influences behavior. Jon Birger Skjærseth shows how international commitments to limit pollution in the North Sea have entrained the participation of a growing array of governmental agencies, target groups, and ENGOs within the Netherlands, Norway, and the UK (Chapter 8). Jørgen Wettestad illustrates a similar process of expanding participation as the same countries sought to implement their international commitments to regulate emissions of nitrogen oxides (NO_x), a leading cause of acid precipitation (Chapter 9). We selected these countries because they would be particularly revealing of whether participation matters. Each country has a markedly different approach to allowing participation of non-state actors in the making and implementation of national policy: the UK's policy style has been relatively closed to participation by non-state actors, especially ENGOs, but is now opening, in part because of pressure by the European Union; the Netherlands has a policy system marked by extensive access and participation; the Norwegian system is open to many participants but participation is structured and the policy process is designed to seek social consensus.

Steinar Andresen shows how participation has influenced the regulation of whaling (Chapter 10). Regulating whaling is the simplest of all the cases of implementation in this book: Andresen shows that whaling in Iceland and Norway is a small, well-organized industry that is easy to control. Nonetheless, when the whaling issue became a matter of "high politics" and exports from whaling nations were targeted for sanctions by the USA and ENGOs, many new government agencies and interest groups whose interests were previously unaffected by whaling became involved. In general, all the studies in this book show that participation rises when policymakers shift from negotiating commitments to implementation—more stakeholders participate as they realize their interest in the outcomes.

Olav Schram Stokke explores how patterns of participation within the USSR (and now Russia) have influenced the making and implementation of policies to regulate dumping of radioactive wastes (Chapter 11).

Second, several studies focus on how participation by target groups influences policy decisions and behavior. We give these groups special attention because it is their behavior that international accords are designed to influence. We ask whether participation by target groups in the making of international commitments and national policies has any impact on the *extent and thoroughness of implementation.* This proposition has been extensively tested in many areas of public policy. In developing projects to promote economic and social development, for example, it is now widely agreed that when the targets of policy participate in making decisions, they "buy in" to the outcome and are more willing to change their behavior. Such a finding supports policies of the World Bank and other institutions to promote participation by targets in project design and implementation.[5] However, that robust finding might not apply to environmental regulation. The experience in economic and social development policy concerned projects in which targets favored assistance and therefore had an incentive to participate. In contrast, international environmental commitments that seek to regulate or redirect behavior typically engage targets that do not want to be regulated.[6]

Third, we explore whether participation by non-state actors leads to decisions and actions that are based on better information about what can be implemented—what we call *implementation expertise*. As noted in one branch of theory on policy implementation, government decision makers often have limited access to useful information; more participation by non-state actors may help fill the gaps.[7] In particular, we expect that increased participation by target groups will result in decisions that better reflect what the target groups can implement. In turn, more realistic content and design should yield policies that have a stronger influence on behavior.[8]

In general, the studies suggest that "buy in" does not, in itself, lead to greater implementation and effectiveness. However, the studies do show that target group participation often leads to policy decisions that are based on more implementation expertise—they better reflect industry's interests and capabilities of target groups. Thus, when target groups participate, international environmental commitments can be more effective. However, target group participation carries risks. Notably, extensive participation by target groups can lead to "regulatory capture"—public policy decisions that merely mirror the interests of the regulated, not the public good.[9] For example, prior to the adoption of international commitments, regulation and monitoring of Soviet nuclear dumping was practically controlled by the military—the targets of dumping policy. The openness of the London Convention to other groups, including ENGOs, is part of the reason policy decisions have increasingly focused on prohibiting dumping. As the USSR and Russian policy processes opened to environmental interests and ENGOs, international prohibitions against dumping were increasingly reflected in national practice.

While exclusive participation can lead to capture, expanding participation also carries risks such as "gridlock," the inability to make decisions because too many participants vie for influence and block progress. Much has been written on participation, capture, and gridlock in domestic regulatory settings. Here, analysis of these issues is extended to the process of making and implementing international commitments.

Target groups are not the only sources of implementation expertise. The studies also examine ways that scientists and other experts contribute to implementation expertise. Much of the literature has assessed expert roles in policy formation;[10] of special interest in this study are the types of expert assessments that are most influential in the implementation process. For example, the NO_x study suggests that when expert assessments focus on environmental damages (what we call "damage science") policies tend to be more stringent than when assessments focus on options (and costs) for implementing abatement policies (what we call "abatement science"). Implementation expertise is often sobering. In this sense, experts and target groups may play complementary roles in gathering and interpreting useful information on which policy decisions depend. A sharp distinction between "experts" and other actors is typically not possible. Often target groups and some ENGOs possess the greatest expertise, creating the danger of regulatory capture if reliance on their knowledge is too exclusive. The studies explore how these actors with implementation expertise are engaged.

In general, the studies suggest that target group participation can be a helpful source of implementation expertise and thus lead to greater implementation and effectiveness of international environmental commitments, but only when groups with other interests also participate. Studies in the first part of this book confirm this finding. For example, target group expertise was crucial for implementation of the prior informed consent (PIC) system, but equally important was the participation by well-informed ENGOs that balanced the influence of the pesticides and chemical industry associations. In the Montreal Protocol (Chapter 3), the Baltic Sea regime (Chapter 5), and the PIC system, independent experts also contributed implementation expertise which, at times, also limited the influence of target groups.

These three broad propositions—whether participation matters and the motivational and informational advantages of target group participation—focus on actors and the roles they play in the implementation process. In each case study, we also examine factors that influence patterns of participation. We study the influence of *access structure*—the rules and procedures that govern who can participate in policy processes. Much policy attention is focused on ways to open the access structure, such as by allowing observer status for non-state actors and granting access to information. However, as these studies show, an open access structure merely allows groups to participate. It is not the only factor that determines participation patterns. Thus, we also examine other factors that determine when and how stakeholders decide to participate, such as the costs and benefits of different modes of participation, the costs of gaining access to usable information, the possibility of joining with other actors to form a group to represent common interests, and the resources that are available or can be tapped.[11] The studies show that these other factors often vary markedly, and thus dramatic changes in participation are often observed even without any change in formal access rules.

Finally, although the focus here is on participation within the national implementation process, several studies also examine participation at the international level. They examine the influence of participation by non-state actors in international fora. They also examine participation by states, the only formal members of international treaties.[12] Treaties require the consent of their members and thus the commitments that have been adopted are highly sensitive to the interests of the participating states. When commitments are determined by voting—as in the International Whaling Commission—the commitments reflect voting rules and the interests of voting coalitions. These points are well known.[13] However, our studies examine some ways that commitments have been affected by altering patterns of state participation. In the North Sea regime, active efforts were made to exclude Spain and Portugal (which had been part of early, ineffective efforts to protect the North Sea) and thus reduce the number of laggards, making it possible for the smaller group that remained to adopt more ambitious commitments. In that case, the use of nonbinding instruments made it easier to exclude these countries, whose participation was not needed to address the environmental problem at hand. The NO_x study shows that a nonbinding declaration allowed a small group of leader countries to adopt more ambitious commitments. In this and the whaling case, efforts to restrict participation were essential to overcome the tendency for international commitments to fall to the level acceptable to the least ambitious state. In the whaling case, active efforts by the opponents of whaling, including ENGOs, to increase participation of like-minded states produced a voting bloc that adopted the whaling moratorium.

Implementation Under Transition

Domestic implementation is a complex process even in well-functioning and stable legal and political systems like those of Norway or the UK. In the former centrally planned countries of Eastern Europe, the transition to a market-based economy has entailed significant disruption and flux in regulatory and legal institutions.

Although transition has been highly disruptive, international environmental governance often requires the participation of countries undergoing transition. These transition countries face, and produce, some of the most severe environmental problems, some of which cross borders and affect other countries. Nuclear fallout from the Chernobyl accident is the most notorious example, but the centrally planned countries have been among the largest contributors to acid precipitation in Europe, pollution of international rivers and seas, emissions of greenhouse gases, and dumping of hazardous wastes. The most serious failures to comply with the Montreal Protocol on stratospheric ozone depletion are all in countries that are undergoing transition from central planning.

Most analyses of the transition process have focused on economic issues. Some studies have addressed domestic environmental policy, but few analysts have examined how transition influences the implementation of international environmental commitments.[14] Yet research on this issue is important for policy and theory. Government officials and interest groups in the West and East alike are keen to improve implementation of international environmental commitments within transition countries. The West is interested if only because improved implementation will deliver environmental benefits downwind and downstream in the West. Even when international environmental protection yields few direct benefits, policymakers in the East often favor improved implementation because many sources of international pollution are also the cause of more immediate domestic environmental problems. In addition, compliance with international environmental commitments by transition countries is often a condition for other benefits of East-West cooperation.

Our studies explore the present situation and the prospects for improving implementation in transition countries, particularly Russia. We begin with a discussion of the main elements and consequences of transition. We then present several case studies that explore how the transition process has affected policy decisions and outcomes.

Transition entails rapid political and economic changes. The political system is being decentralized and opened to new influences. Power is being shifted from the center to regional and local levels; the functions of law making and regulation are being distributed between the executive and independent legislatures that have the power to scrutinize executive decisions. In the economic system, there is a rapid shift away from central planning toward market allocation of goods and services. In short, these political and economic changes entail a transition to a "liberal" state.

The political and economic changes under way in these countries have three major consequences that are particularly important to how international environmental commitments are implemented.

- Rapid political and economic changes have caused serious economic disarray; the emergence of new systems for distributing goods and services has not kept pace with the destruction of the old ones. Resources for administering environmental regulations and changing production processes are often limited. The extent of disarray varies widely but is particularly acute in Russia, our main focus.

- Rapid shifts in the economic and political structure produce uncertainty about current and future sources of control. Transition is not an overnight process, and it is often unclear who the owners of capital are and whether new market rules and laws will be implemented. Because of this uncertainty, priority has been given to near-term economic growth rather than to managing more distant, cumulative environmental problems. Moreover, instability and uncertain regulation may make investors and other suppliers of capital resources (e.g., development banks) less willing to transfer or lend resources that are needed for investment in modern, less-polluting facilities. Such investments give a positive return on investment only after long periods of economic growth and only when the likelihood that polluters will be required to heed environmental regulations is high.

- Long-suppressed facts about environmental degradation are being disclosed. The values emerging in the public sometimes include concern for environmental protection but also reflect a desire for greater material rewards. More open decision making potentially increases the importance of these values. Values, although difficult to assess, are fundamental: they affect what consumers and voters demand.

At times, the consequences of transition work at cross-purposes. In particular, the very decentralization that allows the public to voice demands for environmental protection within the political process also weakens the state's ability to respond to these demands.

The complicated nature of implementation in countries undergoing transition leads us to focus on a small number of cases concerning the process of implementation: Russian emissions of acid pollutants into the atmosphere (Chapter 12); the control of pollutants from the vast nickel-smelting operations on the Kola Peninsula (Chapter 13); and control of Baltic Sea pollution in Russia and the Baltic states (Chapter 14). One chapter also reviews how Poland has controlled water pollution that flows into the Baltic Sea (Chapter 15), which allows a comparison with the experience of Russia and the Baltic states. In addition, the study of nuclear dumping in the USSR and Russia (Chapter 11) evaluates how external political attention and changes in the openness of domestic society have affected dumping policies.

The cases presented here explore the practical impact that transition has had on the process of transmitting regulatory incentives from the international level to national governments, to regional and local authorities, and finally to target groups. The chains of decisions required to implement policies have grown more complex during transition; consequently, the opportunities for implementation failure have increased.[15] Currently, far more actors are relevant to policy action than under central planning. An extreme case is found in St. Petersburg, where a single, giant polluting operation has divided into 60 smaller polluting enterprises. The shift from central control has suddenly presented these countries with the same challenge that Western regulators have faced for several decades: how to change the behavior of large numbers of dispersed actors. We describe the design of pollution fee systems and regulations designed to influence polluters; we explain how the shift to local and regional control has brought regulated firms into closer contact with regulators, which has probably further weakened the influence of public policy on target group behavior. We also explore how instability of property rights and uncertain regulatory intervention influence the behavior of Russian firms, especially their willingness to make investments in environmental protection. In the Russian approach to privatization, property has generally been transferred to insiders (managers and workers) who have strong incentives (their wages and benefits) to pursue short-term production rather than long-term capital accumulation.[16]

These chapters also investigate how the transboundary impacts of pollution can result in international pressure—and financial inducements—to implement domestic policies. (Indeed, both acid precipitation and pollution of the Baltic Sea were put on the international policy agenda by downwind and downstream countries in the West.) Since the end of the Cold War, the West has been willing to transfer money and other resources to pay for pollution control in the East. Financial transfers are often essential when countries that are the source of environmental damage are unwilling or unable to implement the level of environmental protection sought by downwind and downstream countries.[17] Several of the chapters analyze the conditions under which financial transfers occur and are effective. Of particular interest is how international financial transfers are coupled with domestic resources, regulation, and other actions to form package deals. The findings are relevant to designing better transfer mechanisms and, more generally, to developing innovative approaches to controlling international environmental problems such as the much-discussed notion of "joint implementation."[18]

Russia receives the bulk of our attention because it is the largest of all the transition countries in terms of population, natural resources, geography, and economy. Consumption of fossil energy in the Russian Federation is more than twice that in all the other transition countries combined and exceeds the total consumption in France, Germany, and the UK.[19] Nonetheless, Russia's transition is marked by special characteristics that make generalizing our results to other countries and types of transition difficult. Notably, Russia's economy has been among the most severely disrupted by transition, and thus its citizens remain especially focused on the effects of economic decline; environmental protection generally ranks low on the public agenda.

Our ability to generalize may also be limited by our focus on *pollution*. In the absence of outside pressure, polluters will rarely internalize the costs of pollution. Hence much of our discussion of implementation in Russia examines the government's ability to implement regulations, taxes, and other incentives to internalize externalities. In principle the dynamics could be different in cases of resource management, such as fisheries, where users of the resource have a direct incentive to manage the resource for maximum gain over time. In practice, however, there is considerable evidence that natural resources are massively mismanaged for the same reasons: poorly defined property rights, short-term investment horizons, and poor enforcement of rules designed to promote effective resource management. Much of what our case studies find, using pollution control as an example, is likely to be relevant for other types of environmental problems as well.

To close, we note that in principle liberalization should bode well for international environmental governance. Transition to a liberal society can make governments more responsive and accountable to the public. This could lead to more implementation of international environmental commitments, especially when international commitments regulate the same activities that cause local environmental problems and thus are likely to be of direct concern to local populations. Moreover, liberal states may be more willing and honest participants in international mechanisms for reporting data and scrutinizing national implementation (see the first part of this book). The case studies on transition explore whether this liberal hope has any support in practice.

Notes

The editors and authors thank Alexandre Bim, János Gács, Peter Sand, Arild Underdal, and Oran Young for extremely helpful comments on earlier drafts. The focus on "participation" within implementation emerged from a think piece written by members of the research team; see Andresen, S., Skjærseth, J.B., and Wettestad, J., 1995, Regime, State and Society: Analyzing the Implementation of International Environmental Commitments, WP-95-43, International Institute for Applied Systems Analysis, Laxenburg, Austria.

1. Indeed, research on policy implementation has largely failed to identify results that can be generalized across sectors within countries; thus, the difficulty of identifying conclusions that can be generalized across countries is particularly acute. For a critique of policy implementation literature that remains valid today, see O'Toole, L.J., 1986, "Policy Recommendations for Multi-Actor Implementation: An Assessment of the Field," *Journal of Public Policy* 6:181–210. See also discussion and references in Chapter 1.

2. We have avoided the term that is now standard within the United Nations to denote these countries: countries with economies in transition (CEIT). The process of transition has many diverse elements, in addition to economic change.

3. For recent policy statements of the importance of participation, see Principle 10 of "The Rio Declaration on Environment and Development," reprinted in *The Earth Summit*, edited by S.P. Johnson, 1993, Graham & Trotman/Martinus Nijhoff, London, UK, p. 119; see also Declaration by the Ministers of Environment of the region of the United Nations Economic Commission for Europe, Sophia, Bulgaria, 25 October 1995, see paragraphs 41 and 42, p. 7. Similar statements can be found, for example, in the 1982 World Charter for Nature. See also World Commission on Environment and Development, 1987, *Our Common Future* ("Brundtland Report"), Oxford University Press, Oxford, UK.

Statements advocating wide participation are now found in many agreements and decisions adopted by international organizations at the regional and global levels. For a compact review see Sand, P.H., 1997, "Public Participation," draft, Independent World Commission on the Oceans. For a helpful review of domestic (mainly US) experience with participation of non-state actors and proposed application at the international level, see Wirth, D., 1994, "Reexamining Decision-Making Processes in International Environmental Law," *Iowa Law Review* 79:769–802.

Virtually every study of international environmental governance gives prominent attention to the fact that involvement of stakeholders, notably NGOs, has expanded over the past two to three decades. Such groups influence outcomes by participating in international fora and working transnationally (e.g., by working with counterparts in other countries). See, for example, the comprehensive review of actors involved in international environmental law in Sands, P., 1995, *Principles of International Environmental Law I: Frameworks, Standards and Implementation*, Manchester University Press, Manchester, UK, chapter 3. Other reviews include Finger, M., and Princen, T., 1994, *Environmental NGOs in World Politics: Linking the Local and the Global*, Routledge, London, UK; Stairs, K., and Taylor, P., 1992, "Non-Governmental Organizations and the Legal Protection of the Oceans: A Case Study," in *The International Politics of the Environment*, edited by A. Hurrell and B. Kingsbury, Clarendon Press, Oxford, UK; Peet, G., 1994, "The Role of (Environmental) Non-Governmental Organizations at the Marine Environment Protection Committee (MEPC) of the International Maritime Organization (IMO), and the London Dumping Convention (LDC)," *Ocean and Coastal Management* 22(1):1–8; Reed, D., 1993, "The Global Environment Facility and Non-Government Organizations," *American University Journal of International Law and Policy* 9:191–213; Raustiala, K., 1997, "The 'Participatory' Revolution in International Environmental Law," *Harvard Environmental Law Review*, Spring (forthcoming); Hägerhäll, B., 1996, "The Evolving Role of NGOs," in *International Environmental Negotiations*, edited by G. Sjöstedt, U. Svedin, and B. Hägerhäll Anniansson, Swedish Council for Planning and Coordination of Research and The Swedish Institute of International Affairs, Stockholm, Sweden, pp. 50–76. For a longer-term view and review, see Charnovitz, S., "Two Centuries of Participation: NGOs and International Governance," *Michigan Journal of International Law* 18:183–286.

Since at least the late 1960s, public fear that regulatory agencies were being "captured" by regulated interest groups (e.g., industry) led virtually all liberal countries to enshrine new rights of participation in the policy process for a wider range of (non-industry) stakeholders. In the USA, which is often used as a model for reforms in other countries, the result was a legalistic approach that guaranteed participation for many interests, even individual citizens. The styles and timing of expanded participation varied in other countries. Today, extensive participation by non-state actors is a regular feature of domestic environmental policy, at least in liberal countries. Thus the relevant literature on "participation" is huge. "Negotiated rule making" and similar concepts convey that regulatory rules are complex and, in practice, negotiated through administrative processes marked by extensive stakeholder participation, not merely passed down from a detached government decision maker. See, for example, Stewart, R., 1975, "The Reformation of American Administrative Law," *Harvard Law Review* 88:1667–1813; and Perritt, H.H., 1986, "Negotiated Rulemaking in Practice," *Journal of Policy Analysis and Management* 5:482–495. On the trends and consequences of wider participation and policymaking through negotiation see, for example, chapter 6 in Weale, A., 1992, *The New Politics of Pollution*, Manchester University Press, Manchester, UK. The consequences of extensive participation is a topic that has been extensively discussed in the analytical literature on national policy implementation. For example, see the Habermas-inspired "communication model" of policy implementation discussed in Goggin *et al.*, 1990, *Implementation Theory and Practice*, Scott, Foreman/Little, Brown Higher Education, Glenview, IL, USA. See also the literature on implementation through bargaining, which emphasizes that the practical influence of policy is strongly shaped through regular contacts between enforcers and the targets of enforcement. See, for example, Ingram, H., 1977, "Policy Implementation through Bargaining: The Case of Federal Grants-in-Aid," *Public Policy* 25:499–526. In a similar spirit, see Schön, D.A., and Rein, M., 1994, *Frame Reflection: Toward the Resolution of Intractable Policy Controversies*, Basic Books, New York, NY, USA. Bargaining during implementation is a major theme in the comparative study Downing, P.B., and Hanf, K., eds., 1983, *International Comparisons in Implementing Pollution Laws*, Kluwer-Nijhoff, Boston, MA, USA. Downing suggests that this bargaining is one way the impact of regulatory institutions is moderated such that the regulatory outcome reflects mainly the status quo and the basic economics of environmental regulation (the magnitude and distribution of costs and benefits)—regulatory institutions matter, but not much; see Downing, P.B., 1979, "Implementing Pollution Laws: Observations from the American Experience," *Zeitschrift für Umweltpolitik* 4:357–392. Many other studies of implementation of environmental laws underscore that bargaining between enforcers and targets (not the strict application of the law) has a large influence on outcomes. For at least one study that laments that such bargaining (and leniency) is declining, exacerbating the impact of political processes that produce excessively strict environmental laws see Bardach, E., and Kagan, R.A., 1982, *Going by the Book: The Problem of Regulatory Unreasonableness,* a Twentieth Century Fund Report, Temple University Press, Philadelphia, PA, USA.

For a selection of reviews on participation in the environmental policy process see, for example, Gauna, E., 1995, "Federal Environmental Citizen Provisions: Obstacles and Incentives on the Road to Environmental Justice," *Ecology Law Quarterly* 22:1–87; Führ and Gerhard Roller, eds., 1991, *Participation and Litigation Rights of Environmental Associations in Europe: Current Legal Situation and Practical Experience*, Peter Lang, Frankfurt am Main, Germany. For a recent assessment of European litigation which emphasizes the difficulty of public interest groups influencing Community courts directly, see Krämer, L., 1996, "Public Interest Litigation in Environmental Matters before European Courts," *Journal of Environmental Law* 8:1–18.

Specific examples of policies designed to expand participation include the "Target Group Policy" adopted by the Dutch government in the mid-1980s (see Chapters 8 and 9). Similarly, in the USA the Environmental Protection Agency's new "Project XL" gives firms, communities, governmental agencies, and industry sectors "the flexibility to develop common-sense, cost-effective strategies that will replace or modify specific regulatory requirements, on the condition that they produce greater benefits. Based on the premise that these participants know better than the federal government how to reduce their pollution, Project XL reduces the regulatory burden and promotes economic growth while achieving better environmental and public health protection"; Project XL Information Packet (May 20 1996). For more information on XL see http://www.epa.gov/project XL. At the state level within the USA, government and regulatory agencies have increased participation by target groups, for example, by relaxing liability laws and encouraging active efforts by industry to identify and clean up hazardous waste sites; for a review see Anderson, M.D., 1996, "The State Voluntary Cleanup Program Alternative," *Natural Resources and Environment*, Winter 1996, American Bar Association, pp. 22–26. See also the discussion of voluntary regulation in note 5.

Within the European Union, many efforts have been made to increase participation of non-state actors, including the Directive on the Freedom of Access to Information on the Environment (90/313/EEC, 7 June 1990). In practice, the consequences of opening access to information are hardly clear as questions remain about what information must be released and what the public does with information. For one critical assessment, see Rowan-Robinson, J., Ross, A., Walton, W., and Rothnil, J., 1996, "Public Access to Environmental Information: A Means to What End?" *Journal of Environment Law* 8:19–42. In the first part of this book and in Chapter 16, we also examine the utility of released information.

Expanding participation of non-state actors in public decision making is seen as a major goal of the transition from central planning to a liberal, market-based society. For a review and a useful typology of modes of participation by citizens and public interest groups, and application to transition countries, see Tóth Nagy, M., Bowman, M., Dusik, J., Jendroska, J., Stec, S., van der Zwiep, K., and Zlinskzky, J., eds., 1994, *Manual on Public Participation in Environmental Decisionmaking: Current Practice and Future Possibilities in Central and Eastern Europe*, Regional Environmental Center for Central and Eastern Europe, Budapest, Hungary.

The argument that rising participation by non-state actors represents a new mode of democratic political organization and decision making is latent in most studies that document NGO participation as well as policy arguments that advocate further expansion of participation. Theories of "discursive democracy"—a form of decision making based on extensive communication among well-informed citizens—emphasize that rising participation can lead to more accountable governance. Such theories are often invoked, explicitly or implicitly, to support the need for wider participation. Recent writings (and a review of the literature) in this spirit include Dryzek, J.S., 1996, "Political Inclusion and the Dynamics of Democratization," *American Political Science Review* 90:475–487. See also Cohen, J., 1989, "Deliberation and Democratic Legitimacy," in *The Good Polity: Normative Analysis of the State*, edited by A. Hamlin and P. Pettit, Basil Blackwell, Oxford, UK. For an application to environmental decision making, see Dryzek, J.S., 1995, "Political and Ecological Communication," *Environmental Politics* 4:13–30. For a helpful review see pages 215–223 of Hayward, B.M., 1995, "The Greening of Participatory Democracy: A Reconsideration of Theory," *Environmental Politics* 4(4). For attention to the role of science in the democratic process of making environmental decisions see Jasanoff, S., 1996, "The Dilemma of Environmental Democracy," *Issues in Science and Technology* Fall:63–70. Other relevant studies include Williams, B.A., and Matheny, A.R., 1995, *Democracy, Dialogue, and Environmental Disputes: The Contested Languages of Social Regulation*, Yale University Press, New Haven, CT, USA; Lafferty, W.M., and Meadowcroft, J., 1996, *Democracy and the Environment: Problems and Prospects*, Edward Elgar, Cheltenham, UK; and Renn, O., Webler, T., and Wiedemann, P., eds., 1995, *Fairness and Competence in Citizen Participation*, Kluwer Academic Publishers, Dordrecht, Netherlands. The themes of expanded participation, democracy, and incorporation of ecological values throughout decision making are central in the movement to expand access to the policy process and thus to promote environmental justice, which is often labeled "access to justice." Many theories that emphasize decision making through extensive communication, availability of information, and transparency have been developed to describe (and prescribe) decision making *within* societies and thus may not strictly apply to decision making at the international level; however, some argue that increasingly a form of international society exists and thus it is meaningful to speak of democratic and communicative decision making at the international level as well. Indeed, the rising participation of non-state actors, as well as extensive transnational links among non-state actors, is often cited as evidence of this growing international civil society. Democracy is not only a structure for making decisions but also an institution intended to ensure that decisions are legitimate. For an application of that procedural argument to international law see Franck, T.N., 1990, *The Power of Legitimacy Among Nations*, Oxford University Press, New York, NY, USA. For additional speculation on these issues related to democratic participation, especially in liberal states, see Chapter 16.

Although policy and theory about international environmental politics give much attention to participation by non-state actors, it is important to underscore that a prominent role for non-state actors is neither a recent phenomenon nor one exclusive to the field of the environment. For example, earlier relevant work concerns the influence of multinational corporations on world politics, which has been a topic of great interest since at least the 1960s. (Many environmental NGOs have structures and transnational links that are similar to those of multinational corporations.) Work on the international labor movement and labor unions dates back even earlier; their influence is evident in their formal role as participants (alongside industry associations) in the International Labor Organization, founded in 1919. More generally, there were many pronouncements about the need for broad participation as one prerequisite for civil international society at the founding of the League of Nations. Protection of human rights, notably the regimes established since the Second World War, has generally given a prominent role to NGOs in the identification and prosecution of human rights violations. More generally, the problem of international policy coordination when numerous government entities (functional agencies, levels of government) and other actors interact at the international and transnational levels has long been a topic of research and commentary; for one early review see Kaiser, K., 1971, "Transnational Politics: Toward a Theory of Multinational Politics," *International Organization* 25:790–817. For a detailed application see Keohane, R.O., and Nye, J.S., 1989, *Power and Interdependence*, 2nd edition, Scott, Foresman & Co., Glenview, CA, USA; pp. 259–260.

4. The reader will note that we have implied a three-dimensional typology for participation: actors, modes, and levels (international, national). For simplicity, we do not present this as a typology here; nor do we rigorously describe which combinations of modes, actors, and levels are likely to have certain impacts on policy outputs and outcomes. Rather, we present this as a commonsense typology and focus on a few of the combinations that, we expect, are

of special importance to the implementation process (e.g., participation of target groups; participation of other actors in the oversight process that helps to avoid regulatory capture). Other studies may want to develop and employ this typology further. Useful in the development of our typology is the REC typology of public participation (*Manual on Public Participation in Environmental Decisionmaking: Current Practice and Future Possibilities in Central and Eastern Europe*—see note 3). Like many typologies and studies of public (notably ENGO) participation, the REC framework focuses on "rights" to participation—the "right to know," the "right to be heard," and the "right to affect decisions." Our typology is broader since we focus on many different actors; thus in addition to rights we also focus on responsibilities (i.e., the responsibility to make decisions). Our simple framework could be extended to examine other responsibilities, such as to change behavior, which is the responsibility of target groups. In general, frameworks that include target group and governmental participation (as ours does) give more attention to responsibilities, whereas typologies that focus on public interest groups, which have historically been excluded to different degrees, focus on rights of participation.

5. On the importance of target group (and public) participation and current practice at the World Bank, see *The World Bank Participation Sourcebook*, 1996, The World Bank, Washington, DC, USA. See also the well-written overview to United Nations Center for Human Settlements (HABITAT), 1996, *An Urbanizing World: Global Report on Human Settlements 1996*, Oxford University Press, Oxford, UK, especially sections 9.4 and 9.6. The relevant literature is voluminous. For an important essay that reviews the literature and evaluates early experience see Korten, D.C., 1980, "Community Organization and Rural Development: A Learning Process Approach," *Public Administration Review* (September/October):480–510. Some studies underscore that it is not important merely to achieve "participation," but also that particular institutional arrangements exist to facilitate informed (and influential) participation. See Esman, M.J., and Uphoff, N.T., 1984, *Local Organizations: Intermediaries in Rural Development*, Cornell University Press, Ithaca, NY, USA. In the legal system, controlled studies show that decisions reached by mediation—with participation and consent from all sides—are more likely to be implemented than those imposed by the judicial system. See, for example, McEwen, C.A., and Maiman, R.J., 1984, "Mediation in Small Claims Court: Achieving Compliance Through Consent," *Law and Society Review* 18:11–49. Several of the case studies in this book support the hypothesis that "self-regulation" or "voluntary" regulation—that is, regulation with active participation by target groups—can lead to substantial changes in behavior, in part because targets fear more onerous compulsory regulation. See Chapters 6 and 16.

6. We are mindful that targets may want regulation, on their own terms. See Stigler, G.J., 1971, "The Theory of Economic Regulation," *Bell Journal of Economics and Management Science* 2:3–21. Our interest is regulation that reflects interests beyond only those of target groups.

7. Maloney, W.A., Jordan, G., McLaughlin, A.M., 1994, "Interest Groups and Public Policy: The Insider/Outsider Model Revisited," *Journal of Public Policy* 14:17–38.

8. The proposition that target group participation leads to informational benefits has also been examined in the development literature (see note 4) and the literature advocating participation in environmental policy-making (see note 3).

9. We note that other interest groups, such as ENGOs, can also capture the regulatory process. The whaling case (chapter 10) provides an example. For a review and analysis of "capture," with application to US environmental regulation see, for example: Sabatier, P., 1975, "Social Movements and Regulatory Agencies: Toward a More Adequate–and Less Pessimistic–Theory of 'Clientele Capture'," *Policy Sciences* 6:301–342.

10. Østreng, W., and Andresen, S., 1989, *International Resource Management: The Role of Science and Politics*, Belhaven Press, London, UK; Kimball, L.A., 1996, *Treaty Implementation: Scientific and Technical Advice Enters a New Stage*, American Society of International Law, Washington, DC, USA.

11. Readers will note that part of our interest is in how interest groups form to press their cause. We are mindful of the hypothesis, from Mancur Olson, that diffuse stakeholders are unlikely to form into groups, but narrow and concentrated interests will organize themselves more readily. For more see Olson, M., 1965, *The Logic of Collective Action: Public Goods and the Theory of Groups*, Harvard University Press, Cambridge, MA, USA. Thus, diffuse interests will tend to be under-represented in pluralistic decision-making fora, and concentrated interests will have excessive influence. In other words, the "public interest" often remains latent and not adequately reflected in policy. Some of our studies address Olson's hypothesis, though our analysis was not designed to investigate the issues in detail. Contrary to pessimistic expectations based on Olson's logic, in general we find that diffuse interests–notably the public interest in environmental protection–are often represented because environmental issues are typically adopted by existing organizations and networks of organizations and thus the cost of forming a new group need not be incurred. For one of several models of that apply and extend this perspective to public interest groups see Downing, P.B., and Brady, G.L., 1981, "The Role of Citizen Interest Groups in Environmental Policy Formation," *Nonprofit Firms in a Three Sector Economy*, edited by M.J. White, Urban Institute, Washington,

DC, USA. Downing and Brady analyze many factors, including the role of seed money in forming public interest groups, the role of tax policy, and the tendency of such groups to overstate the "public interest" in environmental protection in order to sustain membership, especially when such groups actually succeed in forcing the adoption of policies that improve the environment. For another analysis, which examines the incentives to join industry associations (termed "target groups" in the present study), see Marsh, D., 1976, "On Joining Interest Groups: An Empirical Consideration of the Work of Mancur Olson Jr." *British Journal of Political Science* 6:257–271. For a critique of Olson's pessimistic hypothesis based on membership data from major US environmental groups see Mitchell, R.C., 1979, "National Environmental Lobbies and the Apparent Illogic of Collective Action," *Collective Decision Making: Applications from Public Choice Theory*, edited by C.S. Russell, published for Resources for the Future by the Johns Hopkins University Press, Baltimore, MD, USA.

12. In recent agreements, such as the Montreal Protocol, the European Community is also typically a signatory and party.

13. Voting and decision rules have been the subject of an enormous amount of research. For a recent discussion of voting and decision-making procedures in international environmental decision-making fora, see Széll, P., 1996, "Decision Making under Multilateral Environmental Agreements," *Environmental Policy and Law* 26:210–214. More generally, the making of decisions by voting is one aspect of the very broad field of "public choice," which has developed mainly through analysis of decision making within societies (states). Notably see Arrow, K., 1951, *Social Choice and Individual Values*, John Wiley & Sons, New York, NY, USA; Downs, A., 1957, *An Economic Theory of Democracy*, Harper and Row, New York, NY, USA; Buchanan, J.M., and Tullock, G., 1962, *The Calculus of Consent: Logical Foundations of Constitutional Democracy*, University of Michigan Press, Ann Arbor, MI, USA. In the huge field, useful reviews and contributions are found, *inter alia*, in Russell, C.S., ed., 1979, *Collective Decision Making: Applications from Public Choice Theory*, Johns Hopkins Press for Resources for the Future, Baltimore, MD, USA; and Mueller, D.C., ed., 1997, *Perspectives on Public Choice: A Handbook*, Cambridge University Press, Cambridge, UK.

14. The relevant literature on the impact of transition on regulation, including environmental regulation, is large, although few studies have focused on the impact of transition on the implementation of international environmental commitments. Some exceptions include Darst, R.G., 1997, "The Internationalization of Environmental Protection in the USSR and Its Successor States," in *The Internationalization of Environmental Protection*, edited by M.A. Schreurs and E. Economy, Cambridge University Press, Cambridge, UK (forthcoming); O'Toole, L.J., 1997, "Networking Requirements, Institutional Capacity, and

Implementation Gaps in Transitional Regimes: The Case of Acidification Policy in Hungary," *Journal of European Public Policy* (in press). For additional discussion and results from the present project, see Kotov, V., Nikitina, E., Roginko, A., Stokke, O.S., Victor, D.G., and Hjorth, R., 1997, "The Implementation of International Environmental Commitments in Countries (mainly Russia) Undergoing Economic and Social Transition," *MOCT-MOST Economic Policy in Transition Countries* 7(2) (in press). For more on financial transfers to transition countries, which aid policy implementation (including implementation of international environmental commitments), see Connolly, B., Gutner, T., and Bedarff, H., 1996, "Organizational Inertia and Environmental Assistance to Eastern Europe," in *Institutions for Environmental Aid: Pitfalls and Promise*, edited by R.O. Keohane and M.A. Levy, The MIT Press, Cambridge, MA, USA; and Hiltunen, H., 1996, "Finnish Strategies to Reduce Transboundary Pollution from the Kola Peninsula: Lessons for Implementing Joint Implementation," WP-96-24, International Institute for Applied Systems Analysis, Laxenburg, Austria. For one of many Western projects aimed at building legal institutions and administrative capacity, see Greenspan Bell, R., 1994, "EPA's International Assistance Efforts: Developing Effective Environmental Institutions," *Environmental Law Reporter* 24:10593–10599. Some selections from the broader relevant literature include Vári, A., and Tamás,, P., 1993, eds., *Environment and Democratic Transition: Policy and Politics in Central and Eastern Europe*, Kluwer Academic Publishers, Dordrecht, Netherlands; Goldenman, G., ed., 1994, *Environmental Liability and Privatization in Central and Eastern Europe*, World Bank, Washington, DC, USA; Kruzíková, E., 1995, "The Environmental Management System in Industrial Enterprises," Final Report, Phase 2 of Privatization and Environment in the Czech Republic, Prague, Czech Republic; Botcheva, L., 1996, "Focus and Effectiveness of Environmental Activism in Eastern Europe: A Comparative Study of Environmental Movements in Bulgaria, Hungary, Slovakia, and Romania," *Journal of Environment and Development* 5:292–308. Studies on the Soviet system are useful because they provide information on what the current transition is leaving behind. In particular, see Jancar, B., 1987, *Environmental Management in the Soviet Union and Yugoslavia: Structure and Regulation in Federal Communist States*, Duke University Press, Durham, NC, USA. See also studies on the environmental legacy of central planning: Goldman, M., 1972, *The Spoils of Progress: Environmental Pollution in the Soviet Union*, The MIT Press, Cambridge, MA, USA; Feshbach, M., 1995, *Ecological Disaster: Cleaning up the Hidden Legacy of the Soviet Regime*, Twentieth Century Fund, New York, NY, USA.

15. Kotov, V., 1994, Implementation and Effectiveness of International Environmental Regimes During the Process of Transformation in Russia,

WP-94-123, International Institute for Applied Systems Analysis, Laxenburg, Austria. See also O'Toole, op. cit., note 14.

16. Russian privatization of large enterprises allowed managers and workers to acquire large shares of enterprises essentially for free. The remaining shares were sold in markets, where those same workers could often purchase additional shares at a discount and/or purchase shares with vouchers that had been issued to all Russian citizens. As a result, inside investors held controlling interests of most large firms and had de facto control even when outside ownership was high. The complete story of Russia's initial privatization efforts is best told in Åslund, A., 1995, *How Russia Became a Market Economy*, Brookings, Washington, DC, USA, chapter 7. Recently, some firms have been privatized through supposedly open public auction, including (in the summer of 1997) the giant Norilsk firm, which is the topic of Chapter 13.

17. See also Keohane, R. and Levy, M., eds., 1996, *Institutions for Environmental Aid*, The MIT Press, Cambridge, MA, USA.

18. "Joint implementation" is a concept employed under the UN Framework Convention on Climate Change to describe the possibility that one country can earn credit for policies that it finances and implements in another country to control emissions. The concept, a limited form of marketable emission permits, is also being considered under the 1994 Second Sulphur Protocol to the Convention on Long-Range Transboundary Air Pollution.

19. Coal, oil, and gas, aggregated according to heat content. See British Petroleum, 1994, *BP Statistical Review of World Energy* 34.

8

The Making and Implementation of North Sea Commitments: The Politics of Environmental Participation

Jon Birger Skjærseth

Introduction

Surrounded by densely populated areas, the North Sea is a zone of intense human activity. Major sources of contaminant inputs to the North Sea are river input, direct discharge, dumping at sea, and atmospheric deposition of pollutants. In spite of the institutions created in the 1970s to regulate North Sea pollution, there were growing indications in the early 1980s that specific parts of the North Sea were becoming severely polluted. Two legally binding conventions were established in the early 1970s to address North Sea pollution—the Convention for the Prevention of Marine Pollution by Dumping from Ships and Aircraft (Oslo Convention) and the Convention for the Prevention of Marine Pollution from Land-based Sources (Paris Convention), together known as OSPAR.[1] Even with existing national measures and the OSPAR legal framework, it was clear that measures necessary to reduce North Sea pollution could not be initiated without additional political impetus. Against this backdrop, several political International North Sea Conferences (INSCs) have been arranged since 1984. The nonbinding North Sea Declarations resulting from these conferences represent a marked change in how North Sea states approach marine pollution: instead of controlling pollution levels at sea, emphasis has been placed on significantly reducing pollutant emissions at their sources. Domestic implementation of these Declarations requires a supreme domestic effort and significant capital outlays. Nonetheless, at the domestic level inputs of regulated substances have been reduced significantly overall, though to varying degrees.

Few studies have focused on this shift from inertia to action at the international level and how international commitments have been implemented domestically, even though North Sea cooperation has existed since the early 1970s and may provide lessons relevant outside this specific issue area.[2] This paper focuses on the significant change in international commitments and domestic implementation. The study examines implementation in three countries—the UK, the Netherlands, and Norway—all of which have been major players with different roles and interests related to the North Sea pollution regime. These countries have also achieved different results in implementing their international commitments to regulate North Sea pollution, and they have markedly different regulatory styles. Thus, a central task of this analysis is to assess whether and how the different regulatory styles have produced different policy ambitions and resulted in different levels of actual performance.

The analysis focuses on whether and how patterns of *participation* have influenced the making and implementation of international commitments, as well as on factors that may explain observed patterns of participation. It examines four main types of participants: states, target groups, environmental nongovernmental organizations (ENGOs), and governmental agencies. Research and the role of scientists at the international level are also considered. In particular, the following issues and propositions are examined. First, there is a quite robust assumption that joint commitments at the international level tend to reflect the interests and preferences of the least ambitious actor when those commitments require unanimous consent and are not linked to other issues.[3] In the North Sea case, excluding the least ambitious states and focusing political pressure at the ministerial level allowed the adoption of stringent international commitments that did not merely reflect the interests and preferences of the least ambitious actors. The shift from participation by lower-level governmental representatives to participation by ministers increased pressure at the highest levels of government, where important policy decisions are made.

Second, this study examines the effectiveness of different types of legal instruments. The North Sea Ministerial Conferences set very ambitious goals, which were acceptable because they were nonbinding. They subsequently became more effective when they were codified into legally binding measures through the Oslo and Paris Commissions as well as in the context of the European Union (EU). The interaction between the two forms of instruments—nonbinding and binding—is explored in the course of this study. From the mid-1980s, international commitments had an increasing effect on national ambitions and performance in all three countries.

Third, decision makers face a dilemma concerning the relationship between participation and effective regulation. Excluding from the policy-formulation process those actors that frequently must bear the cost of regulations (target groups) tends to produce ambitious governmental goals and strong resistance when measures are to be implemented. Conversely, including such actors in the formulation of policies may produce less stringent goals but will ensure cooperation during the implementation phase. As expected, this study shows that the stringency of domestic goals and implementation is very sensitive to the *balance* of different interests. In particular, the involvement of target group interests, which frequently are opposed to stringent regulation, should be counterbalanced by participation by other interests and by enforcement.

Fourth, many observers have criticized the fact that pollution control policies are fragmented among many organizations, administrative procedures, and laws—fragmentation, they argue, is inconsistent with the "holism" of the natural world.[4] The "cure" is integrated policy that penetrates all levels of government and involves all governmental agencies in its execution.[5] Even though the "fragmentation/integration" discourse is perhaps as old as pollution control itself, this study shows that the lack of vertical and horizontal integration of environmental concerns and goals still represents a major obstacle to domestic implementation.

The first section of this chapter aims at describing and explaining changes in international commitments. The second section focuses on the implementation of these commitments at the domestic level and the influence of access and participation. Concluding remarks with a view to the extent to which the problem at hand has been solved are presented in the final section.

The International Dimension

Development of International Commitments and Change in Participation
The 25-year history of cooperation on environmental issues concerning the North Sea and northeast Atlantic is marked by a development from international marine pollution "anarchy" toward international "governance." When the coaster *Stella Maris* left the port of Rotterdam in 1971 carrying 650 tons of toxic waste destined to be dumped in the northern part of the North Sea, there were no international guidelines to give formal weight to the protests that arose.

Today, international guidelines prohibit such dumping and therefore dumping has nearly stopped.

Partly as a consequence of the *Stella Maris* incident, the Oslo Convention was signed in 1972. Other cooperative frameworks covering this area include the 1974 Paris Convention on land-based pollution sources and the INSC process.[6] In addition, the EU has played an important role, both as a party to the Paris Convention and the INSCs and as an independent "supranational" institution with its own water and marine policy. By the end of 1990, 27 items of EU water legislation had been passed. It is even argued that EU water legislation today constitutes a more comprehensive legal framework than many national systems of water regulation.[7] The adoption and implementation of relevant EU Directives are not the main focus of this chapter, although EU developments will be included when they are particularly relevant to issues discussed here.

Two phases can be identified in the development of international commitments within the North Sea pollution regime. From the mid-1970s to the mid-1980s, international commitments were developed within the framework of OSPAR as well as in the EU. With some exceptions, the parties did not succeed in adopting commitments aimed at significant behavioral change at any level. One important reason was a profound disagreement on whether goals should be based on uniform emission standards (UESs) or environmental quality objectives (EQOs). The latter principle—advocated by the UK in particular—is based on the idea that money is not wisely spent until certainty exists as to the causal relationship between inputs of contaminants, concentrations, and resulting environmental effects. The environmental quality approach is based on assumptions about the sea's assimilative capacity; thus it normally allows more inputs of contaminating substances to the sea than the uniform emission approach. Consequently, the approach favored by a country is closely related to its material interests. Due to the counterclockwise direction of the North Sea currents, the UK, in particular, can be categorized as a "net exporter" of marine pollution, not significantly affected by either its own or others' activities. At the other end of the spectrum, the Nordic countries represent "net importers," in no position to affect the UK through their polluting activities. In between are continental countries like the Netherlands, liable to import pollutants from the UK and export them to the southern part of the North Sea (see figure 8.1). Thus, an agreement between the core countries representing these different interests would in many ways represent an agreement for the

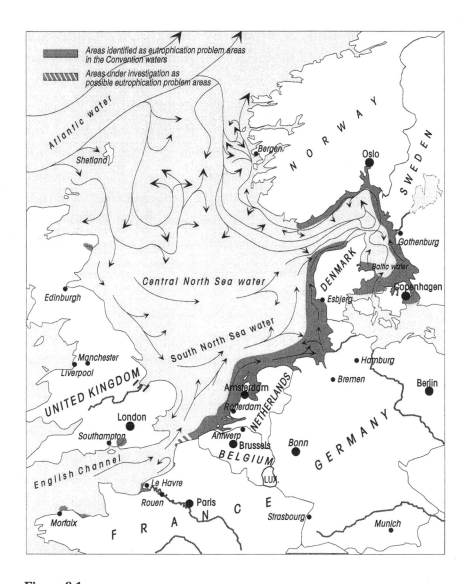

Figure 8.1
The North Sea basin
Arrows show general circulation of water; shaded areas identify eutrophication
problem areas as defined by the parties.

whole North Sea. Moreover, Spain and Portugal, which are parties to the Oslo and Paris Conventions and contribute virtually no pollution to the North Sea, have never favored significant pollution controls. In essence, the states had significantly asymmetrical interests and preferences.

During the second phase of international commitment development, the INSCs took over the task of producing goals for the regime, resulting in a fundamental change in international commitments. The Bremen Declaration of 1984 alluded to the precautionary principle, and the 1987 London Declaration was the first international agreement to explicitly include this principle.[8] During this phase of the regime's development, attention was increasingly focused on technology standards and polluting sources, as emission standards gradually replaced EQOs. These changes paved the way for the adoption of specific international goals on percentage reductions of emissions within fixed time frames. The most important goals in this respect are the following:

- To phase out dumping of industrial waste (by 1989), sewage sludge (by 1998), and incineration at sea (by 1991).
- To reduce emissions of nutrients to sensitive areas in the order of 50 percent between 1985 and 1995.
- To reduce emissions of 37 specified hazardous substances from land-based sources by 50–70 percent between 1985 and 1995.

Given the polarized situation described above, changes in participation had the potential to affect adoption of joint commitments in the following ways. First, the number of participating states could be changed by decoupling the "least ambitious" actors that were insignificant causes of North Sea pollution, thus raising the political pressure on the remaining "laggards." Second, the level at which participation within governments occurred could be raised to generate more political energy to cut through deadlock. High-level conferences may "allow" trade-offs that are far beyond the authority of low-level officials.[9] Third, ENGOs could be included to increase transparency and expose laggards to international pressure. Including target groups would probably counteract these changes, however, as they are the actors that would have to pay the price for more stringent international regulations (see table 8.1). Fourth, including independent scientific bodies capable of producing new and reliable information about the issue could affect the parties' perception of the situation. In short, if participation really matters, a change in these dimensions should be expected prior to significant change in joint commitments.

Table 8.1   Major Sources of North Sea Pollution and Their Regulatory Implications

Type of waste/ activity	Reason for concern	Principal target sectors[a]
Ocean-based sources		
Industrial waste	Toxic, persistent, and liable to bioaccumulate	Manufacturing, industry
Sewage sludge	Same as for industrial waste plus eutrophication	Water, industry
Incineration	Inputs of dioxins under sub-optimal conditions	Manufacturing, industry
Land-based sources		
Hazardous substances	Toxic, persistent, and liable to bioaccumulate	Industry, municipal (plus agriculture in the case of pesticides)
Nutrients	Eutrophication, toxic algae blooms	Agriculture, municipal

[a]Major target sectors may differ somewhat from country to country.

The "OSPAR Decade": A State-Driven Process Sensitive to the "Least Ambitious" Actors.   The Oslo Convention was signed by all 13 West European maritime states in 1972. Its main objective is to take all possible steps to prevent pollution of the sea by substances liable to create hazards to human health, to harm living resources and marine life, to damage amenities, or to interfere with other legitimate uses of the sea. Membership is restricted to European maritime states, although other actors may be invited to participate. As of 1995, all 13 countries that signed the Oslo Declaration have become parties. Geographically, the Convention covers the northeast Atlantic and the North Sea, including the high seas, territorial seas, and internal coastal waters. The Convention includes two annexes that differentiate between substances according to their hazardousness: dumping of substances on the "black" list is banned; dumping of substances on the "gray" list is regulated. The executive body of the Convention is the Oslo Commission, where the parties meet annually. The Commission can adopt decisions, recommendations, and other "agreements" to draw up programs and measures for the prevention of pollution. Until 1984, relatively few decisions and recommendations were actually adopted; those that were adopted mainly concerned the establishment of co-operative procedures.[10] The only exception is a 1980 recommendation to take all possible steps to reduce contamination of sewage sludge by heavy metals at the source.

The Paris Convention, signed in 1974, allowed the EU to join as a contracting party. The Convention's main objective is to take all possible steps to prevent pollution of the sea by adopting, individually and jointly, measures to combat marine pollution and by harmonizing the parties' policies in this regard. Membership is restricted in the same way as in the Oslo Convention. Twelve parties including the EU have ratified the Convention. Like the Oslo Convention, the Paris Convention is structured around a black/gray list system. The Convention originally applied to land-based pollution sources; in 1986 it was amended to include atmospheric sources. Only eight decisions with minor implications for target group behavior were adopted within the Paris Commission up to 1984.

There was no change in state participation in the North Sea pollution regime during the first decade. Belgium, Denmark, the Federal Republic of Germany (FRG), Iceland, Ireland, the Netherlands, Norway, Portugal, Spain, Sweden, the UK, and Northern Ireland were original parties to both the Oslo and Paris Conventions. Finland was a party to the Oslo Convention, but not to the Paris Convention. The EU had only observer status in the Oslo Commission, but was an original party to the Paris Convention. Access procedures for states have not changed substantially over time. The participating states in the conferences leading up to the Conventions as well as states located upstream on watercourses that flow into the maritime area have an automatic right to participate. In addition, the contracting parties can unanimously invite any other state to participate.[11] During this phase delegations to OSPAR meetings were composed of middle-level civil servants from the various countries, representing mainly the environmental sectors.

Nongovernmental organizations (NGOs) did not have formal access to the regime until 1990. The Oslo and Paris Commissions operate under formal procedures. According to Rule 4 of the rules of procedures, the Commission may unanimously invite international organizations and non-contracting states to send observers to the meetings.

Although Rule 4 does not provide for participation by NGOs, at the 1981 meeting of the Oslo and Paris Commissions a decision was made to allow NGOs to attend particular meetings provided there were no objections from the parties.[12] This decision was designed to allow participation by target groups, particularly the refining and offshore industries. Representatives from these industries had already been present at the Paris Commission's Working Group on Oil Pollution; thus in practice important target groups had a voice even when they were formally denied access. This informal practice was stopped at the 1983 joint meeting of the Commissions when Greenpeace applied to become a fully accredited observer. Several options were considered, including changing the procedure and making a special decision on Greenpeace. However, the contracting parties could not agree on a revised procedure and thus no NGOs were allowed to attend. The UK, Finland, the FRG, the Netherlands, and Sweden emphasized that nongovernmental bodies should not be entitled to receive unpublished Commission documents. Denmark was more open to giving NGOs access to information and supported allowing NGOs to submit papers for specific agenda items. As a compromise solution to this deadlock, Greenpeace was allowed to make written and oral statements to the Commissions, but was not permitted to observe negotiations or attend working group meetings.

State control over OSPAR was reinforced by tight control over the flow of scientific and technical information. The Oslo and Paris Commissions were assisted by the Standing Advisory Committee for Scientific Advice (SACSA) and the Technical Working Group (TWG), respectively, as well as by ad hoc working groups and the Joint Monitoring Group (JMG). SACSA and the TWG were composed of civil servants with backgrounds in the natural sciences.[13] Research on the marine environment was conducted in government laboratories that were accountable to the relevant ministries. No transnational networks of scientists existed.[14] Because participants in these advisory groups were drawn from national governments, complaints were made that both the TWG and SACSA were "politicized."[15] In addition, the scientific and technical bodies were given a very limited mandate, covering only a few substances. The main task of the JMG was to assess the level of marine pollution. As late as 1987, the JMG was still preoccupied with developing a monitoring methodology and was unable to present any clear trends to the Commissions with regard to any pollutant in the North Sea.[16] SACSA and the TWG were to discuss and propose practical and technical solutions on the basis of problems identified by scientific research on the North Sea's marine environment. Their main tasks were to keep the process of scientific and technical knowledge under review and to give advice on technical and scientific questions if requested to do so by the Commissions.[17]

The "Conference Decade": Multiple Participation Exceeding "the Least Ambitious" Actors. The Wadden Sea—a vast wetland area in the southeastern corner of the North Sea—was one of the regions becoming severely polluted at the beginning of the 1980s. Motivated by this problem, in 1984 the FRG arranged the first INSC in Bremen. This conference was originally conceived as a onetime event, but political momentum triggered by this conference led to additional conferences in London, UK (1987), The Hague, Netherlands (1990), Copenhagen, Denmark (1993), and Esbjerg, Denmark (1995).

The London Declaration represented a turning point concerning dumping and land-based emissions of nutrients and hazardous substances. For the first time, decisions were adopted to impose ambitious emission targets within fixed time limits. The 1990 Hague Conference clarified and strengthened the London Declaration, particularly concerning land-based sources of pollution. By 1990, at the Hague Conference, it had also become evident that most countries were facing problems reaching the goals on nutrients adopted in the London Declaration. These concerns, among others, led to the intermediate ministerial meeting in 1993.

Some of the "soft law" Declarations from the North Sea Ministerial Conferences have been adopted by the Oslo and Paris Commissions and the EU. An important aim of the INSCs has been to accelerate and intensify the work of these existing international bodies. The goal was to transform the Ministerial Declarations, which are not legally binding,[18] into "hard law" in the form of OSPAR Decisions and EU Regulations, Directives, and Decisions. The 1987 London Declaration made its most direct impact on the Oslo Commission, which transformed soft law commitments to stop dumping into Oslo Commission Decisions. In addition, the initiative taken within the EU to reduce nutrient emissions in the wake of the London Declaration was of major importance.[19] The 1990 Hague Declaration made its strongest impact on industrial sectors within the Paris Commission. In 1992 the Oslo and Paris Conventions were merged into one legal instrument—the new OSPAR Convention, also known as the 1992 Paris Convention—which will replace the two separate conventions when it enters into force. The new 1992 Convention codified some of the earlier achievements.[20] Over time, the process of *international implementation* has led to a comprehensive legal and political international regime aimed at substantial behavioral change by target groups.

The first decade of the North Sea pollution regime was essentially state driven; it was based on a stable number of participating states represented by relatively low-level government officials who controlled the flow of information. In the second decade, however, four principal changes took place that affected the course of collective actions. First, two major laggard states were decoupled from OSPAR by the organization of the first INSC. Second, representation in OSPAR changed, with ministers of the environment replacing low-level civil servants as the state representatives. Third, the regime became more open to NGO participation, which has increased significantly. Fourth, in the second phase, the scientific community has occupied a more independent and prominent role.

The INSCs are ad hoc in the sense that each conference must decide whether there should be a follow-up conference. In practice, INSCs have been held on a regular basis. Each conference is organized by a secretariat, appointed by the host country, and various preparatory groups covering political and scientific and technical issues. In practice, access is determined by the political preparatory group, which sends invitations to those who have shown interest in the work on the North Sea environment and who have something to contribute to the conference. The actors are categorized into observers and participants. One important consequence of these new "soft law" Ministerial Conferences was the decoupling of Spain and Portugal from the North Sea pollution regime. These countries have no borders on the North Sea and contribute virtually nothing to North Sea pollution. Moreover, they have generally behaved as laggards in all areas of international environmental cooperation.[21] Excluding them reduced the number of laggards in the North Sea pollution regime, but did not unify the interests and preferences of the remaining parties. The UK, in particular, remained a laggard in the Oslo and Paris Commissions and in the INSCs. However, the remaining laggards were exposed to increased political pressure. This pressure was reinforced when environmental ministers replaced lower-level civil servants at the conferences, as the ministers were more sensitive to politics and societal pressure because they were accountable to their electorates.

The North Sea states have also gradually opened access to NGOs. In the 1984 and 1987 Declarations the ministers did not mention NGOs, but recognized efforts by intergovernmental organizations. By 1995, the ministers could "note with pleasure that the representatives of industry, agriculture and other

sectors welcome the objectives and are willing to pursue at the national and
international level agreement on instruments and tools for achieving these
objectives between such sectors and authorities, involving the environmental
NGO community."[22] In preparation for the 1984 INSC, expert groups compiled
resolution proposals on the range of subjects to be discussed at the conference.
A special hearing was held to allow international associations and NGOs to
present their suggestions; in effect this was the first official attempt to consult
with NGOs in the North Sea pollution regime. However, NGOs were not
allowed to attend the 1984 INSC. In 1987, NGOs were permitted to attend only
the opening session of the conference and to make brief statements. At the INSC
at The Hague in 1990, NGOs again had the opportunity to give an oral statement
at the beginning of the conference and their access to information was improved.
France and the UK insisted that preliminary reports on implementation of the
1987 Declaration and other preparatory documents should not be sent to any
NGO. However, the Danish Parliament unilaterally decided to provide the
documents to Greenpeace. Consequently, most North Sea states followed the
Danish lead and (anonymously) provided preparatory documents to NGOs
(e.g., Greenpeace).[23] In addition to greater access to information for non-state
actors, the number of ENGOs and target groups participating in INSCs has
increased. In 1995, 36 delegates representing environmental organizations and
32 delegates representing target groups attended the conference.

The conference process also elevated the role of science in the regime, notably through periodic assessments of North Sea quality and policy options.
The first North Sea Quality Status Report (QSR) was prepared for the 1984
Bremen Conference. This report was essentially a compilation of national
reports and opinions of representatives of the North Sea states.[24] During preparations for the 1987 London Conference, it was decided that the conference
should be science based; a Scientific Technical Working Group was established to compile a comprehensive, up-to-date assessment to be used as a basis
for discussing the need for further regulatory commitments. Due to gaps in
knowledge revealed by the QSR, the 1987 conference requested the Oslo and
Paris Commissions and the International Council for the Exploration of the
Sea (ICES) to establish a North Sea Task Force (NSTF). An in-depth study of
ICES has shown that ICES scientists, who operate formally in their personal
capacities, in practice are able to perform their tasks without being strongly

linked to national interests.[25] Thus, ICES' involvement led to more independent participation by scientists. The NSTF completed its task by publishing an updated QSR in 1993. The NSTF, QSRs, and the reviews of implementation compiled for each INSC (see note 41) constitute the North Sea's system for implementation review (SIR), which is a concept analyzed in greater detail in the first part of this book.

The work of the NSTF had three important consequences. First, it provided a consensual and reliable assessment which concluded that additional regulatory action was necessary. Second, it helped to explain observable negative consequences in the marine environment that were caused by pollution and thus increased pressure to strengthen international regulatory commitments. An interim report from the NSTF submitted to the Hague Conference contained results of research on two highly visible incidents in the North Sea: the exceptional algae blooms in 1988–1989 and the sudden death of many North Sea seals in 1988, both of which caused public concern.[26] The NSTF linked the algae blooms directly to nutrient inputs and the seal epidemic was indirectly linked to inputs of hazardous substances. Third, and probably most important, the level of uncertainty decreased in a rather peculiar way. Previously, it was believed that gaps in knowledge concerning the relationship between inputs, concentrations, and effects could be filled through more effective scientific research and monitoring. One of the most important new elements in the 1993 QSR was the acknowledgment that significant uncertainty was probably permanent: "There is now a comprehensive collection of information on the status of the North Sea. However, the North Sea is such a complex system that a thorough understanding of it as an ecosystem will probably never be attained."[27] In other words, it became clear that the prospects for decreasing uncertainty were limited. Accordingly, the argument in favor of precautionary action became more robust. Moreover, this evolving acknowledgment—that uncertainties could not be eliminated and thus precautionary regulation was needed—had consequences for the UK, which had been the most dedicated defender of the environmental quality approach.

Changes in access and participation introduced by the INSCs also affected access and participation in OSPAR during this second phase. The Oslo and Paris Commissions took up the idea of convening high-level conferences. The 1992 meeting of the Oslo and Paris Commissions was convened at a ministerial level, which raised the level of representation. As in the INSCs, the consequences of shifting OSPAR negotiations to a higher political level were apparently quite favorable. The environmental ministers adopted 12 decisions and recommendations on land-based sources at the 1992 meeting, more than twice the annual average from 1984–1991 and nearly twice the annual average from 1993–1995.[28] Ministers were under more pressure than lower-level representatives to have something to show when they returned home.

Greenpeace applied for full OSPAR observer status in 1989 and 1990. The Commissions agreed in 1990 to permit NGOs to be present as observers at their meetings. Following that decision, 12 NGOs applied to be observers; 8 NGOs were invited to participate in the 1991 meetings. Although balanced representation between ENGOs and target groups was not an explicit criterion, this norm has been followed in practice: four ENGOs and four target group organizations were invited. Of the four organizations denied observer status, three were target groups. The new Convention for the Protection of the Marine Environment of the North-East Atlantic has formalized this access procedure in Article 11.[29'] Of interest in this respect is Article 9, which aims at freedom of access to information held by public authorities. It is almost a replica of the 1990 EC Council Directive on freedom of access to information on the environment.[30] Access procedures have since been adjusted, notably to make documents available to NGOs and to allow NGO observers to make oral presentations to meetings of the Commission's subsidiary bodies. The more lenient access structure has had an effect on the NGOs' willingness to participate. The number of documents presented to Commission meetings by ENGOs and target groups increased significantly between 1991 and 1995.[31]

Consequences of and Explanations for Changes in Participation
The most important consequence of the change in state participation was the decoupling from the regime of Spain and Portugal in 1984, which cut the least enthusiastic block in half. With fewer laggards present, the 1987 London and 1990 Hague Ministerial Conferences were able to adopt ambitious joint commitments, which in turn led to more ambitious commitments within OSPAR and the EU. This immediately raises the question of how joint commitments that were impossible to adopt within the frameworks of OSPAR and the EU because of asymmetrical state interests could be adopted by the same institutions following the INSCs. With regard to nutrients, the 1988 algae "invasion"

was particularly important in raising public concern and increasing pressure to limit North Sea pollution. In addition, specific institutional mechanisms helped make the adoption of stringent joint commitments possible. First, the Oslo and Paris Commissions adopted the principle of *regionalization* in 1988. According to this principle, the parties were to continue working for a common goal, but agreement could be reached through different routes and timetables in different parts of the Convention area. This meant that Portugal and Spain were allowed a longer time period to comply with decisions adopted by OSPAR. Second, important institutional changes took place at the EU level in 1987 and 1992, implying more powerful integration and aggregation mechanisms compared with "traditional" environmental institutions. Of particular importance in this respect was the introduction of majority decision making, rather than requiring unanimous consent for all EU policy decisions.[32]

Summits are sometimes used to forge trade-offs that reach far beyond the authority of low-level officials. This was exactly the result when ministerial representation was introduced at the INSCs and at the OSPAR ministerial meetings. Apparently, representation by higher-level officials made the cooperation more sensitive to politics and attention from the media and ENGOs. Hence, the latitude for political pressure increased, implying higher political costs of blocking an agreement. This affected the UK in particular, as it was exposed by ENGOs to the outside world as the "Dirty Man of Europe," especially during the 1987 INSC. Since the late 1980s, the authority of state actors has increasingly been challenged by nongovernmental actors within OSPAR and the INSCs. The limited access of the 1970s and the first half of the 1980s has given way to more openness and broader participation. Moreover, increased participation by target groups has not decreased the stringency of common goals; indeed, the goals have been strengthened. One probable explanation is that representation has been balanced between target groups and ENGOs, thus moderating the effect NGOs have had on the stringency of international commitments.

The role of independent scientific advice has increased due to the involvement of ICES. Of particular importance was the acknowledgment that exact determination of causal links between inputs, concentrations, and effects of all possible hazardous substances would probably never be determined. This admission significantly strengthened the argument for precautionary action based on the principle that hazardous substances should be reduced at the source even though negative effects had not been observed. Accordingly, the UK changed its position. At an ad hoc working group meeting in 1988, the UK presented a paper titled "Up-date of the UK position as regards the use of environmental quality objectives and uniform emission standards." In the paper, the British government reaffirms its view that environmental quality objectives remain a basic principle for water pollution control. However, it also explicitly accepts the uniform emission approach in the following statement: ". . . the UK has modified its position in relation to the most dangerous substances, those which are very toxic, persistent and liable to bioaccumulate. It is now recognized that, particularly in view of the degree of uncertainty about the possible long-term effects of these substances, the precautionary principle dictates that their input from all sources should be minimized."[33] This change in policy had far-reaching implications for the North Sea and northeast Atlantic pollution regime, as the UK remained as the greatest laggard after the decoupling of Spain and Portugal. In 1989 the Paris Commission adopted two recommendations, one on the principle of precautionary action and one on the use of best available technology (BAT). This led to the application of several decisions and recommendations on BAT within specific industrial sectors. These new principles were in turn written into the new OSPAR Convention.

It is extremely difficult to distinguish participation from the rules and procedures (or "access structures") that govern it. However, the change in state participation (i.e., the decoupling of Spain and Portugal) was not entirely caused by changes in access structures. On the one hand, the FRG's initiative to create a "soft law" sub-regime consisting of a subset of the parties should be understood in light of the desire to lead the creation of a more effective pollution control regime.[34] On the other hand, the introduction of the regionalization principle within OSPAR represented a fundamental change in rules and procedures that made it possible to bypass the least enthusiastic actors when the "soft law" declarations were transformed into OSPAR Decisions. The original scope of state membership within OSPAR also illustrates the importance of weighing the number and types of actors against the geographical scope of a new regime. The question remains whether OSPAR would have achieved more in its first decade if Spain and Portugal had not been involved. Excluding these countries would have had no consequences for the state of the North Sea and probably only minor consequences for the wider northeast Atlantic. The parties negotiating the new OSPAR Convention—which will ultimately replace both the Oslo and Paris Conventions—have taken this lesson seriously and have included the regionalization principle in Article 24 in the new Convention. Hence, the North Sea sub-regime has been included and formalized as part of the new northeast Atlantic regime.

The 1990 revision of OSPAR access procedures had an immediate effect on participation by non-state actors: that same year 12 NGOs applied for observer status. However, access rules are not the only factor that governs whether and how NGOs participate. In particular, target groups have sought to influence regulations that significantly affect industrial activities. Thus, the *scope* of regulations seems critical for their motivation to participate. The first decade of the OSPAR regime shows that target groups are able to have their say even when they are formally denied access. Nonetheless, a wide range of industrial confederations applied for observer status when the INSC process and the Paris Commission developed BAT standards within various industry sectors. Previously, few target groups had attempted to observe and influence the North Sea pollution regime. Thus, although being affected by regulations seems to be the crucial motivating factor for target groups, change in access structures is important as well. Participation by ENGOs appears to be more sensitive to changes in access structures than does participation by target groups. ENGOs were not able to participate, even informally, until the access procedures were changed.

The credibility of science may also be improved by including independent scientific bodies. However, changes in scientific and technical participation were only one factor that improved the quality of scientific recommendations in the regime's second decade. Previously, the responsibility of monitoring and assessment work was split between the JMG, the INSC working groups, the TWG, and SACSA. The NSTF brought coherency to this fragmented environment. It enhanced scientific knowledge and understanding by coordinating the activities of diverse organizations responsible for and interested in the "quality" of the North Sea.

Conclusion

Significant changes in participation have taken place in the North Sea pollution regime in the past decade. The INSC process has reduced the number of state actors, higher-level governmental officials have participated in the conferences, participation by target groups and ENGOs has increased significantly, and science has gained a more independent place in the regime. There is strong evidence that the combination of a reduced number of states and higher-level delegations made stronger international commitments possible. Moreover, the acknowledgment that commitments on hazardous substances would have to be based on a high level of uncertainty in the foreseeable future strengthened the argument for a precautionary approach based on uniform emission standards. The consequences of changes in access structures and participation by NGOs have been more ambiguous. Increased participation by target groups has not led to weaker commitments, probably because their influence has been counterbalanced by that of ENGOs, whose participation has also risen. Shifting participation from low-level civil servants to the ministerial level and the creation of a "soft law" institution seem to be the results of intentional political engineering, which indicates that policymakers have a wide scope for influencing participation. Both OSPAR and the INSCs indicate that NGO participation is determined by informal and formal access structures and by whether an NGO is affected by the commitments being discussed.

The Domestic Dimension

Linking the International and Domestic Levels: Implementation in Norway, the Netherlands, and the UK

International and domestic institutions for regulating water and marine pollution developed more or less simultaneously. In Norway, the Netherlands, and the UK, national legislation on land-based pollution was somewhat ahead of international developments on the issue, and international rules and principles on dumping at sea were ahead of national legislation. During the first decade of the North Sea pollution regime, purely domestic concerns about water pollution and regulations were dominant and the transnational aspect of marine pollution was given only minor attention. This general pattern changed in the mid-1980s, and since then international commitments have increasingly influenced the water and marine policies of all three countries.

This section is split into two parts. In the first part, international influence, the level of national ambitions and performance, and explanatory factors with particular relevance for participation are discussed for each country separately. In the second part, observations from the three country cases are used to compare both the consequences of participation and the scope for influencing participation.

In this section, the relationship between international influence, national ambitions, and attainment of goals measured in terms of actual behavioral change, are scrutinized and compared. The analysis explores several assumptions related to how the organization of pollution control affects outcomes. First, it is assumed that including the target groups that must pay the price for regulations tends to reduce the ambitiousness of domestic goals but increase the probability of cooperation during the implementation phase. (Often target groups do not themselves participate, but are "represented" by their counterparts in government.) Conversely, ENGOs tend to push for stringent domestic goals and act as "watchdogs" in the implementation phase. Hence, *balancing* these interests can potentially promote ambitious domestic goals and corresponding performance at the target group level. Second, participation by governmental agencies is scrutinized both horizontally (across sectors) and vertically (across levels of government). Because implementing North Sea commitments concerning land-based pollution sources requires behavioral changes in the municipal, agricultural, and industrial sectors (see table 8.1), it is reasonable to assume that a certain degree of integrated pollution control is crucial for effective domestic initiatives. Moreover, ability and capacity to integrate environmental concerns into other public policy sectors, such as the agricultural sector, are necessary to change behavior to meet national and international goals. It should be noted that patterns of access and participation vary not only between countries, but also between relevant sectors within a country. Hence, analyzing participation in general environmental policy is at best insufficient and at worst misleading. Vertically, the distribution of competence between and participation by regulatory agencies at local, regional, and national levels may be particularly important for implementing international commitments. Representatives from local and regional levels rarely participate in national delegations to international negotiations. Thus, it can generally be assumed that the greater the "distance" between the national representatives who sign international agreements and the local and regional authorities authorized to implement them, the greater the chance of a mismatch between international obligations and domestic performance. In the study of domestic implementation, there obviously is a complex set of factors at work not necessarily directly linked to participation.[35] In particular, the use of different types of policy instruments such as economic, traditional "command and control," and voluntary agreements appears to be particularly important; accordingly, some attention will be paid to policy instruments in the sections that follow.

Norway: Control, Simplicity, and "High" Performance. Until the second half of the 1980s, water pollution legislation and programs in Norway were mainly motivated by domestic concerns. The 1970 Water Act was adopted before any international conventions on the North Sea or the wider northeast Atlantic area were in existence. Domestic pollution was the motivating factor behind the comprehensive "first generation" action program launched by the government in the mid-1970s.[36] Ten years later, the government produced a new report to Parliament on water and air pollution and on municipal waste:[37] only 1 of the report's 93 pages is devoted to international cooperation on marine pollution.

The turning point in the link between international commitments and national goals came shortly after the 1987 London Conference. In 1988, national targets concerning marine pollution were for the first time systematically and explicitly based on international commitments—the London Declaration and the Decisions and Recommendations adopted within OSPAR.[38] Following the 1990 Hague Declaration, the Norwegian government paid considerable attention to implementing the Declarations and developed a comprehensive and detailed domestic program for achieving the emission reduction goals.[39] In particular, the government initiated a comprehensive research program on how to reach goals for limiting nutrient emissions from the municipal and agricultural sectors.[40]

Norway achieved the reduction targets for all hazardous substances included here.[41] There has been significant overcompliance for many of the hazardous substances, amounting to reductions in the order of 80–100 percent between 1985 and 1995, mainly in the industrial sector. Although discharge of these hazardous substances has been reduced significantly as a result of deliberate measures,[42] Norwegian policy in this area has mainly been driven by domestic concerns. The international commitments have mainly influenced the scope of selected substances. Regarding nutrients, the targets for phosphorus substances were reached, but reductions of nitrogen fell short of the 1987 goals because of implementation problems in the agricultural and municipal sectors. In contrast to the reductions of hazardous substances, most of the reductions of nutrients were achieved after 1990. The government had launched comprehensive programs in the municipal sector prior to 1987, but international developments significantly accelerated implementation. Although agriculture was perceived as a problem before 1987, international developments influenced the course of action in the wake of the 1987 Declaration by increasing the ambitiousness of domestic goals and by shifting the focus from improving technical facilities to changing cultivation and fertilization practices. Regarding the INSC Declaration to stop dumping into the North Sea, Norway has never viewed dumping of industrial waste and sewage sludge as an attractive option, and incineration at sea was phased out in 1989 in accordance with the international requirements.

Norwegian environmental policy relies primarily on "command and control" approaches rather than on close cooperation with target groups. Another striking feature of the Norwegian system is the simple and integrated pollution control system in terms of laws and regulatory agencies. Balanced representation of interests combined with legal enforcement may partly explain the general match between ambitions and achievements in Norway, particularly in the industrial sector. However, significant complexities between the levels of government exist concerning the agricultural and municipal sectors, which have made it difficult to develop and implement effective national policies to control nutrient discharges.

There is a single pollution agency in Norway, the State Pollution Control Authority (SPCA), and one principal pollution law, the 1981 Control of Pollution Law covering land, air, and water pollution. The Ministry of Environment has primary responsibility for this law. Although Norway is frequently classified as a neo-corporatist country giving NGOs institutionalized rights of participation in all phases of governmental policy, the system of formal corporate representation in the form of committees and boards is poorly developed in the environmental sector. Between 1981 and 1991 only one pollution council existed, and it was given a very limited mandate. However, a "hearings commission" gives various types of organizations the opportunity to comment on drafts for legal proposals and other governmental documents. The report from the World Commission on Sustainable Development (the "Brundtland Commission," chaired by the past and future Prime Minister of Norway) underlying the 1988–1989 governmental report to Parliament—where the North Sea targets were systematically included for the first time—was developed through extensive "hearings." All major target groups and ENGOs commented on the report. A Norwegian research project recently studied the frequency of actual informal contact between authorities, ENGOs, and several important industrial, agricultural, and transport target group organizations. It concluded that the frequency of contact is similar between ENGOs and target groups and that contacts have remained quite stable since 1982.[43] Thus, both formal access through "hearings" and actual informal participation in the development of environmental policy appear quite balanced in Norway.

Emissions of hazardous substances by industry are regulated through a national system of permits established by the Control of Pollution Law. Authorities at the local and regional levels had no competence in this area until 1993. As mentioned, Norwegian industry has actually overcomplied concerning many of the hazardous substances. Balanced participation in regulation appears to· be one important reason. The permit system is designed to be transparent and inclusive in terms of participation. The SPCA is obliged to distribute information on all permit applications to affected parties. In practice, affected interests avail themselves of these rights to have a voice in, and possibly influence, the process. Approximately 1,500 industrial units currently hold permits. Another important reason for overcompliance is related to enforcement. Since 1981, a wide range of legal and administrative options have been in place to impose sanctions if a polluter fails to comply with its permit. A typical response is to impose penalties. From 1989 to 1990, the SPCA levied fines for lack of compliance in 52 cases; in 48 of these, the companies took remedial action within the given time limits.[44] Although implementation of the North Sea Declarations implies net costs for the industrial sector, there are also indications that Norwegian industry has become less defensive of narrow interests. A certain "greening" of business and industry attitudes is evident.[45]

In the agricultural and municipal sectors, significantly more competence is distributed to the regional and local levels, thus significantly increasing the number of regulatory agencies involved and correspondingly decreasing the central government's control. A comprehensive study of environmental politics and attitudes at the local level shows that local politicians tend to defend local interests rather than serve broader national environmental policies. Moreover, most of the local politicians are generally skeptical of the national government's environmental initiatives, regardless of their political party affiliation.[46] Between 1985 and 1995 the actual reductions of nitrogen and phosphorus substances that flow from the agricultural sector into ecologically sensitive areas of the Norwegian coast were 19 percent and 27 percent, respectively. Thus, significant behavioral changes have occurred, although these changes have not been sufficient to meet Norway's international commitments. The Norwegian agricultural sector has the typical characteristics of a societal block, or "iron triangle." Such triangles have proved quite resistant to policies challenging their core interests. In Norway there is a long tradition of close cooperation between the state and agricultural organizations like the Norwegian Farmers' Union and the Norwegian Smallholders' Union. These two organizations conduct annual negotiations with the state on conditions in the agricultural sector, for example, on prices for agricultural products. This provides the interest groups with the opportunity to influence the integration of environmental concerns into the agricultural sector. Moreover the educational backgrounds of employees in the central administration and in the interest groups are very similar.[47]

The reasons Norwegian farmers have significantly changed their behavior are complex, but are related to changes in participation. Although environmental issues officially became part of agricultural policy in the mid-1970s, agricultural authorities and interest groups did not actively participate in environmental policies until the idea of "sectoral responsibility" was introduced in the late 1980s. The aim was to integrate environmental concerns into other policy sectors, such as agriculture. In accordance with this principle, the Ministry of Agriculture and its subsidiary departments have primary responsibility for regulating agricultural pollution. Since 1987, meetings on agricultural policy have been held twice a year by the agricultural and environmental ministries; in recent years this contact has been further formalized and the meetings have become more frequent. In 1989, the Ministry of Environment was for the first time included in the national committee responsible for agricultural support (e.g., subsidies). Similar developments have taken place at the regional level, and cooperation between the environmental departments and agricultural offices at this level has increased significantly in recent years.[48] Thus, there are clear signs that the social block characteristics of Norwegian agriculture have been weakened, allowing environmental concerns into this sector. Nonetheless, more could probably have been achieved by implementing economic instruments. Norway relies heavily on direct regulations that are hard to enforce because of the large number of targets in the agricultural sector. Various official committees have proposed increasing the 1988 tax on commercial fertilizer. However, economic measures have failed to materialize because of resistance from both agricultural authorities and farmers' organizations.

Investments in wastewater treatment and the operation of treatment plants are mainly in the hands of local authorities—such plants are an important means of removing nitrogen and other nutrients from wastewaters. A law from 1974 gives municipalities the option of financing all investments in wastewater treatment through local taxes. Thus, local participation and general environmental awareness are important determinants of investment at the local level. Municipal involvement in environmental politics has increased. In 1987, the Ministry of Environment and the Association of Local Authorities initiated a joint project, Environmental Protection in the Municipalities, aimed at increasing participation, responsibility, and awareness through the establishment of separate political bodies responsible for the environment. Environmental advisers were appointed in the 90 municipalities that were part of the experiment. In 1992, the experiment was transformed into a fixed system with the establishment of political and administrative units in all municipalities in Norway. An evaluation of the municipality project shows an increase in activities directed at environmental issues at the local level, more cooperation with ENGOs, and higher priority given to environmental questions by local politicians.[49]

In spite of increased awareness at the local level, Norway has fallen short of the nitrogen target. The affected municipalities were unwilling to bear their part of the financial burden, because they saw no local benefits from complying with international commitments. Even though the Ministry of Environment has promised to cover 50 percent of the investment costs, the municipalities, in alliance with various marine researchers and research institutions, claim that the required investments are a waste of money. In contrast, the SPCA and other marine research institutions claim that the investments are needed to combat eutrophication. In 1996 the minister of environment decided to cancel the nitrogen obligations for 21 of 27 municipal treatment plants because of local opposition. Participation and subsidies through the Environmental Protection in the Municipalities project were insufficient to ensure local support in achieving international and national goals.

The Netherlands: Communication, Complexity, and "Moderate" Performance. Prior to 1987, international commitments had a greater influence on Dutch water policy than on Norwegian water policy. The EU and cooperative efforts to clean up the Rhine River were the most important international issues for Dutch environmental action. However, most actions taken in the Netherlands were in response to domestic concerns. Dutch national targets on both hazardous substances and nutrients were more ambitious than international goals, and thus the Dutch needed to do little at the national level to comply with international commitments. As in Norway, this general picture changed after 1987 because of the North Sea Declarations and the adoption of the Rhine Action Programme through a ministerial process similar to that in the North Sea pollution regime.

In the first Water Action Programme (1975–1979), minimum objectives were set for water quality and emissions. Deadlines for some objectives were imposed by EU Directives. National vulnerability due to domestic discharges was the principal motivating factor behind the second Water Action Programme (1980–1984):[50] only one page of the Programme was devoted to international cooperation and consultation. The 1987 North Sea Declaration and the Rhine Ministerial Conferences forced national goals to be linked more closely to international commitments. The goals in the 1987 and 1990 North Sea Declarations were incorporated into the 1988–1989 Dutch National Environmental Policy Plan (NEPP) presented to the Second Chamber of Parliament, as well as into the third National Policy Document on Water Management and the North Sea Action Plan.[51] The 50 percent target on hazardous substances was adopted; for some substances the NEPP envisioned meeting even more ambitious reductions before the year 2000. With regard to nutrients, the 50 percent target was adopted for the year 1995 and a goal was set to balance input and output of nutrients before 2000. Achieving this balance would require a 70–90 percent reduction in emissions of nutrients. In response to the 1990 North Sea Declaration, a specific North Sea Action Plan was developed. All important international goals were included and the responsible regulatory bodies were specified in a detailed list. In short, the Netherlands rapidly and ambitiously incorporated the international commitments into domestic programs.

The Netherlands has fallen short of compliance with regard to nine hazardous substances—four heavy metals and five organic substances. Like Norway, the Netherlands had achieved significant reductions prior to 1985 for reasons unrelated to international cooperation. Although compliance is lower in the Netherlands, the international commitments have had more effect on Dutch policies than on Norwegian policies. The Dutch national targets and implementation programs for industrial sectors were a direct consequence of international developments. The Netherlands, like Norway, falls short of the nitrogen target and probably also the target for phosphorus substances. The agricultural sector is a significant source of these nutrient inputs to the North Sea. Given the ambitious goals concerning these substances, it is interesting to note that there was no reduction in nutrient inputs from this sector between 1985 and 1995. It is hard to distinguish Dutch actions that were domestic in origin from those stemming from implementation of international commitments. With regard to the municipal sector, international developments have initiated and accelerated national abatement programs, particularly concerning nitrogen removal. Concerning the agricultural sector, nutrient inputs into the North Sea actually increased up to 1990 and decreased somewhat between 1990 and 1995. Dutch legislation on surface water did not originally apply to agriculture, and the first environmental legislation to include this sector was adopted in 1986. Since then, the 50 percent reduction target has been central to Dutch policy on agricultural pollution, and data since 1990 indicate that international commitments have had an impact even though total effluents have remained constant. The Netherlands has also phased out dumping and incineration at sea as part of its cooperation with the Oslo Commission.

In contrast with Norway, the Netherlands emphasizes target group consultation, consensus, and compromise in its environmental policy in general and the water sector in particular. The "talking, talking, talking" approach is evident in the formulation of policies, in decision making, and in enforcement.[52] The second important feature of Dutch water policy is complexity and vertical and horizontal fragmentation in terms of laws and governmental agency participation. These features shed light on why the Dutch government has adopted very ambitious goals and why there has been a disparity between these goals and actual performance.

The high level of Dutch ambitiousness suggests that both target groups and affected governmental agencies outside the environmental sector have been excluded from the domestic process of goal formulation. Exactly the opposite is the case—target groups and corresponding government agencies have participated extensively. The Ministry of Environment has primary responsibility for overall Dutch national environmental plans and programs, but water pollution falls under the competence of the Ministry of Transport and Public Works, its powerful Directorate-General for Public Works—the Rijkswaterstaat—and 20 water boards, 7 sewage boards, and 3 provinces. The environmental and transport and public works sectors have developed a consensual approach to environmental regulation. The 1970 Pollution of Surface Water Act introduced water quality regulations into a sector that had previously been dominated by regulations to protect against flooding from seawater through construction of dikes and control of water levels. The water administration's system of effluent charges has given it considerable financial autonomy and the Ministry of Economic Affairs does not intervene in this sector. Moreover, representation has followed the principle that whoever pays effluent charges (i.e., target groups) decides water policy.[53] When the first Water Board Act was passed in 1990, a proposal to allow ENGOs a seat on the board was rejected.[54]

The Ministry of Environment's target group approach was presented in the "Indicative Multi-Year Plans" for the environment, which began in 1984. A source-oriented target group approach was developed and there was a move away from "command and control" toward voluntary agreements between target groups and the government. Throughout, the emphasis was on communication. The target group policy aims at both developing and implementing specific goals in close collaboration with those who control the sources of pollution. By 1994, this strategy had led to approximately 100 covenants covering all major industrial sectors.[55] One striking feature of the covenants is that the negotiations between industrial branch organizations and governmental authorities are quite closed, with limited opportunities for ENGO participation.

Although comprehensive environmental planning started with the first Indicative Multi-Year Plan in 1984, the turning point in Dutch environmental policy came with the publication of the NEPP in 1989, which linked domestic goals to the North Sea Declarations. In contrast to earlier plans, the NEPP was signed by four cabinet ministers: the ministers of environment, transport and public works, agriculture, and economics (industrial ministry). The NEPP has been described as perhaps the most serious attempt to integrate environmental concerns into all aspects of public policy, including the agricultural sector, which is of major importance concerning the North Sea targets.[56] Cooperation has been identified as the most important instrument for implementing the NEPP. The aim is to strengthen cooperation among public authorities and between authorities and target groups.

The experiences of Dutch environmental policy in general and water quality policy in particular do not support the argument that including target groups and governmental agencies outside the environmental sector tends to significantly weaken the agreed goals. The target group policy was developed at the same time as the goals were strengthened. This is not likely to be explained by balanced inclusion of ENGOs and target groups. In relative terms, target groups have participated to a much greater extent than ENGOs, although Dutch ENGOs may have easier access to decision making than ENGOs in other countries. Nonetheless, the involvement of target groups and agencies outside the environmental sector forced the Ministry of Environment to accede to less stringent goals than it otherwise would have proposed.[57] Thus, the goals would have been even more ambitious had they been left solely to the environmental sector.

Because there was widespread consensus among participants on the appropriate pollution control policies, one might expect that all participants would stick to their promises and that the agreed goals would be reached. However, this was not the case: there is a clear disparity between ambitious goals and actual performance in the Netherlands. One important reason the goals have not been met is a lack of enforcement, which has been acknowledged as the weakest link in implementation of Dutch environmental policies since the late 1980s.[58] Lack of enforcement is indirectly related to participation in different ways. First, the consensual target group policy has led to extensive use of voluntary agreements and guidelines that are not legally enforceable, thus authorities are forced to negotiate with target groups whenever violations are detected. Second, the complexity of laws and regulatory agencies involved has made enforcement problematic, even when polluting activities are subject to enforceable permits or regulations. Until 1993, a company required up to four different licenses issued by four different ministries responsible for different legislative acts. Under one of these acts—the Pollution of Surface Waters Act—31 different authorities at the central and regional levels are responsible for the administration of water pollution regulations. The lack of effective enforcement may also shed light on why target groups and sector agencies have agreed to stringent environmental goals: failure to implement the commitments does not have significant negative consequences. In short, there are strong indications that the Dutch faith in an automatic relationship between target group participation and actual implementation has proved to be unfounded. In recent years, legal and regulatory fragmentation has increasingly been dealt with by adopting general environmental acts, but the water sector is still regulated separately from other sectors, with its own legislative act. The 1993 Environmental Management Act (EMA) was adopted to cope with the persistent fragmentation of Dutch environmental law, thus making legal enforcement easier; indeed enforcement has been intensified. The Organisation for Economic Co-operation and Development (OECD) has stated that in those cases where criminal prosecutions have been initiated under the Pollution of Surface Waters Act, the offending discharges have been stopped.[59] Although significant results have been achieved in the industrial and municipal sectors with regard to hazardous substances, behavior still falls short of both domestic and international goals.

An additional important reason for the limited influence of Dutch water policies appears to be the lack of any type of regulation. In the late 1980s, it was revealed that more than one-third of approximately 8,000 highly polluting firms discharging pollutants into state waters that required a license under the Pollution of Surface Waters Act were in fact operating without one.[60] A similar problem was evident at the regional level. The official reason given for this regulatory lapse is lack of administrative capacity—a somewhat strange reason considering the large bureaucracy for administering water policy in the Netherlands.[61] Lack of capacity appears to be closely related to the working style and high number of governmental actors involved in the 1973 Committee on the Pollution of Surface Waters Act, which plays a central role in coordinating water policies and in conducting sectoral studies as a basis for distributing and regulating licenses. The Committee is composed of all relevant water authorities and makes decisions by consensus.[62] In short, the need for hammering out compromises between the many governmental agencies involved, each representing different interests, has protracted decision making, the issuing of licenses, and, consequently, implementation.

Implementation problems have been most severe in the agricultural sector. The environmental authorities in collaboration with the agricultural authorities have agreed to drastic reductions in inputs of nutrients. However, in reality there was no reduction in nutrient emissions between 1985 and 1995. The

Dutch and Norwegian agricultural sectors differ significantly in terms economic magnitude and production methods. Whereas soil erosion and artificial fertilizer are among the most significant problems in Norway, manure surplus is the main problem in the Netherlands.

The use of policy instruments in the form of direct regulations is quite similar in Norway and the Netherlands. Moreover, the Dutch agricultural sector behaves as a "block"—social cohesion is perhaps even stronger than in the Norwegian agricultural sector. The heart of the block comprises the Ministry of Agriculture, the Agricultural Board, and the Agricultural Commission of Parliament. The members of these groups share a common educational background, which has led to extensive interpersonal networks among them. This block was slow to react to researchers' early warnings of environmental problems in the 1970s. Dutch policy on agricultural information relevant to the environment reflects this situation: from 1974 until 1982 the Department of Agriculture discouraged the Central Bureau of Statistics from publishing the calculated manure surplus.[63] When the block finally reacted, too much emphasis was put on technical solutions instead of focusing on low-input agriculture, which is more effective in controlling nutrient runoff. It has also made poor choices of policy instruments. A complex set of direct regulations has been developed as the main instrument to achieve the goals. Enforcement is weak and costly because of the high number of targets—about 124,000 farms. Thus, achieving environmental policy goals in the agricultural sector has relied mainly on faith that farmers will implement environmental standards, though independent monitoring and enforcement are progressing.[64] However, Dutch farmers are interested first and foremost in production growth and competitiveness. The total gross value added in Dutch agriculture in 1993 was about 4 percent of the gross domestic product (GDP) and the intensive production methods have enabled the country to rank consistently among the world's top four exporters of agricultural products. Different studies—including a report from the Scientific Council to the government—have concluded that direct regulations are less suitable in the Dutch agricultural sector than economic instruments, notably taxes. As in Norway, the farmers, the Department of Agriculture, and the Agricultural Board oppose and have been able to block the introduction of economic instruments, fearing that they will lead to a deterioration in the sector's competitiveness.[65] The fact that the Ministries of Agriculture and Environment cosigned the NEPP indicates that the agricultural block's grip on goal-setting is weaker; however, these changes have not yet been sufficient to ensure implementation of national and international goals.

The UK: From Exclusion to Inclusion of Third Parties; Improved Performance. In contrast to both Norway and the Netherlands, in the UK legislation on land-based sources of pollution lagged behind international developments until the late 1980s. A 1985 river quality survey indicated that water quality was actually declining in the 1980s.[66] In the Oslo and Paris Commissions, the UK behaved as a laggard by blocking proposals for stringent commitments.[67] Even though in the EU decisions were made unanimously prior to 1987, and thus could be blocked by the UK, EU Directives significantly influenced British water policy, especially by inducing greater implementation of the UK's 1974 Control of Pollution Act.[68] The Department of Environment responded directly to the London and Hague Declarations by publishing "Guidance Notes" in 1988 and 1990, and a North Sea Action Plan, in which the main international targets were adopted. However, the Notes were not binding, nor were they put before Parliament. In addition, the 1988 Note, in particular, was vague on governmental responsibilities and concrete measures.

Shortly before the 1987 INSC, the British government announced its intention to accept the uniform emission approach.[69] This led to the adoption of the "Red List" in 1989, which included most of the hazardous substances that were also listed in the Hague Declaration. Comprehensive surveys were conducted to identify major sources of "Red List" substances. The UK's dumping policy also changed significantly as a result of the London and Hague Conferences. Because dumping is prohibited by legislation unless a license has been issued by the relevant ministries, implementation of the London Declaration and Decisions adopted within the Oslo Commission did not require legislative action, only a change in the policies of those ministries.[70] Shortly before the 1990 Hague Conference, the minister of agriculture, fisheries, and food declared a firm timetable for ending the dumping at sea of industrial wastes and sewage sludge.[71] These decisions were directly linked to the outcome of the 1987 INSC in London and the upcoming 1990 INSC. The 1987 INSC goal on nutrient emissions was qualified by the phrase "into areas where these inputs are likely, directly or indirectly, to cause pollution." According to the British government, such areas do not exist around the British coast, and thus the agricultural sector has not been affected by any ambitious initiatives.

The UK has phased out both dumping and incineration of industrial waste at sea. Considerable progress has been made on reducing dumping of sewage sludge in line with the London Declaration, and the British government is confident that the reduction target will be met by 1998. British data on hazardous substances are not directly comparable with data provided by Norway and the Netherlands. For many heavy metals 1985 baseline data do exist, but they reflect nonanthropogenic and diffuse sources in addition to point sources—thus compliance is difficult to assess.[72] Although the UK falls short of achieving reduction goals concerning three heavy metals, steady reductions have occurred. With regard to organic hazardous substances, the data are not reliable and cover only the 1991–1993 period. British data on nutrients cover only the 1985–1990 period. Input of phosphorus substances has decreased by 14 percent, and input of nitrogenous substances has increased by 2 percent. Data provided by the National River Authority (NRA) show that river quality has improved since 1990, but has not regained the high standards set around 1980.[73]

Until the late 1980s, the British government's approach to pollution control was marked by a weak legal basis combined with close cooperation between regulators and the regulated and tight restrictions on access to the regulatory process for non-target group constituencies. The UK's collaborative, discretionary, and secretive style of environmental regulation was originally exposed by the Royal Commission on Environmental Protection in 1976.[74] At that time the British made less use of legally enforceable standards than any other industrial society.[75] This system gradually opened up starting in the late 1980s: access for and participation by ENGOs increased, and the use of legally enforceable standards was expanded. Both these changes contributed to more ambitious goals and to reductions of hazardous emissions from the industrial sector, as well as to changes in the UK's dumping policy. Nonetheless, the governmental agencies with competence in water pollution are still quite fragmented, which has created significant problems for the implementation of the North Sea Declarations.

The close link between target groups and regulators was reinforced by the decentralized structure of the water sector. Following major revisions of the water control system introduced by the 1973 Water Act and the 1974 Control of Pollution Act, 10 regional water authorities were given responsibility for all aspects of water management—operation, pollution control, and enforcement.

In addition, there was close cooperation between industry and the water authorities. British policy operated on the idea of "negotiated consent," determined secretly by individual inspectors using very loose national guidelines.[76] The relationship between the water authorities and the government has been characterized as one in which the water authorities determined their own objectives within the financial framework laid down by the government.[77]

In sharp contrast to the close relationship between industry and the water authorities, participation by other public interests in general and ENGOs in particular was very limited, and these groups had little opportunity to influence the outcome. Access for these groups was also restricted by legal procedures concerning restrictions on public access to information and the few opportunities for private enforcement, such as citizen suits, administrative complaints, and other enforcement activities initiated by public interest groups. Ten years after the Royal Commission exposed this tendency to exclude third-party participation in regulation, David Vogel still held that "there is in Britain . . . no significant domestic pressure to change the way . . . pollution control policy is either made or enforced."[78] This can be illustrated by the policy on public access to environmental information. In 1974, Parliament voted in favor of establishing open registers of discharge permits and sampling results. However, ministers from both the Labour and Conservative Parties managed to postpone the installation of this system for 11 years. In 1985, ministers finally moved to make public the findings of the discharge consent system.[79]

This British pollution control system changed significantly in the late 1980s. Environmental protection has primarily been the responsibility of the Department of Environment since 1970. In 1993–1994 this department employed nearly 7,700 people, about 10 percent of whom were involved with environmental protection, planning, rural affairs, and water quality management. It is generally held that, despite the title, few environmental secretaries have shown any particular interest in the environment. Nonetheless, the growing importance of environmental policy in the UK is also evident in the Department of Environment. Civil servants now view a position at the Environmental Protection Division as a promising career move. Moreover, the relationship between the Department of Environment and ENGOs has improved. Perhaps the clearest example is the appointment in 1990 of Tom Burke—formerly director of Friends of the Earth and the Green alliance—as special political advisor to the secretary of the Department of Environment.[80]

Her Majesty's Inspectorate of Pollution (HMIP), established in 1987, was an amalgam of existing inspectorates until the 1990 Environmental Protection Act, which introduced the system of Integrated Pollution Control. The HMIP is responsible for regulating releases to air, water, and land from the most polluting industrial processes. Less-polluting industrial releases not covered by the Integrated Pollution Control system fall under the competence of the NRA for inputs to water and of local authorities for releases to air and land. Thus, although local authorities generally have a wide range of environmental protection responsibilities, water pollution is now mainly in the hands of central agencies. The NRA, initiated by the 1989 Water Act and consolidated by the 1991 Water Resource Act, replaced the previous system of regional water authorities and introduced a consent system for discharges into water. The "softly, softly" approach to enforcement was replaced by a more aggressive control policy that led to more prosecutions for noncompliance.[81] The NRA's focus on legal enforcement started almost immediately. In its first 12 months, it initiated 334 successful prosecutions: 49 percent against industry, 48 percent against farmers, and only 3 percent against water companies. In the next 12 months, the total rose to 908 prosecutions.[82]

Changes have also occurred at the target group level.[83] The British chemical industry is a major emitter of hazardous substances and the sector comprises over 3,500 companies. Around 200 of the largest companies, accounting for approximately 75 percent of the industry's capital expenditure, are members of the Chemical Industries Association (CIA). In 1989, the CIA launched the Responsible Care Program aimed at improving performance in safety, health, and environmental protection. The voluntary program includes specific targets for large chemical plants and has increased reporting on environmental performance. For example, the chemical giant Imperial Chemical Industries (ICI) committed itself to reducing waste by 50 percent by 1995, using 1990 as the baseline year. By 1993, it had achieved a 27 percent reduction in total waste and a 64 percent reduction in hazardous waste.

The Office of Water Services (OFWAT) regulates the 10 private water and sewerage companies established in 1989 and 22 private water supply companies. Thus, although the water pollution control system has become simpler both vertically and horizontally, significant complexities remain. A recent review by the OECD found that there is a general lack of integration of environmental policies in the UK. Fragmentation has affected implementation of national goals related to the North Sea Declarations in the following ways. First, a struggle for competence on hazardous substances between the NRA and the HMIP affected the 1988 Guidance Note on implementation of the 1987 Declaration. The Note did not clarify which body would have principal responsibility for coordinating implementation; it was not clear whether the national plan would be a mere compilation of the plans of the various water authorities, or if the Department of Environment or the HMIP would coordinate these plans to produce a national plan. Consequently, the Guidance Note was vague on concrete action, especially with regard to inputs of hazardous substances. Second, following the privatization of sewerage and water supply in England and Wales, another conflict emerged involving the NRA and OFWAT. Privatization brought a significant change to the financing system. Previously, the Treasury controlled the Regional Water Authorities' investment spending. Due to the recession in the British economy from the mid-1970s to the early 1980s, investments in public water supplies and sewerage systems fell dramatically between 1974 and 1982. This significantly affected the performance of sewage works. Water companies now have increased access to capital and are required to cover all costs through user charges. However, OFWAT and the NRA disagree on the size of these charges, and the Department of Environment has suggested that the NRA delay the introduction of statutory environmental quality objectives, a central measure in the North Sea Action Plan.[84] Lack of implementation can largely be traced back to the disagreement between the NRA and OFWAT over the environmental quality goals that will form the basis of the new system.[85] Because the new act underlying the statutory objectives was proposed by the government and adopted by Parliament, there presumably is political willingness to implement the new instruments. Moreover, the new system is supported by both the ENGOs and the Confederation of British Industry.[86]

Dumping of nonradioactive waste at sea falls under the competence of the Ministry of Agriculture, Fisheries and Food (MAFF). The UK is the only state to have dumped sewage sludge in the North Sea in recent years; it has been responsible for approximately half of all industrial wastes and about a quarter of dredge spoils dumped outside British internal waters. In 1986, the House of Lords Select Committee on the European Communities argued that a proposed EU Directive on strict control of dumping and incineration at sea was ill-conceived and should be dropped.[87] The Committee also revealed that there was virtually no support for the proposed directive in governmental departments, industry, waste management, or water industries, or among marine scientists. All of the groups affected argued that dumping at sea represented the "best environmental option."[88] This consensus was challenged domestically only by the ENGOs, particularly Greenpeace. In 1986, Greenpeace launched its first large-scale North Sea campaign. Although the campaign was directed at the North Sea and the North Sea states in general, dumping and incineration conducted by the UK were among its main targets. Because of the visibility of dumping and incineration operations, dumping and incineration vessels served as perfect targets for direct actions. Greenpeace used these actions to expose the UK to the outside world as the "Dirty Man of Europe." Before the 1987 INSC, a joint Greenpeace and National Union of Seamen campaign was launched. The groups threatened campaigns against vessels operating from the UK if the British government did not change its policy. Moreover, Greenpeace persuaded local authorities to oppose plans for new terminals to serve marine disposal operators.[89] Two months later it was reported that "Ocean Combustion Services (OCS), operators of the incineration vessel *Vulcanus II*, have been losing the public perception battle during a two-week fight in the North Sea with Greenpeace and Danish fishermen . . . ."[90]

This change in public opinion occurred simultaneously with the "greening" of UK's environmental policy.[91] In contrast to both Norway and the Netherlands, in the UK ENGOs have been by far the most important channel of organizing the "greening" of public opinion. To a certain extent, this is related to electoral procedures that are quite insensitive to the organization of new societal demands in the sense that there is a high threshold for access in Parliament. By 1990, approximately 4 million people in the UK, representing nearly 8 percent of the population, had joined the green movement, which has been characterized as the largest social movement that Britain has ever seen.[92] In comparison, all the political parties in the UK had fewer than 2 million members. The ENGOs also gained increased access to MAFF at the end of the 1980s and thus were able to influence dumping policy from within the government.[93] In addition to gaining greater access to the governmental policy process, Greenpeace continued direct action campaigns up to the 1990 INSC, focusing more on its role as a watchdog to ensure that decisions reached in London in 1987 and within the Oslo Commission would be implemented. In 1987, MAFF awarded 20 full and 10 standby licenses for dumping liquid industrial waste. Nine licenses remained in early 1990. In late 1989, MAFF decided to support applications for licensing renewals for four dumping operations through the Oslo Commission's Prior Justification Procedure (PJP), which requires both that there are no available land-based alternatives and that the substances to be dumped are not harmful to the marine environment. Several North Sea states protested the decision and Greenpeace brought the case to the attention of the media. An extraordinary Commission meeting of the ad hoc working group on dumping was convened. Greenpeace submitted a comprehensive paper arguing that the UK had not complied with the PJP procedure. To MAFF's embarrassment, one of the firms involved then withdrew its application because it suddenly "discovered" a land-based disposal option.[94] In the preparations for the 1990 INSC, the British National Power vessel *MVA* was forced by Greenpeace to give up its attempt to discharge power station fly ash in a government-approved zone five miles off the northeast coast of England. Fishermen joined Greenpeace a few days later when 22 ships gathered to harass the *MVA* as she again tried to discharge waste.[95] The government declared that it was revoking British National Power's license to dump 550,000 tons of fly ash.[96]

Some Correlations and Comparisons: Consequences of Participation and Scope for Influencing Participation

The patterns observed concerning international influence on national goals, national ambitions, and level of performance are roughly summarized in table 8.2. It should be noted that performance refers to both behavioral change and compliance. Although the two are not necessarily related, significant behavioral change has been needed to comply with the international commitments. One exception is Norwegian dumping, where compliance has been high but behavioral change has been low to medium as Norway had already banned dumping (but not incineration) in its national policies.

The table indicates that international influence and national ambitions have been sufficient for high performance with respect to international commitments on dumping and incineration at sea. In the case of the UK, high performance has occurred despite "moderate" national ambitions. This pattern appears to be strongly related to the fact that, for the most part, only one well-defined sector has been involved in the activities. Moreover, dumping and incineration activities had been licensed since the implementation of the Oslo Convention

Table 8.2 Level of Ambitions, Level of Performance, and Influence of International Commitments on National Goals in Relative Terms

Commitment	Norway			Netherlands			UK		
	A	P	I	A	P	I	A	P	I
Dumping/ incineration	High	High	Low/ Med.	High	High	High	Med./ low	High	High
Nutrients	High	Med.	High/ med.	High	Low/ med.	High	–	–	–
Hazardous substances	High	High	Med.	High	Med.	High	Med./ high	Med.	High

Notes: A = Ambitions; P = Performance; I = Relative influence.

in the 1970s. Thus, when decisions were made in the late 1980s to phase out dumping and incineration at sea, these activities were already under the full control of national governments and the decisions could be implemented by simply withholding permits. Concerning land-based emissions, high ambitions and high international influence do not constitute sufficient conditions for "high" performance. Problems are more likely to occur when implementation involves different sectors. This is particularly evident in the case of nutrients, where the municipal and agricultural sectors were involved. In addition, the observation that Norway has performed well in the case of land-based inputs of hazardous substances with only "moderate" international influence, whereas the Netherlands has achieved less with higher international influence and ambitious goals strongly indicates that the way pollution control is organized actually matters.

The three countries discussed here have developed quite differently in terms of regulatory styles governing participation of NGOs. The Netherlands has developed a deliberate target group policy based on close cooperation in making, implementing, and enforcing policies. The UK has partially balanced the interests of target groups by allowing the general public and ENGOs to have a voice in the making and implementation of policies, and enforcement has been intensified and left to separate regulatory agencies. The Norwegian system falls between the Dutch and British systems in the sense that it is not based on a deliberate target group policy and does not permit highly institutionalized access for NGOs. In short, the Norwegian system appears to have achieved the most balanced participation in making and implementing policies.

Although these regulatory differences correlate with variances in domestic ambitions and performance, general conclusions should be drawn with caution as other explanatory factors may have had an impact. Nonetheless, differences in societal demands are not likely to explain differences in performance. In all three countries, the societal demands for environmental quality changed when the most important international and national goals were adopted. Public opinion shifted significantly toward "green" values in the latter part of the 1980s in all three countries. This change was mediated by a growth in the green movement and by increased environmental awareness among politicians. The high level of environmental concern has since stabilized in the Netherlands and has dropped significantly in the UK and in Norway.[97] Thus, although the change in attitudes in the latter part of the 1980s went hand in hand with the adoption of more ambitious international and domestic goals in all three countries, this correlation disappeared after 1990 concerning actual behavioral change of target groups in the various countries.

The general tendencies outlined above indicate the following conclusions. The Dutch case does not support the argument that involving target groups in policy-making necessarily decreases the stringency of domestic goals significantly. Nor does it suggest that there is an automatic relationship between target group participation in policy-making and willingness to actually implement agreed international commitments and national goals. The Dutch case indicates that target group participation should be balanced by legal enforcement and/or access for ENGO participation. In the Norwegian case target group interests balanced by legal enforcement and participation by ENGOs during policy-making and implementation led to a relatively close match between ambitions (national policy goals) and actual results. The British case shows that close cooperation between authorities and target groups does not inevitably mean that the making and implementation of environmental policies influences target group behavior. Because of the weak legal basis, close cooperation between these groups may have led to "regulatory capture" until the reorganization of water and environmental institutions in the late 1980s. In the British case, balancing target group interests with legal enforcement and participation by ENGOs led to a positive behavioral change among target groups. Thus, these cases do not suggest that target group involvement has a negative effect on the making and implementation of pollution policies; rather, they suggest that such involvement should be balanced with other interests and combined with legal enforcement.

All three countries have moved from adopting environmental acts covering specific sectors toward integrating various aspects of pollution control. Moreover, environmental policy has increasingly been included in other policy sectors. Together, integrated pollution control and integrating pollution control into other public policy sectors have been used to combat horizontal regulatory fragmentation. Regulatory agency fragmentation within the environmental sector has created implementation problems in both the Netherlands and the UK. Norway apparently has not experienced such problems because it adopted integrated pollution control much earlier (in 1981). These experiences illustrate the advantages of having one general pollution control law, one ministry in charge of that law, and one pollution control agency. Because pollution problems often arise as a by-product of otherwise legitimate activities within society, integrating environmental concerns into other policy sectors is necessary for effective pollution control. Both Norway and the Netherlands have sought to integrate environmental concerns into the agricultural sectors, with some promising results, especially in Norway. However, changes have been slow, largely due to the "social block" characteristics of the agricultural sectors in both countries. Both sectors are characterized by close cooperation with government, Parliament, and interest groups. The actors have been unified by a combination of common goals and similar educational backgrounds, as well as by a tendency to only pay lip service to environmental goals. However, there are clear indications that these segments are starting to break up as new objectives, including environmental protection, are integrated into the sector; however, the pace of change has been incremental and so far has been insufficient to reach international commitments.

With regard to vertical fragmentation and distribution of competence, there seems to be a classic conflict between regulatory efficiency and democratic accountability: the central government's desire for national standardization and regulation often conflicts with the values of representative bodies elected from local constituencies. This dilemma seems particularly evident concerning implementation of international commitments, because of the great distance between international negotiations and local politics and priorities. The Norwegian case, in particular, shows that whenever regional and local perceptions of interests deviate from what the government has defined as the "national interest" in terms of international commitments, significant opposition at regional and local levels can be expected. If local opposition goes hand in hand with decentralization of competence in the relevant sector, there is a risk that support for implementing international commitments will disappear. In the Norwegian case, these factors contributed to minimal local implementation of international commitments and national goals to limit nutrient pollution.

While it is difficult to distinguish between participation in terms of behavior and participation in terms of differences in access structures governing participation at the international level, it is even more difficult to do so at the domestic level. As Vogel has pointed out, national approaches to regulation must be understood within the political and social contexts in which they evolved.[98] This phenomenon is captured by the concept of regulatory *styles*, referring to supposedly distinct national approaches to regulation. In the words of Graham Allison, policy styles may be understood as standard operating procedures evolving not only from explicit rules and principles, but also from tradition and routinization, history, norms, and culture.[99] Against this backdrop, all three countries have shown a remarkable ability to change such procedures.

In the Dutch case, the target group policy, the integration of various pollution acts, and the NEPP appear to have been intentionally initiated from above before the rise of "green" values, which culminated with the 1989 elections. More specifically, the inclusion of the agricultural sector and the cosigning of the NEPP between the Ministries of Agriculture and Environment seem to be direct results of the general redirection of Dutch environmental policy. The idea of extensive consultation between the actors affected and governmental agencies is not new, but is part of Dutch tradition and culture. In the water quality sector, this approach was actually introduced by the Committee on the Pollution of Surface Waters Act in 1973. The Netherlands has shown a remarkable ability to significantly change the standard operating procedures in the environmental sector and to integrate this sector with other relevant sectors. The problem has been that these changes have been made based on the idea that there is an automatic relationship between target group involvement and their willingness to change their behavior.

In contrast to the Netherlands, the redirection of the UK's water policy seems to have been influenced by outside developments (particularly in the EU) rather than steered from above, and thus has been more prone to unintentional consequences. For example, Margaret Thatcher's initiative to privatize the water industry had nothing to do with environmental policy, but was simply aimed at reducing the bargaining power of the national union representing water workers.[100] Moreover, the original intention was to privatize both operation and control. However, private pollution control systems were inconsistent with EU law. Accordingly, the establishment of the NRA was a by-product of privatization and a product of Europeanization. In Norway, the 1987 Environmental Protection in the Municipalities project was designed to increase participation in environmental politics at the local level. Evaluations undertaken so far have concluded that the project increased NGO participation. It was initiated as a joint effort between the Ministry of Environment and the Association of Local Authorities. The policy of integrating environmental concerns into other public policy sectors appears to be a direct result of the Brundtland Commission and the United Nations Conference on Environment and Development (UNCED) process. In Norway, balanced representation in environmental policy-making does not appear to be a conscious policy, but rather a consequence of the lack of both a target group policy and permanent consultative bodies in the area of the environment.

Conclusion and Consequences for the Environmental Quality of the North Sea

To what extent and in what ways have access and participation affected international commitments and domestic implementation? With regard to negotiating international commitments, two groups of mechanisms have been identified. The first centers on the ability and willingness of states to advocate joint action. Exclusion of the least ambitious actors combined with participation by high-level government officials made it possible to adopt commitments that did not merely reflect the interests and preferences of the least ambitious actors. This was accomplished through the creation of a new soft law sub-regime, which led to the adoption of ambitious goals in the North Sea Declarations. Those goals were subsequently codified in legally binding measures within other institutions. Eventually, this process led to a comprehensive international legal and political regime aimed at substantial behavioral change at the domestic level. Second, important changes took place that in effect reduced states' control over the course of action. Of particular importance in this respect was increased participation by NGOs and independent scientists in the international policy process. With regard to the former, balanced inclusion of target groups and ENGOs increased transparency and the latitude for political pressure without decreasing the stringency of the commitments. The involvement of independent scientific bodies increased the robustness and legitimacy of the commitments. In particular, it promoted the recognition that commitments would have to be based on precautionary action in the form of ambitious emission standards because certainty concerning cause-and-effect relationships would probably never be attained.

With regard to domestic implementation of international commitments, there is strong evidence that including target groups in the making and implementation of domestic pollution policies does not automatically lead to changes in target group behavior. This is worth noting in light of the recent trend in pollution control that highlights principles such as "shared responsibility" and measures based on voluntary agreements with target groups. Although a certain "greening" of industry can be witnessed, target group participation should be balanced by participation by other interests and combined with legal enforcement to transform rhetoric into realities. The UK shows that international access structures have affected domestic access structures in reluctant states. Although the countries have different regulatory styles, there has been strong convergence of these styles over the past decade. There appears to be a process toward "Europeanization" of policy on NGO access.

Fragmentation in terms of laws and regulatory agencies has been perceived as a problem inhibiting implementation; thus all countries are attempting to integrate pollution control policies and to integrate these policies into other sectors. The three cases examined here show that both horizontal and vertical fragmentation create problems for implementation, especially when different policy sectors are affected by joint commitments. The agricultural sectors in Norway and the Netherlands illustrate the problem of horizontal fragmentation—the difficulty of integrating environmental policies into other sectors. The agricultural sector has traditionally taken the form of "social blocks" that have been quite resistant to change, including environmental obligations. Nonetheless, as the Norwegian case, in particular, illustrates, other policy sectors reluctant to commit to environmental obligations can be induced to cooperate to combat pollution. Vertical fragmentation is evident wherever significant competence is distributed to regional and local levels. Although local actions are required to meet national goals, the interests of local water authorities are often different from those of the national government. This is closely related to participation in the sense that representatives for local and regional water authorities normally do not participate in negotiations leading up to international agreements. Consequently, even in countries with firm national support for adopting and implementing international commitments—such as Norway—commitments are less effective when officials at the local level pursue other policies.

Participation clearly matters and different participation patterns have different effects on the making of joint commitments and on domestic implementation. However, participation is not all that matters, and changes in outcome occur even when participation patterns remain constant. Complementary and competing explanatory perspectives have not been systematically analyzed here, but the preceding analysis has touched on other perspectives including problem-related interests, exogenous events (in the form of the algae blooms and the seal epidemic), and institutional factors other than those governing participation, such as decision rules at both the international and domestic levels. It is extremely difficult to pinpoint precisely why participation changes and consequently to specify whether and how policymakers can affect patterns of participation. All that is sure is that institutional access, leadership, actor interests, and different formal roles of regulatory agencies apparently play a role. However, given the persistent nature of domestic regulatory systems rooted in tradition, norms, and culture, all three countries have shown a remarkable ability to change their standard operating procedures.

Since the mid-1980s, collective decisions within the EU, OSPAR, and the INSCs have increased in number, stringency, and scope. At the domestic level, there has been a stream of new legislation and administrative directives. It is clear that international commitments have increasingly influenced domestic marine and water policies. Moreover, target groups have actually changed their behavior significantly, and overall emissions of regulated substances have decreased substantially in most of the North Sea states.[101] However, according to the 1993 QSR on the North Sea, it is difficult to discern an indisputable and clear trend pointing toward improvement in the marine environment, despite the fact that the North Sea is among the world's most intensively studied ocean areas.[102] There are various reasons for this situation, spanning from the possibility of unreliable input data to a time lag between emission reduction and actual improvements in environmental quality. However, one particularly important factor is natural variability. The 1993 QSR concludes that natural variability makes it difficult to identify human-induced changes; attributing causes to observed effects is an even more uncertain process. Against this backdrop, the QSR concludes that effects of abatement measures might not be observed and, at the same time, anthropogenic inputs may remain unnoticed due to the large number of substances entering the marine environment. The INSC ministers have taken this lesson seriously by declaring their intention at the 1995 North Sea Conference to phase out all manufactured hazardous substances within one generation (25 years), thus sending a clear message to all those involved in activities causing such emissions.

Notes

1. These Conventions cover the northeast Atlantic including the North Sea.

2. Most studies have focused on the international level: see Sætevik, S., 1988, *Environmental Cooperation between the North Sea States*, Belhaven Press, London, UK; Skjærseth, J.B., 1992, "Towards the End of Dumping in the North Sea," *Marine Policy* 16(2):130–140; Wettestad, J., 1992, "The 'Effectiveness' of the Paris Convention on Marine Pollution from Land-based Sources," *International Environmental Affairs* 4(2):101–121; Haas, P.M., 1993, "Protecting the Baltic and North Seas," in *Institutions for the Earth: Sources of Effective International Environmental Protection*, edited by P.M. Haas, R.O. Keohane, and M.A. Levy, The MIT Press, Cambridge, MA, USA; Pallemaerts, M., 1992, "The North Sea Ministerial Declarations from Bremen to Hague: Does the Process Generate any Substance?" *International Journal of Estuarine and Coastal Law* 7(1); Nollkaemper, A., 1993, *The Legal Regime for Transboundary Water Pollution: Between Discretion and Constraint*, Graham & Trotman, London, UK. To my knowledge, the only study dealing with domestic implementation in any depth is Gibson, J., and Churchill, R.R., 1990, "Problems of Implementation of the North Sea Declarations: A Case Study of the United Kingdom," in *The North Sea: Perspectives on Regional Environmental Co-operation, Special Issue of the International Journal of Estuarine and Coastal Law*, edited by D. Freestone and T. IJlstra, Graham & Trotman, London, UK.

3. See Underdal, A., 1980, *The Politics of International Fisheries Management: The Case of the Northeast Atlantic*, Universitetesforlaget, Oslo, Norway.

4. See Weale, A., 1992, *The New Politics of Pollution*, Manchester University Press, Manchester, UK.

5. Underdal, A., 1980, *"Integrated" Marine Policy: What? Why? How?* R:004-1980, The Fridtjof Nansen Institute, Lysaker, Norway.

6. Other regional and subregional conventions with relevance for this issue area are as follows.

Regional level:

- 1992 Helsinki Convention on Industrial Accidents
- 1992 Espoo Convention on Environmental Impact Assessment
- 1990 ECE Code of Conduct on Accidental Pollution
- 1992 Helsinki Convention on Transboundary Watercourses

Subregional level:

- 1976 Rhine Chemical Pollution Convention
- 1976/1991 Rhine Chlorides Convention
- 1987 Rhine Action Programme

7. Richardson, J., 1994, "EU Water Policy: Uncertain Agendas, Shifting Networks and Complex Coalitions," *Environmental Politics* 3(4):139–167.

8. Cameron, J., 1994, "The Status of the Precautionary Principle in International Law," in *Interpreting the Precautionary Principle*, edited by T. O'Riordan and·J. Cameron, Earthscan Publications, London, UK.

9. Underdal, A., 1990, Negotiating Effective Solutions: The Art and Science of "Political Engineering." Draft, Department of Political Science, University of Oslo, Norway.

10. The two substantial recommendations centered on scrap disposal from offshore activities and contamination of sewage sludge. In addition, five recommendations focused on procedural elements concerning dumping operations.

11. Access procedures are regulated by Articles 20, 21, and 22 of the Oslo Convention; Articles 22, 23, and 24 of the Paris Convention; and Articles 25, 26, and 27 of the new OSPAR Convention.

12. This section is based on archive material from the Secretariat for the Oslo and Paris Conventions in London, UK.

13. Wettestad, J., 1989, *Uncertain Science and Matching Policies: Science, Politics and the Organization of North Sea Cooperation*, R:003-1989, The Fridtjof Nansen Institute, Lysaker, Norway.

14. Haas, P.M., 1993, "Protecting the Baltic and North Seas," in *Institutions for the Earth: Sources of Effective International Environmental Protection*, edited by P.M. Haas, R.O. Keohane, and M.A. Levy, The MIT Press, Cambridge, MA, USA.

15. See Sætevik, op. cit., note 2; and Skjærseth, op. cit., note 2.

16. Ninth Annual Report of the Paris Commission, 1987, Secretariat for the Oslo and Paris Commissions, London, UK, pp. 26–31.

17. Oslo and Paris Commissions' Procedures Manuals, the Secretariat for the Oslo and Paris Commissions, London, UK.

18. Mensbrugghe, Y., 1990, "Legal Status of International North Sea Conference Declarations," in *The North Sea: Perspectives on Regional Environmental Co-operation, Special Issue of the International Journal of Estuarine and Coastal Law*, edited by D. Freestone and T. IJlstra, Graham & Trotman, London, UK.

19. See the Urban Waste Water Directive (91/271/EEC) and the Nitrate Directive (91/676/EEC).

20. Hey, E., IJlstra, T., and Nollkaemper, A., 1993, "The 1992 Paris Convention for the Protection of the Marine Environment of the northeast Atlantic: A Critical Analysis," *The International Journal of Marine and Coastal Law* 8(1):1–76.

21. Skjærseth, J.B., Andresen, S., and Wettestad, J., 1992, EF-landene og Norden i internasjonal miljøpolitikk. Standpunkter, bekgrunnsfaktorer og allianseforhold. Forsker—Notater til Europautredningen, The Fridtjof Nansen Institute, Lysaker, Norway [in Norwegian].

22. Fourth International Conference on the protection of the North Sea (1995), Esbjerg Declaration, p. 20.

23. MacGarvin, M., 1990, *Greenpeace The Seas of Europe—The North Sea,* Collins & Brown, London, UK.

24. Quality Status of the North Sea, Deutsches Hydrographisches Institut, "A Report compiled from Contributions by Experts of the Governments of the North Sea Coastal States and the Commission of the European Communities prepared for the International Conference on the Protection of the North Sea, Bremen, October 31 to November 1, 1984."

25. Founded in 1902, ICES is the oldest intergovernmental organization in the world concerned with marine science. See Fløistad, B., 1990, *The International Council for the Exploration of the Sea (ICES) and the Providing of Legitimate Advice in Fisheries Management,* R:003-1990, The Fridtjof Nansen Institute, Lysaker, Norway.

26. See 1990 Interim Report on the Quality Status of The North Sea, Ministry of Transport and Public Works, The Hague, Netherlands, February 1990.

27. Quality Status of the North Sea, 1993, Secretariat for the Oslo and Paris Commissions, London, UK, p. 111.

28. The annual average from 1985 to 1991 was 5.6 recommendations and decisions, and the annual average from 1993 to 1995 was 6.7 recommendations and decisions. See Procedures and Decisions Manual for the Paris Commission, The Secretariat for the Oslo and Paris Commissions, London, UK.

29. Article 11 on observers reads as follows:

(a) The Commission may, by unanimous vote of the Contracting Parties, decide to admit as an observer: a) any State which is not a Contracting Party to the Convention; b) any international governmental or non-governmental organization the activities of which are related to the Convention.

(b) Such observers may participate in meetings of the Commission but without the right to vote and may present to the Commission any information or reports relevant to the objectives of the Convention.

(c) The conditions for the participation of observers shall be set in the Rules of Procedure of the Commission.

30. OJEC 90/313/EEC.

31. OSPAR Summary Records 1990–1995.

32. See Skjærseth, J.B., 1994, Institutional "Effectiveness" in International versus Supranational Environmental Problem-solving, EED Working Paper, The Fridtjof Nansen Institute, Lysaker, Norway, p. 4.

33. Paper presented by the UK to the ad hoc working group to evaluate the EQO and UES approaches, London, UK, 22–23 November 1988. Title: EQUS 2/3/3-1988:2.

34. See, e.g., Underdal, A., 1991, "Solving Collective Problems: Notes on Three Modes of Leadership," in *Challenges of a Changing World*, The Fridtjof Nansen Institute, Lysaker, Norway.

35. A more comprehensive study of these countries' involvement in the North Sea pollution regime is expected in 1998. See, Skjærseth, J.B., 1998, The Making and Implementation of North Sea Pollution Commitments: Institutions, Rationality and Norms, forthcoming, The Fridtjof Nansen Institute, Lysaker, Norway.

36. St.meld.nr.107 (1974–75). Om arbeidet med en landsplan for bruken av vannressursene. Miljøverndeperatementet, Oslo, Norway.

37. St.meld.nr.51 (1984–85), Om tiltak mot vann-og luftforuresninger og om kommunalt avfall. Miljøverndepartementet, Oslo, Norway.

38. St.meld.nr.46, (1988–1989), Miljø og utvikling. Norges oppfølging av Verdenskommisjonens rapport. Miljøverndepartementet, Oslo, Norway.

39. Report No. 64 to the Storting (1991–92), Concerning Norway's implementation of the North Sea Declarations, Ministry of Environment, Oslo, Norway.

40. Ministerial Declaration on the Protection of the North Sea, Analysis of measures to reduce nutrient inputs, Statens foruresningstilsyn, 1992, Oslo, Norway, p. 34.

41. For all three countries, pesticides and atmospheric emissions are excluded due to low data reliability and the problem of controlling for the effect of other institutions. This leaves us with input to water of 8 heavy metals and 12 organic substances. Input data on hazardous substances and nutrients vary in their reliability and comparability, especially because North Sea states have used different approaches for estimating reductions and different stages of development concerning baseline years. However, input data are sufficiently reliable to allow for cautious comparison at the ordinal level. The main sources used for estimating inputs in all three countries are The Implementation of the Ministerial Declaration of the Second International Conference on the Protection of the North Sea, The Hague, 7 and 8 March 1990, Ministry of Transport and Public Works, The Hague, Netherlands; Progress Report, 4th International Conference on the Protection of the North Sea, Esbjerg, Denmark, 8–9 June 1995, Ministry of Environment and Energy, Danish Environmental Protection Agency, Copenhagen, Denmark; and Nutrients in the Convention Area, 1992, Oslo and Paris Commissions, London, UK.

42. Næringslivets Hovedorganizasjon, 1992, Helse Miljø Sikkerhet, Investeringer og driftskostnader i industrien, Oslo, Norway [in Norwegian].

43. Rommetvedt, H., and Opedal, S., 1995, Miljølobbyisme og næringskorporatisme? Norske miljø – og næringsorganizasjoners politiske p virkning.*Nordisk Administrativt Tidsskrift* 3/1, 76. årgang [in Norwegian].

44. See Norges Offentlige Utredninger (Norwegian Official Publications), 1995, p. 4, Virkemidler i miljøpolitikken, Statens forvaltningstjeneste, seksjon statens trykning, Oslo, Norway [in Norwegian].

45. The Nordic Business Environmental Barometer, 1995, Bedrifts konomens Forlag, Oslo, Norway.

46. Hovik, S., and Harsheim, J., 1996, Miljøvernets plass i kommunepolitikken, Norsk Institutt for by-og regionsforskning, R, p. 6 [in Norwegian].

47. More than 50 percent of employees in the central administration have a university degree in land-use-related subjects and more than 72 percent of regional and local employees have these qualifications. See, Mydske, P.K., and Steen, A., 1994, "Land-use and Environmental Policy in Norway," in *Comparing Nordic and Baltic Countries: Environmental Problems and Policies in*

Agriculture and Forestry, edited by K. Eckberg, P.K. Mydske, A. Niemi.Iilahti, and K.H. Pedersen, TemaNord, Copenhagen, Denmark, p. 572.

48. Ibid.

49. Reitan, M., 1995, "The Deviant Case of Norway," paper presented for the workshop New Nordic Member States and the Impact on EU Environmental Policy, 6–8 April, Sandbjerg, Demark.

50. Water Action Programme (1980–84) The Netherlands, Ministry of Transport and Public Works, The Hague, Netherlands.

51. National Policy Document on Water Management, 1991, Water in the Netherlands: A Time for Action, Ministry of Transport and Public Works, The Hague, Netherlands; North Sea Action Plan, Netherlands Implementation Document, Included in The Implementation of the Ministerial Declaration of the Second International Conference on the Protection of the North Sea, 7–8 March 1990, The Hague, Netherlands; and National Environmental Policy Plan, To Choose or to Lose, Ministry of Housing, Physical Planning and Environment, The Hague, Netherlands.

The new plan (NEPP Plus) developed after the fall of the government in 1989 did not significantly alter national goals relevant to the North Sea pollution regime.

52. Bressers, H.T.A., Huitema, D., and Kuks, S.M.M., 1994, "Policy Networks in Dutch Water Policy," *Environmental Politics* 3(4):25–51.

53. Andersen, M.S., 1994, *Governance by Green Taxes: Making Pollution Prevention Pay,* Manchester University Press, Manchester, UK.

54. Ibid.

55. Liefferink, D., 1995, Environmental Policy in the Netherlands: National Profile, Paper prepared for the workshop on New Nordic Member States and the Impact on EC Environmental Policy, 6–8 April, Sandbjerg, Denmark.

56. Weale, A., 1992, *The New Politics of Pollution*, Manchester University Press, Manchester, UK.

57. Ibid.

58. Environmental News from the Netherlands, 1991–1994, Ministry of Housing, Spatial Planning and the Environment, The Hague, Netherlands.

59. Environmental Performance Review, 1995, *Netherlands*, Organisation for Economic Co-operation and Development, Paris, France.

60. Ibid.

61. The Transport Ministry's powerful Directorate-General for Public Works—the Rijkswaterstaat (Public Works Agency)—is responsible for implementing the Pollution of Surface Waters Act. The Agency has about 10,000 employees working in the central directorate in The Hague, as well as 13 regional executive directorates; Crommelin, D.W.R., 1993, Water Management and Enforcement in the Netherlands, Ministry of Transport, Public Works and Water Management, The Hague, Netherlands.

62. Coordination Committee on the Implementation of Surface Water Pollution Act (COWVU), Study Group XI, Ministry of Traffic and Public Works, 1991.

63. Hegeman, J.H.F., Korver-Alzerda, L., Bourma, J.J., Duijnhouwer, F.J., and Hommes, R.W., 1992, Management of North Sea Eutrophication, Erasmus Centre for Environmental Studies, Erasmus University, Rotterdam, Netherlands.

64. Monitoring and enforcement are the responsibility of the General Inspectorate of the Ministry of Agriculture, Nature Management and Fisheries. Around 150 trained inspectors are available for such activities; OECD, op. cit., note 59, p. 165.

65. Hegeman *et al.*, op. cit., note 63.

66. Kinnersley, D., 1994, *Coming Clean: The Politics of Water and the Environment*, Penguin Books, London, UK.

67. Sætevik, op. cit., note 2; Skjærseth, op. cit., note 2.

68. Haigh, N., Bennett, G., Kromarek, P., and Lavoux, T., 1986, *Environmental Community Environmental Policy in Practice,* Vol. 1, *Comparative Report: Water and Waste in Four Countries*, Graham & Trotman, London, UK.

69. The Implementation of the Ministerial Declaration of the Second International Conference on the Protection of the North Sea, 7–8 March 1990, The Hague, Netherlands, Ministry of Transport and Public Works, The Hague, Netherlands, p. 189.

70. The Ministry of Agriculture, Fisheries and Food (MAFF) and Department of Agriculture, Fisheries and Food for Scotland (DAFF).

71. News Releases, 4 December 1989 and 5 March 1990, Ministry of Agriculture, Fisheries and Food, London, UK.

72. Especially due to the nonanthropogenic element, these data are more sensitive to natural variations than data on point sources. However, the UK produced a list of actions to explain achievements between 1985 and 1990. According to this list, most actions have resulted from implementation of measures, and some actions are due to closures of plants probably unrelated to environmental goals,

United Kingdom Action Plan 1985–1995, Department of the Environment, London, UK.

73. "Advance in River Quality Continues," December 1994, *ENDS Report*, p. 239.

74. O'Riordan, T., and Wynne, B., 1987, "Regulating Environmental Risks," in *Insuring and Managing Hazardous Risks*, edited by P. Kleindorfer and H. Kunreuther, Springer Verlag, Berlin, Germany.

75. Vogel, D., 1986, *National Styles of Regulation: Environmental Policy in Great Britain and the United States*, Cornell University Press, Ithaca, NY, USA, p. 76.

76. Jordan, A., 1993, "Integrated Pollution Control and the Evolving Style and Structure of Environmental Regulation in the UK," *Environmental Politics* 2(3):405–421.

77. Maloney, W.A., and Richardson, J., 1994, *Environmental Politics* 3(4):111—137.

78. Vogel, op. cit., note 75, p. 101.

79. Kinnersley, op. cit., note 66.

80. Rawcliffe, P., 1995, "Making Inroads: Transport Policy and the British Environmental Movement," *Environment* 37(3):16–20, 29–36.

81. Mumma, A., 1993, "Use of Compliance Monitoring Data in Water Pollution Prosecutions," *Journal of Environmental Law* 5(2):191–201.

82. *ENDS Report*, October 1991.

83. This section is based on OECD Environmental Performance Reviews, 1994, *United Kingdom*, Organisation for Economic Co-operation and Development, Paris, France.

84. *ENDS Report*, August 1992.

85. This was also emphasized in an interview with Martin Clarke, Environmental Agency, 4 December 1996.

86. Amanda Bradly, Confederation of British Industries, interview with the author, 4 December 1996.

87. At worst the EU Directive would have obliged the UK to halve the quantities of industrial waste, sewage sludge, and dredge spoil between 1990 and 1995. Moreover, a phaseout of incineration at sea would be required by mid-1991.

88. *ENDS Report*, July 1986.

89. An application for a new waste storage terminal in Sunderland was refused; *ENDS Report*, August 1987.

90. *ENDS Report*, October 1987.

91. Hofrichter, J., and Klein, M., 1991, Evolution of Attitudes Towards Environmental Issues 1974–1991, Report Prepared on Behalf of "Surveys Research Analysis" (Eurobarometer) Unit, Directorate General X Audiovisual, Information, Communication, Culture of the Commission of the European Community, Zentrum für Europäische Umfrageanalysen und Studien, University of Mannheim, Germany.

92. McCormick, J., 1991, *British Politics and the Environment*, Earthscan Publications Ltd, London, UK. Growth in members and income of British ENGOs that are heavily involved in northeast Atlantic affairs and the EU has been dramatic. For example, Greenpeace membership increased from 50,000 in 1985 to 320,000 in 1989.

93. McCormick, J., 1994, "Environmental Politics," in *Developments in British Politics*, edited by P. Dunleavy, A. Gamble, I. Holliday, and G. Peele, Macmillan, London, UK.

94. *ENDS Report*, February 1990.

95. *Marine Pollution Bulletin*, March 1990.

96. *ENDS Report*, February 1990.

97. Comparative data for the UK and the Netherlands up to 1991 can be found in Hofrichter, J., and Klein, M., 1991, Evolution of Attitudes Towards Environmental Issues 1974–1991, ZEUS, Zentrum für Europäische Umfrageanalysen und Studien, University of Mannheim, Germany, December. For data on the Netherlands up to 1994, see Ministry of Housing, Spatial Planning and the Environment, 1995, "Main Results of Environmental Communication Studies," The Hague, Netherlands. The drop in "green" attitudes in the UK has been documented by O'Riordan, T., 1995, "Frameworks for Choice: Core Beliefs and the Environment," *Environment* 37(8):25–29. In Norway, public attitudes have been measured since 1977 as part of an election research program. Seven percent of Norwegians considered the environment to be the most important issue in 1985; this figure increased to 37 percent in 1989 and fell back to 7 percent in 1993. See Aardal, B., and Valen, H., 1995, *Konflikt og opinion*, NKS-forlaget, Oslo, Norway.

98. Vogel, op. cit., note 75, p. 26.

99. Allison, G.T., 1971, *Essence of Decision: Explaining the Cuban Missile Crisis*, Scott Foresman and Company, USA.

100. Vogel, op. cit., note 75, p. 73.

101. Progress Report, 4th International Conference on the Protection of the North Sea, Esbjerg, Denmark, 8–9 June 1995, Ministry of Environment and Energy, Danish Environmental Protection Agency, Copenhagen, Denmark.

102. See North Sea Quality Status Report, 1993, Oslo and Paris Commissions, London, UK.

9

Participation in NO$_x$ Policy-Making and Implementation in the Netherlands, UK, and Norway: Different Approaches but Similar Results?

Jørgen Wettestad

Introduction

In the studies of the Long-Range Transboundary Air Pollution (LRTAP) regime conducted to date, much more attention has been given to the negotiation and implementation of the regime's 1985 sulfur dioxide (SO$_2$) commitments than to its more recent 1988 nitrogen oxides (NO$_x$) commitments.[1] There are several reasons more attention should be paid to the NO$_x$ commitments within LRTAP. First, whereas the 1985 Sulphur Protocol commits parties to reduce sulfur emissions by 30 percent, the NO$_x$ Protocol merely requires parties to stabilize NO$_x$ emissions. Although the NO$_x$ negotiations began with high hopes for adopting similar (30 percent) emission reductions, the final regulatory outcome was much more moderate. Hence, the NO$_x$ Protocol appears to be less ambitious than the Sulphur Protocol. Second, the NO$_x$ negotiations led to more than one international commitment: in addition to the NO$_x$ Protocol, a separate, nonbinding political Declaration calls for the 30 percent reduction that was abandoned in the formal protocol negotiations. Third, implementation performance in the NO$_x$ process has been much more moderate than in the sulfur process. The sulfur process has been marked by considerable overcompliance; in the NO$_x$ process there has been overall compliance, but almost no instances of overcompliance. Finally, the NO$_x$ commitments are currently being renegotiated, and experiences from the first round of policy-making and implementation processes are bound to shed light on the current processes and prospects for implementation success.

How can the differences between the NO$_x$ and sulfur processes and their outcomes be explained? Are they merely the results of differences between the NO_x and sulfur *problems* (e.g., that regulating NO_x is more complex and costly than controlling sulfur)? Or are they caused by different *institutional* approaches to solving these problems? For instance, was the NO_x process more open to sobering scientific inputs and less responsive to participation and pressure from environmental nongovernmental organizations (ENGOs) than the sulfur process? With this general background, the chapter investigates both the factors leading to the international 1988 NO_x commitments and the ensuing domestic implementation processes, with special attention given to how patterns of participation by states and non-state actors have affected these processes.

Domestic policy-making and implementation processes in three countries—the UK, the Netherlands, and Norway—are studied. These countries exhibit some interesting differences and similarities. For instance, the three countries employ different decision-making approaches: the UK uses an "exclusive" system, the Netherlands has a much more "inclusive" system, and Norway's system lies somewhere in between. A second difference is the way these countries approach international environmental commitments. For example, Norway was one of the countries that pushed for the Sulphur Protocol, whereas the UK was in many ways a laggard on the sulfur issue. Was this also true in the case of the NO_x negotiations? Ultimately, the UK did not sign the 30 percent NO_x reduction Declaration; Norway signed it, but only reluctantly; and the Netherlands supported a 30 percent cut throughout the process. With all these differences, there is a basic similarity: despite such different approaches and positions, performance in the implementation phase is on the surface very similar in all three countries, with Norway and the Netherlands achieving around 5 percent emission reductions and the UK achieving slightly lower reductions by 1994.[2]

Three main questions form the point of departure for this chapter: Why was the NO_x Protocol so much less ambitious in scope than the Sulphur Protocol, and why was an additional, nonbinding international NO_x commitment established? What is the reason for the differences in national negotiating positions and acceptance of the international NO_x commitments in the UK, the Netherlands, and Norway? Why have these countries achieved roughly similar results with regard to the development of emissions in the implementation phase despite their different regulatory styles, and do similar results mean that the different national policy-making approaches are equally effective?

The next section examines the international background of the issue and describes and discusses the international NO_x negotiations within LRTAP and their outcome. The third section is devoted to the related domestic-level policy-making and implementation processes in the UK, the Netherlands, and Norway. The final section discusses important findings and lessons.

The International NO_x Process: Development and Outcome

The LRTAP Convention, the Sulphur Protocol, and Related European Community Processes

The LRTAP Convention was established in 1979, both as a result of pressure from a number of Scandinavian countries and as an effort to encourage East-West détente and cooperation.[3] The Scandinavian countries focused on SO_2 emissions and their links to lake acidification, thus this was also the regime's main focus in its early years. The uproar about the death of forests in Germany around 1981–1982 was politically crucial—it changed Germany from a laggard to a leader in international acid precipitation politics. Beginning in the early 1980s, forest damage and the role of substances such as NO_x and volatile organic compounds (VOCs) were added to LRTAP's agenda. An international cooperative program (ICP) on forests was also established in the early 1980s. However, with negotiations on a binding sulfur protocol already under way, most of the attention was initially given to the sulfur issue.[4]

The first Sulphur Protocol, established in 1985, called for a 30 percent reduction of sulfur emissions by 1993, using 1980 emission levels as the baseline. Twenty-one countries and the European Community signed the Protocol; the UK was not among them. Compliance with the Protocol has been very good; in fact, there has been substantial overcompliance, with an overall emission reduction of around 48 percent. The reasons for these high levels of compliance are multifarious. An important factor is the quite long regulatory history of the sulfur issue. Because SO_2 causes local health problems, it had been on several countries' regulatory agenda since the early 1970s; thus policies to regulate sulfur were already beginning to take effect. Consequently, many countries had achieved or were close to achieving the 30 percent reduction when they signed the Sulphur Protocol in 1985. Moreover, it has been relatively simple to regulate the sulfur issue: the bulk of the emissions stem from a limited number of power stations and other large point sources. This has of course facilitated the issue of regulatory consultation and participation.

In comparison, the NO_x issue has been more complicated. Among the complications is the rapidly growing transport sector, which has been something of a regulatory "wild card." In 1985, those responsible for regulating sulfur emissions basically knew what they had to deal with in the years ahead; it is much more questionable whether those who faced the task of regulating NO_x had the same feeling in 1988 when the NO_x Protocol was signed.[5]

It should be noted that in both the Dutch and British cases, relevant NO_x policies have referred not only to LRTAP but also to the European Community. Thus, the issue has been more complicated for the UK and the Netherlands than for Norway, which is not a member of the European Community. The NO_x issue has been part of at least two major European Community policy formulation and negotiation processes: the negotiations on the Large Combustion Plant (LCP) Directive and the negotiations on vehicle emissions regulations. In practice, the influence of the European Community has been more important in the case of the UK, the more reluctant participant, than in the case of the Netherlands, which has been in favor of sulfur and NO_x emission reductions and whose more ambitious goals seem domestically driven. For this reason, the European Community's role is given the most attention in the British case study.

The NO_x Process: Decreasing Ambitions
The international political process to regulate NO_x was initiated at the second session of LRTAP's Executive Body (EB) in 1984. At that session, "the need to reduce effectively the total annual national emissions of nitrogen oxides from stationary and mobile sources or their transboundary fluxes by 1995" was recognized.[6]

The regime's 1985 meeting in Helsinki, Finland, established not only the first Sulphur Protocol, but also a Working Group on Nitrogen Oxides with a mandate to focus on improving knowledge about sources and impacts of NO_x. Canada, the Nordic countries, the Federal Republic of Germany (FRG), and the USA subsequently led groups examining specific scientific and technological aspects of controlling NO_x emissions. The FRG led the legal/political drafting process, which began in the autumn of 1986. At this stage, the FRG, Canada, Austria, the Netherlands, and Sweden called for rapid and substantial reductions in NO$_x$ emissions. It is interesting to note that even during this NO$_x$ negotiation process, substantial attention was already being given to the "critical-loads" approach—that is, setting targets according to ecological vulnerability—whose advocates included the USSR and Canada.[7] "Critical loads" were not used to set the regulatory commitments in the 1988 NO$_x$ Protocol, but more recently they have played a central role in the negotiations for stricter SO$_2$ commitments and in the current NO$_x$ renegotiations.

The Working Group meeting in September 1987 has been characterized as a turning point.[8] A group of five countries—the FRG, Austria, Switzerland, the Netherlands, and Sweden—launched a proposal calling for 30 percent reduction in NO$_x$ emissions by 1995 (using 1985 emission levels as the baseline). Other countries were less interested in reductions: the UK, Norway, and Finland were only prepared to discuss a freeze of NO$_x$ emissions. A third group of countries—those in the Soviet bloc, the USA, Canada, and Italy—were skeptical of even a freeze of emissions.[9]

During the negotiations, there was not enough support for the 30 percent reduction to be written into the Protocol. By early 1988 a general consensus had emerged to stabilize emissions at 1987 levels. However, the parties that had favored a 30 percent emission reduction, together with Denmark and Canada, argued for an 1990 target date, while most of the others favored a target date of 1994. The resulting NO$_x$ Protocol, adopted in Sofia, Bulgaria, in November 1988, called for a freeze of NO$_x$ emissions at the 1987 levels (or other specified baselines, on certain conditions) starting in 1994. Moreover, the Protocol contained general agreements to develop the concept of "critical loads"[10] and to negotiate further reductions, as well as a substantial technical annex. Twenty-five countries signed the Protocol. At the same time the Protocol was adopted, but as a distinct and separate step, a group of 12 European countries signed a political Declaration calling for NO$_x$ reductions "in the order of 30 percent" by 1998, with each country choosing a year between 1980 and 1986 to serve as its baseline.[11]

Causes of Decreased Ambition: Insufficient "Green" Participation or Increasing Realization of a Complex Problem?

It is reasonable to expect that participation in this process has something to do with basic characteristics of the NO$_x$ issue. First, given that NO$_x$ emissions contribute to transboundary "acid cocktails" (i.e., a mixture of several acidifying substances such as SO_2, NO_x, and VOCs), a wide group of countries must cooperate at the governmental level if the problem is to be solved.

Second, compared with sulfur emissions, which mainly stem from power stations and industry, NO_x emissions have a wider range of sources, most notably the transport sector (both inland and offshore). The mix of emission sources of course varies from country to country. However, because transport is generally involved and thus must be targeted by regulations, participation from this sector, as well as from the industrial sector, is crucial.

Access to the LRTAP decision-making processes must generally be characterized as quite open—essentially all "stakeholders" have access to the regime.[12] In the 1979 Convention, LRTAP's formal access structure was very generally formulated in Article 10, which states that the EB can "when it deems appropriate, also make use of information from other relevant international organizations." In practice, LRTAP meetings have been open to intergovernmental organizations (IGOs), industrial groups, and ENGOs. Indeed, because of its wide participation, LRTAP has been referred to as a process of "mutual education."[13] In contrast to the North Sea pollution regime, for example, working group meetings are also open to NGOs, as long as the NGOs have "consultative status" with the UN Economic Commission for Europe (UN/ECE). The NGOs are allowed to participate in discussions, although they seldom do so. The only "closed" fora within the LRTAP regime are meetings of the heads of delegations during negotiation processes.[14]

In the NO_x process, at the governmental level inclusiveness was emphasized from the very beginning. For instance, the "importance of having as many Parties as possible joining the Protocol" was emphasized in the 1986 working group mandate.[15] Hence, governmental participation has been high.

Initially NGOs made only moderate use of this open access, but their participation increased in the concluding phases of the process. For instance, ENGOs failed to attend any of the initial meetings of the Working Group on NO_x. However, several NGOs attended the November 1986 EB session and delivered statements "for the first time in the history of the regime."[16] Moreover, increased interest on the part of ENGOs was evident at the important working group session in September 1987, and these groups began covering the meetings and issuing daily conference bulletins.[17] The International Union for Conservation of Nature and Natural Resources (IUCN) and Greenpeace were especially active in the negotiations.[18] When the final consultations took place during the spring of 1988, these consultations were moved from the working group forum to the heads of delegations level of the EB; hence, observers were excluded and "overly large delegations representing too many sub-national interest groups" were allegedly avoided.[19] This move was intended to increase the negotiators' flexibility and to allow negotiation of particularly sensitive details.[20] Participants in the negotiations have also indicated that NGO activity and pressure, although generally a positive force, went "over the edge" in the concluding phases of the NO$_x$ Protocol negotiations, something that the organizations themselves reportedly have recognized.[21]

Participation by scientific experts was high throughout the NO$_x$ process. This high rate of participation was related to the fact that the knowledge base was quite limited when the negotiations began. Hence, compared with the sulfur process, much of the improvement in knowledge took place *within* the regime and in parallel with the negotiating process over a short period of time. The Working Group on NO$_x$ served as the formal framework for this research. A combination of work produced by task forces, organized by Canada, the Nordic countries, the FRG, and the USA, and subsequent assessment of conclusions in specific "Designated Expert Groups" composed of government-appointed experts from all geographic areas within the UN/ECE, led to considerable progress in a relatively short period of time.[22]

To sum up, a distinctive feature of the international negotiations process has been the gradual decrease in regulatory ambitions over time. One may ask whether this change was related to changes in access and participation. There is an obvious relationship between the decrease in regulatory ambitions and the increase in involvement by scientific and technological experts over time. After an "optimistic" start with little knowledge available, increasing scientific and technological knowledge clearly led to a political "sobering up" and thus to less ambitious targets. (This sobering process will be further elaborated and clarified through the national case studies in the following section.) Moreover, at the same time that international ambitions decreased, the involvement of ENGOs increased. These patterns may be related, because impatient actors may step up their activity when negotiations seem to be going in the "wrong" direction. Another factor is the general "greening" of international and national agendas at the same time that the NO$_x$ Protocol was developed. ENGO pressures were obviously not enough to ensure passage of the original 30 percent reduction commitment. Still, it is possible that NGOs contributed to the adoption of the 30 percent Declaration, which 12 countries ultimately signed. However, it has been indicated that Swiss politics were a more important factor behind the 30 percent Declaration than NGO pressure.[23] Support for the original 30 percent emission reduction came from countries in both the "moderate" group in the negotiations (e.g., Norway and Finland) and the "laggard" group (i.e., Italy). Italy was reluctant to include a stabilization commitment in the NO_x Protocol, yet it signed the 30 percent Declaration. Italy's position is in stark contrast to that of the UK. Although the UK was among the first countries to establish the goal of a 30 percent NO_x reduction by the end of the 1990s, which it set as a domestic goal in 1984, and although it had already accepted a similar target for power stations within the European Community context, the UK was not willing to sign the 30 percent Declaration. The different choices made by Italy and the UK in this situation aptly illustrate the countries' deep-seated differences in regulatory cultures.

On balance, it is reasonable to assume that the gradual moderation of international policy ambitions over time—and the reduced strength of the NO_x Protocol compared with the Sulphur Protocol—was primarily caused by basic issue characteristics. The NO_x issue was less "mature" scientifically, technologically, and politically. Moreover, emission sources were more diverse and regulating them was more complicated. These aspects both influenced participation in the process and, to a great extent, shaped the final outcome. An examination of the domestic processes supports this thesis.

National Policy Formulation and Implementation Processes

The UK: Low Ambitions, Moderate Results
In the sulfur negotiations, the UK was the main laggard in the process leading to the 1985 Sulphur Protocol, which it did not sign. Within the NO_x negotiating process, the UK was something of a reluctant intermediate player. In 1988, it signed the stabilization protocol, but it did not sign the separate 30 percent Declaration. The UK has complied with the 1994 stabilization target: according to the 1995 UN/ECE "Strategies and Policies" report, UK emissions had increased 4 percent by 1993, but a 7 percent reduction was achieved by 1995. The British approach to pollution control has generally been characterized as a selective, shielded consulting process between regulators and those regulated

that relies on voluntary codes of compliance. Access for other interested parties, such as ENGOs, is considered to be limited.[24] Hence, a central question is, How and to what extent did this "exclusive" approach influence NO$_x$ policy formulation and implementation?

Regulatory and Political Background: Institutional Complexity and Complicated Interests. The UK's environmental policy-making structure has been characterized as "confused and piecemeal," and the Department of Environment has been characterized as weak and geared more to local government issues than to the environment.[25] The Department of Environment is also responsible for Her Majesty's Inspectorate of Pollution (HMIP), which was created in 1987 to establish a unified approach to pollution abatement. In that year the HMIP took over routine responsibility for air pollution control from the Industrial Air Pollution Inspectorate. In April 1996, HMIP was absorbed into a new Environment Agency. Another group that has played an important role in air pollution control is the Environment and International Directorate, formerly the Directorate for Air, Noise and Waste (DANW), which is part of the Department of Environment. Its Air Quality Division has been responsible for activities concerning the acid precipitation issue, including European Community and LRTAP negotiations.

Another main actor in the UK's policy-making structure is the Treasury Department, the most powerful department of the British government. It carefully scrutinizes any proposals with public expenditure implications. The Department of Energy has also been characterized as a powerful actor that defends the interests and policy objectives of the energy sector. Likewise, the Department of Transport has strongly defended the transport sector's interests. In addition, the Department of Industry has advanced deregulation and has sought to ensure that environmental controls do not hinder the competitiveness of British industry. The Foreign and Commonwealth Office (FCO) has been concerned about the effect of British air pollution policies on foreign relations, and hence has leaned toward supporting more ambitious environmental policies.

Although in the past Parliament has given low priority to environmental policy-making, the parliamentary Royal Commission on Environmental Pollution, the House of Commons Environment Committee (HOCEC), and the more moderate House of Lords European Communities Committee have all been involved in policy-making concerning the acid precipitation issue. Each of these groups called for cuts in domestic sulfur and NO_x emissions in the mid-1980s.[26]

An absolutely crucial part of this picture is that the Conservative Party was in power from 1979 to 1997 and hence determined environmental and acid precipitation policy throughout the 1980s and most of the 1990s. Britain's Green Party had some success in the 1989 European elections (receiving 15 percent of the votes cast), but is not seen as exerting significant political influence by controlling parliamentary seats due to the country's winner-takes-all electoral system.

On the target group side, the most important actor has been the Central Electricity Generating Board (CEGB), the largest and most important public electricity generating organization. In the 1980s, 60 percent of its power output came from 12 large coal-fired power stations.[27] In 1988 the CEGB was divided into three private energy generating companies—two based on coal (PowerGen and National Power) and one based on nuclear energy (Nuclear Electrics)—and a number of regional electricity distribution companies were created.[28]

Regarding ENGOs, Friends of the Earth (FOE) has been the most active on the acid precipitation issue. It has contributed to parliamentary inquiries and participated in the 1984–1985 international acid rain campaign launched by British ENGOs. Greenpeace has also given some attention to this issue.

With regard to *legislation*, the UK's 1956 Clean Air Act (CAA) was the world's first comprehensive air pollution control act.[29] Still, until 1990, air pollution legislation was poorly integrated and administrative discretion was high.[30] The CAA's central legal acts were the 1972 and 1974 Road Traffic Acts and the 1974 Control of Pollution Act. A process to revise the CAA was started in 1986. One key proposal suggested the introduction of a new two-part schedule listing the industrial processes to be controlled by the HMIP and by local authorities. Local authorities were to gain "prior approval" powers for processes under their control. A system of "consents" to replace the existing certificates of registration for scheduled processes was also proposed. This process was mainly spurred by European Community requirements related to a 1984 European Community directive on air pollution from industrial plants. In the context of this study, a particularly interesting element was the expanded public access, including the creation of public registers of applications for consents.[31]

In 1990, after several rounds of negotiations on the initial 1986 proposals, a new Environmental Protection Act (EPA) was finally established. The EPA gave new powers and guidelines to the HMIP and local authorities, as well as strong regulatory powers to the secretary of state.[32] Nevertheless, vehicle emission regulations, which are generally important in the NO$_x$ context, remained the primary responsibility of the Department of Transport, mainly under the Road Traffic Acts.[33]

A brief look at some important regulatory features from the sulfur policy formulation process will permit some comparisons between the sulfur and NO$_x$ processes. As already indicated, the UK did not join the 1985 Sulphur Protocol. Many factors contributed to this decision not to join, one of which was the imbalance in ministerial participation in the process. The Department of Energy, which assumed a leading role, has been described as more defensive than the industrial interests themselves. The Department of Environment was less organized; at the time it did not even have its own scientists.[34] Important research activities, like the Surface Waters Acidification Programme (SWAP), were funded by the CEGB and the British Coal Board. In general, British scientists found the available acidification evidence "anecdotal and intuitive."[35] Another important factor was access to the decision-making process for representatives of the *target groups*. For example, Lord Marshall, chairman of the CEGB, had entry to Prime Minister Margaret Thatcher's small decision-making circle.[36] The CEGB was also present at the negotiations in Geneva where the Protocol was finalized.[37] As mentioned, British ENGOs tried to influence the process through an international acid rain campaign in 1984–1985. However, the overall impression is that this effort was not very successful.[38]

On balance, the main explanation for the UK's decision not to support the sulfur initiative lies in the basic cost-benefit picture.[39] A crucial element here is the UK's upstream position as a principal "acid exporter," meaning that emission cuts undertaken in the UK would disproportionately benefit other countries. At the time, domestic environmental benefits were perceived as marginal and uncertain; abatement costs, however, were certain to fall on specific and powerful target groups—mainly power stations. These factors worked for governmental and nongovernmental industry and energy actors at the expense of green interests.

NO$_x$ Policy Formulation and Implementation Processes.   In 1985, the UK's main sources of NO$_x$ emissions were road and other transport (responsible for around 50 percent of total emissions), power stations (around 30 percent), and other industry (11–12 percent); various "domestic" sources accounted for the remainder of emissions. In the 1985–1990 period the share of emissions from the transport sector increased slightly.[40] Compared with the sulfur context, where power stations and other point-source industrial processes were the dominant emitters, controlling NO$_x$ emissions from many different sources, especially road transport, promised to be a more complicated task. It is interesting to note that the crucial task of regulating vehicle emissions has remained the primary responsibility of the Department of Transport, mainly under the Road Traffic Acts. As mentioned, British legislation in this issue area has been significantly revised in the past decade, but the independent role of the Department of Transport has not been changed.

Policy formulation: Decreasing domestic ambition and international sobriety. In connection with a report on acid precipitation by the HOCEC, in 1984 the Department of Environment stated that it would aim at reducing both SO$_2$ and NO$_x$ emissions by 30 percent by 1990, using 1980 levels as the baseline.[41] Later, however, the HOCEC recommendations for a 60 percent reduction in SO$_2$ emissions and the installation of low–NO$_x$ burners in power plants were rejected by the British government, which instead opted for the goal of a 30 percent emission reduction by the late 1990s. The minister of environment stated that a 30 percent reduction of NO$_x$ emissions even in this longer time frame would be difficult, because of problems with expanding nuclear power and because of the increase in road transport.[42] Moreover, scientists from the Warren Springs Laboratory emphasized the technological uncertainty with regard to the reduction of vehicle emissions.[43]

Within the LRTAP negotiations, the UK argued for the option of installing low–NO$_x$ burners in major existing sources. Compared with its clear role as a laggard in the sulfur negotiations, in the NO$_x$ context, the UK, together with Finland and Norway, joined the moderate group of negotiating countries. Despite its domestic 30 percent emission reduction target, in the international forum the UK supported only an emission stabilization target.

When the final LRTAP negotiating rounds drew closer, the Department of Environment voiced doubts about the possibility of meeting the domestic 30 percent reduction target. These doubts arose in connection with a follow-up session on air pollution held by the HOCEC. During the HOCEC session, several research reports resulting from increased monitoring and scientific efforts were presented. These reports indicated increasing lake and freshwater acidification in the UK.[44]

At the same time, the CEGB obtained several concessions on air pollution control requirements in a consultative process with the HMIP. For example, with regard to NO$_x$ emissions, a decision was made to aim at "design targets" instead of firm emission targets because of uncertainty about low–NO$_x$ burner technology.[45] However, in April 1987 the CEGB announced that it would retrofit its largest coal-fired power stations with low–NO$_x$ burners over the 1988–1998 period.[46]

In June 1988, the mild softening of the UK's acid stance was confirmed within the European Community context, with some British concessions in European Community negotiations concerning the LCP Directive to limit emissions from power stations—allegedly made without consulting the CEGB.[47] In return, the UK obtained some concessions regarding NO$_x$ emission reduction requirements: the UK was expected to cut NO$_x$ emissions by "only" 15 percent by 1993 and 30 percent by 1998 (with 1980 as the baseline), rather than by 25 percent by 1993 and 40 percent by 1998 as originally formulated in the Commission's compromise proposal.[48] In November 1988 the UK signed the NO$_x$ Protocol, seemingly without any public debate.[49] However, although a 30 percent reduction by the end of the 1990s had been a domestic goal since 1984, and the target of a 30 percent reduction in emissions from power stations had been accepted within the European Community context, Britain did not join the those in favor of the 30 percent Declaration.

The implementation phase: Moderate results. A national plan to reduce emissions under the EPA was first launched in September 1989. Under the LCP Directive, such a plan was required by the end of 1990.[50] In addition to sulfur targets, the British national emission reduction plan contained NO$_x$ emission quotas for three categories of LCPs: power stations, refineries, and "other industry." According to the Directive, more extensive use of low–NO$_x$ burners would reduce emissions. Under the national plan, 12 power stations were to be retrofitted with low–NO$_x$ burners at a capital cost of about 200 million pounds.[51] Moreover, the Department of Transport published a white paper in which it planned a greatly expanded motorway and road-building program to reduce urban congestion.[52]

In February 1992, emission projections published by the Department of Environment caused many experts to seriously question the possibility of achieving the domestic goal of a 30 percent NO_x reduction by the end of the 1990s.[53] Nitrogen oxide emissions from road transport had increased by 44 percent between 1985 and 1991, and the the goal of equipping all cars in the UK with catalytic converters was not expected to be met until 2010 at the earliest.[54] However, NO_x emissions from LCPs developed as anticipated. Such emissions were decreasing and stayed well within the annual European Community quotas.[55]

The overall NO_x performance picture in 1995 indicates a 7 percent decrease in NO_x compared with the 1987 baseline.[56] However, as indicated above, performance has varied in the different sectors. Shipping emissions have increased; NO_x emissions from road transport have also increased in the years up to 1989. Since then, road transport emissions have leveled off at 1,192 thousand tons in 1987 to 1,169 thousand tons in 1994. According to the government, this emission decrease is due to increasing numbers of diesel cars and increases in gasoline taxes.[57] Emission reductions in the power station sector are more substantial than those in the transport sector: NO_x emissions from these sources are down around 40 percent from the 1987 baseline. Switches to new gas-fired power stations and installation of low–NO_x burners in some existing stations are the main factors accounting for the reductions. For instance, electricity generated by natural gas increased from 6.4 terawatt hours (TWh) in 1990 to 145.5 TWh in 1995.[58] As stated in ENDS Report (254/96:21), "The switch to gas has allowed environmental regulation—of both acid gases and carbon dioxide—to go with the grain of the market."

Considering the problem of motor vehicle emissions, the recent increased focus on urban air quality is not surprising. The green movement has stepped up its activism in this area, organizing a number of local transport protests.[59] For these reasons, a specific urban air quality strategy has been developed by the government, with air quality targets for 2005. Motor vehicle emissions have been identified as the most important regulatory challenge.[60] Moreover, the HMIP has formulated new sulfur and NO_x emission limits for PowerGen and National Power.[61] This gradual shift in focus is also reflected in the 1995 Environment Act, which gives power to local authorities to pursue air quality objectives.

Why Low Ambitions and Moderate Results?   Turning first to the *policy formulation* stage, to some extent the UK approached international NO$_x$ commitments much as it had the sulfur commitments. In both situations, weak governmental and ENGO actors lost out to strong transport and industrial counterparts who were backed by scientists who doubted the existence of a problem. However, the NO$_x$ situation was different in several respects. First, from the outset the Department of Environment played a greater role in this process than in the sulfur process. In the LRTAP NO$_x$ negotiations, the UK delegation was led by the Department of Environment, which followed negotiating instructions drawn up after consultation with other departments and industry.[62] However, there is reason to believe that in the interministerial NO$_x$ consultation process within the British government the views of the other ministries and the target groups carried considerable weight. The fact that the UK stubbornly protected power stations and motor manufacturers in the parallel European Community vehicle and LCP negotiations clearly indicates the weight these interests had in the decision-making process. Still, the intensity of these interests' participation was probably decreasing when the final NO$_x$ Protocol negotiations drew closer. Power station commitments taking form within the European Community made the LRTAP stabilization target less threatening. Uncertainty concerning emissions from the transport sector no doubt complicated the issue, but this was a problem for all states involved in the LRTAP negotiations, and likely more severe for other countries such as Norway. Hence, the fact that the UK *could* in fact achieve considerable results by cutting power station emissions meant that, for the UK at least, regulating NO$_x$ was relatively easy compared with controlling sulfur emissions.

In general, ENGO access was probably not much greater in the NO$_x$ process than in the sulfur process, although the general relationship between governmental agencies and ENGOs was closer.[63] Nonetheless, the overall impression is that there was considerably less ENGO activity in the NO$_x$ process than in the sulfur process. There was no specific NO$_x$ campaign from the environmental groups. This may of course be explained by a feeling of frustration over the lack of success with the general acid rain campaign, as well as the general lack of access to governmental processes and information.[64] Moreover the groups found the NO$_x$ issue technically and politically complicated, as attacking the widespread use of the automobile was not very popular.[65] It is possible that the British ENGOs in a way gave up on the domestic scene, concentrating instead on the international forum. The general surge in concern for the environment that was registered in public opinion polls at the time seemingly made no impact in this specific context.[66]

Also, in the UK, early in the policy formulation process science and scientists helped make commitments more realistic by pinpointing technological complications related to the achievement of substantial reduction targets. However, improved monitoring and increasing signs of domestic environmental damage from acid rain led to an overall more nuanced and less politically obstructive role on the part of scientists in the final phase of the NO_x process compared with the sulfur process. In view of the general weight given to scientific evidence by the UK, this development in the final phase of the negotiations no doubt influenced the outcome.

A combination of factors, including specific issue characteristics, a stronger Department of Environment, and greater influence in the intergovernmental policy process by interests favoring more regulation, seems to have led to the UK's acceptance of the NO_x Protocol's stabilization commitment. However, the situation did not prompt the British to accept the 30 percent Declaration target. Public pressure for such a move was almost nonexistent, although interest in the environment as an issue was generally increasing at the time.

Was achieving the stabilization target a real challenge for the British government? Observers who were inside the process have indicated that compliance with the target had already been achieved when the Protocol was signed. For instance, before its privatization in 1988, the CEGB was already installing low–NO_x burners, and the resulting private companies were forced to continue the process.[67] Although achieving the LCP targets was not automatic and transport development was uncertain, the challenge for the UK to stabilize its NO_x emissions must be characterized as moderate. Therefore, in the NO_x process the affected actors have participated less intensely during the implementation phase than they did in the sulfur process.

Overall, access to the policy process and the system of regulation have changed somewhat during the implementation phase, although the influence of these changes remains unclear. The first important factor that should be mentioned is the publication in 1990 of the first comprehensive governmental policy statement on the environment, "This Common Inheritance." This white paper set in progress several institutional reforms, including the introduction of departmental "green ministers" responsible for each department's environmental record. The environment was brought "closer to the heart of decision-making."[68] Hence, it is likely that the relative strengthening of the Department of Environment continued throughout the NO$_x$ process. The strong role of the Department of Transport—nicknamed "the Department of Roads"—has increasingly been challenged, albeit with moderate results so far.[69] Current transport policy often involves institutions and groups not previously included.[70] The government's increasing focus on urban air pollution should be seen in this light.

The general position of ENGOs and their access to environmental information have improved. Both the membership and resources of ENGOs have increased considerably in the past decade. For example, the financial resources of both Greenpeace and FOE increased 10-fold between 1985 and 1993.[71] Increased access to information for ENGOs and other third parties is undoubtedly related to European Community processes, such as the European Community directive on access to environmental information that was adopted in June 1990. However, exactly how much access to information has improved is a matter of dispute. Environmental and legal groups maintain that information is still difficult to obtain because of high prices, obstructive officials, numerous restrictions on "confidential" information, and the lack of an effective appeals mechanism.[72] Overall, within this issue area, ENGOs have increasingly focused on local urban air pollution. Somewhat paradoxically, increased access and influence for ENGOs has developed in parallel with the weakening of domestic NO$_x$ targets. However, the recent upsurge in local activism has contributed to new governmental policy initiatives, and wider effects on national targets are not unlikely.

In summary, the intragovernmental balance between environmental and transport interests has started to change. However, despite some efforts to integrate environmental concerns into transport policy, practical achievements in this regard seem moderate. Emissions from this sector are not "under control." With regard to the power station emissions, much of the activity is related to European Community requirements, and unrelated processes of privatization and energy switching also play a significant role. Thus, processes are becoming more balanced, but so far other factors have been more influential.

The Netherlands: High Ambitions, Moderate Results
Overall, in the LRTAP context the Netherlands has been in favor of ambitious commitments. For instance, the Dutch had a domestic 40 percent target. The Netherlands supported the adoption of a 30 percent emission reduction commitment within the NO_x negotiations and, not surprisingly, signed the 30 percent Declaration. Moreover, it has been a proponent of the "critical-loads" approach. The Netherlands stabilized its NO_x emissions and achieved a 5 percent reduction by 1993; but the 30 percent target has not been abandoned. The Dutch regulatory approach emphasizes consultation, consensus, and compromise; in the 1980s, a significant feature was the development of a formalized target group policy. Hence, among the questions interesting to discuss is, How did this cooperative approach influence NO_x policy formulation and implementation? For instance, did it lead to compromised and "weaker" targets, but fuller implementation?

Before addressing these questions in more detail on the Dutch regulatory process, it is necessary to provide some background information, including descriptions of the central institutional features and important actors, and a brief overview of the Dutch approach to the sulfur process.

Regulatory and Political Background: High Institutional and Political Ambitions.   The political culture in the Netherlands generally has been characterized as a "consensus and consultation" culture.[73] However, the Dutch approach to pollution control has undergone a certain shift in emphasis. In the 1970s, much weight was given to regulation by "command and control" approaches. Pollution control was sector-oriented and fragmented. Periodic indicative multi-year programs (IMPs) were established for the various policy sectors (water, air, soil, etc.). With regard to air pollution, the 1970 Air Pollution Act established the legal framework for regulating emissions from both industry and transport.[74] In the early 1980s, the need for better *integration* was acknowledged; in the absence of integration, regulations in one sector or issue area could induce problems in other sectors rather than an improvement in overall environmental quality.

Beginning in 1984, the sectoral IMPs were gradually replaced by a single, comprehensive IMP. In a related move, environmental goals were formulated around eight priority "themes" (such as acidification), rather than sectors. Moreover, a specific target group policy was developed. Nine identified target groups related to traffic and transport, industry and refineries, agriculture, and households and consumers were to be drawn into the decision-making process with the hope that they would then take environmental consequences into account in their day-to-day activities.[75] In the late 1980s, the planning approach was again revised with the establishment of the first National Environmental Policy Plan (NEPP) in 1988–1989, which established measures and stepwise quantitative pollution reduction targets up to the year 2010. The NEPPs are signed by cabinet ministers from the ministries of environment, transport, agriculture, and economics.[76] Together with a range of specific action programs targeting various environmental problems, a specific Acidification Abatement Plan was produced. Though not formally binding, the NEPPs nevertheless carry considerable political weight. They emphasize cooperative decision making, and the "involvement of target groups for policy change" is stated as a crucial stage of the NEPP approach to analyzing and dealing with environmental problems. By 1994, this approach had led to around 100 covenants (i.e., voluntary agreements) covering all major industrial sectors.[77] On the legislative side, a gradual revision process was completed in March 1993 with the Environmental Management Act (EMA). The EMA covers stationary sources of pollution; the Air Pollution Act remains in force for mobile sources.

Among the most important governmental actors in negotiating and monitoring these covenants is the Ministry of Housing, Physical Planning and Environment (VROM), established in 1971 in connection with the Surface Water Pollution Act and the Air Pollution Act.[78] The VROM has overall responsibility for Dutch environmental plans and programs. The Ministry of Economic Affairs has no direct environmental competence, but coordinates industrial and energy conservation policies. The Ministry of Transport and Public Works is responsible for measures to reduce emissions from the transport sector. The Ministry of Foreign Affairs has the principal responsibility for LRTAP negotiations. It also has a strong position within the central body that coordinated the Netherlands' role in LRTAP negotiations: the Coordination Committee for International Environmental Affairs. Private interests participate in environmental policy mainly through the Council for the Environment. The Council, established in 1981, comprises representatives of public authorities, public utilities, employers' and workers' organizations, various societal interests including environmental and consumer organizations, and experts.[79]

In addition to the important activities at the national level described above, there are 12 provinces and 636 municipalities that are also active on environmental matters. On the one hand, air pollution policy-making is focused at the national level. According to Duncan Liefferink, because the rules and requirements laid down at the national level usually are fairly detailed, little room is left for discretion on the part of local authorities.[80] On the other hand, the provinces and municipalities do have a role to play in the execution and implementation of environmental legislation.[81]

A brief look at some important features of Dutch regulation of sulfur will allow comparisons with the NO_x policy process in the Netherlands. In the 1970s air pollution politics focused on the health effects of pollutants predominantly in local areas. Reports about damage to forests and aquatic ecosystems in Germany and the Netherlands in the beginning of the 1980s led to a reappraisal of existing policies, and concern about the environmental consequences of sulfur emissions began to dominate the agenda.[82]

The sulfur regulatory process in the Netherlands has been described as entailing little social conflict:

> There appears to be no record or memory of fierce competition, negotiation and reluctant acceptance of measures. There were certainly distinct positions, but the extreme standpoints that one may expect from such diverse actors as environmental interest groups and oil refining industries were mediated by the position of the government which was strong and united.[83]

However, Liefferink refers to heated discussions between the Ministry of Economic Affairs and the Ministry of Environment,[84] although in the same account Liefferink states that industry was quite cooperative and the intensity of participation was moderate. How can this apparent contradiction be explained? The availability of natural gas, which represents a clean and cost-effective alternative to coal and fuel oil, is probably an important factor. The Groningen natural gas field was discovered in 1959, enabling a gradual conversion of the energy system from oil to natural gas. However, coal use increased during the 1980s, from providing 15 percent of total electricity generated in 1981 to providing 40 percent in 1988.[85] Thus, it was not merely a matter of uncomplicated energy switching. According to Liefferink,[86] the establishment of strict emission standards in Germany, the Netherlands' dominant trading partner, made it much easier for Dutch industry to accept similar domestic standards.

Moreover, after the initial interministerial conflicts were resolved, much closer involvement in Dutch acidification policy by industrial actors like the employers' association, refineries, and electricity producers was initiated, in line with the general turn toward efforts to involve target groups in the policy process. Hence, the policy process in this issue area increasingly reflected the Dutch consensual model.

The importance of acidification as an issue grew from the mid-1980s, playing an important part in the election debacle in 1989, after which the first NEPP tightened its acidification targets. Against this background, it is not surprising that the Netherlands has consistently complied with its sulfur commitments, reducing sulfur emissions by around 66 percent by 1993.[87]

NO$_x$ Policy Formulation and Implementation Processes.   In many ways the NO$_x$ process was shaped by the Netherland's main emission sources. In the Dutch case, major NO$_x$ emission sources in 1987 were power plants (accounting for 17 percent of NO$_x$ emissions), industry and refineries (14 percent), motor vehicles (50 percent—21 percent from trucks and 29 percent from passenger cars), households (4 percent) and "other" (15 percent).[88] Hence, as in the British case, the policy challenges were more diverse in the NO$_x$ process than in the sulfur process. The special role of transport and distribution activities in the Dutch economy and the related environmental implications should be noted. The Netherlands has been promoted as a distribution country and as the "gateway to Europe." Transport and communications account for more than 7 percent of the Dutch gross domestic product.[89]

Moreover, as in the British case, relevant policies have been related to developments within LRTAP and the European Community. The Dutch approach to international NO$_x$ commitments was relatively relaxed, as its domestic targets were generally more stringent than those being considered in the international processes.[90] Thus, the European Community processes are not discussed in detail here because they did not have much influence on Dutch policy.

As already indicated, sulfur emissions decreased substantially in the 1960s and 1970s, largely because of the change from oil to gas. However, during this same period, a growing transport sector caused large increases in NO$_x$ emissions. Hence, relatively tough NO$_x$ abatement policies were originally developed around 1983–1984, arising in part because of rapidly increasing concern about acidification. The main regulation discussed in this period was the Decree on Emission Standards for Combustion Installations. The Decree's NO_x targets (in the form of emission ceilings) were eventually relaxed, however, because of technological complications, high estimated costs of measuring NO_x emissions, the notion that not all nitrogen compounds lead to acidification, and the international focus on sulfur issues at the time.[91]

In the next couple of years, the feeling that the targets were inadequate gradually increased among policymakers. Several alarming reports were published. First, in 1987 interim results from the Dutch priority program on acidification indicated that more than 50 percent of Dutch forests could no longer be categorized as "vital."[92] Moreover, as part of the preparation for a strengthened policy, the Dutch State Institute for Public Health and Environment Protection (RIVM) carried out a review of the environmental consequences of current policy options. The RIVM discovered that even with the full application of existing end-of-pipe technologies, it would not be possible to prevent a decline in environmental quality. Regarding acidification more specifically, by the year 2010 only 20 percent of woodlands in the Netherlands might be undamaged.[93] In addition, it was realized that several trends were exacerbating the regulatory problem: the growth in production was higher than expected; unforeseen changes in fuel use in power plants were taking place; and the total number of kilometers driven by passenger cars in 1984 turned out to be much higher than predicted.[94] Therefore, to strengthen the domestic NO_x policy, negotiations were started with the main target groups, usually represented by branch organizations: electricity producers, agriculture, the automobile industry, and the oil industry. So-called target group management structures were set up in 1989–1990, overseen by new administrative units in the Ministry of Environment. The outcome was a series of agreements, or covenants, with different structures and degrees of bindingness.[95] This development was part of the preparatory work for the first NEPP. Substantial NO_x reduction targets for the year 2000, such as a 50 percent reduction of power plant emissions and an over 60 percent reduction of motor vehicle emissions (using 1985 as the baseline), were agreed in connection with NEPP and Acidification Abatement Plan discussions.[96]

With their relatively ambitious existing domestic targets and with stricter targets already envisioned under the NEPP, the Dutch could quite confidently travel to the 1988 Sofia Conference and call for a NO_x reduction commitment that would include the largest possible number of countries. Not surprisingly, the Netherlands supported the 30 percent Declaration.

The implementation phase. The NO$_x$ Protocol received little attention in the Netherlands, as the content of the Protocol had no consequences for existing national policy: no new policies were needed to achieve the stabilization target.[97] However, domestic developments in the late 1980s led to more stringent targets anyway. In 1989, in a general political atmosphere marked by sharply increasing environmental concern,[98] the Lubbers Cabinet, having produced the NEPP, collapsed when it failed to gain sufficient support for the abolition of a "car-friendly" tax concession.[99] After winning the general election and reshuffling its parliamentary foundation, the new Lubbers Cabinet then put forward a so-called NEPP Plus, with slightly strengthened targets. Thus, since 1989 NO$_x$ policy implementation has been based on the NEPP Plus and the Acidification Abatement Plan. The NO$_x$ reduction targets that formed the points of departure for implementation processes were a 20 percent reduction by 1994 and a 50 percent reduction by the year 2000 (with 1980 as the baseline year). One of the targets for the year 2000 is a 75 percent reduction of emissions from passenger cars.[100] Environmental targets were also included in the Second Transport Structure Plan (SVV2), presented in 1989. The Transport Structure Plans are efforts to coordinate transport and environmental policies. The SVV2, for instance, set a target of restricting to just 35 percent the increase in vehicle kilometers by 2010.[101] A NEPP 2 was decided on in 1993. It contained emission reduction measures for NO$_x$ in industry and, in addition to the NO$_x$ reduction targets for the year 2000 put forward in NEPP 1, reduction targets per target group for the year 2010. Covenants like the SEP Covenant have been important factors in implementation of NEPP policies. In this "gentlemen's agreement" between the electricity producing companies (SEP), the Ministry of Environment, and the provinces, additional SO$_2$ and NO$_x$ reductions have been agreed upon, although not without complicated discussions.

How has implementation proceeded so far? As indicated earlier, according to the 1995 LRTAP review, by 1993 the Netherlands reduced its NO$_x$ emissions by about 5 percent. Based on figures from the RIVM, the Ministry of Environment claimed a 12 percent reduction by 1995.[102] However, a closer look at different sectors reveals marked differences. The public power sector has achieved 12–13 percent emission reductions. Emissions from industrial combustion processes have increased by 5 percent. Other emissions outside the transport sector have remained roughly stable.[103] Within the transport sector, although the total number of kilometers traveled has increased, passenger car emissions are down by around 20 percent (with 1986 as the baseline), due to the introduction of catalytic converters and cleaner-running vehicles. However, roughly equal increases in emissions from freight transport offset the declining emissions in other sectors such as the public power sector.[104] This is of course related to the important position transport and communications hold within the Dutch economy. Hence, although the Netherlands has easily met the 1994 LRTAP NO_x stabilization target, it is not on track to meet the more stringent domestic targets and the 30 percent Declaration.

Why High Ambitions and Moderate Results?   Turning first to the policy formulation stage, a key question is, To what extent did the Dutch cooperative regulatory approach lead to compromised and "weaker" targets, with environmental interests losing out to strong target groups? Target group inclusion in the NO_x process has clearly been more prominent than ENGO inclusion: a specific target group policy was developed in the mid-1980s, whereas for ENGOs access has mainly come via the Council for the Environment. However, greater access for target groups has not automatically led to weak environmental goals. Compared with other countries the ambitiousness (and sheer number) of Dutch domestic goals is considerable. This can be interpreted in several ways. It is probably related to both Dutch general policy optimism and increasing concern about acidification and the environment. But there are also other possibilities, considered below. Scientists and scientific knowledge surely played a role in the NO_x process, mostly through studies of the damage caused by NO_x emissions, although the Acidification Abatement Plan did include brief sections on technological and political feasibility issues. Overall, the evidence suggests that the general targets that were set were not a sober reckoning of feasible reductions resulting from the target group discussions. Rather, they were viewed more as desirable results to strive for in order to cope with serious, and worsening, problems.

The more modest role of ENGOs in this process must also be seen against the background of the strong general "greening" of the Dutch public, reflected in the governments' giving serious attention to the green administrative and political challenge. The interministerial NEPPs are concrete examples of this attention. Hence, the need for ENGOs to act as vocal and ambitious "watchdogs" was less marked in the Netherlands than in some other countries.

Overall, then, the ambitiousness of Dutch goals cannot primarily be explained by the development of the target group policy or the role of ENGOs. The ambitiousness must be viewed in light of the fact that the Netherlands is one of Europe's most polluted countries because of its geographical location and its high density of inhabitants and industrial activities.[105] Moreover, the domestic independence of the Dutch processes must be emphasized. The policy processes and consultations with target groups were closely related to the domestic agenda; they were not primarily a means to secure implementation of international commitments.

As in the British case, achieving the stabilization target was not a very complicated task. However, the Dutch aspired to cut emissions further. Strict domestic goals allowed the Dutch to sign the 30 percent Declaration with little hesitation. Why then has the Netherlands been unable to achieve its ambitious domestic and international targets? Have efforts been thwarted by complex interministerial battles? Because the evidence at hand is scattered and limited, conclusions must be drawn with due caution. The most reasonable explanation seems to be a combination of the general weight of economic ambitions and interests related to transport and freight and the insufficient attention given to enforcement of environmental policies. As emphasized by Jan van der Straaten and Judith Ugelow,[106] although environmental norms and targets have not been blocked by sector interests, other economic policies regarding transport and the expansion of production and consumption have been executed in such a way that the environmental targets have not been realized: "economic policy [has] swept away environmental interests." The predominance of economic concerns could conceivably be partially explained by a general reduction of attention given to environmental issues in Dutch society, including the issue of acidification. However, during the 1990s, societal pressure and "demand" for effective policies have not declined much compared with the "greener" policy and target formulation phase of the late 1980s.[107]

The need for strengthened air pollution monitoring and enforcement procedures at provincial and municipal levels is pinpointed in the OECD Performance Review report on the Netherlands.[108] Moreover, with regard to weak enforcement, the ambitiousness of environmental targets can also be interpreted as a kind of tactical retreat by target groups: knowing that limited active enforcement of commitments combined with the general weight given to target groups in the policy process would give them ample room for maneuvering during the implementation phase, ambitious targets could be "tolerated." Be this as it may, there is little doubt that the freight transport sector is the main NO_x policy challenge ahead. As noted in the OECD Performance Review, "The growth of road freight transport, a crucial issue both for transport and environment policy, appears out of control . . . ."[109] Hence, in the words of Gary Haq, "The action taken to deal with the increasing environmental effects of the freight sector will illustrate how far the Dutch are prepared to go in placing environmental protection above economic concerns."[110] This raises a crucial question, Is a green "gateway to Europe" possible?

Norway: Moderate Ambitions, Moderate Results

Because it experienced extensive lake acidification that was primarily caused by "imported" sulfur emissions, Norway was an important supporter of the sulfur process and significantly overcomplied with its sulfur commitments. However, because of its transport emissions, Norway ran into far more problems in the NO_x process and was satisfied with the quite moderate stabilization target set in the 1988 NO_x Protocol. Still, Norway also reluctantly signed the 30 percent Declaration. To date, Norway has stabilized its NO_x emissions and achieved a 5 percent emission reduction; the 30 percent target has been abandoned. To a significant degree the Norwegian regulatory system utilizes a "command and control" approach and the system can be characterized as quite simple. How has Norway's approach influenced NO_x policy formulation and implementation? For instance, was Norwegian reluctance during the process based on sobering information from target groups and scientists? If Norwegian interests were so problematic, why did the country accede to the 30 percent Declaration? Why has the 30 percent target been abandoned?

Regulatory and Political Background: Relative Simplicity in Bureaucracy and Initial Interests.   Before discussing the NO_x process, some background is needed on legislative and institutional matters and on the earlier sulfur process.

Institutions and legislation. Norway's Ministry of Environment is responsible for coordinating policy formulation and implementation processes. It operates within the legal framework of the 1981 Pollution Control Act (PCA), which replaced previously separate air and water pollution legislation. The PCA mainly covers pollution from stationary sources. Under the Ministry, there is one main pollution control directorate, the State Pollution Control Authority (SPCA). The SPCA's responsibilities include issuing permits under the PCA and running air pollution monitoring programs. Emission standards for mobile sources are set by the Ministry of Transport. Because Norway is a large country with a widely dispersed population, transportation is important, a fact that is reflected in a powerful Ministry of Transport. Emission standards for ships are set by the Maritime Directorate, which is subordinate to the Ministry of Environment in these matters. In general, the Norwegian regulatory approach can be characterized as quite centralized; industrial emissions are regulated through individual permits issued by the SPCA.[111] This regulatory process has been supplemented by a program initiated in 1975 that offers financial assistance to firms that must pay high costs to implement environmental rules.[112] There is also a tradition of close cooperation between governmental authorities and societal sectors.[113] Parliament's main input to the decision-making processes has been parliamentary reports (and related debates) produced in connection with policy formulation processes or protocol ratification (e.g., the LRTAP Protocols).

The sulfur process. The sulfur issue was relatively simple for Norway: its negotiating positions and the role it played in the negotiations process were closely related to its position as a clear "net importer" of pollution with vulnerable soil characteristics. Norway was a strong leader in the negotiation of the 1979 LRTAP Convention and in the ensuing sulfur regulation process.

The decision-making process related to the Sulphur Protocol was quite centralized. Preparations and negotiations were almost entirely in the hands of the Ministry of Environment, which collaborated with a group of natural scientists. Other ministries were consulted and kept informed through an intragovernmental process. The lack of interest and intervention from other ministries was related to the lack of any obvious new "specific" costs related to the implementation of the 1985 Sulphur Protocol. Part of the reason there were few new costs was that Norwegian domestic regulation of air pollution had begun long before the LRTAP Protocols went into effect.

In Norway sulfur emissions stemmed mainly from various types of industrial processes, and thus the main target groups in the sulfur context were various types of industry. Industry representatives were initially skeptical of the sulfur policy formulation process. However, in the end they were largely indifferent to the process because the costs were being partially compensated by state funding programs related the country's ongoing, more general industrial clean-up program.[114]

Because of the central government's strong sulfur stance in the international negotiating forum, there was little need (or room) for a strong independent non-governmental watchdog. Moreover, NGOs and public opinion were oriented around the central government. The Information Group Against Acid Rain that was established in 1982 as a joint project between five NGOs received most of its financing from the Ministry of Environment.[115] The scientific input to the sulfur process came first and foremost from "damage scientists" documenting the damages to the Norwegian environment caused by acidification. (Hence, they were mainly talking to a European audience.) The input of "abatement scientists" was less extensive. Because of Norway's relatively long history of sulfur regulation, much progress had already been achieved when the Sulphur Protocol drew closer, and thus domestic compliance was taken for granted. Moreover, because the 30 percent reduction had already been achieved in 1985, "implementation" of the LRTAP Sulphur Protocol's 30 percent target was painless for Norway. By 1993, emissions had been reduced by about 74 percent compared with 1980 emission levels—more than double the cut required by the 1985 Sulphur Protocol.

NO_x Policy Formulation and Implementation. Some important background factors that shaped both the policy formulation and implementation processes in terms of access and participation should be discussed first. With regard to *emission sources*, more than 70 percent of NO_x emissions stem from mobile sources; around half of these emissions are from motor vehicles, and the other half are from ships (fishing ships, coastal transport, and mobile drilling rigs). The second largest emitter is the petroleum sector, which accounts for around 13 percent of total emissions.[116] Unlike sulfur emissions, which are emitted from relatively few, mainly stationary point sources, NO_x emissions come from diverse nonpoint sources; thus the policy challenge in the NO_x case was undoubtedly different, and probably more complicated, than in the sulfur context. Second, as has already been indicated, important mobile sources were not covered in the PCA, and hence were not directly overseen by the Ministry of Environment.

Policy formulation. At the LRTAP Executive Body's 1984 session the need to effectively reduce NO_x emissions was recognized. It is reasonable to assume that this also was the official Norwegian position when the NO$_x$ pre-negotiations began in October 1985.[117] The international pre-negotiation working group meetings focused mainly on improving the knowledge basis for the coming formal negotiations. At this stage there seems to have been a general feeling among participants that the development of regulatory commitments was moving quickly—maybe too quickly. As expressed by one of the participants in the negotiations, "Here the politicians decided to go ahead with actual negotiations several years before the necessary scientific basis had been established."[118] International and domestic research carried out in 1986 changed several countries' perceptions of the NO$_x$ problem. Among the main Norwegian conclusions were, first, that there were more sources of NO$_x$ emissions than sulfur emissions and that these sources were less "controllable" than in the sulfur case. Second, there were variations among countries with regard to emission sources; for example, Norway had more emissions from mobile sources than most East European and many West European countries. Also important for the Norwegian negotiating position was the recognition that much more NO$_x$ was emitted from ships in Norwegian waters than had initially been assumed. Third, damaging effects related to the long-range transport of NO$_x$ were primarily felt in Central Europe; only the most southern parts of Scandinavia were affected. Fourth, unlike sulfur, not all nitrogen emissions were necessarily environmentally harmful; thus, tracing the harmful effects was a relatively complicated task. Finally, there were fewer options for installation of abatement technologies at existing emission sources than in the sulfur case.[119]

These findings led to a moderation of the official Norwegian position in the negotiations.[120] However, there was not full consensus within the Ministry of Environment, and a newspaper interview with a dissatisfied bureaucrat created some political turmoil and led to a request from the Municipal and Environmental Committee in Parliament for more information on the matter.[121] Hence, a special Parliamentary Report on "the reduction of NO$_x$ emissions in Norway" was prepared.[122] The report indicated that the anticipated international stabilization goal was attainable through measures such as American-style emission limits for various types of vehicles, stricter emission limits for domestic sea transport, stricter industrial emission limits, and a more environment-friendly transport policy. However, the target of a 30 percent emission reduction *by 1995*, which other countries were advocating in the LRTAP negotiations, was described as "unrealistic" and was said to imply "rapid and very drastic reductions in road and coastal traffic" requiring substantial increases in fuel prices, strict rationing, strict regulation of coastal traffic, etc.[123] Until this point in the process there had been little debate or conflict between the main actors involved: the Ministries of Environment and Transport, the SPCA, and a few well-respected scientists who had also been involved in the sulfur process. These actors agreed on the main points presented in the report. Moreover, the report was circulated in all relevant ministries, and no serious objections were raised.[124]

The subsequent parliamentary debate took place in a changing political climate. As described by Torunn Laugen,[125] starting in the mid-1980s public opinion made a sharp "green turn": 18.8 percent of the public listed the environment as the most important electoral issue in 1989, compared with 2.1 percent in 1985. This shift influenced environmental party politics. Nonetheless, in general, all the participants in the debate were careful to advocate only realistic targets. Representatives from all parties had somewhat reluctantly taken note of the economic and technological complications related to a 30 percent emission reduction that were described by the government. The Conservative Party expressed general discontent with the green ambitions of the governing Labour Party, and thus did not explicitly support the 30 percent reduction goal. The Party's most specific proposal was a tax exemption for car owners who installed catalytic converters in their automobiles. Against this domestic background, it is not surprising that the Norwegian minister of environment signed the stabilization protocol in Sofia. It is a little more surprising that Norway also signed the 30 percent reduction Declaration.

The implementation phase. As indicated in the previous section, measures to stabilize and reduce NO_x emissions were summed up in the 1987 Parliamentary Report. However, as indicated in the Parliamentary Report on ratification produced after the negotiations, the policy challenge with regard to stabilizing emissions at 1986 levels was not very dramatic.[126] According to this report, Norwegian NO_x emissions were around 222,000 tons in 1986.[127] It was estimated that, even without introducing any new measures, 1994 emissions would be around 230,000 tons and 1998 emissions would be around 233,000 tons. Thus, it seemed that stabilization could be achieved quite easily. A 30 percent reduction would require reducing annual NO_x emissions by approximately 75,000 tons. The concluding section of the Report on ratification identified three major measures for meeting the international commitments: (1) emission limits for all new vehicles by the end of 1993; (2) emission limits for domestic ships by the mid-1990s; and (3) new emission standards for some types of industry and for large combustion plants. It should be noted, however, that the plan explicitly envisaged achieving no more than a 20 percent reduction in emissions by 1998.[128]

Partly related to this process, exhaust standards for all types of vehicles were introduced starting in the late 1980s: for gasoline-fueled private cars in 1989; for diesel-fueled private cars in 1990; for trucks in 1992; and for heavy trucks in 1993. Together, these measures were expected to reduce emissions from motor vehicles by almost 50 percent.[129]

Meanwhile, work was initiated within the State Pollution Control Board on a specified implementation plan to achieve the 30 percent Declaration target. Considering that during the policy formulation phase the Board had openly doubted the feasibility of attaining such a goal, one may wonder if this task was embarked upon with very great enthusiasm. Nonetheless, the Board worked on this plan until the autumn of 1991, when a report was delivered to the Ministry of Environment. The Ministry was not interested in publicizing the plan at this stage, and key points were made public only through leaks. The report discussed a long list of possible measures and their cost efficiencies. Several "packages" of measures, each leading to achievement of the 30 percent goal, were introduced and discussed. This phase of the process, which lasted from the end of 1988 until the end of 1991, was dominated by governmental bodies responsible for environmental regulation, notably the Ministry of Environment and the Pollution Control Board. The Board also kept contact with several technological experts, such as MARINTEK/SINTEF in Trondheim, with regard to reducing emissions from ships and offshore platforms.[130] However, according to the Ministry of Environment, the time had now come to embark on a broader consultative process, discussing the different measures and packages with those ministries and social sectors that potentially would be affected.

It should also be noted that the NO_x issue was discussed in connection with several other ongoing policy processes. Efforts to reduce NO_x through car exhaust limits were integrated into a policy package on volatile organic compounds prepared by the Pollution Control Board. Moreover, NO_x effects were also incorporated in the planning process related to the greenhouse gas issue.

There was also an ongoing international process within the International Maritime Organization (IMO) focusing on emissions from ships. On the one hand, the broadness of the process indicated an awareness of possible cost-efficiency gains of addressing several problems simultaneously. On the other hand, it also increased the complexity of the process, opening it up to bottlenecks.

The Ministry of Environment initiated a first, seemingly quite informal, consultation process with the other ministries potentially affected by NO_x regulation.[131] Thus, the consultation process involved potentially important implementing agencies like the Ministries of Transport and Energy and the Directorate of Shipping and Navigation. There are reasons to assume that the response was rather lukewarm in the various agencies,[132] as the Ministry of Environment's next step was to request an additional report from the Statistics Bureau and the Pollution Control Board on the societal benefits of NO_x reductions. In addition, an interministerial committee was established, consisting of the ministries of environment, finance, foreign affairs, agriculture, transport and communication, industry, and energy. The committee was intended to investigate the NO_x process and the issue of greenhouse gas emissions.

The complicated committee work has been aptly described by Laugen:

On one hand the Ministry of Environment has argued that Norway needs to fulfill its international obligations in order to legitimately expect the same from others. On the other hand, the Ministry of Finance has resisted more government spendings, the Ministry of Transport has resisted measures to reduce traffic, the Ministry of Energy has resisted measures towards oil-production and the Directorate of Shipping has resisted regulation of coastal traffic.[133]

Leaks from the interministerial negotiations support this overall description. Although most of the ministries came up with measures related to the initial Pollution Control Board report, these are described as "extra light" versions of the initial suggestions.[134] For instance, the Ministry of Transport suggested only a minuscule change in car taxes and gave no sign of supporting a broader reorientation from car transport toward less-polluting rail transport.[135] The final report contains few specific, new NO_x regulatory initiatives.[136] Instead, the report lists several more general (and partly ongoing) policy processes and initiatives that are expected to bring reductions of up to 12–14 percent by the turn of the century, compared with the 5–7 percent reductions expected without any additional measures.[137] These policy processes and initiatives include revised vehicle emission limits and taxes, developed within the framework of the European Economic Area agreement; continued work within the IMO for the establishment of international NO$_x$ regulations on various shipping activities; some simple "motor technical" NO$_x$ reduction measures aimed at fishing vessels, etc.; consultations with the oil and gas sector concerning installation of new low–NO$_x$ gas turbines; and reductions in energy sector emissions brought about through an emphasis on energy efficiency.

Norway has reached the NO$_x$ stabilization target: emissions were reduced around 5 percent by 1993. According to the government, this reduction was achieved through reduced flaring in the North Sea; reduced gasoline consumption; increased use of catalytic converters; and reduced activity in processes related to fishing, sea transport, and industry.[138] As underscored in the governmental report, it is very difficult to specify the "environmental policy" component of these processes. However, it seems reasonable to assume that the reduced activity level in the sectors mentioned is mainly caused by unrelated factors. Hence, NO$_x$ stabilization has not been very costly. However, in relation to the 30 percent Declaration target, progress is not very impressive. The latest Parliamentary Report estimates reductions in the order of 12–14 percent by the year 2000; the 30 percent target has explicitly been abandoned.

Why Moderate Ambitions and Moderate Results?   There are two central questions: Why was there a "sobering up" of regulatory ambitions in the NOx process compared with the sulfur process? And, despite this general moderation of ambitions, why did Norway sign the more ambitious 30 percent Declaration?

Turning to the first question, it does not appear that the "sobering up" of regulatory ambitions stemmed mainly from the initial organization of the decision-making process in the NO$_x$ process, which was quite different from that of the sulfur process. The ministerial consultation process was probably a little broader and the Ministry of Transport was more actively engaged in the NO$_x$ process. However, the big difference compared with the sulfur process was in the role of scientific and technological expertise and the involvement of Parliament. In the sulfur process, "damage scientists" were involved; their research showing the negative effects of acid rain was mainly used in other European countries to mobilize pressure to regulate sulfur emissions. Due to the quite a long history of sulfur regulation in Norway, much progress had already been achieved by the time the Sulphur Protocol drew closer, and domestic compliance was taken for granted. In the NO_x case, due to the much shorter regulatory history and the greater uncertainty and complexity of this issue, it was natural for the government to give more weight to "abatement science" and technological expertise to assess the costs and feasibility of regulating NO_x. The related moderation of Norwegian negotiating positions caught Parliament's interest. However, it was the potentially high NO_x abatement costs for society that were emphasized and elaborated in the Parliamentary Report; despite a general "greening" of public opinion, Parliament eventually supported only more moderate international commitments to regulate NO_x.

ENGOs do not appear to have been very active in Norway on the NO_x issue at the time the 1988 Protocol and Declaration were adopted.

Given this general picture, why did Norway sign the more ambitious 30 percent Declaration? A combination of several factors probably accounts for this. Pressure from domestic green interests played a role, as did fear of unfavorable media attention. Nordic aspects also played a part. Joining the laggards in a forum (LRTAP) where Norway had once played a leading role was not an attractive option. However, although breaking Nordic unity would be viewed unfavorably, it should be remembered that Finland and Norway had already broken Nordic unity earlier in the process. Moreover, it should be noted that the final Declaration deadline was 1998; the deadline originally set in the failed effort to adopt a binding 30 percent target was three years sooner (1995). Finally, the less-binding nature of the Declaration may also have made it easier to sign.[139]

Was achieving the international commitments a real policy challenge for the Norwegian government? As we have seen, achieving the main NO_x Protocol stabilization target was not a difficult task and would not in itself have activated much opposition. Hence, it is important to keep in mind that the complicated political process in the implementation phase was primarily related to the 30 percent Declaration target.

Why was this process initiated at all, given the gloomy prospects of success emphasized during the policy formulation process? Many of the factors that shed light on why Norway signed the Declaration probably also explain Norwegian attempts to implement it. Among the factors that were probably important were public concern about environmental issues and a related green beauty contest among political parties, and a general ambition to maintain a green international image, both within LRTAP and more generally.

The interministerial follow-up process was bound to be complicated due to the fact that mobile sources of emissions are not covered by the PCA. Thus the various ministries were in charge of the abatement measures that might be implemented in their sectors, and the Ministry of Environment was in the difficult position of brokering and coordinating these activities. In this process, target group representatives from the road transport, shipping, and energy sectors won out over environmental interests. This outcome must be seen against the background of the Norwegian geopolitical landscape. Norway is a country with a scattered population, a long coastline, and huge incomes from the oil and gas industry, giving considerable weight to societal and governmental interest groups in these sectors. Those in the government supporting the emission reduction had the difficult task of arguing for costly measures to fulfill a nonbinding international agreement.[140] Presumably, that task became even more difficult over time, as the public's interest in green issues waned and cost effectiveness became an important consideration in Norwegian international environmental policy.[141]

Environmental publications and ENGOs followed this issue closely for some years in the early 1990s. However, it cannot be said that this has been a major issue in the public debate. Most of the attention has been given to the closely related issue of global warming. Indeed, the NO$_x$ issue and Declaration were hardly mentioned in the recent parliamentary debate on the report from the interministerial climate and NO$_x$ committee.

Concluding Comments

This chapter set out to answer three main questions. First, why was *the NO$_x$ Protocol so much less ambitious* with respect to regulation than the Sulphur Protocol, and why was an additional, nonbinding international NO$_x$ commitment created? Second, what are the reasons for the *differences in national negotiating positions and acceptance of the international NO$_x$ commitments* in the UK, the Netherlands, and Norway? Third, why did these countries have *roughly similar results* with regard to the development of emissions in the implementation phase despite their different regulatory styles and the quite different levels of ambition in their national goals and negotiating positions?

Do similar results mean that the policy-making approaches were similarly effective?

As indicated, with regard to the development of international commitments, a decrease in the stringency of proposed targets can be noted over time. The NO_x process started out with the explicit goal of creating a protocol entailing "effective" reduction targets—in somewhat the same vein as the 1985 Sulphur Protocol, which called for 30 percent emission reductions by 1993. The end result was a protocol that "only" called for emission stabilization by 1994 (with 1987 emission levels as the baseline). The 30 percent reduction target advocated in the negotiations by a group of states that favored stricter regulation was adopted as an additional, nonbinding political Declaration target by a small group of countries. This Declaration set a later target date (1998) and allowed a more flexible baseline (countries were allowed to select any year between 1980 and 1986 as the baseline year).

The access structure of the NO_x process can be characterized as quite open, with only the heads of delegations forum closed to "civil society." However, as access rules were basically the same in both processes, access structure does not throw much light on why there were different outcomes in the sulfur and NO_x processes or what led to the decrease in the ambitiousness of the NO_x process over time.

State participation was similar in both negotiation processes. In the NO_x process the most important attribute of governmental participation was the switch from optimistic initial proclamations to more realistic goals in the final negotiation rounds, which was largely the result of involvement by scientific and technological experts. On the surface, then, the inclusion of scientific and technological expertise and the resultant "sobering up" of political ambitions is important for understanding the decrease in ambitiousness of international commitments. However, the basic underlying factor accounting for the development of the NO_x process and its decreased ambitiousness compared with the Sulphur Protocol is undoubtedly *the characteristics of the NO_x problem.* First, the involvement of scientific and technological experts must be seen as a reflection of the much *less "mature" nature* of the NO_x issue compared with the sulfur issue. The scientific and regulatory history of the sulfur issue dated back to the late 1960s and early 1970s, whereas NO_x regulation began more recently. Moreover, the NO_x issue was in many ways *more complex* than the sulfur issue; for instance, a substantial portion of NO_x emissions in most countries stem from the transport sector, not from a relatively small number of point sources, as is the case for sulfur emissions. Norway, which is heavily affected by transboundary air pollution, was an advocate of stringent regulation of sulfur, but it grew politically pale in the NO$_x$ negotiations when the costly implications for the transport sector became clear. Thus, increased NGO activity and a general "greening" of public opinion could not rescue the initial regulatory ambitions in this issue area. It seems reasonable, however, to conclude that these factors contributed to the establishment of the 30 percent Declaration. Nonetheless, because most of the green pressure was exerted domestically, the importance of green participation in the international forum should not be exaggerated.

How was the adoption of the stricter 30 percent Declaration possible? Only half of those countries that signed the Protocol also signed the 30 percent Declaration. Countries that were the least enthusiastic about NO$_x$ regulation were not involved in setting the relatively stringent 30 percent goal. The less-binding character and more distant target date of the Declaration, as well as pressure from international and domestic green interests, also help explain why the Declaration was adopted.

The UK took up an intermediate position in the NO$_x$ negotiations, supporting a stabilization target. It signed the 1988 NO$_x$ Protocol, but did not sign the 30 percent Declaration. Overall, *the characteristics of the NO$_x$ issue—strong participation by the government's environmental agency*, and *nuanced scientific input*—help explain why the UK accepted the NO$_x$ Protocol. For Britain, controlling NO$_x$ emissions was in a way less complicated than regulating sulfur emissions. Power station commitments taking form within the European Community context made the LRTAP stabilization target less threatening for target groups with good access to decision makers. Uncertainty concerning transport emissions no doubt complicated the issue, but this was a problem for all LRTAP negotiating states; moreover, emissions from the transport sector were relatively more important in other countries, such as Norway. Hence, the UK could achieve considerable results by merely cutting power station emissions. In the interministerial policy negotiations, the Department of Environment played a stronger role in the NO$_x$ process than in the sulfur process. Early in the policy formulation process scientific and technological expertise helped ensure that policy options being considered were realistic. Later in the process, improved monitoring and growing evidence of domestic damage, documented by scientists, helped to catalyze political pressure for more regulation. However, despite this additional pressure, the British government did not adopt the 30 percent Declaration target—even though a similar domestic commitment had been established in 1984. The wider societal and ENGO pressure for such a move was almost nonexistent, although public interest in the environment was generally increasing at the time. Thus, the UK's international NO_x policy ambitions must be characterized as low.

The Netherlands was a strong supporter of emission reductions in the NO_x negotiations, aiming at a binding 30 percent reduction commitment. Thus, it is not surprising that it signed both the NO_x Protocol and the 30 percent Declaration. The Netherlands' ambitiousness must be seen in light of its being *one of Europe's most polluted countries*, due to its geographical location and its high density of inhabitants and industrial activities. Although a specific target group policy was developed in the mid-1980s and target group inclusion in policy processes has clearly been more prominent than ENGO inclusion, domestic targets and international positions have not been weakened to any great extent. The ambitiousness (and sheer number) of domestic goals is considerable. This is probably related to both the general policy optimism of the Dutch and the increasing concern about acidification and the environment that began in the mid-1980s as a result of the country's serious pollution situation. More cynically, the support from industry for ambitious environmental targets can also be interpreted as a tactical move. Because the regulated industries are influential in the policy process and there is little active enforcement by the government agencies, ambitious targets could be tolerated because in practice industry had ample room to maneuver during the implementation phase. Moreover, the domestic independence of the Dutch processes must be emphasized. Because the Netherlands felt it was far ahead of the international process, policy processes and consultations with target groups were closely related to the domestic agenda and were not primarily a means to secure implementation of international commitments.

After initially strongly supporting emission reductions in the NO_x negotiations, *Norway* moved to a more moderate position in support of emission stabilization. Nonetheless, it ultimately signed both the NO_x Protocol and the 30 percent Declaration. Norway did not "sober up" on the NO_x issue because the decision-making process in the NO_x case was vastly different from that in the sulfur case. The big difference compared with the sulfur process was *the role of scientific and technological expertise* and the involvement of Parliament. In the sulfur case, first and foremost "damage scientists" were involved, and mainly talking to a European audience. The main issue in this context was gaining attention for Norway's vulnerable position as a *clear "net importer" of pollution* when its soil characteristics made it particularly vulnerable to damage from acid precipitation. Due to the quite long history of regulating sulfur emissions in Norway, much had already been achieved when the Sulphur Protocol drew closer, and domestic compliance was taken for granted. In the NO$_x$ case, because of the much shorter history of regulating NO$_x$ emissions and the greater uncertainty and complexity of this issue, it was natural for the government to give more weight to "abatement science" and technological expertise. This expertise emphasized *the high share of NO$_x$ emissions from Norway's transport sector and the related high potential costs of NO$_x$ abatement.* This "sober" perspective was given more broad-based support in a specific Parliamentary Report and discussion related to the NO$_x$ topic. Why, then, did Norway sign the more ambitious 30 percent Declaration? First, a domestic "greening" of public opinion and party politics played a role. Moreover, joining the laggards in a forum where Norway had once played a leading role was not an attractive option. Finally, the less-binding nature of the Declaration also played a part.

As indicated above, decision-making processes and regulatory styles vary considerably between the three countries. Nonetheless, NO$_x$ emission reduction performance of these three countries was similar by 1994–1995. To some extent this performance similarity was a *coincidence*: the exact factors and processes that contributed to emission stabilization and even slight reductions vary somewhat between the countries. Reductions of power station emissions contributed to emission stabilization in the UK and the Netherlands; reduced flaring in the North Sea and reduced activity in processes related to fishing, sea transport, and industry led to NO$_x$ reductions in Norway.

To some extent the similarity in abatement performance reflects *the difficulty of dealing with emissions from the transport sector that was common to all three countries.* This difficulty is partly related to the general weight and influence of transport interests in society, but it is also related to the general difficulty of forecasting and regulating the transport choices of millions of individuals. The general similarity in performance also masks some differences. In the Netherlands, the freight transport sector is the most difficult to handle, a fact that is related to the Dutch ambition of being the "gateway to Europe." In

Norway, a country with a long coastline and a scattered population, emissions from ships and from road traffic have been particularly problematic. The UK also has the problem of increased emissions from ships; moreover, the country's road transport emissions have also been increasing, although they have leveled off in recent years.

Do similar results mean that similar efforts have been made in each country? The answer here is no, although the real differences are less marked than a superficial glance may indicate. *The Dutch and Norwegian regulatory efforts seem more advanced than the British processes.* This also correlates well with the fact that the first two countries signed the 30 percent Declaration whereas the UK did not. However, the Dutch effort with its NEPP and interministerial coordination seems driven by domestic priorities and processes. The Norwegian interministerial follow-up process was clearly related to the 30 percent Declaration target; however, it did not lead to many, if any, additional abatement.

Finally, do similar results mean the policy-making approaches were equally effective? This question is of course complicated, as the regulatory and policy-making approaches of a country to a certain extent must be seen in light of that country's specific environmental and political challenges. As noted in another comparative effort: "The Dutch medicine may be good for the Dutch, but is not automatically applicable to the British condition."[142] Nonetheless, given that an air pollution regulation challenge shared by all these countries is the integration of transport and environmental policies, it seems reasonable to conclude that *the Dutch approach seems the most advanced and interesting.* Even if the specific results in the form of emissions reductions have been modest so far, the Netherlands has started on a complicated political integration effort seemingly unparalleled in the two other countries.

Notes

This chapter has benefited from general support and very useful comments in several rounds from the other members of the Fridtjof Nansen Institute–International Institute for Applied Systems Analysis (FNI–IIASA) team, namely, Steinar Andresen, Jon B. Skjærseth, and Olav Schram Stokke, and from David Victor, Co-leader of the Implementation and Effectiveness of International Environmental Commitments (IEC) Project at IIASA. Other members of the IEC Project and Advisory Committee have also provided valuable comments. Peter Sand must especially be mentioned.

Lars Nordberg at the LRTAP Secretariat provided me with useful information on many aspects of the LRTAP regime during a visit to the Secretariat in May 1995. In Norway, Per M. Bakken, Harald Dovland, and Mari Sæther at the Norwegian Ministry of Environment have provided very useful information and comments in several rounds in 1995 and 1996. Regarding the Netherlands, thanks should be given to the Hanf/Underdal SEER1 project for providing me with useful case information (the Raadschelders/Lipman drafts). Thanks to the following persons for taking the time to talk with me on my trip to the Netherlands in July 1996: Julie Raadschelders; H.L. Barbee, Ministry of Environment and Ministry of Transport and Public Works (VROM); W.J. Kakebeeke, VROM; I.B. Abeelen, Ministry of Transport; R. Braakenburg van Backum, Ministry of Transport; D.F. Pietemaat, Ministry of Economic Affairs; and J. van der Kooij, SEP. Volkert Keizer, Ministry of Environment and VROM, deserves special thanks for organizing my interviews and commenting on a draft of this chapter. In the UK, the Department of Environment's Martin Williams and former Department of Environment key acid-rain person Bob Wilson both provided very useful interview information and commented on a draft of this chapter. Sonia Boehmer-Christiansen, University of Hull, also provided very useful interview information. Jens Stærdahl, University of Roskilde, provided useful comments.

I would also like to thank Ann Skarstad, FNI, for invaluable language and editing assistance.

1. For more information, see Wettestad, J., 1996, Acid Lessons? Assessing and Explaining LRTAP Implementation and Effectiveness, WP-96-18, International Institute for Applied Systems Analysis, Laxenburg, Austria.

2. However, it should immediately be noted that, quite naturally, I am more knowledgeable about the Norwegian processes than I am about those of the other two countries. Hence, although I definitely have a comparative ambition, time and resource constraints indicate a basic analytical humility.

3. See, for example, Chossudovsky, E., 1989, *East-West Diplomacy for Environment in the United Nations*, UNITAR, New York, NY, USA; Levy, M., 1993, "European Acid Rain: The Power of Tote-Board Diplomacy," in *Institutions for the Earth*, edited by P. Haas, R. Keohane, and M. Levy, The MIT Press, Cambridge, MA, USA, pp. 75–133.

4. On the knowledge side, the LRTAP regime initially focused on programmatic activities for monitoring and assessing transboundary air pollution. The first protocol (the "EMEP" protocol), signed in 1984, established a funding scheme for these activities (see Chapter 7 in this volume).

5. See e.g., Levy, op. cit., note 3; Wettestad, op. cit., note 1.

6. Gehring, T., 1994, *Dynamic International Regimes. Institutions for International Environmental Governance*, Peter Lang Verlag, Berlin, Germany, p. 156.

7. Probably due to anticipated favorable effects; ibid., p. 175.

8. Ibid., p. 168.

9. ENDS Report 152/87.

10. A "critical load" is defined as "a quantitative estimate of an exposure to one or more pollutants below which significantly harmful effects on specified sensitive elements of the environment do not occur according to present knowledge." See, for example, Levy, op. cit., note 3, p. 24.

11. "Nitrogen Oxides," 1988, *Environmental Policy and Law* 18(6):234.

12. Wettestad, op. cit., note 1, pp. 49–50.

13. Sand, P., 1990, "Regional Approaches to Transboundary Air Pollution," in *Energy—Production, Consumption and Consequences*, edited by J.L. Helm, National Academy Press, Washington, DC, USA.

14. Lars Nordberg, LRTAP Secretariat, communication with the author, May 1995.

15. Gehring, op. cit., note 6, p. 164.

16. Gehring, op. cit., note 6, p. 164.

17. Gehring, op. cit., note 6, p. 168.

18. Anton Eliassen, Meteorological Institute, interview with the author, quoted in Stenstadvold, M., 1991, The Evolution of Cooperation: A Case Study of the NO_x-Protocol, Ph.D. dissertation, University of Oslo, Norway, pp. 121 (in Norwegian).

19. Gehring, op. cit., note 6, p. 170.

20. "Nitrogen Oxides," 1988, *Environmental Policy and Law* 18(3):53.

21. Per Bakken, Ministry of Environment, interview with the author, Fall 1995.

22. Stenstadvold, op. cit., note 18, pp. 91–92; Gehring, op. cit., note 6, pp. 158–159.

23. Peter Sand, IEC Advisory Committee, communication with author, 1996.

24. Hill, M., 1982, "The Role of the British Alkali and Clean Air Inspectorate in Air Pollution Control," *Policy Studies Journal* 11(September):165–174; Vogel, D., 1986, *National Styles of Regulation: Environmental Policy*

in Great Britain and the United States, Cornell University Press, Ithaca, NY, USA; McCormick, J., 1991, *British Politics and the Environment*, Earthscan, London, UK; Boehmer-Christiansen, S., and Skea, J., 1991, *Acid Politics: Environmental and Energy Policies in Britain and Germany*, Belhaven Press, London, UK.

25. McCormick, J., 1989, *Acid Earth*, Earthscan, London, UK, p. 109.

26. Boehmer-Christiansen and Skea, op. cit., note 24, pp. 211–212.

27. Boehmer-Christiansen and Skea, op. cit., note 24, p. 143.

28. Boehmer-Christiansen, S., 1995, The British Case Study: Policy Formulation and Implementation, SPRU contribution for the Hanf project on LRTAP implementation, p. 50.

29. McCormick, op. cit., note 24, p. 9.

30. McCormick, op. cit., note 24, pp. 12, 15. See also OECD Environmental Performance Review, 1994, *United Kingdom*, Organisation for Economic Co-operation and Development, Paris, France, p. 88.

31. ENDS Report 143/86.

32. Boehmer-Christiansen, op. cit., note 28, pp. 53, 55.

33. Boehmer-Christiansen and Skea, op. cit., note 24, p. 165.

34. Bob Wilson, formerly with the Department of Environment, communication with the author, September 1996.

35. Hajer, M., 1993, The Politics of Environmental Discourse: A Study of the Acid Rain Controversy in Great Britain and the Netherlands, Ph.D. dissertation, University of Oxford, Oxford, UK, p. 108.

36. For example, see Boehmer-Christiansen and Skea, op. cit., note 28, p. 216.

37. Bob Wilson, formerly with the Department of Environment, communication with the author, September 1996.

38. Boehmer-Christiansen and Skea, op. cit., note 28, p. 84.

39. Wettestad, op. cit., note 1.

40. "Strategies and Policies for Air Pollution Abatement: 1994 Major Review," 1995, ECE/LRTAP, Geneva, Switzerland, p. 86.

41. Boehmer-Christiansen, op. cit., note 28, p. 46.

42. ENDS Report 130/85, p. 18.

43. ENDS Report 116/85, p. 10.

44. ENDS Report 156/88, p. 17.

45. ENDS Report 158/88, p. 19.

46. Boehmer-Christiansen and Skea, op. cit., note 24, p. 219.

47. Boehmer-Christiansen and Skea, op. cit., note 24, p. 221.

48. ENDS Report 161/88, p. 22.

49. Boehmer-Christiansen, op. cit., note 28, p. 52.

50. ENDS Report 188/90, p. 29.

51. ENDS Report 188/90, pp. 31, 36.

52. Haq, G., 1994, "Transport and the Environment: A Dutch Perspective," in *Rhetoric and Reality in Environmental Policy–The Case of the Netherlands in Comparison with Britain*, edited by M. Wintle and R. Reeve, Avebury Studies in Green Research, Aldershot, UK, p. 57.

53. ENDS Report 205/92, p. 6.

54. ENDS Report 220/93, p. 3; Boehmer-Christiansen, op. cit., note 28, p. 61.

55. ENDS Report 237/94, p. 8.

56. "Strategies and Policies for Air Pollution Abatement: 1994 Major Review," 1995, ECE/LRTAP, Geneva, Switzerland, p. 83.

57. HMSO, 1996, *Digest of Environmental Statistics*, No. 18, Her Majesty's Stationery Office, London, UK.

58. "UK Energy in Brief," 1996, Department of Environment, London, UK.

59. Rawcliffe, P., 1995, "Transport Policy and the British Environmental Movement," *Environment* 37(3):16–35.

60. ENDS Report 240/95; 257/96.

61. ENDS Report 254/96, p. 18.

62. Bob Wilson, formerly with the Department of Environment, communication with the author, September 1996.

63. Bob Wilson, formerly with the Department of Environment, communication with the author, September 1996.

64. This is my own assumption. Unfortunately, I have not been able to track down the relevant persons active in the ENGOs at the time.

65. Sonia Boehmer-Christiansen, interview with the author, July 1996.

66. For instance, in 1988 "a great deal" of concern about air pollution and acid rain was expressed by 45 percent of those polled, compared with 29 percent in 1985; ENDS Report 166/88, p. 3.

67. Bob Wilson, formerly with the Department of Environment, communication with the author, September 1996.

68. Rawcliffe, op. cit., note 59, p. 19.

69. British transport policy has generally been characterized as lacking targets and having little integration with other policy areas like the environment—especially compared with the Dutch processes; Haq, op. cit., note 52, pp. 57–58.

70. Haq, op. cit., note 52, pp. 30–31.

71. Rawcliffe, op. cit, note 59, pp. 20, 29. This report also indicates that the British environmental movement had 4 to 5 million supporters by 1990, compared with less than 2 million members for the political parties.

72. ENDS Report 256/96.

73. Dinkelman, G., van der Sluis, J.., Pleune, R.., and Worrell, C., 1994, "Finding Your Place: A History of the Management of Global Environmental Risks in the Netherlands," draft for the project on Social Learning in the Management of Global Environmental Risks, p. 3.

74. Van der Straaten, J., and Ugelow, J., 1995, "Environmental Policy in the Netherlands: Change and Effectiveness," in *Rhetoric and Reality in Environmental Policy: The Case of the Netherlands in Comparison with Britain*, edited by M. Wintle and R. Reeve, Avebury Studies in Green Research, Aldershot, UK, p. 122.

75. Liefferink, J.D., 1995, Environmental Policy on the Way to Brussels: The Issue of Acidification Between the Netherlands and the European Community, Ph.D. dissertation, Landbouw University, Wageningen, Netherlands.

76. For a thorough discussion of the NEPPs and their cultural, political, and institutional background, see Weale, A., 1991, *The New Politics of Pollution*, Manchester University Press, Manchester, UK, Chapter 5.

77. Liefferink, 1995, Environmental Policy in the Netherlands: National Profile, paper prepared for workshop of New Nordic Member States and the Impact on EC Environmental Policy, 6–8 April, Sandbjerg, Denmark.

78. The VROM was established as the Ministry of Public Health and Environmental Hygiene.

79. Liefferink, op. cit., note 77, p. 9.

80. Liefferink, op. cit., note 77, p. 9.

81. This is further described in the OECD Environmental Performance Review, 1995, *Netherlands*, Organisation for Economic Co-operation and Development, Paris, France, pp. 28–29.

82. Hajer, op. cit., note 35.

83. Raadschelders, J., 1994, Implementation of a Sulphur Dioxide Policy in the Netherlands, BCR Consultants, draft for the Hanf SEER 1 project on LRTAP implementation, p. 15. As a supporting example, Hajer refers to a 1983 symposium where the governmental perceptions and positions met no explicit criticism from ENGO representatives present; Hajer, op. cit., note 35, p. 202.

84. Liefferink, op. cit., note 75, p. 124.

85. V. Keizer, communication with the author.

86. Liefferink, op. cit., note 75, p. 125.

87. According to the OECD Environmental Performance Review (op. cit., note 81, p. 57), this is mainly due to the use of low-sulfur coal and flue-gas desulfurization in the power generation sector. Shifts from oil to natural gas in industry and refineries also contributed.

88. The Netherlands Acidification Abatement Plan, 1989, Ministry of Housing, Physical Planning and Environment, The Hague, Netherlands, p. 43.

89. Haq, op. cit., note 52.

90. Liefferink, op. cit., note 75.

91. Hajer, op. cit., note 35; Lipman, J., 1995, The Dutch Contribution to the SEER Research Project "Domestic Basis of International Environmental Agreements: Modelling National-International Linkages", draft, Bureau for Contract Research BV.

92. Hajer, op. cit., note 35, p. 183.

93. Weale, op. cit., note 76, p. 134.

94. Van der Straaten and Ugelow, op. cit., note 74, p. 125.

95. Somewhat paradoxically, Liefferink (op. cit., note 75, p. 14) indicates that the processes producing covenants were quite closed, limiting the opportunities for public and political participation and control.

96. The Netherlands Acidification Abatement Plan, op. cit., note 88.

97. Lipman, op. cit., note 91.

98. The percentage of the population considering the environment the most important political problem increased from 2 percent in 1986 to 45 percent in 1989. See, for example Tak, T., 1995, "Shades of Green: Political Parties and Dutch Environmental Policy," in *Rhetoric and Reality in Environmental Policy: The Case of the Netherlands in Comparison with Britain*, edited by M. Wintle and R. Reeve, Avebury Studies in Green Research, Aldershot, UK, p. 10.

99. For a more detailed discussion, see, for example, Weale, op. cit., note 76, pp. 143–145.

100. The Netherlands Acidification Abatement Plan, op. cit., note 88, p. 44.

101. Haq, op. cit., note 52.

102. V. Keizer, VROM, interview/communication with the author, July/August 1996.

103. Figures for 1992, "Strategies and Policies for Air Pollution Abatement: 1994 Major Review," 1995, ECE/LRTAP, Geneva, Switzerland, p. 83.

104. Report, Dutch Ministry of Transport, 1994.

105. Van der Straaten and Ugelow (op. cit., note 74, p. 119) go so far as to claim that the Netherlands is the most polluted country in Europe.

106. Van der Straaten and Ugelow, op. cit., note 74, p. 141.

107. According to Barthels and based on opinion surveys, the environment was regarded as the most important social problem in the period from 1988 to 1993, with a slight downward trend starting in 1993; Barthels, G., 1995, Main Results of Environmental Communication Studies, Ministry of Housing, Spatial Planning and the Environment, The Hague, Netherlands, June, p. 9.

108. OECD Environmental Performance Review, op. cit., note 81, p. 208.

109. OECD Environmental Performance Review, op. cit., note 81, p. 151.

110. OECD Environmental Performance Review, op. cit., note 30, p. 60.

111. This approach makes sense, as there are few large combustion facilities, and point-source standards such as those applicable to large combustion facilities in the relevant European Community directives would not apply in Norway's situation. See OECD Environmental Performance Review, 1993, *Norway*, Organisation for Economic Co-operation and Development, Paris, France, p. 68.

112. "Measures against Pollution," Parliamentary Report No. 44, 1975–1976.

113. See for instance Laugen, T., 1995, *Compliance with International Environmental Agreements: Norway and the Acid Rain Convention*, R:003-1995, The Fridtjof Nansen Institute, Lysaker, Norway, p. 69; OECD Environmental Performance Review, op. cit., note 111, p. 88.

114. Laugen, op. cit., note 113, p. 42.

115. Laugen, op. cit., note 113, p. 41.

116. State Pollution Control Authority, 1994, "Pollution in Norway 1994," SPCA, Oslo, Norway, p. 18.

117. Stenstadvold, op. cit., note 18, p. 87.

118. Bakken, P., 1989, "Science and Politics in the Protection of the Ozone Layer," in *International Resource Management, The Role of Science and Politics*, edited by S. Andresen and W. Østreng, Belhaven Press, London, UK, p. 202.

119. Norwegian Parliamentary Report 47, 1987–88, "Om reduksjon av nitrogenutslippene i Norge", p. 8.

120. Stenstadvold, op. cit., note 22, p. 104.

121. Parliamentary information, St.tid:4040.

122. Norwegian Parliamentary Report 47, 1987–1988.

123. Ibid., p. 16.

124. Laugen, op. cit., note 113, p. 44; referring to interview with Sissel Rønbeck, minister of environment in 1988.

125. Laugen, op. cit., note 113, pp. 42–43.

126. Norwegian Parliamentary Report 82, 1988–1989, NO_x Ratification Report.

127. Ibid., p. 4.

128. Ibid., p. 6.

129. State Pollution Control Authority, 1994, "Pollution in Norway 1994," SPCA, Oslo, Norway, p. 19.

130. *NM Bulletin* (green Norwegian bulletin), 1991, p. 24.

131. According to the *NM Bulletin* (No. 15, 1992), the spokesperson for the Ministry of Environment stated that the months after receiving the Pollution Control Board's report were spent on "several informal contacts" with relevant ministries. More generally, as indicated earlier, the mobile sources sector,

which is very important with respect to NO_x issues, is not covered by the PCA; therefore, the various ministries remain in charge of possible measures within their sectors, and the Ministry of Environment is charged with the difficult task of brokering and coordinating of these activities.

132. According to the *NM Bulletin* (No. 14, 1993), the plan from the Pollution Control Board created "sharp reactions" and "fury" in those ministries potentially affected by the NO_x reductions.

133. Laugen, op. cit., note 113, p. 50.

134. *NM Bulletin*, No. 14, 1993.

135. Ibid.

136. Norwegian Parliamentary Report 41, 1994–95, "Om norsk politikk mot klimaendringer og utslipp av nitrogenoksider (NO_x)".

137. Ibid., p. 20.

138. NOU (Norwegian Governmental Reviews), 1995, "Virkemidler i miljøpolitikken", No. 4, p. 288.

139. Per Bakken, Ministry of Environment, interview with the author, October 1995.

140. There is also a complicating technological time factor involved here, related to both the slow turnover of the road vehicle fleet (about 10 years) and the long lifetime of ship engines (about 35 years). Such factors complicated efforts to bring about relatively rapid emission reductions. See, for example, OECD Environmental Performance Review, op. cit., note 111, p. 70.

141. Skjærseth, J.B., and Rosendal, K., 1995, Norges miljø-utenrikspolitikk, chapter in *Norges Utenrikspolitikk*, Cappelen.

142. Wintle, M., and Reeve, R., eds., 1995, *Rhetoric and Reality in Environmental Policy: The Case of the Netherlands in Comparison with Britain*, Avebury Studies in Green Research, Aldershot, UK, p. 7.

10

The Making and Implementation of Whaling Policies: Does Participation Make a Difference?

Steinar Andresen

Introduction: Focus and Perspective

Few international organizations have undergone a more dramatic change than the International Whaling Commission (IWC). The IWC started out as a "whaling club" completely dominated by the short-term economic interests of the whaling industry; more recently, however, it has been turned into a "protectionist club."[1] The IWC was set up to regulate and promote commercial whaling, but for most of the past decade it has maintained a whaling moratorium and allocated no quotas for commercial catch. Aboriginal subsistence whaling is the only type of whaling endorsed by the majority of IWC members.[2] Whether to engage in whaling for scientific purposes is left for the member states to decide, although recently the IWC has sought to strictly limit lethal research as well. Consequently, some nations that favor resumption of whaling are currently working to establish the North Atlantic Marine Mammals Commission (NAMMCO) as an alternative to the IWC.[3]

The "participatory perspective" employed in this book is particularly relevant in the case of the IWC, because one main reason for its transformation from a whaling to a protectionist club was the large influx of new members opposed to whaling. It is often assumed that this transformation was instrumental in "saving the whales." The chapter shows that this is only partly true: conservation of whales started long before IWC membership increased dramatically.

Participation by non-state actors—scientists, environmental organizations, and industry—has also influenced IWC policies. Understanding the interaction between various groups of non-state actors and state actors is crucial for explaining how and why the IWC is one of the few international regimes to have successfully induced behavioral changes among members: practically all whaling nations have stopped their commercial activity and the level of whaling in the remaining whaling states has fallen sharply.

Many other factors also explain the decline in whaling. Resource depletion and the declining role of whale meat in diets are most important. Moreover, a major reason for the transformation of the IWC has been the "'policeman" role of the USA in applying political, legal, and economic pressure within the IWC to end commercial whaling. Of particular importance is the Pelly Amendment to the Fishermen's Protective Act, which requires the US Secretary of Commerce to "certify" any country that diminishes the effectiveness of any international fishery conservation program, including those that protect whales. Once a country has been certified, the president must decide whether or not to impose trade sanctions.[4] Does this mean that the IWC is merely a tool in the hands of its most powerful member, or has the regime had some independent influence on the behavior of whalers and whaling states?

To answer this question, it is necessary to look closely at the domestic level to study why different nations have chosen different strategies in their relations with the IWC. This study examines two whaling states, Norway and Iceland.[5] Iceland has chosen to leave the IWC, but currently is not involved in whaling activities. In contrast, Norway has chosen to remain within the IWC, but has resumed commercial whaling. The different strategies employed reflect the patterns of participation within the policy processes of these two countries.

Although they have reacted differently to the IWC's decision to halt commercial whaling, there are some striking similarities between the processes in the two countries. In both, the links between the international and the domestic levels have been strong and direct, and international reactions have triggered a strong increase in domestic participation in both these societies. In contrast to the long and complex implementation processes that are typical of many regulatory regimes, including most of the regimes discussed in this book, the implementation of whaling commitments has been fairly simple. In both Iceland and Norway, the most complex domestic process has been to decide whether or not to implement the adopted IWC policies. The whaling industry is small, well-known, and relatively easy to regulate. Once a policy decision is made, it is relatively straightforward to put into practice.

International Whaling Commission: History, Goals, and Institutions

Most international environmental and resource treaties are of relatively recent origin. Established in 1948, the IWC is the oldest global organization within this realm. Compared with the long history of whaling, however, the IWC must be considered a relatively recent development. There is written documentation of whaling taking place in Norway as early as the late ninth century.[6] Most important seagoing nations also have a history of whaling, including Spain, the Netherlands, France, Germany, the UK, the USA, Australia, New Zealand, Norway, Japan, Russia, and Canada. Until the end of the nineteenth century the players were the whalers and whaling companies, not states, and the rules were made and implemented by the market, not by governments. The "freedom of the seas" doctrine implied open access for those possessing the will and the ability to engage in whaling. Technological developments and increased demand for whale products, however, turned whaling into a major industry early in the twentieth century, when Antarctic whales became accessible. Whale oil production peaked around 1931.[7] By this time new actors had entered the scene, some governments had introduced licensing systems, and scientists were expressing concern that this "most important source of marine wealth would mathematically be exhausted within a short time."[8] Two international conventions for the regulation of whaling were adopted in the 1930s, largely as a result of the concerted action of the International Council for the Exploration of the Seas (ICES) and the League of Nations. However, because of the combination of an open access system and the dominance of short-term economic interests, neither convention had any significant influence on whaling.[9]

The current international legal instrument for regulating whaling is the International Convention for the Regulation of Whaling (ICRW), adopted in 1946. The ICRW's goal is "to provide for the proper conservation of whale stocks and thus make possible the orderly development of the whaling industry."[10] Thus, conservation was regarded mainly as a means to protect the industry's interests.[11] The basic structure of the IWC is spelled out in Article III of the Convention: "The contracting governments agree to establish an International Whaling Commission . . . to be composed of one member from each Contracting Government. Each member shall have one vote and may be accompanied by one or more experts or advisors." Decisions require a simple majority of votes. However, a three-fourths majority is needed to amend the Schedule (Article V). Whereas the Convention as such deals with the rules for the IWC, the Schedule, an integral part of the Convention, contains the actual regulations, such as the length of the whaling season, catch quotas, which species can be caught, etc. Amendments to the Schedule must "be based on scientific findings" [Article V.2(b)]. Members have the right to object to any amendment (Article III), meaning that if a member lodges an objection to an IWC decision within a certain time period, it is not bound by that decision. Any state can become a member of the IWC, irrespective of its whaling interests. The Commission can set up "such committees as it considers desirable . . ." (Article III.4). The Scientific Committee (SciCom), the Technical Committee, and the Committee for Finance and Administration have been in operation since 1951. Member nations can have as many representatives as they want in the first two bodies, but each nation has only one vote. There has been a vast expansion of the IWC's agenda over the years, and the number of working groups, subcommittees, and special meetings etc., has climbed, but the basic structure of the IWC has remained essentially the same.

Patterns of Participation at the Regime Level: Development, Causes, and Consequences

Below is a short description of changes in the pattern of participation. The following questions are also considered. How do we account for the dramatic change in participation? What are the possible effects of these changes for the policies adopted and their subsequent implementation?

Changing Patterns of Participation

Although membership to the IWC is open to any state, initially only whaling states availed themselves of this right. From its start in 1948 until the mid-1970s, membership in the IWC was stable at around 15 members. From the end of the 1970s to the early 1980s there was a dramatic increase in membership; since then, however, membership has leveled off at around 40 members (figure 10.1). Membership has changed fundamentally in a number of ways. Whaling states used to be in the majority, but currently some 85 percent of IWC members have no whaling interests whatsoever.[12] Developed countries used to dominate, but most new members are developing countries.

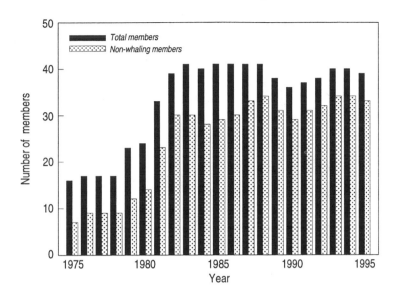

Figure 10.1
Membership of the IWC and changes in the ratio of whaling to non-whaling members, 1975–1995
Dark bars indicate the total number of member states; light bars show the number of states not engaged in commercial whaling, aboriginal whaling, or whaling scientific purposes.
Source: *Reports of the International Whaling Commission*, 1976–1996.

Also, a number of whaling states operated outside the IWC during the 1960s and 1970s, but they eventually all became IWC members.[13]

Over the same time period, there has been an even stronger growth in the number of participating scientists and nongovernmental organizations (NGOs). The number of participating scientists was quite limited during the initial phase (1953–1959), when mean attendance was seven scientists, all appointed by member states.[14] Participation increased gradually until the mid-1970s, and then increased strongly until the mid-1980s, when it leveled off again. The resulting curve is shown in figure 10.2. Another important feature is that a number of different kinds of scientific representatives now take part as observers or full participants, including scientists from related intergovernmental organizations, scientists working for the IWC, those from NGOs, and not least, those invited to participate by the IWC. More recently, around a hundred

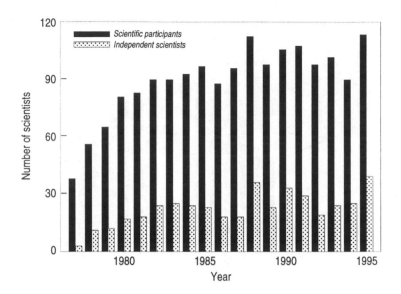

Figure 10.2
Number of scientific participants in the IWC SciCom, 1977–1995
Dark bars indicate the total number of scientists (independent and government appointed); light bars show the number of independent scientists (i.e., appointed by the IWC or other international organizations).
Source: *Reports of the International Whaling Commission*, 1978–1996.

scientists participated in various parts of the SciCom, approximately one-third of whom were "independent"—not appointed by member states. Although the number of participating scientists has been increasing, not all IWC members send scientists to SciCom meetings. In fact, in recent years usually less than half of the state parties make use of this right.[15]

The pattern of participation by NGOs is much the same. No more than a handful participated until the mid-1970s, but thereafter the IWC has proved to be a favorite meeting place for NGOs (see figure 10.3).[16] In contrast to state participation, NGO participation has continued to rise throughout the 1980s and 1990s. Many different types of NGOs participate, including the large international NGOs that work in virtually all environmental fields (e.g., Greenpeace, the World Wide Fund for Nature [WWF], and Friends of the Earth); the general animal rights organizations (e.g., the International Fund for Animal Welfare); groups more particularly preoccupied with the well-being of marine

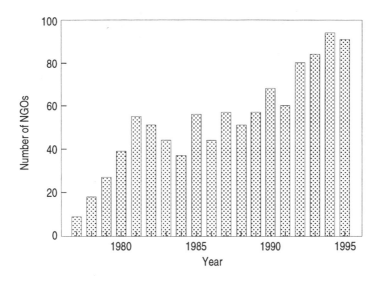

Figure 10.3
Number of nongovernmental organizations (NGOs) participating at IWC meet-
ings, 1977–1995
Data based on registration of organizations with the IWC.
Source: *Reports of the International Whaling Commission*, 1978–1996.

mammals and cetaceans (e.g., the International Cetaceans Society), and finally,
many others with no obvious links to the whaling issue (e.g., A&M Records,
Earth Coexistence Organization, and the Assembly of Rabbis). Although they
are different types of NGOs and have different purposes, they have one thing
in common: their love for whales. Increased participation by groups that lobby
for the target group (whalers) and their allies is a more recent development.
No organization representing commercial whaling interests participated until
1989, but such organizations have become more engaged in the process over
the past few years.

Not only has the number of states and non-state actors participating in the
IWC increased, but some members have also taken considerable advantage of
their right "to bring as many advisors and experts as desired." Over the past
decade, a large majority of IWC members have had either small or medium-
size delegations, with fewer than five delegates.[17] However, there are a few
"participatory giants," especially Japan and the USA, with delegations of up
to 30 people.[18] In this sense the IWC is still strongly dominated by developed

countries. The key members are few and the majority of participants are hardly in a position to play more than a bystander's role.[19]

The IWC has thus been transformed from a small, closed whaling club through the 1960s into a large, open organization with hundreds of participants and considerable media attention. The fate of tens of thousands of whales was once decided by a mere handful of delegates; in the early 1990s, however, the number of participants has risen to a few hundred—roughly the number of whales harvested every year. Although this development to some extent reflects a general trend toward broader and more extensive participation in international environmental and resource regimes, there are few other organizations where this change happened over such a short period of time and in so dramatic a manner. How can this development be explained?

Explaining Patterns of Participation

To what extent have these patterns of participation been shaped by rules of access, and, alternatively, are shifting patterns of participation something that "just happens," due to "external shocks," shifts in popular opinion, etc.? Answers to these questions give an indication of the extent to which policymakers can design international institutions to serve specific purposes.

The ICRW is not open only to state participants, it is also quite open regarding access for various actors concerned with whaling. This is reflected in Article V.2, which states, "Amendments to the Schedule shall not involve restrictions on the number or nationality of factory ships . . . , nor allocate specific quotas to any factory or ships . . . . " Thus, the ICRW actually forbids entry restrictions and specific quotas. Why were these rules included? The ICRW was negotiated immediately after World War II. It was built on a US draft that reflected the contemporary belief in liberal economic principles—that open access and free competition was the most efficient way to manage international common resources.[20] Why was the regime designed to be open to all states regardless of whether they have an interest in whaling? The philosophy is echoed in a statement made by the acting Secretary of State Dean Acheson at the 1946 Washington Conference when the ICRW was adopted: "Whale conservation must be an international endeavour . . . each nation, whatever its direct or indirect interest in whaling, will ultimately participate actively in the great task of fostering and developing this common resource."[21] It is likely that "idealistic" sentiment in the wake of World War II, with the USA as the dominant player, had a strong impact on the drafting of this rule: in the "new" world, everybody should have an equal right to participate.[22] The initial links between the ICRW and the United Nations (UN) (Article III.6) may, to some extent, also account for the openness of the regime. Thus, as a result of deliberate design, the IWC was open to all states, which was in contrast to most international fishery regimes and the Antarctic regime, where either producer interests or some kind of user interests are necessary entry criteria.[23] However, to explain why non-whaling nations suddenly started to take advantage of the open access to become participants, factors other than formal access rules must be considered.

A more general background factor was of course the change in the perception of whales and whaling that took place on the international scene in the 1970s, captured in the following statement by Dr. Sidney Holt, one of the leading authorities on the non-whaling side: "Saving the whale is for millions of people a crucial test of their political ability to halt environmental destruction."[24] The "Save the Whales" movement was necessary for increasing many non-whaling states' interest in participating in the IWC, but it was not sufficient to do so on its own. What were the more specific causal pathways? Quite a few of the developed nations with no previous whaling interests (like Sweden, Finland, and Switzerland) probably joined the IWC simply to improve their green image at the low cost of a membership fee.[25] It has been argued that some of the developing nations may have joined for reasons connected with the concept of the "common heritage of mankind" relevant in connection with the UN Convention on the Law of the Sea negotiations: like deep seabed minerals, whales should belong to all nations. According to one observer, "The IWC provides a decision area to small nations ... an arena on which to hear and be heard," which is important for many small developing countries.[26]

In a sense, the above provides the "rational" base for increased state participation, but it fails to explain why participation skyrocketed starting in the late 1970s. Many able people and organizations within the anti-whaling segment may have played a role, but it appears that some NGOs, most notably Greenpeace, were particularly important. According to some observers, Greenpeace had a deliberate strategy to "pack the IWC" with new non-whaling members, and "the whalesavers targeted poor nations plus some small newly independent countries ... and between 1978 and 1982, the operation added at least half a dozen new member countries."[27] It appears that Greenpeace also often paid the initial membership fees of these new members, and that "this project cost millions."[28] If necessary, NGOs also helped staff the new delegations with scientists and other advisors. A former legislative director of Greenpeace's Ocean Ecology division claims that, "Using the media and the force of public opinion, environmental and animal welfare groups pushed for an end of commercial whaling. With startling speed they carried out what amounted to a coup d'etat in the IWC."[29]

The IWC's development after the adoption of the moratorium on commercial whaling in 1982 lends support to this story, as many newcomers did not take their new membership responsibilities very seriously. Seven of the newcomers, all developing countries, have since left the IWC. Moreover, on average, approximately 20 percent of the "official" members have not participated in the meetings since 1984. In fact, two of the newcomers (Kenya and Costa Rica) have not shown up since 1983, although both are still members. Another indication of this lack of commitment concerns the extent to which membership fees are paid. In 1984, 50 percent of the members had not paid their membership fees. Payment of fees has improved somewhat recently, but over the past five years, some 7–10 members have failed to pay their fees each year. Thus, as many as two-thirds of the countries whose votes were enlisted to adopt the commercial whaling moratorium have either left the organization or have failed to show up or pay the required fees.[30] There are strong indications that most of these countries would never have entered the IWC had they not been actively recruited to pack the Commission with anti-whaling votes.

Active recruitment of whaling nations also took place. In 1979, when the increase in membership started, the whaling nations of Chile, Peru, South Korea, and Spain became parties to the IWC. The USA wanted them to join to reduce whaling outside the IWC and thus applied pressure: if they did not become members, they risked being certified and sanctioned under US domestic law.[31] More recently, Japan has actively recruited new pro-whaling members, but with moderate success; only a few Caribbean nations like St. Vincent and the Grenadines, St. Lucia, and Grenada have joined.[32]

How can increased participation by non-state actors be explained? As mentioned, expanded access rules and increased participation by non-state actors are part of an overall trend within international regimes. More specifically, access rules have actively been changed to effect an increase in participation by non-state actors. Because such changes could be made by a simple majority, this development started some years before the adoption of the moratorium, which required a three-fourths majority to become adopted. Regarding participation by scientists, the IWC has been a pioneer among international organizations, especially with respect to bringing in scientists independent of state members.[33] In general the anti-whaling coalition and the USA in particular have actively worked to change the procedures to broaden the basis for scientific participation, not least to weaken the previous "knowledge monopoly" of the traditional whaling nations. It seems fairly safe to assume that some of the major NGOs like Greenpeace have profited greatly in the form of higher contributions resulting from public concern about whaling. The fact that participation has steadily increased indicates that NGOs and organizations with no links to the environmental movement calculate that there is still something to be gained from taking part.[34] It has been claimed, however, that it is a deliberate strategy of a number of major NGOs to "create" dozens of NGOs that appear at the yearly IWC meetings to give the impression that environmental interest in the whaling issue is still increasing.[35] Why was the whaling lobby so slow to enter the scene? Cultural factors were probably quite decisive. Countries like Japan, Norway, and Iceland did not have the same international lobbying tradition as countries as the USA and the UK. However, there now seems to be increasing understanding among these actors that the "battle over whaling" is not fought only by states and scientists.

In summary, why and how did participation change within the IWC and how does this shed light on possibilities for conscious design of institutions? Clearly, the original access criteria in the IWC were deliberately designed to favor open participation, but until the 1970s there was little interest in whaling, and thus participation was limited to whaling nations. The more recent changes all seem to be related to the changed perception of the whaling issue, which has created pressure for increased and more varied participation. The anti-whaling coalition used the existing open access rules to pack the IWC with new states, which in turn adopted new rules that opened the regime to even more participation by different groups of non-state actors.

International Commitments and their Consequences

Although the main concern in this chapter is domestic implementation, a review of existing international commitments and the factors that explain changes in these commitments must be made.

Participation Patterns and Regime Goals.   The IWC did not embark upon a more conservation-oriented policy until the early 1960s, when it was demonstrated beyond doubt that many whale stocks were seriously depleted.[36] However, contrary to common belief, the IWC introduced many conservation measures long before it became dominated by non-whaling members. To allow for the recovery of stocks, in 1965 the IWC decided that catch quotas should be kept below sustainable yield of whale stocks. The partial introduction of quotas to protect specific species came in 1969. By the mid-1970s, the IWC was managing the catches of four whale species, namely, fin, sei, sperm, and minke whales. Commercial whaling was prohibited for blue, humpback, gray, bowhead, and right whales. Thus, a partial moratorium was already in existence. In 1974 the so-called New Management Procedure (NMP) was adopted. The whale stocks were to be divided into three categories—initial management stocks, sustained management stocks, and protection stocks—on the recommendation of the SciCom according to set criteria. By 1976 all main species and geographical areas were included in the regulatory scope of the IWC, thus allowing better management of commercial whaling and better protection of endangered whale species. It has been rightly argued that there were serious difficulties in applying the NMP: "Unfortunately, although the procedure looked very attractive in principle, the SciCom found that full implementation was difficult."[37] Nevertheless, overall it can hardly be questioned that by the mid-1970s conservation occupied a rather prominent role within the IWC.[38]

One main reason for the more conservation-oriented policies is that as countries quit whaling, some of them tended to adopt strong positions against commercial whaling, notably the USA and New Zealand.[39] This stronger anti-whaling bloc pushed for stricter regulations. The more conservation-oriented policies can also be linked to a stronger and gradually more independent scientific body.[40] As for NGOs, not many were present, but some were very vocal in their protests against whaling, both inside and outside the IWC. As one observer noted, although conflicts mounted in this period (until the mid-1970s), "Since most members had some relation to whaling, voting power was not much used."[41] Traditional "horse trading" between whaling and non-whaling nations predominated. The regulations adopted were compromises between harvesting and conservation interests. The trend was clear, however: the anti-whaling coalition building up outside the IWC was on the winning side. This became evident in 1972 with the adoption of the resolution calling for a 10-year moratorium on commercial whaling at the UN Conference in Stockholm.[42] However, this strong external pressure did not find its way into the IWC prior to 1978.

Following the large influx of new anti-whaling states around 1980, whaling regulations were tightened even more. The moratorium on all commercial whaling was adopted in 1982, when the anti-whaling countries had the three-fourths majority required to amend the Schedule.[43]

Although the new members supplied the votes that were necessary to adopt the moratorium, in practice major policy decisions were controlled by only a few states. Prior to the moratorium, horse trading between the USA and the key whaling members dominated the negotiation process, and in many ways the USA played the leading role.[44] The NGOs lobbied the media, politicians, and the public at both the domestic and international levels: their message was that stopping the "slaughter" of commercial whaling was what mattered, not "cautious" management of whale stocks. The role of the scientists in general was the opposite of that of the NGOs: the SciCom warned against a "blanket moratorium," which it described as "unscientific" and "unnecessary," although some key scientists favored the moratorium's adoption.[45]

The anti-whaling coalition spanned all categories of participants: non-whaling state members of the IWC, NGOs, and some scientists. In this coalition, the dividing lines between the actors' different roles were often blurred; the scientists had very close links to the NGOs, the NGOs had very close links to some national delegations, and some key people operated in different capacities under different circumstances. It was the rare combination of the NGOs' values, the scientists' skills, and the power and leadership of the USA gathered together by the anti-whaling coalition that brought about the moratorium.[46]

The policies of the IWC are still largely controlled by the anti-whaling coalition. However, some long-term and more indirect consequences have been flowing from the scientific work conducted in the period since the moratorium was adopted. Although science was not the driving force behind the moratorium, there was genuine uncertainty about status of many whale stocks. Thus, along with adopting the moratorium, the Commission initiated the process that became known as the Comprehensive Assessment of whale stocks, to be carried out by 1990. The process ". . . was defined by the scientists as an in depth evaluation of the status and trends of all whale stocks in the light of management objectives and procedures."[47] As a direct result of this initiative, research was started to revise and improve the 1975 Management Procedure, and in 1991 the SciCom (with a minority dissenting) recommended that the Commission adopt the Revised Management Procedure (RMP). After some adjustments, the Commission has now formally adopted the RMP. Through this process it became clear that—from a scientific point of view—certain whale species could be harvested commercially without any danger to the status of the stocks, provided the new procedures were followed. This applied both to the northeast Atlantic minke whale stock, especially relevant to Norway, and to the central north Atlantic stock of minke whales, especially relevant to Iceland. However, although the Commission has supported the RMP in principle, the majority of IWC nations have not been willing to implement it, and thus have not allowed resumption of commercial whaling: ". . . [the Commission] accepted the scientific engine that will calculate catch quotas, but added numerous features that need to be in place before the engine is used."[48]

The fact that the Commission in practice did not accept the new scientific procedure prompted the chairperson of the SciCom to resign. In his letter of resignation to the Secretariat he wrote, "The future of this unique piece of work, for which the Commission has been waiting for many years, was left in the air."[49] So far the Commission has not been ready to implement the RMP, although "[t]he procedure is very conservative compared with anything that had gone before, and also by comparison with management regimes for other wildlife or fisheries resources."[50]

The rejection of scientific management has had some important consequences for the IWC's development. First, through this process, scientific consensus has been achieved.[51] Second, whereas the controversies in the IWC used to be cast in scientific terms, this is no longer possible. One of the most clear-cut examples of disregarding the SciCom in recent years is the adoption of the Southern Ocean Sanctuary in 1994, which had no scientific basis.[52] Thus, the IWC majority no longer bases its key decisions on scientific recommendations. Third, the rejection of scientific management has had some important political consequences. According to former US IWC Commissioner John Knauss,

After the 1994 meeting it was clear that it was only a matter of time before the IWC would be faced with either abiding by the implicit premises of the convention and awarding quotas to those nations that elected to continue whaling, or following the wishes of the significant majority of its members to continue the moratorium.[53]

His advice, as well as that of the secretary of the IWC, was that limited commercial catch should be allowed. The anti-whaling IWC majority may continue to refute the use of scientific management, but in the long run their opposition may jeopardize the future role of the IWC, and it may also be detrimental to whale populations, as some states may start whaling within other organizational frameworks with more lenient rules.[54]

Thus, the considerable scientific effort undertaken within the realm of the IWC, initiated as a result of political conflicts and scientific uncertainty, may pave the way for yet another change in the IWC—the resumption of commercial whaling. However, the political interests opposed to that change are strong.

Full Implementation of the Moratorium?   Adopting ambitious commitments is a common phenomenon within international cooperation, not least at the global level. It is less common to see these commitments fully implemented. Because every member has the right to object to decisions made by the IWC, whaling nations did not have to abide by the IWC decisions either before or after the adoption of the moratorium. As shown in figure 10.4, however, catches have been reduced dramatically. Indeed, the whale catch declined by some 60 percent between 1973 and 1979—before the strong rise in the number of non-whaling members.[55] Thus it appears that the whaling nations loyally abided by the more conservation-oriented policies adopted in the 1970s, before the "new" participants arrived. However, not all of this reduction can be attributed to the IWC. Resource depletion is one explanation. Moreover, as large-scale whaling was no longer profitable, many chose to close down their operations. A combination of these "external forces" and IWC regulations is mainly responsible for the reduced catch. However, a look at the domestic implementation processes will yield more detailed insight into this question.

The reduction in whale catch has continued since the adoption of the moratorium, which stated that the whaling nations should end commercial whaling in 1986. In 1985, 12 members of the IWC were still whaling, most of them commercially.[56] Three years later all of them had quit commercial whaling, although whaling for scientific purposes and aboriginal whaling continued. Thus, the very concept of a whaling nation had changed. Although full implementation of the moratorium was delayed two years (until 1988), not least

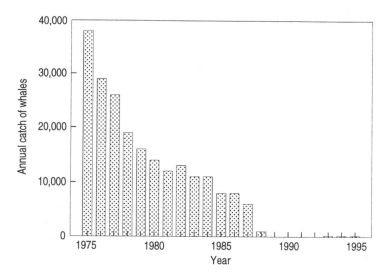

Figure 10.4
Total commercial catch of whales by IWC members, 1975–1996
In accordance with the IWC's moratorium, the commercial catch by IWC members was zero from 1989–1992. In 1993 Norway resumed commercial whaling. In 1996 Norwegian whalers caught approximately 400 minke whales; the quota for 1997 is 580 animals. These data are based on official reports to the IWC; they omit illegal whaling and whaling by non-IWC members, both of which are probably small. Scientific and aboriginal whaling, also not shown, amounts to a few hundred animals per year.
Source: *Reports of the International Whaling Commission*, 1976–1996.

because of resistance from Norway and Japan, in comparative terms it is still quite remarkable that all nations chose to respect the moratorium.

The most significant whaling states were the USSR and Japan, both of which caught most of their whales in Antarctic waters. Most other whaling nations were catching at most only a few hundred animals a year. Some 11,000 whales were caught just after the adoption of the moratorium, but five years later the number was down to approximately 500 animals.[57] Why did the whaling nations quit whaling? For most minor actors it was a combination of pressure brought to bear from the anti-whaling segment, notably the USA, and the fact that whaling was a marginal economic activity. The decisions being made mainly reflected straightforward cost-benefit analysis: the perceived political and possible economic costs of continued commercial whaling were much higher than the economic return from such operations. As to the two major whaling states, both the USSR and Japan objected to the moratorium, but Japan withdrew its objection in 1984, mainly because of pressure from the USA.[58] Russia has not withdrawn the objection, but has quit commercial operations because its decrepit whaling fleet and the country's economic collapse have made whaling unprofitable. The positions and policies of Norway and Iceland, the other countries with fairly large whaling operations, are discussed in the next section.

Making and Implementing National Whaling Policies: Norway and Iceland

For a better understanding of how different factors explain the influence of the IWC on whaling activities, the domestic implementation processes in Norway and Iceland are considered. Norway opposed and formally objected to the moratorium, but quit commercial whaling. It then resumed its commercial whaling activities against the will of the IWC majority, but stayed within the IWC. Iceland exited the IWC. Why did the two countries react differently to the IWC, and what have been the effects of the different strategies chosen?

Norway: Successful Strategy and Low Compliance?
Norway, once a leader in large-scale industrial Antarctic whaling operations, sent its last expedition to the Southern Ocean in 1967.[59] Thereafter, Norwegian whaling was restricted to small type whaling, mainly of minke whales in the northeast Atlantic. This continued until 1987, when Norway stopped its commercial whaling operations. In 1993 Norway resumed commercial catch of minke whales, and over the past couple of years the quota has gradually increased: a quota of 580 minke whales was allowed in the 1997 season.

Premoratorium Whaling.   Small type whalers have always been based in small communities along the Norwegian coast, mostly in the northern part of the country. Whaling has been an important part of the cycle of different kinds of fisheries used to make up a complete man-year for the fishermen. Thus, Norwegian whalers are not a distinct vocational group, but an integral part of the fishing industry.[60] Economically and in terms of the number of jobs, whaling was of marginal importance in the 1970s and 1980s, although it was quite important for a few smaller communities.[61] After World War II whale meat was used mostly for human consumption. The blubber was used mainly for oil or animal feed and was of marginal importance until the Japanese market demanded it for human consumption in the 1980s.[62]

Initially, Norwegian whaling policy was a simple process with participation restricted to the fisheries sector. The Ministry of Fisheries and their operating arm, the Fisheries Directorate, were the regulatory agents; most scientific work was done by the Marine Research Institute, also part of the official fisheries bureaucracy. The target group (fishermen and whalers) had access to the policy process through their organizations, the Norwegian Fishermen's Union and the Norwegian Small-type Whalers' Association. It was a rather consensual process as the rules and regulations adopted in general had a very limited effect on the behavior of whalers; neither the number of whalers participating nor the level of catch was significantly affected.[63] Costs and benefits were perceived to be highly concentrated in the fisheries sector; no other actors saw the need to interfere. The de facto open access system for whalers led to the well-known problem of resource depletion—the tragedy of the commons. Between 1950 and 1975, the average catch was reduced by more than 50 percent, mainly because of resource depletion.[64]

The northeast Atlantic minke whale was included in the scope of IWC regulations in 1976, and from 1976 and until the 1986 season IWC regulations were transformed into Norwegian domestic legislation and for the first time Norway adopted a total quota for its whalers. Quotas were strongly reduced as a result of IWC regulations, and the catch probably would have been considerably higher in the absence of these regulations. When the moratorium went into effect, however, Norway did not abide by the IWC decision and adopted a "unilateral" quota of 400 animals, based on population estimates from the Marine Research Institute. In July 1986, however, Norway announced that it would temporarily halt its commercial whaling after the 1987 season.[65]

National–International Interactions: Norway versus USA, Greenpeace, and the IWC. The Norwegian decision in 1986 to quit whaling came as a result of external actions, or threats of actions. Although the IWC provided the general setting, it was the more specific actions from the USA, Greenpeace, and to some extent anti-whaling scientists that brought about this decision. Greenpeace organized a boycott of Norwegian fish products, mainly in the US market. Initially, the Norwegian government did not succumb to such pressure. This changed in 1986 when the USA threatened Norway with economic sanctions. This threat was the main reason for the halt to Norwegian commercial whaling operations.[66] The IWC as such did not have a significant role in this process.

Along with the decision to halt commercial whaling, Norway announced a large new research program to assess the state of the northeast Atlantic minke whale. The program minimized research that was lethal to whales: altogether only 51 animals were killed in the 1988–1991 period. However, based on information from the research program that showed that minke whales were abundant and based on the specified scientific needs, on 16 April 1991 the Norwegian government decided to escalate the scientific catch considerably. More than 300 animals were taken in the 1992–1994 period. Throughout this period Norwegian researchers worked in close cooperation with other scientists within the framework of the SciCom. At the 1992 IWC meeting, the SciCom endorsed Norway's research and unanimously concluded that the northeast Atlantic minke whale stock comprised approximately 86,700 animals.[67]

Nevertheless, Norway's research catch was strongly condemned in the IWC, even when it was down to five animals in 1990, and Norway was also certified by the USA under the Pelly Amendment.[68] The USA again certified Norway for sanctions in 1992. However, as in 1986, no sanctions were levied, and neither the US certifications nor the IWC resolutions appear to have had any additional effect on the Norwegian policy, as scientific research catch was stepped up considerably in 1992. Moreover, at the IWC meeting in 1992 Norway announced that it would resume commercial whaling in 1993, much to the surprise of domestic and international observers.[69]

On 18 May 1993 the decision to start commercial whaling was confirmed formally when the minister of foreign affairs addressed Parliament and announced that Norway intended to resume limited commercial whaling for the 1993 season.[70] The fourth US certification followed, and consumer boycott actions were again launched by Greenpeace and other NGOs, most notably in Germany and the USA. Although estimates of the effect of such boycotts vary widely, in practice the boycott actions vanished relatively quickly.[71] Greenpeace also made a few attempts to interfere with the Norwegian catch, but the Norwegian Coast Guard intervened promptly; these direct actions were also very short-lived. Moreover, once again the USA proved reluctant to impose sanctions. The USA has continued to protest regularly, but the protests are described as "ritual," containing nothing new, and there are no threats of sanctions even though the quota has increased considerably.[72] Since 1993 the USA and the IWC have more or less tacitly accepted Norwegian whaling.

New Participants and New Policies.   The previous section illustrates the strong direct link between the international and domestic levels; obviously, general political pressure and threats of sanctions and consumer boycotts initially had an effect on Norwegian whaling policy, as Norway suddenly decided to quit commercial whaling. Here the domestic process is considered more closely, showing that Norway has pursued a long-term strategy with the ultimate goal of resuming commercial whaling.

External pressure on Norway to stop whaling triggered an expansion in the type and number of domestic actors involved in the debate over Norwegian whaling policy. At the government level, external pressure shifted whaling from the domain of fisheries to that of foreign policy, thus the Ministry of Foreign Affairs (MFA) became the key actor. The Ministry of Environment was also engaged, as the whaling issue had also become a question of environmental policy. The Ministry of Trade became involved in the whaling issue as boycott actions affected wider Norwegian trade interests. At the sub-national level, external pressure triggered responses from the media, trade and industry organizations, NGOs, scientists, and of course the target group, whalers. An impression was created that continued whaling could hurt important parts of the Norwegian economy.[73] Most of the new domestic actors that became involved perceived the costs of continued whaling to be high; the target group was the only direct beneficiary of whaling, and it seemed to be weak with few allies and thus was "outvoted." However, this was not only a question of a cost-benefit analysis in economic and political terms, it was also a question of what was "right"; did Norway have a good scientific case for resuming whaling?

This question engaged Gro Harlem Brundtland, who resumed her position as prime minister in 1986. She had started her career as minister of environment in the 1970s. She had been appointed head of the UN Commission on Sustainable Development in 1984, and was the principal author of "Our Common Future"—also known as the Brundtland Report—the most important international environmental document of the 1980s. Norwegian commercial whaling could easily turn into an embarrassing issue for Prime Minister Brundtland, a leading advocate of sustainable development, if the critics were right that Norwegian whaling was not being conducted on a sustainable basis. She had been following the scientific controversy between Norwegian and other IWC scientists and had the impression that Norway's scientific case was weak.[74] Thus, with its decision to stop commercial whaling, the Norwegian government declared that Norway would appoint a group of scientists (The "Walløe Group," headed by Professor Lars Walløe) to assess available research on northeast Atlantic minke whale stocks. In an effort to enhance its legitimacy, the group was explicitly international and independent of the institutions that had so far been involved in the whaling issue.[75]

Their assessments were more critical than the government expected. They claimed that the scientific basis for Norwegian whaling was much weaker than Norway had maintained, a devastating indictment of earlier Norwegian whaling: "Over the years a total of more than 100,000 minke whales have been taken by Norway. However, very little data useful for the management of this species has resulted from this catch or from the operations of the whaling vessels."[76] The group also criticized the lack of institutional independence in previous scientific research and recommended that this be changed. All the main recommendations from the Walløe Group were followed and, as mentioned, a large research program was launched in 1988, again under the leadership of Professor Walløe. This program's assessment of the size of the minke whale stocks in the northeast Atlantic was endorsed by the SciCom in 1992.

Given Norway's endorsement of the "scientific strategy," it would have been impossible to consider resuming commercial catch if the scientists had concluded that the stock was in danger. Given the international scientific consensus on the status of the stock, however, the situation was now fundamentally different than when Norway decided to temporarily halt its commercial operations in 1986. The scientific piece of the puzzle was now clarified, but what about the political piece? Internally, the government was under heavy fire from the Norwegian Fishermen's Union and the whalers for its cautious and slow scientific strategy. They claimed that the IWC was completely captured by the anti-whaling segment and saw no possibility for resuming commercial whaling within that organization.[77] Consequently, they wanted Norway to leave the IWC and build up an alternative international management organization. From the end of the 1980s in particular, Iceland had been actively seeking to build up NAMMCO as a possible alternative to the IWC because of frustrations with IWC policies. Norway participated in this process together with the Faroes and Greenland.[78] The target group and its allies were active in this process. Thus, NAMMCO may in part have been seen by the Norwegian authorities as an internal instrument to pacify the fisheries organizations. Externally, NAMMCO was also actively used: if the new Norwegian whaling policy was not accepted, the country might leave the IWC and start whaling within the framework of NAMMCO. It may also be that the pressure from fishermen and whalers, emboldened by the establishment of NAMMCO in 1992, had some effect on the decision to resume whaling, although it probably was not significant—the Norwegian resumption of whaling was more a question of principles than a consideration of the narrower interests of the target groups.

Norway was certified by the USA and condemned by others in 1990 when five whales were taken for research purposes; yet today increased commercial catch can take place in a relatively peaceful atmosphere. How can this change be explained? No doubt it is linked to who participated in the Norwegian decision-making process and in what capacity. Once the scientific piece of the puzzle was clarified, Norway could launch an offensive political strategy. The two most important players in this process were the MFA and the Prime Minister's Office. Although the issue had important internal political dimensions, it was above all conceived of as a foreign policy issue and was carried out at the very highest level. Two ministers of foreign affairs took personal interest in the issue and brought it to the forefront in Norwegian external relations, in close cooperation with the Prime Minister's Office.[79] The prime minister herself was directly involved throughout the process.[80] The Ministry of Fisheries also participated in the process, but the Ministry of Environment did not play an important role.

An informal forum was set up to manage the issue and frequent meetings were held in 1992 and 1993. Apart from the Prime Minister's Office and the MFA, the Ministry of Fisheries was represented and the link to the scientific community was secured through the participation of Professor Walløe, the head of the Norwegian delegation to the SciCom. The USA was considered by far the most important "opponent," and the issue was raised at the highest political level, seemingly with positive results for Norway.[81] The minister of foreign affairs also hired an international consultancy firm to lobby Congress, which was expensive, but was "well-spent money" according to one well-placed source.[82] In general, some of the best people in the MFA were put to work on the issue. It was very easy to involve these people, as the task was considered a real challenge—more interesting work than most diplomatic issues.[83] Several other anti-whaling countries were also visited by high-level Norwegian diplomats, and an expensive international information campaign was conducted. The Norwegian offensive extended to the international media as well as to NGOs, including close direct meetings between Greenpeace and key Norwegian officials. The final decision to resume commercial whaling, however, was not made according to "standard bureaucratic procedure" through the hierarchical process in the MFA (or elsewhere). Rather, the decision was made by the prime minister and the minister of foreign affairs. In fact, members of the MFA's bureaucracy were not informed that the decision had been made until it was announced publicly. The US delegation was informed only half an hour before Norway declared its new policy in Glasgow, Scotland, at the IWC meeting in 1992.[84]

The key decision-making group was small, "elite driven," and quite exclusive, but a wide range of "stakeholders" were consulted. Notably, close links were also established with potential opponents of Norwegian whaling policy, such as the most important Norwegian environmental NGOs, as well as with different key actors representing Norwegian export interests. It appears that these regular contacts have been important in building domestic consensus. Prior to these consensus-building overtures, parts of the media, the NGO community, and potentially affected export and business interests wanted to end commercial whaling altogether. Many of these major actors were now drawn into the decision-making process, and opposition gradually waned.[85] As to the role of Parliament, the Extended Committee on Foreign Relations had been consulted and informed on a regular basis, and when the decision to resume commercial whaling was discussed in Parliament in 1993 there was not a single dissenting vote.[86]

Other Explanatory Factors. This high-level strategy—which included some participants and excluded others—appears to have been successful. The resumption of commercial whaling was tacitly accepted internationally, and domestic consensus was achieved. However, this success cannot be seen solely as a result of how the process was organized and the efforts put into it; other explanatory factors were also at work.

Norway was potentially quite vulnerable on the issue; consumer boycotts and economic sanctions could have hurt the export-oriented economy. However, actions were short-lived and had little effect. If this had not been the case, the domestic consensus might have been destroyed and thus Norwegian policy could have been very different. To some extent the ineffectiveness of boycotts and sanctions may have been due to the Norwegian offensive, but these actions were also due to weakened foreign opposition, not least from the USA. The more cautious US policy may be due to the General Agreement on Tariffs and Trade (GATT), later the World Trade Organization (WTO). The point of departure was the much quoted tuna/dolphin case between the USA and Mexico, where a GATT panel ruled that a US ban on Mexican tuna was not consistent with GATT rules.[87] The US Marine Mammals Commission said in a public letter to the US IWC Commissioner (5 December 1991) that the panel verdict will "prevent the US from utilizing certifications and trade sanctions to encourage compliance with IWC rulings." The fact that the USA has threatened a number of countries with sanctions according to the Pelly Amendment but has never imposed them can be seen in this light; the USA has feared that the sanctions might not stand up against GATT rules.[88] It also seems that Congress has been less aggressive on the whaling issue than it used to be—a change largely linked to the more active role of Alaskan legislators who were not uniformly opposed to all whaling, not least because of their interest in the sound management of the living resources of the sea.

The situation in the IWC was also changing. The establishment of NAMMCO, Iceland's withdrawal from the IWC, threats of withdrawal from Japan and Norway, and the scientific consensus that cautious resumption of whaling of certain species might be justified, have all contributed to a strengthening of the Norwegian position.[89] According to "neutral" observers in the IWC, the USA has recently lost some of its leadership role in the Commission, not least because of its unsustainable position on scientific issues.[90] Due to the broad opposition to whaling in Congress and among the US public, it is not very likely that the USA will change its position on the issue, but at present it seems to accept Norwegian whaling as long as it takes place within the realm of the IWC.[91] For the time being, the USA appears more concerned with preventing the use of an alternative "whaling friendly" international body (such as

NAMMCO) as a basis for future whaling. Some tacit compromise might have been made between Norway and the USA to this effect. The fact that Norway did not vote against the Southern Ocean Sanctuary adopted in 1994, although there was no scientific basis for its adoption, can be seen in this light. A tacit compromise might also explain the somewhat reluctant Norwegian position toward NAMMCO. Norway is a member of NAMMCO, but has been reluctant to support Iceland's efforts to strengthen the organization's role, maybe with the ultimate goal of creating a management alternative to the IWC. Thus, Norway has succeeded with her strategy, but to some extent at the expense of her "whaling allies"—Japan and Iceland.[92]

Unintended links to other issues may also have helped Norway. For instance, the active and secret diplomacy carried out by Norway through the "Oslo Channel" in relation the Middle East Conflict probably had an impact. This successful diplomatic effort made it very difficult for the USA to levy sanctions. However important the whaling issue may be, it is hardly comparable to this development in the Middle East.[93]

Another, at least initially, unintended link that contributed to the hardening of the Norwegian position on whaling was the "EU factor."[94] The whaling issue was a potential stumbling block to Norwegian membership in the European Union (EU). The principal opinion of the Community on whaling was clear: "If it was simply a matter for the Community to decide, all commercial whaling would be abandoned once and for all."[95] Legally, the issue was complicated and will not be dealt with here.[96] The UK in particular, represented by Minister of Agriculture John Gummer, was quite decisive: membership would mean an end to Norwegian commercial whaling.[97] No agreement was reached—the EU and Norway decided to discuss it within two years if Norway became an EU member. The government, which favored EU membership, had little to give on the issue for internal political reasons. If the Norwegian government had "sold out" the whaling interests as a result of pressure from the (much hated) "bureaucrats in Brussels," opposition to the EU would have become even stronger in the many fishing communities in the north, where opposition to the EU was particularly strong; the government had no room for compromise.[98] Thus, instead of softening the Norwegian position on whaling, the EU negotiations tended to harden it.

The Norwegian strategy has been successful in that the goal of sustainable whaling has been achieved. Norwegian whaling is tacitly accepted by the

IWC's key players. Norway's objection to the moratorium has allowed it to remain formally in compliance with IWC rules and decisions. However, there is no doubt that Norway acts in violation of the new protectionist "spirit" of the IWC. Norway has not succeeded in convincing the IWC majority that it has a just cause. As to future Norwegian whaling, the level of catch is now about to reach the limit of the domestic demand. Whether the quota will continue to increase therefore depends on whether it will again be feasible to export minke whale products.

Iceland: Unsuccessful Strategy and High Compliance?

In contrast with Norway, Iceland has never been an Antarctic whaling nation, and thus bears no responsibility for the depletion of the large whales in the Southern Ocean.[99] The use of whales in Iceland as a source of food was documented as early as the thirteenth century.[100] Modern whaling from land-based whaling stations was introduced into Iceland in the late nineteenth century, and Iceland experienced resource depletion early in this century, resulting in strict regulatory measures introduced by its Parliament. Icelandic fishermen have hunted minke whale in coastal waters since the end of World War II, but on a much smaller scale than their Norwegian counterparts.[101] Catch limits were introduced in Icelandic minke whaling in 1977, and a quota of 320 whales was set by the IWC for the central north Atlantic stock.[102] In contrast to Norway, however, Iceland was also hunting larger whales from a whaling station in southwestern Iceland. The fin whale was by far the most important species for this fishery, with an average annual catch of some 200 whales in the decade prior to the adoption of the moratorium, but some sei and sperm whales were also caught.[103] Thus, Iceland not only employed fishing vessels in its whaling activities, it also had its own small whaling fleet, Hvalur Ltd.[104]

Prior to the adoption of the moratorium, whaling in Iceland was a rather marginal economic activity, although it was more important here than in Norway. It accounted for 2 percent of export earnings from the fishing industry.[105] It is important to recognize that whaling had a stabilizing effect on the Icelandic economy that was of great value in a society dependent on fluctuating fish resources. Also, in contrast to other fishing activities, no foreign debts were associated with the whaling fleet. Traditionally, Iceland has exported most of its whale products, most notably to Japan.[106] Before looking at the significance of different patterns of participation within the country, a short outline of the main aspects in "postmoratorium" Icelandic whaling policies is given.

The Whaling Policy of Iceland after the 1982 Moratorium.   In contrast to Norway, Iceland did not lodge an objection to the moratorium of 1982. Thus, if Iceland rejoins the IWC, it is legally bound by the moratorium unless a three-fourths majority of IWC members votes to lift it, which currently is unlikely as most IWC members vehemently oppose commercial whaling. Iceland was the first whaling country to launch a scientific strategy to assess the status of those whale stocks relevant to Iceland as part of the IWC's Comprehensive Assessment of whale stocks, to be used as a basis for the RMP. The program covered the four-year period from 1986–1989. Although the main part of the program dealt with nonlethal research, such as sighting surveys, provisions were also made for killing 80 fin whales, 40 sei whales, and 80 minke whales per year.[107]

The IWC majority strongly opposed the lethal aspects of the research project, which were seen as a disguise for commercial whaling and were judged to be particularly bad because Iceland had not objected to the moratorium. The presentation of the Icelandic research program in the IWC in 1985 triggered a counterstrategy among the IWC majority. First, procedures were changed to give the SciCom more control over domestic research programs, although according to the ICRW this is a matter for the member countries to decide for themselves. Second, procedures were changed so that the (more political) Commission was given more direct control over the work of the SciCom. Third, measures were taken to limit international trade in whale products. The USA played a key role in changing these procedures. As a result, Icelandic research whaling was strongly condemned by the IWC. Moreover, the move to limit trade in whale products was a problem for Iceland because most of Iceland's whale meat was exported.

Iceland was also exposed to pressure from the USA and Greenpeace. The USA contacted Iceland immediately after the 1986 IWC meeting and threatened to certify Iceland if it continued its scientific catch and the sale of whale meat to Japan. Although they disagreed over principles, the conclusion of this conflict was traditional horse trading: the USA allowed Iceland to export 49 percent of the whale meat to Japan, with the rest to be for local consumption only.[108] Another outcome of these bilateral negotiations was that Iceland gradually reduced its scientific catch, ultimately taking less than half the "scientific quota" it had adopted for the 1986–1989 period. In return, Iceland was not certified. The USA and the IWC lifted the pressure when it was made clear in 1988 that there would be no scientific catch after the 1989 season. Nonetheless, in 1988 Iceland was still catching whales, and as this was unacceptable to Greenpeace, boycott actions were launched early in 1988 in the USA. The main arena for the boycott actions, however, was Germany, where large supermarkets and warehouses stopped buying tinned seafood from Iceland. Although uncertain and disputed, total losses were probably more substantial in Iceland than in Norway, perhaps reaching US$30 million by the time research whaling stopped one year later.[109] Protests waned and boycotts were cancelled in the USA and Germany in the autumn of 1989.

Based on its research, Iceland presented stock estimates at the 1990 SciCom meeting, where it was agreed that the previously unclassified minke whales of the central north Atlantic stock could be classified as an initial management stock.[110] Understandably, Iceland considered this a victory and argued that commercial catch could be reopened. But, as accounted for previously, the IWC majority thought otherwise; it argued that commercial harvest of one stock could not begin before the entire management system was in place. Thus, Iceland's request for interim procedures to resume commercial whaling was rejected. This was the same answer that Norway had received in 1992, but because Iceland had not formally objected to the moratorium, it had less room to maneuver. Iceland strongly condemned what it saw as deliberate postponement tactics concerning implementation of the RMP and decided to leave the IWC. It formally left the IWC during the 1992 session and since then has only been represented by an observer. In 1993 the USA still considered Iceland a potential whaling nation and threatened retaliation against any future commercial whaling.[111] The issue remains an unresolved problem in US–Icelandic relations.[112]

Unilateral whaling is not an option for Iceland because it has ratified the United Nations Convention on the Law of the Sea, which states that whaling must be based on international cooperation. This explains why NAMMCO is so important to Iceland, although so far NAMMCO has not substantially advanced Iceland's interests.[113] Even though Iceland was the first of the whaling nations to confront the IWC, and in a manner that paved the way for the subsequent Norwegian offensive, it nevertheless has adopted a rather cautious strategy.

Limited scientific catches were taken for a short period of time. Iceland has never been certified by the USA—when such threats were made Iceland reduced catches to avoid an escalation of the conflict. No whaling has been conducted by Iceland since 1989. It will need to take some risks and adopt a more offensive strategy if it is to resume commercial whaling within the existing political and legal framework, which may activate underlying domestic controversies.

Different Actors: Roles, Interests, and Influence.   As in Norway, external pressure to quit whaling has caused an expansion in the domestic actors participating in the decision-making process in Iceland. The process has been an open one with seemingly easy access for all key parties. This is amply illustrated by looking at the decision-making process that led to Iceland's decision not to object to the moratorium. Normally this question would be one for the government executive to decide, as was the case in Norway. However, because Iceland's coalition government was unable to agree on the issue, it was decided to put the issue before Parliament, thus opening up, and making more uncertain, the decision-making process.[114] Although formally it was the government that made the decision, the minister of fisheries made it clear that he would listen to the majority view of Parliament. Export interests, NGOs, and officials from the US embassy lobbied heavily and stood against pro-whaling arguments for the principle of self-determination and sustainable harvest. The debate was heated, all parties were split on the issue, and the majority for accepting the moratorium was the closest possible (29–28).

Since the adoption of this decision the Ministry of Fisheries and the MFA have been the dominant players at the government level. When external conflicts have been high, Iceland's prime ministers have also played active roles; even the president, usually more of a symbolic figure, has expressed support for Iceland's whaling policy. Throughout the 1980s, all governmental actors generally favored the same approach: a scientific strategy as a means to pave the way for commercial whaling. The Ministry of Fisheries seems to have had a very strong position during this period.[115] Although the relevant ministries were unified in their whaling strategy during the 1980s, their roles have since diverged in response to external pressure and shifting perceptions of the whaling issue. Iceland has thus pursued a dual strategy. In relation to the IWC and NGO pressure, the issue has been framed in narrow terms: whales are marine living resources where science and sustainability should guide policy. The scientists of the Marine Research Institute and the Ministry of Fisheries have been the main players in this context. In relation to the USA, the MFA and the prime minister have played key roles, as it has been of vital significance for Iceland to make clear to the USA that whaling is a matter of general foreign policy as well as security policy. Iceland has deliberately linked whaling to other foreign policy issues, with some success. In 1986, Iceland's minister of foreign affairs wrote directly to his US counterpart, George Schultz, and set the whaling issue in a broader context: "... it threatens to severely damage the relations between the two countries ... [and] also affect other relations ... with unforeseen consequences."[116] In 1987 this was taken a step further when the minister of foreign affairs told high-ranking US counterparts that US certification might make Iceland reconsider its North Atlantic Treaty Organization (NATO) membership.[117] Because of Iceland's significance as a NATO member and host to the Keflavik air base, the US State Department and the National Security Council were more favorable toward Iceland's whaling interests. They were inclined to see the whaling issue as a peripheral concern that threatened to disrupt overriding common security interests with Iceland. In contrast, the Department of Commerce, which has direct responsibility for the whaling issue (because they have responsibility for implementing sanctions under the Pelly Amendment), strongly opposed Iceland's whaling policy, and Iceland actively sought to exploit these differences of opinion within the US government.

The making of Iceland's policy was not, however, left to government players alone. Parliament continued to play an active part after deciding not to oppose the moratorium. Moreover, it did so in quite an unpredictable way because all the political parties were split on the issue, a rare occurrence in Icelandic policy. Parliament is also very open to lobbies both in favor and opposed to whaling. This openness is a part of Icelandic culture and reflects Iceland's small population (270,000 inhabitants), most of whom live in the Reykjavík area. The "distance" between the people and the authorities is small. Overall, Parliament was a more cautious player than the government, very much concerned about international reactions from the USA and from international NGOs. Nevertheless, it did not seem to have had a major impact on Icelandic whaling policies in the 1980s after the moratorium decision—the minister of fisheries (1983–1991) maintained an extremely strong position in favor of whaling, which was supported by nearly all parties.[118]

The science-based Icelandic strategy failed in the sense that it did not pave the way for commercial whaling. More recently, reluctance and uncertainty have characterized Iceland's whaling strategy. It may also have been more difficult to maintain the ministerial consensus after Iceland left the IWC. An indication of this came in 1993, when a report published by the MFA concluded that, overall, losses resulting from resuming whaling could outweigh the benefits. The Ministry of Fisheries strongly disagreed. It seems that the MFA, in line with its more general foreign policy objectives, is more concerned with the overall interests of Iceland, while the Ministry of Fisheries represents the fisheries segment, which is generally keen to resume commercial whaling. More recently, it appears that the prime minister is also reluctant to act on the issue.[119] The main impression conveyed by various Icelandic players, however, is not disagreement but uncertainty. The procedures for dealing with this issue over the past couple of years give ample illustration of this. Neither the government nor Parliament is ready to take the responsibility for making a decision. The "decision crisis" seems to be linked to the frequently weak, split, and changing coalition governments, which have been unable to make a long-term coherent strategy. Thus, over the past couple of years, three different committees have been discussing the future of Iceland's whaling policy, but a substantive conclusion remains elusive. One committee was composed solely of parliamentarians, the second was composed of only bureaucrats, and the third and current one is composed of participants from both camps.

Considering the results of opinion polls taken between 1986 and 1995, this indecisiveness may seem somewhat surprising, as by and large the people of Iceland—even more than in Norway—have favored an offensive whaling strategy.[120] Thus, it seems there is quite a bit to gain politically from taking a "tough" stance on the issue. However, public opinion has been volatile, and during boycott actions support for the official policy declined drastically. Although few groups are openly against resumed whaling, large fish exporters, the tourist industry, airline companies, and others are afraid that a resumption in these activities might harm their interests.[121] The bottom line is that there is no unity in Iceland on the issue. It should also be remembered that it has been more than a decade since commercial whaling was halted. The issue is about to become history. According to one key player in Iceland's whaling process, a resumption of commercial whaling would mean "war," especially against the USA, and "you do not go to war if there is not domestic unity on the issue."[122]

Although Iceland challenged the USA and the IWC in the 1980s, overall it complied with IWC rules and decisions until it left the organization when the IWC refused to allow resumption of commercial whaling. Future Icelandic whaling seems uncertain. Not only will it be difficult to resume whaling within NAMMCO (or the IWC if Iceland rejoins it), but Iceland will also need foreign markets to which to export most of its whale products.

Conclusion

The main driving forces in the transformation of the IWC are not linked to access structures or to patterns of participation. The fundamental change that has taken place within the IWC was brought about by the "adoption" of the whale by the environmental movement in the 1970s. At that time the whaling industry had already been considerably weakened, primarily because of previous depletion of large Antarctic whales, and thus proved to be a fairly easy target. However, whaling nations would not have given in so easily had it not been for pressure mobilized within the IWC. An anti-whaling coalition was able to "capture" the IWC through a combination of the skills of a number of scientists, the values of NGOs, and the power of the USA.

Access and participation and the institutional setup of the ICRW and the IWC help shed light on the IWC's transformation. First, the fact that the ICRW actually prohibits both entry restrictions on factory ships and the allocation of specific quotas paved the way for the "whaling olympics"—the rampant whaling that depleted the stock of Antarctic whales in the 1940s and especially the 1950s. Second, the fact that, in contrast to most international resource regimes, the IWC had no entry restrictions on state members made it possible to "pack" the IWC with non-whaling states, which led to the moratorium. The fact that voting was frequently used, which is quite rare within international organizations, is also important in this context. This open access regime provided a "window of opportunity" for clever entrepreneurs, not least within parts of the NGO community, to change the IWC. Thus, it is the interaction between the more basic "background factors" and institutional features linked to access and participation that brought about the change in the IWC. More recently, the massive research effort conducted within the framework of the

IWC in response to scientific uncertainty and political conflicts has the potential to once again change the IWC—this time into a body for sustained harvest of whales.

Turning to the domestic level, the pressure the anti-whaling coalition put on nations that had previously been involved in whaling, such as Norway and Iceland, completely changed the nature of the whaling issue. A number of other actors, including scientists, NGOs, the business community, the media, and various ministries, became involved in what originally was a narrow issue within the fisheries sector. Both countries launched large scientific programs to learn more about the status of the relevant stocks, and the whaling issue, once a peripheral concern, became a matter of "high politics," with the MFA as a key player in each country. In this process, it was not the IWC as such that was considered the main opponent, but the USA and some major NGOs, most notably Greenpeace. Norway has succeeded with its strategy in the sense that its commercial whaling activities have resumed, and are escalating, while protests have almost disappeared. Iceland, on the other hand, has failed in that it has conducted no whaling since 1989. This difference can in part be explained by who participated in each process and in what capacities.

In Norway the process was firmly in the hands of a small group of people in the MFA and the Prime Minister's Office, where the prime minister herself played a key role. Although the process was quite "elite driven" and exclusive, it was also inclusive in the sense that all key actors were consulted, which was instrumental to bringing about a domestic consensus on the issue. After the Commission rejected Iceland's request for resumed whaling, Iceland left the IWC; since then it has not been able to agree on a coherent long-term strategy. The decision-making process has been very open, and it has not always been clear who is responsible for it—Parliament or the government. It should be noted, however, that Iceland faces a more difficult situation than Norway, because it did not lodge an objection to the moratorium and is also probably more vulnerable to external boycotts and sanctions. Both Norway and Iceland consciously pursued scientific strategies to successfully demonstrate that whaling could be sustainable. While Norway was also successful with its political strategy and has resumed whaling, Iceland has not adopted a political strategy and its whaling operations remain dormant.

Notes

This chapter could not have been written the way it is without very useful information from a number of people. On the Norwegian side, first and foremost, Associate Professor Alf Håkon Hoel, University of Tromsø, member of the Norwegian delegation to the IWC, should be mentioned. Professor Lars Walløe, chief scientist of the Norwegian delegation, also provided very useful information. On the Icelandic side, I am particularly indebted to Jóhann Sigurjónsson, Deputy Director, Marine Research Institute, for providing information as well as detailed comments. Very useful information was also provided by Arnór Halldórsson, adviser in the Ministry of Fisheries, Kristján Loftsson, Director of Hvalur Ltd. I also benefited from talking with Jóhann Vidar Ívarsson on the issue of Icelandic whaling policy. I am also in debt to the Secretary of the IWC, Dr. Ray Gambell, for information relevant to this chapter. On the more traditional academic side, very useful comments have been provided by my colleagues at the Fridtjof Nansen Institute, Jon Birger Skjærseth and Jørgen Wettestad. Finally I would like to thank David Victor for very good and helpful comments and not the least his patience in reading the various drafts of this chapter.

1. Andresen, S., 1993, "The Effectiveness of the International Whaling Commission," *Arctic* 46(2):108–115; Sigvaldsson, H., 1996, "The International Whaling Commission: The Transition from a 'Whaling Club' to a 'Preservation Club,' Cooperation and Conflict," *SAGE* 31(3):311–352.

2. The first Schedule to the ICRW already distinguishes between commercial and aboriginal catch: although it was forbidden to kill gray and right whales, an exception was made when the meat and products of such whales were exclusively for local consumption by aboriginal populations. For further elaborations on this distinction, see Gambell, R. 1993, "International Management of Whales and Whaling: An Historical Review of the Regulation of Commercial and Aboriginal Subsistence Whaling," *Arctic* 46(2):97–107.

3. Hoel, A.H., 1993, "Regionalization of International Whale Management: The North Atlantic Marine Mammals Commission," *Arctic* 46(2):116–123.

4. DeSombre, E.R., 1995, "Baptists and Bootleggers for the Environment: The Origins of United States Unilateral Sanctions," *Journal of Environment and Development* 4(1):53–75.

5. For an analysis of the whaling policy of Japan, the third major whaling state, see Friedheim, R., 1996, "Moderation in Pursuit of Justice: Explaining Japan's Failure in the International Whaling Negotiations," *Ocean Development and International Law* 27(4):349–378.

6. Stenseth, N.C., Hoel, A.H., and Lid, I.B., eds., 1993, *The Minke Whale—The Difficult Choice* ad Notam, Gyldendal, Norway [in Norwegian].

7. Tonnesen, J., and Johnson, A., 1982, *The History of Modern Whaling*, C. Hurst & Co., London, UK.

8. Birnie, P., 1985, *International Regulation of Whaling,* 2 volumes, Oceana Publications, New York, NY, USA.

9. Elliot, G.H., 1979, "The Failure of the IWC, 1946–1966," *Marine Policy* (April):149–155; McHugh, J.L., 1974, "The Role and History of the Whaling Commission," in *The Whale Problem: A Status Report*, edited by W.E. Schevill, Harvard University Press, Cambridge, MA, USA.

10. Preamble to the 1946 International Convention for the Regulation of Whaling.

11. M'Gonigle, R.H., 1980, "The 'Economizing' of Ecology: Why Big, Rare Whales Still Die," *Ecology Law Quarterly*:120–137.

12. This means that 15 percent of the IWC members are whaling nations. This figure, however, includes the USA (for aboriginal whaling), which is not usually considered a whaling nation, as well as St. Vincent and the Grenadines, where one old man is allowed to catch one or two whales a year. Apart from Norway, the rest of the whaling nations are either whaling for scientific purposes or engaging in aboriginal whaling.

13. In 1982, only Portugal was whaling outside the realm of the IWC.

14. For a detailed account of the role of science during the early years of the history of the IWC, see Schweder, T., 1995, Intransigence, Incompetence, or Political Expediency? Dutch Scientists in the International Whaling Commission in the 1950s, University of Oslo, Norway.

15. *Reports of the International Whaling Commission*, 1984–1996.

16. Among the well-known NGOs, the World Wide Fund for Nature (WWF) entered the scene in the mid-1960s; Greenpeace did not show up until 1978, the year that marked the beginning of the explosive growth in NGO participation.

17. Most nations have small delegations (one to two persons), some have medium-sized delegations (three to five perons), and only seven developed nations have delegations with more than five participants; *Reports of the International Whaling Commission*, 1984–1996.

18. During the past decade, on average the countries with the largest delegations (Japan, the USA, Norway, and Denmark) combined have had almost as many delegates as all the rest of the participants combined. Japan alone has more than twice the number of delegates as the 17 states with small delegations combined. The USA and Japan together account for almost half the total number of scientists participating, while few developing countries send scientists to

the SciCom meetings at all; *Reports of the International Whaling Commission*, 1984–1996.

19. The very active role played by the Seychelles until the mid-1980s indicates that the size of the delegation is not always decisive; Andresen, S., 1989, "Science and Politics in the International Management of Whales," *Marine Policy* (April):99–117. Doubts have also been expressed regarding Japan's ability to make use of its enormous delegation; Friedheim, op. cit., note 5.

20. Elliot, op. cit., note 9.

21. Birnie, op. cit., note 8.

22. Japan was initially excluded because of its role in World War II, but was admitted in 1951.

23. Andresen, S., and Wettestad, J., 1992, "International Resource Cooperation and the Greenhouse Problem: Lessons and Learning," *Global Environmental Change*:277–291.

24. Holt, S., 1985, "Whale Mining, Whale Saving," *Marine Policy* (3): 192–214.

25. A complex formula for calculating membership fees was adopted. A basic fee is paid for membership only (2 shares). Additional shares (fees) are allocated for various types of whaling activities and according to the size of the delegation. Thus, while the minimum contribution is approximately £14,000, Japan pays the highest membership fee, almost £80,000. *Reports of the International Whaling Commission* 42:50, and Provisional Estimates of Financial Contributions 1996/97 and 1997/98, IWC, 23 April, 1996.

26. Hoel, A.H., 1985, The International Whaling Commission 1972–1984: New Members, New Concerns, R:003, The Fridtjof Nansen Institute, Lysaker, Norway.

27. Spencer, L., with Bollwerk, J., and Morais, R.C., 1991, "The Not So Peaceful World of Greenpeace," *Forbes* (November 11):174–180.

28. Ibid.

29. Wilkinson, D.M., 1989, "The Use of Domestic Measures to Enforce International Whaling Agreements," *Denver Journal of International Law and Policy* 17(2):271–291.

30. *Reports of the International Whaling Commission*, 1984–1996.

31. Hoel, op. cit., note 26.

32. According to NGO sources, such as the International Wildlife Coalition, "these four islands have sold their IWC votes to Japan for foreign aid considerations and personal favors . . . ." Accordingly, the Wildlife Coalition organized a tourist boycott of these islands; MARMAM@UVVM.BITNET, 13 March 1994.

33. It soon became apparent, however, that some of these scientists had very close ties to the environmental movement. Thus, it is doubtful whether all of them can be labeled "independent" scientists.

34. Especially in the USA, a number of celebrities of various kinds have made a point of their love for whales. This may explain why A&M Records, for example, participates.

35. Personal communication.

36. McHugh, op. cit., note 9.

37. Gambell, op. cit., note 2.

38. Compared with some management "ideal," it may well be that the IWC should have been more conservation oriented in this period. However, compared with other international fisheries management bodies, the IWC was probably more conservation oriented than most of them. For a thorough analysis of one fisheries management body that failed, see Underdal, A., 1980, The Politics of International Fisheries Management: The Case of the Northeast Atlantic, Universitetsforlaget, Oslo, Norway.

39. Animal Welfare Institute, 1981, Whales vs. Whalers, Washington, DC, USA.

40. Andresen, S., Skodvin, T., Underdal, A., and Wettestad, J., 1994, "Scientific" Management of the Environment? Science, Politics and Institutional Design, R:006, Fridtjof Nansen Institute, Lysaker, Norway.

41. Hoel, op. cit., note 26.

42. The resolution was adopted with a vote of 53–0, with only Japan, Brazil, and South Africa abstaining. The USSR did not take part at the Conference. The fact that so many whaling nations voted in favor of the resolution may indicate that it was not taken all that seriously, or that different ministries were involved in the two processes.

43. Even how to refer to the 1982 decision to set a zero-catch quota, pending a comprehensive assessment of the whale stocks to be completed no later that 1990, is controversial. The anti-whaling forces prefer to label it a moratorium while the pro-whaling side refers to it a temporary zero-catch decision.

44. According to an animal rights source, the USA held the leadership position during most of the 1970s, but lost it for some time when it had to trade with the whaling nations to retain the controversial bowhead quota. When it achieved a three-year quota in 1981, this trading was no longer necessary, which once more paved the way for US leadership; Animal Welfare Institute, op. cit., note 39.

45. Gulland, J., 1988, "The End of Whaling?" *The New Scientist*, 29 October, 120(1636):42–48.

46. Although this coalition managed to change the de facto goal of the IWC, formally the goal of the ICRW is still the same. There have been frequent discussions of revisions, but more recently the winning coalition has seen no need for any as they can accomplish their goals without them.

47. Gambell, op. cit., note 2.

48. Cherfas, J., 1992, "Key Nations Defy Whaling Commission," *New Scientist* 4(July):7–11. Although RMP has been adopted, the anti-whaling majority of the IWC has invented a new arrangement—the New Management Science—which they have made a new prerequisite to the resumption of commercial whaling.

49. Hammond, P., chairperson of SciCom, Letter to R. Gambell, secretary of the IWC, 26 May 1993.

50. Gambell, R., 1995, "Management of Whaling in Coastal Communities," in *Whales, Seals, Fish and Man*, edited by A.S. Blix, L. Walløe, and O. Ulltang, Elsevier Science, Amsterdam, Netherlands, pp. 699–708.

51. Typically a limited, but diminishing number of scientists with close links to the environmental movement have made footnotes or reservations to reports of the IWC SciCom. At the last IWC meeting, all believed that there was scientific consensus on the status of the northeast Atlantic minke whale stock, but one scientist—Justin Cook, an "oldtimer" in the IWC with undisputable skills but close links with the environmental movement—suddenly changed his mind.

52. Burke, W.T., 1996, "Memorandum of Opinion on the Legality of the Designation of the Southern Ocean Sanctuary by the IWC," *Ocean Development and International Law* 27(3):315–327.

53. Knauss, J., 1997, "The International Whaling Commission: Its Past and Possible Future," *Ocean Development International Law* 28(1):79–99.

54. Motluk, A., 1996, "Blood on Water," *New Scientist*, July 23.

55. This figure is based on official IWC statistics. This may not be a reliable source, however, not least because of recently exposed massive Russian cheating regarding catch of whales. Nevertheless, it is still such official statistics, based on national reporting on catch or emissions, that usually must be relied on within resource and environmental regimes. For an elaboration of the Russian "cheating story," see Stoett, P., 1995, "The International Whaling Commission: From Traditional Concerns to an Expanding Agenda," *Environmental Politics* 14(1):130–135.

56. Brazil, Chile, Peru, Korea, Spain, the Philippines, Japan, Norway, Iceland, and the USSR were all conducting commercial whaling. Denmark and the USA were conducting aboriginal whaling.

57. More recently catches have again increased somewhat, mainly because Norway has resumed commercial whaling and Japan has increased scientific catch. From an economic or ecological point of view this is an insignificant development, but from a political perspective it is interesting as it may indicate a reversal of the trend toward complete protection of whales.

58. Peru also objected to the moratorium, but its objection was soon withdrawn. The USA and Japan concluded an agreement in late 1984 in which the USA agreed not to invoke the legal provisions on Japan during a three-year period. In return, Japan withdrew its objection to the moratorium, effective in April 1984. In the meantime, the USA "allowed" Japan a catch of a considerable number of sperm whales, clearly in violation of the moratorium resolution. Traditional horse trading was the name of the game; Birnie, P., 1986, "Are Whales Safer than Ever?" *Marine Policy* 10(1):63–64.

59. Tonnesen, J., 1970, Den moderne hvalfangsts historie, fjerde bind. Den pelagiske fangst 1937–1969 (The history of modern whaling, 4th volume, The Pelagic catch 1937–1969), Sandefjord, Norway.

60. The Norwegian fishing industry is tightly integrated—the setting of prices, sales, and processing are all performed by the same organizations.

61. In 1985 there were 192 whalers. As the season is four months long, this equals approximately 60–70 man-years. If processing, sales, and direct and indirect effects of different kinds are included, it has been calculated than somewhere between 300–700 man-years were related to the whaling industry. As to economic value, first-hand value carried between 32 and 45 million Norwegian krone (1980–1985), while the wholesale value was approximately 130 million Norwegian krone; Hoel, A.H., 1987, Norway, the US and the Catch of Minke Whales: The Difficult Choice, R:002, The Fridtjof Nansen Institute, Lysaker, Norway [in Norwegian].

62. Export of whale meat and blubber has been forbidden by law since 1986. Since Norway has resumed commercial whaling, almost all the blubber has been stockpiled, although rumors say that some of it is still finding its way to the Japanese market. Japan is willing to pay a price of approximately US$15 per kilo, and pressure from whalers to resume exports is building. Norway does not export whale products because the minke whale is on the CITES list of prohibited products. The discussion over (re)classification of the minke whales within CITES, at the upcoming CITES meeting in June 1997, may be important in this context.

63. Anderson, R., Beverton, R., Semb-Johansson, A., and Walløe, L., 1987, *The State of the Northeast Atlantic Minke Whale Stock*, Økoforsk, Norway.

64. Ibid.

65. For the full content of the government decision of 3 July 1986 to temporarily halt commercial whaling see Anderson *et al.*, op. cit., note 63, p. 92.

66. Personal communication.

67. Cherfas, op. cit., note 48.

68. It appears that one reason for the certification was that Norway had not consulted the USA properly when deciding to take the five whales. At the same time, the USA hunted a much larger number of bowhead whales, making use of the IWC exemption on aboriginal whaling.

69. Skåre, M., 1994, "Whaling: A Sustainable Use of Natural Resources or a Violation of Animal Rights?" *Environment* (September):13–34.

70. MacLeod, D., 1994, "International Consequences of Norway's Decision to Allow the Resumption of Commercial Whaling," *The Dalhousie Law Journal* 17(1) Spring:83–103.

71. Bjørndal, T., and Toft, A., 1994, Economic Consequences of Boycott Actions against Norwegian Business Interests due to Norwegian Whaling, Commissioned Report from the Norwegian Ministry of Foreign Affairs, Norway.

72. *Aftenposten*, 27 June 1996.

73. Some of the newspaper headlines were quite alarmist and the minister of trade also went a long way in this direction. It appears, however, that the actual effect was quite moderate and Norwegian exports to the USA increased very strongly during the period; Hoel, op. cit., note 61.

74. Personal communication.

75. The government also declared that scientific surveys would continue and that the halt in commercial whaling was linked to the completion and outcome of the IWC comprehensive assessment (1990). The group responsible for the assessment consisted of two British and two Norwegian professors with backgrounds in zoology and biology. An American professor was also appointed but chose not to participate. For further details on their credentials and backgrounds, see Anderson *et al.*, op. cit., note 63 (Terms of ref., Royal Resolution No. 6 of August 8, 1986).

76. Anderson *et al.*, op. cit., note 63.

77. ME'A, 9/89 (Magazine for the Norwegian Fishermen Association). Hvalfangsten må gjenopptas (Whaling must be resumed, editorial) [in Norwegian].

78. Some countries also participate as observers, e.g., Russia, Canada, Japan.

79. The two ministers of foreign affairs were Thorvald Stoltenberg and Johan Joergen Holst, both well known on the international scene and both closely involved in the Middle East negotiations through the so-called Oslo Channel.

80. There have been examples of direct communication between her and the Norwegian delegation to IWC meetings when thorny issue have appeared (personal communication).

81. The personal communication between the Norwegian prime minister and US Vice President Al Gore seems to have been particularly useful for Norway.

82. Personal communication.

83. Some might of course question the use of administrative and political resources on this issue, but that question is outside the scope of this paper.

84. Personal communication.

85. Major business firms in Norway supported the Norwegian position because they saw it as a precedent-setting case. If a decision were to be made in this case based on emotions and external pressure, not science, it might be that they would be affected in a similar manner another time.

86. According to an opinion poll at the time, some 20–25 percent of the population was against the resumption of commercial whaling, but this "silent minority" does not seem to have had an organizational or political outlet. MacLeod, op. cit., note 70.

87. The case was not followed up within the GATT Council because it was assumed that the USA would use its veto. It has been argued that within the WTO, the possibilities of using international law to prevent unilateral action like this are increasing; Gudmundsson, 1995, Presentation at the Roundtable

Discussion on Sustainable Use of Wildlife and International Regimes: With Special Reference to Cetaceans, The Fifth International Whaling Symposium, Institute for Cetaceans Research, pp. 52–56.

88. Hoel, A.H., 1994, The Whaling Issue and Economic Sanctions: Actors and Processes [in Norwegian].

89. These facts are reflected in the Marine Mammals Commission's communication with the US IWC delegation advising a more cautious policy.

90. The US Commissioner at the time, J. Knauss, stated that he would defend the US position on ethical grounds but could not do so on a scientific basis. To refute science as a management principle for the world's leading scientific nation is clearly problematic in a wider perspective.

91. In a survey of public attitudes toward whales in six countries, including the USA, 48 percent said they were opposed to whaling under any circumstances and 55 percent said they were against whaling even when properly regulated; Freeman, M.R., and Kellert, S., 1992, Public Attitudes Towards Whales, Results of a Six Country Survey, University of Alberta/University of Yale, Alberta, Canada.

92. Norway has probably done what any country would do in the same situation by acting in its perceived self-interest. In this process, the USA has been considered the key to resuming commercial whaling, not potential alliances with Japan and Iceland; this would explain Norway's NAMMCO policies and the fact that it did not vote with Japan on the sanctuary issue. This having been said, Japan and Iceland first must decide whether they want to resume commercial whaling within or outside the IWC.

93. Strong American actions may have been made even more difficult as the same ministers of foreign affairs that worked with the Oslo Channel (Holst and Stoltenberg) were also personally involved in the whaling issue.

94. Davies, P.G., 1994, "Legality of Norwegian Commercial Whaling Under the Whaling Convention and Its Compatibility with European Community Law," *International and Comparative Law Quarterly* 43(April):270–295.

95. Ibid., p. 291.

96. Two pieces of legislation were particularly relevant: the Habitat Directive (1992) and the CITES Regulation (1982).

97. Recall that Mr. Gummer was given the honorary title of "shitbag" by the Norwegian minister of environment.

98. It may be recalled that the Norwegian minister of fisheries got the nickname "No-Fish Olsen" in the negotiations with the EU.

99. Most of the "raw material" and the facts on Icelandic whaling policy are based on Ivarsson, J.V., 1994, Science, Sanctions and Cetaceans, Iceland and the Whaling Issue, Center for International Studies, University of Iceland, Reykjavík, Iceland. This source is supplemented by some other written materials and by interviews with actors from the Icelandic authorities (Ministry of Fisheries and the Institute of Marine Research), the NGO community, and the (previous) whaling industry.

100. Sigurjónsson, J., 1989, "Whale Research and Management in Iceland, To Icelanders Whales Were a Godsend," *Oceanus Magazine* 32(1) Spring:29–37.

101. While some 2,000 minke whales were caught annually by Norwegian fishermen well into the 1970s, the catch in Iceland rose from an average of 50 animals (1914–1950) to some 200 animals annually in the 1970s and early 1980s; ibid.

102. In a bilateral agreement with Norway, Iceland was allocated 200 whales per year; Sigurjónsson, J., 1982, "Icelandic Minke Whaling, 1914–1980," *Reports of the International Whaling Commission* 32:287–296.

103. Sigurjónsson, J., 1988, "Operational Factors of Icelandic Large Whale Fishery," *Reports of the International Whaling Commission* 38:327–334.

104. This fleet of four whaling boats is still intact, although it has not been used for whaling since 1989. Two of the boats were sunk by the Sea Shepards in 1987, but were repaired. According to the owner of the fleet, the yearly cost of maintaining the fleet and related facilities is approximately US$40,000–50,000.

105. As Iceland's exports are completely dominated by the fishing industry, it also accounted for 1.5 percent of the country's total exports. This figure has been rather stable over time.

106. The modest catch of minke whales has been consumed domestically but the more significant catch of the larger whales has been exported.

107. Nevertheless, this scientific catch represented a fairly high proportion of its previous commercial catch as in the early 1980s Iceland was catching some 200 fin whales, about 100 sei whales, and some 200 minke whales annually; Sigurjónsson, op. cit., note 102.

108. However, no mechanisms were elaborated to control this agreement, so it is an open question what it meant in practice.

109. According to Ivarsson, op. cit., note 99, pp. 107, ". . . the estimated annual losses sustained by seafood exporters stood at about USD 29 million. The value of whale product exports in 1987, by comparison, was about USD 4 million."

110. In simple terms, this means that previously not enough knowledge existed to determine whether this stock could be harvested or not; now, however, the SciCom agreed that it could be harvested.

111. Ivarsson, op. cit., note 99.

112. There are still high-level meetings between the USA and Iceland on the whaling issue, although, as mentioned, Iceland has not been whaling for almost eight years (personal communication).

113. As mentioned, Norway has been reluctant to strengthen NAMMCO because it can conduct whaling within the IWC. Thus Iceland is the only state member that potentially wishes to use NAMMCO as a basis for harvesting whales (Greenland and the Faroe Islands, the other two members, are not independent states). However, Canada and Russia participate in NAMMCO as observers, and there are rumors that Canada may join in the near future. This may increase NAMMCO's legitimacy considerably; Andresen, S., 1997, The IWC, NAMMCO and the Nordic Countries, Paper presented at the Conference on Whaling in the North East Atlantic: Economic and Political Perspectives, Reykjavík, 1 March 1997, to be published in forthcoming Proceedings.

114. At an open meeting on the whaling issue the day before the vote in Parliament, where some 10 members of Parliament were present, the antiwhaling lobby was very active. Thus this meeting may well have been decisive for the decision not to oppose the moratorium (personal communication). It should also be noted that Mr. Halldor Asgrimsson, the current minister of foreign affairs, was the spokesperson for the majority view in Parliament in February 1983. A few months later he entered the scene in the capacity of minister of fisheries, and has taken a very firm stand on the issue (personal communication).

115. On one occasion, a new and less experienced prime minister gave a statement that could be understood as an inclination to give into the external pressure, hinting at a "softer" Icelandic position. Immediately the minister of fisheries publicly corrected him, there was a Cabinet meeting, and the official position was confirmed; Ivarsson, op. cit., note 99.

116. Ivarsson, op. cit., note 99.

117. Ivarsson, op. cit., note 99.

118. Personal communication.

119. Personal communication.

120. Ivarsson, op. cit., note 99.

121. Personal communication.

122. Personal communication.

11

Nuclear Dumping in Arctic Seas: Russian Implementation of the London Convention

Olav Schram Stokke

Introduction

In 1990, bits and pieces of information emerged concerning hitherto unknown, if not unsuspected, Soviet dumping of radioactive waste in the Barents and Kara Seas. Such dumping had been conducted since the 1960s by the USSR's Northern Fleet and by the Murmansk Shipping Company, a civilian operator of nuclear-powered icebreakers in the Northern Sea Route. A number of actors in and outside Russia helped uncover this information, including individuals in target groups, nongovernmental organizations (NGOs), and to some extent parliamentary committees. By current estimates, the waste dumped into Arctic seas by the USSR had, at the time of disposal, a total radioactivity twice as high as that of all previously known dumping.[1] Of this waste, the nuclear vessel reactors that still contain spent fuel are the most intensely radioactive.

Some of this dumping violated Soviet commitments to the 1972 London Convention on the Prevention of Marine Pollution by Dumping of Wastes and Other Matter,[2] as well as Soviet domestic legislation in this area. To a substantial extent, therefore, this is a clear-cut case of implementation failure. Implementation is understood here as the process of converting international agreements into behavioral adaptation on the part of target groups. The purpose of this chapter is to make use of that failure in order to understand when and how international regimes affect the domestic implementation game in member states—that is, the vying for influence by different groups with stakes in the behavior addressed by the regime. In particular, we will focus on the significance of changes in coalition patterns and access rules in Russian nuclear politics and trace the extent to which such changes result from rules and programs of the London Convention.

Because Russian nuclear dumping in the Arctic, like that of the USSR before it, is related to the operational needs of naval submarines, and thus to core national interests, behavioral adaptation is presumably particularly difficult to achieve. This case is therefore attractive in methodological terms: in this context, any changes resulting from certain regime features will strongly indicate that regimes matter. Yet, there are obvious limits to the causal claims that can be substantiated within a single case. Typically, several potential explanatory factors vary simultaneously, making it difficult to render firm conclusions on the precise contributions of rules and activities generated by the international regime. The case at hand allows a longitudinal breakdown into four fairly distinct stages in terms of access and participation patterns in the Soviet and Russian implementation game: a long period of military self-regulation; a stage of gradually expanding participation; a stage marked by acute politicization; and, finally, the current, somewhat ambiguous situation in which domestic involvement in nuclear affairs is contracting while foreign participation is on the rise.

The core of the argument here is that Soviet and Russian management of nuclear waste in the north has been significantly influenced by regulations and programs generated under the London Convention. As a result of the regime, scientific surveys and monitoring of the radiological situation around the dumping sites have been stimulated; responsibility for regulatory tasks has been shifted from operators of nuclear facilities to independent agencies; domestic rules have been tightened; and, in recent years, cooperative technology programs coordinated under the London Convention have led to improvements in treatment and storage facilities, which will enable Russia to cut its dumping of radioactive waste.

The Dumping of Radioactive Waste

Radioactive waste has been called the Achilles' heel of nuclear activity:[3] more than five decades after the first controlled nuclear fission, there is still no widely accepted method for dealing with the most radioactive by-products, so-called high-level waste and spent nuclear fuel.[4] Although globally the amount of spent fuel produced in the military sector is modest compared with that from the civilian sector, the nuclear waste dumped by the USSR in Arctic seas is chiefly of military origin. As documented in the Yablokov Report,[5] a governmental white paper published in 1993, as many as 16 nuclear reactors have been disposed of in the Kara Sea since 1965. Seven of these reactors are especially danger-ous because spent fuel was not removed prior to their disposal. In addition, the Northern Fleet has dumped large amounts of low- and medium-level solid waste in flimsy metal containers that are highly vulnerable to corrosion. Low-level liquid waste, such as water used in cooling, incineration, or deactivation of radioactive installations, has been disposed of in the Barents Sea since the mid-1960s. This past dumping is a matter of substantial concern in both Russia and the West, and various remedial measures have been considered, including sealing, capping, and retrieval of waste for storage on land.[6] Such action, how-ever, may itself involve great hazards and would unquestionably be very costly. Measurements at a number of sites in the Barents and Kara Seas, including the dump sites for the hazardous reactors in some of the bays in Novaya Zemlya, indicate that thus far there has not been a significant release of radioactivity into the marine environment.[7] Indeed, the levels of radioactivity in these seas are comparatively low, certainly much lower than those in the Black and Baltic Seas.[8] Simulation models suggest that even the worst-case scenario, a rapid release of all the dumped radioactivity, would not result in significant exposure to humans through marine food chains, although local-scale effects would need to be studied more.[9] These conclusions should be seen as preliminary because of the considerable uncertainty regarding both the transport models underlying them and the rate of release.[10]

This past dumping is not the only disturbing aspect of the nuclear waste sit-uation in the Russian Northwest. Even more alarming is the current imbalance between the steady generation of new waste and Russia's capacity to properly dispose of it. First, the more than 100 nuclear-powered vessels currently oper-ated by the Northern Fleet regularly generate large amounts of both solid and liquid waste, yet adequate storage or treatment facilities are lacking. As for spent nuclear fuel, the highly deficient temporary storages for removed fuel assemblies are already filled to capacity. Second, the accumulation of waste will accelerate in the coming years as more submarines are decommissioned because of old age or to comply with commitments under the Strategic Arms Reduction Treaty regime. Sixty Northern Fleet vessels were removed from service between 1989 and 1993, and it is expected that another 30 will be scrapped within the next few years.[11] Only a fraction of the vessels retired so far have had their reactor fuels and reactor sections removed. According to Western sources, in the early 1990s the Northern Fleet was able to dismantle

submarines at a rate of only one per year.[12] In part, the slow pace was due
to a lack of storage facilities for the reactor cores and an inadequate system
for transporting the waste out of the region,[13] but it was also a result of the
tendency to allocate scarce dockings for reloading operative vessels rather than
unloading inactive ones.

Thus, the backbone of radioactive waste management, a key problem addressed by the London Convention, is adequate storage. This involves interim
storage at the site where waste is generated and a satisfactory system for transporting high-level waste and spent nuclear fuel for final deposition or, in the
case of spent fuel, for reprocessing.[14] In practice, adequate storage also involves the capacity to concentrate or solidify liquid waste and to compact solid
waste to facilitate storage. Since the 1960s the Murmansk Shipping Company
and the Northern Fleet in particular have experienced a widening gap between
actual and required capacity. This gap is the fundamental reason both have
resorted to dumping some of the waste generated by the nuclear complex in
the Russian Northwest.

The International Dumping Regime

The core of the international dumping regime is the 1972 London Convention.
Although radioactive waste is only one of the substances dealt with in this
Convention, it has been the most politicized of the issues involved. The
Convention's main decision-making body is the Consultative Meeting of the
Parties, usually held every year. The Convention uses a system in which
dumping of items on the "black list" is forbidden and dumping of items on
the "gray list" requires special permits from a designated national authority;
permits must be reported to the secretariat of the Convention,[15] which is located
at the International Maritime Organization (IMO). There is also a waiting
list composed of items identified as potentially harmful.[16] Unlike many other
international agreements, the London Convention does not require a unanimous
vote to pass regulatory decisions; amendments to the lists can be passed by
a two-thirds majority. There is, however, an "opting out" clause that allows
states to avoid being legally bound by provisions they do not wish to adhere
to.[17] In addition to legally binding amendments to the Convention, the Meeting
can adopt nonbinding resolutions with a simple majority. As to enforcement,
the London Convention sets out a broad range of provisions for the prevention,

discovery, and punishment of violations, obliging members to enforce rules in their capacities as flag states, port states, or coastal states. At the 1988 Consultative Meeting, the parties concluded that coastal states could apply the Convention not only within their territorial seas, but in their exclusive economic zones (EEZs) as well.[18] A dispute-settlement arrangement providing for arbitration or submission to the International Court of Justice was adopted in 1978,[19] but has yet to enter into force.

In terms of *access and participation*, the regime set up by the London Convention is comparatively open. In accordance with Article XVIII, any state may accede to the Convention. In principle the Convention allows not only relevant international organizations, such as specialized agencies of the United Nations (UN) or the International Atomic Energy Agency (IAEA), but also a range of NGOs to attend Consultative Meetings as observers and to make statements, submit documents, and participate freely in plenary and working discussions.[20] Friends of the Earth International was the first NGO to attend a Consultative Meeting, where it immediately targeted the radioactive waste issue.[21] In 1981, more detailed procedures were established for NGOs wishing to take part in Consultative Meetings.[22] The same year, Greenpeace International achieved observer status, having just started its campaign against the dumping of low- and medium-level nuclear waste in the Atlantic Ocean.[23] Between 8 and 10 NGOs attend the Consultative Meetings on a regular basis; typically, half represent environmental organizations and half participate on behalf of various target groups, such as the International Dredging Association.

Regulative Developments
The general trend in international law is that radioactive dumping is gradually being defined as unacceptable.[24] Dumping of high-level waste has been prohibited since the London Convention entered into force in 1975; step-by-step this prohibition is being extended to low- and medium-level waste as well.

The tendency over time has been to extend the scope of the London Convention's regulations. For example, according to Article VII provisions do not apply to military vessels, although states are required to adopt measures to ensure that even military vessels act in accordance with the "object and purpose of this Convention." No consultative party objected in 1989, however, when a working group, citing Article VII, concluded that disposal of decommissioned naval submarines was covered by the prohibition on dumping of high-level waste.[25] Moreover, as noted, some of the Soviet and Russian dumping activities in the Arctic were conducted by the nonmilitary Murmansk Shipping Company, and civilian companies usually do not enjoy sovereign immunity under international law. Also, although the geographic scope of the Convention is limited to the high seas, the EEZs, and territorial waters,[26] since 1992 the Consultative Meetings have discussed extending the provisions to internal waters, as well.[27] In an earlier Consultative Meeting, after years of debate and deliberations, the parties decided that disposal of radioactive waste in seabed repositories accessible from the sea constitutes dumping.[28]

As to the behavioral adaptation prescribed by the regulations, two points are of particular interest in the context of this discussion.

• Members are obliged to *monitor* and keep a record of the nature and quantities of matter permitted to be dumped, as well as when, where, and how the dumping occurred and the conditions of the seas where it occurred (Article VI, paragraph 1).

• Because high-level radioactive waste was placed on the original black list in 1972, members are also obliged to *abstain* from any dumping of such material. This was a highly controversial decision, at first strongly opposed by the UK and the USA. For its part, the USSR favored an even more comprehensive prohibition, including not only high-level waste but also low- and medium-level waste.[29] The parties to the London Convention designated the IAEA as the competent international advisory authority on whether given nuclear materials are unsuitable for dumping.

Subsequent regulatory discussion on nuclear waste has revolved around sharpening regulations concerning dumping of low- and medium-level waste. Accordingly, the IAEA set up *geographic criteria* for the localization of such dumping,[30] including requirements that it should only occur in the belt between 50 degrees north and 50 degrees south latitude, beyond the continental shelf, and at depths greater than 4,000 meters. In contrast to these requirements, the Barents and Kara Seas are located roughly between 70 and 80 degrees north, and most of the area is on a continental shelf with depths rarely exceeding a few hundred meters. Although a proposed ban failed to gain sufficient support in 1983, Spain, closely backed by several South Pacific and Nordic countries, successfully sponsored a resolution on a *voluntary moratorium* on all dumping of radioactive materials until an expert meeting could present their final report to the contracting parties.[31] Although it did not join the six states that voted against the resolution, the USSR abstained from voting.[32] It abstained again when the moratorium was prolonged in 1985. The reasons cited were that the moratorium lacked adequate scientific basis and that it violated the spirit of consensus underlying the Convention.[33] Four years later, however, the Soviet delegation officially declared that it had not dumped such materials in the past and would not do so in the future.[34] In 1993, a binding *prohibition* on the dumping of low- and medium-level waste was established by a unanimous decision to amend the annexes accordingly.[35] Russia was among the five states that abstained from voting.[36] After a failed attempt to obtain a two-year delay, Russia filed a formal reservation to the amendment, implying that it is currently not formally bound by this prohibition.[37]

Programmatic Activities

Efforts to enhance the *knowledge base* for decisions form the core of the programmatic activities under the London Convention. Since the adoption of the Convention, a three-component system for providing scientific advice has been elaborated. The broadest advisory mechanism is the Scientific Group on Dumping, made up of experts nominated by the contracting parties. The Group, which achieved permanent status in 1984,[38] meets intersessionally. It gives important support for the regulatory work of the Consultative Meetings, primarily by responding to direct requests for scientific evaluations and by continually reviewing existing provisions and annexes in light of new scientific information.

A second scientific component is a range of ad hoc groups of experts set up to compile information and make recommendations on particularly vital or controversial matters, such as the Group of Legal Experts on Dumping formed at the first Consultative Meeting, or the Panels on Sea Disposal of Radioactive Waste set up in 1983 and 1985.[39] In 1987, the Inter-Governmental Panel of Experts on Radioactive Waste Disposal at Sea (IGPRAD) embarked on a process of addressing the wider political, legal, economic, and social aspects of radioactive waste dumping; the comparative costs and risks of dumping at sea versus land-based disposal; and the possibility of proving that radioactive dumping is not harmful to human life or the marine environment.[40] IGPRAD's final report in 1993 presented the Consultative Meeting with seven options, one of which was to prohibit all dumping of radioactive waste at sea.[41]

A third component of the knowledge-related activities generated by the London Convention is the work conducted by external organizations at the request of the Consultative Meetings. The significance of being able to trigger or forward investigations conducted by others becomes clear when we note that in 1990 the London Convention had a budget of only US$0.76 million, and that a mere five IMO staff members were allocated to it.[42] The IAEA, with a budget of roughly US$200 million and a staff of approximately 2,000,[43] has conducted a number of specialized technical and scientific studies that have been vital to the work of IGPRAD.[44] As discussed below, it was at the request of the Consultative Meeting of the London Convention that the IAEA initiated its International Arctic Seas Assessment Project after information emerged concerning Soviet dumping activities in the Barents and Kara Seas.[45]

Monitoring and assessment of member compliance with the regulations of the London Convention largely rely on self-reporting. Because so few IMO staff members are designated to work on this Convention, their ability to assist the consultative parties in critically assessing the implementation of international commitments is necessarily limited. To make matters even more difficult, the rate of submission of reports is fairly low; typically, as many as two-thirds of the contracting parties fail to lodge reports in any given year.[46] In an effort to strengthen the information about compliance included in national reports, the consultative parties, after considerable debate, passed a resolution in 1989 that redefined "monitoring," as required by the Convention, from "assessments of changes in the marine environment caused by dumping operations"[47] to "measurements . . . to demonstrate the compliance of their permitted at-sea dumping and incineration practices with the overall intent of the Convention and the requirements of the Annexes."[48] To some extent and in some situations, the Convention's formal reporting system is complemented by information made available to the Consultative Meetings by NGOs with access to the deliberations. Thus, at the 1991 Consultative Meeting a document presented by Greenpeace International triggered the animated discussion on Soviet dumping in Arctic seas that produced a Soviet pledge to submit more information on the matter to the Secretariat.[49]

Inter-regime Linkages
In terms of regulatory linkages to other regimes, the obligation to control dumping is confirmed by the global 1982 United Nations Convention on the Law of the Sea, which in Article 210 refers implicitly to the London Convention and

its annexes when requiring national regulation to be at least as stringent as the rules and standards set globally.[50] This obligation is also confirmed by decisions made under a number of conventions more geographically confined than the London Convention; Article VIII of the Convention encourages members to enter into regional conventions to give life to its objectives. Thus, dumping of radioactive waste is prohibited in treaties for the Baltic Sea and for the South and Southeast Pacific, and the International North Sea Conference agreed in 1990 that the North Sea is unsuitable for radioactive dumping.[51] Similarly, the Nuclear Energy Agency of the Organisation for Economic Co-operation and Development (OECD) has overseen a long-term monitoring program concerning a dumping site in the northeast Atlantic.[52]

However, the most significant inter-regime linkage of the London Convention is the designation of the IAEA as a pertinent authority in scientific and technical matters. This move not only endows the IAEA's technical guidelines with some legal force as minimum standards for national regulation,[53] but, as mentioned above, it also generates significant programmatic activities relevant to the London Convention. Moreover, the fairly ambitious Arctic Monitoring and Assessment Programme under the 1991 Arctic Environmental Protection Strategy has singled out radionuclides as a priority area; a state of the Arctic environment report was published 1997.[54] Regarding the Barents and Kara Seas in particular, the Kirkenes Declaration on the Barents Region in 1993 identified radioactive contamination in these waters as a key priority, although no legally binding commitments were involved.[55] At a bilateral level, four Russian-Norwegian research cruises into the Barents and Kara Seas have been launched since 1991. These cruises have been endorsed, rather than initiated, by the London Consultative Meetings to gauge nuclear contamination in water masses and subsoil sediments in areas close to dumping sites.

Thus, on both the regulatory and the programmatic sides the London Convention is interrelated with a range of other cooperative processes, largely on regional and sometimes bilateral levels. From the viewpoint of effectiveness, these regime linkages are supportive of the London Convention. Methodologically, they remind us that any analysis of regime consequences must acknowledge the existence of other cooperative processes able to affect outcomes independently of the regime under scrutiny.

Summary: International Implementation of the London Convention

If implementation is a matter of putting provisions into practice, it may be useful to break the *international* aspect of implementation into three activities: the collective generation of knowledge needed to make informed choices; the production of a set of agreed-upon regulatory measures that give life to the principles and make use of existing knowledge; and the implementation of a collective system to stimulate compliance, including verification of whether international commitments are matched by behavioral adaptation.

The principle of the regime based on the London Convention is that, unless other options are demonstrated to be more harmful, disposal of radioactive waste in the sea cannot be allowed if it is hazardous on the grounds of toxicity, persistence, bioaccumulation, and the likelihood of significant widespread environmental exposure.[56] These issues have been under systematic scientific scrutiny since the first Consultative Meeting of the contracting parties. Studies conducted by the various expert groups and panels on radioactive waste have been particularly relevant in this respect, as have the programmatic contributions of the International Atomic Energy Agency and a number of related international cooperative ventures. It can therefore be concluded that the knowledge-gathering aspect of international implementation has been addressed with considerable vigor by the parties to the London Convention. A similar conclusion seems warranted for the regulatory task: since the regime's creation, the Consultative Meetings have been able to cut through the differences among members and establish increasingly strict and binding regulatory measures on the dumping of nuclear materials.

The principal weakness of the London Convention's current international implementation profile relates to the system designed to stimulate compliance on the part of members. As shown, this system relies in large part on self-reporting of data, and in addition to a widespread inclination to ignore existing obligations to file reports, there is very little opportunity for the Secretariat or other members to subject reports to critical assessment. Moreover, the regime cannot directly provide significant positive incentives to comply with its requirements. It should be pointed out, however, that relatively undeveloped compliance systems are quite common for environmental and resource-management regimes.[57]

Coalitions and Access in the Russian Implementation Game

Moving from the international to the domestic aspect of implementation, we now look more closely at how, and the extent to which, the London Convention has affected Soviet and Russian decision making in the matter of radioactive waste dumping. In particular, the focus is on patterns of access and participation in key decisions pertaining to this matter. Like its international counterpart, the domestic implementation game can be discussed along three lines. Concerning knowledge, various domestic players engage in or try to influence the process of collecting and disseminating information on dumping activities and the effects of those activities on humans or marine ecosystems. With respect to regulation, state and societal actors try to shape national standards on how radioactive waste should be handled. Finally, on the matter of compliance stimulation, various types of actors often differ in their notions of how target group adherence to such national standards can be enhanced—for instance, through measures such as intrusive verification mechanisms linked to sanctions or, more positively, through the enhancement of behavioral alternatives to dumping.

To discuss the impact of the London Convention on Soviet and Russian decision-making processes regarding nuclear waste, we must understand *how* international regimes can affect behavior that contributes to the problem. As elaborated by Oran Young and Marc Levy,[58] international regimes can affect the behavior of state and non-state actors through many different mechanisms.[59] The mechanism most frequently resorted to is a *carrot-and-stick* approach. For example, when the effectiveness of resource-management regimes is discussed, attention is usually focused on the adequacy of monitoring or sanctioning provisions. A second type of mechanism is *learning*; international regimes frequently promote scientific activities that generate learning regarding the consequences of current behavior. A third general type of mechanism can be called *obligation*, in the sense that states and targets adhere to rules simply because they regard it to be the right and proper course of action. There can be several reasons for such obligation. From an international-law point of view, Thomas Franck discusses four features of an international rule or institution that can enhance its legitimacy: historical track record; determinacy; connectedness to principles underlying other rules; and adherence to a normative hierarchy, including secondary rules of lawful procedure.[60] The latter two features refer to regulatory linkages between regimes. From an organizational point of view, the obligation mechanism can be seen as inertia or routinized behavior on the part of national bureaucracies, which, at least if the issue is not a matter of dispute among various domestic groups, may tend to see international commitments as directives for everyday administrative decisions.[61] Other mechanisms can be elaborated as well;[62] although they will not be equally relevant in each case, having a broad range of mechanisms can be useful for substantiating the impacts of international regimes on behavior.

In this chapter, we analyze how regulatory or programmatic activities under the London Convention have affected Soviet and Russian implementation with respect to dumping of radioactive waste. This analysis focuses on how three mechanisms—reward or punishment, learning, and obligation—have changed the interaction of various interested actors in Russia concerning decisions associated with scientific *monitoring* of the radiological situation, the setting of *national standards and regulations*, and the *behavior of target groups* such as the Northern Fleet, including measures designed to enable target groups to manage nuclear waste without resorting to dumping.

Targets, Regulators, and Intervenor Groups

It may be useful here to distinguish between three types of domestic actors that engage in the implementation of international commitments: targets, regulatory agencies, and societal intervenor groups.[63] The *targets* of regulation are those organizations that must adapt their behavior if the state is to comply with international commitments. The Soviet, now the Russian, Northern Fleet, based on the Kola Peninsula, has been and continues to be the principal source of radioactive waste dumped into Arctic seas. Thus it is the key target for international regulations in this field. The second main target in the region is the Murmansk Shipping Company, which operates seven nuclear-powered icebreakers engaged in keeping the Northern Sea Route open, especially its western part, between Murmansk and the Siberian city of Dudinka on the banks of the Yenisey River.[64]

Turning from targets to *regulatory agencies*, three sets of distinctions may be relevant. The first is the classical differentiation between legislative, executive, and judicial powers. In matters directly related to foreign affairs and international commitments, in most countries the executive branch is in charge unless the matter becomes politicized enough to engage one or both of the other powers. In the Soviet and Russian cases, the judiciary has failed to play an independent role and for the purposes here can be ignored. For most of its lifetime, the Soviet political system was marked by a strong executive branch: although formally the apex of power was the legislative Supreme Soviet, the real power resided in the Communist Party and was wielded primarily through the huge bureaucratic apparatus coordinated by the Council of Ministers.[65] Jeffrey Canfield notes that, in 1990, when a decree was issued on measures to improve implementation of previous legislation to protect the northern environment, the cognizant Supreme Soviet committee was not even consulted.[66] The introduction of presidential rule that same year implied some executive separation from the Communist Party,[67] and that institution survived the dissolution of the USSR. The 1993 Constitution of the Russian Federation endowed the president with extensive powers, including the rights to overrule legislative initiatives and to issue legally binding decrees. However, during the period between the dissolution of the USSR and the 1993 assault on Parliament by troops loyal to President Boris Yeltsin, the legislative branch was very active on nuclear matters in the north, especially regarding nuclear tests on the Novaya Zemlya site.[68]

The second set of distinctions regarding regulatory agencies can be considered territorial. In the Soviet and Russian contexts, it is generally helpful to scrutinize both federal and regional levels of government.[69] However, in the case of nuclear waste management, not much is lost by disregarding the latter, because the few recent attempts on the part of regional governments to regulate the nuclear safety practices of the military have been futile. In 1991, for instance, the governor of Murmansk set up operational rules for the removal of spent fuel from nuclear reactors in naval bases.[70] Those rules were stillborn, however, because physical access to the bases is still controlled by the military. The Northern Fleet flatly refused a 1993 request from the environmental committee in the Murmansk oblast administration for information on nuclear waste management at the bases, although a visit was granted to one base two years later.[71] When in 1992 President Yeltsin decreed that the lands on which the Novaya Zemlya nuclear test site is located were to be federalized, authorities in Arkhangel'sk were neither consulted nor informed prior to the decision.[72]

The third set of distinctions in the regulatory dimension can be considered functional. From the outset, the main bureaucratic segments involved in the management of radioactive waste in the USSR were the defense segment, the nuclear energy segment, and to a limited extent the health segment, all represented by agencies under the pertinent ministries. As we shall see, after passing legislation to implement the London Convention, the interagency State Committee on Hydrometeorology (Goskomgidromet) and later the State Committee on Environmental Protection became involved as well.

Thus, regulatory players in the implementation game associated with international regimes can be found across the various branches, levels, and functional segments of government. In situations where authority relationships between the various political institutions are fluid or in doubt, as they were in Russia right before and after the dissolution of the USSR, conditions are favorable for new players to enter the process.

The political significance of the third category of players, societal *intervenor groups* such as NGOs, remained insignificant until the late 1980s. In broad terms, the domestic Soviet and Russian implementation game regarding marine disposal of radioactive waste falls into four more or less distinct stages, each with its own pattern of participation and coalitional dynamics. The next section considers the shifting role of the London Convention in these stages, which respectively are marked by military self-regulation, cautious expansion of regulatory agencies, politicization, and ambiguous contraction regarding participation in decision making.

Before London: The Period of Military Discretion
Throughout the 1960s and 1970s, Soviet regulation of the dumping of nuclear waste was a closed matter, with few access points and a pattern of inclusion clearly biased in favor of the navy. Twelve of the sixteen reactors disposed of in the Kara Sea were dumped during this period, before the London Convention entered into force.[73] In addition, the low- and medium-level waste dumped annually during this period fluctuated between a low of close to zero terabecquerel (TBq) and a peak of approximately 300 TBq.[74]

Largely because of their military significance, most aspects of the Soviet nuclear programs were shrouded in a thick veil of secrecy. The years immediately after World War II were marked by a determined effort to catch up with the American nuclear program. At that time, the nuclear program was placed under the minister for state security, Lavrenti Beria, who directed the construction of a number of closed nuclear laboratories in secluded cities.[75] In 1990, more than 100 such "secret cities" existed, some with tens of thousands of inhabitants, yet they were omitted from official maps and access to them remained strictly controlled. A number of them, such as Arzamas-16 and Chelyabinsk-65, are key components of the Russian nuclear complex today. Except for a short period in the late 1950s, when Andrei Sakharov corresponded with Nikita Khrushchev on the matter and was allowed to publish several critical articles, public discourse on nuclear issues in the USSR before the explosion at Chernobyl was either nonexistent or remained silent on the problems and hazards involved. Fears about nuclear radiation, it seems, were expressed only through morbid jokes or indirectly and poetically, as in Andrei Tarkovsky's *Stalker*.[76] Yet another illustration of the traditional difficulty of gaining access to information about the Soviet nuclear complex is the way crises and accidents were handled by Soviet officials at home and abroad. An explosion at the nuclear facility in Kyshtym in the Urals in 1957, for instance, was denied by Soviet officials until 1989,[77] although details of the accident had been published in the West a decade earlier.[78]

It should be noted that secrecy in nuclear affairs is not uncommon. Even in the USA, which has a greater tradition of openness, organized opposition to nuclear waste management has for the most part been limited to the civilian sector, largely because in this sector there is some access to information.[79] Thus, in a North Atlantic Treaty Organization (NATO) report on international environmental problems associated with military installations, before detailing the situation in Russia, the authors note that little is known about the temporary storage of spent nuclear fuel from Western naval vessels.[80] Indeed, there is evidence suggesting that Western intelligence learned about the Kashtym explosion in 1957, but failed to make the information public. It is speculated that their odd reluctance to publicize the explosion was related to the fire in the Windscale Piles in the UK the same year and a perception that news of two such accidents occurring simultaneously might undermine domestic support for nuclear programs.[81]

Throughout the 1960s and most of the 1970s, *regulation* of dumping and implementation of safety precautions for the personnel involved in the operations were largely left to the Northern Fleet itself. The first sanitary requirements were established in 1960 under the control of the navy and the Ministry of Medium Machine Building,[82] which was once the hub of the Soviet nuclear complex, operating the network of closed nuclear research cities.[83] In addition, although it had no regulatory authority,[84] an agency under the Ministry of Health was included in the drafting of these sanitary standards throughout the Soviet period.[85] These three agencies made the regulations more specific in 1962 and 1966.[86] However, the navy alone was responsible for key decisions in 1965 and 1967 that permitted dumping of liquid waste 10 miles from shore and dumping of solid waste in thin metal containers (or even without containment), and that designated the Barents Sea for liquid-waste disposal and the bays of Novaya Zemlya for disposal of solid waste.[87]

In 1979, three years after Soviet ratification of the London Convention, the Council of Ministers passed Resolution 222 on Measures to Ensure Performance of the Soviet Side's Obligations Following from the 1972 [London] Convention, which prohibited dumping of high-level waste and made Goskomgidromet responsible for granting permits regarding dumping of low- and medium-level waste and for reporting these permits to the IMO.[88] This resolution was the kickoff of the Soviet implementation game; for the first time, radioactive waste management was extended beyond the military complex and, at least formally, naval self-regulation was brought to an end. Since the resolution introduced a new regulatory agency into the nuclear waste arena, it is likely that this change was the result of commitments under the London Convention rather than Soviet domestic processes. Radioactive waste was only one of a large number of substances regulated by the London Convention, and with its multi-sectoral nature and extensive environmental monitoring responsibilities, Goskomgidromet was the natural coordinating unit. Thus, the regime-generated mechanism involved here was obligation, not so much in the sense of defining the parameters of appropriate behavior as in the sense of generating routinized bureaucratic decisions regarding division of labor that were largely based on past responsibilities.

The London Convention's role in altering Soviet behavior regarding generation and reporting of *scientific knowledge* was very similar to its role in the regulatory component of implementation. Under the early regulations of the 1960s, the Northern Fleet was responsible for mapping the environmental situation around the sites used for dumping solid nuclear waste. The mapping was conducted by four research institutions administered by the Ministry of Defense; all investigations proved very reassuring for the military.[89] In the most significant failure to fulfill obligations under the London Convention, after 1967 no water or sedimentary measurements were taken closer than 50 kilometers from the solid-waste disposal areas around Novaya Zemlya.[90] This respectful distance from the most hazardous dumping sites was kept even after Goskomgidromet began monitoring the sites following the 1979 Council of Ministers resolution. Moreover, Goskomgidromet was never allowed to monitor the situation inside the military bases or repair yards.[91]

Even during this period of military self-regulation, Soviet authorities made some efforts to stimulate *alternatives* to dumping radioactive waste. For the Arctic waste problem, elaboration of alternatives to marine disposal means constructing adequate interim storage facilities to be combined with either onsite treatment facilities and a permanent repository or a system for transporting some of the waste out of the region for reprocessing. As noted, Soviet authorities selected the latter option quite early on, primarily in order to generate plutonium for use in weapons. The first interim storage facility for spent fuel was ready for operation by the Northern Fleet in 1962, but it experienced considerable problems right from the outset.[92] Major leaks from the pools occurred from 1982 to 1983, resulting in a gradual closing of this storage facility.[93] Fuel assemblies were transferred to nearby storage tanks meant for low-level liquid waste.[94] Three other main interim storage facilities for fuel assemblies were also built.[95] In 1973, the Northern Fleet and the Murmansk Shipping Company began transporting spent nuclear fuel to Murmansk by barge, and from there to a reprocessing plant in Mayak, near Chelyabinsk in the Urals.[96] From a waste perspective, the catch to reprocessing is that the separation process generates considerable volumes of high-level liquid waste that cannot be returned to the fuel cycle and that are more hazardous to store than spent nuclear fuel.[97] In the case of the Mayak complex, this catch created one of the gravest environmental disaster areas in the entire USSR. Thus, the early investments in infrastructure to permit reprocessing of spent fuel can hardly be seen as an indication of a Soviet desire to avoid nuclear contamination.

To summarize, until the 1979 implementing resolution of the Council of Ministers, Soviet regulation of nuclear dumping activities was, for all practical purposes, left to the navy. For reasons of their own, the target groups alleviated the need for dumping by creating a system to transport spent fuel assemblies to other regions for reprocessing. They also built interim storage facilities. Three years after it was ratified by the USSR, the London Convention transformed this implementation game by shifting executive involvement to other levels of government, by prohibiting the dumping of high-level waste, and by introducing a regulatory newcomer regarding low-and medium-level waste. That agency, Goskomgidromet, also gained a role in monitoring the environmental situations in dumping areas. All these measures were in line with the regulatory provisions of the London Convention and would be very difficult to account for in the absence of that Convention. The causal process involved here is obligation in the special sense of bureaucratic adaptation to noncontroversial commitments: the obligations set down by the London Convention to regulate, monitor, and report on dumping activities required greater bureaucratic integration in this area to present a coherent report to external agencies.

The Expansion Stage

The decade following the passage of Resolution 222 was marked by a gradual broadening of regulatory agencies participating in the Soviet implementation of international dumping commitments. As in the previous stage, it was the regulatory rather than the programmatic components of the London Convention that affected developments. In particular, the IAEA guidelines on geographic criteria for dumping sites, according to which the Barents and Kara Seas are particularly poorly suited for the purpose, acquired considerable significance by generating discord in the Soviet implementation process. In accordance with the new access rules, in 1983 Goskomgidromet participated in the elaboration of new standards on dumping of radioactive waste. However, its endorsement of these regulations, which permitted continued dumping of low- and medium-level waste, was given on the understanding that the Northern Fleet would realize plans to build installations for treatment (i.e., concentration and solidification) of that waste in order to phase out the dumping operations.[98] In the meantime, the Murmansk Shipping Company, which had far smaller volumes of waste to handle in the first place, built a treatment installation at its Atomflot base outside Murmansk and was able to discontinue dumping of liquid waste in 1984 and solid waste two years later.[99] When the Northern Fleet failed to build similar installations, Goskomgidromet first expressed disagreement with the selection of dumping sites, citing the IAEA guidelines, and then in late-1987 withdrew its endorsement of the permit to dump radioactive waste in the sites used by the Northern Fleet.[100]

The key target of regulation, however, was not impressed with the stricter policy line assumed by Goskomgidromet: in 1988, the year after Goskomgidromet withdrew its endorsement of the dumping permits, the Northern Fleet dumped more low- and medium-level waste than it had in any of the previous 12 years.[101] Even more serious in terms of potential release into the environment, two reactors were dumped the same year in a bay at Novaya Zemlya.[102] Once again, dumping was regulated by the navy alone, just as it had been prior to 1979.[103]

Although dumping continued, developments under the London Convention appear to have made a difference in the Soviet process of regulating it. Again, obligation appears to have been the most relevant mechanism. Goskomgidromet, which had headed the Soviet delegations since the third Consultative Meeting of the London Convention, tried in vain to persuade the navy and the Ministry of Defense of the need to adopt the international standards at the national level. The Ministry of Defense was represented in the Soviet delegation to the first Consultative Meeting in 1976, but was not represented thereafter; in contrast, the Ministry of Merchant Marine, which administered the Murmansk Shipping Company throughout the Soviet period, was usually represented.[104] As noted above, in the early 1980s radioactive waste came under increasing scrutiny in the London Convention meetings, and although the USSR was not legally bound by the voluntary moratorium on dumping introduced in 1983 and confirmed two years later, it did not appear insensitive to the growing opposition to nuclear dumping.[105]

Although the regulatory discord between Goskomgidromet and the navy was clearly related to the obligating force of the London Convention, it is not fully explained by it. It is important to recall that in 1985 Mikhail Gorbachev ascended to power in the USSR and rapidly embarked on his project of gradually loosening restrictions on access to bureaucratic decision making.[106] Also, the Chernobyl accident the following year channeled much of the public's disapproval of the government into the environmental arena, particularly into activities involving nuclear risks. Thus, although Goskomgidromet voiced its concern about the 1983 regulations because they deviated from the IAEA criteria, the boldness of its move four years later must be seen in the context of a rapidly changing society concerned with radioactive contamination and managed by a modernizing leadership that encouraged criticism of bureaucratic malfeasance.

Gorbachev's reshuffling of the Soviet apparatus produced another regulatory agency in the implementation of dumping commitments: in 1987 a State Committee on Nature Protection (Goskompriroda) was established. Two years later Goskompriroda took over from Goskomgidromet the leadership of Soviet delegations to the London Convention.[107] The domestic influence of this agency rose steadily—culminating in the adoption of a new Russian Environmental Law in 1991—and then receded. One might have expected that its emergence would strengthen those actors in the Soviet system who opposed the dumping practices of the Northern Fleet and encourage the formation of an effective coalition to counter the resisters in the implementation game. Instead, Goskomgidromet and Goskompriroda reportedly clashed in a disruptive power struggle regarding responsibility for *monitoring* the radiological situation in the north.[108] The official Yablokov Report notes that although these two institutions held a series of closed meetings between 1988 and 1990 regarding the flagrant disregard of the IAEA guidelines, they were unable to generate action at the government level.[109]

Thus, the 1980s saw a cautious expansion in the number of regulatory agencies involved in Soviet implementation of the London Convention. For several years, however, the practical implications were moderate. None of the newcomers were granted permission to inspect the military bases, and monitoring of the radiological situation around the dumping sites remained nonintrusive—that is, measurements were still not made within 50 kilometers of the areas where high-level waste had been dumped. Furthermore, despite the hardening of Goskomgidromet's attitude concerning regulation, the Northern Fleet continued, even increased, its disposal of radioactive waste in Arctic seas. Moreover, no new attempts were made to develop alternatives to dumping in the form of improved storage or treatment facilities.

The London Convention's effect on the Soviet implementation game during this second stage remained largely limited to regulatory aspects, with obligations stemming from the London regulations as the main mechanism at work. That these obligations played a significant role in Soviet implementation of the Convention, at least as far as Goskomgidromet is concerned, is suggested by the fact that Goskomgidromet built its criticism and subsequent denouncement of Northern Fleet dumping operations explicitly on guidelines elaborated by the IAEA under the London Convention. While internal change in the USSR provided the political energy for a transformation of the Soviet regulative process concerning dumping, the London Convention provided the direction. For its part, the Northern Fleet continued dumping radioactive waste as if nothing had happened.

Politicization of Dumping

In the late 1980s, dramatic changes occurred regarding both access rules and patterns of participation in Soviet environmental affairs. Unlike in the past, the impact of these changes was also felt in the nuclear arena. Although the preceding stage of cautious expansion had involved alterations in the mix of regulatory agencies, during this politicization stage the political weight of a third type of actor was added—the range of societal *intervenor* groups interested in the process, especially environmental organizations. Although semi-official organizations for the protection of nature thrived throughout the Soviet period, a critical environmental movement independent of state authorities did not emerge until the mid-1980s. Its eventual emergence was stimulated in large part by the fear of nuclear contamination. During the early 1990s, these so-called informals were able to organize large street demonstrations and public hearings on the ecological situation in the Russian Northwest.[110] A survey conducted in 1990 in 850 cities throughout the USSR suggested that more than half of those surveyed were unhappy with the environmental situation; moreover, radiation was among the top three worries cited.[111] Quite predicatably, the economic hardships of the 1990s have made it more difficult for the environmental movement to command the political attention of the average citizen in the Russian Northwest. However, such fluxes have been observed in the West as well, and they do not imply that the Russian Greens are a thing of the past.

It is actually not until this third stage, beginning in the late 1980s and early 1990s, that real competition among coalitions engaged in a game of implementation could be seen in the domestic processes generated by the London Convention. With the 1993 publication of the Yablokov Report, a coalition of actors critical of nuclear dumping was able to take advantage of the fluid authority situation prevailing during the transition from the USSR to the Russian Federation to tip the balance of influence in their favor, at least temporarily. During this politicization stage, the international dumping regime's effect on Soviet and Russian nuclear politics was at its greatest: not only regulatory but also programmatic activities under the London Convention fed into the domestic implementation process and helped shape the outcome.

A former radiation safety engineer in the Murmansk Shipping Company, Andrei Zolotkov, who was also an activist in the NGO Toward a New Earth,[112] played an important role in the disclosure of Soviet dumping activities in the Arctic Ocean.[113] At that time, Zolotkov was also a delegate from Murmansk to the Congress of People's Deputies,[114] an assembly set up in the Gorbachev era as part of the effort to vitalize the legislative branch of government.[115] Zolotkov's stature and his experience in the northern nuclear complex gave his detailed account of past and ongoing dumping activities sufficient credibility to generate a huge scandal both domestically and internationally. When his allegations were neither withdrawn nor rejected by competent Soviet authorities, Greenpeace International compiled a report, primarily based on Zolotkov's information, that was presented at a press conference in Moscow in September 1991.[116] The report was circulated informally at the 1991 Consultative Meeting under the London Convention, complementing a Soviet-Norwegian information paper on plans for cooperative investigations into the radiological impacts of the alleged dumping.[117]

These environmental activists were helped considerably by the fact that nuclear dumping became politically linked to the even more salient issue of nuclear tests on Novaya Zemlya. Indeed, the establishment of the Yablokov Commission, which proved so important to the subsequent Russian implementation game, resulted from a struggle between Yeltsin and the Congress of People's Deputies regarding access to information on dumping conducted by the test site authority.[118] Yeltsin's 1991 decision on a unilateral moratorium on nuclear tests, one of the early accomplishments of the nuclear activists, had been widely interpreted as a strategic move to match Gorbachev's Soviet-level decision to the same effect.[119] This interpretation is supported by certain subsequent decisions seen as favoring the nuclear complex, especially the federalization of the test site area in 1992.

The significance of the London Convention for the creation of the Yablokov Commission and the subsequent increase in the amount of information available on the Russian nuclear complex should not be exaggerated. It is true that the 1991 Consultative Meeting encouraged the compilation of information on past dumping operations,[120] but in 1992, when the Meeting shifted from encouraging data reporting to making an actual request for information, the Russian delegation was able to respond by outlining the composition and tasks of an already established fact-finding commission headed by the distinguished scientist Alexei Yablokov.[121] On balance, internal Russian dynamics were far more important than international requests in generating support for the Yablokov Commission. Interinstitutional rivalries during the transition period were especially useful as they could be exploited by activists from intervenor groups and regulatory agencies favoring adherence to the London Convention and greater openness on nuclear affairs.

Despite the fact that leading representatives from the nuclear complex took part in its preparation, the Yablokov Report was highly critical of both the dumping and the secrecy surrounding it. Indeed, the Yablokov Commission used the obligating force of the London Convention for all it was worth. The fact that Soviet commitments under the Convention are systematically exaggerated may be suggestive of the Commission members' belief in the domestic political force of the London regulations. The Report itself makes no mention of the distinction between resolutions and amendments to the London Convention, nor of the Convention's opting-out clause. Thus, it does not highlight the fact that the Soviet abstentions from voting on the voluntary moratoria on radioactive waste dumping in 1983 and 1985 make it difficult to argue that the country was legally or even politically bound by them in this period. Likewise, although the Commission boldly stated that the dumping of low- and medium-level waste in the Barents and Kara Seas was illegal,[122] in reality the IAEA guidelines have only quasi-legal status.[123]

The norms developed under the London Convention were obviously perceived by members of the Yablokov Commission as potent in the Russian context. However, an important change during the politicization stage was that *programmatic* activities associated with the London Convention gradually became more important to the Russian implementation process. This implies that financial and technical rewards, and to some extent learning, replaced obligation as the international regime mechanisms that most influenced domestic outcomes. In terms of monitoring, starting in 1991 four Russian-Norwegian cruises, with participation from the IAEA Marine Environment Laboratory, among others, took measurements in the fjords where reactors still containing spent fuel had been dumped.[124] Encouraged by the Consultative Meeting of the London Convention,[125] the IAEA was quick to establish its International Arctic Seas Assessment Programme.[126] The causal mechanisms at work in this process, affecting Russian monitoring practices, were rewards and obligation. The rewards included equipment, expertise, and attractive trips to conferences and cooperative working groups financed by Western participants. For its part, obligation occurred through continuous pressure in a range of international fora, including the Consultative Meetings under the London Convention,[127] to fully disclose available information and to allow physical access to the bays of Novaya Zemlya where reactors have been dumped.

The most important *regulatory* change that occurred in the area of nuclear waste during the politicization period was the adoption of the new Russian Environmental Act in 1991. This act generally gave pride of place to Goskompriroda, which was elevated and renamed the Russian Ministry of Environmental Protection and Natural Resources.[128] However, since being raised to ministerial status in 1991, this agency has lost several important struggles for regulatory competence. For instance, regarding live marine resources, the old hands in the bureaucracy overseeing fisheries have regained control over quota allocation and compliance control operations.[129] Also, although for a short time Goskomgidromet and the State Committees on Water, Forestry, and Cartography were placed under the Ministry of Environmental Protection and Natural Resources,[130] they are now once again separate federal agencies.[131] In the area of nuclear safety, as well, the Ministry is now seen as having very limited enforcement powers, and its regulatory role is limited by the fact that it is a new agency with very limited financial backing, an inadequate informational basis for making environmental decisions, and poorly defined internal structures.[132]

In contrast, the Ministry of Atomic Power appears to have gradually recovered much of its strength after the setbacks associated with the explosion at Chernobyl. A merger with the Ministry of Medium Machine Building in 1989 brought both the military and the civilian parts of the nuclear complex into its portfolio.[133] In subsequent years, new reactors were put on line in the Russian nuclear program, partly to compensate for the loss of control over nuclear plants in Ukraine. On matters related to nuclear issues in general, a sense grew in the environmental movement that Yeltsin was increasingly yielding to the demands of the Ministry of Atomic Power and the nuclear lobby.[134] Western observers now describe the Ministry as "extremely large and powerful," and note that the minister, Viktor Mikhailov, was appointed to the Russian Security Council in July 1995.[135]

In summary, during the period marked by the politicization of dumping, the barriers to involvement in these affairs were dramatically lowered, resulting in a sharp increase in societal participation in the decision-making process. Interinstitutional rivalry during the transition from the USSR to the Russian Federation enhanced this development, and the implementation game was transformed from a process involving a few regulatory agencies into a high-level issue including some of the most salient figures in Russian politics. At the same time, the domain of the game shifted from regulation to monitoring. Consequently, the primary significance of the London Convention shifted from its regulatory to its programmatic activities, in that the various international programs to measure the extent of nuclear contamination came into focus. Still, the activist coalition that supported this development was also very deliberate in mobilizing and even overselling the obligating force of the London Convention, as well as Russian commitments in other fora, to press for greater openness regarding nuclear waste management in the Russian Northwest.

It would be difficult, however, to uphold the view that the London Convention itself was decisive for these developments. As for the Russian scandal generated by news of past dumping, domestic institutional processes were more decisive than the Convention. Regarding the subsequent launching of international cooperative programs to map nuclear hazards in the Arctic, processes other than the London Convention have been at least as important. As noted, the bilateral Russian-Norwegian ties in the nuclear era preceded the politicization of this issue in the London meetings,[136] and the cruises themselves were organized under that bilateral umbrella. The IAEA investigations probably could also have been conducted even in the absence of the London Convention. In short, as to international participation in the nuclear monitoring efforts in the Barents and Kara Seas, which took off after the disclosure of past dumping, the London Convention provided only one of several cooperative fora, all of which tend to be mutually supportive and complementary. Furthermore, the limits of progress regarding capacity to monitor and enforce regulations in the Russian nuclear complex have been noted. Even in the politicization period, access to the military bases, including the nuclear test site on Novaya Zemlya, remained under military control.

Ambiguous Contraction

In Russian decision making concerning nuclear waste, the scope of participation has leveled off since its peak with the publication of the Yablokov Report. There are several reasons for this decline. At the level of societal organization, there currently is less enthusiasm for environmental matters than in the late 1980s, in part due to disillusionment with the early experiments with political activism and direct democracy. Perhaps more significant have been the economic hardships and political turmoil of the 1990s, which have pushed environmental affairs down the agenda.

During this contraction phase, there has also been political consolidation of presidential power, including stronger authoritarian features in the governing style,[137] and a reduction in the number of access points for those still interested in affecting nuclear developments. Along with the Ministry of Environmental Protection and Natural Resources' failure to assert its authority in areas formally placed under its jurisdiction and the gradual recuperation of the Ministry of Atomic Power, there has been a return to secrecy in the nuclear waste arena. In 1992, the Ministry of Atomic Power and the nuclear industry managed to convince the Supreme Soviet to extend the classified status of governmental information on nuclear programs.[138] Also in that year, Yeltsin reversed a decision to open up the nuclear city of Severodvinsk, home of one of the principal military shipbuilding complexes during the Soviet era. Another indication of this trend toward less openness on nuclear matters is that Gosatomnadzor, the Federal Nuclear and Radiation Safety Authority of Russia, which in 1991 was assigned the task of regulating and inspecting safety practices at both civilian and military facilities,[139] lost the military part of its portfolio through the Presidential Decree of July 1995 after it published a critical inspection report.[140] An even more direct indication that access rules are being tightened is the new and tougher policy pursued regarding environmental organizations in the nuclear field. In 1992, a representative of Toward a New Earth was included as a senior expert and author in the Yablokov Commission, despite, or perhaps because of, that organization's association with Andrei Zolotkov, who was the first source of information on military dumping practices. Three years later the institutional framework proved far more hostile: in late 1995 the Federal Security Bureau raided the homes and offices of a number of people involved in the preparation of a report on the Northern Fleet's management of nuclear waste. The Bureau later arrested one of the authors, a Russian citizen formerly with the Northern Fleet but currently employed at the Moscow office of the Norwegian environmental organization Bellona, accusing him of espionage and high treason.[141] Thus, the period after the publication of the Yablokov Report can be considered contractive in terms of participation because the level of secrecy surrounding nuclear and military affairs is again markedly on the rise and because societal attention to nuclear matters, indeed to environmental affairs in general, is waning in Russia.

At the same time, there is an element of ambiguity here because this contraction does not extend to foreign relations: Russian institutions and authorities continue to maintain close contacts with foreign counterparts seen as capable of playing a role in solving practical problems in the Russian nuclear complex. After having ascribed a 1993 incident in which liquid radioactive waste was dumped in the Sea of Japan to irresponsibility on the part of the navy and the nuclear industry, the Russian Minister of Environmental Protection and Natural Resources informed the Consultative Meeting of the London Convention that Western technology and financial resources would accelerate the process of acquiring the capacity to do without such dumping in the future.[142] In response, an international technical advisory assistance team was set up to develop projects on treatment and storage facilities.[143] The next year, this team was able to report to the Consultative Meeting that Japan and Russia had signed an agreement to build a treatment facility in the Far East for low-level liquid waste, and that there had been progress regarding a project to enhance the liquid-processing capacity at Atomflot, the base of the Murmansk Shipping Company.[144] Furthermore, they reported that Norway and Russia had reached agreement on a two-year assessment program on the nuclear waste challenges in the Mayak plant.[145] In 1995, experts from six NATO countries were invited to an international scientific symposium in Moscow on decommissioning nuclear submarines involving leading figures in the State Committee on Defense Branches of Industry (Goskomoboronprom), the Ministry of Atomic Power, and the Northern Fleet.[146] That same year, 32 representatives of 13 ministries or major organizations in Russia responsible for radioactive waste participated in an IAEA meeting on international cooperation on nuclear waste management.[147] In the present situation, it seems that the groups that once composed the backbone of resistance to openness on nuclear matters, including the navy and the Ministry of Atomic Power, have consolidated their control over domestic decision making and are becoming increasingly involved in cooperative programs generated by the London Convention as well as in other fora. Consequently, the domain of the implementation game is shifting again, from domestic regulation and environmental monitoring toward the third implementation task, the enhancement of *capacity to avoid* dumping in violation of international commitments.

In the present stage of ambiguous contraction, the level of domestic participation is on its way down, whereas international contacts continue to thrive.

With the international focus shifting from regulating and mapping radioactive contamination to developing practical measures to avoid it, yesterday's resisters of have become today's supporters of international coordination in the nuclear waste arena. The regime mechanisms that affect behavior remain the same as in the previous stage: with growing attention to programmatic, rather than regulatory, regime components, causal mechanisms such as rewards and to some extent learning crowd out obligation, which was so important in the first and second stages of Soviet and Russian implementation of the London Convention.

Again, there is little reason to assume that this coordination of foreign assistance on nuclear waste would have been impossible to achieve without the support of Consultative Meetings under the London Convention. The Governing Council of the IAEA could have been another vehicle for this purpose; moreover, on a bilateral level, Russian-Norwegian cooperation in the nuclear area is a result of region-building aspirations quite independent of the global dumping regime.[148] It would be more accurate to say that it is the cluster of international arenas involved in this field that is now activated on the matter of treatment and storage facilities in Russia, as it previously was on the matter of monitoring.

Conclusion

This part of the book highlights the role international regimes play in altering access and participation patterns in member states, and traces the impacts of those patterns for implementation and regime effectiveness.. The fact that a single implementation case is portrayed in this chapter obviously places some limits on making generalizations based on the findings and the range of causal processes that can be substantiated. The issue area studied here is difficult because military security concerns loom large, implying that enhanced access and participation are particularly difficult to effect. By implication, processes shown to accomplish this in the case of military dumping activities are presumably robust. Causal linkages between the international regime and the process of domestic implementation in Russia are substantiated here by tracing, over time, the processes of obligation, learning, and reward among regulatory agencies, targets, and intervenor groups, and by trying to determine whether these processes result from regulatory or programmatic activities under the London Convention.

In this chapter it is argued that the regime set up by the London Convention on dumping has helped reduce domestic access barriers in the USSR and Russia regarding decisions on the disposal of nuclear waste and has promoted a stepwise broadening of actual participation by regulatory agencies and societal intervenor groups. Closing a two-decade period of military self-regulation, Soviet legislation implementing the Convention in 1979 elevated the nuclear waste issue to the cabinet level and added a nonmilitary regulatory agency, Goskomgidromet, for the management of low- and medium-level waste. This change served to reduce an access bias that had to that point clearly favored the target groups, primarily the Northern Fleet. The role of the regime was to generate a set of routinized bureaucratic responses to uncontroversial but explicit responsibilities defined internationally. Although secrecy continued to shield military dumping from broader public scrutiny, this change brought about a cautious regulatory competition that in the mid-1980s was further nurtured by the political turnabouts of *glasnost* and *perestroika*. Institutional outcomes of particular significance in this stage of cautious expansion were an environmental bureaucracy, Goskompriroda; a more active legislative body, the Congress of People's Deputies; and a radiotoxically attentive green movement independent of the state apparatus.

During the politicization stage in the early 1990s, the international dumping regime aided critics of dumping, both among regulatory agencies and intervenor groups, in their successful efforts to enhance transparency on nuclear activities. Access to information on nuclear safety in the military sector, as well as participation in the associated policy-making processes, reached a high point with the publication of the 1993 governmental Yablokov Report. Although this report itself was largely the result of internal Russian processes, it also responded to demands articulated by the Consultative Meeting of the London Convention. Moreover, the various prescriptions set forth in the Convention appear to have enhanced the political clout of those critical of dumping. Such prescriptions figure prominently in the unequivocal arguments made in the Yablokov Report on the severity of past dumping and the need to invest more in storage and decontamination facilities to avoid future dumping.

Since the end of this stage of increased politicization, access to military information, including nuclear waste practices, has been tightened at a time when public attention to environmental problems is ebbing. Also, the limited funds, personnel, and experience of the environmental bureaucracy are becoming apparent, with the nuclear complex currently regaining much of its previous political strength and prestige. Significantly, the civilian regulatory apparatus does not have physical access to military bases or shipyards. This contraction in terms of domestic access and participation is the result of internal Russian developments, but it is to some extent balanced by steadily widening international participation in programs designed to monitor the level of radioactivity in Arctic seas and to subsequently alleviate the Northern Fleet's need to continue dumping. These international programs have required the consent and, increasingly, the active participation of the navy itself. This support has been secured primarily because the navy believes that such programs will be conducive to the transfer of Western technology and financial resources to Russia. The causal significance of the London Convention in this context should not be overstated, however, as the programs are supported by a range of other cooperative vehicles, both bilateral and regional, as well as the IAEA. The role of the London Convention has been partly to coordinate and partly to encourage and legitimize programmatic activities initiated or financed within other such processes.

The *consequences* of these changes in access and participation for the effectiveness of the international dumping regime have been measured along three dimensions: monitoring, regulation, and compliance stimulation, including enhancement of target group capacity to avoid dumping. The entry of Goskomgidromet, and later Goskompriroda, into the arena implied somewhat enhanced *monitoring* of the environmental situation, but until their internationalization during the politicization stage, these activities remained remarkably nonintrusive, as until 1993 measurements were not taken near the dumping sites. The same is true for behavioral monitoring of compliance: as noted, inspection of nuclear waste management in military facilities was, and remains, largely the responsibility of the Northern Fleet itself.

As for *regulations*, the entry of nonmilitary agencies into the radioactive waste arena during the period of cautious expansion after 1979 prepared the groundwork for controversy, as Goskomgidromet was increasingly critical of naval practices and, in 1987, withdrew the navy's permit to continue dumping low- and medium-level waste. However, this regulatory discord did not force the Northern Fleet to halt dumping. On the contrary, unlike the civilian

Murmansk Shipping Company, which with its better treatment capacity had been able to stop dumping in the mid-1980s, the navy has continued to dump nuclear waste well into the 1990s. We have seen that the extent to which regulations were contested was partly determined by the guidelines set forth under the London Convention. However, the articulation of those guidelines in the regulatory process remained fairly limited until the nuclear complex, including its military component, was thoroughly, if temporarily, enfeebled by the ecological disaster of the explosion at Chernobyl and the political reshuffling of *perestroika*. Thus, the international regime provided the direction but not the energy for this change in regulatory implementation.

Regarding *behavior of targets*, the entry of foreign participants into the implementation process in the late 1980s and especially after the turn of the decade, has been significant, not so much by penalizing dumping as by helping to enhance the Northern Fleet's ability to avoid dumping. This is achieved through cooperative international programs designed to estimate the hazards involved and to elaborate practical ways to enhance treatment and storage facilities for liquid and solid radioactive waste.

Thus, whereas the routinizing and obligating forces of international rules impacted implementation the most during the expansion and politicization stages, during the current phase the programmatic regime components, and thus learning and reward rather than obligation, are becoming increasingly important. Such foreign contribution is probably decisive to the realization of Russian capacity to adequately treat and store radioactive waste, as domestically the navy and Russian authorities more generally are again shrouding waste management in secrecy.

In the case discussed here, the *conditions* under which such regime-generated processes have been able to affect domestic implementation in a highly sensitive issue area have been quite straightforward. The target groups' self-regulation ended in the late 1970s, because those involved believed that only an intersectoral agency such as Goskomgidromet would be able to manage the wide range of materials besides nuclear waste that are included in commitments under the London Convention. As long as this civilian agency failed to challenge the target groups on either monitoring practices or dumping operations, such a solution was hardly controversial in the domestic context. For its part, the IAEA operational guidelines on dumping generated regulatory discord and subsequently broad politicization of the dumping issue only because conditions were highly favorable due to the combination of *glasnost* and Chernobyl and the interinstitutional rivalry associated with a state apparatus in transition. Similarly, the shift in emphasis from the regulatory to the programmatic activities of the regime was conditioned on the fact that Western partners, especially the USA, Norway, and the European Union, were ready to define nuclear contamination of Arctic seas as a high-priority issue worth significant financial investment.

Although those favorable conditions emerged independently of the international dumping regime, the latter put certain components into place that proved highly instrumental in making use of the window of opportunity they provided. The relative openness of the regime to participation by NGOs is seen as part of the reason for regulatory developments under the London Convention,[149] especially the moratoria on radioactive waste dumping in the 1980s. It is true that, as discussed above, those moratoria did not play any role in the cautious broadening of regulatory participation in that particular stage of the Soviet implementation game. Later, however, Greenpeace's ability to present its report on Soviet military dumping to the 1991 Consultative Meeting of the London Convention probably enhanced the domestic scandal and subsequent politicization of the nuclear waste issue in the Soviet and Russian contexts. Long before this occurred, a second regime feature had served to end target group self-regulation, that is, the Convention's requirement that a domestic regulatory body be designated to manage a permit system guided by the annexes to the Convention and report compliance to the Secretariat. A third regime feature, one that prompted regulatory discord in the Soviet implementation game, was the very specific operational guidelines developed by the IAEA, which provided Goskomgidromet and later the Ministry of Environmental Protection and Natural Resources with clear standards to invoke when they found the time ripe for challenging existing domestic regulations. Finally, the Consultative Parties have been able to link the Convention with other international activities, especially the mobilization of international organizations with greater financial and technological muscle, such as the IAEA. This ability prepared the international dumping regime to use the unexpected opportunity that arose in the early 1990s to channel international expertise and funds into the highly sensitive area of military dumping of nuclear waste in the Arctic.

Notes

I would like to thank Steinar Andresen, Olav Berstad, Frode Fonnum, Alf Håkon Hoel, Helge Hveem, Kal Raustiala, Magne Røed, Eugene Skolnikoff, Anita Sørlie, Arild Underdal, David Victor, Davor Vidas, and Oran Young for very helpful comments.

1. Of a total radioactivity of 136,682 terabecquerel (TBq), Soviet dumping in Arctic seas from 1960 to 1991 accounted for 90,152 TBq; Sjoeblom, K.-L., and Linsley, G., 1994, "Sea Disposal of Radioactive Wastes: The London Convention 1972," *IAEA Bulletin* 2:12–16. These figures include only items that have been deliberately disposed of at sea.

2. *International Legal Materials*, Vol. 11, pp. 1291 ff., The American Society of International Law, Washington, DC, USA. The London Convention was adopted 13 November 1972 and entered into force 30 August 1975; the USSR ratified the Convention in 1976. The official name of the Convention was changed from the London Dumping Convention (LDC) to the London Convention (LC) in 1992.

3. Blowers, A., Lowry, D., and Salomon, B.D., 1991, *The International Politics of Nuclear Waste*, MacMillan Press, London, UK.

4. According to the International Atomic Energy Agency (IAEA), high-level waste comprises irradiated reactor fuel, liquid or solidified wastes from the first solvent extraction cycle of chemical reprocessing (or equivalent processes) of such fuel, or any other matter of activity concentration exceeding certain limits specified for alpha, beta/gamma, and tritium emitters; IAEA Safety Series No. 78, reproduced in International Maritime Organization (IMO), 1991, *The London Dumping Convention: The First Decade and Beyond*, IMO, London UK, Annex 18.

5. Yablokov, A.V., Karasev, V.K., Ruyantsev, V.M., Kokeyev, M.Y., Petrov, O.I., Lystsov, V.N., Yemelyanenkov, A.F., and Rubtsov, P.M., 1993, Fakta og problemer forbundet med deponering av radioaktivt avfall i havet som omgir den russiske foderasjons territorium. Materiale fra rapporten til regjeringskommisjonen for sporsmål forbundet med deponeringen av radioaktivt avfall i havet, oppnevnt ved forordning fra Den Russiske Foderasjons president, av 24. oktober 1992, forordning nr 613 (Facts and problems related to radioactive waste disposal in seas adjacent to the territory of the Russian Federation: Materials for a report by the government commission on matters related to radioactive waste disposal at sea, created by decree no. 613 of the Russian Federation president, October 24, 1992. Unofficial Norwegian translation of Russian original), Office of the President of the Russian Federation, Moscow, Russia.

6. Office of Technology Assessment (OTA), 1995, Nuclear Wastes in the Arctic: An Analysis of Arctic and Other Regional Impacts from Soviet Nuclear Contamination, Congress of the United States, Washington, DC, USA, pp. 68–69.

7. Secretariat of the Joint Russian-Norwegian Export Group for Investigation of Radioactive Contamination in the Northern Areas, 1996, *Dumping of Radioactive Waste and Investigation of Radioactive Contamination in the Kara Sea: Results from 3 Years of Investigations (1992–1994) in the Kara Sea,* Østerås, Norway, pp. 42–49.

8. North Atlantic Treaty Organization (NATO), 1995, Cross-Border Environmental Problems Emanating from Defense-Related Installations and Activities: Volume 1, Radioactive Contamination (Final Report), NATO, Brussels, Belgium, p. 287.

9. Baklanov, A., Bergman, R., and Segerstahl, B., 1996, Radioactive Sources in the Kola Region: Actual and Potential Radiological Consequences for Man, Final Report of the Kola Assessment Study of the RAD Project, International Institute of Applied Systems Analysis, Laxenburg, Austria.

10. OTA, op. cit., note 6, pp. 79, 108.

11. Figures cited are from St.meld. 34, 1993–1994 (Report to the Storting), Atomvirksomhet og kjemiske våpen i våre nordlige nœrområder (Nuclear activity and chemical weapons in our northern proximities), Ministry of Foreign Affairs, Oslo, Norway. For Russia as a whole, the total number of decommissioned vessels will be 170 by the year 2000; the comparable figure for the USA is 120. See NATO, op. cit., note 8, p. 276.

12. NATO, op. cit., note 8, p. 283.

13. Yegorov, N.N., 1995, "Plenary Address," *International Cooperation on Nuclear Waste Management in the Russian Federation,* International Atomic Energy Agency, Vienna, Austria, pp. 15–26.

14. Although a number of states currently have programs for final disposal under way (most of which opt for deep underground sites in stable geological strata), the first operative repository is still at least 20 years away. See International Atomic Energy Agency, 1995, *IAEA Yearbook,* Vienna, Austria, p. C83.

15. Article IV, paragraphs 1–2, and Article VI, respectively. Since the eleventh meeting in 1988, a Working Group of the Annexes has considered ways to update this system; see Report of the 11th Consultative Meeting of Contracting Parties to the Convention on the Prevention of Marine Pollution by Dumping of Wastes and Other Matter, International Maritime Organization (LDC

11/14:13), London, UK. This Working Group is also to elaborate a New Assessment Procedure (LDC 13/15:11–13), subsequently renamed the Waste Assessment Framework (LC 15/16:18–20). The new framework, which is still being created, will basically imply more detailed guidance of the domestic decision-making process before dumping permits are issued (LC 18/11:12; see also Annex 6).

16. International Maritime Organization (IMO), op. cit., note 4, p. 118.

17. Article XV, paragraphs 1 and 2.

18. LDC 11/14:32.

19. LDC 3/12:11; Annex 4.

20. See Rules 3 and 4 of the Rules of Procedure (LC 1/16, Annex II); each Consultative Meeting is left to decide whether or not to invite given international or nongovernmental organizations (Rule 3).

21. LDC 4/12:18.

22. LDC 6/12:3–4. Resolution LC 30 (11), adopted in 1988, further requires NGOs to keep delegations small, to refrain from obstructing the meeting or communicating with the media in a manner prejudicial to the discussion, and to respect any specific requirements agreed to by the contracting parties. See LDC 11/14, Annex 2.

23. Blowers *et al.*, op. cit., note 3, p. 79.

24. Birnie, P., and Boyle, A.E., 1992, *International Law and the Environment*, Clarendon Press, Oxford, UK, p. 322.

25. LDC 12/16:40.

26. Article III, paragraph 3; see also LDC 11/14:33.

27. LC 15/16:14–16.

28. LDC 13/15:39–40.

29. Ringius, L., 1992, "Radwaste Disposal and the Global Ocean Dumping Convention: The Politics of International Environmental Regimes," Ph.D. dissertation, European University Institute, Florence, Italy. This view was repeated by Soviet delegations on later occasions; see, for instance, LDC 5/12:12.

30. International Atomic Energy Agency, 1978, IAEA INFRCIRC/205/Add.1/ Rev.1, Vienna, Austria.

31. LDC 7/12:19–30. The voluntary moratorium was established by Resolution LDC 14 (7), reproduced in LDC 7/12, Annex 3.

32. The states voting against were Japan, the Netherlands, South Africa, Switzerland, UK, and USA. LDC 7/12:29.

33. LDC 9/12:41; also Annex 5.

34. Yablokov *et al.*, op. cit., note 5, p. 10.

35. The resolution amending the annexes is LC 51 (16), reproduced in LC 16/14, Annex 5.

36. The other abstainees were the UK, Belgium, France, and China; LC 16/14:17.

37. LC 17/14:6.

38. IMO, op. cit., note 4, p. 117.

39. See, respectively, LDC 7/12:19–30, also Annex 6; LDC 8/10:19–20, also Annex 4; and LDC 9/12:19–29.

40. LDC 10/15, Annex II.

41. LC 16/14:19–20. Other similar expert groups set up under the Convention are the Ad hoc Group of Experts on the Annexes, the Ad hoc Working Groups on Dredged Materials Disposal and on Incineration at Sea, and the Task Team on Liability.

42. Sand, P.H., ed., 1992, *The Effectiveness of International Environmental Agreements: A Survey of Existing Legal Instruments*, Grotius, Cambridge, UK, p. 16.

43. Bergesen, H.O., and Parmann, G., eds., 1995, *Green Globe Yearbook*, 1995, Oxford University Press, Oxford, UK, pp. 233–235; of those, more than 800 are professional scientists.

44. LDC 13/15:32.

45. LDC 15/16:38–40.

46. LC 17/14:13.

47. LDC 5/12:8–9.

48. LDC 12/16:13.

49. LDC 14/16:36–37.

50. Birnie and Boyle, op. cit., note 24, p. 320. For a condensed analysis of the relationship between the London Convention and United Nations Convention on the Law of the Sea, see also Canfield, J.L., 1994, "Soviet and Russian Nuclear Waste Dumping in the Arctic Marine Environment: Legal, Historical, and Political Implications," *Georgetown International Environmental Law Review* 6(2):353–444.

51. Birnie and Boyle, op. cit., note 24, p. 324.

52. See Ringius, op. cit., note 29, p. 11; and Templeton, W.L., 1989, "Disposal of Low-Level Radioactive Wastes in the Ocean," in *Marine Waste Management: Science and Policy: Oceanic Processes in Marine Pollution*, Vol. 3, edited by M.A. Champ and P.K. Park, Robert E. Krieger, Malabar, FL, USA, pp. 75–83. Relations with the Nuclear Energy Agency have been a regular theme since the second Consultative Meeting in 1977 (LDC 2/11:10–11).

53. Birnie and Boyle, op. cit., note 29, p. 324.

54. Arctic Monitoring and Assessment Program, 1997, Arctic Pollution Issues: A State of the Arctic Environment Report, The Arctic Monitoring and Assessment Program Secretariat, Oslo, Norway. A discussion of the relevance of the Arctic Environmental Protection Strategy (AEPS) for nuclear waste management in the Arctic is given in OTA, op. cit., note 6.

55. On the Barents Region process, see Stokke, O.S., and Tunander, O., eds., 1994, *The Barents Region: Cooperation in Arctic Europe*, Sage, London, UK.

56. Birnie and Boyle, op. cit., note 24, p. 321.

57. Andresen, S., 1992, "International Verification in Practice: A Brief Account of Experiences from Relevant International Cooperative Measures," in *Achieving Environmental Goals: The Concept and Practice of Environmental Performance Review*, edited by E. Lykke, Belhaven Press, London, UK, pp. 101–121. See also the first part of this book.

58. Young, O.R., and Levy, M.A. (with G. Osherenko), 1997, "The Effectiveness of International Regimes," in *The Effectiveness of International Regimes*, edited by M.A. Levy and O.R. Young, Cornell University Press, Ithaca, NY, USA (forthcoming).

59. For an application to the Antarctic Treaty System, see Stokke, O.S., and Vidas, D., eds., 1996, *Governing the Antarctic: The Effectiveness and Legitimacy of the Antarctic Treaty System*, Cambridge University Press, Cambridge, UK.

60. Franck, T.M., 1990, *The Power of Legitimacy Among Nations*, Oxford University Press, Oxford, UK.

61. Chayes, A., and Chayes, A.H., 1993, "On Compliance," *International Organization* 47(2):175–205, Spring.

62. See in particular Young and Levy, op. cit., note 58, which elaborates a number of general mechanisms, including those mentioned in the text. These mechanisms imply different causal pathways between an international regime and the solution to the problem addressed. A similar attempt is made in

Haas, P.M., Keohane, R.O., and Levy, M.A., eds., *Institutions for the Earth. Sources of Effective International Environmental Protection*, The MIT Press, Cambridge, MA, USA.

63. O'Riordan, T., 1985, "Approaches to Regulation," in *Regulating Industrial Risks: Science, Hazards and Public Protection*, edited by H. Otway and M. Peltu, Buttersworth, London, UK, pp. 20–39.

64. In addition, the nuclear icebreaker *Lenin* has been taken out of operation; Berkov, A.E., 1995, "Ministry of Transport of the Russian Federation (Mintrans)," *International Cooperation on Nuclear Waste Management in the Russian Federation*, International Atomic Energy Agency, Vienna, Austria, pp. 63–66. The civilian nuclear power plant in Polyarnyye Zori in Murmansk oblast has not dumped waste in Arctic seas and is not among the target groups in this context.

65. For a portrait of the Soviet political system, see Kerblay, B., 1983, *Modern Soviet Society* (translated by Rupert Swyer; original version, La société soviétique contemporaire, 1977, by Armand Colin, Paris), Methuen, London, UK. On the power relations between the various branches of government and the Communist Party, see in particular pp. 242–248.

66. Canfield, op. cit., note 50, p. 371.

67. Egge, Å., 1993, "Fra Aleksander II til Boris Jeltsin. Russlands og Sovjetunionens moderne historie," Universitetsforlaget, Oslo, Norway, p. 270.

68. On the role of the legislative Supreme Soviet in this matter, see Canfield, op. cit., note 50, pp. 375–379.

69. Under the 1993 Constitution of the Russian Federation, Russia has a total of 89 subjects, which may be either republics, provinces (*oblast*), territories (*kray*), or autonomous areas (*okrug*).

70. Castberg, R., and Stokke, O.S., 1992, "Environmental Problems in Northwest Russia: Regional Strategies," *International Challenges* 12(4):33–45.

71. Nilsen, T., Kudrik, I., and Nikitin, A., 1996, "Den russiske Nordflåten: Kilder til radioaktive forurensning," Bellona rapport nr. 2, Oslo, Norway, p. 87.

72. Canfield, op. cit., note 50, p. 376.

73. Yablokov *et al.*, op. cit., note 5, pp. 33–36.

74. Because of very large discharges of liquid waste in the Kara Sea, 1976 was a peak year. The total activity of low- and medium-level waste dumped by the USSR in Arctic seas, measured at the time of disposal, is 1,342 TBq; NATO, op. cit., note 8, pp. 17, 33. The total activity dumped by the USSR, including reactors with spent nuclear fuel, is about 90,000 TBq.

75. Weart, S.R., 1988, *Nuclear Fear: A History of Images*, Harvard University Press, Cambridge, MA, USA, p. 122.

76. Ibid., pp. 204, 239.

77. Feshbach, M., and Friendly, A., Jr., 1992, *Ecocide in the USSR: Health and Nature under Siege*, Aurum Press, London, UK, p. 174.

78. Medvedev, Z., 1979, *Disaster in the Urals*, Angus and Robertson, London, UK.

79. Blowers *et al.*, op. cit., note 3, p. 240.

80. NATO, op. cit., note 8, p. 282.

81. Blowers *et al.*, op. cit., note 3, p. 41.

82. Yablokov *et al.*, op. cit., note 5, pp. 20–21.

83. In 1989, the Ministry of Medium Machine Building was merged with the Ministry of Nuclear Power to become the Ministry of Atomic Power and Industry, which was renamed the Ministry for Atomic Power in 1992; OTA, op. cit., note 6, p. 218.

84. OTA, op. cit., note 6, p. 219.

85. This situation continues today; see Shamov, O.I., 1995, "Ministry of Health Care and the Medical Industry of the Russian Federation," *International Cooperation on Nuclear Waste Management in the Russian Federation*, International Atomic Energy Agency, Vienna, Austria, pp. 43–50.

86. Yablokov *et al.*, op. cit., note 5, p. 22.

87. Yablokov *et al.*, op. cit., note 5, p. 22.

88. Yablokov *et al.*, op. cit., note 5, p. 22. Where appropriate, Goskomgidromet was to consult with the Ministry of Fisheries.

89. Yablokov *et al.*, op. cit., note 5, pp. 48, 53–54.

90. Yablokov *et al.*, op. cit., note 5, p. 54.

91. Yablokov *et al.*, op. cit., note 5, p. 49.

92. Nilsen, T., Kudrik, I., and Nikitin, A., 1995, "Zapadnaja Litsa," Bellona Arbeidsnotat 5, Oslo, Norway, pp. 12–13.

93. Lystsov, V.N., 1994, "The Yablokov Commission Report on Soviet Radioactive Waste Dumping at Sea: Additional Comments," *Arctic Research of the United States*, Vol. 8 (Spring), pp. 270–272.

94. Nilsen *et al.*, op. cit., note 92, pp. 16–17.

95. These other main storage facilities for spent fuel assemblies are at the naval base at Gremikha, at the naval shipyard at Severodvinsk, and at the Atomflot base of the Murmansk Shipping Company; Nilsen, T., and Bohmer, N., 1994, "Sources to Radioactive Contamination in Murmansk and Arkhangel'sk Counties," Bellona Report, Vol. 1, Oslo, Norway. Spent fuel is also stored on several other bases and on barges operated by the Murmansk Shipping Company.

96. However, the Mayak plant cannot reprocess spent fuel in defective assemblies or from reactors that are liquid-metal cooled or that have damaged fuel assemblies; Bergman *et al.*, op. cit., note 9.

97. NATO, op. cit., note 8, pp. 266–267. In 1987, a pilot vitrification facility was opened at the Mayak complex, which by 1993 had solidified 5000 cubic meters of high-level liquid waste; Bibilashvili, Y.K., and Reshetnikov, F.G., 1993, "Russia's Nuclear Fuel Cycle: An Industrial Perspective," *IAEA Bulletin* 35(3):28–33.

98. Yablokov *et al.*, op. cit., note 5, p. 25.

99. Berkov, op. cit. note 64, p. 65.

100. Yablokov *et al.*, op. cit., note 5, p. 25.

101. NATO, op. cit., note 8, pp. 17, 33.

102. Yablokov *et al.*, op. cit., note 5, p. 36.

103. Yablokov *et al.*, op. cit., note 5, p. 25.

104. List of Participants to the First Consultative Meeting of Contracting Parties to the Convention on the Prevention of Marine Pollution by Dumping of Wastes and Other Matter, 1976, International Maritime Organization, London, UK (LDC 1/INF.1); (LDC 2/INF.1); (LDC 3/INF.1); (LDC 4/INF.1); (LDC 5/INF.1); (LDC 6/INF.1); (LDC 7/INF.1); (LDC 8/INF.1); (LDC 9/INF.1); (LDC 10/INF.1); (LDC 11/INF.1); (LDC 12/INF.1); (LDC 13/INF.1); (LDC 14/INF.1); (LC 15/INF.1); (LC 16/INF.1); (LC 17/INF.1).

105. LDC 5/12:12; LDC 9/12:27.

106. Egge, op. cit., note 67, p. 265.

107. LDC 13/INF.1; LDC 14/INF.1; LC 15/INF.1; LC 16/INF.1; LC 17/INF.1. With the exception of 1991. Goskompriroda had been represented in the delegation since 1988; in 1992 it was elevated to ministerial status.

108. Canfield, op. cit., note 50, pp. 371–372.

109. Yablokov *et al.*, op. cit., note 5, p. 26.

110. Andreev, O.A., and Olsson, M.-O., 1992, The Ecological Situation and Environmental Organizations in the Russian North-West, CERUM Working Paper No. 15, Umeå, Sweden.

111. Feshbach and Friendly, op. cit., note 77, p. 238.

112. In Russian, Novaya Zemlya means new earth.

113. Yablokov *et al.*, op. cit., note 5, p. 6.

114. Canfield, op. cit., note 50, p. 386.

115. Egge, op. cit., note 67, p. 268.

116. Yablokov *et al.*, op. cit., note 5, p. 6.

117. LDC 14/16:36–37.

118. Canfield, op. cit., note 50, p. 379.

119. Canfield, op. cit., note 50, p. 375.

120. LDC 14/16:37.

121. LC 15/16:38–40.

122. Yablokov *et al.*, op. cit., note 5, p. 26.

123. Birnie and Boyle, op. cit., note 24, p. 324.

124. Secretariat of the Joint Russian-Norwegian Export Group for Investigation of Radioactive Contamination in the Northern Areas, op. cit., note 7. A fourth cruise was conducted by the Norwegian Akvaplan-NIVA and the Murmansk Marine Biological Institute in 1992; see Sjoeblom, K.-L., and Linsley, G.S., 1995, "The International Arctic Seas Assessment Project: Progress Report," *IAEA Bulletin* 37(2):25–30.

125. LC 15/16:38–40.

126. Sjoeblom and Linsley, op. cit., note 124.

127. See in particular LDC 14/16:36–37; LC 15/16:38–40; and LC 16/14:19, 23–24.

128. As noted, prior to the dissolution of the USSR the Council of Ministers passed a 1990 Decree on Measures to Secure Implementation of the 1984 Edict on Intensifying Nature Protection in the North; however, in the fluid political situation, this decree failed to be of practical significance. Canfield, op. cit., note 50, p. 371.

129. Stokke, O.S., Anderson, L.G., and Mirovitskaya, N., 1997, "The Barents Sea Fisheries," in *The Effectiveness of International Regimes*, edited by M.A. Levy and O.R. Young, Cornell University Press, Ithaca, NY, USA.

130. Vsya Moskva: Informatsionno-reklamny ezhegodnik 1992/93, 1992, (All Moscow: Information and advertisement yearbook 1992/93), Vsya Moskva, Moscow, Russia.

131. Novaya Rossiya: Informatsionno-statistichesky almanakh '94, 1994, (New Russia: Information and statistical almanac '94), Vsya Moskva/ Mezhdunarodnaya akademiya informatizatsii, Moscow, Russia, pp. 53–55.

132. OTA, op. cit., note 6, p. 217.

133. OTA, op. cit., note 6, p. 218.

134. Canfield, op. cit., note 50, p. 425.

135. OTA, op. cit., note 6, p. 218.

136. LDC 14/16:36–37.

137. Baranovski, V., 1995, "Russia and Its Neighbourhood: Conflict Developments and Settlement Efforts," *SIPRI Yearbook 1995: Armaments, Disarmaments and International Security*, Stockholm International Peace Research Institute, Stockholm, Sweden, pp. 231–264.

138. Canfield, op. cit., note 50, p. 429; at that time, this agency was named the Ministry of Nuclear Energy.

139. Zubkov, Y.I., and Kislov, A.I., 1995, "Federal Nuclear and Radiation Safety Authority of the Russian Federation (Gosatomnadzor)," *International Cooperation on Nuclear Waste Management in the Russian Federation*, International Atomic Energy Agency, Vienna, Austria, pp. 27–36.

140. Roginko, A., 1996, Environmental Security Issues in the Russian Arctic in the Context of INSROP, IMEMO, Moscow, Russia. Thus, Zubkov and Kislov (op. cit., note 139, pp. 27–28) note that Gosatomnadzor had withdrawn permits from three enterprises engaged in processing of radioactive waste, including Mayak, due to a ". . . very complicated situation in radwaste management . . ."; the conference where this article was presented was held one month prior to the decision to reduce the area of competence of Gosatomnadzor itself.

141. Bellona Press Release, 7 February 1996, The Bellona Foundation, Oslo, Norway.

142. LC 16/14, Annex 6.

143. LC 16/14:25.

144. LC 17/14, Annex 5. A facility to concentrate and solidify low-level liquid waste was built in 1991–1992; Castberg and Stokke, op. cit., note 70. p. 35.

145. LC 17/14:30.

146. *NATO Science and Society Newsletter,* No. 45, 3rd Quarter 1995.

147. Proceedings of the conference are published by the International Atomic Energy Agency (IAEA), 1995, International Co-operation on Nuclear Waste Management in the Russian Federation, Proceedings of a seminar organized by the International Atomic Energy Agency at the request of the Nordic states and held in Vienna, 15–17 May 1995, Vienna, Austria.

148. The assignments of a new Task Force on Environmental Matters under the Barents Council in the nuclear waste area were reported to the 1994 Consultative Meeting under the London Convention (LC 17/14:29).

149. Birnie and Boyle, op. cit., note 24, p. 321.

12

Implementation and Effectiveness of the Acid Rain Regime in Russia

Vladimir Kotov and Elena Nikitina

Introduction

The Convention on Long-Range Transboundary Air Pollution (LRTAP) addresses transboundary airborne pollution, primarily in Europe. Under the LRTAP regime a sophisticated monitoring system has been set up and four substantive subagreements have been negotiated: two on sulfur oxides (SO_x) and one each on nitrogen oxides (NO_x) and volatile organic compounds (VOCs). The shift from Cold War politics toward détente played an important role in the development of the regime. The creation of the LRTAP regime marked the turning point in the evolution of Soviet attitudes toward cooperation between East and West. After the 1975 Helsinki Conference, Soviet President Leonid Brezhnev pushed to have the topic of transboundary air pollution included in the discussions of international cooperation designed to promote détente and ease East-West tensions. Traditionally rather uncooperative and reserved toward cooperation with the West during the Cold War, in the late 1970s the USSR was enthusiastic in its support of the LRTAP process. It even favored a 1977 initiative by the Nordic countries on the reduction of emissions causing transboundary air pollution in Europe that contained binding reduction commitments; curiously, this initiative was rejected at that time by most countries in the West.

The origins of Soviet support for acid rain control were quite different from those in Western countries. Whereas the Nordic states supported these control efforts for environmental reasons, the East bloc countries were primarily concerned with "high politics."[1] Soviet goals and approaches to the LRTAP regime were shaped by factors that were both endogenous and exogenous to the LRTAP process. These factors led to national compliance with the regime's commitments at a relatively low cost. The USSR's level of adherence to this international regime appeared to be much higher than its level of adherence

to other international environmental agreements, a disparity that continues in
Russia today. The high degree of compliance did not, however, stem from
concern about solving the problems of acidification. At the time the LRTAP
regime was formed, combatting acid precipitation was mainly regarded as part
of the general air-protection policy; the issue was not placed on the national
environmental agenda until the late 1980s. It is doubtful that before the 1980s
the Soviets would have undertaken international environmental obligations
that might have resulted in severe restructuring of the national economy. Soviet political goals—principally maintaining détente—largely defined national
strategies on the issue, and domestic energy and air-protection policies affected
patterns of national behavioral changes and, subsequently, the variations in the
LRTAP regime's effects in the country.

During the negotiations of LRTAP's first Sulphur Protocol, the USSR insisted that parties be allowed to choose between controlling national emissions of acidifying pollutants and controlling the transborder fluxes of those
pollutants.[2] The USSR chose the narrower goal of decreasing transboundary
pollution for several reasons. During the era of secrecy, the USSR was reluctant to submit to the international community domestic regional emissions data
that "would reveal sensitive economic, energy, and military information."[3] But
a more important reason was that reducing transboundary fluxes would cost
considerably less than controlling national emissions, given that only a small
percentage of Soviet emissions of air pollutants were transported to other countries (between 1.8 and 2.1 percent of its total sulfur emissions and between 1.3
and 1.5 percent of its NO_x emissions crossed national European borders during
the period from 1985 to 1989). Today, about 190,000 tons of sulfur from
European Russia—i.e., Russian territory west of the Ural Mountains—flows
over borders and is deposited in other countries (table 12.1). Most emissions
from European Russia are deposited within the country; about 48 percent of the
sulfur deposition on European Russia comes from foreign sources.[4] The option
of reducing transborder SO_2 fluxes meant the Soviets had to control only those
industrial sources of pollution that posed the greatest problem for neighboring
countries; these industries were mostly located along the USSR's western border. Because only the European part of the country was included in the purview
of the LRTAP regime (see figure 12.1), some heavily polluting industries were
moved eastward, redistributing acid deposition within the country. Thus, an
unintentional negative consequence of the LRTAP agreements may have been

Table 12.1 Balance of Sulfur Deposition in European Russia, in 10^6 g

	Deposition of sulfur		Balance
	Exported to Russia	Imported from Russia	(net deposition in Russia)
Ukraine	395	37	358
Germany	129	0	129
Poland	128	5	123
Belarus	87	14	73
Romania	69	0	69
Czech and Slovak R.	62	0	62
Estonia	46	2	44
Bulgaria	40	0	40
Finland	39	28	11
England	38	0	38
Yugoslavia	28	0	28
Caucasus region	11	4	7
Lithuania	9	4	5
Sweden	8	6	2
Moldova	6	0	6
Latvia	4	2	2
Turkey	4	4	0
Norway	0	10	−10
Kazakstan	4	74	−70
Other sources	97	0	97
Total transboundary deposition	1,204	190	1,014
Total transboundary and domestic deposition	2,506	1,696	−

Source: Gosuidarstvennyi Doklad, 1995, "O Sostoyanii Okruishayshei Prirodnoy Sredy v Rossiiskoy Federacii v 1994 gody" (The state of the environment in the Russian Federation in 1994), Moscow, Russia, MOOSPR, p. 13.

an increase in air pollution in Siberia: while sulfur dioxide (SO_2) emissions in the European part of the USSR decreased, they increased by 12 percent in the Asian part of the country.

The signing of the LRTAP Convention coincided with significant developments at the national level. The first development was the restructuring of the national energy policy in the late 1970s. This policy supported the transition to natural gas, an increase in nuclear power production (especially in European USSR), the development of an energy complex in Siberia, and a shift toward low-sulfur coals. Another was the adoption, in 1980, of a new national

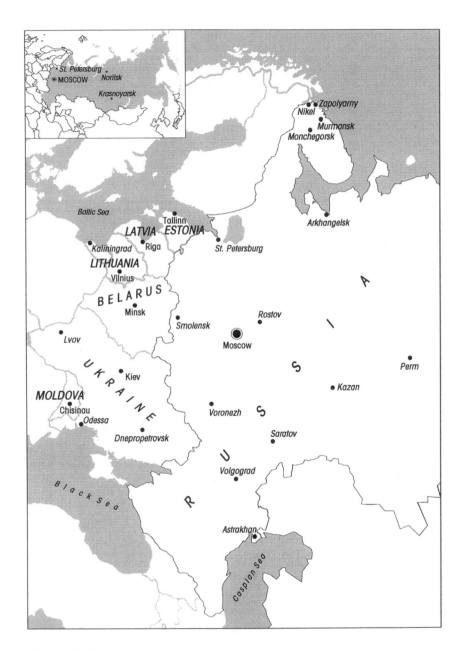

Figure 12.1
The European part of the former Soviet Union

law on air pollution and the introduction of a set of standards and rules on air protection and air quality. These developments contributed significantly to limiting emissions and transboundary flows of pollutants controlled by the LRTAP regime.

The disintegration of the USSR and Russia's subsequent shift toward democracy and a market economy have had a considerable impact on the implementation of LRTAP agreements. A new environmental policy has been formed in Russia that includes the introduction of economic mechanisms for environmental management, decentralization of power, transfer of authority to regional and local levels, wider participation in decision making by nongovernmental actors, and modifications in the patterns of implementation of international agreements. The recent economic crisis and decreases in industrial production in Russia have led to an increase in compliance with LRTAP agreements.

Russia has maintained the high degree of compliance with the LRTAP regime established by the USSR. The USSR was notorious for declaring but not implementing its international environmental commitments. Thus, it is quite remarkable that Soviet and Russian compliance with LRTAP has been high. By the late 1980s the USSR had already met the targets set for SO_2 emissions and for reductions in transborder fluxes according to the first Sulphur Protocol. By 1993, Russia had significantly surpassed the Protocol's commitment to cut sulfur 30 percent below 1980 levels. An important question is whether this high level of national compliance with LRTAP agreements has been due to domestic implementation of the Protocol or to other factors. This chapter assesses which controls on emissions and transborder fluxes can be attributed to LRTAP implementation efforts and which reflect other factors. The real impact and significance of the LRTAP regime on the USSR and Russia are evaluated here. This chapter also examines how the process of transition has influenced Russian implementation of and compliance with LRTAP agreements.

Russia and the Acid Rain Regime

Russia is both an exporter and an importer of transboundary air pollution (see table 12.1). According to scientific evaluations at the time the LRTAP Convention was signed, due to prevailing westward air currents 5 to 10 times more sulfur and nitrogen pollutants were carried into the USSR from Western Europe than flowed out of the USSR to Western Europe.[5] The primary foreign sources of air pollution were in Poland, East Germany, Czechoslovakia, West Germany, and Romania. The Scandinavian countries—especially Finland—were net importers of Soviet pollution (Finland imported more SO_2 from the USSR than it exported to the USSR, but it exported more NO_x to the USSR than it imported).[6] Since the collapse of the USSR, Ukraine and Belarus have become major exporters of transborder air pollution to Russia. The USSR frequently used its position as a victim of transborder acid deposition in negotiations and political bargaining, a practice that continues in Russia today. This position has been rather important in the formulation of national approaches to the acid rain regime.

In addition to regulatory commitments on emissions and their transborder fluxes, the LRTAP regime contains programmatic commitments concerning the formation of national monitoring systems as parts of the Cooperative Programme for Monitoring and Evaluation of the Long-Range Transmission of Air Pollutants in Europe (EMEP). EMEP has two international monitoring centers, one located in Norway, the Meteorological Synthesizing Centre–West (MSC-W), and one located in Russia, the Meteorological Synthesizing Centre–East (MSC-E). Through EMEP, Russia participates in international data exchange and compiles national inventories of emissions of acidifying compounds.

The USSR entered into the LRTAP regime primarily for political, rather than environmental, reasons. But the USSR, and later Russia, became rather proud of its active participation in this regime and of its high level of national compliance with the regime's standards and rules. Data on dramatic reductions in sulfur emissions were widely used to illustrate compliance with LRTAP provisions and the efficacy of domestic air-protection policies. The exemplary results were often cited as examples of national willingness to participate in international environmental efforts on the global change agenda. Extensive participation in scientific activities under the LRTAP regime illustrated the Soviet and Russian scientific community's role in addressing the acid rain problem.

Although Russia exceeded its international obligations on emission reductions under the Sulphur Protocol, acidification of the environment remains rather high in certain regions of European Russia. The LRTAP regime has not been effective in solving problems of acidification in these areas or in some regions of other countries.

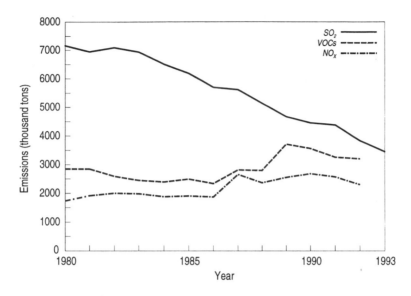

Figure 12.2
Emissions of acidifying substances from European Russia
Sources: Russian Federation National Environmental Report and EMEP.

Compliance with Sulphur Protocols

In accordance with the 30 percent reduction target of the 1985 Helsinki Sulphur Protocol, by 1993 SO_2 emissions in European Russia had decreased 51.7 percent from their 1980 level (see figure 12.2). Only part of this reduction, however, arose from policies implemented as a result of the LRTAP regime. Since the end of the Soviet era, some reductions have been due to economic decline, not to policy actions, and some reductions have been the result of changes in domestic energy and environmental policies.

Russia signed the second Sulphur Protocol in 1994 (it has not yet been ratified). The Protocol calls for reductions in sulfur emissions in European Russia by 38 percent in 2000 and by 40 percent in 2005 and in 2010, using 1980 levels as the basis for calculating the reductions.[7] Although a recent official report finds that international obligations "to reduce sulfur dioxide emissions fixed by the second Sulphur Protocol had been already achieved during 1990–1992,"[8] it is too early to assess complete compliance with the second Sulphur Protocol: Russian emissions may increase when the economy recovers.

Compliance with the 1988 NO$_x$ Protocol

The USSR signed and ratified the NO$_x$ Protocol, which requires a freeze of emissions or transboundary fluxes at 1987 levels by 1994, but subsequent domestic action was rather modest. Nitrogen oxide emissions are considerably more difficult to control than sulfur discharges. Compared with the 1987 level, NO$_x$ emissions from stationary sources and from automobiles decreased by 13.4 percent in 1992 in European Russia (figure 12.2). This decrease was mainly the result of a reduction in discharges from stationary sources caused by the decline in industrial production in the country. Emissions from mobile sources, which have proved more difficult to deal with, continue to grow. As with sulfur, NO$_x$ emissions may increase further in the near future once the economy recovers from the current economic recession.

VOC Protocol

Russia is not a party to the VOC Protocol. Volatile organic compounds do not contribute to acid rain; rather, they are a precursor to tropospheric ozone and smog—primarily national, not transboundary, problems. By 1993 emissions of VOCs (including methane) in European Russia had decreased 1.5 percent from their 1988 level; this was the domestic target set by Russia after the elaboration of the VOC Protocol.[9]

Until recently, domestic standards for VOCs were based on the pollutants' toxicity to humans, not on their contribution to tropospheric ozone.[10] Inventories of VOC emissions from enterprises are compiled using this approach. Recently, domestic goals for VOC emission reductions were expanded to include transboundary environmental effects. Targets were set to cut emissions or their transborder fluxes by 30 percent by 2000, using the 1988 level as a basis for measuring the reductions.

Domestic Implementation of the LRTAP Regime

Institutional Framework

After the USSR ratified the LRTAP agreement, a governmental interdepartmental commission was created to regulate domestic implementation; the commission was headed by the State Committee on Hydrometeorology (Goskomgidromet).[11] In the absence of a specialized environmental agency,

Goskomgidromet was also responsible for the management of national air-protection activities. The main functions of the interdepartmental commission were to coordinate domestic efforts to comply with LRTAP requirements and to elaborate measures to prevent transboundary pollution. It had to create an infrastructure to facilitate exchange of information, processing of monitoring results, and adherence to established targets.

There were two categories for membership in the interdepartmental commission: one included representatives from the Soviet republics that contributed to westward transborder fluxes of air pollutants (Russia, Ukraine, Moldova, Belarus, Estonia, Latvia, and Lithuania); the other included representatives from the central ministries and organizations involved in solving this environmental problem, including those responsible for the main emission-producing industries.

As was typical in the Soviet system, the interdepartmental commission issued commands to the industrial ministries (ministries of energy, ferrous and nonferrous metallurgy, coal, oil-processing industry, etc.) that controlled polluting enterprises. Industrial ministries then established and enforced standards for emission reductions for these enterprises. These LRTAP-induced standards were incorporated into a broader system of domestic environmental regulations that were imposed on each polluter by the industrial ministries. The industrial ministries also incorporated these standards into their annual and five-year plans on air protection. The standards were introduced into the national plans of economic and social development, and thus implementation became obligatory. In this way, the national economic plan served as an instrument for the implementation of LRTAP agreements. The central industrial ministries also issued commands to their western (republic) branches.

Most of the pollutants flowing west originated along the USSR's western border. For example, 85 percent of the SO_2 emissions that drifted to the West originated in sources situated within a 300-kilometer belt along the border. About 50 percent of Soviet SO_2 transborder emissions originated in the Murmansk, Leningrad, Kaliningrad, and Karelia oblasts (provinces) of Russia and in Estonia, Lithuania, Latvia, and Moldova, and about 35 percent were from Ukraine and Belarus. Therefore, reduction measures concentrated on these areas. For the most critical sources of transborder pollution—for instance, from nonferrous smelters on the Kola Peninsula (see Chapter 13)—the interdepartmental commission participated in setting targets at the micro level for specific industries; together with the responsible industrial ministries, it designed programs for emission reductions from these plants.

This was the institutional framework for LRTAP implementation in the USSR during the 1980s, when the first LRTAP Sulphur Protocol was first incorporated into domestic planning. Since then, significant institutional changes have taken place, including the restructuring of environmental management and the formation of a new institution. This institution was initially established in 1988 as the State Committee on Environmental Protection; in 1991 it became the Federal Ministry of Environmental and Natural Resources Protection. The responsibility for coordinating LRTAP implementation, together with other functions in the environmental sphere, was transferred from Goskomgidromet to the new ministry. However, a new interdepartmental commission responsible for LRTAP implementation has not yet been created, although bureaucrats in the environmental agency have been pushing for its establishment.[12] Without such a commission, bureaucrats in the environmental ministry are unsure about the future of LRTAP implementation.

The division of institutional responsibilities for implementation of the LRTAP regime remains uncertain. Goskomgidromet is still responsible for air-pollution monitoring, but the main functions for air-quality control have been transferred to the Ministry of Environment. In practice, this division is unclear. Institutional responsibilities for LRTAP implementation at the central, regional, and local levels also have not been clarified. With the general decentralization of power, regions and separate enterprises are increasing their roles in the decision-making process regarding implementation of LRTAP policies. Formerly powerful, centralized industrial ministries are losing their authority; they can no longer totally control the activities of producers that are becoming increasingly independent through privatization. Socialist central plans for social and economic development—special mechanisms to move tasks, orders, and targets from top to bottom and from center to periphery—are no longer binding. In short, the institutional framework for implementing LRTAP in Russia is being completely revised.

Surprisingly, it appears that the old institutional structure of the interdepartmental commission will be replicated in the new system. The old institutional form fit perfectly with the centralized system of economic management. However, in the wake of the radical political and economic changes that have taken place in Russia, including decentralization and reduction of federal power, the authority and effectiveness of this kind of institutional organization have diminished dramatically. In the old system, the interdepartmental commission controlled substantial financial resources and had power and authority over other institutions; the commission could provide effective implementation of international commitments. In contrast, the Ministry of Environment (which was reduced to a state committee in 1996) does not possess such resources, nor does it have direct control over other actors involved in implementation of the LRTAP regime. The extreme difficulties in implementing LRTAP-related programs are due not only to a lack of funds, but also to a lack of control over those funds that are available. Moreover, although the Ministry of Environment has been given the authority to supervise the environmental activities of industrial ministries, in practice it has not been able to influence the behavior of some of the resistant powerful industrial ministries. The finance issue has frequently been used by industrial ministries as an excuse for implementation failures.

National Strategies and Programs

Before the LRTAP regime, the acid rain issue was treated domestically as part of the general air-pollution problem. Soviet participation in the LRTAP regime helped to transfer the acid rain issue from general air-protection management to an independent element within domestic air-protection policies. This evolution became evident starting in the late 1980s with the development of ecological *glasnost*, the formation of a new environmental policy, and the creation of a specialized institution on environmental protection. The first widely disseminated official document (previously they were circulated only internally) that indicated national strategies and goals for the LRTAP regime was the first national (and the last for the USSR) middle-term environmental program. This program contained a general strategy for LRTAP implementation, quantitative national goals, and concrete measures to achieve them. The program, published in 1990, included the following goals:

- To reduce SO_2 discharges by 30 percent from the 1980 level in European USSR by 1993, and to reduce them by 50 percent by 1995 in the regions bordering Finland; to stabilize NO_x emissions at the 1987 level by 1994, with further reductions to be determined.
- To reduce SO_2 emissions from all stationary sources by a factor of 2.3 (compared with the 1988 level) by 2005; to decrease NO_x emissions by a factor of 1.5 (compared with the 1988 level) by 2005; to reduce NO_x

emissions from mobile sources in cities by 44 percent (compared with the 1987 level) by 1995; to decrease NO_x emissions in the most polluted cities and resort areas by 7 percent (compared with the 1987 level) by 1995.

• To provide low-sulfur fuels to cities with high levels of air pollution; to provide non-ethylene gasoline to Moscow, Leningrad (now St. Petersburg), capitals of Soviet republics, resort areas, and service stations along international roads; to provide 70–80 percent of total gasoline production by 1995.

• To replace liquid motor fuel with compressed and liquid gas (annual production to be no less than 6.5 million tons by 1995).[13]

The USSR compiled this list but did not have time to deal with any individual items before its collapse; all the pollution problems were inherited by Russia. The goal of adherence to LRTAP targets was stressed again in the early 1990s by the Russian Ministry of Environment, and quantitative targets for emission reductions were set for European Russia. The National Plan of Actions to Implement UNCED Decisions envisions many measures including shifts to condensed and natural gas for use in cars, increases in the use of non-ethylene gasoline, introduction of neutralizers, establishment of a network of stations for technical control, introduction of automobile emission standards similar to those in the West, use of alternative sources of energy (solar, thermal, and wind power), and installation of purification facilities for flue gases from stationary sources.[14] A special item was a 50 percent reduction of SO_2 emissions in the Karelia, St. Petersburg, and Murmansk oblasts by 1995 to comply with a bilateral agreement with Finland.

In 1994 a set of long-term goals to reduce acid rain was established within the program entitled Concept of Environmental Security of the Russian Federation. Another state program called Clean Air of Russia, which is currently under development, envisages measures to reduce emissions of acidifying pollutants. Currently, attention is increasingly being paid to the problem of acidification at the national level. However, despite the progress that has been made in the formulation of goals and strategies, not much has been realized in practice. For example, in the Murmansk oblast the goal of a 50 percent decrease in SO_2 emissions has not been met; emissions were curtailed in 1993 by only 30.5 percent of the 1980 level.[15] Today, a serious gap exists between declared goals and their achievement; Russia's implementation of programs has not improved considerably over that of the USSR.[16]

Governmental Management and Regulations in Transition

Starting in the early 1990s, the system of environmental management in Russia, particularly its air-protection policies, was modified considerably. On the basis of the first national environmental law (nothing comparable to it existed before), a new system of environmental management is being introduced. The law calls for shifts to economic instruments (namely, charges for pollution and resource use), the establishment of environmental funds independent of the national budget, and the introduction of new mechanisms to transfer financial resources. Institutional changes include the decentralization of environmental management, the creation of a specialized environmental ministry, and the introduction of obligatory environmental impact assessments. Efforts are being made to develop environmental *glasnost*. The present system is in transition, and several old rules and regulations currently exist together with new ones. A new law on air protection is under development; this law will consolidate all recent changes in environmental management in Russia.

Thus, decentralization of environmental management is under way. Regional and local organs are becoming increasingly involved in environmental control, and the role of industrial ministries has diminished. Most decisions regarding the implementation of international rules are still made at the federal level, although wider decentralization is evident here, as well. Enterprises are gradually becoming direct participants in decision making. Regions and enterprises are usually unaware of what particular international or domestic regulations they are expected to implement. As a rule, local environmental inspectors of enterprises are also unaware of the relevant international standards. There is, however, one group that is very aware of air-pollution regulations. This group is made up of enterprises that contribute considerably to transborder flows of air pollution—such as the Kola enterprises of the Norilsk Nickel nonferrous company (see Chapter 13)—and that are critical sources of transboundary SO_2 emissions. In these cases, federal and regional environmental organs jointly determine the targets for these enterprises, define strategies according to international obligations, and incorporate these targets into national environmental programs. These enterprises receive considerable pressure from federal organs to comply with international regulations.

Currently, notable shifts in the process of implementing international standards are taking place in Russia.[17] These changes, which are reviewed below, coincide with the evolution of the LRTAP regime itself, specifically with the development of second-generation protocols such as the 1994 Sulphur Protocol. This Protocol presupposes the change to a critical-loads approach in setting international targets and in domestic implementation of this international regime. Russia intends to apply this approach in the future not only to European Russia, which is within the purview of LRTAP, but to the entire country. Thus, the international regime is having a growing impact on domestic air-protection policies.

Norms and Standards.   Russia's current system of air-protection regulation and standards is based on meeting domestic standards of air quality: stationary sources of pollution must not exceed maximum allowable emissions (MAEs) calculated on the basis of the standards of maximum allowable concentrations (MACs). Over the past 10–15 years MAE standards have been established for about 13,000 industrial enterprises, including those contributing to transborder pollution; they contribute more than 80 percent of the total air emissions from stationary sources. Currently, the established emission standards are met by a small group of enterprises contributing only 10 percent of air discharges in the country.

As in the Soviet era, Russia's national legislation establishes MAE levels for stationary sources of pollution. For each source of pollution the MAE level is fixed to ensure that urban surface concentrations of pollutants do not exceed established MACs.[18] Harmful emissions in combination with other sources of pollution, air dispersion of harmful matter, and prospects of industrial development in the area are taken into consideration when determining this level.

Current criteria for air quality are based on protecting human health, although in practice they are often adjusted and in many cases relaxed. The current goal is to define new MAC standards that also protect organisms and ecosystems. Ten years ago a provision was introduced to set standards to protect sensitive fauna and flora. In practice, however, these standards were not widely used. Moreover, in some areas they were applied only on an experimental basis. In the near future, a gradual shift from MAE and MAC standards toward critical loads is expected. Studies have been conducted to estimate levels of critical loads in European Russia; these loads have been used to compute SO_2 emission reductions.

Standards for fuel produced in Russia are also being fixed. Efforts to develop new types of gasoline that are environmentally friendly and that meet international standards are currently under way.[19] The sulfur content in diesel fuel was set to be limited to 0.3 percent by 1995 and to 0.005 percent by 2000.

Permits. Permits for air emissions are provided to polluters by special regional environmental organizations of the Ministry of Environment. The permits fix MAE standards for each pollutant and are valid for one year when emissions exceed the allowable standards and for five years when emissions comply with the MAE standards. Violations can result in administrative sanctions and, ultimately, court proceedings, which in turn may result in the closing of an enterprise or its plants.

Payments for Pollution. In 1992 the new system of environmental management introduced payments for pollution;[20] during the Soviet era polluters were not charged. This system can be considered one of the important domestic mechanisms for LRTAP implementation.

Under the new system, a polluter must pay for air pollution emitted within allowable MAE limits; payments increase fivefold for air pollution exceeding MAE limits. Payments for pollution within allowable limits can be deducted as a cost of production, but payments above allowable limits are taken from the polluter's income. Rates of payment for each air pollutant are fixed by the Ministry of Environment, and its regional branches set individual charges for each enterprise in the region. This system is also used for water pollution (see Chapter 14) and for waste disposal. The system is designed to incorporate changes due to inflation, but in practice the real level of payments for pollution has decreased more than fivefold since the early 1990s.

Although the system of pollution payments is an important step toward creating economic incentives for polluting enterprises to decrease their emissions, under current conditions it is not very effective: it does not create adequate incentives for enterprises to increase their environmental investments. Payments are not fully based on an economic analysis of environmental measures, and the rates of payment are underestimated. The result is that polluters often prefer to pay for pollution above the allowable standards rather than invest in environmental facilities. Such a situation creates an incentive for enterprises to be prompt in environmental payments, but to be lax about implementing antipollution measures.

In many cases, emissions of air pollutants greatly exceed the MAE levels fixed for enterprises; consequently, the pollution charges are considerable. Sometimes the required payments even surpass the revenues from an enterprise's economic activities, which can result in its bankruptcy. In practice, authorities are not able to close down an enterprise, especially when the enterprise is economically or socially important to the region. A compromise solution must be sought: allowable limits for emissions are increased by introducing provisionally coordinated emissions (PCEs) for a certain period of time; the firm still pays fees that are higher than those for emissions within MAE limits, but it can deduct all of the fees as costs.[21] In return for this privilege, the enterprise sets up a program of measures to reduce its emissions to MAE limits, and environmental authorities monitor its adherence. Use of PCEs is increasing, and the effectiveness of the payment system is decreasing.

Financial resources derived from environmental charges, payments for use of natural resources, and environmental fines are deposited into the government's non-budget environmental funds. These funds finance environmental activities, such as implementation of ecological projects, programs, and research. According to Russian national legislation, the financial resources of the environmental funds are to be distributed as follows: 60 percent to the local level, 30 percent to the oblast and republican levels, and 10 percent to the Federal Ministry of Environment. With the current deficit in state financing for environmental purposes, the environmental funds, together with enterprise investments, are expected to be a major source of domestic financing.[22] Unfortunately, environmental funds make up only a small share of the financing of environmental protection; according to a recent annual national environmental report, they accounted for only 1 percent of domestic environmental financial transfers in 1992 and 2.4 percent in 1994.[23]

Verification and Control.   Special inspectorates within the Federal Ministry of Environment and its regional branches regularly supervise polluters' activities. Inspectors collect environmental information, verify compliance with emission limits, and monitor the operation of abatement equipment. In cases of violations, negotiations with enterprises are initiated, sometimes followed by fines or court proceedings. In cases of serious violations, environmental authorities, together with the regional administration, can close an enterprise. In practice, this approach is often not possible: powerful interest groups usually enter the scene to stop the closure.

Role of Regional Government

With the transition from Soviet planning, all aspects of Russian governmental activities are being decentralized, and environmental policy is no exception. Participation in the environmental decision-making process, including implementation of international commitments, is expanding at the oblast and local levels. Formerly, regional participation in discussions of international issues was perfunctory. Today, the opinions of regional participants are being considered in the decision-making process at the federal level.[24]

In the past, officials at the oblast level did not take part in discussions of the regional consequences of USSR entry into LRTAP Protocols. The central government passed general standards of emission reductions, as well as specific international obligations, down to the oblast level. This procedure has started to change. For instance, during Russia's entry into the 1994 Sulphur Protocol, the Ministry of Environment conferred with all regions potentially involved in its domestic implementation. The text of the second Sulphur Protocol was sent in advance of its adoption to all of Russia's European oblasts and republics for consideration. The Ministry has also begun to bargain with regions and to lobby for support from them when dealing with other federal institutions. In turn, regional authorities in areas such as Karelia and Leningrad have argued that they will be able to meet international obligations only if support and financing are provided by the federal government. At times regions have suggested direct quid pro quos, telling officials at the federal level, "If you provide additional financing for implementation of international environmental commitments, then we will discuss this issue," or, "If you lay a gas pipeline and provide support from the Ministry of Fuel and Energy, then we will adhere to international provisions." Sometimes territories ignore instructions from the federal level, arguing that the central government should implement the agreements it has signed.

Explaining Compliance and Domestic Implementation

Domestically, the LRTAP regime has contributed to a range of behavioral changes. The most significant changes have been in the development of goals and strategies to reduce transboundary air pollution, in research and monitoring activities, and in air-pollution protection in general. These changes most likely would not have occurred without the LRTAP agreements. However, the LRTAP regime's impact on emission reductions has been quite modest. The main objectives of this section are to describe and evaluate the impacts of the LRTAP regime.

Russia's striking overcompliance with LRTAP's sulfur commitments appears to be predominantly due to exogenous factors. The sharp decrease in SO_2 emissions beginning in the early 1990s is explained in part by domestic antipollution measures and changes in the energy sector, but mainly by curtailed industrial production during the economic crisis. Reductions in NO_x emissions from stationary sources can also be attributed to this factor. These reductions are examples of complying with international agreements without undertaking any domestic implementation measures.

In the 1980s, shifts in domestic air-protection and energy policies caused significant decreases in emissions. These decreases were correlated with, but were not caused by, the LRTAP regime. Beginning in the 1990s, however, the process of economic restructuring—and the attendant economic collapse—had more of an impact on reducing air emissions than activities on implementation of LRTAP provisions and other antipollution measures.

A major portion of the SO_2 emissions decline brought about during implementation of the 1985 Helsinki Sulphur Protocol occurred in the energy sector. Between 1985 and 1992, SO_2 emissions from power stations and boilers decreased nearly 50 percent. Sulfur dioxide emissions from nonferrous metallurgy (another major source of SO_2) declined by 13 percent.[25] Over most of the period, structural changes in the national energy sector were the primary reason for reductions of pollutant emissions and their westward transborder fluxes in European Russia. During this period, coal was replaced by natural gas in many areas. In 1970 coal accounted for 35 percent of total fossil fuel production; its share had decreased to 20 percent by 1988. The share of natural gas increased from 19 percent to 39 percent during this period, and is currently 44 percent; in 1955 the share of natural gas in total USSR fuel consumption was 2.4 percent.[26]

During the 1980s restrictions were imposed on the construction of electric power stations in European Russia. The use of alternative energy sources, particularly nuclear energy, was expanded. Since the accident at Chernobyl, national opposition to reliance on nuclear power has increased. Despite this high level of opposition, however, the current national energy program suggests the need to double the share of nuclear energy in the national energy balance by 2010, on the condition that safety is improved in nuclear power stations.[27] Market reforms in Russia since the early 1990s have raised energy prices and thus decreased energy and electricity consumption, lowering SO_2 emissions still further.

The Russian economic depression has caused industrial production and gross national product (GNP) to decline considerably (by about 55 percent and 50 percent, respectively, from 1990 to 1995). Fuel production and consumption declined, with considerable curtailment in production by ferrous and nonferrous industries. Consequently, SO_2 emissions (as well as NO_x emissions from stationary sources) dropped sharply. However, the decrease in emissions has not been in proportion to the decline in industrial production.[28] An important question is how emissions will be controlled when the economy recovers. Industrial production appeared to be stabilizing at the end of 1995. The decline in GNP slowed, as did price inflation. Both domestic and international experts predict a shift from recession to growth in 1997. The effect on implementation of LRTAP commitments is likely to be mixed. Economic stabilization in Russia will result in more resources available for pollution control, but will simultaneously yield higher emissions.

In sum, many actions undertaken during the 1980s and 1990s to reduce air-pollution emissions in accordance with the LRTAP regime were part of large-scale domestic air-protection policies. They were initiated in the early 1980s with the adoption of the national law on air protection,[29] about the time the LRTAP regime entered into force. Standards were set for allowable concentrations of air pollutants and allowable emissions from enterprises, including acidifying substances. Regulations on fuel quality, especially its sulfur content, were introduced and then tightened by the late 1980s, and enforcement was strengthened. These measures all contributed to implementation of LRTAP's regulatory commitments, though none was explicitly brought about by the LRTAP regime's first Sulphur Protocol.

The timing of these developments may give the impression that the LRTAP Convention and the Sulphur Protocol had a significant impact on Soviet air-pollution and energy policies. However, it appears that the USSR successfully tailored its international commitments within the LRTAP regime to coincide with domestic energy policies and activities in industrial sectors. Almost none of the actions undertaken to adhere to LRTAP provisions were induced by the treaty; thus, the LRTAP regime had less of an effect on the reductions of polluting emissions than on development of research and monitoring.

However, there was one exception to this generalization. The *net effect* of LRTAP's regulatory commitments on sulfur is evident in the changes that led to the reductions of emissions and their transborder fluxes from stationary sources along the country's western border. The majority of SO_2 transborder flows from the USSR to the West originated in a 300-kilometer belt along the border, and much of the domestic action taken to comply with the Sulphur Protocol concentrated on pollution sources in this zone.

The shorter history of the implementation of the 1988 NO_x Protocol makes the claims about its effectiveness difficult to prove. The implementation of concrete measures to reduce NO_x discharges from mobile sources can be attributed mainly to national policy developments, rather than to the impact of the Protocol. Similar to SO_2 reductions, the decrease in NO_x emissions from stationary sources since the early 1990s is a result of the decline in industrial production in the country.

Currently, discharges from automobiles account for 44 percent of the total volume of emissions in cities and towns, and this trend is increasing. Automobile emissions are supplemented by discharges from air, water, and rail transport. Russia's 1994 State Environmental Report indicates that the annual growth of average NO_x concentrations (up 9 percent) was due to an increase in the number of cars, including those in need of repair.[30] Today, the framework of the national air-protection policy emphasizes measures to decrease air emissions from transport—an area in which progress is slow and difficult.

Effects of the LRTAP Regime on Science and Monitoring

Scientific Learning
Although the LRTAP regime has had little impact on the behavior of polluters, it has contributed to scientific learning and the dissemination of information on acid rain and long-range pollution in Russia. Soviet meteorology and climatology were already well advanced in the late 1970s. At the start of the LRTAP negotiations, Soviet scientists tried to integrate into the international scientific community and participate in the international scientific exchange

on related issues. At the time, these contacts were encouraged by domestic policymakers because establishing contacts with the West was a major political goal of Soviet participation in the LRTAP process.

Prior to the LRTAP regime, scientific understanding of damage from acidification was poorly developed. There were no regular assessments of damage from acid deposition. Random and uncoordinated attempts to estimate damage were made by some Russian scientists, but methods varied and the quality of results was poor. The LRTAP agreements definitely stimulated coherent studies in this field through joint research programs and regular monitoring and analysis of acidification. As a result of such efforts, in the late 1980s maps of damage from acidification and regional levels of acidity in different ecosystems were published for the first time; since then, maps of this type have been produced on a regular basis.

Monitoring

The USSR initiated the development of the EMEP system in the country, and Russia has continued this activity. This is a unique example of Soviet and Russian receptiveness not only to the regular international exchange of data but to an international division of labor in this field. Although it preferred not to provide information on regional distribution of emissions, the USSR showed more openness in terms of information exchange in EMEP than in other environmental agreements.

Under the LRTAP regime a special system of 12 observation stations along the western border of the USSR was created. Today, the EMEP monitoring network in Russia consists of three monitoring stations; air pollution is also monitored in 138 cities and 390 stations in European Russia. The LRTAP regime helped to improve the national system, and the observation programs were expanded and calibrated within the EMEP scheme (see also Chapter 7). Consequently, data on export-import fluxes, deposition, and concentrations of pollutants within European Russia are now available.

One effect of the LRTAP regime is progress in national participation in international data compiling and processing. Officials report that EMEP's MSC-E (in Moscow) is ready to expand its network of observation stations eastward to create a system of grids east of the Ural Mountains.[31] MSC scientists have developed a computerized model to calculate long-range transport and deposition of air pollutants in the Northern Hemisphere. Recently, MSC-E advanced to modeling and calculating transborder fluxes of air pollutants to the Arctic. Transborder fluxes between Russia and other former Soviet republics are also evaluated. Within the recently adopted federal program on the formation of a national environmental monitoring system, a special section has been set up to deal with the control of transboundary air pollution. Despite efforts to develop national environmental monitoring systems beginning in the late 1970s, such initiatives seem unlikely without the LRTAP regime.

New Approaches: Critical Loads

As a consequence of the LRTAP regime, the concept of critical loads has gained prominence in Russian environmental management and is expected to replace the MAC and MAE concepts not only in European Russia but throughout the country. Critical loads are the pollution threshold above which sensitive ecosystems experience significant damage; such loads allow calculation of allowable pollution loads, based on rational scientific management. Russian scientists believe that there are regional differences both in acid deposition and in the allowable critical loads. Such differences are particularly important for countries like Russia with diverse environmental and climatic conditions. Based on critical loads, a differentiated approach to the optimization of pollutant emissions (or their fluxes) has been developed. The research is initially concentrating on the methodology of estimating allowable critical loads common to all LRTAP parties.

Since 1994 Russian scientists have been defining and mapping critical loads for European Russia. Using Western methods, critical loads were calculated for 1,315 grid points according to the 60 percent scenario of 1994 Sulphur Protocol. The final results and methodologies should be compatible with those used by researchers working in the East and the West. The results have been used to estimate critical loads for European Russia as well as the levels of SO_2 reductions necessary within regions.[32]

Inventories

The effects of the LRTAP regime on emission inventories have recently become apparent. A number of serious problems exist in Russia in this sphere, mainly associated with the character of the domestic system of statistical data, but also with the need to alter the national system of environmental reporting. The sectoral principle of economic management, inherited from the USSR, is still functioning in Russia. Government statistics from all sectors of economic activities and the compilation of data on air pollution are based on the sectoral principle, as well. It has proved difficult for Russia to shift from the Soviet system of sectoral statistics to the new geographic system classified according to EMEP requirements. An additional aggravation is the inadequate supply of financial resources available for restructuring. Nonetheless, a new system, made possible by general changes in environmental management, is currently under development. It is unlikely that such changes in domestic inventories could have occurred a decade ago.

In sum, EMEP standards and programmatic commitments and activities under EMEP have led to considerable improvement in knowledge about Soviet and Russian sources and effects of acid deposition. In this area, the LRTAP regime has had its largest impact on Russian national policy. The influence of EMEP is most evident in the application of the critical-loads concept to pollution management in Russia.

Conclusions

For the USSR, the political effects of the LRTAP regime were more important than the environmental effects. As has been shown, Soviet implementation was focused on transboundary fluxes and emission sources along the western border. Other, unrelated trends in energy use and industrial production, as well as domestic activities in air protection, helped ensure compliance. The effects of the LRTAP regime on the scientific community were much stronger than its effects on emission reductions. Russia made a number of substantial changes in its environmental policy in the early 1990s; consequently, considerably more attention is being paid to acidification issues; the knowledge base for addressing these issues has improved substantially because of LRTAP, especially EMEP. The effects of the LRTAP regime on science and monitoring continue to grow, including new approaches to compiling inventories of acidifying substances and the gradual shift to a critical-loads approach.

Transition from the Soviet system and the introduction of new mechanisms in environmental protection have had varied effects on the implementation of LRTAP's regulatory commitments. The elimination of the central planning mechanism has made it more difficult for the central government to influence the behavior of emitters. With decentralization of environmental policies, regions are increasingly involved in decision making in this field. Economic decline and local control have made public authorities unwilling to fully apply emission standards and pollution charges. Nonetheless, compliance with the Sulphur Protocol has increased and domestic commitments under it have been overfulfilled. However, the main cause for overcompliance has been economic depression, not implementation.

The future of policy coordination for LRTAP implementation between Russia and the other states of the former Soviet Union is uncertain. The USSR entered into the LRTAP regime representing all of the republics except Ukraine and Belarus, which were autonomous participants in the negotiation process as United Nations members and formal members of the agreement.[33] However, the republics' actions in the implementation of the LRTAP regime were coordinated by the central Soviet government. Variations in the republics' interests— suppressed by the central government—were caused by regional differences in emissions of acidifying pollutants from industrial sources, as well as by differences in contributions to transborder air pollution across the western border of the USSR.

The distribution of SO_2 sources and NO_x pollution within the USSR was very uneven. About 50 percent of total Soviet SO_2 fluxes originated in the Murmansk, Leningrad, Kaliningrad, and Karelia regions of Russia and in the republics of Estonia, Latvia, Lithuania, and Moldova; about 35 percent originated in Ukraine and Belarus.[34] Before the LRTAP initiative, these regional differences were intentionally disregarded in the decision-making process. The regime, especially the EMEP system, contributed significantly to improved understanding of these differences in levels of regional emissions and transborder fluxes. Virtually all data and evaluations came from EMEP's Synthesizing Centres. Strategies, response options, and patterns for implementation of the international regime were determined and coordinated by the central government. However, there were large differences in SO_2 reductions across regions between 1980 and 1989.[35]

The breakup of the USSR has had immense consequences for domestic implementation of the LRTAP regime. Russia declared its succession to all international obligations of the USSR. Ukraine and Belarus, previously parties to the 1979 LRTAP Convention and the Sulphur and NO_x Protocols, are expected to continue to participate in the LRTAP process. Estonia, Latvia, and Lithuania have declared their intentions to become parties to the LRTAP regime, but it is unclear whether Moldova will assume treaty obligations. The issue of the rights and obligations of the newly independent states is important, as these countries have many sources of transborder fluxes to the West.

The LRTAP regime emphasizes both the need for the newly independent states to establish new relations with the countries of Western Europe and the need for them to interact with one another, as well. Thus, the regime could have significant implications for the regulation of transboundary pollution among newly formed states, whose previous differences in "national" interests were skillfully subdued by the central authority in Moscow to avoid regional conflicts. Flows of air pollutants that were classified as internal when they crossed borders between the Soviet republics now qualify as international fluxes. Establishing new patterns of interrelations between these republics as polluters and victims of pollution could negatively affect their already unstable and conflictual interactions, not only on environmental problems but on a broader scale as well.

Russia, for instance, may look to the LRTAP regime to seek redress for a situation in which it receives 10 times as much air pollution from Ukraine and Belarus as it directs toward them. A major contributor to transborder flows between the former republics is Ukraine, which exports the same amount of pollutants as Germany and Poland together (in 1992 its SO_2 and NO_x exports to Russia were 393,000 and 110,200 tons, respectively). To its disadvantage, Russia may now be expected to reduce the large volumes of SO_2 and NO_x emissions that flow across its now national border with Kazakstan (about 149,000 and 762,000 tons, respectively, in 1992 from European Russia); these amounts are higher than those exported to Finland, Norway, and Sweden together (47,000 and 6,100 tons, respectively).[36] It is interesting to note that official data on transborder flows of air pollutants between the former republics were widely published for the first time in the 1992 National Environmental Report of Russia. It seems that not only environmental *glasnost* but the LRTAP regime itself have contributed greatly to the development of transparency between the newly independent states.

In 1992, an environmental agreement was adopted by 10 countries in the Commonwealth of Independent States. Among other items, the agreement presupposes coordination of the air-pollution policies of the member states. In the short term little cooperation can be expected in domestic efforts to reduce transboundary pollution, given the disarray of the economic and political transition in the countries of the former Soviet Union and the myriad other divisive issues that have accompanied the disintegration. Nevertheless, some initial steps have been taken to coordinate actions to model and monitor transborder fluxes. Russia and especially the EMEP center based in Moscow are taking the leading role in coordinating these efforts.

Notes

1. For details see Levy M., 1993, "European Acid Rain: The Power of Tote-Board Diplomacy," in *Institutions for the Earth: Sources of Effective International Environmental Protection*, edited by P. Haas, R. Keohane, and M. Levy, The MIT Press, Cambridge, MA, USA, p. 82; Chossudovsky, E., 1988, *East-West Diplomacy for Environment in the United Nations: The High Level Meeting within the Framework of the EEC on the Protection of the Environment: A Case Study*, New York, NY, USA; McCormick J., 1989, *Acid Earth: The Global Threat of Acid Pollution*, 2nd edition, Earthscan, London, UK; Lammers, J., 1991, "The European Approach to Acid Rain, in *International Law and Pollution*, edited by M.D. Barstow, University of Pennsylvania Press, Philadelphia, PA, USA.

2. Izrael, Y., 1984, Ekologia I Kontrol Sostoyania Prirodnoy Sredy, 2nd edition, Gidrometeoizdat, Moscow, Russia, p. 465.

3. McCormick, J., 1986, *Acid Earth: The Global Threat of Acid Pollution*, Earthscan, London, UK, p. 64.

4. Gosuidarstvennyi Doklad O Sostoyanii Okruizhauishei Prirodnoy Sredy v Rossiiskoy Federacii v 1994 gody, 1995, Ministry of Environment, Moscow, Russia, pp. 12-13; Barret, K., Seland, O., Foss, A., Mylona, S., Sandnes, H., Styve, H., Tarrason, L., 1995, European Transboundary Acidifying Air Pollution: Ten Years Calculated Fields and Budgets to the End of the First Sulphur Protocol, Cooperative Programme for Monitoring and Evaluation of the Long-Range Transmission of Air Pollutants in Europe (EMEP), Meteorological Synthesizing Center–West, Oslo, Norway.

5. Insarov, G., Fillipova, L., 1981, Model vlyania fonovych koncentracyi sernistogo angidrida na rastenya, Problemy Ekologicheskogo Monitoringa I Modelirovanya Ekosystem, Vol. 4, Gidrometeoizdat, Leningrad, Russia, p. 235–250.

6. EMEP, 1991, Estimation of Airborne Transport of Oxidised Nitrogen and Sulphur in Europe—1988, 1989, Meteorological Synthesizing Center–East, Moscow, Russia; Erdman, L., Dedkova, I., Rozovskaya, O., Stryzhkina, I.,

1994, Transgranichnyi Perenos Soedinenyi Sery I Azota v 1992 Godu na Territorii Rossiiskoy Federacii, Ukrainy, Belarusy, Moldovy, Kazahstana, stran Baltii, Zakavkazya i Sredney Azii, Report 12/94, EMEP, Meteorological Synthesizing Center–East, Moscow, Russia.

7. Protocol to the Convention on Long-Range Transboundary Air Pollution on Further Reduction of Sulfur Emissions, Annex II, EB.AIR/R.94, Oslo, Norway, 1994.

8. Gosuidarstvennyi Doklad O Sostoyanii Okruizhauishei Prirodnoy Sredy v Rossiiskoy Federacii v 1994 gody, 1995, Ministry of Environment, Moscow, Russia, p. 11.

9. The 1990 State Environmental Program envisaged VOC emission reductions of 1.7 percent from the 1988 level for the whole country by 2005.

10. Discharges of methane were included in the estimates until recently. Currently, inventories of VOC discharges, apart from methane emissions, are being performed that permit analysis of the feasibility of measures to decrease VOC emissions.

11. Postanovlenye Soveta Ministrov, No. 416, O Merach po Obespecheniy Vypolnenya Obiazatelstv Sovetskoy Storonoy Vytekauishih iz Konvencii o Transgranichnom Zagriaznenii Vozduiha na Bolshie Rastoyania ot 13 noyabria 1979 Goda, Moscow, Russia, 18 May 1982.

12. Interviews with officials at the Russian Ministry of Environmental and Natural Resources Protection, Department of Air Protection, 12 November 1995.

13. The 1990 USSR State Program on Environmental Protection and Rational Use of Natural Resources During 1991–1995 and Until 2005, Ekonomicheskaya Gazeta, No. 41, October 1990.

14. Zelenyi Mir, 1993, No. 19–21.

15. Annual Report of the Murmansk Oblast Environmental Committee, 1994.

16. Nikitina, E., 1995, National Implementation of International Environmental Commitments: A Review of Soviet Literature, WP-95-26, International Institute for Applied System Analysis, Laxenburg, Austria.

17. Kotov, V., 1994, Implementation and Effectiveness of International Environmental Regimes During the Process of Economic Transformation in Russia, WP-94-123, International Institute for Applied Systems Analysis, Laxenburg, Austria.

18. Until recently, general rules of introduction of MAE and MAC were regulated by the 1980 national standard entitled Environmental Protection, Atmosphere: Rules for Establishing Levels of Maximum Allowable Emissions of Harmful Substances from Industrial Enterprises.

19. Gasoline with lead content not higher than 0.01 g/cubic decimeter, sulfur content not higher than 0.05 percent, mercaptan not higher than 0.01 percent, VOCs not higher than 40 percent, and benzene not higher than 5 percent.

20. The 1991 National Law of Russian Federation On Environmental Protection, Article 20.

21. Postanovlenye Pravitelstva RF, 28 August 1992, No. 632.

22. The Effectiveness of International Financial Instruments for Environmental Investment in CEE Countries: Recipients' Perspectives, Final report, 1995, Band 37/1995, Bundesministerium für Umwelt Österreich/UK Department of the Environment, Vienna, Austria, p. 32.

23. Gosuidarstvennyi Doklad "O Sostoyanii Okruizhauishei Prirodnoy Sredy v Rossiiskoy Federacii v 1994 gody," 1995, Ministry of Environment, Moscow, Russia, p. 43.

24. Interviews with officials from the Environmental Committee of Novgorod Oblast, 20 February 1995; the Murmansk Oblast's Environmental Committee, 2 December 1994; and the Ecological Committee of Moscow, 27 April 1995.

25. Zelenyi Mir, 1994, No. 24, p. 64.

26. Expert reports show that, despite the absence of flue-gas desulfurization facilities in many power plants, during the 1980s SO_2 emissions dropped by about 40 percent because of the increased share of natural gas in power production, as well as increases in consumption of low-sulfur coals and cheap open-pit coals; Varnavsky, V., Gromov, B., Kovyliansky, J., 1989, Teplofikacia i ee Rol v Reshenii Socialnyh I Ekologicheskyh Problem, Elektricheskye Stancii, No. 8, p. 38–40.

27. Izvestia, 14 July 1992.

28. Kotov, V., and Nikitina, E., 1996, "To Reduce, or to Produce? Problems of Implementation of the Climate Convention in Russia," in *Verification Yearbook 1996*, edited by J.B. Poole and R. Guthrie, Westview Press, Boulder, CO, USA, p. 339.

29. Zakon SSSR Ob Okhrane Atmosfernogo Vozduiha, in Ob Okhrane Okruizhauishei Sredy, 1986, Politicheskaya Literatura, Moscow, Russia, p. 333–337.

30. Gosuidarstvennyi Doklad O Sostoyanii Okruizhauishei Prirodnoy Sredy v Rossiiskoy Federacii v 1994 gody, 1995, Ministry of Environment, Moscow, Russia, p. 9, 201.

31. Interview with officials at the EMEP Meteorological Synthesizing Center–East, Moscow, Russia, 2 September 1994.

32. Ten categories of emissions sources were determined: power and heating stations, facilities for burning fuel, industrial equipment engaged in burning fuel, technologies that are not engaged in burning fuel, mining and distribution of fuel, solvents use, automobile transport, waste disposal, agriculture, and natural sources.

33. Currently, Ukraine, Belarus, Lithuania, and Latvia participate in the LRTAP Convention.

34. The primary Soviet sources of SO_2 transborder air pollution were situated in Ukraine (transborder fluxes across the western border in 1989 were about 111,000 tons), Russia (46,000), Belarus (14,000), Moldova (13,000), Estonia (7,000), Lithuania (7,000), and Latvia (2,000). Data on NO_x fluxes indicate that the primary exporters to Western Europe were Ukraine (25,900), European Russia (9,400), Belarus (6,600), Moldova (2,700), Lithuania (1,800), and Estonia (1,400). Calculations are based on EMEP/MSC-E data.

35. The percentages of SO_2 emission reductions between 1980 and 1989 were the following: Estonia, 58 percent; Lithuania, 18 percent; Latvia, 2 percent; Leningrad oblast, 34 percent; Murmansk oblast, 13 percent; Karelia, 8 percent; Ukraine, 16 percent; Belarus, 13 percent; Moldova, 6 percent; Russia, 35 percent.

36. EMEP, MSC-E Report, No. 12/94, Moscow, Russia, 1994, pp. 32, 68.

13

Regime and Enterprise: Norilsk Nickel and Transboundary Air Pollution

Vladimir Kotov and Elena Nikitina

Introduction

Norilsk Nickel, a recently privatized firm, is one of Russia's leading producers of nonferrous and platinum-group metals. It controls one-third of the world's nickel deposits and accounts for a substantial portion of the country's total production of nickel, cobalt, platinum, and palladium. It is also Russia's largest air polluter. Pechenga Nickel and Severo Nickel, its subsidiaries on the Kola Peninsula in the northwestern part of the country, emit large quantities of sulfur dioxide (SO_2), which is responsible for acid precipitation throughout the region. This situation has led to a long-standing dispute between Russia (and before it the USSR) and the countries downwind from the Kola Peninsula—principally Finland, Norway, and Sweden. Domestic, bilateral, and international efforts have not yet been able to resolve that dispute.

As part of a new effort to address environmental problems, the Russian government recently approved a project to refurbish Pechenga Nickel's obsolete plant. This project, in which Scandinavian companies are slated to participate, should reduce the facility's emissions of SO_2 by 95 percent. Actually implementing the project, however, will be complicated by the sweeping economic and political changes now occurring in Russia. Among the most important of these changes are the recent (unfinished) privatization of Norilsk Nickel and the resulting nature of the firm's management.

In this chapter the environmental behavior of Norilsk Nickel is examined. The chapter also traces how the USSR and Russia have attempted to implement multilateral and bilateral commitments to reduce pollution, notably pollution from Norilsk's smelters on the Kola Peninsula, which flows into Scandinavia and Finland. The study explores how Russia's transition to a market economy, privatization, and devolution of power upon regional levels have influenced Norilsk. It shows that instruments such as regulation and environmental fees have had little influence on this firm; on balance, Norilsk Nickel has enjoyed greater autonomy during the transition phase than it did during the central planning era.

This paper also examines Western efforts to finance pollution reduction efforts at Norilsk. These efforts, which exemplify the types of projects envisioned under the concept of joint implementation (JI), have been marked by high transaction costs exacerbated by ambiguous property rights. They suggest that workable JI packages depend not only on external funding, which has been the subject of most theoretical research on JI, but also on domestic financing and institutions. The study underscores that when transaction costs are high, property rights are insecure, and host country participation is unstable, JI transfers are unlikely to be successful. In November 1996, a decade after negotiations on financing pollution control efforts at Norilsk Nickel began, the Norwegian government pulled out of the scheme and the project has, for now, collapsed.

Norilsk Nickel

Norilsk Nickel has been called the "diamond in the crown of Russian privatization."[1] It has a virtual monopoly on the production of nonferrous and precious metals in Russia, and it is one of the world's biggest producers of certain metals (see table 13.1). The company employed 162,000 people in 1995 and has had annual sales of about US$2 billion in recent years.[2]

Norilsk Nickel has a fairly elaborate corporate structure, with four main operations: a mining and metal-processing facility at Norilsk in northeastern Siberia (see inset map, figure 12.1 in this volume); a metal-processing facility at Monchegorsk on the Kola Peninsula in the Murmansk region (Severo Nickel); mining and metal-processing facilities at Zapolyarnyy and Nikel on the Kola Peninsula (Pechenga Nickel); and a precious-metals-processing plant at Krasnoyarsk in central Siberia. The company also has a research institute, Gipronickel in St. Petersburg, and a construction facility on the Kola Peninsula. Furthermore, the company has erected entire towns near its facilities, complete with homes, schools, hospitals, shops, and roads; about 500,000 people living in these towns are dependent on Norilsk Nickel.

Because the Soviet government did not release data on the production of nonferrous and precious metals and Norilsk Nickel has only recently begun to do so,

Table 13.1 Market Shares of Major Nonferrous Metal Producers, 1994

Metal	Norilsk Nickel (% of Russian market)	Norilsk Nickel (% of world market)	INCO (% of world market)	Falconbridge (% of world market)
Nickel	80	27	26	18
Copper	40	4	3	3
Cobalt	70	19	9	24
Platinum	100	22	2	1
Palladium	n.a.	62	2	2

Notes: INCO and Falconbridge are both based in Canada; n.a. = not available.
Sources: "Norilsk Nickel," *Segodnya*, 6 February 1995; "Commodities and Agriculture: Russian Smelter Clean-Up Stalled by Cash Shortage," *Financial Times*, 29 September 1994, p. 36; and *Delovoy Mir*, 14 June 1995, p. 3.

the precise scale of the company's operations is difficult to determine.[3] However, recent estimates of the company's nickel output range between 155,000 and 180,000 tons, about 45 percent of which comes from the facilities on the Kola Peninsula.[4]

During recent years, Norilsk Nickel has increasingly oriented its production toward export: its exports of nickel have risen significantly in recent years, from 87,000 tons in 1993 to 120,000 tons in 1995. They now account for more than 50 percent of the company's sales and for 84 percent of all Russian exports of nickel (in 1994 Russia exported 79 percent of its domestically produced nickel).[5] World nickel prices have been stable, and the company has gained an important position in world markets. Currently, Russia supplies one-third of the nickel consumed in Europe. Norilsk Nickel significantly influences the world nickel market, and world prices for nickel are sensitive to the situation at the company. For example, at the end of 1994, as soon as it became known that a breakdown in the energy supply to Norilsk plants had occurred, world nickel prices on the London Metal Exchange increased by about US$400 per ton (approximately 5 percent).[6] The world nickel market has also been sensitive to recent developments in the privatization of Norilsk Nickel.

The financial revenues of Norilsk Nickel stem mainly from its exports. The company has consolidated its economic position considerably during recent years, despite the country's deep economic crisis. Like other natural resource companies in Russia, Norilsk Nickel has weathered the crisis fairly successfully, although its condition deteriorated markedly in 1996. Because export earnings have become an important source of tax revenues, the Russian government also has a vested interest in the company, which paid about 3 trillion rubles (US$670 million) in taxes in 1995.[7]

Norilsk Nickel was privatized in 1993 with the issuance of 126 million shares at 250 rubles per share. The offering attracted approximately 300,000 purchasers, even though 51 percent of the voting shares were to remain in government hands for three years. Norilsk Nickel's balance income in 1994 was 2,108 billion rubles; its net income was 1,543 billion rubles. In 1994, Norilsk paid dividends of 3,314 rubles per share of preferred stock and 1,000 rubles per share of common stock.[8] Experts believe that the current cost of Norilsk Nickel shares is greatly undervalued because it fails to reflect the large deposits of state-owned ore that the company controls (it has 20-year leases on state ore deposits). The attractiveness of this company is closely associated with its unique resource base.

Major Environmental Polluter

Norilsk Nickel and its subsidiaries are the largest source of air pollution in Russia. Its factories rank first on the list of domestic industrial air polluters: the city of Norilsk, in Siberia, is the most polluted in the nation; the city of Monchegorsk has the nineteenth highest level of air pollution in Russia (see figure 12.1 in this volume). The company is responsible for about one-tenth of the total air pollution from all stationary sources in Russia. According to official figures, which most likely understate Norilsk's environmental impacts, the parent company in northeastern Siberia emitted about 1.9 million tons of air pollutants in 1994; that same year, Severo Nickel on the Kola Peninsula emitted approximately 111,000 tons and Pechenga Nickel emitted 132,900 tons.[9] Sulfur dioxide made up about 92 percent of these emissions. The Norilsk facilities, for example, account for 26.4 percent of the SO_2 emissions from stationary sources in Russia. The facilities of Norilsk Nickel play a key role in air pollution reported by the domestic nonferrous sector. That sector emitted 3,502,000 tons of pollutants in Russia in 1993; emissions from Norilsk Nickel plants made up about 66 percent of this total figure.

Norilsk Nickel's facilities have a great impact on overall environmental conditions in the areas where they are located. For example, the Kola plants contribute about 84 percent of the Murmansk region's SO_2 emissions. Moreover, the specific locations of these facilities compound the problem. With the exception of the plant at Krasnoyarsk, all of them are situated north of the Arctic Circle, a region where ecosystems are relatively fragile and lack the assimilative capacity of those in lower latitudes. As a result, Norilsk Nickel's industrial activities have led to wide-ranging environmental degradation and acidification.

On the Kola Peninsula, for instance, an estimated 8,100 hectares of land have been damaged beyond rehabilitation. An additional 126,000 hectares of forested lands, including one-third of a nature reserve in the Murmansk region as well as areas inhabited by indigenous peoples, have suffered. Health problems have also appeared. For example, according to official statistics, Monchegorsk and Norilsk are among the 11 Russian cities with the highest rates of disease among children under 14 due to air pollution. The situation in northeastern Siberia is even worse. In that region, acid precipitation has destroyed 180,000 hectares of forests and damaged an additional 382,000 hectares. Trees have ceased to reproduce and primary productivity is at a minimum within a 120 kilometer radius of the Norilsk facility.[10]

The SO_2 emissions from the Norilsk Nickel Kola facilities are not just an internal problem for Russia, however. A significant portion of these emissions flow across the border into Finland and the Scandinavian countries and contribute to transboundary air pollution. In fact, data for 1992 indicate that the releases from the company's two smelters vastly exceeded the total releases from Norway, Sweden, and Finland combined (they were 10.8, 4.2, and 2.2 times higher than in each of these countries, respectively). In that year, approximately 21 percent of the sulfur deposited in Finland, 12 percent of that deposited in Norway, and 5 percent of that deposited in Sweden originated in the European part of Russia. Large percentages of the deposits came from the Murmansk region, which includes the Kola Peninsula (see table 13.2). In the early 1990s, about 6–7 percent of the annual SO_2 emissions from the Murmansk region were transported to Scandinavia. Facilities in the Murmansk region are responsible for about 70 percent of the SO_2 originating in Russia and deposited in Scandinavian countries in general, and for about 91 percent of that deposited in Norway in particular. Not all the air pollution problems in the region originate in Russia, however. The flows of nitrogen oxides (NO_x) from Finland, Norway, and Sweden into Russia are 8 to 15 times greater that those flowing in the opposite direction.[11]

Table 13.2 Emissions and Transborder Fluxes of Sulfur Dioxide, 1992 (in 1,000 tons)

Source	Emissions	Deposition[a]		
		Finland	Norway	Sweden
European Russia	4,400	30 (20.9)	11 (11.9)	6 (4.9)
Murmansk region	514	19 (13.2)	10 (10.8)	4 (3.3)

[a]Numbers in parenthesis are the percentages of sulfur deposits in each country attributable to sources in Russia.
Sources: Tuovinen, J.P., Barrett, K., and Sryve, H., 1994, "Transboundary Acidifying Pollution in Europe: Calculated Fields and Budgets 1985–93," EMEP/MSC-W Report 1/94, p. 22; Erdman, L.K. et al., 1994, Transgranichnyi perenos soedinenyi sery i azota v 1992 godu na territorii Rossiiskoy Federatsii, Ukrainy, Belarusi, Moldovy, Kazakhstana, Stran Baltii, Zakavkazia i Sredney Azii (Transboundary air pollution involving sulfur and nitrogen compounds in the Russian Federation, Ukraine, Belarus, Moldovia, Kazakhstan, the Baltic states, the Caucasus, and central Asia in 1992), EMEP/MSC-E, pp. 31–32; *Okruizhayuishaya Prirodnaya Sreda Rossii (Russian Environment)*, EKOS, Moscow, Russia, pp. 38–39.

Failure of International and Domestic Regulatory Efforts

Starting in the late 1970s, efforts to address the problem of acid precipitation originating from Norilsk Nickel's nonferrous facilities on the Kola Peninsula have been undertaken both internationally—on the multilateral and bilateral levels—and domestically. They were pursued by the USSR before its collapse, and have subsequently been taken up by Russia. However, none of these regulatory efforts have had much influence. Only since the early 1990s has the influence of regulation become more evident.

Multilateral Accords

In 1979, the USSR signed the international Convention on Long-Range Transboundary Air Pollution (LRTAP) (see Chapter 12). That agreement and the 1985 Sulphur Protocol required the country to reduce SO_2 emissions in its European part, or their transboundary fluxes, by 30 percent (relative to the 1980 level) by 1993. Despite the fact that the revised 1994 Sulphur Protocol requires even greater reductions and establishes emission ceilings for European Russia,[12] Russia has already met the emission reduction goals of both Protocols.

Although not specified directly in the first Sulphur Protocol, Norilsk Nickel's nonferrous smelters on the Kola Peninsula, together with some other critical sources of transboundary air pollution situated mainly within the 300 kilometer

belt along the western border of the USSR (where about 85 percent of transborder SO_2 flows originate), were among the Protocol's main targets in the
USSR. During the 1980s, the Kola facilities frequently "endangered" national
compliance with this international regime, and experts considered them to be
the problem most likely to result in a violation of international obligations.[13]

Bilateral Accords
In addition to the multilateral commitments adopted to address the problem of
transboundary air pollution, there have also been efforts at the bilateral level
between Scandinavian countries and the USSR, and later Russia.

Cooperation on environmental protection began in the 1980s between the
USSR and Finland as part of their active bilateral economic and technical cooperation. In 1985 the USSR entered into an environmental agreement with
Finland, and by 1989 the two countries had adopted an action program for
reducing air pollution along their common border and a protocol for cooperation on the Kola Peninsula.[14] These agreements went further than the LRTAP
Protocol, requiring each country to reduce its SO_2 emissions in border regions
by 50 percent (relative to the 1980 level) by 1995. Russia has not met that
goal. In 1992, Finland and newly independent Russia adopted a framework
environmental agreement and an agreement on cooperation in several different
spheres that affects Russia's entire northwest, not just the Kola Peninsula.[15]

Since the late 1980s there has also been greater environmental cooperation
with Norway. In 1988, the USSR signed an agreement with Norway for the
protection of nature, which Russia affirmed in 1992.[16] Although the agreement
focused on the Kola Peninsula, it did not include targets for reductions in air
pollution. The emphasis of this agreement was on a broad range of environmental problems and on development of monitoring and scientific research on
acid rain impacts.

The 1980s were marked by active public pressure in the Scandinavian countries on the issues of transboundary air pollution and acid rain: Norilsk Nickel's
facilities on the Kola Peninsula were the main targets of public and political
campaigns, which identified them as principal sources of acidifying substances
deposited in Scandinavia. Local public protests in Russia on this issue began
only in the early 1990s with the introduction of *glasnost* and the development of
the green movement in Russia. During the Soviet period, accurate information
about the environmental situation on the Kola Peninsula was withheld from the

public; under *glasnost*, more information on the sources and consequences of Kola pollution was available to the public.

Domestic Measures

Several responses were undertaken at the governmental level to implement these international commitments to reduce air pollution. The Soviet government imposed severe restrictions on SO_2 emissions within the country. Norilsk Nickel's two smelters on the Kola Peninsula were prime targets of this effort. In the mid-1980s, the government ordered the Kola plants to reduce their emissions to 204,000 tons (from 590,000 tons in 1980) by 1993, the target date of LRTAP's first Sulphur Protocol. Following the adoption of bilateral commitments with Finland, the 1990 Soviet governmental program "On environmental protection and rational use of natural resources" envisaged a 50 percent reduction in SO_2 emissions in the northwest regions of Russia bordering Finland by 1995. Once again, the targets for emission reductions were passed along to Severo Nickel and Pechenga Nickel; in keeping with the practice of the Soviet command economy, there were no consultations with the enterprises involved, and those enterprises had virtually no voice in these decisions.[17] Partly for this reason, and partly because the USSR lacked the technology and resources to achieve such emission reductions, the government's ambitious goals went largely unmet and a serious gap existed between the goals and strategies formulated and their implementation.

It is expected that after the 1994 Sulphur Protocol is ratified by Russia, domestic measures to reduce SO_2 emissions from Norilsk Nickel facilities on the Kola Peninsula will be adopted by the environmental protection organs. These measures will be based on the Protocol's scheme on levels of sulfur deposition within each Cooperative Programme for Monitoring and Evaluation of the Long-Range Transmission of Air Pollutants in Europe (EMEP) grid on the Kola Peninsula.

International Measures

Because Soviet domestic measures had little influence on implementation, there were several international attempts to modernize Norilsk's facilities on the Kola Peninsula to help the USSR reduce its transboundary air pollution. Attempts were made to reconstruct the obsolete production process of the Kola facilities with the help of Western participation, especially that of Finland. In the early

1980s, for example, the Finnish company Outokumpu Oy began negotiating with the Soviet government on a proposal to modify the plant at Pechenga Nickel and to partially reconstruct Severo Nickel; the goal of this modernization was a 15-fold reduction in SO_2 emissions in 1994.[18] The Finnish government suggested a 3 billion markka credit (approximately US$700 million) for this project (with the participation of Norwegian and Swedish financial institutions) on the condition of extensive participation by Finnish companies.[19] In this case, the environmental concerns of both parties coincided with their economic interests: the Soviet government was interested in expanding the production of nickel and other metals, and the Finns were interested in increasing their technology-based trade with the USSR and in creating additional jobs for Finland. In the end, however, the project fell through because the USSR objected to its high price (US$600 million, which some experts thought was inflated by a factor of three).[20]

Later, the focus of international measures between the USSR, and then Russia, and the Scandinavian countries shifted. Since the late 1980s, Norway has begun to play a comparatively more active role. Negotiations between the Norwegian and Soviet and Russian governments on environmental upgrading of the Kola smelters developed as part of the implementation process of the intergovernmental environmental agreement. As noted above, another effort to revamp Pechenga Nickel is now in progress in Russia. In 1993, the Russian government solicited bids from foreign companies and selected a proposal from a group of Norwegian and Swedish firms. The project, which was supposed to begin in 1996 but instead collapsed that year, was estimated to cost less than US$300 million. In addition to being less costly than the proposed Finnish-Russian project, if the project is restarted it would benefit from the massive economic and political changes that have taken place in Russia since the breakup of the USSR, as well as from Russia's stronger commitment to the environment and its adoption of a new system of environmental management.[21]

Causes of Emission Reductions

Because Soviet efforts to curb the air pollution emanating from the Kola Peninsula were largely unsuccessful, the problem was inherited by Russia. During the initial stages of implementation of the LRTAP Convention in the USSR, these mechanisms had some effect, at least on the formulation of national goals

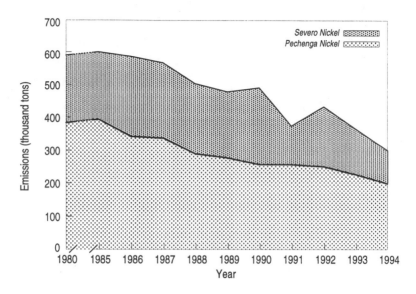

Figure 13.1
Changes in SO₂ air emissions from the Kola enterprises of Norilsk Nickel,
1980 to 1994
Source: Norilsk Nickel; data for 1981–1984 not available.

and strategies on acid rain abatement (see Chapter 12). Later, the impact of this
Convention diminished as it became clear that the targets of the first Sulphur
Protocol would be met. By 1993, the company's two facilities on the Kola
Peninsula—Pechenga Nickel and Severo Nickel—were in nominal compliance
with the initial goal of reducing SO₂ emissions by 30 percent: their emissions
in 1993 were down 40 percent and 34 percent, respectively, from the 1980
levels. There was a stable trend in emission reductions from the second half
of the 1980s, and from the late 1980s the rates of these reductions increased
considerably, to about 50 percent by the mid-1990s (see figure 13.1). The
fact that the plants have met commitments on emission reductions is used as a
powerful bargaining tool in the company's negotiations with the government;
Norilsk Nickel also uses evidence of declining emissions to give the public the
impression that environmental prospects are favorable.[22]

Sulfur dioxide emissions from Norilsk Nickel's facilities on the Kola Peninsula have decreased for several reasons. About 12 percent of the improvement
is the result of operational changes, primarily the installation of scrubbers.

According to official data, Norilsk Nickel currently captures about 7 percent of its sulfur emissions (the level of dust absorption, for example, is much higher, about 94 percent).[23] Further increase in the absorption capacity is scarcely possible for technological and economic reasons.

The principal reason for recent SO_2 emission reductions is a downturn in production at Norilsk Nickel as a result of the country's economic crisis (according to some estimates, nickel consumption in Russia has decreased fivefold since 1990).[24] This reflects the overall economic situation in Russia, where industrial production during recent years has fallen by about 50 percent. Interestingly, these emission decreases have not been in proportion with Norilsk's decline in nickel output. At the Severo plant, for instance, SO_2 emissions have declined 31 percent, while output has decreased 50 percent from the 1989 level.[25]

The implications are that Norilsk Nickel's environmental problems have merely been masked, not solved, and that this trend in declining emissions does not indicate a long-term improvement in the environmental situation, especially if production recovers. On the contrary, until the company invests in cleaner technology, its environmental gains will be largely a mirage. Moreover, once economic growth returns to Russia, production by Norilsk Nickel will increase, and hence pollutant emissions will rise as well.[26]

Why has the Russian nickel industry not made more of an effort to curb its pollution? Are there policy measures—regulatory and otherwise—that the country can use to ameliorate the situation? Are existing regulatory instruments ineffective? To answer these questions, it is necessary to examine the different factors that affect nickel production and environmental policy in Russia.

Technological Options and Prospects

Nickel is processed from sulfide ores, which contain a certain amount of sulfur. This sulfur is released when the ore is processed to extract the nickel. Norilsk Nickel's main base for raw materials is located in Norilsk, which currently produces about 90 percent of the ores used by all of the company's facilities. Before shifting to consumption of Norilsk ore, the Kola facilities obtained all of their ore locally, exploiting extensive ore deposits with relatively low sulfur contents. These deposits were the basis for the development of the nonferrous metal industry on the Kola Peninsula in the late 1940s. As they declined, however, Kola plants turned to Norilsk's mines in northeastern Siberia, which produce an ore with a high sulfur content.[27]

During the Soviet era Norilsk shipped approximately 1 million tons of ore from Siberia to its Kola facilities every year. Transportation costs, which were quite high due to the length of the sea route and the severity of the climate through which it passed, were not an issue during this era. With the shift to a market economy, however, the company has been forced to contend with these costs, which in effect have risen several hundredfold. This cost increase and the decline in Norilsk's production have led the company to rely more heavily on its deposits on the Kola Peninsula; shipments from Siberia have fallen to 400,000 to 500,000 tons per year.[28]

This development is not as favorable for the environment as it might seem, however. The method that Norilsk Nickel uses to remove sulfur from flue gases entails converting a part of it into sulfuric acid. For the equipment to function properly, however, the concentration of sulfur in the flue gases must be at least 3 percent; otherwise, most of the sulfur will not be absorbed but will simply be emitted into the atmosphere. For this reason, a certain percentage of the ores smelted must be high in sulfur.[29] Of course, more advanced technologies for desulfurization could be obtained from foreign companies, and steps in this direction have already been taken (including the planned reconstruction of Pechenga's smelter). The real questions, however, relate to the availability of financing and to Norilsk Nickel's incentives to invest in cleaner technology. In this regard, the regulatory climate in Russia is extremely important.

Domestic Environmental Regulations

Under the Soviet regime, the government exercised complete control over industrial operations such as those of Norilsk Nickel. The Ministry of Non-ferrous Metals made all the important decisions, including those pertaining to environmental quality. Other industrial ministries issued numerous directives regarding air pollution control, but they had little effect. Unlike most other countries, the USSR had no agency devoted entirely to the environment with the authority to issue and enforce regulations. Environmental quality was simply too low a priority for the government, which lacked the resources to invest in cleaner technology and could not provide incentives for plants to behave differently. Underlying these failings, of course, was the inability of a command economy to operate efficiently or to make significant technological progress. Limited information about the environment, low levels of public concern, and even lower responsiveness by the central government to these public concerns also contributed to this situation.

The collapse of the USSR brought about a complete change in environmental management in Russia. In 1992, the new Ministry of the Environment instituted a system of pollution charges under which firms may emit various types of pollutants (up to specified limits) but are required to pay fees for the privilege. As reviewed in Chapter 12, these fees are increased fivefold when a firm exceeds the allowable limits. Severo Nickel paid 19 billion rubles (US$4.2 million) in such fees in 1995, compared with 12.5 billion rubles (US$6.3 million) in 1994; these fees were for emissions of air pollutants, water pollutants, and solid waste. Pechenga Nickel paid 20.5 billion rubles (US$4.5 million) in 1995, compared with 9.7 billion rubles (US$4.9 million) in 1994; more than 80 percent of its fees were for emissions of air pollutants, virtually all of which were in the form of SO_2.[30]

These pollution charges were intended to provide incentives for firms to reduce their emissions. In practice, however, they have not had much influence on the behavior of polluters, because the fees being assessed are much lower than the cost of investing in more environmentally responsible technology. For instance, experts from the World Bank recently concluded that it would be 1,000 times more expensive for Severo Nickel and Pechenga Nickel to invest in new equipment than to simply pay the fees.[31]

Lenient enforcement is another factor that lowers the effectiveness of these pollution charges. Many Russian firms currently exceed their allowable emissions and incur the fivefold increases in fees. According to the law, the additional charges are to come out of profits and cannot be deducted as a business expense.[32] However, when a firm significantly exceeds its allowable emissions, another standard is applied—so-called provisionally coordinated emissions. In this case, the firm still pays the higher fees, but can deduct all of them as costs. Under current circumstances, the Russian government must allow such concessions or face the possible bankruptcy of firms in which it has an interest and which employ many workers. Severo Nickel and Pechenga Nickel both fall into this special category.[33]

The general weakness of the Russian government offers producers another way to avoid pollution charges: they can simply not pay them. As incredible as it may seem to people in the West, and despite the nominal existence of penalties, the practice of not meeting one's financial obligations is widespread in Russia. Firms have evaded taxes, defaulted on bank loans, and failed to pay their suppliers and employees.[34] Executive salaries are often paid out of separate bank accounts, and black market transactions are rampant. Under these conditions, market incentives such as environmental fees and fines often have little influence.

The shift to a market economy has greatly reduced the power of the state vis-à-vis major companies, thereby constraining its ability to enforce environmental regulations. At the same time, the state must rely on entities such as Norilsk Nickel for a significant portion of its revenues. The complexity and conflicting pressures inherent in this situation make it difficult for the Russian government to wield much influence in the environmental arena.

Enterprise and Regional Authorities

Compounding the problem of governing is Russia's shift to a more federal system with greater regional autonomy. During the Soviet era, all decisions related to industrial production and environmental protection were made in Moscow, with largely pro forma participation by regional authorities. Now, however, regional and local authorities are playing increasingly larger roles in the formulation and implementation of policy. In Norilsk Nickel's case, for instance, both the authorities in Murmansk and the Murmansk regional environmental committee (a branch of the Ministry of the Environment) are involved in making decisions about the company's operations. Today the regional state authority, in particular, provides and enforces actual regulations on the environmental behavior of enterprises. The Murmansk environmental committee allots emission permits to the Kola Peninsula facilities of Norilsk Nickel. Using the uniform national standards as a starting point, the committee officials determine the amount of pollutants Norilsk may emit and the fees it must pay. They also monitor the company's compliance with environmental regulations. Murmansk authorities play an active role in disseminating the funds collected through pollution charges, 90 percent of which are paid into regional funds (60 percent are transferred to the local environmental organs of the Murmansk regional environmental committee and 30 percent go to the Murmansk region); the remaining 10 percent are given to the federal environmental ministry. Although these funds are supposed to be spent on projects to enhance the environment, the Murmansk administration sometimes diverts them to other activities such as building churches or roads, or buying fuel.[35]

In such an economically depressed region, where many other firms have become completely insolvent, Norilsk Nickel is clearly important to economic development. The company's two facilities also account for nearly three-fourths of the tax revenues collected in the Murmansk region.[36] In a sense, then, the entire region is dependent on the health of this company. There are no other major employers, and the company's earnings provide much of the region's social infrastructure—including schools, hospitals, libraries, shops, transport facilities, and food and water supplies.[37] In fact, social considerations are the primary reason that authorities at all levels have been unwilling to close Norilsk's Kola Peninsula facilities.[38]

The Corporate Environment and "Nickelgate"

Why have Russia's new efforts to protect the environment not been more successful? Why do policy measures that work in the West—such as pollution charges, decentralized management, and transfer of authority to the local level—apparently not work in this country? Why do standard methods of environmental regulations not result in standard reactions from the targets of these regulations? Is it likely that the problem lies not with new environmental instruments but with their targets?

The answers to these questions may lie in the fact that Russia's market economy remains relatively undeveloped. The process of privatization is not yet complete; property rights are not fully defined. An enterprise in Russia is not yet completely comparable with a market producer in the West: it has a different internal organization of interests, different distribution of control rights, and a different property structure. Few owners or managers (many of whom are holdovers from the Soviet era) have any long-term commitment to the enterprises in their charge. On the contrary, they are often interested only in enriching themselves as quickly as possible, an attitude that has serious implications for the country's environment. This combination of factors leads to nonstandard reactions and responses to standard methods of environmental regulation.

The recent struggle for control of Norilsk Nickel and the behavior of its leadership during this period illustrate the problem perfectly. As noted above, under the Soviet regime Norilsk's operations were entirely controlled by the state through the Ministry of Nonferrous Metals.[39] In 1993, President Boris Yeltsin signed a decree that turned Norilsk Nickel into a shareholder-owned company. (Although Russians call such an act "privatization," in reality it is just the first step in the privatization process.) According to the decree, the Russian government was to retain a majority of the voting shares for three years, but it soon lost actual control over the company as a result of the general chaos of the period. Largely free from shareholder control, Norilsk's directors consolidated their hold on the enterprise and restructured it to further their own interests.

In November 1995 Norilsk held a so-called loan-for-shares auction in which the shares held by the government were offered as security for a one-year loan. Uneximbank, a relatively new but quite successful commercial bank based in Moscow, made the winning bid of US$170.1 million (the minimum bid was US$170 million) and assumed control of Norilsk Nickel. Another bank, which reportedly was ready to bid US$355 million, was not allowed to participate in the auction.[40] According to some experts, the real value of the shares was as much as US$3 billion.[41] A power struggle broke out after the shares were transferred. Uneximbank wanted to control Norilsk's finances directly, a move the company's board of directors naturally resisted. In response, the bank attempted to convene an emergency meeting of the shareholders. The board objected, claiming that the bank had no authority to do so. The board also filed a lawsuit to invalidate the privatization of the company.[42]

At the beginning of 1996, a state prosecutor initiated criminal proceedings against Norilsk officials for allegedly selling metal at below-market prices (a practice that usually implies concealment of hard-currency revenues).[43] Meanwhile, another contender entered the struggle for control of the company: its employees. In early 1996, they held a large public meeting to express their distrust of Norilsk's management and to demand payment of salaries, which had been delayed for several months.[44] Facing a growing scandal, the Russian Duma (Parliament) began an investigation into Norilsk's affairs. In April, the government forced the company's president to resign and reorganized the board to include four representatives of Uneximbank.

The real significance of these events lies in a statement by Anatoly Filatov, the company's ousted general director: "We are against any interference with the affairs of Norilsk Nickel."[45] By "interference," of course, he meant the legitimate involvement of owners and creditors. In the chaotic period following the company's privatization, neither the Russian government nor the other nominal owners of Norilsk Nickel were able to exercise effective control over the enterprise. Largely unaccountable to anyone, Norilsk's management (the so-called red directors) ran the company for personal profit rather than long-term viability. Naturally, they were not interested in making capital-intensive investments to benefit the environment.

This situation highlights the crucial distinction between Norilsk's leadership and its owners. In the West, ownership implies that a company's managers are ultimately accountable to the company's owners, and thus will pay attention to promoting that company's long-term interests. Managers whose primary goal is to increase the value of their company will make the investments (including environmental investments) necessary to enhance its prospects. In Norilsk's situation, however, exactly the opposite occurred.[46]

Ownership and Control of Norilsk Nickel: Incentives for Long-Term Environmental Investments

As noted, in 1993 a special governmental decree signed by President Yeltsin put reconstruction of Pechenga Nickel up for international tender. The aim of the project was to reduce the plant's SO_2 emissions to the level of maximum allowable emissions with minimal reconstruction costs. The offer from a consortium of Swedish and Norwegian companies for upgrading the facilities at Pechenga Nickel was accepted. Estimates of the project's cost range between US$250 million and US$297 million.[47] The project's purpose is not merely to cut Pechenga's SO_2 emissions by as much as 95 percent (as a result of changes in the company's production process), but also to enable Pechenga to use locally mined, low-sulfur ore in its operations.[48]

What are the prospects for implementation of this international project? The project will not be carried out unless Norilsk Nickel's management actively supports it. As a result of its partial privatization, the company has acquired considerable independence from the state, and its bargaining power has increased tremendously. The state is no longer able to make enterprises such as

Norilsk Nickel follow its orders and participate in costly reconstruction projects. For a long time the company claimed that it simply could not afford such a large investment. Conditions concerning financial transfers and governmental participation in the reconstruction project are still among the most important items in the company's bargain with the government. Norilsk Nickel's final decision on whether to take part in reconstruction was entirely tied to the Russian government's decision on financial assistance. During the bargaining process, two main possibilities for financial support emerged: the government could directly finance a part of the reconstruction, or it could grant certain economic privileges for Norilsk Nickel during the period of reconstruction.

The Russian government finally decided to support reconstruction of Pechenga Nickel. In the summer of 1995 a law "On measures of the state support of reconstruction of metallurgical process of shareholding company Pechenga Nickel of Norilsk Nickel"[49] was enacted, authorizing the Russian government to contribute US$42 million. The government of Norway has pledged the same amount.

Even more important, at the company's insistence the Russian government granted Norilsk substantial tax concessions for the reconstruction. As of 1 April 1996, the company is exempt from paying duties on its exports of metals.[50] In addition, the duties it must pay on imports of technical equipment (mining, ore-dressing, metallurgical, and electric power equipment; means of transportation; and road-construction equipment not manufactured in Russia) have been reduced. These provisions were fixed in a governmental law enacted in the summer of 1996 that provides tax breaks and gives governmental guarantees for foreign bank loans. The law also allocates funds from the federal budget to help deliver seasonal products to the Norilsk industrial area in Russia's far north and to help the company move the unemployed and those unable to work to other locations. The government's assistance is not specifically aimed at modernizing Norilsk's facilities on the Kola Peninsula, however, and a considerable portion may be used by the enterprise elsewhere. Most experts agree that these concessions will, in principle, enable Norilsk to finance the upgrades at Pechenga. According to these experts, this decree relieves Norilsk Nickel of some 6.9 trillion rubles (US$1.3 billion) of financial and tax burdens.[51] However, one question remains: How will the federal budget be financed if companies such as Norilsk Nickel cannot pay their taxes? The bargaining process is still under way, and the enterprise has not yet made a final decision regarding implementation of the reconstruction project.

The real problem has been management's unwillingness to invest Norilsk's sales revenues in the company instead of diverting them to their own pockets. That Norilsk has substantial financial resources is demonstrated by the fact that, in order to maintain their control, the board of directors even proposed using company funds to purchase the government's shares.[52] They then used their bargaining power with the Russian government to avoid paying for the refurbishments at Pechenga. Their recalcitrance has endangered the natural beauty of Russia's far north.

The situation appears to be settling now (late in 1997). Uneximbank has consolidated its ownership and control over the company by purchasing all shares of Norilsk offered by the government in the summer of 1997. The company should now behave more like a normal profit-seeking firm under coherent management—presumably it will make long-term investments, for example. However, poor enforcement of environmental laws is still rampant, and external financing to upgrade the Kola facilities has stalled. The situation still does not bode well for the environment on or downwind from the Kola Peninsula.

Some Final Observations: Why Russian Regulation Has Little Influence

At the most basic level, the Norilsk case indicates that Western environmental policy instruments will not necessarily be effective in a country undergoing a major economic and political transition. Corruption, lack of motivation, an inability to impose sanctions on those who violate the law, and a decrease in the ability of the state to regulate activity within its borders all work against attempts to solve environmental problems through public regulation.[53] Compounding the problem, of course, is the absence of effective ownership in Russian industry, which reduces management's incentive to make long-term environmental investments. As a result, governmental regulations that have been effective in the West produce unexpected outcomes in Russia, ultimately resulting in low responsiveness of polluters to environmental rules and incentives.

The solution to environmental problems such as those caused by Norilsk Nickel appears to lie in further implementation of market mechanisms in Russia and in the creation of a truly democratic government that is sensitive to public interests and has real powers of regulation to replace the weak and corrupt government that currently exists. It is technologically and economically feasible to refurbish Norilsk's plants on the Kola Peninsula so that they will pollute less. The Russian government has already allocated considerable resources—in the form of foregone tax revenues—that are nominally directed toward these aims. One major impediment to reconstruction of Kola's facilities is the unsettled state of property rights in Russia, which eliminates the incentive to make environmental investments. If that impediment is removed, the way will be open for such investments, both by individual firms and through joint implementation projects.

Of course, there are those who oppose this type of approach, preferring to simply close highly polluting facilities.[54] On the whole, however, this view seems shortsighted. First, closing Norilsk's Kola Peninsula facilities would not necessarily benefit the environment. Other firms would simply take over the market, expanding their production to meet world demand. Because nickel production tends to cause severe environmental damage wherever it is located, the goal should be to overhaul existing plants. Closing enterprises would only result in redistribution of the world nickel market; it would not solve environmental problems. Second, there is no compelling reason for the Russian government to close Norilsk's facilities on the Kola Peninsula: the country is technically meeting its international obligations under LRTAP with respect to reducing SO_2 emissions, and closing the facilities would entail high economic and social costs. Third, joint implementation—receiving assistance from downwind countries to pay the costs of abatement—would be a good way to achieve plant reconstruction. As the transition to a market-based society continues, joint implementation and other market-based mechanisms for pollution control should become more feasible.

Recent changes in Russia's political situation make the prospects for environmental improvement somewhat unclear, however. One positive development is the government's decision to provide additional financial support to Norilsk Nickel. A significant negative development is the recent elimination of Russia's Ministry of the Environment. From now on, environmental protection in Russia will be in the hands of a state committee rather than a full ministry. Thus, far less emphasis will be given to environmental issues, because the chair of the committee will have no input in high-level decisions affecting it. In some senses this replicates the Soviet system, where environmental protection was a subordinate part of industrial ministries. The company's new management, in which share owners have greater representation, may improve the situation by taking a longer-term view of the firm's development.

Notes

The authors thank Rune Castberg of the Fridtjof Nansen Institute, Norway, for advice and thought-provoking discussions of the issues raised in this chapter. They also thank Kal Raustiala, Boris Segerståhl, Marvin Soroos, David Victor and Oran Young; thanks also to all those at Norilsk Nickel, in the Russian and Norwegian Ministries of the Environment, and in Bellona for useful suggestions and insights. We thank Robert Nicholson for editorial assistance. A version of this chapter was published in *Environment* 38(9):6–11, 32–37 (November 1996); portions reprinted with permission of the Helen Dwight Reid Educational Foundation, published by Heldref Publications, 1319 18th Street, NW, Washington, DC 20036, Copyright 1996.

1. Anatoly B. Chubais, former First Deputy Prime Minister of Russia, quoted in Kovalev, A., 1994, "Aktsii Norilskogo Nikelya khoroshi dlya lyubykh investorov (Norilsk Nickel's shares are good for investors)," *Kommersant Daily*, 5 October, p. 4.

2. *Delovoy Mir*, 14 June 1995, p. 3; *Kommersant Weekly*, 13 February 1996; *Segodnya*, 6 February 1996.

3. In the spring of 1995, the Russian government released data on the country's production and consumption of nickel at a meeting of the International Nickel Group in the Netherlands. Since then, however, "information regarding the production of nonferrous and rare metals, and other metals of strategic importance" has been declared confidential. Sobranye Zakonodatelstva RF (Code of the Russian Federation), article 8830 (1995).

4. See *Nezavisimaya Gazeta*, 17 January 1996; "Russian Nickel Exports Seen Down Slightly in 1994," *Reuters News*, 11 October 1994; "Metal Analysts Expect Fall in Russian Nickel Exports," *Financial Times*, 2 May 1995, p. 29; "Norilsk Meets Copper Export Deals but Output Lower," *Reuters News*, 2 August 1995; and "Norway/Russia Pechenga Deal Delayed but Intact," *Reuters News*, 18 July 1995.

5. *Segodnya*, 17 October 1995.

6. "Russia's Norilsk Has No Plans for Force Majeure," *Reuters News*, 7 December 1994.

7. Lukianov, S., 1996, "Yeltsin Gives Bounty of Tax Breaks to Norilsk," *Moscow Times*, August, pp. 1–2. The ruble-dollar exchange rate changes constantly because of inflation in Russia. Hereinafter, when providing US dollar

equivalents for ruble figures, the following approximate mid-year exchange
rates for the corresponding years are used: 50 rubles/dollar for 1991, 150
rubles/dollar for 1992, 1,000 rubles/dollar for 1993, 2,000 rubles/dollar for
1994, 4,500 rubles/dollar for 1995, and 5,000 rubles/dollar for 1996.

8. *Kommersant Weekly*, 28 November 1995, p. 51.

9. Russian Ministry of the Environment, 1995, Gousudarstevennyi doklad o
sostoyanii okruizhayuishei prirodnoy sredy v Rossiiskoy Federatsii v 1994
gody (National report on the state of the environment in the Russian Federation
in 1994), Moscow, Russia, p. 192; also see sources listed in note 2 above.
According to the company's own data, Severo Nickel and Pechenga Nickel
emitted 364,000 tons of air pollutants in 1993, nearly two-thirds of them in the
form of SO_2; representatives of Norilsk Nickel, personal communication with
the authors, 3 May 1995.

10. USSR Ministry of the Environment, 1991, Nacionalny doklad SSSR k konferentsii OON 1992 goda po okruizhayuishei srede i razvitiy (National report
of the USSR to the 1992 UNCED conference), Moscow, Russia, pp. 283–
289; Feshbach, M., 1995, *Environmental and Health Atlas of Russia*, Paims,
Moscow, Russia; Russian Ministry of the Environment, 1992, Gousudarstevennyi doklad o sostoyanii okruizhayuishei prirodnoy sredy v Rossiiskoy Federatsii v 1992 gody (National report on the state of the environment in the Russian
Federation in 1992), Moscow, Russia, pp. 51, 60, 65.

11. See Erdman, L.K. et al., 1994, Transgranichnyi perenos soedinenyi sery
i azota v 1992 godu na territorii Rossiiskoy Federatsii, Ukrainy, Belarusi,
Moldovy, Kazakhstana, Stran Baltii, Zakavkazia i Sredney Azii (Transbound-
ary air pollution involving sulfur and nitrogen compounds in the Russian
Federation, Ukraine, Belarus, Moldova, Kazakhstan, the Baltic states, the
Caucasus, and central Asia in 1992), Cooperative Programme for Monitor-
ing and Evaluation of the Long-Range Transmission of Air Pollutants in
Europe/Meteorological Synthesising Center-East (EMEP/MSC-E), Moscow,
Russia, p. 31.

12. According to the revised Protocol, Russia must reduce its SO_2 emissions
by 38 percent (relative to the 1980 level) by 2000 and by 40 percent by 2005
and 2010; see Protocol to the Convention on Long-Range Transboundary Air
Pollution on Further Reduction of Sulfur Emissions, EB.AIR/R.94, Oslo, 1994,
annex II.

13. Interview with a member of the USSR State Committee on Environmental
Protection, 2 February 1989.

14. Agreement between the Government of Finland and the Government of the
USSR on Cooperation in the Field of Environmental Protection, 1985; Action

Program Agreed between the Republic of Finland and the Union of Soviet Socialist Republics for the Purpose of Limiting and Reducing the Deposition and Harmful Effects of Air Pollutants Emanating from Areas Near Their Common Border, 1989; and Protocol between the Government of Finland and the Government of the USSR on Cooperation in the Kola Peninsula Region, 1989. *Finland's International Environmental Agreements*, 2nd edition, Ministry of the Environment, Helsinki, Finland, 1993.

15. Agreement between the Government of Finland and the Government of the Russian Federation on Cooperation in the Field of the Environment, 1992; Agreement between the Government of the Republic of Finland and the Government of the Russian Federation on Cooperation in Murmansk, in the Republic of Karelia, in St. Petersburg and the Leningrad Area, 1992, *Finland's International Environmental Agreements*, op. cit., note 14.

16. Russian Ministry of the Environment, 1994, unpublished documents.

17. Norilsk officials consider the commitments made by the government to be unrealistic and say they should never have been made without consulting the company. Personal communication with the authors, 4 March 1996. Russia's Ministry of the Environment now engages in extensive negotiations with firms concerning environmental goals.

18. Shmyganovsky, V., 1990, "Milliardy na ekologiy (Billions for Ecology)," *Izvestia*, 10 October, p. 4.

19. For details see Hiltunen, H., 1996, Finnish Strategies to Reduce Transboundary Pollution from the Kola Peninsula, Interim Report, International Institute for Applied Systems Analysis, Laxenburg, Austria.

20. *Mining Journal*, 27 November 1987, p. 443; *Metal Bulletin*, 2 June 1987; Kuznetsov, U., 1990, "Na 'strannom kholme' i vokrug nego (On a Strange Hill and Around It)," *Pravda*, 30 August, p. 3.

21. This commitment is reflected in Russia's adoption of more sophisticated environmental management strategies and a general increase in environmental *glasnost*. See Kotov, V. and Nikitina, E., 1993, "Russia in Transition: Obstacles to Environmental Protection," *Environment*, December, p. 10.

22. Officials from Norilsk Nickel, interview with the authors, 4 September 1995.

23. Russian Federation Ministry of Environment, 1995, O Sostoyanii Okruizhauishei Prirodnoy Sredy RF v 1994 Godu, Gousudarstevennyi Doklad, Moscow, Russia, p. 192.

24. Lennon, J., 1995, "Fact and Fiction Merge in Cold Siberia," *American Metal Market*, 19 January, p. 10A.

25. *Sovetsky Murman*, 12 January 1993, p. 1.

26. See Kotov, V., and Nikitina, E., 1996, "To Reduce, or to Produce? Problems of Implementation of the Climate Convention in Russia," in *Verification Yearbook 1996*, edited by J.B. Poole and R. Guthrie, Westview Press, Boulder, CO, USA, p. 339.

27. These deposits are particularly rich (with known reserves of nickel and copper amounting to about 1 billion tons) and account for 90 percent of Norilsk Nickel's annual ore production. At current rates of utilization (approximately 11 million tons per year), the deposits should last for at least another 100 years. *Segodnya*, 6 January 1996.

28. Representatives of Norilsk Nickel, personal communication with the authors, 29 September 1995.

29. *Evrasia*, No. 9, 1993, p. 50; officials from Norilsk Nickel, interview with the authors, 18 January 1995.

30. Committee on the Environment and Natural Resources, Murmansk region, unpublished documents.

31. World Bank, 1993, Project Document for the Pilot Project to Be Implemented as a Part of the World Bank Supported Environmental Management Project of the Russian Federation, Murmansk Oblast, October 1993, World Bank, Washington, DC, USA, p. 28.

32. Resolution of Russia's Government N 632, Moscow, 28 August 1992.

33. Pechenga, for instance, is effectively allowed to emit five times as much SO_2 as it otherwise would.

34. According to a recent press report, Norilsk Nickel has failed to pay US$56 million in environmental fees; the company denies this report, however. See sources in note 2.

35. Representatives of Norilsk Nickel, interview with the authors, 14 March 1995.

36. Representatives of Norilsk Nickel, personal communication with the authors, 29 September 1995.

37. Norilsk officials often complain that a large part of their capital spending goes toward such infrastructure, which lowers the company's profitability and its capacity to make other investments. According to these officials, the company spent 1 trillion rubles on housing, utilities, and other amenities for its workers and the local population in 1995; Kotov, V., Kux, S., and Nikitina, E.,

1996, "Ecology and Subsidiarity: The Role of Russia's Regions in Environmental Policy," in *Proceedings of the Regional Science Association European Congress*, Zurich, Switzerland.

38. Representatives of Norilsk Nickel, personal communication with the authors, 29 September 1995.

39. In principle, all firms in the USSR were owned by the people, but in practice such ownership was clearly a fiction. Even those with nominal rights of control, such as boards of directors and regional authorities, played quite limited roles.

40. "Russia: Battle for Control of Norilsk Nickel," *Reuters News*, 14 May 1996.

41. "Russia: Norilsk Nickel Rises as Other Russian Shares Slip," *Reuters News*, 4 March 1996.

42. "Norilsk Nickel to Appeal Against Court Ruling on Auction," *Interfax*, 28 February 1996.

43. *Segodnya*, 1 March 1996.

44. *Segodnya*, 20 February 1996.

45. See sources in note 2.

46. It is questionable how responsible Uneximbank will be in its management of Norilsk Nickel. Some experts believe that the bank is primarily interested in the profits it can earn from trading in Norilsk's undervalued stock; *Segodnya*, 6 February 1996.

47. The companies involved are Kvaerner A/S, a Norwegian shipbuilding and industrial group; Elkem A/S, a Norwegian ferroalloys and technology group; and Boliden AB, a Swedish mining and metals group. Penson, S., 1995, "Prime Minister to see Yeltsin on Makeover Approval," *American Metal Market*, 10 April, p. 2; *Izvestia*, 8 July 1995, p. 1; Velichko, O., 1995, "Russia Plans Reconstruction of Nickel Plant near Norway," *Tass On-line Service*, 10 May; and Shuvalov, A., 1995, "Norwegian Ecology Minister to Visit Russia," *Tass On-line Service*, 23 January.

48. New geological surveys are now under way on the Kola Peninsula. One vein being explored is estimated to contain 11 million tons of ore. "Russia Holds Tender for Arctic Nickel-Copper Field," *Reuters News*, 14 November 1994.

49. Sobranye Zakonodatelstva RF (Code of the Russian Federation), No. 28, 1995, Article 2689.

50. Russia imposes duties on the export of many types of metals and minerals.

51. "No. No. No.," *The Moscow Times*, Issue 1024, 28 August 1996, p. 1; *Rossiiskaya Gazeta*, 17 August 1996.

52. *Segodnya*, 6 February 1996; *Financial Times*, 3 February 1996.

53. Government bureaucrats in Russia have shown a strong tendency to pursue their own interests instead of fulfilling their duties, a phenomenon that has been called the "privatization of the state." See Kotov, V., *Privatization in a Privatized State*, University of Fribourg Press, Fribourg, Switzerland (forthcoming).

54. Darst, R., 1996, "Subsidies and Transboundary Pollution: Another View," *Environment* 38(November):36.

14

Domestic Implementation of Baltic Sea Pollution Commitments in Russia and the Baltic States

Alexei Roginko

Introduction

The countries that have emerged since the collapse of the USSR are now undergoing a painful process of transition to democratic political systems, more decentralized governance, and market economies. This process affects the ways that these countries implement their international environmental commitments. Many of the commitments were adopted long before the current transition process started and were initially implemented in an entirely different economic and social situation. By tracing changes in implementation patterns over time, we can identify how transition has influenced the process of implementation.

This study concerns implementation of commitments to regulate Baltic Sea pollution by Russia and the three newly independent Baltic states—the republics of Estonia, Latvia, and Lithuania. These four countries face somewhat similar economic and environmental problems inherited from the USSR, but each is now following a different transition path. The policy instruments, institutional structures, and impact of economic decline vary across these countries, as does the extent to which international commitments have been translated into action at the domestic level. For these reasons, many quasi-controlled comparisons of these countries' experiences are possible.

The international commitments in question are those under the Convention on the Protection of the Marine Environment of the Baltic Sea Area (the 1974 Helsinki Convention), which has been in force since 1980, and those set forth at the Ministerial Conferences of the 1980s and 1990s and in the Baltic Sea Joint Comprehensive Environmental Action Programme (JCP) and some bilateral agreements. Together these conventions, agreements, and programs make up the Baltic Sea environment protection regime. The regime existed long before the current transition process began and has changed with the transition in the East: it has progressed from limited technical and scientific cooperation during the Cold War to a "program strategy" linking environmental cooperation to economic reforms in the former Soviet republics and Poland. The regime thus includes two types of commitments—regulatory and programmatic. The current study primarily examines how the regulatory commitments have been implemented in Russia and the Baltic states. The first section of this chapter outlines the evolution of the regime's regulatory and programmatic commitments. It serves to introduce the regime for this analysis and for the analyses in other chapters that address the Baltic regime, including Chapter 15 on implementation of regulatory commitments in Poland and Chapter 5 on implementation of programmatic activities related to implementation review. The overview also evaluates the interests Russia and the Baltic states have in participating in the Baltic Sea environment protection regime and implementing its commitments—those interests provide the context for the implementation analysis that follows.

The analysis presented here considers all major aspects and pathways of implementation in all four countries, although many of the comparisons are limited by incomplete data. It examines regulatory mechanisms in these countries and finds that, to date, programs adopted to implement the Baltic pollution controls have lacked priorities, cost-benefit analysis, and funding sources. Environmental bodies responsible for implementation of international commitments have been plagued by coordination problems and a lack of both a clear line of authority and well-defined roles and responsibilities. Financial mechanisms such as pollution taxes and environmental funds have been used in each country; however, the study results indicate that the failure to index taxes and fines to inflation, among other basic failures, has severely limited the influence of such market-based mechanisms. Fines typically are not enforced by the legal and administrative system, which is overburdened with other tasks.

The study explores issues concerning mobilization of domestic and international financial resources for implementing the Baltic pollution controls, especially the role of external resource transfers. It finds that in all four countries little budget financing has been available for environmental purposes, and enterprises have relied primarily on their own very limited funds for financing environmental investments. External resources have flowed primarily to the more stable Baltic states, but an increasing share is now shifting to Russia. There have been few commercial loans for implementation of Baltic commitments within the region, especially in Russia. The main source of Russia's external funding is bilateral arrangements with Western nations; however, donor countries are still reluctant to commit themselves to large-scale projects under conditions of economic and political instability.

The study also examines how the principal societal actors, in addition to the state and its regulatory apparatus, have responded to Baltic Sea commitments in each country. It examines the role of "target groups," the polluting firms and enterprises whose behavior is the target of the regime. It finds that the number of relevant actors has increased sharply since the transition: previously monolithic state enterprises are being privatized and broken into many units. These changes have substantially reduced the environmental authorities' ability to enforce regulations. In each of the countries, the courts and the legal system have played only a minor role: even when sanctions for environmental offenses have been applied, they have been clearly inadequate to change the behavior of polluting firms. Many incentives for environmental investments, including tax incentives, have been developed by federal and local authorities, but they have rarely been used by state-owned enterprises, especially those in the defense industry. Public participation is also examined in the study. The public, especially in the Baltic states, has many new voices and potential avenues of influence; however, in practice few environmental nongovernmental organizations (ENGOs) have been well organized and active on the Baltic Sea issue in these countries.

The analysis presented here examines the process of implementation in detail. A final section assesses the process of implementation in these countries as a whole and examines the principal explanations for changes in the levels of pollution originating from these countries. Until the mid-1990s virtually all changes in pollution levels reflected factors other than implementation of international commitments. Even when commitments have been written into domestic policy they generally have not been enforced and have had little influence on the behavior of target groups. Notably, decreases in pollution since the late 1980s have mainly reflected economic decline. In recent years many projects have been initiated to limit pollution, mainly by building water treatment plants or by updating those plants already in place. Western financing has been crucial to these projects, although in many cases the countries are implementing the projects primarily to address local, not regional, water pollution problems. The need to match the interests of Western donors (who are concerned about the Baltic Sea) with those of Eastern recipients (who have more immediate local concerns) has been a major part of this recent phase in Baltic Sea cooperation and illustrates the overlap between international and domestic environmental protection.

The Baltic Sea

The Baltic Sea, with a surface area of about 400,000 km^2 and a volume of 21,000 km^3, is one of the largest brackish water areas in the world. The shallow, narrow Danish Straits allow only a very slow water exchange between the Baltic and North Seas. As a result, water in the Baltic Sea has an extremely long residence time, on the order of 35 to 40 years, leading to accumulation of pollutants in water, sediments, and biota.[1] The Baltic Sea is one of the most severely polluted bodies of water in the world; eutrophication and oxygen depletion in bottom layers are the most serious problems.

Nine states border the Baltic Sea: Denmark, Estonia, Finland, Germany, Latvia, Lithuania, Poland, Russia, and Sweden (see figure 14.1). The land area of the Baltic drainage basin covers 1.7 million km^2 and is home to 75 million people. Sweden and the former Soviet republics occupy over 60 percent of the basin's land area; Poland accounts for over half the area's population and is the single largest polluter (see Chapter 15).

About half the Baltic pollution is transported through the atmosphere; the other half comes from land-based sources. The following sources are most important:

- Poor treatment of municipal and industrial waste (mainly from the Gulf of Finland, the Gulf of Riga, and the Bay of Gdańsk).
- Outdated pulp and paper mills that discharge sulfur dioxide (SO_2) and organic substances (mainly in Karelia, the Baltic republics, and Poland).
- Destruction of solid and hazardous wastes without proper incineration (mostly in Russia and the countries of Eastern Europe).
- Runoff of nitrogen (30 to 35 percent of the total load) and phosphorus (about 10 percent of the total load) used as agricultural fertilizer (predominantly in Denmark, Sweden, and East European countries).[2]

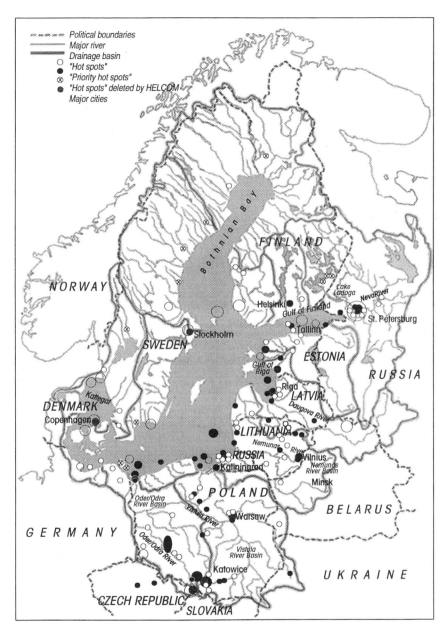

Figure 14.1
Baltic Sea catchment basin including "hot spots" and "priority hot spots" defined by 1992 Joint Comprehensive Environmental Action Programme (JCP).
Source: Adapted from HELCOM data.

The Baltic Sea Environment Protection Regime

The Convention on the Protection of the Marine Environment of the Baltic Sea Area (the 1974 Helsinki Convention) was adopted in Helsinki on 22 March 1974 and signed by all seven of the Baltic countries in existence at that time. The Convention was the first comprehensive regional marine environment protection agreement to address all sources of marine pollution, including land-based sources. Over time, the Baltic Sea regime has evolved to include Ministerial Conferences, which have set ambitious targets for controlling major pollutants. In 1992, member countries adopted the overarching JCP, which linked environmental cooperation to economic reforms in the formerly communist countries of the region and facilitated an integrated approach to control pollution in the basin.

The 1974 Helsinki Convention
The Helsinki Convention entered into force on 3 May 1980. The Baltic littoral states that are currently signatory to the Convention are Denmark, Estonia, Finland, Germany, Latvia, Lithuania, Poland, Russia, and Sweden. Belarus, Ukraine, the Czech and Slovak Republics, and Norway also drain into the Baltic Sea, but are not parties to the Convention.

The 1974 Helsinki Convention sets an ambitious goal—to "individually or jointly . . . prevent and abate pollution and to protect and enhance the marine environment of the Baltic Sea area." Additional goals are listed in an annex concerning land-based pollution. These include appropriate treatment of municipal sewage, minimization of the polluting load of industrial waste, employment of low-waste technologies, and recirculation of water. No intermediate objectives or timetables for the attainment of these goals are provided by the Convention or by its annexes.

Similar to many other marine pollution control agreements, the Convention distinguishes between hazardous and noxious substances. Hazardous substances (listed in Annex I) are essentially banned. Among the banned substances are dichlorodiphenyltrichloroethane (DDT) and its derivatives, polychlorinated biphenyls (PCBs), and polychlorinated terphenyls (PCTs). Noxious substances, listed in Annex II, include heavy metals, phenols, halogenated hydrocarbons, persistent pesticides, radioactive materials, oil and petrochemical waste, etc. Parties are supposed to require special permits, issued by national authorities, if a significant amount of any noxious substance is to be dumped into the marine environment.

The Convention has established a permanent working body, the Helsinki Convention Baltic Marine Environment Protection Commission (HELCOM), comprising representatives from all state parties and served by a small Secretariat. HELCOM has become the organizational nucleus of the environment protection regime in the Baltic, even for activities not formally required under the Convention.[3] HELCOM meets once a year in Helsinki. Each member country has one vote, and HELCOM Decisions must be reached unanimously at all stages. HELCOM's meetings are attended mostly by high-ranking officials from the national environmental ministries concerned; they take place at the ministerial level only in exceptional circumstances. The preparatory work for HELCOM's Decisions and Recommendations is done by HELCOM's four major committees,[4] their subcommittees, and ad hoc working groups that report to the committee in question.

The most important "product" of HELCOM activities are Recommendations related to various aspects of monitoring, organization of research programs, and prevention, control, and abatement of pollution. More than 160 Recommendations have been issued since 1980: about one-third of these Recommendations pertain to problems of control and prevention of pollution from ships; 18 Recommendations concern monitoring and reporting; and 63 pertain to the control of land-based pollution.[5] Eighty percent of the latter have been adopted since 1990, which is indicative of the growing awareness of this major source of pollution. Some of the Recommendations contain specific targets and time-tables for their achievement, but because none of them are amended to the text of the Convention, they are not considered legally binding; in other words, the Convention operates on a "voluntary" basis. However, because all of the Recommendations are adopted by unanimous vote, they are considered to be at least "morally binding."[6]

Although all HELCOM Recommendations have the unanimous consent of the parties, there are usually considerable delays before they are implemented, if they are implemented at all.[7] Furthermore, because many of the Recommendations are vague, it is not easy to determine whether they have been implemented.[8]

Institutional Change in the Regime

During the 20 years of its existence, the Baltic Sea environment protection regime has demonstrated its ability to adjust over time. Martin List describes the regime as evolutionary, implying new organizational setups, new procedures, and above all new rules.[9] Almost all the rules established by the Helsinki Convention are technical in nature. Foreseeing that technical knowledge might change rapidly, the parties to the Convention wanted to keep adoption and adaptation of rules relatively easy. This goal was achieved by placing the technicalities to be regulated in annexes (and appendices thereto) to the Convention right from the start. These annexes can be changed by the HELCOM decision-making procedure, which does not require ratification by national Parliaments.

HELCOM itself has evolved over time. In one of its most important procedural innovations, in 1988 observer status was granted to nongovernmental organizations (NGOs), putting them on the same level as relevant intergovernmental organizations, which have participated since 1980. This reform reflects the state actors' increased awareness of the importance of public involvement in marine pollution matters.[10] Greenpeace International was the first NGO to take advantage of the wider access to the regime. Representatives of other international NGOs (e.g., the World Wide Fund for Nature and Coalition Clean Baltic) are also invited to working group meetings when HELCOM decides their attendance is appropriate.

The most far-reaching procedural change was the introduction of Ministerial Conferences, the first of which took place in March 1988. The idea for such conferences came from the North Sea regime (see Chapter 8); it was hoped that the high amount of political attention generated by the Conferences would result in increased domestic implementation of HELCOM Decisions. The Ministerial Conferences also set ambitious targets for future pollution controls. The "Declaration on the protection of the marine environment of the Baltic Sea Area," adopted at the ministerial level during the ninth meeting of HELCOM in 1988, called for a 50 percent reduction of total discharges of listed pollutants (heavy metals, toxic chemicals, and nutrients) as soon as possible, but no later than 1995.[11] However, the Declaration did not provide for the measurement of the discharge reductions or for their distribution among the countries involved; a reference year was not even selected. In the Ronneby Declaration of 1990, the rather vague goal of a 50 percent emission reduction proposed in 1988 was somewhat clarified by the addition of a reference year, 1987, thus placing it on a par with the goals adopted by the International North Sea Conference in 1987 and clarified in 1990. In addition, according to the Declaration, biological treatment for nutrient removal must be installed no later than the year 2000.[12]

The ministerial meetings spearheaded a fundamental shift from a reactive approach based on assumptions about the Baltic Sea's ability to assimilate pollution to a proactive approach based on the principle of precautionary action. The 1988 Ministerial Declaration introduced the concept of best available technology (BAT); the Ronneby Declaration of 1990 introduced the concept of best environmental practice (BEP) and the principle of precautionary action.[13]

The most potentially significant regime change was the adoption, in April 1992, of the revised Helsinki Convention on the Protection of the Marine Environment of the Baltic Sea Area (the 1992 Helsinki Convention). When it enters into force, it will supersede the 1974 Convention. The new Convention contains major expansions in purpose (to prevent and eliminate pollution rather than to just control or minimize it), in scope (such as inclusion of internal waters and the entire Baltic Sea catchment area), and in regulatory aggressiveness (such as invoking the precautionary and "polluter pays" principles, and shifting to a uniform regime for all substances by requiring the use of BAT and BEP). New provisions for notification and for dealing with noncompliance have also been introduced. However, because implementing the new provisions will not be required for several years, these provisions are not analyzed in this chapter.

The Baltic Sea Joint Comprehensive Environmental Action Programme (JCP)

By the late 1980s, the Nordic countries had already implemented substantial pollution control programs. The success of these efforts meant that additional pollution control in these countries was increasingly costly.[14] In contrast, the countries of Central and Eastern Europe had done little to control pollution; their past inaction meant that many sites remained where Baltic pollution could be limited at relatively low cost. The end of the Cold War eased barriers to funding projects in the East and made an integrated East-West approach to pollution control possible.

With this economic and environmental logic in mind, the 1990 Ministerial Conference in Ronneby, Sweden, called for the elaboration of the JCP "to restore the Baltic Sea to a sound ecological balance"[15] and established an ad hoc high-level task force, followed in 1992 by the Programme Implementation Task Force (HELCOM PITF).[16] To outline priorities for action, seven pre-feasibility studies were carried out in the former Soviet Union (FSU) and Poland, financed by national governments through multilateral banks. The findings indicated that there were 132 pollution "hot spots"; 47 of them were designated "priority" hot spots. Of the 132 hot spots, 95 were located in the formerly centrally planned economies of the Baltic basin, including 60 hot spots (44 percent of the total) in former Soviet republics (see figure 14.1).[17] Of the 37 hot spots in the West, one-third have since been taken off the list because water treatment facilities have been completed.[18] In short, the inventory of hot spots underscored that the next steps to clean up the Baltic had to take place mainly in the former centrally planned economies.

The JCP approach has several novel features. First, the countries have developed concrete national plans, which has forced them to scrutinize the wide range of activities that have an impact on the Baltic Sea environment. Second, because the JCP is a joint program, as far as possible priorities for its implementation are set for the catchment area as a whole, not just within a national context. Third, to the extent possible, the program is worded so as to provide for participation by new actors—development banks as well as other financing agencies, including those involved in bilateral assistance programs.[19] The ultimate goal of the program is to comply with the environmental standards of the European Union (EU) or, where applicable, with other stricter standards.

The May 1996 Baltic Sea States Summit Meeting held in Visby, Sweden, recommended that HELCOM update and strengthen the JCP, as well as increase the pace of its implementation. It also suggested that the JCP become an important element in the elaboration of Agenda 21 for the Baltic Sea region. Finally, it strongly recommended that special attention be given to water supply and the treatment of wastewater in the St. Petersburg, Pskov, and Kaliningrad areas, and in the Vistula and Odra River basins. HELCOM has been called to develop an action program for phasing out discharges and emissions of hazardous substances, including persistent organic pollutants.[20]

To sum up, the Baltic Sea environment protection regime started by adopting a "technical-scientific" strategy consisting of three major tasks: conducting research and gathering information, formulating principles for emission limitations, and specifying rules and procedures. This strategy functioned well in the bipolar security system of the Cold War: cooperation was primarily technical and uncontroversial, and did not threaten the member states' security concerns.[21] Two factors have since contributed to the regime's development: better scientific understanding of the pollution problem and rising public concern fueled by media reports. The regime has progressed from limiting emissions of substances to identifying the best available technologies for across-the-board cuts of those and other emissions from a variety of industrial branches or sectors.[22]

Because of the massive political changes occurring in Europe and the emergence of new conditions for cooperation through East-West funding and technology transfer, a new "program strategy" has largely replaced the regime's previous strategy. The central characteristics of the new strategy are the linkage of environmental cooperation to economic reforms, an emphasis on long-term planning, and high-level political involvement. Overarching, action-oriented programs—notably the JCP—now guide HELCOM's activities. The scope of these programs has been expanded by linking them to regional cooperation in other areas, such as industrial development, energy, transportation, and agriculture. The number of actors involved has also increased dramatically with the inclusion of new member countries, international financial institutions, local-level authorities, private businesses and independent professional experts.[23]

National Interests and Approaches to the Regime

When evaluating whether and how the USSR and its successor states have implemented the Baltic Sea commitments, it is crucial to consider their interests in participating in the regime. Soviet interests help explain both why there was no pollution control in the past and why these countries are now engaged in the regime. Furthermore, the interests of each of the successor states help to explain that country's particular pattern of interaction with the regime. The principal interests of these states are considered here; they provide the context for the types of commitments that apply to these states and how they have been implemented, which is the topic of the remainder of the paper.

For the USSR as a whole, environmental problems in the Baltic area remained of secondary importance as long as pollution did not affect the country's economic interests, particularly fishing and recreation. There is now evidence of some impact from pollution, but during the Soviet era either there was no appreciable impact or this information was concealed from the public. Compared with other Baltic littoral countries, the amount of the total land area within the Baltic drainage basin held by the USSR was relatively insignificant (2.5 percent), and a mere 4 percent of the total Soviet population lived in the region.[24]

Because the Baltic environment was peripheral, security interests largely determined the Soviet position in Baltic environmental cooperation. The USSR and its East European allies were extremely distrustful of any provisions or formulations in the 1974 Convention that might imply a limitation of their sovereignty.[25] This distrust probably explains both the fact that practically the only binding obligations in the Convention referred to pollution from ships, and that through the 1980s implementation of the Convention mainly dealt almost exclusively with this issue. Control of land-based pollution sources was virtually nonexistent.

Soviet participation was clearly responsible for several of the Convention's important drawbacks. One of them, the exclusion of internal waters from the sphere of application, resulted from the USSR's sensitivity to sovereignty issues. Although the full proceedings of the negotiations have never been made public, and thus this conclusion cannot be proved with certainty, many analysts and observers suggest that this was the reason.[26] The exclusion of internal waters has hindered control of land-based pollution, most of which is discharged into internal waters.

Because the Soviets feared interference in their domestic affairs, Article 6 of the Convention, which requires parties to take appropriate measures to control and minimize land-based pollution, was interpreted differently in the USSR than in the West. Western countries understood it to mean that these measures had to be applied to all discharges, whereas Soviet administrators held that the minimization measures only had to be applied to pollution flowing over the border. However, no technical methods to measure the pollution load transported over the border existed at that time, which in effect eliminated any possibility of verifying the implementation of domestic obligations, as any information on the volume of discharges and environmental quality was classified for official use only. The Soviet authorities took a similar approach to control acid rain (see Chapter 12).

Concerns about interference in its domestic affairs also made the Soviet government reluctant to release data.[27] It seems plausible that the Soviet military were unwilling to release exact emission figures because they feared that this knowledge could lead to information on Soviet military industries.[28] Even more plausible is that this protection of so-called security interests was actually a ploy to classify (and hence to conceal from the domestic and international public) all environmental data to conceal the inadequacy of domestic pollution abatement efforts.

The USSR regarded international environmental protection in the Baltic as a continuation by other means of the policy of "The Baltic—A Sea of Peace" that was repeatedly proposed by the USSR's East European allies from as far back as 1957. According to List, "although this policy originally was directed toward a different goal, namely ending North Atlantic Treaty Organization military presence in the area, it was not difficult to integrate the new task of environmental cooperation into this perspective."[29] Environmental cooperation in the Baltic was viewed as a means of maintaining good relations with the West, and the USSR never considered itself bound to honor any obligations.[30]

In the early years of *perestroika*, Soviet rhetoric and approaches to pollution control did not change much. Even in 1988, the USSR remained reluctant to admit that there were severe environmental problems in the Baltic area and to accept a more action-oriented strategy for dealing with the issue. Moreover, there was no official indication that the USSR was unable to cope with its own problems for financial or technological reasons.[31]

However, by the end of the Gorbachev era, it became clear that the factor that most limited Soviet efforts to improve the Baltic environment was a lack of financing. According to the vice chairman of the Council of Ministers, under whose authority the State Committee on Nature Protection (Goskompriroda) fell, the USSR was technically, scientifically, and morally ready to participate in the measures proposed at Ronneby; however, because they could not finance the necessary changes, the USSR was forced to re-orient its priorities.[32]

With the advent of *perestroika*, the USSR abandoned its position of strongly defending its national sovereignty. During this period, Baltic environmental cooperation became less of a priority in the overall Soviet (and later Russian) foreign environmental policy, particularly once the Baltic republics acquired their independence. In 1990 and 1991, after the Ronneby Conference, the USSR did not attend many subcommittee meetings and was not very active within HELCOM. (In contrast, during the period between 1977 and 1982, the Soviets participated more actively than any other party.) Harald Velner, a prominent Estonian scientist who has held many positions at HELCOM, received no instructions from Moscow during this period, although he was still officially representing the USSR.[33]

Russia as it exists today has lost most of its former Baltic coastline and is troubled with many pressing social and economic issues. For these reasons, environmental problems in the Baltic would probably receive even less attention from the Russian government than they did from the Soviet government were it not for two factors: the strong transboundary impact of the pollution generated, particularly that originating in St. Petersburg; and the perceived need to demonstrate compliance with international obligations. Moreover, in Russia some environmental problems are regarded as "first class" problems because they attract the attention of the West. The significance of such problems within Russian policy is determined primarily by the response they cause abroad, and to a much lesser extent by their domestic impact.[34]

St. Petersburg is the heart of the Russian military-industrial complex, but it lacks up-to-date municipal and industrial water treatment for the more than 500 enterprises that discharge wastewater into the Neva River through nearly 400 outfalls.[35] Moreover, although the Neva River is only 74 kilometers long, it also collects water from a highly industrialized area slightly smaller than Italy encompassing the Leningrad province and parts of the Novgorod, Pskov, and Vologda provinces.[36] According to the results of the Second Baltic Sea Pollution Load Compilation undertaken by HELCOM, in 1990 Russian municipal sources (primarily those in St. Petersburg) accounted for 74 percent of the total BOD_7 (organic matter),[37] 70 percent of the nitrogen, and 85 percent of the phosphorus load in the Gulf of Finland.[38]

The three newly independent Baltic states have a much higher stake in the Baltic Sea environment than Russia. Apart from peat and forest lands, their most valuable natural resources are fish from the Baltic Sea and coastal recreational resources, both under severe threat from pollution. Public concern about the environment has been greatly enhanced by the perception that most of the environmental problems in the Baltic states are the result of economic mismanagement by Moscow during the Soviet era, which together with the expansion of heavy industry and the state's political monopoly led to ineffective environmental policies.[39] Each of the three countries is its own largest source of pollution. However, much of the domestic pollution flows into the Baltic, and thus cooperation in the Baltic is also a way to address domestic environmental treaties.

As during the Soviet era, Baltic cooperation is a way to engage with the West, although now the goals are to solidify Western relations (and eventually join the EU) and to weaken Moscow's influence. HELCOM activities were important in gaining international recognition for these three former Soviet republics. The HELCOM platform gave them some of their earliest opportunities to participate in international fora as independent entities. This participation was made possible by a progressive attitude on the part of the Nordic countries, especially Denmark and Sweden, which enacted several measures to prepare the way for the Baltic states' future recognition. Participation in HELCOM activities is currently among the new states' top international environmental priorities.

Estonia is noted for its especially high levels of air pollution resulting from the concentration of power plants in the northeastern part of the country, which account for three-quarters of Estonia's total air pollution load. Estonia's emissions of 140 kg of SO_2 per capita per year are probably the highest in the world; in comparison, Latvia, for example, emits 23 kg of SO_2 per capita annually, and Sweden emits 12 kg SO_2 per capita each year.[40] Estonia's capacity to purify industrial and urban wastewater is limited but improving: the proportion of insufficiently treated wastewater declined from 78 percent in 1987 to 12 percent in 1994. Nonetheless, about 10 percent of Estonia's sewage is not treated.[41] Many smaller cities and towns have no water treatment at all. In Latvia, the situation is even bleaker. Reports indicate that the fishing industry is threatened because Riga, a city of about 1 million inhabitants, had no wastewater treatment plant until 1991. There have been serious outbreaks of hepatitis.[42] About 45 percent of the wastewater is inadequately treated or untreated, and about 30 percent of Latvia's municipalities lack treatment plants.[43] In Lithuania, Kaunas, with a population of 500,000, has no primary sewage treatment plant; all industrial and residential waste enters the Neman and Neris Rivers and is carried to Kursiu Lagoon and into the Baltic. Of the three Baltic states, the percentage of wastewater treated in accordance with existing standards is the lowest in Lithuania, where only 75 percent of wastewater is treated.[44] In both Latvia and Lithuania, beaches have been closed to swimming several times since the summer of 1989 because of concern about health risks.

Implementation of the Baltic Sea Commitments

Government Regulation

The balance of this chapter considers how Russia and the Baltic states have implemented commitments to clean up the Baltic Sea. This section adopts a state-centered approach: it examines the mechanisms by which Baltic pollution controls have been implemented by central and regional or local *governmental* bodies in Russia and the Baltic republics; it identifies the instruments used to modify the behavior of target groups and rates their success; and it determines the importance of the governments' ability to mobilize domestic and external financial resources to pay the cost of implementation. This section emphasizes two aspects of the implementation of these controls: the effectiveness of market-based instruments such as pollution charges and taxes, and the ways that decentralization of authority and uncertainty in the division of rights and responsibilities between regulatory subjects brought about by the transition have affected the states' ability to translate international commitments into domestic action. Here, implementation by governmental bodies is organized into three components: national programs and plans, regulatory activities, and sources of financing.

National Programs.   The USSR established its first environmental program for the Baltic Sea region in 1988. The program encompassed about 500 of the most significant land-based sources of marine pollution and required an investment of 1.2 billion rubles. It aimed at meeting the targets set in the 1988 Ministerial Declaration, and thus also required the construction of treatment plants for municipal sewage for the region's main cities, to be carried out by 1993.[45] The program was incorporated into the State Environment Protection Program for 1991–1995, which had a special chapter on the Baltic region. However, because of the deterioration of the USSR's economic situation and the ensuing disintegration of the Union itself, the program was never adopted.

In 1992, Finland and Russia signed an agreement on environmental cooperation that included an action program for limiting water and marine pollution in areas adjacent to the Finland-Russia border.[46] In 1993, Russia adopted a draft National Action Plan to implement the decisions of the United Nations Conference on Environment and Development (UNCED). The draft Plan contained a section devoted to the Baltic Sea that envisaged implementing the JCP, the HELCOM Conventions, Ministerial Declarations, and the Soviet-Finnish agreement.[47] However, these plans and programs followed a tradition that prevailed during the communist period: they were merely an uncoordinated listing of investment needs for a number of specific projects. No priorities were set, no cost-benefit analysis was made, and no funding sources were identified. The National Action Plan, for example, included 149 "priority measures and directions for environmental rehabilitation," although it was estimated that domestic resources could at best cover only one-tenth of the required investment needs for the Plan's implementation.[48]

No specific programs for implementing the JCP or the Helsinki Convention have yet been developed in the Baltic states. A partial exception is Estonia, where a national plan for the protection of the Baltic Sea was adopted in 1991, shortly after the country gained its independence. However, this plan was modeled on its Soviet predecessors and thus lacked specific priorities and funding sources.[49] Also, Estonian cooperation with Finland is based on a bilateral agreement signed in 1993. The reduction targets in this agreement are somewhat less ambitious than those in a similar agreement between Russia and Finland.[50] Nonetheless, in all three Baltic states national environmental strategies or programs, including short- and medium-term action plans, are in various stages of drafting or development. Development of these plans and strategies is usually funded by foreign sources, mainly from the EU's PHARE program.[51]

Regulatory Structures.   Environmental programs have helped to set goals and strategies. In turn, governments have used regulations to control emissions. The effectiveness of those regulations has depended on the standards adopted as well as the administrative mechanisms by which standards are applied. Both are considered here.

Divergent Systems of Standards.   Historically, two major types of water pollution control strategies have been applied. In the first type, the aim is to control the environment that receives discharged pollutants; in the second, attempts are made to control the sources of pollution. In the first case environmental quality standards are applicable, whereas in the second case emission (or technological) standards are used. The first approach has the advantage of minimizing environmental protection costs, because it is primarily based on the ultimate environmental objective and does not necessarily mandate that particular sources be controlled in particular ways. In contrast, the second type of strategy leads to specific requirements for specific plants, based on economic and technological capabilities. Frequently, combinations of the two approaches are employed.

In an attempt to reduce expenditures for wastewater treatment, in the 1960s the USSR chose the first strategy. Focusing on the self-purification capacity of the water environment,[52] the USSR built several deep-sea sewage outfalls for the cities of Tallinn and Kohtla-Järve, among others.[53] The strategy was put into law by the USSR Water Code of 1970, according to which discharges of wastewaters were permitted provided that the concentration of pollutants at a control site did not exceed the maximum permissible concentrations (MPCs) established for sanitary protection of the water bodies. The volumes of permitted discharges were calculated on the basis of MPCs, taking into account the effects of dilution, mixing, and self-purification. However, in spite of the growing body of knowledge about these processes and the use of contemporary theories of water treatment systems management, the state of the water environment in the USSR, including the Baltic basin, continued to deteriorate.

One reason for this deterioration was the difficulty of monitoring the water quality of water bodies to determine whether it met the environmental quality standards, which was both costly and technically complicated. First, the standards were too numerous and the resources for environmental monitoring too limited. Furthermore, no reliable analytical control methods were available for the majority of pollutants with established MPCs (currently totaling 1,345). Moreover, the MPC-based system did not take into account the synergistic or cumulative effects of pollutants. Finally, the rates of developing new MPCs lagged behind the introduction of new chemical substances.[54]

All the Baltic coastal countries except the USSR and Poland opted for the second type of water pollution control strategy. In this strategy, emission or technological standards were used which led to the direct control of discharges from industries and municipal treatment plants.[55] The differences in the two approaches complicated the work of HELCOM, which had to establish unified standards for all Baltic littoral countries. Efforts to negotiate the differences failed. Largely because of pressure from Sweden, Finland, and Germany, however, HELCOM adopted several Recommendations on limiting discharges from specific industries and municipalities, all of which established emission standards. HELCOM has never adopted an environmental quality standard.[56]

Article 6(6) of the Helsinki Convention requires parties to adopt common criteria for issuing permits for discharges (i.e., emission standards). In 1985, after prolonged discussion, a compromise approach was developed and the first criteria for issuing discharge permits for oil refineries were adopted. In practice HELCOM moved to emission standards long before the collapse of the USSR. This shift caused problems for implementation in that country, because Soviet legislation was based on environmental quality standards. However, for political and economic reasons, the USSR did not change its internal rules, and domestic implementation of HELCOM-developed emission and technological standards was uncommon. HELCOM Recommendations were translated into Russian and distributed to local environmental authorities, but the authorities were instructed to merely take them into account.[57]

In the newly independent Baltic states there has been some movement away from the old Soviet system of environmental quality standards. In Lithuania, new regulations on the procedure for determining environmental pollution standards were enacted in January 1991. They are generally based on international agreements, whereby two types of standards are distinguished: maximum permissible emissions (MPEs) and temporary permissible emissions (TPEs). The latter are still considered necessary due to current difficulties in meeting the international obligations.[58] In Latvia, a new system of environmental standards is expected to be developed in connection with the ongoing institution-building project financed by PHARE.[59]

The 1992 Helsinki Convention has overcome the problem of discordant systems of environmental standards by adopting the "precautionary principle" based on BAT or BEP. How this principle will be implemented in practice remains to be seen.

State Regulatory Mechanisms.   In the USSR, the regulatory apparatus for implementing Baltic Sea controls had two main forms. From 1971 to 1976, authority was vested in the Ministry for Land Reclamation and Water Management (Minvodkhoz); from 1976 until the USSR's dissolution, authority was vested in the Interdepartmental Commission on the Protection of the Marine Environment of the Baltic Sea. The latter had the right to control the implementation of the 1974 Convention by Soviet ministries and agencies, but in practice this right was hardly ever used. The Commission did conduct environmental impact assessments of large-scale industrial projects, such as the construction of a ferry link in Klaipeda and the mining of phosphates in Estonia. In light of the Commission's recommendations, the ferry-link project was modified 'and the mining operations were never begun.[60] Exploratory drilling for oil and gas on the continental shelf in the ecologically sensitive area of the Kursiu Lagoon, off the Lithuanian coast, was also stopped for environmental reasons.[61] In many cases, the Commission produced recommendations concerning the introduction of up-to-date (mostly imported) technologies. However, the recommendations generally were not complied with because of the USSR's lack of hard currency resources and the general inadequacy of its economic mechanisms.[62] Overall, the Commission's major efforts prior to 1985 focused on providing environmental equipment for vessels operating in the Baltic, establishing services for combatting oil spills at sea, and installing port reception facilities for oil residues and wastes from ships.[63]

In 1988, the newly established Goskompriroda took over most of the responsibilities of Minvodkhoz. As of August 1996, apart from the Ministry of Environment,[64] which succeeded Goskompriroda, three other agencies have participated in HELCOM activities: the Federal Service of Hydrometeorology and Environmental Monitoring (Rosgidromet), the Committee on Fisheries (Roskomrybolovstvo), and the Department of Marine Transportation in the Ministry of Transport. In practice, according to the national UNCED report, the responsibility lies in the hands of "ministries, departments, and the bodies of local self-government,"[65] an extremely diffuse and unclear model of the division of responsibilities. At the federal level alone, at least six agencies are responsible for water use and protection.[66]

In Russia and all three Baltic states, transition from central planning has shifted responsibility for implementing the Convention to the local level. In Russia, for example, a great deal of responsibility for implementation falls not only on federal bodies but also on local environmental protection committees (e.g., the Committee on Ecology and Natural Resources for St. Petersburg and the Leningrad Province, Lenkomekologiya), subordinated to the Ministry of Environment, and on local and municipal authorities. However, this transfer of responsibilities in Russia and the Baltic states usually has not been accompanied by a corresponding transfer of resources and implementation competence or by the establishment of appropriate local infrastructure. In Russia, responsibility for environmental management is divided between the subjects of the Federation (republics, provinces, territories, autonomous areas and provinces, and the cities of Moscow and St. Petersburg) and the Federation itself, which maintains control of the majority of management and control bodies, with "the only reason for their existence being to justify the existence of the controllers themselves."[67] The situation is exacerbated by the unclear division of responsibilities between local divisions of federal environmental bodies and local or municipal authorities.

Because the drainage basin of the Neva River and the Lake of Ladoga includes the territories of 11 provinces in northwestern Russia, the state of the environment in the Gulf of Finland depends on the environmental protection activities of each province. There have been many efforts to coordinate the environmental activities of various agencies on the principle that the basin should be managed as a single unit. Lenkomekologiya has established a coordination council of representatives from the 11 northwestern provinces, with working groups to coordinate inspection activities and analytical and expert assessment services.[68]

In practice, however, there has been little coordination even between the city of St. Petersburg and the surrounding Leningrad province, two subjects of the Federation that share a common environment and are obvious partners in the collective effort to protect the Baltic. The Leningrad province has even established its own Ministry for Environmental Protection and Ecology, with a staff of 15. The confusion in environmental administration within the region has been exacerbated by a fierce struggle for power and jurisdiction between the city of St. Petersburg and the Leningrad province. Lenkomekologiya is supposed to service both, which is often difficult.[69]

Vertical connections between various levels of government regarding program implementation are very loose, which impairs the transmission of regulatory signals between them. The officials at Lenkomekologiya have repeatedly complained that the flow of information is predominantly one-way—that is, bottom-up—and that the federal ministry sends them back mostly orders and instructions. HELCOM documents and Recommendations also reach St. Petersburg mostly via Moscow, often after lengthy delays.[70]

The situation is well illustrated by the monitoring issue. In Russia, every agency concerned with natural resource use has its own environmental monitoring system; by law, each is required to regularly submit all monitoring data to the federal Monitoring Center for processing. In practice, however, the Center produces only aggregated data; moreover, the Ministry of Environment does not supply detailed data to regional committees. Consequently, despite extensive Russian monitoring, regional authorities lack a comprehensive view of the local environmental situation. In 1994 St. Petersburg's environmental authorities established a comprehensive regional monitoring system that is supposed to supply all the relevant information to government authorities; however, it is still too early to assess whether this new approach is working.

Following independence, the Baltic states completely reconsidered their institutional structures for environmental protection. In all three countries, executive departments have been transformed into environmental ministries that provide overall management and control of environmental pollution and natural resources. Environmental management has also been decentralized. A number of regional environmental protection departments (19 in Estonia, 9 in Latvia, and 8 in Lithuania) are entrusted with issuing and enforcing permits for pollution discharges and use of natural resources. However, coordination problems, the absence of a clear line of authority, and poorly defined roles and responsibilities detrimentally affect the performance of these bodies. For example, in Lithuania the Republican Hygiene Center is responsible for the enforcement of recreational and drinking water standards, but coordination between the Center and local environmental agencies is hampered by the fact that the agencies are organized on the basis of 8 regions, whereas the Hygiene Center is organized on the basis of 44 municipalities and 8 cities.[71]

On the positive side, all major activities in Estonia and Latvia aimed at implementing the JCP with respect to priorities and time schedules are currently related to the EU PHARE program and to PHARE management units (PMUs) in Tallinn and Riga, respectively. The Estonian representative at HELCOM PITF is the head of the PMU office, which functions as an administrative unit of the Bureau of International Relations within the Ministry of Environment.[72] Thus in practice PHARE has significantly facilitated planning and coordination of JCP implementation in these countries.

Nevertheless, the Baltic states show a growing appreciation of the need for closer cooperation in environmental protection and in coordination of scarce resources in the issue field. This appreciation has been evident in the emergence of a plethora of new bilateral agreements that include, but are not limited to, the issue of Baltic environmental protection. Among these agreements are those between Russia and Lithuania on Kaliningrad (1991); between Latvia and Estonia (1994); between Lithuania and Belarus (1995); between Latvia, Estonia, and Lithuania (1995); between Estonia and Poland (1995); and most recently (January 1996) between Estonia and Russia.

Financial Mechanisms and Investments.   The investments in water pollution control in the Baltic region required to implement the JCP are immense and will far outstrip available funding. Estimated expenditures for the 132 identified hot spots are some 10 billion ECU (US$13.4 billion), including about 6.5 billion ECU (US$8.7 billion) for the 47 sites deemed "priority" hot spots.[73] The formerly communist countries of the region account for over 80 percent of the total investment needs. The country with the greatest investment requirements is Poland, which accounts for 41 percent of the total estimated expenditures (see Chapter 15). However, the needs of Russia and the Baltic states taken together exceed the figure for Poland. Of these, Estonia comes first, requiring nearly 16 percent of the total,[74] followed by Russia with 14 percent of the total. In Russia alone, total investment requirements for implementing the JCP have been estimated by HELCOM to be approximately 1.5 billion ECU (US$2 billion).[75]

The JCP is expected to be phased in over a period of at least 20 years to keep pace with the gradually increasing capacity to mobilize financial resources. In the first phase (1993–1997), at a total cost of about 5 billion ECU (US$6.7 billion), efforts will be concentrated on creating institutional arrangements. Limited investments will be made in the highest-priority projects, including mainly rehabilitation and expansion of existing municipal and industrial wastewater treatment plants in Poland, Russia, and the Baltic states. Reducing water pollution from 29 hot spots during this stage is expected to contribute to a decrease in the overall annual pollution load by 300,000 tons of BOD_5, 33,500 tons of nitrogen, and 8,200 tons of total phosphorus. The second phase of the JCP (1998–2012), with a total investment estimate of about 13 billion ECU (US$17.4 billion), will focus on developing specific investment projects for each remaining hot spot.[76] Cost estimates continue to change as more information is gathered in these countries.[77]

Even during the initial stage of the JCP's development, it has been widely understood that availability and quantity of funds are the main barriers to implementation. This section analyzes the collection and spending of local and foreign resources.

Domestic Resources.   Estimates of funds spent on Baltic environmental protection in the FSU are few and their reliability is questionable. In 1992, the Russian Ministry of Environment estimated that overall Soviet expenses for this purpose reached 2.5 billion rubles by the mid-1980s: about 1 billion rubles were spent on preventing pollution from vessels and on constructing port reception facilities, and about 1.5 billion rubles were spent on capital investments in land-based facilities. Due to a lack of funding, by the mid-1980s only 70 percent of the Soviet enterprises and cities affected had fulfilled the planned targets for controlling land-based pollution envisaged by the 1976 Council of Ministers' Resolution.[78]

With the transition to a market economy, financing of environmental programs in Russia has undergone radical changes. Federal budget funds are available only for financing some measures that were included in state programs, such as the Chernobyl program. Thus, since 1992 funds from enterprises have been the primary source of financing for capital investments. However, high inflation rates and a lack of funds have prevented adequate allocation of resources for investment in production, let alone environmental measures.

Over the course of economic and political transition, the system of pollution charges has become the most significant financial innovation for environmental protection. All pollution charges paid by enterprises are earmarked for environmental funds: 10 percent to the federal fund, 30 percent to regional funds, and 60 percent to local funds. However, not only was the federal environmental fund "consolidated" into the federal budget in both 1994 and 1995, but attempts to use earmarked resources from the environmental funds for purposes other than environmental protection are widespread at the local level. In theory, environmental funds are independent of local authorities; in practice, however, they are typically controlled by regional administrations. Consequently, financial resources frequently do not reach the funds, are spent for other purposes, and are rapidly devalued by inflation.[79]

Pollution charges are based on federal norms of emissions and discharges established by the Ministry of Environment for 198 polluting substances. The rate charged for above-limit pollution discharges is five times that charged for within-limit emissions; the fines for above-limit discharges are to be paid directly from the after-tax profit. (A similarly structured system of charges is applied to air pollution—see Chapter 12.) In practice, payments for above-limit discharges account for about 80 percent of the total.[80] At the same time, the system allows for a large degree of flexibility. Local authorities are empowered to increase or reduce payments depending on the local environmental situation. For example, pollution charges in St. Petersburg have been increased by 100 percent since April 1996, a decision motivated by the need to raise revenues for city environmental construction projects.[81] However, sums spent by enterprises for priority environmental purposes can be deducted from pollution charges; in the Baltic Sea basin, these include water protection measures aimed at reducing the emissions of phosphorus, nitrogen, oil, heavy metals, and other pollutants determined by HELCOM.[82]

Flexibility has decreased the effectiveness of the system of pollution charges. In the majority of instances, local authorities have made use of their right to reduce the amount of payments, usually limiting them to 7 to 10 percent of a firm's after-tax profits to prevent the firm's going out of business. When charges are kept this low, they have little effect on the polluting firms. In addition, pollution charges have persistently lagged behind inflation.[83] Calculated in constant prices, the charges in 1993 were several times lower than those in 1991.[84] As a result, pollution charges, which account for just 0.1 percent of the consolidated federal budget revenues, are too low to stimulate rational environmental management by polluters, nor do they raise sufficient money for environmental investments. This drawback is gradually being rectified, however: compared with basic charges, all charges were increased by a factor of 10 in 1994, by a factor of 17 in 1995, and by a factor of 35 in 1996.[85]

Before 1993 no funds were appropriated from the federal budget for implementation of the JCP in Russia. However, the allocation of about US$15 million throughout 1993 and 1994 allowed the completion of the second phase of construction of the northern wastewater treatment plant in St. Petersburg, extending its daily capacity from 0.6 million to 1.25 million cubic meters (corresponding to additional wastewater treatment for about 1 million inhabitants). Eventually, almost one-third of the city's wastewater load will be treated at this facility at a total cost of US$77 million.[86] The 1995 federal budget allocated US$16 million for upgrading water treatment and sewerage systems in the St. Petersburg area, including US$13 million for dealing with the JCP-designated hot spots.[87] These measures have allowed 40 percent of the sewerage floodgates to be switched to the centralized city sewerage network and the proportion of untreated municipal discharges to be reduced from 40 percent in 1990 to 20 percent in 1995.[88] It is likely that without the existence of international commitments, these federal investments would have been substantially lower or nonexistent.

Apart from the federal budget, domestic financial resources for implementing the municipal and agricultural elements of the JCP in the St. Petersburg area originate from the city itself, from the State Environmental Fund, and from the state enterprise Vodokanal (St. Petersburg's municipal water and sewerage works).[89] Because federal funds constitute only a part of the financing required, the city has had to increase allocations from its own budget on a regular basis. Although the share of financing from the Federal Environmental Fund has increased somewhat, it remains very low, representing 1 percent of total Russian environmental spending in 1992 and 2.4 percent in 1994.[90]

Vodokanal, which previously was completely dependent on funding from the St. Petersburg City Council, is currently financed in part by municipal subsidies and in part by user fees. However, the proportion financed by user fees is increasing and is expected to reach 100 percent in the near future. In theory, the development of autonomous, self-financed water utilities should result both in their being operated more efficiently and in reductions in industrial and domestic water consumption and water losses.[91] These changes, however, involve raising user fees to adequate levels, which will result in increased difficulties with fee collection, especially from domestic consumers.[92]

A total of 80 million ECU (US$106 million) was invested between 1991 and 1995 to renovate the water supply and water treatment infrastructure in St. Petersburg.[93] The planned investment for the city is 200 million ECU (US$264 million). No matter how large these investments may seem by Russian standards, they are still substantially below the investment needed to meet HELCOM standards at just four priority hot spots in the St. Petersburg area, the costs of which have been estimated at about 1.6 billion ECU (US$2.1 billion), with US$ 713 million required for sewers in St. Petersburg alone.[94]

Compared with St. Petersburg, the situation is more serious in the Kaliningrad area where, apart from primitive mechanical treatment, wastewater treatment plants are virtually nonexistent. In 1976, construction began on a number of combined water treatment facilities, which are now 50 percent completed; even as late as 1994, none of the 45 facilities under construction had been put into operation.[95] In that year, from a total of US$12.5 million allocated for the completion of wastewater treatment facilities in Kaliningrad, actual disbursements from centralized funding sources provided only US$1 million. The quality of construction, especially that done in previous periods, is so poor that it is doubtful whether these plants will ever be useful. As no additional investments are planned from domestic or international sources,[96] the attainment of HELCOM requirements in Kaliningrad in the foreseeable future is highly questionable.

As in Russia, the domestic economic situations in the newly independent Baltic states still preclude significant national investments in environmental projects. As a result, many of the projects concerning designated hot spots have experienced delays or have not been started. Even in Lithuania, where the construction of wastewater treatment plants at priority hot spots has been treated as a matter of national importance, and where the 1993 and 1994 state budgets allocated 3 percent of total government expenditures (about US$36 million) for this purpose, available funds at best are able to cover only a small percentage of the total estimated investments. Moreover, these funds are being allocated on a year-by-year basis, and there is uncertainty as to whether and when funding will be available for completing long-term projects.[97] Moreover, environmental outlays have tended to decline, rather than increase, over time. In 1995, Latvia spent 45 percent less on environmental protection than in 1994.[98]

In general, funds from state budgets currently play relatively minor roles in financing environmental investments in the Baltic states: at best they cover only the operating costs of the central and regional administrations.[99] Based on a sample from Estonia, Latvia, and Lithuania, the actual funds available are well below 1 ECU per capita.[100]

Environmental funds, which are supplied with the revenue from pollution taxes, have been much more important sources of financing in the Baltic states than in Russia. In Estonia, for example, resources from the Environment Fund covered 24 percent of total environmental expenses in 1994.[101] The environmental funds are built on the principle that all natural resources are the property of the state, and their use is therefore subject to a fee. Consequently, all three Baltic states have introduced economic incentives to implement environmental policy. Taxes are levied on the use of state-owned natural resources and on each ton of a polluting substance that is discharged (the tax rate is dependent on the type of pollutant discharged).[102] In Estonia, penalties can be added to the pollution taxes if permitted discharge levels are exceeded. Enterprises that invest in environmental protection can obtain a tax reduction. The taxes collected are shared equally between the state and regional environmental funds.[103]

Pollution taxes in Lithuania are also directly related to environmental standards. The funds obtained through these taxes amount to about 0.6 percent of Lithuania's national income, or 1.2 percent of total budget expenditures. Seventy percent of the collected fees go to the municipalities and 30 percent go to the State Environmental Fund. State financial support for environmental projects in Lithuania is channeled primarily for construction of wastewater treatment plants.[104] As in Russia, the effectiveness of this system of economic incentives is questionable, because the tax rates are fixed and do not reflect the inflation rate. Moreover, in various regions the amount of the pollution charges depends on the polluters' ability to pay, and only about 50 percent of the anticipated income is actually collected. So far there has been little evidence that pollution taxes in Lithuania have actually had an impact on reducing emissions.[105]

Nevertheless, despite limited domestic resources, several investment projects at hot spots in the three Baltic countries have taken place since 1991, some of which have progressed significantly.[106] Overall, between 1991 and 1994 more than US$13 million was invested in abatement projects in the Baltic states, with financing from both local and external sources. This figure should, however, be seen in light of the additional investment of almost US$400 million that will be required if HELCOM Recommendations are to be met in full: US$120 million is needed for sewers in Riga alone.[107] In Russia, the imbalance between the investments required and those incurred already is even greater.

External Resources.   The experience of implementing the JCP in the formerly communist countries of the Baltic region since 1991 has demonstrated that external resources are vital if HELCOM standards are to be met, and that they will remain at least as important as local funding in both the short and medium terms. In Estonia, for example, foreign resources accounted for 44 percent of the financing for water management projects in 1994;[108] in St. Petersburg foreign sources currently make up an estimated 10 percent of total financing, and this figure is gradually increasing.[109] The principal external sources currently available include grants and concessional funding provided by bilateral donors, loans provided by international financial institutions (IFIs) and commercial banks, direct investments by foreign companies, and export credit guarantees.

Grant and concessional resources from the EU and bilateral donors have been the scarcest but also the most important source of financing because they do not require repayment. Under the PHARE and LIFE programs, the EU committed 1 million ECU to each of the three Baltic states in 1992 (these figures are dwarfed, however, by the EU's 75 million ECU contribution to Poland's environmental sector in the same year). PHARE environmental budgets in Latvia for 1992 and 1993 amounted to 1.1 and 1.6 million ECU, respectively; in 1994 PHARE's budget in Lithuania was 1.6 million ECU.[110] The LIFE program has provided support for two Environmental Centers for Administration and Technology (ECATs), one in St. Petersburg and one in Riga. Both centers were designed as cofinanced twinning arrangements between the municipalities of St. Petersburg-Hamburg and Riga-Bremen.[111] EU assistance to Russia is distributed primarily through the TACIS program; however, unlike PHARE, TACIS has not given high priority to environmental issues, and thus only a few EU-assisted environmental projects (mainly related to energy issues) have been implemented in Russia.[112]

The main source of external financing for JCP implementation, including all pre-feasibility studies, has been grant or concessional funding from bilateral donors, mainly Nordic countries. In 1991 and 1992, about 37 percent (US$10 million) of Finland's total assistance to Russia and 40 percent (US$8 million) of its assistance to the Baltic states was allocated to the environment.[113] In 1993, Sweden dedicated about US$37 million to measures within the JCP framework—the greatest amount of support (US$16 million) was provided for investments in wastewater treatment plants in Estonia, Latvia, and Lithuania.[114]

Bilateral environmental assistance to the Baltic countries and northwestern Russia has been allocated according to a "geographical division of labor" among the Nordic donor countries. Although assistance from virtually every Nordic country can be found in each of the former Soviet republics under study, Finnish aid is primarily concentrated in Estonia, Karelia, St. Petersburg, and the Leningrad province; Norwegian assistance is centered on the Kola

Peninsula; Sweden is most active in Latvia; and Denmark concentrates on Lithuania.[115] Among the Baltic states, Estonia has received more international environmental support than Latvia or Lithuania (if the support for nuclear safety at the Ignalina nuclear power plant is excluded).[116] In some cases the choice of a recipient country or region is explained by its geographic location "upstream" or "upwind" from the donor country (Finland, Norway, and Sweden). In other cases other variables, such as type of project, political situation, influence of pressure groups (e.g., immigrants from the region), investment needs, or, most often, domestic companies' interests in transferring equipment or knowledge linked to such investments, play a major role.[117]

Although exact numbers are not available, rough calculations of the amount of bilateral and multilateral environmental support (including loans) provided to the Baltic states and northwestern Russia (excluding the Murmansk region) seem to indicate that significantly less external environmental assistance has gone to Russia than to the Baltic states. Since the fall of the communist regimes, Estonia has received US$97.6 million in foreign environmental assistance, Latvia US$32.9 million, and Lithuania US$36.7 million (in addition, loans for about US$30 million are in the discussion stage); in comparison, northwestern Russia has received only US$24.7 million.[118] The difference can be explained by the greater political and economic stability in the Baltic countries compared with the situation in Russia. Furthermore, enterprises and municipal facilities in Estonia, Latvia, and Lithuania are better positioned to purchase foreign technology because their domestic currencies are convertible.[119] An additional factor is the difference in attitude toward the use of imported technology: Russian officials have repeatedly emphasized their preference for Russian technology— which is generally less costly and even, on occasion, more effective—to solve domestic environmental problems. Thus the condition of using imported technology, which is typically tied to foreign assistance, has met more criticism in Russia than in the Baltic states.[120]

Most bilateral agreements require the recipient country to match foreign funding with funding in the local currency, which is financed mainly with the earnings of the company or plant in question. Grant and concessional financing from bilateral sources is normally conditional on special procurement procedures that tie its use to equipment, consulting services, and training from sources within the donor country itself.[121] Thus, domestic resources and technology remain underutilized, and at times donors conceal technical information from their foreign partners.[122] In addition, the provision of foreign environmental assistance to Russia has been hampered by the imposition of customs duties on imported environmental equipment: according to Finnish sources, between one-fourth and one-third of total Finnish appropriations for environmental assistance to Russia is spent on duties and other taxes, thus reducing the funds available for environmental investments and jeopardizing the implementation of several JCP programs.[123]

The interests of donors and recipients in these bilateral agreements have been compatible in the sense that pollution affects all those involved. However, there are differences in how these groups prioritize various environmental issues; for instance, although most local decision makers in St. Petersburg emphasize purification of drinking water, offers from Finnish companies have generally focused on sewage treatment systems. The Finnish Ministry of Environment has offered financial support for projects that contribute to improving the water quality in the Gulf of Finland. Thus, Finland's interest in improving the sewerage system has not always been met with equal enthusiasm in St. Petersburg. The same is true of Estonia, where public attention is focused on environmental issues caused by the Russian military and on groundwater pollution, rather than on the pollution of the Baltic.[124] Often, evaluations and conclusions produced by foreign experts do not adequately account for local conditions. As several projects have shown, recommendations can rapidly become outdated as a result of political and economic developments, thus requiring new pre-feasibility studies before implementation can begin.[125]

In addition to grants and concessional funding from bilateral donors, financing for environmental projects also comes in the form of loans from IFIs and commercial banks. Funds from multilateral financial institutions are lent at market rates, and their effective use is contingent upon the borrower's willingness to agree to service the resulting loans. Many multilateral institutions also require state guarantees for repayment from recipient countries. The World Bank and the European Bank for Reconstruction and Development (EBRD) have recently begun to act as coordinators or leaders of projects where investments are too large to be financed by a single source and therefore several donors are involved.[126] This is often the case for major municipal projects concerning mostly combined industrial and municipal wastewater treatment.[127]

In May 1995, the World Bank announced a major program to support the JCP by financing seven projects at a total cost of US$240 million. Lithuania and Latvia are each undertaking two projects, and Estonia, Russia, and Poland are undertaking one project each. Five of the projects had been approved by the Bank's Board of Executive Directors as of March 1996.[128] The World Bank became active in Russia much later than in the Baltic states. Its project in St. Petersburg, part of a larger housing project, is short-term in nature and aims at strengthening water and wastewater services in the northern part of the city, including completion of the northern wastewater treatment plant.[129] The World Bank is preparing a water and sanitation loan for four or five cities, including St. Petersburg and Kaliningrad; investments will probably begin in 1997 at the earliest.[130]

The EBRD, which was established specifically to distribute loans for investments in Central and Eastern Europe, has been somewhat less active in the environmental field than the World Bank. The EBRD's first, and so far its only, loan for environmental infrastructure—a loan of US$26 million for renovating the Tallinn wastewater treatment plant—was approved in 1994. Recently, the EBRD and Vodokanal of St. Petersburg entered into negotiations for loans totaling US$73.5 million to improve the reliability and quality of drinking water in the city.[131] The EBRD is also preparing a Riga Environment Project (with funding totaling US$82 million) to finance short-term priority investments in the Riga waterworks.[132]

The Nordic Investment Bank (NIB) has not supported many projects in Central and Eastern Europe because of the credit risks. However, it has created the Nordic Environment Finance Corporation (NEFCO), a facility connected to the NIB, to make it possible to provide loans to the environmental sectors in these countries. According to its charter, NEFCO funds should be invested only in commercially sound projects in which a Nordic company is a partner.[133] Within the JCP, the NIB has financed pre-investment and pre-feasibility studies for designated hot spots and has provided some technical assistance. In Russia, most of these studies were connected with Finnish investment projects and were financed through the NIB's Finnish Trust Fund.[134]

Overall, because multilateral institutions arrange loans at around market rates rather than use concessional funding, and because the countries want to create as little foreign debt as possible, few such loans for JCP implementation have been used within the region. This is particularly true in Russia, where the general opinion among the authorities is that they cannot afford to take foreign loans under the current loan conditions, which are considered to be too strict.[135]

To sum up, despite good will and high-level political confirmation of the willingness to support the JCP financially, little external financing actually took place until about 1994. Many investment proposals have been developed and pre-feasibility studies have been conducted, but most of these have tended to be oversized and costly; in many cases, they have not coincided with the priorities of municipal governments and water enterprises. Municipal governments undertaking some of these proposals have committed their scarce resources to expensive ventures that could be achieved at a much lower cost.[136] Whatever foreign funding has been provided has primarily been oriented toward technical assistance, and the role of investment projects has tended to be minimal.

Recently, however, the trend has been changing. Recipient countries are now demanding that pre-feasibility studies be followed by investments. Several donors (Finland, Sweden, Norway, and EU PHARE) are now turning to a more investment-oriented approach, and some of the big investment projects led by the World Bank and the EBRD have now reached the implementation stage.[137] Although the bulk of international environmental assistance is still channeled to the countries of Central and Eastern Europe, there is also a distinct (albeit slow) trend toward more environmental support for Russia.

Still, attempts to mobilize large-scale financial resources for JCP implementation on a multilateral basis have had mixed results. Apart from a few multilateral projects, virtually all external funding for JCP hot spots comes through bilateral arrangements with Western nations. Donor countries have been reluctant to commit themselves to large-scale projects in situations of economic and political instability. For the time being, only Finland and to a limited extent Denmark have provided tangible financial support to Russia for implementing priority projects identified in the JCP. Moreover, the progress achieved to date has been mainly in the municipal sector. In the industrial sector, some on-site research has been conducted and some pilot and demonstration units have been installed, but full-scale investment programs do not yet exist.[138]

Courts
The role of courts in the implementation process has been minimal. Since 1994, arbitration courts in St. Petersburg have often refused to accept environmental

cases, arguing that the courts are overburdened with other, more important cases. Another reason the courts have played such a small role is that the whole process of enforcing fines has become almost meaningless due to inflation. In 1994, courts in St. Petersburg were recovering damages on suits filed in 1989, without any adjustment for inflation (which reduced the real value of payments by a factor of at least 2,000).[139] Even if damages are assessed promptly by court action, they generally cannot be recovered: most enterprises are officially insolvent, though in practice many operate through subsidiary companies that make profits but cannot be held responsible for the environmental violations of the parent company.

Administrative fines for enterprises prescribed by the 1992 Law on Environmental Protection (which is currently being revised) range between 50,000 and 500,000 rubles (roughly US$10 to US$100) per violation—values so low that they are not felt by any company. Recovering administrative fines from legal persons is nearly impossible. Fines are generally paid on a practically voluntary basis, as almost no court will accept claims to this end made by local environmental protection committees.[140] Not surprisingly, penalties levied for violations of emission limits produce little effect. However, in addition to fining the enterprises, courts can fine the officials responsible for the violation (from 3 to 20 months' minimum-wage earnings), as well as private persons violating emission limits (from 1 to 10 months' minimum-wage earnings). The latter fines reportedly have a greater effect, but are not believed to have much influence on major polluters, as the size of the fines (currently from about US$13 to US$260) is still insignificant compared with the cost of implementing measures to meet emission standards.[141] Although some criminal sanctions are possible, criminal law is almost never applied for environmental offenses: 90 percent of the offenses are punished by administrative means.[142] However, the new criminal code, which entered into force 1 January 1997, envisages tougher sanctions for environmental crime if the actions have caused damage to human health or the death of animals, including fines of up to 500 months' minimum-pay wages (currently over US$6,000) or a prison term of up to three years.

Because most state efforts are directed at countering violent and economic crime, by some estimates unregistered environmental crime makes up over 90 percent of the total number of environmental offenses. The number of criminal lawsuits for the most serious environmental offenses is currently 50 to 70 percent lower than it was in 1987.[143] Environmental offenses are still regarded as "insignificant," presenting little social danger; the law on responsibility for environmental offenses is still in the early stages of drafting. Such "tolerance" stimulates negligence and irresponsibility among managers and entrepreneurs.

Target Groups

So far this analysis has concerned mainly governments and their agents. However, domestic implementation of international environmental commitments requires the participation of many other actors: target groups (industries, municipal water authorities), ENGOs, the public, the courts, the media, etc. This section attempts to demonstrate how changes in the number and composition of these "stakeholders" caused by transition have affected implementation. It incorporates the material discussed above and addresses the central questions of interest in this book: What impact did the policies to implement Baltic Sea commitments have on the behavior of target groups, and how has behavior been influenced by other stakeholders?

A critical element in this story is that the transition from central planning has dramatically increased the number and changed the composition of actors involved; control and the functions of governance have been dispersed. In the majority of cases, privatization of formerly state-owned enterprises has resulted in their splitting into smaller independent firms. As a rule, these new companies have been unwilling to take full responsibility for the costly, capital-intensive requirements to update obsolete environmental infrastructure—such as old wastewater treatment plants, sewerage systems, or waste dump sites— nor have they planned any serious investments in environmental protection. In many cases, smaller privatized firms are unable to pay the costs of water treatment at new, "private" wastewater treatment plants, resulting in repeated "accidental" discharges into water bodies.[144] In the privatization process itself, the State Committee for the Management of State Assets (a federal agency set up to plan, organize, and oversee the process of privatization) does not take into account the environmental situation at a given firm or the costs of environmental measures, nor does it provide for "environmental rehabilitation" of the enterprises involved. No environmental audits are included in the privatization process, and no liability questions related to polluted sites are addressed. "Thus, enterprises already privatized are becoming more and more environmentally dangerous."[145]

In the past, environmental protection authorities in St. Petersburg, for example, had to deal with a single gigantic industrial enterprise, Kirovskiy Zavod, which ranked first among the country's defense industry plants in terms of volume of polluted wastewaters discharged and accounted for 13 percent of the industrial discharges in St. Petersburg. Today, the authorities are faced with controlling approximately 60 companies that have emerged since the enterprise was dissolved. Similarly, the Izhorskiy Zavod enterprise has splintered into 11 independent firms. In 1993, the number of registered "environment users" in St. Petersburg was growing at a rate of three to four per week.[146]

Furthermore, one of the potentially most difficult pollution control problems in the Leningrad province is managing pollution from over 20,000 new small private farms: environmental control mechanisms modeled on those that existed under socialism are ill-suited for controlling the behavior of numerous small actors.[147] In addition, there is no legislative basis for such control, nor are there sufficient resources for exercising it: the entire St. Petersburg Lenkomekologiya staff numbers around 200 people, of whom only 6 are actually involved in water sampling.[148] Most of the employees are grossly underpaid, resulting in high personnel turnover, and there are acute equipment shortages.[149] Specialized marine inspections have been limited to the territory of the port and to small-sized vessels because the last specialized inspection vessel was sold in 1995.[150]

Thus, by simultaneously increasing the number of relevant actors participating in the implementation process, introducing instability and uncertainty in ownership rights, and reducing the administrative capacity of the central and local state authorities, transition has dramatically increased regulatory uncertainty and substantially weakened Russia's ability to implement environmental policies.

The analysis seems to indicate that on the Russian domestic scene participation by targets is virtually nonexistent, at least at the policy-making stage. The crucial target group in the implementation process in St. Petersburg, the defense industry (about 70 percent of the city's industry is defense-oriented), continues to play a very passive role in making and implementing rules. Federal and especially local laws and regulations provide for numerous tax and other privileges, such as the option of spending up to 30 percent of the profit tax on construction of environmental infrastructure instead of remitting it to the state and the right to reduce pollution charges by the amount spent on environmental protection.

The striking fact is that state-owned and even newly privatized large enterprises make very little use of any of these privileges. This is especially true of the defense industry: in 1994, only three defense enterprises in St. Petersburg applied for reductions of pollution charges equal to the amounts they spent on environmental protection.[151] For many years the defense industry operated solely on governmental orders, outside the sphere of market relations, and it remains largely insensitive to cost-benefit calculations. Furthermore, many of these enterprises do not pay any taxes at all and thus do not care about claiming a part of the remittance. By comparison, new private companies have rapidly learned to make use of these privileges, for example, by establishing small subsidiary businesses which are exempt from the profit tax paid to local budgets for two years provided that they invest (even if only on paper) in environmental protection.[152]

Nonetheless, the application of the polluter pays principle in Russia has clearly had a discernible effect on the behavior of polluting enterprises: today they must take environmental standards into account when formulating production policies.[153] In 1993, the approximate sum of pollution payments for an average-size pulp and paper mill amounted to no less than 1 billion rubles (about US$1 million), a sizable figure by Russian standards.[154] Even the defense industry, despite substantial economic hardships, has been forced to react promptly to the application of pollution charges. In 1994 the huge Kirovskiy Zavod enterprise in St. Petersburg paid 2.5 billion rubles (about US$1.3 million) for discharges above the allowed levels. In 1995 it was compelled to complete the construction of its water treatment facilities in just six months, after a construction period stretching back two decades.[155] Attempts to evade payments of pollution charges are widespread, but some of the money is being recovered by the state. In 1992 alone, arbitration courts in Russia considered almost 6,000 claims and recovered 2.8 billion rubles (about US$19 million).[156]

The use of tax incentives in combination with the system of pollution charges has also had a discernible stimulating effect on environmental investments in St. Petersburg and has positively affected the behavior of a key target group—industrial polluters. Several industrial wastewater treatment plants were completed in 1994 in the St. Petersburg/Leningrad area, including the largest one at Kirovskiy Zavod with expenditures totaling US$630,000, and several plants at pulp and paper mills with total investment costs of US$700,000.[157] As a result, after remaining almost unchanged for about 10 years, in 1994 the share of total investments in St. Petersburg devoted to environmental purposes increased to about 7 percent of total investment, compared with the country average of 3.9 percent.[158]

ENGOs and Public Participation

Public environmental movements acquired far greater importance in the former Baltic states than in Russia because of a unique linkage that developed in these states between environmental advocates and national independence movements in the late 1980s. What began as local environmental actions grew into calls for national independence. For example, the "Singing Revolution" in Estonia began in 1988 when public groups protested against plans to exploit phosphorite mines on the republic's northeastern coast.[159] The Latvian independence movement was born out of the Environmental Protection Club (VAK), which organized the first antigovernment demonstrations in Latvia in 1987 and 1988. Following Mikhail Gorbachev's shift to an emphasis on environmental issues in the wake of the Chernobyl accident, nascent Baltic NGOs concerned with the environment began to view these issues in the context of local control over national resources.[160] Baltic ENGOs focused attention on the role the Soviet system, especially the military, played in the degradation of natural resources.[161]

Within Europe, the Baltic states tend to associate themselves with the Nordic countries that lead Europe in environmental protection initiatives. Since public participation there has enjoyed a strong tradition as an important component of environmental protection, the Baltic states are also among the most active FSU countries in public participation initiatives, although such initiatives are still in the early stages.[162] Most national and many local ENGOs cooperate with foreign and international ENGOs, which helps to raise the standards of the domestic organizations. Some national NGOs are members of international networks and international NGOs, such as Coalition Clean Baltic and Friends of the Earth. All the ENGOs face similar difficulties concerning financing (especially from domestic sources), membership development, and declines in popularity.[163] Funding for NGO activities mainly comes from foreign NGOs, institutions, and foundations, including the EU's PHARE programs, rather than from national and local funds.[164] During the struggle for independence environmental protection actions were a major part of a broader political movement; once independence was gained, however, cooperation between ENGOs weakened. Few regular fora and joint actions have been organized in recent years, a notable exception being the open annual meeting of the Estonian Green Movement.

Green parties were founded in all three Baltic states in 1990; following independence in 1991, green party deputies were elected into the first Parliaments of all three countries. Formed as a protest against communism, the green parties in the Baltic states have been more nationalistic than their Western counterparts. They are concerned mostly with domestic problems, which they hope market mechanisms will be able to solve. In the 1992–1993 elections, no green candidates were elected to Parliament in any of the Baltic states. Membership in the green parties is declining as the public increasingly turns its attention to economic and political problems rather than the environment.[165]

All three Baltic countries encourage extensive public participation on environmental issues. Rules that require access to environmental information and allow public participation are provided in constitutions and environmental laws. However, these provisions are broad and difficult to translate into practice. Notably, existing legislation provides few mechanisms by which the public can influence individual decisions of governmental authorities.[166] For example, access to information and the right to know are two constitutional rights that are not fully realized in practice: environmental laws in Latvia and Lithuania do not clearly define when and how information should be made available to the public.[167]

No laws or rules exist that require public participation in the drafting of laws or in deliberations concerning such laws. Parliamentary commissions rarely hold public hearings on environmental laws and regulations; NGOs occasionally have been invited as experts in the field, but not as representatives of the public.[168] In one of the few cases of public participation in legislation and rule making, the Estonian Green Movement participated in the drafting of the procedure for environmental impact assessment. Public participation can be more substantial at the local level. In Estonia, the public has sometimes been consulted or invited to take part in the decision-making process, but only when a foreign source of financing for a particular project has demanded that this be done.[169] Overall, regular cooperation or dialogue on environmental issues between ENGOs, the government, and Parliament has not yet fully developed in any of the Baltic countries. The public and NGOs are not involved in discussions at the parliamentary and governmental levels on international programs and projects financed by IFIs.

Regarding access to the courts, which has been a major means of public participation in the West, every citizen of these countries has a right to participate in court cases individually or through NGOs. However, in Estonia, for example, NGOs do not have the right to initiate a court case: with respect to environmental offenses, only state authorities have the right of standing.[170] The courts are heavily overworked and only limited legal assistance is available—lawyers are usually unfamiliar with existing environmental laws and show little interest in environmental issues.[171] The general image of the courts is poor compared with the images of other state institutions; they are perceived as instruments of government policy and are rarely used by NGOs as a tool for public participation.[172]

Thus, many legal mechanisms remain unused or rarely used, perhaps in part because the public is more accustomed to extralegal approaches, such as letters of protest, complaints, petitions, lobbying, and demonstrations, which have been successful in the past.[173] An example of one such grass-roots effort aimed at protecting the Baltic Sea was the blockade of the Sloka paper pulp factory in Latvia in 1992. Built a century ago, the factory is the largest polluter of the resort in Yurmala. VAK demonstrators blockaded the factory for several days and, with public opinion behind them, managed to have it closed down until reconstruction of the water treatment system was completed.[174] In Lithuania, NGOs mounted a successful campaign in 1988–1990 to force the government to support the construction of biological water treatment plants in five main cities as a matter of national importance.[175]

Yet the record of public participation in the Baltic states has been mixed. On the one hand, progressive legal mechanisms for public participation have been adopted; cooperation with foreign organizations seems to be stable; relatively free access to media channels has been assured; discussions between NGOs and governments on a number of important policy issues are under way; and several protests and petitions against environmentally harmful activities have brought positive results. At the same time, the public makes little use of formal provisions expected to facilitate public participation, which is low in environmental law and decision making and in the enforcement of laws and regulations. A lack of trust between the authorities and the public still exists.

Social and economic problems have pushed environmental awareness off the agenda of many ordinary citizens, and pressure for increased public participation has declined substantially since the late 1980s. Only a "small segment of society . . . continues to push for a more active role in decision-making."[176]

This trend is very much in evidence in Russia, where economic reforms have resulted in much greater economic hardship for the population. Core economic and social concerns such as wages, high prices, and crime understandably dominate the political agenda. Although environmental issues consistently ranked very high—second or third—among public concerns in the years of *perestroika*, they had slipped to between tenth and thirteenth place by the mid-1990s.[177] Letters on environmental problems account for less than 1 percent of all the letters received by the government and the presidential administration.[178] Environmental issues are practically absent from the campaign promises of the major political parties and presidential candidates.

With this shift in the public agenda since the late 1980s, the number of ENGOs and their influence have declined dramatically. In 1990, ENGOs in the Russian Northwest numbered more than 130; by March 1992 that figure had dropped to 91, and in 1995 it probably did not exceed 30.[179] Apart from a decade-long fight against the construction of a dam in the Gulf of Finland, ENGO activities oriented toward Baltic protection are currently very few and not widely publicized. The Coalition Clean Baltic, currently the only collective ENGO that is consistently active at HELCOM, includes only one NGO from Russia (Neva River Clearwater), which educates school children about the environment using financial assistance from an American NGO. Lenkomekologiya does not cooperate with any NGOs whatsoever,[180] and is often severely criticized by the St. Petersburg greens.

Russia has almost no experience with public involvement in any facet of governance, including environmental decision making. The very concept of public participation is virtually unknown among public servants and the general public alike. As in the Baltic states, existing legislation provides citizens and NGOs with the basic rights for public participation, such as access to information. However, the legislation provides only general principles and no direct mechanisms to encourage public involvement; moreover, the responsibilities of the government and the business sector with respect to access to information and decision making are unclear.[181]

There are practically no instances of private citizens or NGOs using legal action to uphold their right to a clean environment, despite the fact that the 1992 Russian Law on the Protection of the Natural Environment granted citizens "the right to file lawsuits in court, demanding termination of environmentally harmful activities damaging the health and property of citizens, the economy, and the environment." One case, however, has set a historic precedent as Russia's first civil lawsuit concerning environmental pollution. The lawsuit filed in 1993 by the NGO Russian Center for Environmental Law in St. Petersburg, with the assistance of the US National Resources Defense Council, claimed that Vodokanal's lack of adequate water and sewage treatment facilities violated key provisions of the Helsinki Convention. According to the director of the Center for Environmental Law, Vodokanal was legally required to ensure adequate processing of 70 percent of the untreated water flowing through the Neva River out into the Baltic Sea.[182] Although the case was lost because Russia had not ratified the 1992 Helsinki Convention,[183] the fact that it was brought to court at all signals that the Russian public, traditionally passive before government bureaucracy, is becoming aware of concepts such as individual responsibility and "people power."

Concerning public participation, perhaps the most challenging task ahead for Russia and the Baltic countries is to improve the transparency of decision making. This lack of openness contributes to a high level of corruption and the making of arbitrary decisions, both of which are persistent legacies of the last decade of Soviet power.[184]

Assessment of Implementation

The implementation record is complicated and trends are mixed. This section provides an overview of the answers to three questions. What was the degree of compliance with the regime requirements (primarily reductions of discharges)? What factors, both endogenous and exogenous to Baltic Sea cooperation, were responsible for it? To what degree have changes in the behavior of target groups contributed to the improvement of the environmental state of the Baltic Sea? The first two questions examine the interaction between compliance and effectiveness (see Chapter 1). The last question explores the degree to which the Baltic pollution problem is being solved.

Compliance with International Standards

Because no information on Soviet era discharges was published until 1992, it is difficult to evaluate the extent to which the country implemented its commitments, notably HELCOM Recommendations and the 1988 and 1990 Ministerial Declarations to cut pollution by 50 percent.[185] However, there are indications that many of these commitments have not been reached to date. The 1990 data on the state of municipal and industrial wastewater treatment in the city of Leningrad indicate that about 60 percent of municipal wastewaters were treated biologically and the remainder were discharged into the Gulf of Finland untreated. Industries purified about 60 percent of their wastewaters chemically, only 1 percent were treated biologically, and 9 percent were treated mechanically; 30 percent were not treated before discharge.[186] These practices exceed international standards and also contravene national goals—in 1976 the USSR Council of Ministers pledged to end all untreated sewage discharges by 1985.

Similar problems existed in other Baltic cities as well. Facilities for biological treatment of wastewater, usually the second phase after mechanical treatment, still have not been finished in Tallinn, although construction started in 1968 and was scheduled to be completed by 1980.[187] By May 1991, only 5.6 percent of the total sewage from Riga was treated. In Lithuania, 25 percent of sewage was not treated at all in 1990, of which some 90 percent came from the second largest city, Kaunas.[188] In all these cases the USSR obviously did not comply with HELCOM Recommendations.

Over the past four or five years, emissions of most major pollutants in Russia, such as those from St. Petersburg, have declined. By 1994, loads of organic substances (BOD_{total}) in the Leningrad province had declined by 12 percent, those of nitrogen by 14 percent, those of phosphorus by 39 percent, and those of copper (in St. Petersburg proper) by 67 percent, compared with 1990 levels.[189] HELCOM statistics, which are based on different data, largely confirm these trends. Nonetheless, even had all planned remedial works been in full operation, the 1994 loads for BOD, phosphorus, and nitrogen would have greatly exceeded the levels required to meet the HELCOM Recommendations.[190]

HELCOM data for Latvia and Lithuania indicate that the decrease in pollution loads of BOD and especially nitrogen from priority hot spots since 1991 has been greater in these two countries than in Russia.[191] Lithuanian nitrogen loads in 1994 were lower than required by HELCOM standards. Although no comparable data for Estonia are available, statistics on pollution loads in the country reveal a similar, even more pronounced, trend: since 1991, BOD loads here have declined by a factor of almost 8, phosphorus loads by a factor of 2.5, and nitrogen loads by a factor of 2.3.[192]

What factors have accounted for such pollution-load dynamics? It has been widely acknowledged that any implementation of the Helsinki Convention that has occurred in Russia and in the Baltic states since 1991 has been largely coincidental, resulting mainly from a drastic decrease in production levels in both industry (especially in military-related industries) and agriculture.[193] The latter decrease is particularly significant from the viewpoint of the markedly fewer farm animals and decreased rates of fertilizer and pesticide application. HELCOM Recommendations have already been met for the agricultural priority hot spots in the Baltic states and in Russia, but only because of the sharp decline in agricultural activities.[194] The situation is different for the majority of municipal hot spots, which would not meet the HELCOM Recommendations even if all planned abatement measures were enacted in addition to those already in place. However, improved wastewater treatment has markedly reduced pollution in some cases, such as in Riga with the completion of a new wastewater treatment plant in 1992, and in Tallinn, where the wastewater treatment plant has been upgraded.

Many industrial sources in St. Petersburg have also cut their emissions of pollutants by 50 percent without implementing any environmental policies, primarily because of a decrease in production. It is impossible to estimate how much of the pollution-load decrease in St. Petersburg was due to industrial decline and how much is attributable to pollution abatement efforts within the framework of the JCP. However, the available data indicate that while industrial production in the city has declined by about 50 percent over the course of the past five years, the water pollution loads have declined by only 10 percent during the same period.[195] Thus, even allowing for a degree of generalization, it can be safely assumed that declines in water pollution loads have been not been in proportion to industrial declines, and that if it were not for a tremendous production decline, pollution levels during the same period would most probably have increased rather than decreased.

One side effect of this situation is that some of the pollution problems that were deemed most important at the time the JCP was developed are now less of a priority. For instance, effluents from several pig farms in the Leningrad region that were chosen as priority hot spots have undergone a dramatic reduction because the number of pigs has fallen sharply—leading Lenkomekologiya to informally propose switching them to the category of "cold spots" (similar to what has been done with "hot spots" in Finland and Sweden).[196] The situation in Russia, however, is obviously very different from that in Scandinavia, where compliance has been due to technological change (implementing HELCOM Recommendations), not to declines in production.

The newly independent Baltic states, especially Estonia and Latvia, have fared slightly better than Russia because of better regulation and stronger economies. In Lithuania, less progress in wastewater treatment has been achieved than in the other Baltic states, despite the high priority given to the expansion of wastewater treatment plants by the government. In all three countries, plans for concrete measures to reduce pollution loads at virtually all municipal priority hot spots are at an advanced stage or are being implemented. Consequently, a significant reduction of the pollution load can be expected following implementation of these plans: BOD_5 is expected to be reduced by about 75 percent, nitrogen loads by approximately 40 percent, and phosphorus loads by 60 percent.[197] These anticipated cutbacks mostly reflect investments rather than declines in production.

Problem Solving

Because there are no comparable long-term data for any part of the Baltic Sea, especially for Russian coastal waters, no definite conclusions on environmental quality can be reached. The biological state of the Neva River stabilized to some extent in 1993, and the Neva estuary has been reclassified as only "moderately polluted." However, the long history of industrial and municipal waste discharges has resulted in the accumulation of heavy metals in fish tissues at levels close to or exceeding MPCs.[198] The data for 1994 also indicate elevated average concentrations of nitrogen (1.8 MPC), phenols (3 MPC), and copper (4.4 MPC) in the estuary.[199]

At the 1994 HELCOM meeting, the Russian delegation acknowledged that neither the environmental situation in the Russian part of the Baltic Sea nor the environmental impact of economic activities in this area had changed significantly since 1988. Although a considerable reduction in pollution load has taken place with respect to BOD and oil products, discharges of phosphorus and nitrogen have remained practically constant; the concentration of heavy metals in the coastal waters also has not changed appreciably in recent years.[200] In short, it is still too early to tell whether the measures taken by Russia between 1991 and 1994 to implement the HELCOM Recommendations have resulted in an improvement of the environmental situation in Baltic coastal waters.

Summary and Conclusions

The Baltic Sea environment protection regime initially adopted a "technical-scientific" strategy; this approach functioned well in the sense that cooperation was primarily technical and uncontroversial with respect to the member states' security concerns. In the 1980s, participating in the regime was more important for the USSR than actually achieving environmental goals, which were loosely formulated. Security concerns overruled environmental interests and played a decisive role in determining the Soviet approach to Baltic cooperation. Major Soviet implementation efforts were focused on the control of pollution from ships, and so-called security interests were used as a pretext to keep environmental data from the public to conceal the inadequacy of efforts to control domestic land-based pollution.

Massive political changes in Europe and in the USSR allowed the Soviets to reconsider their national interests and provided a new context for Baltic cooperation, including East-West funding and technology transfer. The new "program strategy" of Baltic cooperation, which replaced the previous technical-scientific strategy, is reflected primarily in the development and adoption of the JCP. The JCP has adopted an approach of using environmental investments where they can produce maximal environmental benefits at minimal costs, namely, in the countries of Central and Eastern Europe.

Despite the increased possibilities for cooperation and a perceived need to demonstrate compliance with international commitments, Baltic environmental issues became less of a priority in the overall Soviet (and later Russian) foreign environmental policy in the early 1990s. This shift in priorities was partly the result of the Baltic states' acquiring their independence and Russia's losing much of its Baltic Sea littoral territory. In contrast, for the newly independent Baltic states, participation in HELCOM activities played an important role in their international recognition, providing them with some of their earliest opportunities to participate in international fora as independent entities.

In the waning years of the USSR, the availability of domestic resources and the ability to mobilize them had already become critical factors limiting Soviet (and later Russian) efforts to implement Baltic pollution controls. The staggering economic crisis that accompanied the transition from central planning prevented allocation of any federal funds for this purpose until 1993; enterprises had to rely primarily on their own very limited funds for financing capital investments, including investments for pollution control. Several national plans and programs have been adopted, but at best they merely represent uncoordinated listings of investment needs for a number of specific projects, without specification of priorities or sources of funding.

Despite the fact that economic incentives to implement environmental policy (e.g., pollution charges and taxes) have been introduced both in Russia and in the Baltic states, the effectiveness of these systems remains questionable, because despite periodic adjustments, tax rates lag behind the inflation rate. Consequently, pollution charges generally have been too low to play an important stimulating role. Earmarked resources from environmental funds have been widely used at local levels for purposes other than environmental protection. Some effects, however, have been noticeable: enterprises in the region, even those in the defense industry, have had to take environmental standards into account when formulating their production policies.

Because of the huge imbalance between the investments required and the costs already incurred, the need for very significant resource transfers has been paramount for implementation of the JCP. Little money flowed before 1994. Since then, the trend has started to change. Pre-feasibility studies are now being followed by investments. Most of the money has flowed to the relatively stable Baltic states, but Russia now receives an increasing share. The multilateral banks, above all the World Bank and the EBRD, have begun coordinating several projects in designated hot spots where the investments needed are too large to be financed by a single donor. However, because the banks provide loans at market rates, few commercial loans for JCP implementation have been used within the region, especially in Russia. The main source of external funding for projects in hot spots is bilateral arrangements with Western nations. However, donor countries are still reluctant to commit themselves to large-scale projects in situations of economic and political instability.

One of the most important changes that the political and economic transition in Russia and the Baltic states brought to environmental regulatory policies was the decentralization of authority—the shift of implementation responsibilities from federal to regional and local levels. However, in a country where "parades of sovereignties" and "wars of jurisdiction" are commonplace and the division of rights and responsibilities among regulatory subjects is unclear, the ability to translate international commitments into domestic action has been limited.

By introducing new patterns of private ownership of capital, the transformation has also radically decentralized the targets of public policy—the firms and enterprises that pollute—and changed their composition. Privatization has yielded many small specialized companies that are unable to acquire costly, capital-intensive environmental infrastructure, such as wastewater treatment plants. Privatization has also dramatically increased the number of relevant actors, substantially limiting the environmental authorities' ability to enforce regulations. This problem is exacerbated by a lack of resources and the absence of a legislative basis for controlling a large number of small actors.

The courts and the legal systems in Russia and the Baltic states have not played a prominent role in environmental issues. Overburdened with other cases, arbitration courts in Russia often refuse to accept claims for environmental damages. The process of recovering fines was almost meaningless with inflation at high levels. Even when sanctions for environmental offenses have been applied, they have been clearly inadequate to change the behavior of polluting enterprises. The attitude, inherited from the Soviet system, that environmental offenses are a minor matter and present little social danger has stimulated negligence and irresponsibility among managers.

Little public pressure to implement Baltic environmental controls exists in Russia. Russia has almost no experience with public involvement in any facet of governance, let alone environmental decision making. The number and influence of green NGOs have fallen sharply since the late 1980s. Their relations with governmental authorities remain strained. Even in the Baltic states, where environmental advocates were linked to the popular national independence movements in the late 1980s, public participation in environmental law and decision making is low. In Russia and the Baltic states, public environmental awareness has declined as other issues, such as crime and unemployment, have gained attention.

Overall, the impact of state regulatory policies on the behavior of target groups and on domestic implementation has been mixed. Tax and other incentives for environmental investments developed by federal and local authorities have rarely been used by state-owned enterprises. Many newly emerged private companies have made use of such tax privileges without actually making environmental investments. The application of pollution charges, to be paid directly from after-tax profit, has had, at least in some important cases, a more stimulating effect. By the mid-1990s, the proportion of environmental investments in St. Petersburg had grown considerably compared with the country average after remaining practically unchanged for about 10 years.

This growth, however, has not yet led to complete implementation of Baltic Sea commitments. A decline in discharges of most major pollutants has resulted in compliance with obligations made at the 1988 and 1990 Ministerial Conferences. However, the compliance has been predominantly coincidental, resulting mainly from a drastic decrease of production levels in both industry and agriculture. Pollution loads have been declining at a much slower rate compared with the rate of decline of industrial production. If it were not for a tremendous economic collapse, pollution in the first half of the 1990s would most probably have increased rather than decreased.

In sum, for many commitments there has been compliance without implementation. However, in some localities international commitments and programs—notably those that entail building wastewater treatment facilities—have influenced behavior although full compliance with the relevant commitments has not been achieved.

Although the effects induced by the Baltic Sea environment protection regime and the results of its implementation in Russia remain mixed at best, the Baltic Sea regime has markedly improved its management efforts over time. By taking advantage of political developments, the regime has been able to evolve into a system that employs more rational, demanding, and effective approaches. It has also been able to deal successfully with bottlenecks such as low implementation capacity and to play a central role in coordinating complicated Western resource transfers. These successes, combined with future economic and political stabilization in Russia and the other formerly communist countries of the Baltic basin, inspire hope for long-term efficiency of the regime, which is already evident in many projects.

Notes
This chapter is primarily based on a more detailed study published as Roginko, A., 1996, Domestic Implementation of Baltic Sea Pollution Controls in Russia

and the Baltic States, WP-96-91, International Institute for Applied Systems Analysis, Laxenburg, Austria.

I am grateful to several people who facilitated access to primary sources of information and provided insights into the implementation of Baltic pollution controls in Russia, in particular Vassily Rodionov (Helsinki Commission), Dmitri Zimin (Ministry of Environment, Russian Federation), Nikolai Sorokin, Valery Kulibaba, and Tatiana Sokornova (Committee on Ecology and Natural Resources for St. Petersburg and Leningrad Region). I am extremely grateful for the many thoughtful and useful comments on various drafts of this paper provided by my International Environmental Commitments (IEC) Project colleagues David Victor, Kal Raustiala, and Ronnie Hjorth. The structure of the chapter was inspired by a research protocol developed by my colleagues from the IEC Project, Elena Nikitina and Vladimir Kotov. Any omissions or shortcomings are the sole responsibility of the author.

1. Voigt, K., 1983, "The Baltic Sea: Pollution Problems and Natural Environmental Changes," *Impact of Science on Society*, No. 3/4, pp. 413–420.

2. The Baltic Sea Joint Comprehensive Environmental Action Programme, Diplomatic Conference on the Protection of the Marine Environment of the Baltic Sea Area. Helsinki, Finland, 9 April 1992 (Conference Doc. No. 5/3).

3. Broadus, J.M., *et al.*, 1993, Comparative Assessment of Regional International Programs to Control Land-Based Marine Pollution: The Baltic, North Sea, and Mediterranean, Marine Policy Center, Woods Hole Oceanographic Institution, Woods Hole, MA, USA.

4. The Environment Committee deals with technical questions of environmental quality and oversees monitoring and data collection programs. The Technological Committee formulates measures and standards for controlling pollution from a variety of land-based sources. The Maritime Committee is responsible for the prevention of operational pollution from vessels and related maritime safety issues. The Combatting Committee is responsible for the prevention and combatting of accidental pollution caused by spills of oil and other harmful substances.

5. Several recommendations have been exchanged between the North Sea and Baltic regimes, brokered by Denmark, Germany, and Sweden, which are parties to both regimes. With only minor phrasing changes, arrangements for offshore installations, mercury and cadmium emissions, and dumping practices for dredging spoils were initially adopted in the North Sea regime and subsequently adopted by HELCOM. Standards for oil emissions from refineries were first adopted by HELCOM and then transferred to the Paris Commission. See Haas, P.M., 1993, Protecting the Baltic and North Seas, in *Institutions for the Earth: Sources of Effective International Environmental Protection*, edited by P.M.

Haas, R.A. Keohane, and M.A. Levy, The MIT Press, Cambridge, MA, USA, p. 151.

6. Rijsberman, F.R., Koudstaal, R., and Wijtfels, A.T.M., 1990, Review of the Effectiveness of the Helsinki Convention as a Tool for Integrated Coastal Resources Management, Report for the Organisation for Economic Co-operation and Development (OECD) project "Integration of Environmental Considerations into Coastal Zone Management," Doc ENV/NRM/90.1.

7. To deal with the problem of implementation delays in the countries under transition, in 1993 HELCOM endorsed a differentiated approach in formulating implementation timetables; these countries were offered extended implementation time limits to bring the discharges and emissions from existing enterprises into conformity with HELCOM Recommendations. However, no exemptions were made for new enterprises, *HELCOM News*, March 1993, No. 2, p. 4.

8. Hjorth, R., 1992, *Building International Institutions for Environmental Protection: The Case of Baltic Sea Environmental Cooperation*, TEMA, Linköping Studies in Arts and Science, No. 81, Linköping, Sweden, p. 216.

9. List, M., 1990, "Cleaning up the Baltic: A Case Study in East-West Environmental Cooperation, in *International Regimes in East-West Politics*, edited by V. Rittberger, Pinter, New York, NY, USA, pp. 90–116.

10. Ibid.

11. HELCOM, 1988, Activities of the Commission 1987, Baltic Sea Environment Proceedings, No. 26.

12. Baltic Sea Declaration by Heads of Government and High Political Representatives of the Baltic Sea States, Norway, the Czech and Slovak Federal Republics and the Representative of the Commission of the European Communities, Assembled at Ronneby, Sweden, 2–3 September 1990, s.l., 1990 (mimeo).

13. Broadus *et al.*, 1993, op. cit., note 3.

14. Per unit of pollutant it is 16 times more economical to remove the first 80 percent of the pollution load than the last 20 percent.

15. Baltic Sea Declaration, op. cit., note 12.

16. In addition to the seven Baltic states, Norway, Czechoslovakia, and the European Commission, representatives from five international financial institutions (IFIs) also participated in the Ronneby Conference: the European Bank for Reconstruction and Development (EBRD), the European Investment Bank (EIB), the Nordic Investment Bank (NIB), the World Bank, and the Nordic Environment Finance Corporation (NEFCO).

626   *Alexei Roginko*

17. The percentage of "priority" hot spots designated in the FSU is even higher: 26 of 47 "priority" hot spots (55 percent) are located in the FSU.

18. *HELCOM News*, June 1996, No. 3, p. 9.

19. *HELCOM News*, 1994, No. 2, p. 3.

20. *HELCOM News*, June 1996, No. 3, p. 3.

21. Hjorth, op. cit., note 8.

22. See Haas, op. cit., note 5.

23. See Hjorth, op. cit., note 8; Ringius, L., 1995, The Environmental Action Plan Approach: A Milestone in Pollution Control in the Baltic Sea, Working Paper No. 1995-1, Center for International Climate and Energy Research, University of Oslo, Norway.

24. Broadus *et al.*, op. cit., note 3, p. 49.

25. Füllenbach, J., 1977, Umweltschutz zwischen Ost und West, Bonn, Schriften des Forschungsinstituts der Deutschen Gesellschaft für Auswärtige Politik e.V., p. 230.

26. A Soviet decision maker on the Baltic Sea issues from Minvodkhoz, Arkady Izvolsky, stated that the exclusion of internal waters was caused by Soviet security considerations and the closed nature of the USSR. See Van der Weij, E., 1993, Soviet International Environmental Politics, Ph.D. dissertation, University of Amsterdam, Department of International Relations, and the Institute of Central and Eastern European Studies, p. 30.

27. Füllenbach, op. cit., note 25, p. 230.

28. Van der Weij, op. cit., note 26, p. 32.

29. List, op. cit., note 9, p. 108.

30. Hjorth, op. cit., note 8, pp. 153–154.

31. Hjorth, op. cit., note 8, pp. 155.

32. Baltiku eshche mozhno spasti, 1990, *Izvestiya*, September 4, p. 7.

33. Van der Weij, op. cit., note 26, p. 102.

34. See, for example, Minin, A.A., 1996, Produkt vtoroi svezhesti, *Nezavisimaya gazeta*, No. 5, January 11.

35. Gosudarstvennyi doklad, "O sostoyanii okruzhayushchei prirodnoi sredy v Rossiyskoi Federatsii v 1994 godu." *ZM*, 1995, No. 31, p. 4.

36. Tsvetkov, S., 1990, "Neva: Solution Begets Pollution," Glas:en.marine, April 20.

37. Biochemical oxygen demand (BOD) is the measure of concentration of organic matter in sewage. It reflects the amount of dissolved oxygen consumed by microbial life while assimilating and oxidizing the organic matter present within a specific time period (usually 5 or 7 days—BOD_5 or BOD_7). For measuring BOD_{total}, a longer time period, usually no less than 20 days, is used.

38. Second Baltic Sea Pollution Load Compilation, 1993, Baltic Sea Environment Proceedings, No. 45, p. 68.

39. See Eckerberg, K., 1994, "Environmental Problems and Policy Options in the Baltic States: Learning from the West?" *Environmental Politics* 3(3): 445–478.

40. Ministry of the Environment of Estonia, 1992, National Report of Estonia to United Nations Conference on Environment and Development, Tallinn, Estonia, p. 26.

41. Ministry of the Environment of Estonia, 1995, Estonian Environment 1994, Environmental Information Center, Tallinn, Estonia, pp. 61–62.

42. Canfield, J.L., 1993, "The Independent Baltic States: Maritime Law and Resource Management Implications," *Ocean Development and International Law* 24(1):1–39.

·43. *REC Bulletin*, 1995, Vol. 5, No. 3.

44. Environmental Protection Department of Lithuania, 1992, National Report of Lithuania to United Nations Conference on Environment and Development, Vilnius, Lithuania, p. 75.

45. Gosudarstvennyi doklad "Sostoyaniye Prorodnoi Sredy i Prirodookhrannaya Deyatelnost' v SSSR v 1989 godu," 1990, Goskompriroda, Moscow, Russia, p. 167.

46. In June 1994, the territorial scope of the program was expanded to include the Pskov and Novgorod provinces; Gosudarstvennyi doklad ... v 1994 godu, ZM, 1996, No. 16, p. 6.

47. Natsionalny plan deistviy po realizatsii resheniy Konferentsii OON po okruzhayushchei srede i razvitiyu: Proekt. ZM, 1993, No. 19.

48. Maksimov, A., 1995, Vnedrenie planovoi ekologii v Evrope – delo neskoroe, Segodnia, December 7, p. 9.

49. Baltic Sea Environment Programme, 1994, "Hot Spot Review," Prepared for the HELCOM Programme Implementation Task Force by I. Krüger Consult AS, COWIconsult, Carl Bro Environment a/s, and Vandkvalitetsinstituttet, Copenhagen, Denmark, November 1994, Vol. 2, Country Reports, p. 17.

50. Hiltunen, H., 1994, Finland and Environmental Problems in Russia and Estonia, The Finnish Institute of International Affairs, Helsinki, Finland, p. 39.

51. See Baltic Sea Environment Programme, op. cit., note 49.

52. The decision was based on the hypothesis that the world's oceans have a limitless capacity to accumulate, dilute, and purify anthropogenic wastes. This theory, however, has not proved to be practically feasible: the smaller the water body, the sooner its purification capacity becomes exhausted. In this situation, the only viable option is to reduce pollution loads to an economically justified minimum. This fact forced most industrialized countries to switch in the 1980s from a "release and dilute" strategy to a pollution-prevention strategy based on emission or technological (BAT, etc.) standards.

53. Lääne, A., 1992, Vodookhrannaya strategiya i podkhody k normirovaniyu, Scientific Center for Environmental Protection TTU, Tallinn, Estonia, p. 6.

54. Ibid., pp. 61–62.

55. Ibid., pp. 7–10.

56. Lääne, A., 1995, Political Impediments to Implementing International Waterway Agreements: The Example of the Baltic States, paper presented at the International Studies Association Conference, Chicago, IL, USA, 21–22 February.

57. Ibid.

58. Environmental Protection Department of Lithuania, op. cit., note 44, p. 107.

59. Baltic Sea Environment Programme, op. cit., note 49, pp. 32.

60. "Otvety na voprosnik po mezhdunarodnym soglasheniyam i programmam," informal working document, Ministry of Ecology and Natural Resources of the Russian Federation, Moscow, Russia, May 1992.

61. Baltic Marine Environment Protection Commission, Report of the 15th Meeting, Helsinki, Finland, 8–11 March 1994, p. 76.

62. "Otvety na voprosnik...", op. cit., note 60.

63. Baltic Marine Environment Protection Commission, op. cit., note 61, p. 76.

64. The name and functional scope of the Russian environmental agency have changed several times since 1992; for simplicity we use the term Ministry of Environment. After the presidential elections in 1996 and the ensuing governmental reform, the Ministry of Environment lost its cabinet status and became the State Committee on Environmental Protection (Goskomekologiya), which by law does not determine state policy in the issue area. At the time of this writing, the responsibilities of the newly formed state committee with regard to implementation of international commitments are unclear.

65. Natsionalny Doklad SSSR k Konferentsii OON 1992 goda po okruzhayushchey srede i razvitiyu, 1991, Minpriroda SSSR, Moscow, Russia, p. 233.

66. Apart from the Ministry of Environment and Rosgidromet, these include Roskomvod (a successor to Minvodkhoz), Roskomnedra (State Committee on the Earth's Interior), Minselkhozprod (Ministry of Agriculture and Agricultural Products), and Goskomsanepidndzor (State Committee on Sanitary and Epidemiological Inspection).

67. Bratashov, V., 1996, Organizatsiya upravleniya ratsionalnym prirodopol' zovaniem i okhranoi prirody na munitsipal'nom urovne, *ZM*, No. 7–8.

68. Frolov, A.K., ed., 1995, Sostoyaniye okruzhayushchei sredy Severo-Zapadnogo i Severnogo Regionov Rossii, Nauka, St. Petersburg, Russia, pp. 6–7.

69. For details, see Roginko, A., 1996, Domestic Implementation of Baltic Sea Pollution Controls in Russia and the Baltic States, WP-96-91, International Institute for Applied Systems Analysis, Laxenburg, Austria.

70. Valery Kulibaba, head of Department of Complex Analysis, Committee on Ecology and Natural Resources for St. Petersburg and Leningrad Region, personal communication with the author, 30 May 1995.

71. Baltic Sea Environment Programme, op. cit., note 49, p. 42.

72. Baltic Sea Environment Programme, op. cit., note 49, p. 14.

73. Hereinafter, when providing US dollar equivalents for ruble figures, the following approximate mid-year exchange rates for the corresponding years are used: 50 rubles/dollar for 1991, 150 rubles/dollar for 1992, 1,000 rubles/dollar for 1993, 2,000 rubles/dollar for 1994, 4,500 rubles/dollar for 1995, and 5,000 rubles/dollar for 1996. The conversion of ECU figures into US dollars is made at the approximate mid-year rate for the year of the assessment: 1.34 ECU/dollar for 1992, 1.13 ECU/dollar for 1993, 1.19 ECU/dollar for 1994 and 1.32 ECU/dollar for 1995.

74. However, over two-thirds of Estonia's estimated investment needs are required for the reconstruction of oil and shale power plants at Narva to reduce atmospheric emissions of dust and SO_2.

75. The Baltic Sea Joint Comprehensive Environmental Action Programme, op. cit., note 2.

76. The Baltic Sea Joint Comprehensive Environmental Action Programme, High Level Conference on Resource Mobilization, Gdańsk, Poland, 24–25 March 1993, Conference Document No. 2, Background Paper (Doc. HELCOM TC 4/3d, 29 June 1993).

77. For details, see Roginko, op. cit., note 69.

78. "Otvety na voprosnik...", op. cit., note 60.

79. See Golub, A., and Strukova, E., 1995, "Financing Environmental Investments in the Russian Federation," in *Financing Environmental Quality in Central and Eastern Europe: An Assessment of International Support*, edited by G. Klaasen and M. Smith, International Institute for Applied Systems Analysis, Laxenburg, Austria; Ledov, A., and Zhukov, B., 1995, "Ekologicheskie fondy rastvorilis' v 'obschem kotle' budzheta," *Segodnia*, May 18, p. 6.

80. Fomin, V.G., 1995, Proekt novogo federal'nogo zakona, *ZM*, No. 34, pp. 6–7.

81. *TEN*, 1–15 May 1996, Vol. 2, No. 9.

82. Mamin, R., 1993, Plata za zagriaznenie okruzhayushchei sredy v Rossiyskoi Federatsii (prakticheskie voprosy vzimaniya), *ZM*, No. 9, pp. 8–9.

83. Ibid.

84. Yablokov, A., 1993, *Minprirody* Rossii: opasnye tendentsii, *ZM*, No. 14, pp. 1, 4.

85. Gosudarstvennyi doklad ... v 1994 godu, *ZM*, 1996, No. 13, p. 11.

86. Initially it was planned to put the northern wastewater treatment plant into operation prior to the construction of the dam in the Gulf of Finland; however, due to a lack of financing, the plant's construction was frozen in the early 1980s.

87. Implementation of the Baltic Sea Joint Comprehensive Environmental Action Program in St. Petersburg and Leningrad Region. Submitted by Russia (Doc. HELCOM PITF 6/2/3, 31 May 1995).

88. Kulibaba, op. cit., note 70.

89. Vodokanal in St. Petersburg is the largest water supply and sewerage enterprise in Russia, incorporating 18 subordinate departments with more than 7,000 employees; Baltic Sea Environment Programme, op. cit., note 49, p. 6.

90. Gosudarstvennyi doklad ... v 1994 godu, *ZM*, 1996, No. 15.

91. See Stottman, W., 1993, "World Bank Activities in the Municipal Water/Wastewater Sector," in High Level Conference on Resource Mobilization, Gdańsk, Poland, 24–25 March 1993, Compilation of Presentations and Statements, Baltic Sea Environment Proceedings, 1993, No. 47, pp. 112–125.

92. Because production and sewage volumes in St. Petersburg have fallen drastically over the past few years, industrial sewage today accounts for only 12 percent of all waste; moreover, the tariffs are now too expensive for most enterprises to pay. This situation forced Vodokanal to abolish higher tariffs for industries starting from 1 March 1996; this loss was compensated by raising household consumers' user fees by 30 percent; *TEN*, 1996, Vol. 2, No. 3.

93. Swedish Environmental Protection Agency, 1996, The Baltic Sea Joint Comprehensive Environmental Action Programme, Combined Municipal and Industrial Discharges: Lead Party Report, Stockholm, Sweden, p. 18.

94. Baltic Sea Environment Programme, op. cit., note 49, Vol. 1 (Executive Summary), p. 5.

95. *ZM*, 1993, No. 17, p. 3.

96. Baltic Sea Environment Programme, op. cit., note 49, Vol. 7 (Basin Report for Kaliningrad), p. 15.

97. Baltic Sea Environment Programme, op. cit., note 49, p. 45.

98. *TEN*, 1996, Vol. 2, No. 8.

99. Eckerberg, op. cit., note 39, p. 463.

100. The Baltic Sea Joint Comprehensive Environmental Action Programme, op. cit., note 76, p. 36.

101. Ministry of the Environment of Estonia, op. cit., note 41, p. 98.

102. Eckerberg, op. cit., note 39, p. 463.

103. Ministry of the Environment of Estonia, op. cit., note 40, p. 36; Baltic Sea Environment Programme, op. cit., note 49, p. 18.

104. Environmental Protection Department of Lithuania, op. cit., note 44, p. 112.

105. Baltic Sea Environment Programme, op. cit., note 49, pp. 44–45.

106. For details, see Roginko, op. cit., note 69. See also Niels-J. Seeberg-Elverfeldt, 1995, "Hot Spotting, in Estonia, Latvia and Lithuania," *HELCOM News*, No. 1, March, pp. 9–17.

107. Baltic Sea Environment Programme, op. cit., note 49, pp. 6–7.

108. Ministry of Environment of Estonia, op. cit., note 41, p. 64.

109. Valery Kulibaba, written communication, 21 July 1996.

110. Baltic Sea Environment Programme, op. cit., note 49.

111. In March 1996, the ECAT project in St. Petersburg was terminated and a new project in Kaliningrad was started. The Russian part of the ECAT team in St. Petersburg was transferred to the environmental administration of the mayor's office. ECAT has been successful in implementing several projects between 1993 and 1995, including supplying equipment for recovering spilled oil, aiding firms in reducing toxic waste, and a range of public awareness programs; *TEN*, 1996, Vol. 2, No. 6.

112. Berg, C., 1995, The Environmental Support to the Baltic States, Poland and Western Russia, Swedish Environmental Protection Agency, Stockholm, Sweden, p. 11.

113. Hiltunen, op. cit., note 50, p. 41.

114. High Level Conference on Resource Mobilization, Gdańsk, Poland, 24–25 March 1993, Compilation of Presentations and Statements, Baltic Sea Environment Proceedings, No. 47, p. 44.

115. Hiltunen, H., 1996, "The Politics of Environmental Aid Programs: The Case of Finland, Russia, and Estonia," in *Baltic Environmental Cooperation: A Regime in Transition*, edited by R. Hjorth, Linköping, Sweden, p. 98; Berg, op. cit., note 112.

116. Berg, op. cit., note 112, p. 19.

117. Berg, op. cit., note 112, pp. 47–49. For details of projects, mainly wastewater treatment plants, see Roginko, op. cit., note 69, pp. 38–39.

118. Calculations are based on project data presented by Berg, 1995, op. cit., note 112. The data are incomplete and the amounts of foreign contributions to some of the projects are not available. Included in the calculations are environmental (investment and technical) assistance to industry, water protection, waste management, agriculture and forestry, nature conservation, and monitoring, as well as public administration (institutional) support. Support for the energy sector, for the phasing out of ozone-depleting substances, and for nuclear safety is not included. The figures given here differ from those supplied

by HELCOM, because the latter refer to investments only and are compiled on the basis of information supplied by countries.

119. The problems related to financing the Russian share of the projects are especially grave in St. Petersburg, where the majority of investments needed for reducing pollution to the Gulf of Finland come from municipal sources; in comparison, in the Russian republic of Karelia, local enterprises are able to pay for environmental technology with natural resources, such as timber; see Hiltunen, op. cit., note 115, p. 101.

120. Hiltunen, op. cit., note 115, pp. 100–101.

121. The Baltic Sea Joint Comprehensive Environmental Action Programme, op. cit., note 76, pp. 21, 40.

122. See Kaminskaité, A., and Liubiniené, V., 1996, "Managing Environmental Aid Programs: Experiences from Lithuania," in *Baltic Environmental Cooperation: A Regime in Transition*, edited by R. Hjorth, Linköping, Sweden, p. 116.

123. *ZM*, 1995, No. 3, p. 2.

124. See Hiltunen, op. cit., note 50, pp. 18–19.

125. See Kaminskaité and Liubiniené, op. cit., note 122.

126. Most donors have strict limits on the proportion of project costs they are willing to meet, hence matching funds, guarantees against loans, etc., are normally needed. For Russia and the Baltic states, matching funds or guarantees are not usually readily available internally, leading to complex arrangements with outside donors.

127. Seeberg-Elverfeldt, op. cit., note 106, p. 10.

128. *ECB*, March 1996, Vol. 4, No. 5.

129. "World Bank Aids Baltic Sea Environment Program," World Bank News Release No. 95/S88ECA, 1995.

130. Swedish Environmental Protection Agency, op. cit., note 93, p. 13.

131. *HELCOM News*, 1996, No. 1, p. 8.

132. *ECB*, March 1996, Vol. 4, No. 5.

133. Since 1996, NEFCO has been administering a new soft-financing facility set up on a trial basis by the Nordic countries, which is intended to provide concessional financing to environmental projects in the Central and East European countries of the Baltic and the Barents regions. In 1996, the facility disposed of about US$5 million; the first proposals are being analyzed; "NEFCO's

activities in relation to the JCP," Doc. HELCOM PITF 8/96/INF.8, 14 May 1996.

134. Berg, op. cit., note 112, p. 41.

135. Baltic Sea Environment Programme, op. cit., note 49, p. 11.

136. Stottman, op. cit., note 91.

137. Berg, op. cit., note 112, p. 49.

138. A report on JCP industrial point sources prepared by Finland has even found out that more financial aid is provided to the industrial sector for projects that do not involve hot spots than for those that do. Thus, it is easier to find local motivation to invest in small enterprises and relatively modern facilities than to invest in the most difficult sites. Obviously, this is also justified economically, especially in the Baltic countries, where markets for products from the former Soviet production facilities are limited; Lead Party Report on the JCP Point Source element "Industry". Submitted by Finland. Doc. HELCOM PITF 8/96/7.3/1, 20 March 1996, p. 4.

139. Kulibaba, op. cit., note 70.

140. Fomin, op. cit., note 80.

141. Baltic Sea Environment Programme, op. cit., note 49, p. 7.

142. Sukharev, A.Y., 1996, Ekologicheskaya prestupnost, *ZM*, No. 1, p. 8.

143. Ibid.

144. Kulibaba, op. cit., note 109.

145. Fomin, op. cit., note 80.

146. Sorokin, N.D., ed., 1993, Ekologicheskaya obstanovka v Sankt-Peterburge v 1992 godu (analiticheskiy obzor) (Committee for environment and natural resources of St. Petersburg and Leningrad Region), Lenkomekologiya, St. Petersburg, Russia, pp. 150–151.

147. Kulibaba, op. cit., note 70.

148. The maximum number of water samples that can be taken and analyzed within one month is reported to be about 10, since every analysis takes about three days to complete. The Kirovskiy Zavod association alone had about 1600 sources of wastewater discharge. Understandably, only the most toxic sources are controlled at random. Previously, these sources were controlled by the industry's own laboratories, but their number has been reduced more than twice since 1992; N.D. Sorokin, First Vice-Chairman, Committee on Ecology and Natural Resources for St. Petersburg and Leningrad Region, personal communication with the author, 2 June 1995.

149. T.V. Sokornova, Chief Expert, Department of Complex Analysis, Committee on Ecology and Natural Resources for St. Petersburg and Leningrad Region, personal communication with the author, 2 June 1995.

150. Kulibaba, op. cit., note 70.

151. Sokornova, op. cit., note 149.

152. Sorokin, op. cit., note 148.

153. Kozeltsev, M., 1993, Nalogi i stimuly, *ZM*, No. 1, p. 7.

154. Danilov-Danilyan, V.I., 1993, Tochki nad "i", *ZM*, No. 14, pp. 5–10.

155. Sokornova, op. cit., note 149.

156. Danilov-Danilyan, op. cit., note 154.

157. Implementation of the Baltic Sea Joint Comprehensive Environmental Action Program in St. Petersburg and Leningrad Region, op. cit., note 87.

158. Sorokin, op. cit., note 148.

159. Merisaar, M., 1995, "Estonia," in *Status of Public Participation Practices in Environmental Decisionmaking in Central and Eastern Europe*, Regional Environmental Center for Central and Eastern Europe, Budapest, Hungary.

160. Canfield, op. cit., note 42.

161. Eckerberg, op. cit., note 39, p. 468.

162. Stec, S., 1995, Manual on Public Participation in Environmental Decisionmaking: Current Practice and Future Possibilities in Central and Eastern Europe, Baltic Supplement, Regional Environmental Center for Central and Eastern Europe, Budapest, Hungary.

163. Vainius, L., 1995, "Lithuania," in *Status of Public Participation Practices in Environmental Decisionmaking in Central and Eastern Europe*, Regional Environmental Center for Central and Eastern Europe, Budapest, Hungary.

164. Blumberga, U., and Ulme, A., 1995, "Latvia," in *Status of Public Participation, Practices in Environmental Decisionmaking in Central and Eastern Europe*, Regional Environmental Center for Central and Eastern Europe, Budapest, Hungary.

165. See Eckerberg, op. cit., note 39.

166. Stec, op. cit., note 162.

167. Vainius, op. cit., note 163; Blumberga and Ulme, op. cit., note 164.

168. Blumberga and Ulme, op. cit., note 164.

169. Merisaar, op. cit., note 159.

170. Merisaar, op. cit., note 159.

171. Vainius, op. cit., note 163.

172. Stec, op. cit., note 162.

173. Stec, op. cit., note 162.

174. Latvia: Green Tribunal, in Glas:pns.baltic, 26 September 1993.

175. Vainius, op. cit., note 163.

176. Stec, op. cit., note 162.

177. Baiduzhiy, A., 1995, "Interview with Alexei Yablokov," *Nezavisimaya gazeta*, March 24, p. 3.

178. Gosudarstvennyi doklad "O sostoyanii okruzhayushchei prirodnoi sredy v Rossiyskoi Federatsii v 1993 godu", 1995, *ZM*, No. 4, p. 12.

179. Frolov, op. cit., note 68, p. 325.

180. Sorokin, op. cit., note 148.

181. Ponizova, O., 1995, "A View from Moscow," *REC Bulletin* 5(2).

182. Browning, L., 1993, "Environmental Lawsuit: First of Its Kind in Russia," *The Moscow Times*, 19 January, p. 5.

183. The court has determined that HELCOM Recommendations, in the absence of specific domestic legal norms, do not create any binding obligations for enterprises.

184. Stec, op. cit., note 162.

185. For the USSR, the implementation of the 1988 Ministerial Declaration reportedly did not prove to be so "difficult," because little was known about actual emission levels. Professor Harald Velner, a key player in the Soviet delegation to HELCOM, pointed out that until 1988 the censorship agency Glavlit prohibited scientists from providing any data on discharges; Van der Weij, op. cit., note 26, p. 99.

186. Second Baltic Sea Pollution Load Compilation, 1993, op. cit., note 38, p. 67, 71.

187. Van der Weij, op. cit., note 26, p. 108.

188. Nordic Investment Bank, Pre-Feasibility Study of the Lithuanian Coast and the Nemunas River Basin. Synthesis Report, Baltic Sea Environment Programme, Stockholm, Sweden, May 1992.

189. The data are calculated on the basis of Sorokin, op. cit., note 146; Implementation of the Baltic Sea Joint Comprehensive Environmental Action Program in St. Petersburg and Leningrad Region, op. cit., note 87.

190. For details, see Baltic Sea Environment Programme, op. cit., note 49, Vols. 1 and 3 (Basin Report for Gulf of Finland).

191. Baltic Sea Environment Programme, op. cit., note 49, Vols. 1 and 5 (Basin Report for Gulf of Riga) and 6 (Basin Report for Nemunas River Basin).

192. Ministry of the Environment of Estonia, op. cit., note 41, p. 54.

193. See, for example, Baltic Marine Environment Protection Commission, op. cit., note 61, pp. 76–77; Baltic Sea Environment Programme, op. cit., note 49.

194. Baltic Sea Environment Programme, op. cit., note 49, p. 5.

195. *TEN*, 1996, Vol. 2, No. 8.

196. See paragraph on Baltic Sea Joint Comprehensive Environmental Action Programme (JCP) in this chapter.

197. Baltic Sea Environment Programme, op. cit., note 49, Vol. 1, p. 6.

198. Gosudarstvennyi doklad ... v 1993 godu, *ZM*, 1994, No. 27.

199. Gosudarstvennyi doklad ... v 1994 godu, *ZM*, 1996, No. 3. In the Kursiu Lagoon, some improvement of environmental quality has also been observed in the course of 1993; "Gosudarstvennyi doklad ... v 1993 godu," op. cit., *ZM*, 1994, No. 27.

200. Baltic Marine Environment Protection Commission, op. cit., note 61, pp. 76–77.

15

Implementation of Baltic Sea Pollution Commitments in Poland: A Review of the Literature

Ronnie Hjorth

Introduction

This chapter reviews how Poland has implemented international commitments and initiatives to clean up the Baltic Sea. Based mainly on documents and previously published literature, the chapter focuses on how the process of economic and social transition from a communist state to a liberal market-based society has influenced the country's ability to control pollution.

The chapter begins with a survey of Poland's commitments and initiatives regarding Baltic Sea pollution control and relevant domestic policies, primarily in the field of wastewater treatment. The main international commitments and initiatives are related to the Convention on the Protection of the Marine Environment of the Baltic Sea Area (1974 and 1992), referred to here as the Helsinki Convention, and the Baltic Sea Joint Comprehensive Environmental Action Programme (JCP), signed in 1992. (See Chapter 14 for a more detailed review of the Baltic Sea commitments and institutions.) Poland's efforts to implement these international commitments are then reviewed and illustrated. Finally, the ways that economic and social transition have influenced the implementation process are examined. Particular attention is given to the decentralization of public administration, to resources from local, regional, and national funds, and to international bilateral and multilateral funding.

International commitments and domestic Polish environmental policy have had a significant influence on the behavior of polluters. The shift to a market economy has been accompanied by the emergence of regulatory institutions; power has devolved upon regional and local levels. During the communist period laws were on the books but had little influence; today more attention is paid to enforcing laws, levying pollution taxes, and targeting funding to assist with costly pollution abatement projects. On balance, political and economic transition have had a positive effect on implementation in Poland. In contrast, Russia and the Baltic states have demonstrated much less implementation activity (see Chapter 14). However, although the behavioral impact in Poland has been substantial, the environmental problems are still enormous. Nevertheless, current implementation efforts indicate that Poland is moving in the right direction.

The Context: Domestic Politics, International Commitments, and Initiatives

The development of environmental policy in Poland and the country's ability to implement international commitments must be seen in the context of the prevailing political and economic conditions. The transition process started much earlier in Poland than in Russia and the Baltic republics of Estonia, Latvia, and Lithuania, where central planning remained largely unchallenged until the collapse of the USSR. During the 1970s and 1980s, Polish society experienced a marked evolution toward greater openness and increased opportunities for private enterprise. A more moderate version of a command-and-control economy was introduced. Although no multiparty democracy existed, independent trade unions and interest groups were tolerated, including grass roots environmental protection organizations. Following the imposition of martial law in 1981, the climate hardened. However, the sweeping reforms that began in 1989 resulted in the peaceful and orderly dismantling of the communist state and, among other things, sparked the hope that more effective pollution control policies would be implemented.

Environmental commitments regarding the Baltic Sea were specified in the 1974 Helsinki Convention. (See Chapter 14 for an overview of the Baltic Sea environment protection regime.) Poland assumed an active role in the early phase of international cooperation on protecting the Baltic Sea by hosting the negotiations on the Gdańsk Convention on Fishing and the Conservation of Living Resources in the Baltic Sea and the Belts. That step, however, was not accompanied by any concrete initiatives to control the pollution flowing into the Baltic. Poland remained largely inactive within the Helsinki Convention Baltic Marine Environment Protection Commission (HELCOM) in the 1980s, making no effort to help shape its policy. It presented few documents at

HELCOM meetings and did not take part in the so-called lead party procedure, under which the parties to the Helsinki Convention agreed to distribute the preparatory work for HELCOM Recommendations.[1]

At the same time, however, the Polish government's candor about the extent of the environmental pollution in Poland was unparalleled in the Soviet bloc. Poland's minister of environment told the 1984 and 1988 Ministerial Meetings of the Helsinki Convention that, because his country suffered greatly from transboundary as well as domestic pollution, international cooperation was a key aspect of the country's environmental policy. Authorities in the USSR and the German Democratic Republic (GDR), by contrast, consistently refused to concede the severity of their domestic and international pollution. Polish diplomats also pointed out that Poland accounted for nearly 50 percent of both the population and the farmland in the Baltic Sea drainage area.[2]

Thus, the Polish position on environmental issues in the 1980s was marked by both a low level of activity and a policy of official acknowledgment of the existing problems that went far beyond those instituted by other communist authorities in the region.[3] This relative openness reflected the comparatively liberal climate in Poland, where some economic reforms had been undertaken and where there was less state control than in the neighboring USSR and the GDR. However, environmental protection was never a government priority, which explains the country's minimal commitment and initiative.

Environmental Regulation in Poland Before 1990

As in the other countries of communist Eastern Europe, pollution control policies were certainly not a core concern of the Polish government. Nevertheless, environmental legislation has long been part of Polish law. Poland's first water law was passed in 1922 and revised in 1962; a new water law was issued in 1974.[4] Furthermore, principles now considered to be vital components of a modern environmental protection policy were implemented in Poland long before the current transition period began. For example, the "polluter pays principle" (PPP) was introduced in Poland with the levying of fines for wastewater discharges in 1970 and the introduction of effluent charges in 1975. In theory, the charges and penalties were to be placed in environmental protection funds to be invested in environmental protection projects. However, as in many other communist countries with stringent laws on the books, implementation was weak.[5] In Poland's case, the funds had little effect on behavior, because charges often remained uncollected and inflation devalued the resources that had been set aside for investment.[6] Although the government often stressed the need for environmental protection, natural resources were mainly viewed as a production factor to be utilized for industrial purposes.[7] Thus, new laws and regulations were adopted but had minimal influence on the behavior of polluters. Monitoring systems and emission standards were established, but violations, if detected, were rarely punished.[8] In part, the lack of implementation during the 1980s was a result of inadequate legal and institutional frameworks for policy implementation. Other causes included the structure of domestic production, which emphasized polluting industries and placed no value on clean water.[9]

The New Environmental Policy
The situation changed when Poland's democratic opposition came to power. Swedish Prime Minister Ingvar Carlsson and Polish Prime Minister Tadeusz Mazowiecki organized a ministerial conference in Ronneby, Sweden, in 1990. One of several motives for holding the conference was Sweden's desire to extend Baltic Sea cooperation beyond the HELCOM framework.[10] The conference gave high-level political recognition to the struggle for independence by the Baltic states. In terms of environmental protection, the Baltic Sea Declaration presented in Ronneby established a cooperative framework that led to the JCP and a new era of more substantial collaboration among the Baltic littoral countries (see Chapter 14).

The report on Poland's National Environmental Policy issued in 1991 by the Ministry of Environmental Protection, Natural Resources and Forestry was a key document that guided the development and implementation of environmental policy as Poland embarked on market reforms. Adopted by the government and Parliament, the report signaled a new approach to pollution control in a period of economic transition. As in Polish economic policy in general, the new environmental policy was based on a separation between production and state administration. One of the core objectives was to fully implement the PPP. There was to be no opportunity to circumvent environmental rules and regulations due to "circumstances outside one's control," "public interest," or "impossibility." In the past, such exceptions had been among the main reasons for the failure to implement the PPP. In some years, these "exceptions" led authorities to excuse (or not collect) nearly 80 percent of the penalties for wastewater discharges.[11]

The National Environmental Policy report prescribed a three-pronged approach to pollution control. In the short term (3 to 4 years), point-source emissions were to be limited using an "end of pipe" approach. The aim was to limit further environmental degradation where technical solutions were available. The Policy envisioned the need for new economic and legal instruments in the medium term (4 to 10 years) to influence polluters' incentive structures. This market-based approach was also to give priority to improving environmental protection institutions. Finally, in the long term (2 to 3 decades), new measures were to be adopted, including the use of clean technologies and the conservation of nature, and there was to be an attempt to achieve sustainable development.[12]

Implementation of Baltic Sea environmental commitments under the JCP was ranked among the short-term priorities. Most of the hot spots are point-source emissions that can be tackled by end-of-pipe solutions. Other short-term priorities included constructing or modernizing wastewater treatment plants, reducing water consumption, improving the water balance through reservoirs and leakage reduction, reducing solid-waste production, and introducing quality standards for fuel. The medium-term goal is a 50 percent reduction of wastewater discharges from municipalities, a 30 percent reduction of sulfur dioxide (SO_2) emissions (compared with 1988 levels), and a parallel 10 percent reduction of nitrogen oxide (NO_x) emissions. Among the long-term priorities is an 80 percent reduction of the total pollution load discharged into the Baltic Sea.[13]

In addition to the introduction of the National Environmental Policy, various international commitments have contributed to the new environmental direction in Poland. One international document that has been especially influential is Agenda 21, adopted at the Rio Summit. As a consequence of Agenda 21, Poland established an intersectional governmental national committee and introduced the environmental sustainability approach, which is now widely used for setting long-term environmental goals. Furthermore, Poland's desire to become a member of the European Union (EU) has prompted efforts to adjust national regulations to EU standards—an activity that is partly financed by the EU, notably through the program for Assistance for Economic Restructuring in the Countries of Central and Eastern Europe (PHARE). So far the impact of the Helsinki Convention and JCP has been evident mainly in the setting of short-term priorities. The Environmental Action Programme for Central

Table 15.1 Cost Estimates and Number of Hot Spots and Priority Hot Spots, by Country

Country	Hot spots	Priority hot spots	Cost estimates (million ECU)
Poland	34	18	4,023.0
Russia	17	7	1,372.0
Lithuania	15	5	497.0
Estonia	12	4	1,545.0
Sweden	12	0	451.0
Finland	10	0	424.7
Latvia	9	6	417.3
Germany	8	0	350.0
Denmark	4	0	312.5
Belarus	3	0	31.0
Czech R.	2	2	113.6
Ukraine	1	1	214.0
Russia/Poland*	1	1	20.0
Poland/Germany*	1	1	20.0
Lithuania/Russia*	1	1	30.0
Estonia/Latvia*	1	1	20.0
Czech R./Poland*	1	0	–

*Indicates a hot spot that spans a border area.
Source: HELCOM Third Activity Inventory, 1995, Tables 9 and 11.

and Eastern Europe (EAP), launched by the Organisation for Economic Co-operation and Development (OECD), has had important structural effects on Polish environmental regulation. The EAP covers programs in three areas: policy reform, institutional strengthening, and financing.[14]

Implementation

Environmental Problems and Priorities

Although it is well established that Polish environmental policy during the 1970s and 1980s had little influence on behavior, one cannot assess the effectiveness of Polish policy without considering the severity of the country's environmental challenges. One of Poland's most urgent problems is water pollution. Between 1984 and 1988, the Ministry of Environment surveyed the water quality of 161 lakes: only four met the water quality standards required for drinking water. Similar conditions were observed for Poland's rivers, especially the Vistula. According to a 1991 ministry report, the surface water

Table 15.2 Municipal or Combined Municipal/Industrial Wastewater Systems and Larger Treatment Plants

Country	Number of hot spots	Number of priority hot spots	Number of treatment plants within hot spots
Poland	22	16	41
Finland	1	0	1
Russia	7	6	9
Estonia	7	4	9
Latvia	3	3	3
Lithuania	10	5	10
Belarus	3	1	4
Ukraine	1	1	1
Czech R.	1	1	16
Germany	8	1	9
Denmark	1	0	1
Sweden	2	0	6
Total	66	38	110

Source: The Swedish Environmental Protection Agency, 1996, Lead-Party Report on Combined Municipal and Industrial Discharges, February, Stockholm, Sweden, p. 10.

quality of 57 percent of the river length was below the standard required for industrial use or irrigation.[15]

Nearly every report on the Polish environment paints a similarly dark picture. Water quality ranks among the worst problems, but forest damage due to air pollution and large amounts of hazardous and industrial waste also pose severe challenges to planners who must decide on the allocation of scarce resources.

Implementation of the Joint Comprehensive Programme (JCP)

Two of the JCP's central tasks were to evaluate the principal sources of Baltic Sea pollution—so-called hot spots—and to identify "priority" hot spots. The JCP survey found more hot spots and priority hot spots in Poland than in any other country in the region. Moreover, Poland accounts for 40 percent of the total cost of implementing the JCP (see table 15.1). A particularly urgent problem, and the largest source of Baltic pollution, is inadequate wastewater treatment (see table 15.2).

A 1996 JCP lead party report provides examples of how Poland is implementing controls on wastewater treatment.[16] According to the report, in the Polish area of the Vistula lagoon, 12 of a required 19 wastewater treatment plants have been installed. The plan is for all plants to treat waste biologically and mechanically by the year 1998. A new treatment plant was completed in 1995 in Koszalin; an extension of the plant's biological treatment facilities is planned for 1997. Biological treatment facilities will be constructed in Gdynia-Deborgóze in a project being financed by local authorities and by loans from national environmental protection funds. In Gdańsk-Wschod, biological treatment facilities are scheduled to be completed by 1998 in a project being financed by both local and national sources.

In the Vistula River basin, 75 percent of the wastewater in Bygoszcz-Fordon and Bygoszcz-Kapusciska is currently left untreated. A new treatment plant is planned for 1999. The feasibility study is being financed by the EU's PHARE program. Similarly, Toruń lacks wastewater treatment, but a new plant under construction will provide mechanical and biological treatment. Three-quarters of the project is being financed through environmental protection funds, and the rest by the municipality. In Włocławek there are plans to extend the mechanical and biological treatment facilities; however, funds have not yet been secured for this project.

The three hot spots in the Warsaw region concern plants treating the water supply for more than 1.6 million people. Only the Warsaw-Czajka treatment plant has biological and mechanical treatment facilities; the other two, Warsaw-Sierkierki and Warsaw-Panceerz, have no treatment facilities whatsoever. The European Investment Bank has granted a loan for building the necessary treatment facilities, but the additional funding needed has not been forthcoming. The two hot spots in Krakow are also very serious: the Krakow-Plaszów plant has mechanical and biological treatment facilities, but the Kujawy wastewater is released untreated. A new plant at Krakow-Kujawy is due to be completed between 1998 and 2001; the project is being financed by local and national sources, and by a small contribution from the EU.

The situation in the Odra River basin is also serious. In Szczecin, only 15 percent of the wastewater is treated. There are plans for building a new treatment plant there, to be financed by provincial and national environmental protection funds and foreign aid. In the city of Poznań, with 580,000 inhabitants, there are only mechanical treatment facilities; 30 percent of the wastewater is left untreated. There are preparations under way for constructing a new treatment plant in the city, but no financing is available. Similarly, Łódz, with a population of 830,000, only mechanically treats its wastewater.

In Zielona Góra, urban wastewater and wastewater from a food-processing plant are left untreated. A project currently under way there is being funded by municipalities and environmental protection funds; completion is scheduled for 1997. In Wrocław wastewater treatment is limited to mechanical treatment methods and irrigation fields. Large amounts of Wrocław's wastewater come from industrial sources. Here, a project to upgrade treatment facilities, begun in 1976, is being funded by municipalities, environmental protection funds, and the state budget; it was scheduled to be finished in 1996.

The overview of Polish implementation provided in the 1996 lead country report is incomplete due to a lack of comparable data. However, these examples show that much implementation activity is under way at several of the hot spots in Poland. Funding for these projects has predominantly come from national sources. Nevertheless, very few plans have been fully implemented. Even if the programs are fulfilled, the treatment plants constructed will not be of the highest standard available.[17] Some of the projects have been under way since the 1970s: these projects were launched without adequate financing before the country's transition and thus provide additional evidence that Poland was not lacking in policies but that implementation failed because the necessary institutional framework and regulatory pressure were absent.

The general conclusion of the 1996 lead party report is nevertheless that Poland has succeeded in taking steps in the direction of significantly reducing pollution that flows into the Baltic. Three pollution spots, Bygoszcz-Fordon, Toruń, and Warsaw-Czajka, are now considered "cold spots"—former hot spots that now meet HELCOM standards.[18] Funding has been significant, notably from domestic sources, but there will have to be considerable additional investment if all the projects that are needed are to be implemented. Nevertheless, there has been substantially more implementation, as well as domestic and international funding, in Poland than in Russia (see Chapter 14).

Effects of Transition on Policy Implementation

A major reason policy implementation has improved during the recent economic and political transition is that Poland has redesigned and rebuilt its administrative institutions. Attempts to bring the environmental policy instruments into line with Western models were made as early as the 1970s and 1980s. However, the instruments introduced (e.g., pollution charges) were designed to influence interest-based calculations made within the context of a market economy. The political system and bureaucracy of communist Poland could not provide the institutional setting required to transmit such market-oriented signals to their ultimate targets (e.g., polluting enterprises). As a result, policy's failure to influence target behavior could only be overcome by a radical change in the country's fundamental legal, administrative, and economic institutions. This change had to wait until 1989.

Poland was the first Soviet bloc country to make a graceful exit from communism. Roundtable negotiations between the communist government and opposition parties led to elections in June 1989. The new system of government was codified in revisions to the Stalinist constitution, which completely reshaped Poland's political, legal, and economic institutions. The changes included separation of powers, popular election of the president, devolution of some powers upon local levels, and the introduction of a market economy and the concept of universal human rights.[19]

These reforms transformed Poland from a communist state into a society organized on liberal democratic principles. The transition was a prerequisite for receiving international assistance in the form of financial aid and loans. It also led to fundamental changes in the institutions overseeing environmental policy implementation. Changes in at least three institutional areas have had a direct impact on the implementation of pollution controls in Poland: public administration, environmental protection funds, and foreign assistance.

Decentralized Public Administration
The administration of environmental regulations in Poland occurs at the national, voivodship (province), and municipal levels. The Ministry of Environment, the highest national authority, is responsible for formulating policy and coordinating the activities of other authorities, mainly other ministries and voivodships. Several ministries have become involved in implementing and financing environmental commitments within their respective sectors.[20] At the voivodship level, environmental administration is oriented mainly toward control and coordination of provincial environmental activities. Each voivodship has its own department for environmental protection; among its tasks are issuing permits, setting emission and discharge levels, and collecting fees.[21]

As a consequence of the revisions to Poland's constitution, in 1989 and 1990 administrative responsibilities were shifted from the central government down to local governments. Polish municipalities now enjoy a greater degree of self-governance, including the right of taxation. Among the tasks that have shifted to local levels is responsibility for wastewater treatment and other infrastructure. Voivodships also play a more active role in implementing policies. Although many functions have been decentralized, central authorities have retained the power to make and supervise legislation.[22] Decentralized administration and increased participation by local governments have enabled municipalities to handle pollution controls in relatively flexible ways. In practice, however, without mandatory control by national authorities, coordination problems among levels of government have arisen.[23]

Decentralization has allowed local governments to pursue their own initiatives, including improvements in environmental protection. Polish municipalities can reach agreements directly with foreign or domestic companies on environmental investments. Municipalities can even approach international institutions for assistance.[24] Similarly, there has been a marked increase in foreign aid targeted at local projects. Such projects already provide ample evidence of the influence of international commitments and institutions. However, as in many federal systems, the success of local environmental policies in Poland varies from region to region.

Environmental Protection Funds

Poland has the ability to mobilize substantial domestic resources to finance environmental investments. According to the Ministry of Environment, environmental expenditures rose from 0.6 percent of the gross national product (GNP) in 1989 to 1.4 percent of the GNP in 1994.[25] This ability to secure domestic financing is often attributed to the system of environmental protection funds.

Environmental protection funds were a prominent part of Poland's environmental policy long before the country's transition took place. The system was initiated during the 1970s with the introduction of financial penalties and effluent charges, and has since been adjusted for the conditions of a market economy. One of the early problems with these funds was the difficulty of collecting revenues; this is no longer a problem in post-transition Poland. The revenues of the Polish National Fund (the largest of the funds) have increased from US$12.9 million in 1990 to US$284 million in 1993.[26]

Charges and penalties for discharges that exceed effluent standards are placed in environmental protection funds. The funds give loans and grants for environmental investments. There is one national fund, the National Fund for Environmental Protection and Water Management, and several regional environmental protection funds.

The Polish National Fund is an independent financial institution that was established as a corporate entity by an act of Parliament in April 1989. In contrast to similar funds in other countries in transition, the Polish National Fund is not organized within the Ministry of Environment.[27] The National Fund made environmental expenditures of US$198.5 million in 1993, which amounted to 22.3 percent of Poland's total environmental expenditures in that year.[28] The main spending areas for the Polish National Fund are air pollution control (47 percent) and water pollution control (35 percent).[29]

The Ecofund is another type of fund institution that was established by Parliament in February 1992 for the conversion of Polish foreign debts into environmental aid. Four objectives are mentioned in the Ecofund charter: (1) to prevent transboundary air pollution by reducing emissions of sulfur and NO_x; (2) to reduce flows of polluting and eutrophying substances into Baltic waters; (3) to reduce emissions of greenhouse gases, particularly carbon dioxide; (4) to protect biological diversity.[30]

Western governments agreed to reduce Polish debts by 50 percent and to add an additional 10 percent reduction in exchange for Poland's creating a domestic fund for environmental investments. Thus, the debts were converted into aid handled by a domestic fund institution. A total of US$460 million has been guaranteed until the year 2010. In accordance with agreements with Western donor countries, the Ecofund finances projects with international and transboundary significance. Such agreements also include technology transfer and purchases from donor countries.[31]

Because the funds can be targeted at particular areas, they can help industry finance environmental investments that would be too costly for a firm to justify under a strict interpretation of the PPP. Another important factor is that regional and local governments can pursue specific environmental protection policies according to their priorities. Provincial funds were established in the 49 provinces in 1993; they are organized according to principles similar to those of the Polish National Fund and thus are independent legal entities. In addition, independent local funds have been established.[32] Thus, regional environmental funds are able to direct resources to local and regional concerns without having to wait for signals from the central administration. In Poland, in particular, local authorities are important for the formulation of priorities and projects to be financed by environmental funds.[33] Local communities can now influence the construction of sewage treatment facilities; previously, such decisions were the prerogative of industry and the central government.[34]

Several recent reports on the implementation of environmental commitments in Poland have attributed considerable influence to these environmental funds. According to a 1994 HELCOM publication, "especially the Polish National Fund for Environmental Protection plays an important role."[35] According to HELCOM's 1994 *Hot Spot Review*, "Poland has succeeded in establishing a dynamic legal, administrative and financing system to support and promote ambitious environmental policies."[36] The *Review* notes that Poland's ability to secure domestic sources of financing for investment in wastewater treatment is the most important reason for its implementation success. A 1996 lead country report on the implementation of the JCP on combined municipal and industrial discharges concludes that rehabilitation of old wastewater treatment plants and building of new ones have been made possible in part because of the new legislation and in part because of the funds.[37] As a rule, around 50 percent of total costs are covered by a national fund in conjunction with a voivodship fund, normally in the form of loans or grants.[38] Generally, the Polish National Fund or the Ecofund finances no more than half of any particular project. Thus, an applicant must finance the rest of the project through its own resources or through funds from other financial institutions, for example, commercial banks.[39] Roughly 50 percent of Poland's environmental expenditures are channeled through fund institutions (national, provincial, and local).[40]

Thus, the funds provide vital help in securing domestic financing of environmental projects. In a sense, such financial assistance prevents full application of the PPP. However, in reality the PPP cannot be fully implemented because too many Polish companies cannot afford pollution control equipment. The technical improvements needed to combat such high pollution levels are simply beyond most companies' means without government support or other forms of financial aid. Thus, the contribution of the PPP (e.g., taxes on effluents) is complemented by that of the environmental funds, which enable mobilized resources to be concentrated on the most urgent investments for pollution prevention.[41] The issue of whether the funds violate the PPP has been discussed in the OECD context: the environmental funds are subsidies that are contrary to the PPP; however, because they are derived from pollution charges, the funds have been accepted by several OECD countries.[42] It is also argued that the funds may be necessary during the transition process, but that they should not hinder market solutions.[43] The fact that the Polish funds are independent institutions and are not controlled by government is promising in this sense.

Although the funds have had much influence, they are unable to bear the full costs of Poland's protection of the Baltic Sea. In 1994, the Polish National Fund's provision covered only one-quarter of the yearly investments needed to fully implement the JCP.[44] Clearly, the enormous needs cannot be met by national financial institutions alone. An additional source might be foreign aid.

Foreign Assistance

Limited domestic resources can be augmented by external assistance. In practice, direct foreign aid so far has contributed only a minor share of the financing for Poland's environmental projects. According to HELCOM, 95 percent of the financing for the Baltic Action Plan in Poland is covered by domestic sources; very few hot spots have received foreign aid, with the exception of pre-feasibility studies. Only about 4 or 5 percent of Poland's environmental investments are financed through foreign assistance. A 1996 report put the figure for foreign aid at 15 percent in the field of wastewater treatment.[45]

The largest provider of foreign assistance is the EU's PHARE program, from which Poland received a total of 75 million ECU between 1990 and 1996. The largest sources of bilateral assistance are the USA, Denmark, Germany, and Sweden.[46] The breakdown of Poland's environmental investment financing in the early 1990s is shown in table 15.3. Private investors covered one-quarter of the total costs. However, these data should be interpreted in light of the fact that many pollution activities are still within the public sector and are financed via national or local budgets. Roughly 50 percent of the financing is provided by the Polish National Fund or by voivodship and local funds, a fact that underscores the importance of domestic funds.

Although the amount of direct foreign aid allocated to environmental projects makes up only about 5 percent of total financing, the transfer of resources to Poland has doubtless contributed greatly to the improvement of Polish environmental policies. Foreign assistance involves more than direct financing: Polish

Table 15.3 Financing of Environmental Investment Expenditures from 1991 to 1993

	1991	1992	1993
Environmental funds	40	58	58
Enterprises	30	20	23
Municipalities	20	13	10
State budget	5	5	5
Foreign assistance	5	4	4
Total	100	100	100

Sources: Data for first and second columns are from OECD/CCEET, *Environmental Performance Reviews: Poland*, OECD, Paris, France, p. 93; data for third column are from Regional Environmental Center for Central and Eastern Europe, *National Environmental Protection Funds in Central and Eastern Europe*, Budapest, Hungary, p. 57.

experts are cooperating with their Western counterparts to implement a number of projects. One such project was the construction of a district heating plant in Gdańsk.[47] The project not only produced a new district heating plant, it also enlarged capacity and allowed Polish experts to upgrade their skills. Moreover, efforts were made to establish new and less pollution-intensive practices.[48] Foreign assistance also helped shape the new environmental policy in the early 1990s. Rafal Milaszewski argues that Poland's National Environmental Policy was the result of cooperation with international experts at conferences.[49]

Concluding Remarks

A major factor behind Poland's improved capacity to handle environmental problems has undoubtedly been the changes in domestic institutions that accompanied the transition from central planning. The new democratic constitution, local government participation, and basic market and regulatory institutions have all contributed to more effective environmental management. Poland's more active role in international environmental institutions and its strong desire to join the EU have also been important. Although constitutional and economic changes in Poland are aimed at creating an open society with a decentralized government, political initiatives and planning remain prominent elements of Polish policies. In the environmental sector, policies and regulatory activities by local authorities play an important role, and environmental funds provide roughly 50 percent of the funding. Despite ambitions to implement a market-oriented, interest-based style of regulation, environmental policy in Poland is still predominantly controlled by governmental authorities. Nonetheless, Poland has made great strides toward a functioning market-economy policy style.

Understanding how national institutions can affect the transition process is crucial when considering environmental policy implementation in Poland. On the one hand, the constitutional changes are intended to yield a complete and radical transition of Poland's economy and government. On the other hand, the maintenance of certain institutions has modified that impact. The key issue is whether such modifying institutions jeopardize the transition or contribute to stability by adjusting programs to national traditions and practices.

Poland's distinctive style of making and implementing environmental policies has not disappeared as a consequence of its participation in international environmental cooperation to limit Baltic Sea pollution. The Polish case illustrates that existing institutions are not renounced, but are adjusted for the new conditions. Although environmental hot spots, as defined by the Baltic Action Plan, are identified and assessed using a single transnational process (HELCOM and the JCP), the financial and regulatory arrangements to implement international objectives are organized nationally, and thus follow national policy styles.

Poland is not following a radical path toward market-based environmental policy in which property rights and a full application of the PPP are the core elements. Instead, implementation efforts have relied, in part, on adjustments to existing institutions. The introduction of property rights and other market institutions has provided the institutional framework that is necessary if environmental protection funds are to work. The ineffectiveness of the funds during the communist era has been overcome by the new institutional framework, which is based on a wider application of market principles. Despite the improvement of institutions, the extent to which direct interests, in terms of costs and benefits for regulated enterprises, explain the behavior of polluting agents is still uncertain.

High-level Polish officials argue that there may be a conflict between economic transition and environmental protection.[50] Nevertheless, during transition there has been an increase in the share of the Polish GNP allocated for environmental protection due to the activity of environmental protection funds. The fund concept has been partially responsible for successes in tackling environmental pollution problems during the transition. However, the element of collectivism in the fund concept may lead to politically motivated environmental investments rather than to investments that strictly serve the interests of investors. The debate over possible conflicts between the PPP and the use of national environmental funds is relevant for all transition countries that have established environmental protection funds. However, the fact that the Polish funds function well and are independent make them promising. Unless the funds threaten the evolution of a market economy, they may be an adequate form of transition institution.

Notes
1. Hjorth, R., 1992, *Building International Institutions for Environmental Protection: The Case of Baltic Sea Environmental Cooperation*, Tema, Linköping Studies in Arts and Science, No. 81, Linköping, Sweden.

2. Ibid., pp. 140, 146.

3. Ibid., Chapter 5.

4. Milaszewski, R., 1994, "Water Protection Policy in Poland" in *Environmental Policies in Poland, Sweden and the Netherlands: A Comparative Study of Surface Water Pollution Control*, edited by M. Löwgren and R. Hjorth, Tema, Tema V Report No. 19, p. 63, Linköping, Sweden.

5. Mikosz, J., 1996, "Water Management Reform in Poland: A Step towards Ecodevelopment," *Journal of Environment and Development*, 5:230–253. For comparisons with other East European states, see Jancar, B., 1987, *Environmental Management in the Soviet Union and Yugoslavia*, Duke University Press, Durham, NC, USA.

6. Löwgren, M., and Hjorth, R., eds., *Environmental Policies in Poland, Sweden and the Netherlands: A Study of Surface Water Pollution Control*, Tema, Tema V Report No. 19, p. 105, Linköping, Sweden.

7. Ibid., p. 99.

8. Kamieniecki, K., and Salay, J., 1994, Beauty and the East: An Evaluation of Swedish Environmental Assistance to Eastern Europe, Secretariat for Analysis of Swedish Development Assistance (SASDA), Working Paper No. 7, Stockholm, Sweden, p. 7.

9. Löwgren and Hjorth, op. cit., note 6, p. 105.

10. The creation of the Baltic Sea Council as well as the 1996 Visby Conference are other results of that desire.

11. Milaszewski, op. cit., note 4, pp. 56–57. The information originates from Poskrobko, B., 1987, "Is a System of Environmental Protection Management Possible?" *Gospodarka Wodna*, 47(5) (in Polish).

12. Baltic Sea Environment Programme, 1994, *Hot Spot Review*, Vol. 2, Copenhagen, Denmark, p. 57. The *Hot Spot Review* is prepared by I. Krüger Consult AS; COWIconsult; Carl Bro Environment a/s; and Vandkvalitetsinstituttet.

13. Ibid., pp. 59–60.

14. "The St. Petersburg Guidelines on Environmental Funds in the Transition to Market Economy," 1995, Environmental Funds in Economies in Transition, OECD/CCEET, Paris, France.

15. Milaszewski, 1994, op. cit., note 4, pp. 51–53.

16. Swedish National Environmental Protection Agency, 1996, Lead Party Report on Combined Municipal and Industrial Discharges, February, Stockholm, Sweden.

17. Such wastewater treatment plants would have mechanical, biological, and chemical treatment methods.

18. Swedish National Environmental Protection Agency, op. cit., note 16, p. 8.

19. Sokolewicz, W., 1995, "The Relevance of Western Models for Constitution-Building in Poland" in *Constitutional Policy and Change in Europe*, edited by J.J. Hesse and N. Johnsson, Oxford University Press, Oxford, UK, pp. 245–246.

20. The following ministries are involved: Ministry of Industry and Trade; Ministry of Agriculture; Ministry of Physical Planning and Buildings; Ministry of Transportation and Maritime Management; Ministry of Health and Social Welfare; and Ministry of Privatization. See Baltic Sea Environment Programme, op. cit., note 12, p. 54.

21. Environmental Performance Reviews: Poland, 1995, OECD/CCEET, Paris, France, p. 26.

22. Swedish National Environmental Protection Agency, op. cit., note 16, p. 16.

23. For instance, voivodships cannot plan the development of entire river basins; see Mikosz, op. cit., note 5, p. 236.

24. Interview with Polish officials, December 1995. The author would like to thank Mr. Wojciech Szrubka for his help with the interviews conducted in Poland.

25. Interview with officials at the Polish Ministry of Environment, December 1995.

26. Kruszewski, J., 1994, "Polish National Fund for Environmental Protection and Water Management" in *National Environmental Protection Funds in Central and Eastern Europe*, edited by P. Francis, Regional Environmental Center for Central and Eastern Europe, Budapest, Hungary, p. 59.

27. Similar funds are organized in Bulgaria, the Czech Republic, Hungary, and the Slovak Republic. See Francis, P., ed., 1994, *National Environmental Protection Funds in Central and Eastern Europe*, Regional Environmental Center for Eastern and Central Europe, Budapest, Hungary.

28. The Slovak Fund, which is much smaller, covers 20 percent of the country's environmental expenditures. For the other countries, the figures range between 7 and 11 percent; ibid., p. 44.

29. Ibid., p. 14.

30. Ecofund Charter, section II, paragraph 5.

31. Francis, op. cit., note 27, p. 36.

32. Kruszewski, op. cit., note 26, p. 56.

33. Francis, op. cit., note 27, p. 10.

34. Francis, op. cit., note 27, p. 10.

35. *HELCOM News*, 1994, No. 2, p. 17.

36. Baltic Sea Environment Programme, 1994, *Hot Spot Review*, Vol. 1, Copenhagen, Denmark, p. 18.

37. Swedish National Environmental Protection Agency, op. cit., note 16, p. 16.

38. Baltic Sea Environment Programme, op. cit., note 12, p. 61.

39. Anderson, G., and Zylicz, T., 1995, "The Role of Environmental Funds in Environmental Policies of Central and Eastern European Countries" in *National Environmental Funds in Economies in Transition*, OECD/CCEET, Paris, France, pp. 94–95.

40. Kruszewski, op. cit., note 26, p. 57.

41. Kamieniecki and Salay, op. cit., note 8, p. 9.

42. Anderson and Zylicz, op. cit., note 39, p. 99.

43. Francis, op. cit., note 27, p. 20.

44. Baltic Sea Environment Programme, op. cit., note 12, p. 61.

45. Swedish National Environmental Protection Agency, op. cit., note 16, p. 16.

46. In 1993 the assistance from these countries was as follows (in million US dollars): Denmark, 30.6; Germany, 26.3; Sweden, 19.2; and the USA, 36.3. Baltic Sea Environment Programme, op. cit., note 12, p. 63.

47. Kragh, P., 1996, "The Role of Expert Knowledge in the Implementation of Regional Environmental Commitments: Cases from Poland," in *Baltic Environmental Cooperation: A Regime in Transition*, edited by R. Hjorth, Tema, Tema V Report No. 23, Linköping, Sweden.

49. Milaszewski, op. cit., note 4, p. 56.

50. Interview with Polish officials.

16

Conclusions

Kal Raustiala and David G. Victor

The chapters in this volume describe and analyze a wide range of international environmental regimes and implementation experiences. As they demonstrate, there is no standard model for the implementation process. The outcomes of implementation are often uncertain, especially when implementation requires influencing the behavior of a large number of social actors. Such challenging implementation requirements are increasingly common—they are an indication that countries are tackling a growing array of international (increasingly global) environmental problems that require pervasive economic and social changes.

Even when implementing the same international commitments, different national circumstances have led countries to take different approaches. Norwegian efforts to regulate nitrogen oxide (NO_x) emissions have focused in part on ships, because many vessels sail through Norway's vast territorial waters; the Netherlands and the UK have focused on emissions from automobiles and combustion plants. Sweden has complied with most international commitments to protect the Baltic Sea because Swedish domestic standards have been more stringent than those of the Baltic Sea environment protection regime; Sweden used the regime to induce other polluters to implement stronger measures, not to induce additional activity in Sweden.[1] In contrast, for Poland, which until recently had done little to control Baltic effluents, membership in the Baltic Sea regime has required substantial implementation activity.

Implementation activities also vary with the commitments themselves. Formal differentiation of commitments is typically minimal or nonexistent. More common is differentiation through interpretation and practice. The USSR interpreted international commitments to cut sulfur dioxide (SO_2) emissions by 30 percent to apply only to transboundary flows, not to emissions nationwide. Thus it focused its modest implementation activities on controlling emissions from power plants located near its western border, where emissions readily flowed into Western Europe. Similarly, the role of interpretation is evident in the North Sea regime, where commitments concerning land-based sources of nutrient pollution apply only to "sensitive areas." The British government declared that no areas proximate to the UK were sensitive to nutrient pollution, and thus has made virtually no effort to implement nutrient controls. In contrast, sensitive areas are abundant in Dutch and Norwegian waters, and thus a central aspect of those countries' efforts to implement North Sea commitments has focused on regulating the agricultural practices that are a principal cause of nutrient pollution. Often the exact implications are unclear when international commitments are negotiated. For example, only after the North Sea nutrient commitments were adopted did the Norwegian Parliament, under pressure from environmental nongovernmental organizations (ENGOs), declare that all Norwegian coastal waters were "sensitive."

Implementation experiences also vary by nation and locality because international commitments typically overlap with other goals of domestic policy. Limiting land-based sources of pollution flowing into the Baltic, for example, is only one element of national and local efforts to protect water quality. Similarly, controlling NO_x helps limit the international problem of acid rain and also reduces urban smog. Where the resonance between international environmental commitments and other policy goals has been recognized and exploited, political support for implementation of international commitments and actual changes in behavior have been greater. Because most pollution problems have a common source—the cycling of materials and energy through the economy—control efforts are often synergistic. In the cases in this book, direct conflicts between international commitments and other environmental objectives have arisen mainly when international commitments have merely resulted in the relocation of pollution: for example, the Soviet strategy of focusing SO_2 controls only in the western part of the country contributed to a net shift of pollution to the Arctic, and British regulation of North Sea dumping shifted some pollution to land-based dumps and incinerators.

The most evident characteristic of the implementation processes studied in this book is that when national implementation is a demanding task, both the means and the outcomes of implementation are typically varied and uncertain. Often, a country adopts an international accord without a clear plan for putting the commitments into practice. Moreover, when national implementation is complex, more political and economic interests are likely to be affected, leading to political mobilization and shifting coalitions. Typically these coalitions become more complicated, with less predictable outcomes, as international commitments become more stringent. The uncertainty of outcomes from the implementation process has three important consequences.

First, governments cannot ensure that national performance will conform with international commitments. Even highly responsive governments can find themselves unable to comply with international commitments.[2] Our studies suggest that noncompliance is typically the product of incomplete planning and miscalculation rather than a willful act, though distinguishing between intentional and incidental noncompliance is difficult. Implementation is an evolutionary process, often shrouded in uncertainty.[3] Consequently, nations find it difficult to pursue their interests in a unitary, strategic fashion because their interests and capabilities, as well as the demands of international commitments, are often shifting and unclear.[4] Only when implementation is trivial—such as in the regulation of whaling—is it possible for nations to clearly calculate the consequences of membership in an international environmental agreement.

Second, the studies in this book confirm what is often claimed: almost all countries comply with almost all of their binding international commitments.[5] However, the inability to ensure particular outcomes from the implementation process has led most governments to be very conservative in the international commitments that they adopt. It is crucial to distinguish legal compliance with an international commitment from the extent to which the commitment has actually influenced behavior in a way that advances the goals that inspired the commitment—what we call *effectiveness*. Compliance is the formal aim of international commitments. However, compliance depends on the stringency and scope of the legal standard, as well as on behavior. Thus compliance is not the same as effectiveness. Compliance with the 1985 Sulphur Protocol to the Convention on Long-Range Transboundary Air Pollution (LRTAP) has been nearly perfect—most parties have overcomplied with the modest commitment to cut SO_2 emissions 30 percent by 1993. But studies that trace the Protocol's influence on behavior find that its effectiveness has been low in most countries.[6] In Russia, emissions of major air and water pollutants are sharply lower today than a decade ago—and thus Russian compliance with international regulatory commitments has been very high—but nearly all of that drop is a consequence of economic decline, not implementation of international environmental commitments.[7] Formal compliance with treaties is also often high when countries take reservations against particular treaty requirements, as in the case of Norway with respect to the commercial whaling ban and in the case of Russia with respect to the London Convention's ban on dumping of radioactive waste into the ocean.

Whereas many analysts have seen high compliance as a sign that commitments are influential, our cases suggest that compliance often simply reflects that countries negotiate and join agreements with which they know they can comply. Before they adopt an international commitment, most governments engage in extensive internal review to determine whether they can comply with it, especially if the agreement is legally binding. Thus compliance is high because proposed commitments that could lead to noncompliance do not earn the consent of most governments. When implementation is complicated and uncertain, the necessary margin of error to ensure compliance is large. Ambitious proposals to cut NO_x emissions were abandoned when the NO_x Protocol was adopted in 1988 because few governments thought they could comply with them. The USSR was especially careful to negotiate and interpret its international commitments to enable high compliance with minimal change in behavior. In short, legally binding agreements often codify what is already under way or reflect actions that parties are confident they can implement.[8]

Although effectiveness is what matters most, the concept of compliance is not irrelevant. Mechanisms that improve the effectiveness of international agreements, such as the Non-Compliance Procedure of the Montreal Protocol, are typically triggered only when noncompliance exists. Those mechanisms can help deter and reverse situations of noncompliance. However, determining whether such mechanisms actually influence behavior requires careful tracing of cause and effect and not merely examining compliance levels.

Third, implementation uncertainty creates a strong demand for information about implementation options and for periodic reviews to ensure that countries are putting their international commitments into practice. We show that this demand can be satisfied through participation by "target groups" (e.g., regulated industries) and other nongovernmental organizations (NGOs) with implementation expertise and through the operation of systems for implementation review (what this volume terms "SIRs"). The result is a context rich in information on implementation, which in turn can yield more effective agreements by reducing uncertainties, allowing the negotiation of more realistic international commitments and making it easier to assess implementation performance.

These three consequences of implementation uncertainty set the scene for the rest of this chapter. In the next section we focus on national implementation and examine some sources of and responses to implementation uncertainty. We then focus on the international level, where the primary response to the difficulty of ensuring national implementation has been the emergence of decentralized SIRs. Subsequently we show how the use of nonbinding legal instruments can reduce the conservative behavior of governments caused by implementation uncertainty; increased use of nonbinding instruments, we suggest, can make demanding regulatory regimes more effective. Finally, we speculate on the broader context: the ongoing integration of national economies and the fact that the industrialized countries that adopt the most demanding international environmental commitments are mainly liberal states. Throughout, we suggest some ways to design international agreements, institutions, and national implementation activities to better contend with pervasive implementation uncertainties.

Implementation at the National Level

The case studies in the second part of this book examine in detail how international commitments are implemented domestically. They explore how that process of domestic implementation interacts with the negotiation and evolution of international commitments. The studies devote particular attention to the role of participation and the ramifications of the transition from central planning.

Participation in the Implementation Process

The need for greater transparency, openness, and participation in the policy process is virtually a mantra of modern governance.[9] At the national level, the demand for participation is reflected in legal provisions such as citizen-suits and information-access statutes. Similarly, in international fora, NGOs have been granted greater access and participate more intensely in environmental regimes than ever before.[10] But despite more extensive participation in both national and international settings, until now there has been little systematic investigation of the actual influence that patterns of participation have on the content and implementation of international environmental commitments. Does participation matter? If so, what can be done to alter patterns of participation?

The Influence of Participation.   In light of the extensive attention that policymakers have given to participation, we expected that patterns of participation by stakeholders would affect both the policies adopted and their actual results. If that expectation were found to be invalid, then one of the strongest rationales for expanding stakeholder participation—that it leads to different (more democratic) policies that better serve the interests of many stakeholders—would also be invalid. The evidence from the studies is ambiguous. In most cases, expanding participation *has* affected policy outputs. In general, the result has been more demanding environmental policies because, relative to other groups, ENGOs and other public interest NGOs have expanded their influence the most. In an extreme case, the Netherlands' approach to policy-making, based on extensive consultation, has produced ambitious policy statements that increasingly reflect the interests of ENGO participants. British policy statements have also become more green, in part because ENGOs now have greater access and participate more actively in policy formation. However, in neither country can all of the change be traced to wider participation. Other factors also explain the shift to green policies; notably, public environmental concern has risen at the same time. In the UK, for example, the adoption of stringent policies against dumping in the North Sea occurred before ENGOs gained substantially greater access to decision-making fora and to information.

The influence of participation on policy outputs is strongly evident in the transition countries. Declared policies to limit marine dumping of nuclear waste in Russia have been a direct consequence of greater participation in policy-making processes and wider availability of information. When dumping policy was controlled by the military (the source of dumping) the resulting policy matched military interests; as the voice of nonmilitary interests has risen, regulations on dumping have been tightened. The creation of an independent parliament with investigative powers has helped to expose dumping hazards and has spurred much tighter regulation. Inside Russia, some ENGOs have been active on the issue and have influenced dumping policies in ways that were not possible in the Soviet system. Outside Russia, Western ENGOs have publicized Russian dumping practices; their access to international policy-making fora aided the mobilization of international pressure against Russian dumping practices.

Although participation has clearly affected declared policies, its impact on the implementation process and the behavior of target groups has been far more ambiguous. In the case of NO_x regulation, different declared policies and patterns of participation in the UK, the Netherlands, and Norway have led to remarkably similar outcomes: all three countries achieved roughly a freeze on growth in NO_x emissions. The factors that had the largest impact on emissions were unrelated to environmental policies: in the UK and the Netherlands, emissions were easier to control because of a restructuring of the power sector (the UK) and the availability of natural gas (the UK and the Netherlands). In Norway, emissions proved more difficult to control because NO_x effluents from ships were unexpectedly high. In both the NO_x and the North Sea cases, ambitious Dutch policy statements—which were clearly the result of the participatory Dutch policy style—had little effect on behavior. The gap between policy declarations and behavior by target groups in that country has been wide; poor enforcement has allowed bold policy goals with few penalties for implementation failure.[11] In sum, the general proposition that participation matters is not sustained in all cases. Participation has clearly had an influence on declared policies, but not always on the behavior that follows.

Participation by Target Groups Leads to More Effective Commitments and Implementation. We expected that participation by target groups— associations of industries and individuals whose behavior must change if environmental goals are to be met—could lead to more effective regulation in two ways. First, we expected that target groups that participate might be *motivated to implement commitments more thoroughly* because they develop a stake in the outcome. None of the cases supports this hypothesis—by itself, target group participation has not led to more thorough implementation. Often, participation has been a necessary condition for target groups to change their behavior, but in none of our studies was it sufficient in itself. In Norway, for example, target group participation has been a crucial part of the consensus-oriented policy process. Even extensive participation by Norwegian municipalities did not significantly increase their willingness to install the costly wastewater treatment facilities necessary to reduce North Sea pollution. Our studies reveal instances where target group participation appears to have resulted in extensive implementation, but only because it was directly in the target groups' interest. Participation in itself did not motivate target groups to implement international commitments. In the case of chemicals and pesticides trade, industry actively and voluntarily implemented the nonbinding system of prior informed consent

(PIC) because it feared that failure of the scheme would lead to a more onerous binding system.

Second, we expected that target group participation would *provide better information* on the range of possible policy options, technical feasibility, and costs and benefits—what we call "implementation expertise." The evidence strongly supports this proposition. Target groups frequently have the most timely, accurate, and complete implementation information. Thus, enhancing their participation can increase the supply of useful information and lead to better-crafted decisions. In the UK and Norway, target group participation has substantially increased the flow of useful information to decision makers on North Sea and NO_x policy options. In the Montreal Protocol and in the PIC system, industry has supplied vital information on chemical hazards. Without industry's participation, it would have been nearly impossible to implement the Montreal Protocol's "essential uses" exemption. That exemption was critical to the effectiveness of the Protocol because it allowed the adoption of stringent regulatory commitments while ensuring that important uses for which no substitutes were (yet) available could be maintained. In short, target group participation has led to substantial informational benefits that have made international cooperation more effective. The informational benefits of target group participation appear to have been greatest when policy options have been complex and uncertain—the conditions that we argue will become more common as countries engage in deeper cooperation to regulate a wider range of activities that cause environmental problems.

The Risk of Regulatory Capture.   We expected to find that policy systems open to participation by target groups would be prone to regulatory capture, leading to public policy decisions that mirror the interests of the regulated target groups, not the public good. The studies confirm that while regulatory capture is a risk, the capturing influence of target groups has been offset through informed participation by countervailing groups.[12] For example, in the PIC case, oversight and expert information provided by consumer and development organizations helped to scuttle industry efforts to restrict the PIC system to chemicals and pesticides that were already closely regulated. Indeed, information and pressure from public interest groups even helped extend PIC to include pesticides that posed the greatest hazards in developing countries.

We also expected to observe many instances of ENGOs monitoring the implementation of and compliance with international commitments. By exposing implementation failures, ENGOs could induce governments and target groups to implement international commitments more fully. It is now widely asserted that such oversight and "enforcement" are among the ENGOs' crucial contributions to environmental governance.[13] Our cases suggest that ENGOs perform these functions relatively rarely: Greenpeace actions against British dumping in the North Sea and Greenpeace-organized boycotts of products from the whaling nations Iceland and Norway are among the few examples in this volume. The rarity of oversight and enforcement by ENGOs or other non-state actors likely reflects costs and benefits. Oversight and enforcement are expensive because they require timely information on the behavior of target groups. Target groups themselves typically have that information, but often have little incentive to use it for enforcement purposes or to share it with others. Improving public access to information could lower the costs to ENGOs of gaining such information, but typically such transparency has not, in practice, yielded nearly as much useful, complete, or timely information as hoped.[14] Moreover, often few benefits flow directly to the public interest groups that pay the costs of oversight, except where media-friendly images result (ships in blockade, stymied officials, and so forth). ENGO "enforcement" efforts do not always focus on failures to comply: neither Iceland's lethal scientific whaling research nor Norway's commercial whaling was in formal violation of international commitments, but both were attractive targets for ENGOs.

Enforcement by ENGOs has been quite extensive in at least one area of international cooperation: wildlife law. Decades of engagement by ENGOs have led to their extensive involvement in setting the agenda for international wildlife negotiations, managing negotiations, and performing many functions of implementation. The quasi-NGO International Union for Conservation of Nature and Natural Resources (IUCN) gathers and assesses vital information on the status and effectiveness of national wildlife management programs, including programs that are mandated by international commitments. The World Wide Fund for Nature (WWF) serves as the "lead party" for managing wetlands and bird habitats in the Baltic Sea, a responsibility that includes making proposals for commitments and taking the lead in overseeing their implementation. By performing such functions in the negotiation and operation of international legal instruments, these ENGOs have made possible greater oversight and enforcement by themselves and other ENGOs. These cases show that public interest NGOs can engage in effective oversight and enforcement if they devote the resources, over a long period of time, to build the needed technical capacity, information base, and reputation.[15]

Policy Instruments for Altering Participation Patterns: The Access Structure. Although we find that participation does not always influence declared policies and actual outcomes, at times it is important and thus policymakers may seek to alter patterns of participation. Policymakers may especially seek specific forms of participation—such as by target groups and countervailing interests during the implementation process—that our studies suggest could make international environmental regimes more effective. Moreover, whether or not participation has a substantive impact, many now argue that participation should be wider for procedural and normative reasons—so that policy is more fully democratic and better reflects a wider range of stakeholder interests. In light of these benefits and pressures, what factors govern patterns of participation?

Much policy attention has focused on access rules, and we expected that those rules would strongly affect—and could be adjusted to alter—patterns of participation. The studies suggest that permissive rules are a necessary, but not a sufficient, condition. A striking example is the policy decisions of the International Whaling Commission (IWC), where the rules of access have been open and unchanged for decades. Until "whales" were adopted as an environmental concern, practically the only participants were those nations directly engaged in whaling. In the past two decades, participation by non-whaling states and like-minded non-state actors (scientists and ENGOs) has risen with their interest in whaling, not in response to changing rules of access. Changes in international whaling policy were clearly the result of these new participants—once the anti-whaling coalition had enough votes, the IWC adopted a moratorium on commercial whaling. The anti-whaling coalition has also used its access to block adoption of a Revised Management Procedure (RMP) that would allow resumption of commercial whaling, although reasonable scientific assessment confirms that the RMP is adequate to achieve its function—protecting whale stocks. Previously, the IWC was a forum run by and for whalers; now its many functions have been captured by preservationists.

In nearly all the cases discussed in this book, participation has risen over time at both the international and national levels whether or not access rules have changed. In general, as an issue matures a greater number of stakeholders realize their interests in the issue and thus seek to influence policy. Several cases suggest that participation contracts only when political attention to the issue at hand wanes. In only one of the cases in this book—Russian dumping of radioactive waste—has participation declined because of active efforts by a government to restrict participation.

We began this study with the expectation that many differences in national implementation would be attributable to systematic differences in institutions and culture—national "styles" of regulation[16]—including differences in participation. Two studies in this volume (Chapters 8 and 9) examine three countries—the Netherlands, Norway, and the UK—selected for systematic differences in regulatory style. Chapter 10 compares the whaling policies of two countries—Iceland and Norway—mindful of differences in national styles of policy-making. The studies on transition countries (Chapters 11–15) were undertaken in part because we expected that transition would affect participation and might cause a particular style of implementing regulatory commitments. Although the styles vary significantly across these many cases, there has been a remarkable convergence in national policy style vis-à-vis participation. In all these cases there currently are, to different degrees, permissive access structures even though some had been tightly closed as recently as the mid-1980s. (However, actual NGO participation in the policy process in transition countries has often not followed more liberal access rules in the cases examined in this volume: where NGOs are active on the environment, their concerns typically are not focused on the issues that are the subject of international commitments.)

In sum, the most obvious tool in the hands of policymakers—altering rules of access—has been employed to allow ever-wider participation. In practice, however, open access has allowed, not caused, more participation. In some cases, more open access rules have followed, not caused, expanding participation by non-state actors. Moreover, while wider participation has clearly affected many policy declarations—making them systematically greener—the impact on actual behavior has been mixed. Influence is often correlated with implementation expertise. Thus, in practice, only a few of the new participants have proved influential. Becoming an influential participant in the implementation phase is a costly undertaking that bears fruit only after years of investment.

Implementation During Transition[17]

Chapters 11–15 concentrate on implementation of environmental commitments by societies undergoing extensive change. Public decision-making processes are becoming more open and decentralized; politics is more pluralized; the economics of these "transition" countries are increasingly market-based.[18] All of these changes are occurring simultaneously and rapidly. Consequences include varying degrees of economic instability and decline, greater availability of information on environmental hazards, and increased civil capacity to pressure government to respond to environmental hazards. In this book, special attention has been paid to transition because it is the central feature of many environmentally significant industrial economies. We focus on Russia because it is the largest of these: Russia burns more fossil fuels, a major contributor to many air pollution problems, than all other transition countries combined; its fuel consumption also exceeds that of France, Germany, and the UK together.[19]

Economic Decline Leading to High Compliance. The experiences of transition countries underscore why it is crucial to look beyond compliance to assess the effectiveness of international commitments. Soviet and Russian compliance has been generally high, but this largely reflects what Alexei Roginko (Chapter 14) terms "compliance without implementation." During the Soviet era, compliance was high because Soviet authorities carefully designed international commitments so that compliance was possible with minimal change in domestic activities. The few changes that were needed could be implemented readily through the state's central planning powers. During transition, compliance with regulatory commitments has remained high because most pollution is correlated with industrial activity, which has declined sharply. The remarkable emission reductions in Russia, including a 52 percent decrease in SO_2 emissions and a 10 percent decline in NO_x emissions, and the fact that most transition countries have met most international commitments to cut pollutants flowing into the Baltic Sea mainly reflect economic decline.[20] However, during the period of the sharpest economic decline, 1989 to the present, the drop in pollutants has not been commensurate with the drop in economic activity; per unit of gross domestic product, economic activity is "dirtier" than ever.[21]

Economic decline has not always resulted in compliance, especially when compliance has been more expensive than inaction. Russian compliance with data-reporting requirements in the Baltic Sea regime, the LRTAP Convention, and the Montreal Protocol has been poor. Dumping of high-level radioactive waste in the Barents and Kara Seas in violation of international commitments occurred as recently as 1988, partly because the Soviet military lacked cheaper disposal alternatives and was not compelled to change its behavior. Dumping of low-level radioactive waste has not been a formal violation of international law only because the Soviet government lodged a reservation against the international moratorium on such dumping. And the Baltic states, Russia, and Poland are not on track to meet the Baltic Sea regime's wastewater treatment commitments by the year 2000, although Poland is making considerable progress toward that goal.

In short, international environmental commitments have had little influence in the former Soviet republics. Compliance has resulted mainly when rules have happened to conform with existing trends in behavior. The studies investigated several possible explanations for this observation.

Low Public Pressure.   Minimal implementation of international environmental commitments in these states mainly reflects low public pressure for environmental protection. Under communist central planning, public information on environmental dangers was limited. International environmental issues were put on the agenda primarily by the West; the communist countries participated in international environmental accords chiefly to further East-West diplomacy. Public influence should be higher under the new system, but in practice more pressing issues, such as crime and unemployment, have overshadowed environmental concerns and corruption has reduced the public's ability to influence policy decisions and implementation. ENGOs working on international issues are few, and in the case of radioactive waste dumping, Russian government crackdowns have limited the activities and influence of ENGOs working inside the country.

Decentralization and the Devolution of Power.   Transition is marked by the opening of politics and society, and on most issues transition countries are also shifting the functions of government from the center to regional and local levels.[22] Our studies show that decentralization and devolution of power have weakened the ability of government to implement international environmental commitments in three interrelated ways. First, most international environmental commitments require some form of government action to give them influence at the domestic level. Decentralization and devolution have generally lengthened and weakened the links of the chain by which government regulatory decisions are then transmitted to their targets, a situation further complicated by the participation of many new actors.[23] In contrast, the Soviet state had greater control over actors within its borders and was better able than its Russian successor to ensure compliance with international environmental commitments.[24]

Second, implementation now takes place primarily through the decentralized market system, not via commands. Ironically, while the goal of transition is to weaken the state's grip on society, successful social regulation through markets makes enormous demands on the state apparatus. It requires that the state be able to design and implement policies that influence highly decentralized actors (through markets) while minimizing distortions of markets. On the surface, transition countries employ an impressive array of market-based incentives such as fees, taxes, and marketable permits. However, in practice, in the former Soviet states market instruments are neither designed nor implemented in a way that has much influence on behavior. Taxes and fines have not kept pace with rampant inflation. Resources in funds earmarked for environmental projects have been spent for other purposes. There are indications, however, of improved tax structures and enforcement in all these transition countries. After having stalled construction for decades, one of the largest polluters in St. Petersburg rapidly completed a wastewater treatment plant after local authorities fined it US$1.5 million for excess discharges. Incidents like this are rare, but they indicate that fuller application of market incentives is possible in Russia. The design and application of market-based pollution controls is systematically better in Poland.

Third, the devolution of power has blurred the distribution of authority among federal, regional, and local authorities. In general, transition has given regional and local authorities more responsibility for making and enforcing environmental rules.[25] But those authorities face many other pressures that decrease their zeal to enforce environmental standards. For some enterprises, full assessment of fines would mean bankruptcy and unemployment, which would undermine the votes and tax base that local officials are keen to sustain. Thus, in practice, officials make extensive adjustments when applying pollution charges. For example, in water pollution control, Russian authorities regularly issue waivers that reduce pollution fees and allow firms to deduct a large portion of fees as operating expenses. In air pollution control, authorities can negotiate "provisionally coordinated emissions" that blunt the market signal.

As in the West, much policy is made from the "bottom-up" through negotiations between targets and regulators. In stable regulatory systems, such "negotiated implementation" often takes place in the shadow of a judicial stick that can be used in rare cases when more stringent enforcement is needed. But courts have played only a small role in the transition countries because they are burdened with other cases and, especially in Russia, high inflation makes the collection of past fines meaningless. Anecdotal evidence also suggests that negotiated implementation and the shift to regional and local control have allowed increased corruption because targets have more direct and exclusive contact with, and thus greater ability to influence, the officials who enforce rules.

The Impact of Privatization. Privatization appears to have exacerbated the challenges of decentralization and devolution and reduced the ability of government to implement international accords. State-owned monoliths have been privatized into many discrete firms: the St. Petersburg industrial association Kirovskiy Zavod, which was the largest single source of polluted wastewater in the Soviet defense sector, has been dissolved into 60 individual companies. Privatized firms have been acutely sensitive to short-term costs that affect profits. In Russia, in particular, the method of privatization has increased the control over firms by managers, who have been able to dominate production decisions even when outside owners have a controlling interest. Managers have run firms for their immediate benefit rather than for long-term profitability. Poorly defined and uncertain ownership of property rights has also contributed to short time horizons.[26] Although weak public pressure and poor public regulation appear to be most significant, low profits and managerial control also help to explain why private firms have had little incentive to make long-term, environmentally beneficial investments. Some of these factors can be overcome. For example, the use of collective environment funds, financed by pollution charges, has helped to finance costly investments that profit-sensitive firms will not make on their own. In the Baltic states and especially in Poland such funds appear to have been particularly important in facilitating implementation of environmental regulations, including regulations that implement international environmental commitments.

Roles for Financial Transfers. The antiquated capital stock in transition countries yields enormous pollution but also offers wide scope for inexpensive pollution controls. Western countries are often downwind and downstream and thus have a strong incentive to transfer the resources needed for pollution control in the transition countries. In recent years such transfers have grown. Without Cold War ideological and geopolitical barriers, the West has been able to focus on practical ways to achieve low-cost environmental protection. With the desire to achieve benefits from integration with the West, fears of sovereign intervention in the East have waned, making it easier to accept external scrutiny and verification, which are conditions of most Western assistance.

Although much Western attention is focused on what the West can do externally through financial transfers, the studies in this book underscore that under most conditions the domestic resources of the recipient nations themselves are actually larger and more important. About 90 percent of all environmental spending in St. Petersburg and about 95 percent of total environmental spending in Poland is financed domestically. While Western aid and technology would have been crucial to the (now stalled) agreement to reduce emissions from Norilsk Nickel on the Kola Peninsula, the largest contribution to the package would have been relief from taxes, totaling as much as US$1.3 billion, provided by the Russian federal government.

As expected, the relative role of Western financing is higher for effluents that affect environmental quality in the West. The West is providing 32 percent of the resources allocated to clean up Polish "hot spots" that are the main sources of Baltic Sea pollution.[27] For matters where there is little domestic benefit, such as compliance with the ozone accords, the share of Western financing is even higher. Forty percent of the funding for a recent project to phase out ozone-depleting substances, as required under the Montreal Protocol, is being paid by the Western-funded Global Environment Facility (GEF). Although external resources have been crucial to Russia's full implementation of the Protocol, Russia is still expected to pay most of the cost itself. Our studies demonstrate that the need for international financial transfers has been tempered when domestic public pressure has been high: much of Polish water pollution regulation reflects local public pressure to stop the fouling of local waters, which also happens to limit Baltic pollution. In contrast, recently Russia has been able to stifle domestic opposition to marine dumping of radioactive waste;

in doing so, it has been able to credibly demand that outsiders—Japan, Norway, and the USA—pay the costs of finding alternative disposal sites.

The transaction costs of international transfers can be very high. In an extreme example, the negotiation to transfer money and technology to Norilsk Nickel in exchange for limiting emissions from the largest source of air pollution on the Kola Peninsula took nearly a decade. Eventually, Western donors withdrew in frustration. When domestic regulatory and market institutions are poorly developed, it is especially difficult for recipients to assure donors that financial transfers will be spent as intended. Thus, as expected, donors have focused on countries where transaction costs are lower and domestic assurances are higher. Consequently, in the Baltic Sea regime donors have favored Poland over Russia; the fraction of resources sent to Russia has risen only slowly.[28] In both the regime to limit dumping of radioactive waste and the regime to protect the Baltic Sea, programmatic commitments and activities, such as to report and analyze data, have improved knowledge about national situations and made it easier to target aid.

Overall, the studies in this book cast doubt on some of the more sanguine predictions of schemes to transfer resources in exchange for pollution controls, which are often termed "joint implementation" (JI). Such schemes depend not only on the donors' interests in controlling transboundary pollution, but also on compatible domestic institutions in recipient countries that allow for secure and efficient contracts. Even when opportunities for JI-like transfers are numerous—as in Russia today—the absence of compatible domestic institutions makes practical implementation of JI projects difficult or impossible.

Only Bad News? The above is a generally dismal story. For Russia, in particular, the outcome—lack of implementation—is overdetermined: low public pressure, lack of regulatory enforcement, a scarcity of resources that can be tapped for expensive capital improvements, the Russian style of privatization, poorly defined property rights, and barriers to efficient financial transfers are all factors that have caused low implementation. But the long-term picture may be brighter. Private ownership and control of firms, real pricing of natural resources, stable and transparent regulation, and access to capital markets all facilitate long-term planning and investment—including planning and investments for environmental purposes. By pluralizing political processes, the transition countries have also made possible the fuller expression of environmental values. The factors that underpin a prosperous liberal, market-based society do not necessarily lead to more international environmental protection, but they appear to often have that effect, especially when local and national environmental regulation overlaps with international environmental objectives. Our review of the literature on Poland's implementation of the Baltic Sea accords shows that the transition to a liberal society can also yield new regulatory mechanisms that successfully influence behavior.[29] Even the Baltic republics, notably Estonia, demonstrate some partial implementation successes.

Systems for Implementation Review (SIRs)

At the national level, in most well-functioning polities institutions are in place to monitor, assess, and enforce the implementation of laws. The international system lacks such extensive structures, but the need for these functions remains. Some states attempt to translate their international obligations into action but fail. Others attempt to "free ride." Still others have the will and capacity to implement environmental commitments but are reluctant to adopt costly measures without assurance that other societies are bearing similar costs. Often, effective international cooperation also requires the ability to assess and adjust commitments in light of new information. These situations can be addressed when procedures exist to collect and assess data on whether countries are meeting their commitments; to handle the implementation problems that are identified, such as by mobilizing technical assistance, political pressure, or sanctions; and to assess the adequacy of existing commitments and future options. The actors and institutions that perform these functions comprise what we term *systems for implementation review* (SIRs). The first part of this book focuses on how SIRs operate and the ways that they contribute to making international cooperation more effective.

The Systems View

At the outset of this project we expected to find only a modest amount of implementation review. The few existing studies on the topic showed that little monitoring and review (often termed "verification") of implementation took place.[30] That monitoring and review which did occur was generally poor. We expected efforts to handle problems of noncompliance would be few and modest because we expected, as many scholars had argued, that compliance would be high. We also expected that sticks wielded in response to violations—also termed " enforcement"—would be practically nonexistent because they are rare in international law.[31]

The cases show that implementation review is, in fact, quite active and effective. Typically, the functions of implementation review have been performed by a decentralized array of institutions and procedures; only a small fraction (in some cases, none at all) were formally dedicated to that purpose. In all cases, most functions of implementation review evolved informally, after the agreement entered into force. Thus analysts who look only at formal legal procedures, especially those enshrined in original treaty texts, will draw a highly narrow and inaccurate picture of how implementation review is actually practiced. They will see few dedicated procedures for implementation review and will observe that those dedicated procedures often do little, although in practice much review occurs. They will also see many formal mechanisms for dispute resolution that perhaps could be used to handle implementation problems, but in practice such mechanisms have never been used.

In contrast, studies show that implementation review within each regime is performed by numerous institutions and procedures that operate together as a *system*. That system is decentralized, and many of its components are not dedicated to the task nor even formally mandated to perform functions of implementation review.

Even the most extensive formal mechanism for implementation review—the Montreal Protocol's Implementation Committee—is only one part of a larger decentralized system. Questions about whether India's and China's plans to build chlorofluorocarbon and hydrochlorofluorocarbon production facilities were consistent with their obligation to implement the Montreal Protocol were raised and debated within the Multilateral Fund (MLF) in the context of those countries' MLF funding programs, not in the Protocol's Implementation Committee. Regular reviews of the implementation of the Montreal Protocol's "essential uses" exemption have taken place within a Technical Options Committee, which is the same group that recommends when a use is no longer "essential." In the Baltic Sea regime, the Helsinki Commission's review activities have even reviewed implementation of standards for oil pollution, which are formally established by another legal instrument (MARPOL) under a different international organization (the International Maritime Organization).

This decentralization has resulted in many benefits. The dispersion of functions has yielded useful redundancy. In some cases, non-state actors have provided data that are independent of official government reports and have filled gaps when official data have been absent. Decentralization has allowed extensive review even in the absence of formal procedures. In the Baltic Sea regime there have been extensive reviews of projects funded under the Joint Comprehensive Programme (JCP) and reviews of the adequacy of the JCP itself, yet until recently no formal procedure for reviewing implementation existed.

Informal and non-dedicated procedures have been effective in handling some aspects of implementation review that are politically sensitive, such as making funding conditional upon performance. In the Montreal Protocol, most funding is part of the MLF, but the financing necessary for Russia and several other countries to comply with the Protocol flows from the GEF, which has no formal connection with the Protocol. In practice, the GEF has made its funding for projects contingent upon these countries handling their cases through the Protocol's Non-Compliance Procedure. The GEF has thus ensured that the regime's mechanism for implementation review is active and effective. Because the GEF was not formally established by the Montreal Protocol's parties, it has been able to apply conditionality to its funding relatively easily. In contrast, formal efforts to make funding from the Montreal Protocol's MLF conditional upon performance—even concerning modest topics such as compliance with data reporting—have been more difficult and controversial.

The multiplicity of institutions and actors has raised fears of duplication and poor coordination. Indeed, the need for more coordination is now widely discussed and many activities are under way, especially in the United Nations, to improve coordination. Yet in practice, levels of coordination have been relatively high, in part because the same actors operate in multiple fora and in part because special (often informal) attention is given to ensuring that dispersed activities operate as a coordinated system.

The studies suggest that the effectiveness of each component to the system for implementation review has multiplied as the system has become more integrated. For example, data reporting in the Montreal Protocol has been more complete when backed up by the Secretariat's and Implementation Committee's regular review of whether the required data are actually submitted. In turn, data reporting has improved because the MLF funds capacity-building projects for that purpose. Moreover, as the system has become more integrated the data and review processes have become more useful for assessing whether existing regulatory commitments are adequate and for proposing adjustments. In the Baltic Sea regime, the development of the system for reviewing implementation has been integral to the assessment and adjustment of HELCOM Recommendations to limit land-based pollution.

The nature of implementation review, and the decentralized way in which it so often operates, also allows SIRs to shift participation patterns within regimes. The many decentralized bodies that contribute to implementation review under the Montreal Protocol, for example, rely upon and indeed transfer considerable power to expert groups. As regimes develop and tackle more complex implementation issues, they are likely to include a larger number of such expert bodies. These experts, however, are not always natural scientists, who traditionally have been the focus of studies of the role of experts and expertise.[32] Rather, they are individuals with implementation expertise often drawn from the regulated targets themselves. In the PIC case, representatives from both industry and consumer groups have played major roles in providing information and assessments related to implementation. All these groups have made a substantial investment in the issue area, measured in terms of field activities, regular attendance at meetings, and projects related to implementation. As noted earlier, groups that had not given sustained attention to an issue did not build up the necessary implementation knowledge—they had little that was substantial to offer and thus had low influence.

Trends in SIRs. SIRs are becoming more common and more elaborate. In at least one major subset of environmental accords—fauna and flora agreements—SIRs have steadily become more complex and appear to be making an increasing contribution to the effectiveness of agreements. Early agreements included no provisions for reporting and review; since the 1950s, nearly all agreements do. Today, the "standard" wildlife agreement includes regular reporting, regular reviews of implementation, regular reviews of the adequacy of commitments, and opportunities for non-state actors and experts to contribute information and participate in implementation review. With such a relatively high level of implementation review as the standard, it has been easier for some agreements to go even further: 4 of the 19 wildlife agreements concluded since 1970 even have provisions for on-site inspections.

In addition to John Lanchbery's study of a large sample of fauna and flora agreements (Chapter 2), the other case studies in the first part of the book also show that SIRs have become more extensive and intensive over time. As parties have become more intent on addressing the environmental problems at hand, they have responded both by making commitments more stringent *and* by enhancing SIRs. However, parties that have been wary of international commitments have also been wary of implementation review. The Montreal Protocol illustrates a tradeoff between the stringency of possible commitments and the extent of implementation review: developing countries opposed adoption of a rigorous review procedure but accepted commitments to sharply cut consumption of ozone-depleting substances.[33] But in other cases, when parties have favored deeper cooperation, more stringent commitments and extensive implementation review have gone hand-in-hand. In the Baltic Sea regime, donors have made financial and technical assistance conditional upon extensive implementation review; in the European air pollution regime, the 1994 Sulphur Protocol includes a noncompliance procedure to help ensure that its more stringent, costly emission controls are implemented fully.

Data Quality.   Data are the backbone of SIRs. Without data on the environmental problem at hand and the extent of implementation activities it is impossible to review implementation, identify and handle implementation problems, and assess the adequacy of existing commitments. The main source of such data is the typical requirement in an international environmental agreement that each party report data on its own behavior. Previous studies have demonstrated that such national data reports are typically late and incomplete.[34] We found that many international agreements now benefit from extensive efforts to improve reporting rates; financial assistance has helped many countries to report data and the end of the Cold War has reduced the political barriers to data reporting in transition countries.

However, all of our case studies demonstrate that a more intractable problem of data *quality* remains: national data often are not comparable, and their accuracy is often low or unknown. In the Baltic Sea regime, the quality of reported data was initially low and improved only through several rounds of active efforts to compare and apply data to the assessment of Baltic Sea quality and regulatory priorities. In the best-developed systems, the quantity and quality of data that are collected typically fall well short of what is needed for

SIRs to reach their full potential. Even in the most extensively developed data collection system—that of the European air pollution regime (Chapter 7)— it took nearly two decades of effort among countries with high administrative capacity to build up an integrated scheme for collecting data for use in models of the transport and chemistry of European air pollution. That experience shows that data collection can be useful for designing more effective international regulatory regimes, but if policymakers want such capacity, they must begin early. In that case, data collection efforts began even before the first round of substantive commitments was negotiated.

Addressing Implementation Failures and Noncompliance: Management versus Enforcement. Finally, the studies have considered many of the ways that the operation of SIRs has contributed to the effectiveness of international environmental accords. Of particular interest is what happens when an SIR uncovers an instance of inadequate implementation. Often such scrutiny of implementation failure has been triggered by formal noncompliance with international commitments, which underscores that while compliance is often a poor measure of whether an international agreement is effective, it is nonetheless important. Here, we briefly consider the two most important hypotheses: one, that failures to implement international environmental commitments are best "managed" in a nonconfrontational manner; the other, that coercive "enforcement" techniques are needed. The two schools of thought reflect different visions of how the international system works, the possibilities for governance with international law, and the policy tools that are available and should be used to handle implementation problems.

The "managerial" approach to compliance holds that states have a propensity to comply. Instances of noncompliance, for the managerialists, are seldom deliberate and usually result from problems of capacity, treaty ambiguity, and/or uncontrollable social or economic changes. Noncompliance is a problem to be solved, not an action to be punished. Solutions include greater transparency, nonadversarial forms of dispute resolution, and technical and economic assistance.[35] Conversely, the "enforcement" school builds on traditional realist models of state behavior and argues that states in fact calculate the costs and benefits when they choose whether to comply.[36] Hence the proper policy response to extensive noncompliance is to increase costs through enforcement measures. Proponents of enforcement strategies argue that when cooperation has historically been at its deepest, enforcement measures have played important roles. Moreover, successful instances of intensive cooperation—such as the General Agreement on Trade and Tariffs–World Trade Organization system and the European Union (EU)—contain enforcement provisions that have grown stronger as the regime has grown deeper.

Our research provides a mixed message for this debate. The studies suggest that most implementation problems are not willful violations. We find little evidence of states strategically calculating whether to comply with extant international obligations, in part because states that adopt the most stringent international commitments—usually advanced industrialized countries—typically face domestic pressure to address environmental problems. The only cases that illustrate such strategic behavior are those that concern the USSR before transition, when the government suppressed facts and public influence, thus limiting domestic pressure to address pollution, and when the command system facilitated a unitary approach. Moreover, as the managerialists expect, the most serious failures to meet international commitments identified in this study clearly stemmed from unanticipated factors. The failure of Russia and a few other transition countries to eliminate ozone-depleting substances reflects that these countries have limited ability to control the firms within their borders. Similarly, the Norwegian central government does not have direct control over municipalities, whose cooperation has been needed (but not forthcoming) to reduce nutrient pollution flowing from wastewater treatment plants into the North Sea. However, classifying these implementation problems as willful or accidental is difficult; arguably, they merely reflect that governments have not given sufficient priority to implementation and compliance.

Fundamental to this question of whether noncompliance is mostly an unanticipated or a calculated phenomenon is the fact, noted earlier, that compliance rates for binding commitments, which are the instruments most extensively used in international environmental governance, are generally very high. Few of the implementation problems identified in this study actually constitute formal noncompliance. The practice of adopting binding international commitments with which compliance is possible explains why those few violations reflect miscalculation rather than mischief—states do carefully calculate their interests when negotiating and joining international agreements. High compliance may also explain why it is often difficult to mobilize international responses to implementation problems—because few such problems have actually yielded noncompliance few have triggered response mechanisms such as noncompliance procedures.

Regarding the instruments used, we find support for both managerial and enforcement models. Most cases of actual or possible noncompliance are "managed" through discussions and negotiations. Increasingly, resource transfers ("carrots") have been part of the management approach. Managerialists claim that stronger responses to implementation problems, such as sanctions and other "sticks," typically are not available in the international system; they also argue that, even if they were, such techniques would not be as effective as the management approach. Our studies only partially confirm that expectation. The regimes examined in this volume that have been marked by the most extensive cooperation, such as the Montreal Protocol, have had at their disposal powerful incentives and disincentives—tools of enforcement. When such tools have been used, they have worked, especially when the sanction has been to withdraw assistance (i.e., to stop supplying "carrots"). Under the Montreal Protocol, funding for developing countries is withheld if those countries do not report their baseline data within one to two years of their first funded projects. Meeting that standard is relatively easy; nonetheless, all failures to report data have been met by a threat to cut funding, and almost immediately the needed data have been supplied by the delinquent governments. Similarly, the threat of denied GEF funding played a major role in the effective handling of the Russian and East European noncompliance cases. In practice, however, the operation of the Protocol's Non-Compliance Procedure generally has been nonconfrontational and has followed the management mode. "Sticks" have rarely been used and, perhaps, are rarely needed because the occasional use of strong measures may send a signal that deters other potential violators, although properly evaluating their deterrent role is difficult.

Other cases confirm that sticks can be essential for handling poor implementation. ENGOs enforced the implementation of whaling norms by mobilizing consumers against whaling countries, with some influence on whaling practices, especially in Iceland. In the Convention on International Trade in Endangered Species of Wild Fauna and Flora (CITES), multilateral sanctions have been applied. Trade in CITES specimens with Thailand and with Italy was temporarily banned after those parties repeatedly failed to implement domestic legislation and control trade as required by CITES. The United Arab Emirates was expelled from CITES, and thus excluded from trade in CITES specimens, because it persistently violated controls on trade in ivory.[37] These cases also confirm that it has been much easier to trigger the mechanisms for applying such sticks when there has been a formal verdict of noncompliance.

The means for handling compliance problems at the international level shares some features with domestic regulatory enforcement. Studies on the implementation of domestic air pollution regulations in the USA, for example, show that compliance schedules are often negotiated between government agents and polluters; many penalties that are authorized by statute are actually never applied and few violations are strictly punished.[38] That is, compliance with domestic regulatory law is also mostly managed, not strictly enforced. A critical difference between international and domestic regulation is that at the international level the range of international enforcement measures is typically much narrower. The ability of international institutions to apply large sticks or carrots to specific instances of noncompliance, as evident in the Montreal Protocol, is still unusual. As at the domestic level, the need for such measures may also be rare, but some instances do arise, and thus the ability to credibly threaten strong responses to violations makes other, softer management responses more effective. In contrast, at the international level the compressed range of available responses to implementation problems suggests that the ability to deter implementation failures may be small. Moreover, the management approach may be weakened because there are few stronger tools available when management fails. Indeed, the Russian case of noncompliance with the Montreal Protocol is one such instance where management efforts had repeatedly failed and were rejuvenated only because stronger measures were available and used.

The Choice of Legal Instruments[39]

Although this book focuses on the implementation process, the case studies have allowed us to speculate about which types of legal instruments induce the most implementation activity and thus are likely to be the most effective. The choice of instruments is a central issue facing negotiators of international agreements; our analysis of the choices builds on several other studies that have explored which instruments are most effective under different conditions.[40]

Conventional wisdom holds that the most effective international commitments are legally binding.[41] Yet our cases point to many instances where nonbinding agreements have had greater influence on behavior, especially when parties have sought the benefits of international cooperation but have been uncertain of their ability to implement commitments. Four cases—regulation of NO_x, protection of the Baltic and North Seas, and regulation of trade in hazardous chemicals and pesticides—show how the effectiveness of international cooperation rose with the adoption of nonbinding instruments. In none was the improvement a sole result of the choice of legal instrument: nonbinding instruments allowed but did not directly cause more effective cooperation.

Nonbinding commitments have aided cooperation and implementation in several crucial ways. States appear to have been more willing to adopt commitments that are both clear and ambitious when they have been codified in nonbinding form. Clear commitments have been more effective because they are more easily translated into specific actions, regulations, and other incentives for target groups. They are also more readily reviewed and evaluated by the international community. The ambitious nonbinding North Sea commitments to cut major pollutants 50–70% were highly specific and thus it has been easy to assess whether national performance has met the goals. The Baltic Sea JCP has produced highly detailed priorities for action, making transparent the principal causes of Baltic pollution and the cost of necessary policy responses. JCP priorities have not been followed fully, but they have helped to direct and coordinate funding, which would not have been possible if goals had been vague.

Ambitious commitments have spurred wider and more intensive efforts to change the behavior of target groups. When the legally binding Protocol to freeze emissions of NO_x was signed in 1988, a small group of countries simultaneously adopted a more ambitious nonbinding Declaration to cut emissions by 30 percent. While it is difficult to ascribe a strong impact to either agreement, at least in the Netherlands and Norway the existence of more ambitious nonbinding commitments forced governments to explore the need for additional regulations that they otherwise would not have considered. Norway has since rejected the Declaration, but only after serious efforts to make additional cuts in NO_x emissions. The flexibility of the Declaration allowed Norway to consider deeper cuts that it clearly was not contemplating under the binding NO_x Protocol, without fear that it would be locked in if the additional cuts proved infeasible. The ambitious nonbinding Ministerial Declaration to cut the main Baltic Sea pollutants by 50 percent has required Finland and Sweden to implement additional measures, whereas earlier international commitments required little additional action.[42]

Both these benefits—clarity and ambition—have been most evident when parties have been uncertain what they can implement. When uncertainty has been high, most governments have approached binding commitments with caution: they have signed only what they could implement, and thus binding commitments have typically required only modest, if any, change in behavior ex ante and have been accompanied by high compliance rates ex post. In contrast, governments have been less hesitant to adopt clear and ambitious commitments if they are nonbinding, even when implementation uncertainty creates risks of noncompliance. Indeed, compliance with nonbinding commitments has been low, but in many cases the influence of those commitments on behavior has been high. In short, contrary to popular wisdom, compliance and effectiveness are often inversely related.[43]

Another attribute of nonbinding agreements that allows for more effective cooperation is flexibility in participation. In both the NO_x and North Sea cases, a small "club" of countries used nonbinding instruments to move forward with deeper cooperation. In both cases, nonbinding agreements allowed the benefits of "minilateralism"—focused cooperation among a small number of motivated parties—when it was politically or symbolically difficult to exclude laggards from formal, binding agreements.[44] In the North Sea regime, ministerial-level conferences oriented around nonbinding declarations made it easy to exclude laggards Spain and Portugal. Neither state contributed significantly to North Sea pollution, but both had been formal participants (and slowed work) in the legally binding conventions. Without those two states, the only remaining laggard was the UK. Isolated, branded the "Dirty Man of Europe," faced with a growing domestic green movement, and under high-level pressure at the North Sea Ministerial Conferences, the UK switched positions and North Sea cooperation moved forward rapidly. Nonbinding instruments made it easier to isolate and pressure the UK and made it easier for the UK to adopt the stringent commitments once it had changed its position.

Our studies also demonstrate that nonbinding instruments can be effective in cases where the environmental problem at hand has been ambiguous but stakeholders nonetheless have wanted to start the process of international co-operation. In the case of regulating trade in hazardous chemicals and pesticides, when the nonbinding PIC system was adopted it was unclear which substances should be included in PIC and how PIC should work in practice. The non-binding instrument created a voluntary scheme that could be adjusted easily and rapidly. None of the important rules was formalized; rather, the system evolved as the participants—industry, public interest groups, government officials, international organizations, experts—gained experience. In 1989, when PIC was adopted, advocates of tight trade regulations saw the adoption of a nonbinding system as a setback. They favored a binding alternative, but many exporting nations would not have consented to a binding PIC system in the late 1980s. (At this writing a binding treaty, modeled closely on the nonbinding system, is being negotiated.) In retrospect, the benefits of wide participation and "learning by doing" have been extremely important and probably would not have been nearly as abundant if PIC had been binding in its early stages. Once industry support was assured (which often occurs when nonbinding measures are backed by the credible threat of binding law), the nonbinding instrument yielded effective international environmental governance at the early learning stages of the regime.[45] The presence of a system for implementation review provided information feedbacks and facilitated "learning by doing."

In sum, while prior studies have extolled nonbinding instruments because they enter into force immediately, without ratification,[46] our cases point to other benefits that are more important. Such instruments have allowed parties to adopt clearer and more ambitious goals, especially when they are unsure of what they can implement. This central benefit of nonbinding instruments has also contributed to two other benefits. Parties that have wanted deeper cooperation have used nonbinding instruments to create a smaller club of like-minded enthusiasts. Moreover, the flexibility of nonbinding instruments has facilitated learning by doing, which has allowed more effective cooperation when it has been unclear how best to cooperate.

Taken together, these benefits suggest a new approach to international environmental governance that makes more extensive use of nonbinding instruments, especially at the early stages of cooperation. It is contrary to the current conventional wisdom, which leads diplomats and policy advocates to focus on negotiating binding commitments and to resort to nonbinding commitments only when binding efforts fail. Our evidence does not apply under all conditions: notably, if the goals, means, and ambitions of cooperation are clear then a binding instrument may be more appropriate (or, perhaps, the choice of instrument does not matter).

While advocates of binding measures fear that parties to nonbinding commitments will readily defect, the perils of defection have been reduced through transparency and extensive implementation review. The North Sea case provides an example and points to two important elements of the review process. First, effective reviews have looked at policies and plans, not only at simple indicators of compliance. Such reviews have made it possible to assess whether countries are on track to meet international commitments and whether existing commitments are adequate. In contrast, simple compliance reviews focus on ex post assessments. Second, in the North Sea case, reviews have been part of the Ministerial Conferences and thus have been backed by periodic high-level political attention. The presence of high-level government officials has made scrutiny of national performance more effective because such officials often have the power to change policies that are criticized in reviews and have the authority to forge agreements with their counterparts in other countries, including agreements that require extensive and costly implementation. Review procedures—SIRs—are likely to be critical for ensuring that noncompliance with ambitious nonbinding commitments, which is common, is not merely a sign of inaction.

Legally binding commitments nonetheless retain an important role as one of many international policy instruments. Indeed, the benefits of nonbinding instruments often have been most evident when applied in tandem with legally binding measures. The North Sea Ministerial Declarations and the NO_x nonbinding Declaration were conceived as part of a broad complex of instruments that includes both nonbinding and binding commitments. Domestic efforts to pressure governments and target groups to implement international commitments may be more effective when they can refer to a binding instrument, even if its commitments are modest while more ambitious commitments are found only in nonbinding instruments. The existence of a core binding commitment may serve as a necessary rite of passage, helping to raise the profile and effectiveness of all efforts—binding and nonbinding, formal and informal. Binding commitments can also serve as a backstop if ambitious nonbinding commitments are abandoned, such as in the case of Norway's efforts to regulate NO_x.

This new approach to international environmental governance, which places greater emphasis on nonbinding instruments and on regular and extensive implementation review, can and should become more common in handling the new generation of environmental problems. These problems are marked by the need for costly but uncertain changes in behavior as well as ambiguity as to the best means of achieving such changes. In that category today are problems such as climate change and loss of biological diversity, which may require fundamental changes in the ways that modern economies use and value natural resources. Fundamental changes are difficult to plan and implement according to exacting, binding targets.

Some Speculation on Current and Future Cooperation: Deep Integration and Liberalism

In the preceding sections we have focused on specific propositions concerning the factors that influence the implementation and effectiveness of international environmental commitments, based on the empirical studies in this book. Here we examine the broader international context. We focus on two central contextual changes. First, as economic liberalization expands, a wide range of policies are becoming deeply integrated across countries and thus increasingly interdependent. A core zone of integration centers on the member states of the Organisation for Economic Co-operation and Development (OECD), but the zone is rapidly expanding. Second, the states that undertake the most extensive international environmental commitments, the highly industrialized OECD members, are similar in their domestic structures: they have representative (elected) governments, constitutional protection of individual rights, independent judiciaries, and market economies based on private property. They are broadly "liberal."[47] That zone of liberalism is also expanding, most notably into the transition countries. The states in these zones of integration and liberalism are industrialized (leading to many serious, shared environmental problems, as well as the capacity to recognize them) and wealthy (providing the resources with which to address these problems).

As others have argued, interdependence and liberalism affect how states view and pursue their interests and how they perceive the roles of international institutions.[48] Yet scholars have given little attention to the implications for international environmental regulation. Rather, the literature on international environmental politics has largely developed without close attention to the broader international context. We suggest that the context can make international environmental cooperation more effective. Liberal states are more supportive of international institutions needed for effective international environmental governance, and the demand for environmental regulation is higher in liberal states than in nonliberal states. Regulation of externalities that are pervasive in the economy, such as pollution, is also easier when nations are already coordinating and integrating their national policies. But taking account of this context also requires changing some notions about international cooperation—for example, decreased emphasis on compliance and increased attention to implementation. It also requires careful assessment of the tradeoffs incurred through participation by nonliberal states.

Deepening Integration of Liberal States

Many of the international regimes explored in this volume address areas of policy traditionally considered "domestic," such as agricultural policy, energy use patterns, and municipal waste treatment. Increasingly, international regimes are used to harmonize, coordinate, or strengthen diverse national policies. In many cases, as these chapters demonstrate, such international commitments require significant and novel action—extensive implementation of new international commitments. As a result, domestic policy is critically shaped by international decisions.[49] The opposite is also true: the implementation of international environmental commitments relies heavily on, and is implemented through, existing national regulatory structures. Extant domestic policy can thus greatly influence the scope and terms of the international measures that states seek and will accept; domestic policies of powerful states can be major determinants of international regime rules.[50]

Following a multivolume assessment of all major aspects of national economic policy, the concluding volume to The Brookings Institution's project on "Integrating National Economies" argues that the process of domestic policymaking is undergoing radical change:

> Viewed separately, the measures that have been taken [by international agreement] on financial regulations, regulatory matters, and environmental protection can be seen simply as incremental expressions of

international concerns over issues once regarded as domestic. Viewed together, they reflect a new threshold in global economic relations and in the relations between governments and their citizens .... [P]ressures from divergent national practices, international spillovers, and the erosion of the global commons are leading to direct challenges to national sovereignty. National governments and international negotiations must increasingly deal with deeper, behind the border integration.[51]

The authors argue that an essential part of "deep integration" is the progressive synthesis and coevolution of domestic and international affairs. "Shallow integration" is marked by the simple elimination of barriers to commerce and interaction; for example, the progressive reduction of border impediments to the movements of goods, such as tariffs and quotas under the General Agreement on Tariffs and Trade. Of the cases in this book, shallow integration marks the adoption of quotas for emissions of SO_2, the catch of whales, and the dumping of radioactive waste at sea, which have required only simple governmental actions (or no action at all), and thus little interdependence of domestic policies. Deep integration, by contrast, is an active political and economic program; it promotes integration because only with integration are certain benefits possible. In trade, those benefits include greater flows of goods and services through reduced nontariff barriers to trade, requiring active integration of national policies on patent protection, subsidies, health and safety regulations, and so on. In the environment, the goal of deep integration includes the reduction of transboundary pollution resulting from pervasive economic activities, such as the burning of fossil fuels and growing of crops. In other words, deep integration both reflects and furthers interdependence.[52]

The most complex cases of international regulatory cooperation—and the deepest integration—occur primarily among the liberal states of the West. These states share a desire to address the environmental problems of industrialization. Yet the extensive ties, transnational relations, and liberal precepts that exist among their societies militate against blunt or unilateral regulatory responses. The result is a zone of collective management, marked by shared environmental problems and shared preferences for managing those problems through institutions that operate according to liberal principles—they must be broadly participatory, rule-bound, and transparent.[53]

Some Consequences of Deep Integration and Liberalism

The phenomenon of deepening integration and the concept of a zone of collective management help to explain some important characteristics of cooperation among liberal, integrating states. Here we speculate on three: (1) the meaning of compliance; (2) the role of SIRs; and (3) cooperation with states outside the zones of liberalism and deep integration. All three concern the design of international institutions as well as the tactics and strategy of international environmental governance.

The Meaning of Compliance. Efforts to solve international problems through deep integration frequently require reconfigurations of domestic laws and policies; the success of such initiatives depends on thorough implementation. While international environmental policy represents only one of several core areas ripe for deeper integration, the cases we explore in this volume provide cautionary lessons. The implementation of international commitments faces serious obstacles, ranging from low administrative capacity (and overcapacity)[54] to political indifference and interest-group counterpressures. While analysts concerned with deep integration have largely focused on the costs and benefits of and prospects for a program of deeper integration,[55] in fact the most important issue may be the feasibility of implementation. As we have shown, implementing "deep" commitments is no easy matter.

Deep initiatives are likely to critically depend on implementation and how implementation failures are handled. Often, implementation problems are expressed as failures to comply. However, as we have shown, the relationship between compliance and effectiveness is neither direct nor simple: high compliance is not equivalent to effectiveness. An ambitious agreement may induce marked behavioral change that nevertheless fails to match commitments. Indeed, perfect compliance is rarely a central goal of collective management; rather, it is more typically a by-product of collective efforts to solve shared problems by adopting international agreements and building institutions to review performance. Compliance is not irrelevant, however, because often those institutions focus on compliance as an indicator of performance. Moreover, compliance with international commitments is an important value for liberal states, because it also indicates good-standing membership in the international community.[56] But what matters most, as we have stressed throughout this book, is performance. Expected performance is difficult to achieve when international cooperation is demanding—when international regimes include commitments that require extensive, costly, and often complex political, legal, and behavioral changes that are characteristic of deep integration.

Demanding regimes for environmental cooperation among liberal states may need to be especially tolerant of implementation failures. Because they are particularly responsive to domestic pressures, liberal states will face pressure to deviate from international commitments. Because international cooperation is demanding it is often uncertain exactly what policies will be needed to implement international environmental commitments. And because sectors and nations are interdependent, many factors other than those policies affect the behavior of target groups and thus compliance with international targets. These factors partially explain why many international agreements contain escape clauses allowing bounded deviations. (Nonbinding "voluntary" agreements allow similar flexibility because they are more permissive of noncompliance.) For many observers escape clauses undermine cooperation because the proliferation of escape clauses "debases" compliance by effectively lowering collective standards. In a recent book, Downs and Rocke argue conversely that states may respond to the problems of deepening cooperation—such as domestic political backlash—by purposively developing enforcement provisions that allow some deviation from regime disciplines.[57] The ability of a regime to bend, but not break, gives it strength and resiliency over time and allows for deeper commitments.[58] The deeper the cooperation, therefore, the more escape clauses may proliferate. The research in this volume supports this view of escape clauses. That they at times debase compliance is relatively unimportant, because compliance is not the primary goal of collective environmental management. What matters is long-term performance and progressive resolution of the problem at hand in a way that does not unduly burden integration in other areas and that does not provoke backlash and extreme political dissent. This is a process that requires extensive efforts over long periods of time. Derailment is more dangerous than deviation.

As a result, escape clauses, nonbinding instruments, and other forms of institutionalized flexibility should often be welcomed, not lamented. Such flexibility in international legal instruments aimed at deep integration allows the balance between domestic autonomy and international collaboration to be adjusted to particular circumstances, electoral cycles, and economic conditions. Many analysts fear that nonbinding recommendations and extensive escape clauses are a recipe for symbolic and ineffective international cooperation. The enormous amount of attention devoted to compliance, to dispute resolution, and to agreements with "teeth" reflects a belief that states must be forced to move in lockstep with one another toward cooperative solutions. In contrast, our view is that flexible modes of cooperation allow cooperative states to take two steps forward and one step back, to move at different speeds and at different times, but in broadly the same direction. This process may actually result in increased noncompliance, extensive use of escape clauses, or both. As cooperation deepens, the incidence of noncompliance and the use of escape clauses may even increase. While often cited as evidence of the failure of cooperation, in our view noncompliance and the use of escape clauses are also indicators of the challenges faced, even by strongly supportive states, in implementing deep, demanding, and intrusive commitments. Because noncompliance often triggers responses that can lead to fuller implementation, in some cases extensive noncompliance can be an indicator that international cooperation is becoming deeper and more effective. Most important is that it is vital for analysts and policymakers to look beyond simple indicators of compliance when determining whether and how international commitments are being put into practice, especially as cooperation deepens among liberal states.

The Crucial Role of SIRs.   Because states will at times face unavoidable pressures to deviate from regime rules, international cooperation will depend crucially on the ability to assess whether parties are nonetheless broadly contributing to solving common problems. Simple indicators of compliance, we have shown, often say little about performance. Thus a prerequisite for deep integration is the operation of extensive SIRs and the availability of a wide array of feasible responses to implementation failures. Implementation review helps to ensure that behavior remains transparent and bounded, and forces states to defend irregularities in performance. In contrast, shallow integration can proceed even when SIRs and enforcement are weak or nonexistent. Indeed, to date most international environmental cooperation has focused on compliance and SIRs are much weaker than they could be. Of the cases in this book, the North Sea regime has done most to allow deep integration, through ambitious nonbinding commitments and extensive implementation review. The Baltic Sea regime is moving in that direction. In both cases, attention to implementation review has grown as political pressure to solve environmental problems has increased and as the international commitments have become more challenging to implement—integration has deepened, and more demanding (nonbinding) commitments have often led to more noncompliance. The SIR in each of the North and Baltic Sea regimes has intensified its scrutiny and has helped to ensure that implementation is under way and that noncompliance is not merely a sign of inaction. The active SIR in the Montreal Protocol is indicative of what is needed for deep integration, though the substances and activities regulated under it have not required such deep integration of national policies—implementing the Protocol's regulatory commitments has not required pervasive changes in the economy.

The studies in this book suggest that increasing attention is being given to the practice of implementation review. A culture of implementation review is developing, akin to the "compliance culture" in arms control.[59] The trend is starkly evident in the countries undergoing transition, which previously had opposed nearly all monitoring and implementation review activities. We speculate that this trend is a reflection of the opening of domestic politics to multiple influences and the expansion of commercial linkages among countries; it is the result of liberalization and desires to achieve deeper integration. These states increasingly accept that institutions, including intrusive international bodies, play an important role in addressing the shared environmental problems of industrialization. This trend is especially important for data reporting, the backbone of SIRs. The only known cases of egregious misreporting of data in environmental regimes have concerned nonliberal states, such as the falsification of whaling data by Panama and the USSR.[60] Misreporting of data is more difficult in liberal countries, which face more intense internal and external review of national policies. In short, at the national and international levels the trend is toward greater openness and greater acceptance that the benefits of international cooperation often require external scrutiny of national policies. That trend bodes well for the development of SIRs and the ability of these institutions to yield more effective international cooperation.

The Participation of Nonliberal States.   Increasingly the international environmental agenda includes global problems; such problems intrinsically involve all types of states. At present, demanding commitments are often limited to the advanced industrialized democracies—generally liberal states whose economies are integrating in many ways—but at some point this bifurcation is likely to change.

For many agreements, gaining the participation of nonliberal or developing states has required paying their participatory costs: the cost of sending diplomats to meetings as well as the costs of implementing any agreed measures. Indeed, every new global environmental agreement includes provisions for industrialized (and mostly liberal) states to pay the "agreed incremental costs" incurred when developing (and mostly nonliberal) states implement international commitments. Virtually all the existing literature focuses on the fact that developing countries are less able to pay the costs of implementation. While that is surely true, our approach emphasizes that the internal characteristics of states may also lead to a reluctance to become substantively engaged in international institutions unless the narrow calculation of benefits and costs favors membership. It also helps to explain, for example, why Turkey—the least liberal of all OECD members—has joined fewer international accords than any other OECD member.[61] Not only do nonliberal nations respond to different incentives when deciding whether to participate, they also greatly constrain the process of cooperation within those regimes that they do join. Nonliberal states appear less inclined to allow international institutions to scrutinize performance and may block efforts to expand the range of tools available to respond to poor implementation. In the Montreal Protocol, for example, efforts to strengthen the powers of the Non-Compliance Procedure were scuttled by nonliberal countries; nonliberal countries have also been the cause of the Protocol's most egregious data-reporting violations. Wariness of scrutiny means that nonliberal states are less likely to allow deep integration to evolve. They may block the commitments that require deep integration as well as the institutional innovations—SIRs—that make it possible.

Universal accords for global issues are often cited as essential for legitimacy: because all nations are part of the problem, all must be part of the solution. But universal participation is not without drawbacks, and among them may be the perpetual shallowness of cooperation. Solutions that allow deep cooperation may include dealing with nonliberal nations on their own terms, for example by using sanctions and benefits to directly and explicitly change the structure of costs and benefits. The Montreal Protocol best illustrates these propositions: the most serious cases of noncompliance to date are being addressed only because the industrialized nations are paying much (but not all) of the incremental costs of compliance; wide participation by nonliberal countries reflects that the incremental costs of their participation are paid; and the regime includes the credible threat of trade sanctions to exclude nonparticipants from valuable markets. Antidotes to shallow cooperation may also include more attention to subagreements among committed liberal members, such as the nonbinding approach supported by extensive SIRs proposed earlier.

In sum, the most active environmental cooperation has occurred among a particular type of polity—the liberal state. Compared with cooperation involving nonliberal states, cooperation among liberal states is *deeper*, in the sense of involving greater attention to domestic activities, *more demanding*, in terms of substantive commitments, and *more intrusive*, in that cooperation among liberal states is more likely to feature scrutiny behind the border as well as limitations on the externalities that liberal states can impose on each other. This form of cooperation is likely to be necessary for the global environmental management challenges of today and of the future. That more states appear to be liberalizing, both politically and economically, is thus a positive trend. Of course, many other factors also affect the behavior of liberal states besides their liberalism. Notably, a polity's degree of liberalism, the level of integration, and public concern about the environment are all correlated with income. As incomes rise, so does the demand for environmental protection and the resources to supply it. While these other correlated factors are important, the program of deep integration and the character of liberal states lead to a capability for collective management and a particular style of cooperation. That style helps to explain some of the phenomena uncovered in this book, such as the importance of looking beyond simple measures of compliance, the growing participation of nonstate actors, the need for flexible measures such as nonbinding instruments, and the importance and operation of SIRs.

Conclusion: Commitments, Implementation, and Effectiveness

Implementation often is a complex and difficult process. The difficulty is compounded when policies are negotiated internationally, requiring coordination and at times integration of already complex political and economic elements. At times, international commitments yield none of the intended changes in behavior: officials do not anticipate that some activities will need regulation, they make efforts but choose ineffective policy instruments, or they simply

698   Kal Raustiala and David G. Victor

do not have adequate control over their subjects. Although the sources of implementation failure are numerous, the cases in this volume also show that international environmental commitments have induced substantial implementation activities within nations.

To close, we return to the question of effectiveness posed in the introduction to this book: how much variance in target group behavior is explained by international commitments and institutions? The authors of the 14 studies have been mindful of the myriad factors that potentially explain the outcomes, although they have focused on only a few, especially those related to how institutions help the process of implementing international environmental commitments. Our interest is hardly new or unique; social scientists in general have turned their interest to the roles of institutions in shaping social behavior and outcomes, as reflected in the literature dubbed the "new institutionalism." But how much do institutions really matter?

In virtually all of our studies, the most important turning points and fundamental pressures that have caused regulatory action have not been institutions. Regulation of North Sea pollution became more stringent after the shocking appearance of dead seals and algae blooms. In the whaling regime, the critical turning point was caused by the spread of organized anti-whaling sentiment. In the Baltic Sea regime, the critical event that led to improved cooperation was the end of the Cold War, which dramatically unencumbered the East-West cooperation that was necessary to address Baltic pollution. But in these cases, institutions have helped policy advocates to take advantage of opportunities. For instance, expert groups analyzed North Sea pollution and attributed the seal deaths and algae blooms to it, which helped to convince national leaders to adopt and implement costly decisions. Institutions have also set standards for data reporting, helped to target financial resources, and made possible international reviews of national performance. Such institutional functions have made international cooperation more effective, but they were not the critical element.

Although the main driving forces are found elsewhere, we have focused on institutions because they are among the few factors that participants can change—that is, they are the most amenable to policy. Most of the other important factors—diffusion of environmental values, focusing events such as environmental catastrophes, and economic collapse—affect environmental quality and the prospects for effective international cooperation but are beyond the direct control of policy. In the end, however, decision makers and analysts are faced with a common problem: often the factor of greatest interest to them is only one of many. This weak position should not cause despair. For analysts, these studies show that research can isolate the ways that institutions influence the implementation of international environmental commitments. For stakeholders, our research shows how institutions are important and how to make them more effective.

Notes

1. Hjorth, R., 1997, "Development and Implementation of Baltic Sea Pollution Commitments: The Case of Sweden," in *North European and Baltic Sea Integration Yearbook 1997*, edited by B. Lindström and L. Hedegaard, Springer International Verlag, Berlin, Germany.

2. In arms control this has long been an issue in strategic analysis. For a current discussion see, e.g., Chayes, A., and Chayes, A.H., 1995, *The New Sovereignty: Compliance with International Regulatory Agreements*, Harvard University Press, Cambridge, MA, USA.

3. This temporal dynamic is also suggested in Young, O., 1989, "The Politics of International Regime Formation: Managing Natural Resources and the Environment," *International Organization* 43:349–375. Young notes that uncertainty is often high during the early stages of negotiation and, consequently, it is often easier to reach agreement because parties are unclear about their interests. Our studies suggest that that is true, but a different outcome is observed: governments behave conservatively, especially because when interests are unclear so are capabilities to comply with commitments. The discussion below outlines some ways to use nonbinding instruments to reduce that conservatism.

4. As numerous studies have shown, domestic interest groups are rarely unified in their interests and perceptions. Such groups can strongly influence outcomes, and thus international commitments reflect at least two levels of negotiation: international and domestic. Evans, P.B., Jacobson, H.K., and Putnam, R.D., eds., 1993, *Double-Edged Diplomacy: International Bargaining and Domestic Politics*, University of California Press, Berkeley, CA, USA.

5. The most cited statement is from L. Henkin: ". . . almost all nations observe almost all principles of international law and almost all of their obligations almost all of the time." Henkin, L., 1979, *How Nations Behave: Law and Foreign Policy*, 2nd edition, Columbia University Press, New York, NY, USA, p. 47. We are mindful that Henkin's famous quote concerns all commitments— demanding and trivial—and thus was not intended to reflect that compliance is merely the result of tailoring commitments to reflect behavior. Indeed,

Henkin has often been quoted to underscore that international law does have influence. We have examined compliance in part because evidence supporting the proposition that compliance is high has been thin. However, we have been careful to separate "compliance" from actual influence on behavior and are critical of other research that has not done this as explicitly. See, for example, Jacobson, H.K., and Weiss, E.B., 1995, "Strengthening Compliance with International Environmental Accords: Preliminary Observations from a Collaborative Project," *Global Governance* 2:119–148.

6. Levy, M.A., 1993, "European Acid Rain: The Power of Tote-Board Diplomacy," in *Institutions for the Earth: The Sources of Effective International Environmental Protection*, edited by P.M. Haas, R.O. Keohane, and M.A. Levy, The MIT Press, Cambridge, MA, USA, pp. 75–132. See also Chapters 9, 12, and 13 of this book.

7. Russian compliance with programmatic commitments has been much lower—installing and operating monitoring equipment is expensive and reporting data raises concerns about sovereignty.

8. The distinction between compliance and effectiveness does not hold under one special condition: when international commitments require the *elimination* of an environmental threat, such as the Montreal Protocol on Substances that Deplete the Ozone Layer, which requires elimination of chlorofluorocarbons that deplete the stratospheric ozone layer. Yet few international agreements eliminate environmental threats; most manage environmental problems. Thus, except for this special case, any assessment of whether increased compliance is evidence of more influential international commitments also requires an evaluation of the standard against which compliance is assessed.

9. The Rio Declaration on environment and development, Principle 10, in Johnson, S.P., ed., 1993, *The Earth Summit*, Graham & Trotman/Martinus Nijhoff, London, UK; Declaration by the Ministers of Environment of the region of the United Nations Economic Commission for Europe, Sofia, Bulgaria, 25 October 1995, see paragraphs 41 and 42, p. 7. For additional citations, see note 3 in the short text that introduces the second part of this book.

10. Many studies of international environmental governance give prominent attention to the fact that the involvement of stakeholders, notably NGOs, has expanded over the past two to three decades. Such groups influence outcomes by participating in international fora and transnationally (e.g., by working with counterparts in other countries). For extensive references, see note 3 of the short text that introduces the second part of this book.

11. There is some evidence that enforcement is beginning to improve. However, the shift from binding regulations to nonbinding covenants between industry and government has made it difficult for ENGOs to compensate for poor

oversight and enforcement by government—the covenants typically are not transparent and their legal status is ambiguous. Similarly, in the UK the system of negotiated pollution consents has often led to little change in behavior by polluters and has made it difficult for other stakeholders to participate.

12. See also an analysis of these issues at the national level: Sabatier, P., 1975, "Social Movements and Regulatory Agencies: Toward a More Adequate—and Less Pessimistic—Theory of 'Clientele Capture'," *Policy Sciences* 6:301–342.

13. Interviews with many ENGO representatives confirm that they view this "watchdog" role as one of their chief functions. For application to the Montreal Protocol, see Barratt-Brown, E., 1991, "Building a Monitoring and Compliance Regime Under the Montreal Protocol," *Yale Journal of International Law* 16:519–570.

14. Within nations there have been some successful efforts, notably the US Toxic Releases Inventory. However, the difficulties of the European Environment Agency, which has the mandate to assemble and make public useful and comparable information within the European Union, illustrate the problems that arise when countries have different statistical systems and when information that is released is not useful. Hearne, S.A., 1996, "Tracking Toxics: Chemical Use and the Public's 'Right-to-know'," *Environment* 38(6):4–9, 28–34; Bureau of National Affairs, 1996, "Conservation Information Submitted to EEA Incomplete; Lack of National Inventories, Low Priority of Data Collection Cited," *International Environment Reporter*, pp. 992–997.

15. For documentation of these functions see, for example, Sand, P.H., 1997, "Commodity or Taboo? International Regulation of Trade in Endangered Species," in *Green Globe Yearbook of International Co-operation on Environment and Development*, Oxford University Press, New York, NY, USA, pp. 19–36; see also Chapter 2 in this book and note 3 in the short text that introduces the second part of this book.

16. Brickman, R., 1985, *Controlling Chemicals: The Politics of Regulation in Europe and the United States*, Cornell University Press, Ithaca, NY, USA; Vogel, D., 1986, *National Styles of Regulation: Environmental Policy in Great Britain and the United States*, Cornell University Press, Ithaca, NY, USA.

17. For additional details on the project's findings related to transition countries see Kotov, V., Nikitina, E., Roginko, A., Stokke, O.S., Victor, D.G., and Hjorth, R., 1997, "Implementation of International Environmental Commitments in Countries in Transition," *MOCT-MOST Economic Policy in Transition Economies* 7(2):103–128.

18. We have generally avoided the term that is now standard within the United Nations to denote these countries: "countries with economies in transition

702 Kal Raustiala and David G. Victor

(CEIT)." The process of transition has many diverse elements, in addition to economic change.

19. Coal, oil, and gas aggregated to *fossil energy* according to heat content. See British Petroleum, 1994, BP Statistical Review of World Energy, London, UK.

20. SO_2 and NO_x data are for 1980–1993; Baltic Sea data are for 1990–1994; strictly, compliance with the ambitious nonbinding commitments to cut Baltic Sea pollutants by 50–70 percent should be measured from 1987–1995. However, data are especially unreliable prior to 1990; at the time of this writing 1995 data were not available.

21. We make this statement cautiously, mindful of the fact that measurements of economic output in the transition countries are flawed and probably under-represent, perhaps massively, the true level of economic activity.

22. Dumping of radioactive waste, which remains largely under the control of the central government and the military, is an exception.

23. In other terms, the policy networks under central planning were relatively stable and closely linked. Transition has caused many gaps and failures in policy networks. For one study that applies the policy network concept to the transition in Hungary, see O'Toole, L.J., 1997, "Networking Requirements, Institutional Capacity, and Implementation Gaps in Transitional Regimes: The Case of Acidification Policy in Hungary," *Journal of European Public Policy* (in press).

24. Darst, R.G., 1997, "The Internationalization of Environmental Protection in the USSR and Its Successor States," in *The Internationalization of Environmental Protection*, edited by M.A. Schreurs and E. Economy, Cambridge University Press, New York, NY, USA (forthcoming).

25. An exception is Russian policy on marine dumping, which is still centrally controlled.

26. The role of property rights is obviously important and has many dimensions, which we have not examined in detail. Notably, rules concerning liability for environmental damage strongly affect the ownership and stability of property rights and the systems of privatization in the transition countries. Among the useful studies and overviews on this topic is Goldenman, G., ed., 1994, *Environmental Liability and Privatization in Central and Eastern Europe*, The World Bank, Washington, DC, USA.

27. Helsinki Commission, 1995, "The Baltic Sea Joint Comprehensive Environmental Action Programme, Third Activity Inventory," February, table 11.

28. Russia has accounted for only 10–15 percent of the Western money spent on Baltic Sea projects in the former Soviet republics, despite the fact that many hot spots in Russia would be ideal candidates for Western assistance. Eleven percent is the figure suggested by data summarized and analyzed in Roginko, A., 1996, Domestic Implementation of Baltic Sea Pollution Controls in Russia and the Baltic States, WP-96-91, International Institute for Applied Systems Analysis, Laxenburg, Austria. A similar figure (13 percent) is suggested by other data on funding activities: Helsinki Commission, 1995, "The Baltic Sea Joint Comprehensive Environmental Action Programme, Third Activity Inventory," February. The share of resources now targeted for Russia has been increasing since 1995, partly because difficulties in contracting with Russia are slowly being overcome and partly in response to political pressure (from West and East) to ensure that Baltic Sea cooperation fully engages Russia. As during the Cold War, such cooperation is aimed not only at cleaning up the environment but also at extending East-West contacts.

29. While Poland is seen as a success story in comparison with Russia, much remains to be done, especially on non-point sources of pollution. Moreover, some analysts have emphasized the need for more attention to cost-effective solutions; for example, Zylicz, T., 1994, "In Poland, It's Time for Economics," *Environmental Impact Assessment Review* 14:79–94.

30. See references in the text that introduces the first part of this book.

31. See note 3 in the short text that introduces the first part of this book.

32. See, for example, the special issues of *International Organization* (Volume 46, No. 1, 1992) on epistemic communities; see also Haas, P.M., 1990, "Obtaining International Environmental Protection through Epistemic Consensus," *Millennium* 19:347–363.

33. Széll, P., 1995, "The Development of Multilateral Mechanisms for Monitoring Compliance," in *Sustainable Development and International Law*, edited by W. Lang, Graham and Trotman, London, UK; see also Chapter 4 of this book.

34. General Accounting Office, U.S. Congress, 1992, International Environment: International Agreements Are Not Well Monitored, GAO/RCED-92-43.

35. In particular, see Chayes and Chayes, op. cit., note 2.

36. Downs, G.W., Rocke, D.M., and Barsoom, P., 1996, "Is the Good News About Compliance Good News About Cooperation?" *International Organization* 50(3):379–406. A review of game theoretic approaches to the analysis of international cooperation, which implies a similar *enforcement* approach of adjusting costs and benefits, is Oye, K.A., ed., 1986, *Cooperation Under*

Anarchy, Princeton University Press, Princeton, NY, USA (see chapter 1 in particular).

37. We do not consider the difference between multilateral and unilateral enforcement in depth here. The "managerial" argument—that sanctions are difficult to mobilize—applies especially to sanctions that require multilateral cooperation. However, in the area of wildlife law there have been several examples of unilateral sanctions, notably by the USA under the Pelly Amendment and the Packwood-Magnuson Acts. For their relevance to the whaling issue, see Chapter 10. For an overview, see Charnovitz, S., 1994, "Encouraging Environmental Cooperation through the Pelly Amendment," *The Journal of Environment and Development* 3:3–28; DeSombre, E.R., 1995, "Baptists and Bootleggers for the Environment: The Origins of United States Unilateral Sanctions," *Journal of Environment and Development* 4:53–75. For more on the effectiveness and difficulties of sustaining cooperation needed for multilateral sanctions, see Hufbauer, G.C., Schott, J., and Elliott, K.A., 1990, *Economic Sanctions Reconsidered*, Institute for International Economics, Washington, DC, USA; Martin, L.L., 1992, *Coercive Cooperation: Explaining Multilateral Economic Sanctions*, Princeton University Press, Princeton, NJ, USA.

38. For studies that emphasize the role of negotiation between regulators and targets, rather than simple and strict application of statutory penalties see Lipsky, M., 1980, *Street-level Bureaucracy*, Russell Sage Foundation, New York, NY, USA; Ingram, H., 1977, "Policy Implementation through Bargaining: The Case of Federal Grants-in-Aid," *Public Policy* 25:499–526; Melnick, R.S., 1984, "Pollution Deadlines and the Coalition for Failure," *The Public Interest* 75(2); and other works cited in note 3 of the short introductory text to the second part of this book.

39. The influence of instrument choice is addressed in greater detail, with illustrations from the research presented in this book, in Victor, D.G., 1997, "The Use and Effectiveness of Nonbinding Instruments in the Management of Complex International Environmental Problems," *Proceedings of the American Society of International Law, 91st Annual Meeting* (forthcoming).

40. Among the few studies that have examined nonbinding instruments are Contini, P., and Sand, P.H., 1972, " Methods to Expedite Environment Protection: International Ecostandards," *American Journal of International Law* 66:37–59; Schachter, O., 1977, "The Twilight Existence of Nonbinding International Agreements," *American Journal of International Law* 71:296–304; Handl, G., 1988, "A Hard Look at Soft Law," *Proceedings of the American Society of International Law, 82nd Annual Meeting*; Donoghue, J.E., 1993, "Environmental Law: When Does it Make Sense to Negotiate International Agreements?" *Proceedings of the American Society of International Law, 87th*

Annual Meeting; Roht-Arriaza, N., 1995, "Shifting the Point of Regulation: The International Organization for Standardization and Global Lawmaking on Trade and the Environment," *Ecology Law Quarterly* 22:479–539.

41. Although this claim is conventional wisdom, it is rarely analyzed. Most studies on the use of nonbinding instruments have emphasized especially their speed of entry into force and their flexibility. The present analysis suggests that, in addition to those benefits (especially flexibility), nonbinding instruments have other attributes that allow for more effective regulation.

42. Similarly effective was the ambitious nonbinding "Action Plan" to reduce pollution in the Rhine River, which is not considered in this book but has been analyzed by other scholars. See Bernauer, T., and Moser, P., 1996, "Reducing Pollution of the Rhine River: The Influence of International Cooperation," *Journal of Environment and Development* 5:389–415.

43. Furthermore, if one "controls" for legal status then compliance and effectiveness of international commitments are often not correlated at all. An example from Chapter 14 illustrates the point with two sets of nonbinding commitments: The Baltic Sea regime has induced significant implementation activity—behavioral change—in Riga, Latvia, yet HELCOM Recommendations (nonbinding standards) will not be met "even if planned abatement measures were enacted in addition to those already in place." In contrast, industrial sources in St. Petersburg have cut emissions of pollutants by half—thus meeting the ambitious nonbinding commitments of the 1990 Ronneby Declaration— "without implementing any environmental policies, primarily because of a decrease in production." In the former case, noncompliance is the result, despite significant action; in the latter, zero implementation activity still yields compliance.

44. Kahler, M., 1992, "Multilateralism with Small and Large Numbers," *International Organization* 46(3):685–691.

45. We are mindful that a firm determination of the effectiveness of the nonbinding PIC system is severely hampered by the lack of relevant data (see Chapter 6).

46. Some of this concern with the speed of entry into force was caused by long delays of many accords in the 1970s and 1980s while waiting for the requisite number of ratifications. Recent experience points to the opposite problem: negotiating schedules are so compressed that accords leave many loose ends. The accords on trade in hazardous waste (1989), biodiversity (1992), and climate change (1992) have actually entered into force rapidly, which suggests that time delays of ratification are now a less severe obstacle to the operation of international accords.

47. Burley (Slaughter), A.-M., 1992, "Toward an Age of Liberal Nations," *International Law Journal* 33; Slaughter, A.-M., 1995, "International Law in a World of Liberal States," *European Journal of International Law* 6(4):503–538; Moravcsik, A., 1992, "Liberalism and International Relations Theory," Center for International Affairs Working Paper, Harvard University, Cambridge, MA, USA; Moravcsik, A., 1997, "Taking Preferences Seriously: A Liberal Theory of International Policies," *International Organization* 51:513–553; for a survey of the current situation and application to policy, see Zakaria, F., 1997, "The Rise of Illiberal Democracy," *Foreign Affairs* 76(6):22–43.

48. See references in this section, especially notes 47, 51, and 52.

49. Gourevitch, P.A., 1978, "The Second Image Reversed," *International Organization* 32(4); Rogowski, R., 1990, *Commerce and Coalitions: How Trade Affects Domestic Political Alignments*, Princeton University Press, Princeton, NJ, USA; Evans *et al.*, op. cit., note 4.

50. Raustiala, K., 1997, "Domestic Institutions and International Regulatory Cooperation: Comparative Responses to the Convention on Biological Diversity," *World Politics* 49(4).

51. Lawrence, R., Bressand, A., and Ito, T., 1996, *A Vision for the World Economy: Openness, Diversity, and Cohesion*, The Brookings Institution, Washington, DC, USA, pp. 14 and 22.

52. Keohane, R.O., and Nye, J.S., 1989, *Power and Interdependence*, 2nd edition, Scott, Foresman & Co., Glenview, IL, USA (see Chapter 2 in particular).

53. Others have noted similar processes at work. Chayes and Chayes, op. cit., note 2, argue that extensive regulatory cooperation is a distinguishing feature of what they term the "New Sovereignty." The nature of sovereignty itself, they suggest, has changed. For many states today, membership in good standing in the panoply of extant regulatory regimes is central to sovereign statehood. In some ways this resembles an old approach to sovereignty: the nineteenth century *standard of civilization* defined the legal and political requirements necessary ". . . for a non-European country like China to gain full and *civilized* status . . . . Included in these requirements were the ability of the country to guarantee the life, liberty, and property of foreign nationals; to demonstrate a suitable governmental organization; to adhere to the accepted diplomatic practices; and to abide by the principles of international law." Gong, G., 1984, "China's Entry into International Society?" in *The Expansion of International Society*, edited by H. Bull and A. Watson, Oxford University Press, Oxford, UK, p. 179.

54. See Chapter 7.

55. Lawrence *et al.*, op. cit., note 51.

56. Chayes and Chayes, op. cit., note 2.

57. Downs, G.W., and Rocke, D.M., 1995, *Optimal Imperfection: Domestic Uncertainty and Institutions in International Relations*, Princeton University Press, Princeton, NJ, USA, especially Chapter 4 (on tolerance of deviations and compensation for deviations as part of an enforcement strategy) and Chapter 5 (on the relationship between enforcement strategies and certainty about a state's capacity to implement collective commitments). Much of their argument focuses on the availability and reliability of information about a country's future implementation of collective (international) commitments. They show (Chapter 5) that cooperation among a few reliable partners can be more effective than cooperation among many parties, even if such narrow cooperation excludes some parties that cause common problems (e.g., pollution). They suggest that this finding may explain why "developing and politically volatile states . . . are rarely members of international institutions with strongly enforced norms of cooperation" (p. 137). We support the benefits of "minilateralism" (see note 44 and discussion in main text), but here we suggest that low participation by such countries is also a consequence of their nonliberal status.

58. See, for example, Ruggie, J.G., 1983, "International Regimes, Transactions, and Change: Embedded Liberalism in the Postwar Economic Order," in *International Regimes*, edited by S.D. Krasner, Cornell University, Ithaca, NY, USA.

59. We acknowledge W. Lang as the source of the insight that a "compliance culture" has developed in arms control regimes and has resulted in greater attention to ensuring that compliance is monitored and implementation problems (often "noncompliance") are handled.

60. On Panamanian statistics see Birnie, P., 1985, *International Regulation of Whaling: From Conservation of Whaling to Conservation of Whales and Regulation of Whale Watching*, Oceana Publications, Dobbs Ferry, NY, USA; on Soviet data, see Freeman, M., 1995, "Whale Numbers," *Nature* 276:11; and, Yablokov, A.V., 1994, "Validity of Whaling Data," *Nature* 367:108.

61. Data on membership compiled as part of the OECD Environmental Performance Reviews. See, for example, the compendium of OECD membership in multilateral treaties in OECD, 1996, *Environmental Performance Reviews: United States*, OECD, Paris, France, Annex III. The data exclude Poland and South Korea, which became OECD members only recently.

Index

critical loads concept. *See* European
air pollution regime
Czech Republic, 111, 148, 173, 181,
301, 325, 580, 625, 657
Czechoslovakia, 524, 625

data
quality 680–681
Baltic Sea environment
protection regime, 189,
193–194, 196–203
European air pollution
regime, 293–294
improvement due to linkage
with modeling programs,
19, 199–201
Montreal Protocol, 106–107,
144, 159,
trade in hazardous chemicals
and pesticides regime, 265
reporting by governments
Baltic Sea environment
protection regime,
188–189, 196–198, 203
European air pollution
regime, 289–294
marine dumping of nuclear
waste regime, 481–482
Montreal Protocol, 106–108,
111–113, 143–144
role of nongovernmental
organizations in providing,
667, 683
Baltic Sea environment
protection regime, 201
fauna and flora protection
regimes, 67–74
Montreal Protocol, 109–110
trade in hazardous chemicals
and pesticides regime,
244–247, 262–263
use in assessing adequacy of
commitments, 18–19, 50,
67–74, 198–203, 339, 680
Decision Guidance Document (DGD).
See trade in hazardous

chemicals and pesticides
regime
deep integration. *See* economic
integration
democracy, 21, 305, 320–321. *See
also* participation
dependent variable. *See* methodology.
See effectiveness
Designated National Authority
(DNA). *See* trade in
hazardous chemicals and
pesticides regime
détente, 178, 179, 210, 383, 520
dichlorodiphenyltrichloroethane
(DDT), 207, 215, 217, 269,
274, 580
Directorate for Air, Noise and Waste
(DANW), 389. *See* United
Kingdom
dumping permits. *See* marine
dumping of radioactive
waste regime

Ecofund, 650, 651, 657
ecoglasnost. *See* transition countries,
definition of
Economic Commission for Europe
(ECE). *See* United Nations
Economic Commission for
Europe
economic integration, 689–697
definition, 689–691
impact on implementation,
692–697
meaning of compliance,
692–694
economic sanctions. *See* sanctions.
See enforcement of
implementation. *See*
United States of America,
certification for sanctions
under Pelly Amendment
and the
Packwood-Magnuson Act
economies in transition. *See* transition
from central planning

The International Institute for Applied Systems Analysis

is an interdisciplinary, nongovernmental research institution founded in 1972 by leading scientific organizations in 12 countries. Situated near Vienna, in the center of Europe, IIASA has been for more than two decades producing valuable scientific research on economic, technological, and environmental issues.

IIASA was one of the first international institutes to systematically study global issues of environment, technology, and development. IIASA's Governing Council states that the Institute's goal is: *to conduct international and interdisciplinary scientific studies to provide timely and relevant information and options, addressing critical issues of global environmental, economic, and social change, for the benefit of the public, the scientific community, and national and international institutions.* Research is organized around three central themes:

- Global Environmental Change;
- Global Economic and Technological Change;
- Systems Methods for the Analysis of Global Issues.

The Institute now has national member organizations in the following countries:

Austria
The Austrian Academy of Sciences

Bulgaria*
The Bulgarian Committee for IIASA

Finland
The Finnish Committee for IIASA

Germany**
The Association for the Advancement
of IIASA

Hungary
The Hungarian Committee for Applied
Systems Analysis

Japan
The Japan Committee for IIASA

Kazakstan*
The Ministry of Science –
The Academy of Sciences

Netherlands
The Netherlands Organization for
Scientific Research (NWO)

Norway
The Research Council of Norway

Poland
The Polish Academy of Sciences

Russian Federation
The Russian Academy of Sciences

Slovak Republic*
The Slovak Committee for IIASA

Sweden
The Swedish Council for Planning and
Coordination of Research (FRN)

Ukraine*
The Ukrainian Academy of Sciences

United States of America
The American Academy of Arts and
Sciences

*Associate member
**Affiliate member